THE GOULBURN NORWICH DIARIES

THE GOULBURN NORWICH DIARIES

Selected Passages from the ten remaining
Norwich Diaries of

EDWARD MEYRICK GOULBURN

M.A., D.C.L., D.D.
Dean of Norwich, 1866–1889

Chosen, Edited and Introduced
(together with a brief biography)

by

S. J. NOEL HENDERSON, M.A.

The Canterbury Press
Norwich

© S. J. Noel Henderson 1996

First Published 1996 by The Canterbury Press Norwich
(a publishing imprint of Hymns Ancient & Modern Limited,
a registered charity)
St Mary's Works, St Mary's Plain,
Norwich, Norfolk, NR3 3BH

*All rights reserved. No part of this publication which is copyright may
be reproduced, stored in a retrieval system, or transmitted, in any form
or by any means, electronic, mechanical, photocopying, recording, or
otherwise, without the prior permission of the publisher.*

Noel Henderson has asserted his right under the Copyright, Designs
and Patents Act, 1988, to be identified as Author of this Work

British Library Cataloguing in Publication Data

A catalogue record for this book is available
from the British Library

ISBN 1-85311-125-2

*Typeset by David Gregson Associates, Beccles, Suffolk
Printed and bound in Great Britain by
Antony Rowe Ltd, Chippenham, Wiltshire*

To Phyllis
our Children
and Grandchildren

CONTENTS

Acknowledgements	page viii
Preface	ix
Cathedral Personnel	xi
Brief Biography	1
1867 Journal	41
1868 Journal	67
1869 Journal	96
1873 Journal	118
1874 Journal	156
1881 Journal	206
1882 Journal	244
1883 Journal	292
1886 Journal	330
1887 Journal	377

Appendices:
1. Published Writings and Sermons of Dean Goulburn (and his First Letter) — 417
2. Select Bibliography — 421
3. Goulburn Family Tree — 423
4. Thomas Family Tree — 424
5. Goldsmid-De Visme Family Tree — 425
6. Cartwright Family Tree — 426
7. Open Letter 'Eight Directions' (See p. 17 of Brief Biography) — 427
8. 'The Argumentative Discourses' 1871–1876 (See pp. 33 and 36 of Brief Biography) — 428
9. A note on the costs and prices in the Diary — 430

ACKNOWLEDGEMENTS

My grateful thanks are due to:

The Dean and Chapter of Norwich for allowing me the free use of the Goulburn Diaries, and access to the Photocopying Machine in the Cathedral Office, with its helpful staff.

Mr Tom Mollard, Sub-Librarian of the Dean and Chapter Library, who spent a very great deal of time compiling a booklist of all the works of Dean Goulburn held in the Library. These consisted not only of all titles recorded in the Library Catalogue, but also a list of all the material, previously unlisted, which was stored in five pamphlet boxes.

He also obtained the full list of Dean Goulburn's works held by the Local Studies Library, since tragically devastated by fire in 1994. It is not yet known if any, or all, of these works survived.

In many other ways Mr Mollard, and his Assistant, Miss Barbara Smith, willingly and cheerfully helped, and sought to answer the queries I often put to them.

Mr Bryan Gipps, of Egerton House, Kent, a fourth Cousin, three times removed, of Dean Goulburn. Most generously, he lent me some 70 personal family letters written by the Dean; gave me 32 letters written to the Dean by leading Ecclesiastics of the day – these I have passed on to the Library of the Dean and Chapter; lent, and also given me, a number of contemporary family photographs of the Goulburn period, as well as a scrapbook of newspaper cuttings relating to the Dean, and a bound set of ten large mounted photographs of the Cathedral. Most willingly and cheerfully, he has answered my many queries about the Goulburn family, and checked the Family Trees I had compiled.

The Theodore Trust (a Registered Charity set up by the late Reverend Alan Carefull for the Advancement of the Christian Religion) for the generous financial help towards the publication of this book.

Barrie and Jenkins, Publisher of *Lili at Aynhoe* (1989) by Elizabeth Cartwright-Hignett, for permission to quote two extracts from Lili's Diary. This is a delightful book containing interior paintings of Aynhoe Park (The Great House) and the village, by Lady Elizabeth Cartwright ('Lili') in the 19th Century. The book also contains much information about the Cartwright family.

Miss Janet Smith for information about the Thorpe area and its estates in the 19th Century, with accompanying maps.

Mrs Audrey Talks for permission to quote from *An Historical Guide to Norwich Cathedral* (Revised Edition 1994) by Ethelreda Sansbury.

The Norwich Diocesan Office for allowing me to borrow copies of the *Norwich Diocesan Calendar* for the years 1858 to 1900.

Unfortunately, some years are missing from this set. (Happily the complete set in the Local Studies Library survived the fire).

Mr D. J. M. Armstrong for permission to quote from B. J. Armstrong, *A Norfolk Diary* (Edited by H. B. J. Armstrong) (G. G. Harrap and Co., Ltd. 1949).

The Revd Philip Barrett for information about Cathedral legislation learnt from his book *Barchester – English Cathedral Life in the Nineteenth Century* (SPCK 1993).

The Very Revd Alan Webster for valuable help and advice.

S.J.N.H.

PREFACE

The Goulburn Diaries (those which remain) have, probably, been on the shelves of the Library of the Dean and Chapter of Norwich for almost 100 years. During that time, they have been dipped into, but I doubt if they have been read from cover to cover. Until 1993, I had found no reference being made to them. Dean Goulburn wrote a well-formed even script which is easy to read. But with some of the ink beginning to fade, I decided that my first task was to make a typed copy of the 14 volumes, thus making reading and reference easier. This copy will be available in the Dean and Chapter Library alongside the original volumes. In editing and selecting, I have cut out much of the repetitive matter – time of getting up in the morning, meal times, luncheon and dinner parties, Service times, sentences unnecessary to the sense of the entry. Goulburn included in a very large number of his entries, two sums – his cash in hand, and his expenditure of that cash. This was an almost continuous process from one entry to another. Except for one or two examples left in, I have excluded these entries. *But*, in Appendix 7, I have given a selection of prices for goods and services being charged in the 1860s to 1880s, taken from the Diaries.

Goulburn was meticulous in the preparation of his Sermons and writings. He checked and revised again and again. The Diaries, on the other hand, give the impression of once written, not re-read. They are full of the names of his relations (both Goulburn and Cartwright), of his friends, acquaintances, correspondents – more often than not, Christian or surnames only. Even within his family circle, it is difficult, for example, to decide to which of the three Louisas, or the three Sophias, he is referring. He also loved giving people nicknames, without mentioning their proper names; he relates an incident or poses a problem, without revealing the outcome; certain words he almost always abbreviates. So it has often been necessary to add explanatory notes after an entry. The text of the Diaries has necessarily been reduced to between one-fifth and one-sixth of the original number of words, but, nevertheless, I think I have kept the authentic atmosphere and aura.

The Diaries build up a picture of the personality of Goulburn; of the life and activities of the Cathedral and Close, of the Diocese and City; and of some of the people who lived there at that time. Strangely enough, although 13 of the Diaries are missing for his 23 years in Norwich (and this is very regrettable) one is still on familiar ground when they resume after a gap. Fortunately, the ten are spread over the years from 1867 to 1887.

Reading the Diaries, three things should be kept in mind:

(1) Goulburn normally rose in the morning between 6am and 8am – more often nearer to the earlier time. He frequently worked at a Sermon, or other matter, before Breakfast; he received, and promptly answered, a large number of letters (he had no official Secretary or Typewriter) almost daily.

(2) He was quite often ill, and in considerable pain, during the night, and unable to sleep. Yet, surprisingly, he was usually able to fulfil his daily work and duties; until his latter years, he rarely missed his long daily walks, accompanied or unaccompanied.

(3) Normally, he attended the Daily and Sunday Services in the Cathedral. If unable to attend, he read the Service at home, either alone or with his wife, Julia (Ju).

The first three Norwich Diaries are the shortest of the ten. Goulburn had a relatively poor start as Dean of Norwich. Although living in the Deanery from February 27th, officially he also remained as Incumbent of St John's, Paddington, until June 1867 (his two Curates being in charge), to oblige his successor; he had an accident on October 7th, 1867, which incapacitated him until February 26th, 1868, and there are no Diary entries for this period of 4½ months; and then his rather difficult and demanding father, for whom he had a very great care and concern, was terminally ill for some months before he died on August 24th, 1868, and Goulburn was frequently in London to see him. From then on the Diaries begin to reflect a more normal, active and integrated Cathedral life.

The Dean's spelling of names is sometimes inaccurate and variable.

Where square brackets appear in the diary entries, these contain my own insertions or comments.

NOEL HENDERSON

CATHEDRAL PERSONNEL

The Bishop and his Family
The Hon. and Rt. Revd John Thomas Pelham, M.A., D.D. (1811–94). Bishop 1857–93.
m. Henrietta, 2nd d. of Thomas Tatton, of Wythenshawe Hall, Cheshire.

Family
Henry Francis (1846–1907): Camden Professor of Ancient History at Oxford and President of Trinity College, Oxford.
m. Laura, 3rd d. of Sir Edward North Buxton.
Sidney (1849–1926): V. of St. Peter Mancroft; Hon. Canon; Rural Dean of Norwich; Archdeacon of Norfolk for 14 years.
m. (1897) Caroline d. of Canon J. Patteson, R. of Thorpe.
Fanny (18??–1916): 1885–90 Vice-President Diocesan G.F.S.; 1890 President.
After her father's death, she lived at 16, The Close.
Herbert (1855–81): C. of St Philip's, Heigham. (Had been an Oxford Rowing Blue).
Died from a fall when mountain climbing in Switzerland.

The Dean
The Very Revd Edward Meyrick Goulburn, M.A., D.C.L., D.D. (1818–1897). Dean 1866–89.
m. Julia ('Ju'; 'Auntie'; 'Judy') youngest daughter of William Ralph Cartwright, of Aynhoe Park, Northants.
Guardian (from 1864) of Augusta ('Gussie', etc.) Cartwright (1853–1949).
m. (1880) Gerard de Visme Thomas (1848–1900).

Residentiary Canons:	In office
Professor Adam Sedgwick	1834–73
George Archdall-Gratwicke	1835–67
James W. L. Heaviside	1860–97
Charles Robinson	1861–1909
John Majorbanks Nisbet	1867–92
Arch. Henry R. Nevill	1873–1900

Precentors:	In office
Henry Symonds ('Pinseter'; 'Pin')	1844–74
E. S. Medley	1874–77
G. W. Barrett ('Bartie')	1877–93

Chapter Clerks
John Kitson   d.1869
W. T. Bensly, LL.D   1869–

Minor Canons   *In office*
J. C. Matchett   1824–79 Sacrist
Henry Symonds   1844–74 Precentor
E. Bulmer   1865–1900 Sacrist
W. T. Moore   1874–94
E. S. Medley   1872–77 Precentor (1874–77)
G. W. Barratt   1877–93 Precentor

Organists   *In office*
Dr Zechariah Buck   1819–77
Dr F. E. Gladstone   1877–81
F. C. Atkinson, Mus. Bac.   1881–85
Dr Frank Bates   1885–1928

Choir School Masters   *In office*
W. H. Alden   1866–74
Tompson   1874–78
J. H. Brockbank   1878–1921

Archdeacons
Norwich   *In office*
R. E. Hankinson   1857–68
A. M. Hopper   1868–78
T. T. Perowne   1878–1913

Norfolk   *In office*
W. A. Bouverie   1850–69
Ralph Blakelock   1869–74
Henry R. Nevill   1874–1900

Suffolk   *In office*
R. H. Groome   1869–87
J. Woolley   1887–92
R. H. Gibson   1892–1901

BRIEF BIOGRAPHY

Brief Biography

THE VERY REVEREND EDWARD MEYRICK GOULBURN, M.A., D.C.L., D.D. (1818–1897)

Knowledge of Goulburn has been based largely on the Memoir (published in 1899) by Prebendary Berdmore Compton, one of his assistant masters at Rugby, and his lifelong friend; the entry in the *Dictionary of National Biography*; the obituaries in *The Times* and *Guardian*, and in Norfolk newspapers in May 1897; some perhaps, of the very long list of his publications and printed Sermons. But, until the appearance, in 1993, of Philip Barrett's excellent study of *Barchester: English Cathedral Life in the Nineteenth Century*, little, or no, reference had been made to Goulburn's surviving *Diaries*.

The Diaries

Fourteen volumes of these Diaries are in the Library of the Dean and Chapter of Norwich. They are the equivalent of some 1,300 A4 typed pages. The first is for 1861, and the fourteenth for 1887; so that, in this sequence of Diaries thirteen are missing. The indications are that other Diaries preceeded 1861, and followed 1887. The first four cover four of the seven years when he was Vicar of St John's, Paddington; and the remaining ten when he was Dean of Norwich. When he resigned in 1889, it is most unlikely that he would have left the Diaries in the Cathedral Library. So it must be assumed that, in the course of his retirement moves between 1889 and 1897, the missing Diaries somehow vanished. This carelessness, together with the uncorrected mistakes, the abbreviations, the many Christian names and nicknames only, often the lack of explanation, which the Diaries contain, surely indicate that he was not writing intentionally for posterity. But they do give a portrait of the day to day life of a fairly conservative, scholarly, and conscientious Victorian Dean and his Cathedral.

When he died in 1897, his widow, Julia (who outlived him by six years), sent a gift of books from his Library to the Norfolk and Norwich Library. She also sent to the Dean and Chapter Library, the collection of 85 volumes of the Fathers of the Church (in

Latin) with which he had been presented on leaving St John's, Paddington. It is more than likely that, at the same time, she also sent the 14 remaining Diaries.

Family Background

There is a tradition, for which no evidence can be found, that the Goulburn's came, originally, from Scotland. The name 'Goulburn' (an uncommon one) can be traced back as far as the 13th Century, to a small township 'Golborne', in the Parish of Winwick, on the Lancashire-Cheshire border. From this area it is historically certain that Goulburns emigrated to Jamaica in the 17th Century, some time after the British capture of the island from the Spaniards in 1655. They amassed a 'considerable property' in Jamaica, the Amity Hall estate. For more than a hundred years they lived there in Amity Hall, until Munbee Goulburn (1756–1793), Dean Goulburn's grandfather, was sent to Eton and Oxford. He remained in England, married, on June 6th, 1782, the Hon. Susannah Chetwynd, eldest daughter of the impoverished Viscount Chetwynd, and lived in Portland Place, London.

Munbee and Susannah had three sons: Henry (1784–1856); Edward (1787–1868), the Dean's father; and Frederic. It was thought that Munbee and Susannah were on the point of separating, when Munbee died suddenly in 1793, at the age of 37. He had incurred heavy debts, and he died intestate. Eventually, his widow was granted a jointure of £800 per year, but was debtor 'to a large amount' on the Jamaican estate. Henry went to Cambridge in 1801, and when he came of age in 1805, inherited the Amity Hall estate, worth 'only' £20,000. He married Jane Montagu, daughter of Lord Rokeby. Eventually, he became Chancellor of the Exchequer under the Duke of Wellington, and Home Secretary, and again Chancellor of the Exchequer, under Sir Robert Peel.

His brother, Edward, became a Barrister. He married Harriette de Visme, 3rd daughter of Philip Nathaniel de Visme of Nottinghill House, Kensington. They had two sons – Edward Meyrick (1818–1897), and Frederic Anderleet (1820–1877); and also two daughters Harriette, who died in 1830, and Susan who died in 1836. Edward (Senior) became a D.C.L., a Sergeant-at Law, for a time a Welsh Judge, Tory M.P. for Leicester from 1835–37, and from 1842 until his death in 1868, Commissioner of the Court of Bankruptcy. He was also an Ecclesiastical Commissioner.

When his mother, Harriette, died in 1823, Goulburn (the future Dean), his brother and two sisters, were sent to live with their Aunt Louisa Goldsmid and her family for a time. He came to regard his Cousin Louisa, eight years his senior, as an adopted sister. In retirement in the 1890s they wrote long letters of reminiscences about those days to each other. She lived to 1911 to be 101.

Two years after his first wife's death, Edward (Senior) married his cousin, the Hon. Esther Chetwynd, daughter of the 5th Viscount Chetwynd, and they had one daughter, Esther. When his second wife died in 1829, the children once again were sent to their Aunt Louisa and her family, now living in Bedford Square, Brighton.

Two years later, Edward (Senior) married, thirdly, another connection, the Hon. Catherine Montagu, daughter of the 4th Lord Montagu, and this marriage lasted for some 35 years. In the Diaries, Goulburn refers to her frequently as 'my mother'. So, throughout the Diaries, we have large numbers of de Visme, Chetwynd, Montagu, and Goulburn relations appearing regularly and confusingly (sometimes with the same Christian names); as well as, perhaps even larger numbers of Cartwrights, his wife, Julia's family and relations; for *her* father had been married twice and had thirteen children.

School and University

At school, first at Rottingdean (because he was living in Brighton at the time) and then at Eton, Goulburn did not play games, apparently because he was short-sighted. Probably this is why he made so much of his regular, almost daily, long walks throughout his life. But he was a voracious reader, scholar and academic. By the age of 16 he had won a scholarship to Balliol College, Oxford, and went up the following year, 1835.

In view of later controversy, it is interesting to note that Goulburn and Arthur Penryn Stanley (who had come up to Balliol the year before) became close friends. While they were still at Oxford, Stanley's father, in 1837, became Bishop of Norwich. In 1841, after they had both become Fellows of Colleges (Goulburn of Merton, Stanley of University College), they spent the summer holiday together in Northern Italy and Greece. Stanley was going on a ten month's trip abroad, and he left on July 10th. As arranged, he met Goulburn in Geneva and they set off together on September 3rd in a britschka (an open carriage with a folding hood top and space for reclining) with the bags and trunks in front of them. After five weeks in Northern Italy, they sailed for Corfu. In alternate weeks each composed a Sermon and preached it to the other. After Corfu, they went on to Patras where, on disembarking, Goulburn fell into the hold and severely bruised his leg. Because of this, shortly afterwards he decided to return home, leaving Stanley to continue his tour.

Ordination
Achieving a First in Classics, Goulburn became a Fellow of Merton in 1841, and was ordained a year later, continuing his work as a Tutor. He had been brought up as an Evangelical, but gradually he was influenced by the Tractarians, and especially by W. G. Ward, Fellow of Balliol from 1834 to 1845 who, having been deprived of his degree for heresy (he wrote a Romanist treatise) became a Roman Catholic in that year. For the rest of his life Goulburn remained a moderate High Churchman. He loved, and always aimed for, liturgical order and perfection, good music and well-trained choirs, but he was never (in 19th Century terms) a 'Ritualist'. In June 1875, when Goulburn came to preach for the local Church Schools at Dereham, the Revd B. J. Armstrong, the Vicar, noted in his Diary: 'He is a very reverent man, bowing at the Sacred Name and the Glorias.[1] Some forty years after Ward had become a Roman Catholic (and had died in 1882), Goulburn suddenly got a strong desire to write a Memoir of his former Tutor. He got in touch with his son Wilfrid, also a Roman Catholic, and later to become Editor of the 'Dublin Review', and a biographer. In December 1886, Wilfrid stayed for two nights at the Deanery in Norwich. Goulburn 'lionised' him round the city and took him for one of his long walks.

In 1844, Goulburn accepted the Merton College Living of Holywell in the city of Oxford, continuing to live in College, and attracting undergraduates by his preaching.

Marriage and the Cartwrights
On December 11th, 1845, Goulburn married Julia Cartwright, of Aynhoe Park, Northamptonshire. The Cartwrights had been at Aynhoe Park since 1615. Enlarged over the years, it was an enormous house by the 19th Century, and needed some 20 to 30 servants to run it. Julia's father, William Ralph (who died in

---

1. H. B. J. Armstrong, (Ed.), A *Norfolk Diary* G. G. Harrap & Co. Ltd. 1949, p. 192.

1847) had been a Tory Squire and M.P. for South Northamptonshire. He had been married twice; first, to Emma Maude, daughter of the 1st Lord Hawarden. They had five sons and three daughters. When Emma died, William Ralph married, in 1810, Julia Aubrey, daughter of a Welsh Squire. This was Julia Goulburn's mother. There were three sons and two daughters from this second marriage.

It is worth pursuing the Cartwright family in more detail, because, every year, the Goulburns spent part of their holidays at Aynhoe and in neighbouring villages where Cartwright relations lived. Aynho[e] is in the southern corner of Northamptonshire, between Banbury and Bicester. In the 19th Century, the Post Office dropped the 'e' from the name, but the 'Great House' refused to do this; and so it is Aynho Village and Aynhoe Park. Edward and Julia were so fond of it, that they called their retirement houses in Brighton and Tunbridge Wells 'Aynhoe'.

Thomas, the eldest son of the first marriage was a diplomat, knighted in 1835. In 1824 he had married Countess Elizabeth von Sandizel, eldest daughter of a Bavarian nobleman. She was 19, tiny, and weighed only 6½ stone. Known always in family circles as 'Lili',[2] she was a dominant figure for the rest of the 19th Century, dying in 1902 at the age of 97. Her husband did not take her on his diplomatic business in Europe, and so she spent the early days of her marriage doing the most detailed paintings of the main rooms at Aynhoe Park, and in the Rectory, and in one or two local cottages. She also kept a Diary from 1828 to 1902. Initially, she did not like Eward Goulburn when he married Julia. In her Diary for November 8th, 1845, she wrote: 'He ... has imperfections which inspire no confidence for the future happiness of this excellent and angelic Julia'.[3] Many years later, the Goulburn Diaries reveal a very happy and affectionate marriage. Lili (now living in Leamington) spent many holidays at the Deanery in Norwich, she and Goulburn often exchanging presents of books. When the Goulburns visited Aynhoe each year, usually she came over from Leamington to be there at the same time. While going occasionally to an Anglican Service, she remained, all her life, a very faithful Roman Catholic. In Norwich, Goulburn would invite to dinner the Roman Catholic

---

2. Elizabeth Cartwright-Hignett, *Lili at Aynhoe* (Barrie & Jenkins 1989). This delightful book contains the paintings at Aynhoe of Lady Elizabeth Cartwright ('Lili'), and gives much information about the Cartwright family. Lili's Diary was written in French. Aynhoe Park is now a home for retired people.
3. Ditto, p. 62.

Priest of the Church which she attended when visiting the Deanery.

Thomas and Lili had two sons, William and Thomas. 'Willy' inherited Aynhoe from his father in 1850, when his mother moved to Leamington Spa. But, with the estate so much in debt, he let Aynhoe Park for most of the remainder of the Century. 'Tommy' married Lady Elizabeth Leslie-Melville, heiress of the 8th Earl of Lever and Melville, and took the name 'Leslie-Melville-Cartwright'. In the Goulburn Diaries they are usually referred to as 'Tom and Bitta'.

Julia (Goulburn) had been named after her mother. Of her mother-in-law, Lili writes in her Diary for 1828 (on her first visit to Aynhoe): 'I was enchanted with everything and especially with Mrs Cartwright. She is the second wife of my father-in-law who lives with her in perfect happiness. She brings up all the children with extreme care, and loves them all as if they were her own. To all the qualities of the heart she adds those of the mind. She is well-educated, of a charming gaiety and always of an equitable temper'.[4] When Goulburn was Headmaster of Rugby School in the 1850s, Mrs Cartwright died while on a visit to them. Goulburn gave a set of stained glass windows to the School Chapel in memory of his mother-in-law.

In 1847, while continuing in charge of the Parish of Holywell, Goulburn became a Chaplain to the Bishop of Oxford, Samuel Wilberforce (son of William, the great anti-slavery campaigner), who was noted for his eloquence and pastoral efficiency.

Headmaster of Rugby

At the end of 1849, at the age of 31, and seven years after Thomas Arnold, Goulburn became Headmaster of Rugby.[5] His immediate predecessor, Archibald Campbell Tait, became Archbishop of Canterbury in 1868; Edward White Benson, one of only four Assistant-Masters whom he appointed during his eight years as Headmaster, became Archbishop of Canterbury in 1882, while Goulburn was still Dean of Norwich. It was to Benson, then Chancellor of Lincoln Cathedral, that, in 1876, he dedicated one of his major publications: 'The Ancient Sculptures of Norwich Cathedral'. And Goulburn's successor as Headmaster was Frederick Temple, who went to Canterbury in 1896. Goulburn

---
4. Ditto, p. 16.
5. I am indebted to J. B. Hope Simpson, *Rugby Since Arnold* (Macmillan 1967), for information about Rugby School in Goulburn's time.

found a remarkable body of Assistant-Masters at Rugby. Four became Headmasters of other leading Public Schools; one of them later became Bishop of Calcutta; another Dean of Westminster; two became University Professors, one of whom went to be Principal of United College, St Andrew's, and then Professor of Poetry at Oxford.

Goulburn was never completely happy as a Schoolmaster, often wishing that he had remained in Parochial work. His rather conservative convictions and the moderate ritualism he introduced in the Chapel (he was Chaplain as well) were considered to be the reason for falling numbers. He deeply regretted this reduction, because it also meant a reduction in the salaries of his Assistant-Masters (based as they were upon the number of boys in the School). Arnold, in 1842, had left a School of 362 (more than, theoretically, he wished to have); Tait left Goulburn about 400 (and large classes). By 1857, numbers had dropped to 316. Nevertheless, Goulburn made his own positive contribution to the School. He was able to have smaller classes; the academic standards of the School continued, and probably increased; for in the year before he resigned almost all the Open Awards at Oxford and Cambridge were won by Rugbeians, and numbers were climbing to 365.

His two predecessors, to some extent, excluded unpromising boys. Goulburn thought that a Public School should do its best for all, encouraging the dull boy. There had been virtually no Science taught in the School since 1834. Goulburn appointed Berdmore Compton (who in 1899 wrote his 'Memoir') to be teacher of Natural Science, and he made it a regular subject in 1851. He offered to employ, at his own expense, an Architect to design a Natural Science Room; he improved the Chapel, building a South Transept, to balance the North Transept, and removed the flat ceiling to give greater height. The Organ Gallery, which had blocked the West Window, was also removed and built on the North side in 1855; an ante-Chapel was erected, with windows presented by Goulburn. Shortly after coming to Rugby, he had built, at his own expense, a new Boarding House; and, in 1854, he had presented a new field to the School, mainly to be used for Cricket. Strangely enough, in spite of the criticism he received as Headmaster, he looked back, in later years, to the Rugby period as among the best years of his life. He always enjoyed meeting Old Rugbeians, some of whom wrote to him, or called at the Deanery in Norwich, or asked him to be Godfather to their children; and, occasionally, he returned to the School, by invitation, to preach. During this Rugby period, he had also given the Bampton Lectures ('The Resurrection of the Body') for 1850; published A *Manual of Confirmation* in three parts in 1855 (which reached its 11th, Edition in 1883), and *The Book of Rugby School* in 1856. He resigned in 1857.

Parish Priest

Goulburn returned to parochial work as Incumbent of Quebec Chapel (later known as the Church of the Annunication, St Marylebone), close to Seymour Street, where his father lived. He and Julia lived at 21, Sussex Gardens, Hyde Park, which would appear to be their own house, because they did not vacate it when he resigned from Quebec. 'One of the foremost preaching positions in the Church of England', says Berdmore Compton. Writing to his Aunt Louisa, he commented: 'Quebec Chapel is all very well, but a little *popular preacherish*, which neither of us quite like'.[6] During this period he became a Prebendary of St Paul's Cathedral, and a Chaplain to the Queen.

Vicar of St John's, Paddington

In 1859, the Incumbent of Paddington Parish Church (St James') offered him the Parish of St John's. He wrote to his Cousin, Louisa Thomas (daughter of his Aunt Louisa): 'Mine will be a wealthy district; tho' not as wealthy or as aristocratic as the congregation I am leaving ... but the work is heavy, and being studious, and loving my leisure, I cannot say I *coveted* it ... I shall stalk about as proud as a peacock with three Curates ... there are 10,000 people – 4,500 poor. The chief parishioner (tho' he never comes to the Church), the celebrated A. J. B. Beresford Hope'.[7] (Beresford Hope *was* a strong Churchman; he had founded St Augustine's Missionary College, Canterbury in 1848, and played a large part in building All Saints' Church, Margaret Street in 1849). It is during this Incumbency that the first of the Diaries we possess (1861) begins.

Goulburn *did* have an equally wealthy and generous member of the congregation of St John's – William Gibbs, who had made his fortune from guano. His London house was 15 Hyde Park Gate; his country estate was Tyntesfield, near Bristol. He liked

---

6. Letter dated March 17th, 1858, lent by Mr Bryan Gipps.
7. Letter written from his London Club, probably in 1859, lent by Mr Bryan Gipps.

Goulburn, and he wanted to build, and largely furnish, a Chapel of Ease within the Parish. Goulburn entered with enthusiasm into his project, and together they spent many hours planning the building which became St Michael and All Angels. He funded other projects within the Parish, and continued his generosity to Goulburn after he had become Dean of Norwich. For example, he gave £1000 to St John's, Timberhill in 1873; and, in 1874, £500 to increase the endowment of St James', Pockthorpe, and repair its Vicarage – both Dean and Chapter Livings. The Goulburns were often invited to Tyntesfield, which had an Oratory in which the Daily Services were said. Among a wide range of gifts, William Gibbs was the donor of the Chapel of Keble College, Oxford; his sons gave the Hall and Library. It is more than likely that, when Mr Gibbs died, he left Goulburn a legacy, for, when Mrs Gibbs died some years later, in 1887, she left him £500.

Augusta

Goulburn was very fond of children, but he and Julia, to their great regret, had none of their own. He loved to give presents to the children of his relations and friends, and, when he came to Norwich, to the children of his Residentiary and Minor Canons, and others living in the Close. The children of the Close were often invited to parties at the Deanery, and also felt free to call of their own accord. Julia was involved with Sunday School classes, with the Jenny Lind Infirmary for sick children, and, after its formation in 1875, with the G.F.S. She often entertained the members of these groups in the Deanery. While the Dean, deeply involved in the work of the Cathedral Choir School, organised parties and fireworks and outings for his Choirboys.

One of Julia's step-brothers, Stephen, was Rector of the family Living of Aynhoe. In 1838 he had married Lady Fanny Hay, daughter of the 15th Earl of Erroll (an ancient Scottish family in Perthshire, going back to the 1st Earl in the 12th Century). They had no children until, on July 18th, 1853, a daughter, Augusta Emma, was born. But, a few weeks later, on August 28th, her mother died. When Augusta was nine, her father, Stephen, after a very short illness, died on August 9th, 1862, while the Goulburns were on holiday – and drinking the waters – at Homburg in Germany. Augusta was now an orphan, and homeless. She had visited the Goulburns from time to time, and, soon after returning, they offered to take her into their home, to be brought up and treated as their own daughter. Berdmore Compton says that they 'adopted' her, but the entry in the Diary for March 7th, 1864 reads: 'Joined Robert at Proctor's at 3.15; there made myself guardian "ad litem" to Gussey, and became guarantee for Robert in administering to Gussy's mother's will'. (Robert Cartwright, a Barrister, was another step-brother of Julia's). Stephen appears to have left debts, and little, if any, money, but Augusta had been provided for by her mother. She had already come to live with the Goulburns at 21 Sussex Gardens, on February 9th, 1863, and, in every possible respect, she became their loved and loving daughter. Goulburn, who had a great liking for nicknames, called her, variously, 'Gussie', 'Little Dustkins', 'Little Buskins', etc., even when she grew up, and was married, and had children of her own.

When Augusta was 26, she married, on January 29th, 1880, a relative of the Goulburn side of the family, Gerard de Visme Thomas, of Eyhorne House, Hollingborne, Kent. He was the son of Goulburn's cousin, Louisa (nee Goldsmid), and was five years older than Augusta. From time to time, he had quite serious illnesses, about which Goulburn expressed concern in the Diaries. He had been at Harrow and Magdalene College, Oxford; he became a Barrister of the Inner Temple in 1875; a J.P. for Kent; was employed in Foreign Civil Service Commissions; and was an Attache to Maj.-Gen. Frederick Goldsmid's Special Mission to Persia. He and Augusta had seven children. The eldest, Louise Fanny de Visme Thomas, born in 1880, died in infancy, and was buried at St Mark's Churchyard, Lakenham, Norwich. The other six, four girls and two boys, born between 1882 and 1891, and who died in the 1950s and 1960s, were all buried at Hollingbourne. The eldest surviving daughter, and the two sons, married, but the latter left no sons to carry on the name of Thomas. Gerard died in 1900, aged 52; but Augusta lived until February 2nd, 1949, aged 95. The widow of one of Augusta's sons died in 1994, aged 96.

Stephen was succeeded as Rector of Aynhoe by Julia's youngest *full* brother, Frederick, who, for the previous 18 years had been Vicar, and Rural Dean, of Oakley, Bucks. He was to be Rector of Aynhoe for the next 44 years, dying in 1906 at the age of 88. He and Goulburn had been born in the same year (1818), and they were particularly close friends, Goulburn always referring to him as 'the Dean', probably because he had been a Rural Dean for so long. Later, in Norwich, the Goulburns appointed a German lady to be Governess to Augusta. Formerly, she had been a governess in the house of Goulburn's friend, William Alexander, then

Bishop of Derry (husband of Frances, the Hymn writer, and later to be Archbishop of Armagh). The Alexanders had recommended her, and she always said that Goulburn was the kindest of men, and his life the best commentary upon his favourite subject, 'Holiness'. Long after Augusta no longer needed a governess, Fraulein was always a welcome visitor at the Deanery in Norwich, spending many a holiday there.

Dean of Norwich
At the beginning of March 1861, the rumour spread, and was even published, that Goulburn had been offered the Deanery of Exeter. Although he himself denied it, congratulations kept flowing in, to his great embarrassment, for the next few weeks. Then Goulburn heard that the Bishop of Exeter (Henry Phillpotts) had objected to him. Finally, in mid-June, it was announced that the new Dean of Exeter would be Charles Ellicott, Professor of New Testament Exigesis at King's College, London, who, two years later, became Bishop of Gloucester and Bristol.

On November 4th, 1866, Goulburn was offered the Deanery of Norwich, on the death of the Hon. George Pellew, who had been Dean for 38 years. He was installed on December 4th; but he then returned to London to make arrangements for the move to Norwich, and also to make arrangements with his Curates about the care of St John's, Paddington, the Incumbency of which he retained officially until June 4th, 1867, paying his Curates' stipends until then. He had delayed his resignation in order to facilitate his successor, Emilius Bayley. Being now Dean of Norwich, he was also ex officio, a Member of Convocation: and so, while still in London, was able to attend the meeting of Convocation from February 12th to 15th.

The move to take up residence in Norwich was on Wednesday, February 27th, The Goulburns arrived by train about 4 p.m. 'the house was very nice and comfortable; of course, a bundle of letters, one from the Bp. asking me to preach at his Ordination ... Can. Heaviside came in before dinner, and put me up to several things.'

(a). *The Chapter*
He was fortunate to find a friendly and learned Chapter, who welcomed him cordially as a person and as a fellow Academic. Two of them, J. W. L. Heaviside and Charles Robinson, were to be with him for the whole of his 23 years as Dean.

In order of seniority, the four Residentiary Canons were:

(1) Professor Adam Sedgwick, B.A., LL.D, F.R.S. had already been a Residentiary Canon for 33 years. He was a very famous Geologist; he had been Woodwardian Professor of Geology at Cambridge since 1818; President of the Geological Society; President of the British Association; and he had received Honorary Doctorates from Oxford and Cambridge. He found it difficult to bear the modest innovations which Goulburn began to introduce. The idea of a weekly Holy Communion shocked him. He continued to read the Lessons from his Stall, instead of from the Lectern, as Goulburn had asked the Canons to do. Goulburn writes: 'He was exceedingly narrow in his religious opinions. I do not think I ever came across a man so intellectually powerful, and so very highly cultivated, who was equally so'. Nevertheless, Sedgwick remained friendly and loyal in general to Goulburn and the Chapter. In January 1873, hearing that Sedgwick was too ill to travel to Norwich to the Chapter Meeting, Goulburn took the Chapter to Cambridge, and held it in Sedgwick's rooms in Trinity College. A week later, Sedgwick died at the age of almost 88. A stained glass window, the gift of Goulburn, was placed in St Luke's Chapel in his memory, and on the brass tablet below it an inscription in Latin, written by Edward White Benson (then Chancellor of Lincoln Cathedral, but ten years later to be Archbishop of Canterbury). In order to give more light in the Chapel, the window was later removed to the South Transept, and is the top centre window above the door. The brass tablet remains in place.

(2) George Archdall, D.D. (also known as Archdall-Gratwicke) had been master of Emmanuel College, Cambridge since 1835, and a Residentiary Canon of Norwich for 25 years. There appeared to have been some difficulty about his 'residence' just after Goulburn arrived, and in August 1867, Archdall resigned.

(3) James William Lucas Heaviside, M.A., was the only one of the four Canons then residing permanently in the Close. He had been a Fellow and Tutor of Sidney Sussex College, Cambridge; Professor of Mathematics and Natural

Philosophy at the Imperial Service College; an examiner in the same two subjects at London University and, later, for the Council of Military Education; and Tutor in Mathematics to HRH the Duke of Connaught. He had become a Residentiary Canon in 1860, and was more involved in local activities outside the Close than any other member of the Chapter. He was a Governor (as Goulburn also became) of King Edward VI Grammar School, Norwich; a Trustee of the Norman Endowed School; a Charity Trustee; the first Chairman of the Norwich School Board; and also involved in many Charitable and Benevolent Institutions. He was a main link between Cathedral and City. The Prince of Wales, on one occasion, invited him to Sandringham for a week-end, and to preach in Sandringham Church; and, on November 3rd, 1874, the Prince dined at Heaviside's house in the Close to celebrate the Canon's birthday. He was also 'an admirable man of business', and relieved Goulburn of much of the secular work inevitably connected with the Cathedral. He was the ideal person to be Goulburn's Vice-Dean. And when the Dean retired in 1889, he wrote to Heaviside: 'Your friendship, counsel, and affection have been so great a support to me during my stay in Norwich that I really do not think that I could have stood my ground without them'.

(4) Charles Robinson, M.A., D.D., became Master of St Catherine's College, Cambridge, in 1861, and by virtue of the Mastership, also a Residentiary Canon of Norwich. He made a point of residing in Norwich as much as possible, and being fully involved in Chapter affairs. When Mrs Robinson died of pleurisy in Cambridge early in January 1882, the burial was in Norwich; and, on the following Sunday (8th) Goulburn preached a Memorial Sermon for her entitled 'The Spheres and Duties of Christian Women', which was printed in full in the *Norfolk Chronicle* of January 14th. The Choir sang the Anthem, 'The souls of the righteous are in the hands of God'; the Bishop gave the Blessing; and the 'Dead March' in Saul was played on the organ as the congregation left. Goulburn was always very attentive to, and caring for, those who were ill, or had been bereaved. When he had heard from Cambridge about Margaret Robinson's death on the 4th, he wrote immediately to 'the

Master' that morning, and then another letter in the afternoon. He spent the whole of the 5th preparing the Sermon, and still worked at it next morning. On the 6th at 12.45, he, Archdeacon Nevill, and Canon Heaviside went to the Railway Station to await the arrival of the funeral. Afterwards he took Robinson and his two sons to the Deanery for luncheon, where they remained until 4 p.m. And, on the Sunday evening, he wrote another letter of sympathy to Canon Robinson.

With the resignation of Archdall in August 1867, another Canon had to be appointed. This was to be:

(5) John Majorbanks Nisbet, M.A. He had been Rector of Deal (1856–61); Vicar of Ramsgate (1861–67); and Chaplain to Archbishop Sumner. Now, in 1867, he had just become Rector of St Giles-in-the-Field, London. When not in residence in Norwich, he lived at 16 Bedford Square, London. He remained as a Residentiary Canon until his death in 1892.

And when Professor Sedgwick died in 1873, the new Residentiary Canon was:

(6) Henry Ralph Nevill, M.A. He had been Curate of Gt Yarmouth (1848–50); of St Martin-in-the-Fields, London (1850–51); Priest-in-Charge of St Mark's, Lakenham, Norwich (1851–58); and Vicar of Gt Yarmouth (1858–73); both of these last two parishes were Dean and Chapter Livings. He had been an Honorary Canon since 1860; he became a Residentiary Canon in 1873, and, in the following year, Archdeacon of Norfolk as well. In addition, from 1881 to 1884, he was Vicar of St Peter Mancroft.

So from 1873 until his resignation in 1889, Goulburn had his team of four Residentiary Canons, two of whom lived permanently in the Close.

(b) *The Place of a Cathedral*
For a number of years, Goulburn had been a Parish Priest. Now, at the age of 49, he was a Dean of a Cathedral. He saw a clear distinction between the two, and between the function of a

Parish Church, and that of a Cathedral. The two were complementary to each other, and the two, with their separate roles, were necessary to carry out the Church's mission.

In 1869, the two Archbishops sent a letter to all Deans of Cathedrals in England and Wales. It followed a meeting which the Archbishops had had with a large number of the Deans (Goulburn had not been able to go). The object of the Meeting had been to consider what improvements could be made to the Cathedral system. The Archbishops now wanted each Dean to tell them what changes he may consider to be of great importance for his particular Cathedral, and also what the views of the Chapter were.

Goulburn had strong views on this subject, and he replied to the Archbishops with an Open Letter. The Christian Ministry, and every building for Christian Worship, has a twofold object, 'a face towards God and a face towards man'. Neither Parish Church nor Cathedral is exempt from this twofold object. But, he said, it is 'natural and reasonable that there should be ministers and Churches more particularly devoted to the one, and also ministers and Churches more particularly devoted to the other'. Cathedrals should be devoted to the cultivation of worship in its highest form; they should lead the way for other churches in the perfection of music and song; and they should be places for meditation and deep study. In this respect, he said, it was very important that the right people should be appointed to the various offices, so that there should be no abuse of such privileges.

He said that he was not necessarily against reform of the Cathedral system; but that he was against it *at this particular time*. For the present, he was strongly in favour of continually improving and perfecting the Cathedral system *as it existed*. And he believed in being painstaking in the choice of people for Cathedral offices, whether of a junior or of a senior nature. The Diaries contain many instances of such thoroughly vetted appointments.

He ends his letter by listing eight directions in which he thinks improvements to the present Cathedral system should aim. These are listed in Appendix 7.

(c) *The Building*
Goulburn wanted the building in his care to be a fit and seemly place for the worship of God, and an attractive place for those who came to it. In 1867 the Cathedral was in a considerable state of dilapidation. In April, the well-known Architect, George

Gilbert Scott (later Sir George) was asked to give an estimate of the *essential* work to be done, and he gave a figure of £12,000 (probably not less than £240,000 at today's values). Goulburn was faced with a gigantic task and one which he would only partially be able to accomplish. Throughout the years he was in Norwich, the thanks of the Chapter kept recurring for work done at the Dean's expense. It is calculated that he spent about £10,000 of his own money on Cathedral restoration, largely the earnings from the books he wrote.

But first, he must do something immediately for the congregations who came to the Services. The Cathedral was cold for them (and he was only too conscious of this himself). He intended to increase the number of Services – three on Sunday (sometimes four on Festivals) instead of two; more frequent Celebrations of Holy Communion; special Courses in Advent and Lent; and then there were the daily Services and special occasions. Many Services lasted for two hours, or more. Sermons could be up to an hour. So it was decided that the building should have a hot water heating system, costing the considerable sum of £1,100. The Revd B. J. Armstrong wrote in his Diary for Sunday, November 12th, 1871 (when he was staying with the Bishop for the weekend): 'A clear frosty morning, but the Cathedral well warmed'.[8] At the same time, £200 was to be spent on 'fittings' in the Nave which would benefit the congregation. The doors were to be kept open on weekdays between the Services for admission and private devotions; a corner of the west end of the building was to be converted into School for the Choristers, and prizes given to encourage their learning. Goulburn was appalled at the building in which the Choir School was at present housed, 'a poor mean cottage on the way to the ferry'. It was not until 1951 that the Cathedral Choir School was incorporated into the Norwich School (King Edward VI's).

He then began to tackle the generally dilapidated state of the building, an ongoing task for all his years in Norwich. St Luke's Chapel was restored, so that the congregation of St Mary-in-the-Marsh could hold its Services there again. The ancient Parish Church of St Mary, which had stood on the south side of the Close, had been pulled down in the reign of Queen Elizabeth I, and the Cathedral authorities had allowed the parishioners to use this Chapel. The ceiling of the Nave had been covered with a

---

8. H. B. J. Armstrong (Ed.), *A Norfolk Diary*, G. G. Harrap & Co. Ltd., 1949, p. 163,

thick yellow wash, blotting out the ancient colouring. This was removed at a cost of just over £1,000; the Apse was restored; as was the Jesus Chapel which had been in great disrepair. On Friday, April 18th, 1873, Goulburn writes in his Diary: 'After Mg. Service ... went with the Pin into the Jesus Chapel to see the relics of an Early English (plaister) reredos, which have been discovered there by Bensly'. At his own expense, he restored the Reliquary Chapel. On August 6th, 1873, there was a long discussion at the Chapter Meeting on how far the Cloisters should be restored, The meeting was adjourned to the following Friday, when the Diary states: 'Ordered restoration of the Upper Arcade, a new roof (oak and lead) for the vacant space over what was once the Master's house at a cost of £705; and I ordered the restoration of the old refectory staircase at a cost of £61. 17s ... also agreed to go to Q.A.B. for a loan for Nevill's house on security of Corporate Property'. (This needed some £600 work of repair). To the east of the Cathedral, Goulburn had excavations carried out to determine the exact foundations of the Norman Lady Chapel. It is here that the present St Saviour's Chapel was built in the 1930s. Permanent desks were placed in the Nave for the Choir Boys; Goulburn gave a present of the High Altar Rails; and Julia a Choir Organ and the Cathedral Clock with its chimes. Outside work was done to strengthen the buttresses on the North side; and there were repairs to the Erpingham Gate. In December 1881, the foundations of the Campanili, or separate Bell Tower, opposite, I think, 71, The Close, and abolished in the 16th Century were uncovered.[9] Towards the end of 1883, after consulting a London engineer, it was discovered that considerable immediate repairs were needed to the Cathedral Tower.

(d) *The Pulpits*
It is highly appropriate that Goulburn's name should be linked with the *two* pulpits in the Cathedral; it rarely happens that a Cathedral receives the gifts of two pulpits within six weeks of each other. The carved oak Pulpit in the Presbytery, designed by Mr J. P. Seddon, FRIBA, was given as a memorial of Goulburn's 23 years as Dean. On May 14th, 1891, two years after he had retired, he returned to be the first to preach from it. The occasion was the annual Diocesan Anniversary of S.P.G. The newspaper account

---

9. See A. G. G. Thurlow, M.A., 'The Bells of Norwich Cathedral' in Vol. 29 (Centenary Vol.) of *Norfolk Archaeology*, p. 89.

says that 'there was an enormous assembly'. Some six weeks later, the stone Pulpit in the Nave, a gift *from* Goulburn, was formally dedicated. He himself was unable to be present. On his behalf, Mr R. H. Carpenter, F.S.A., one of the designers of the pulpit, made the formal presentation. Canon Robinson (now Vice-Dean) accepted it on behalf of the Dean and Chapter. The Mayor (Edward Wild) – the Deputy-Mayor was also present – spoke on behalf of the City. Finally, Canon Hinds Howell spoke on behalf of the Honorary Canons. The Dedication Service then followed, the Revd G. W. Barrett, who had been Precentor for the past 14 years, intoning the prayers. The cost of the Nave Pulpit was almost £1000.

Goulburn had been a preacher very much in demand, both within and beyond the boundaries of the Diocese, and he had to refuse more invitations than he was ever able to accept. Quite often, while at Norwich, he preached in other Cathedrals – St Paul's, Peterborough, Chichester, Salisbury, Wells. Frederick Hibgame, writing his 'Recollections' said: 'Dean Goulburn was the most beautiful reader I ever heard in my life, and was admirable in every way'.[10] Unfortunately, his singing voice was not so good, and as he wanted to intone the Services when he came to Norwich, he spent much of his first year having lessons from Dr Zechariah Buck, the Cathedral Organist. Buck had spent virtually the whole of his life at the Cathedral, as Choir-boy from the age of nine, Assistant-Organist from the age of 19, and Organist from the age of 21 for a further 58 years. Goulburn spent a very long time preparing his Sermons, writing them, correcting them, revising them, until he was satisfied that they were the best he could do. Most were written in full, but at times he also preached from notes, and a few were extempore. Indoors or outdoors, in the garden, or when alone on his long walks around Norwich, he would 'meditate' a Sermon (that is, if not reading *The Times* as he walked). If he felt it necessary to refresh his memory or increase his knowledge, he would use Biblical Commentaries, or read the relevant books. He was often his own critic, especially if, after delivering the Sermon, he realised that it was too long. He appreciated good Sermons from other preachers, and said so, and commended them. As was the custom of the time, he had many of his Sermons printed as little booklets, and sent them to other clergy or lay people (as occasion offered),

---

10. F. T. Hibgame, *Recollections of Norwich Fifty Years Ago*, p. 21.

or had them on sale for one penny. In return he received the Sermons of others. Often his published books or booklets went into several editions. On January 8th, 1874, he heard from his London publisher, Rivingtons, 'that 3000 of the *Gospel of the Childhood* had sold, and 2000 of the *Catholic Church* – gave instructions for new edition of former' (5000 of each had been printed). His *An Introduction to the Devotional Study of the Holy Scriptures* had reached its 10th edition by 1878. His Sermons and Theological writings must have reached a large number of readers, both at home and abroad.

(e) *The Three Major Writings*
The Revd Henry Symonds, M.A., had been Precentor and Minor Canon of the Cathedral since 1844. Like Goulburn, he was a graduate of Oxford, probably also in Classics, and was only three years younger. A common interest, and a common ability to translate Latin made them close colleagues for at least the next twelve years, even though Symonds became Rector of Tivetshall in 1874. April 30th, 1867, is the first entry in the Diary in which Goulburn refers to him as the 'Pinseter' (did it originate with a Choir boy getting 'Precentor' wrong?), and he continues to call him this until eventually he abbreviates it to the 'Pin'.

On May 3rd, 1867, he went with Symonds to examine the contents of the Dean and Chapter Library (it was then, and until 1913, in the Audit Room, adjacent to the house of the Organist, Dr Buck). By June 12th they had begun to work on a card description of the Cathedral for visitors; and over a week later they went round checking on what they had written. But, more significantly, Goulburn, that afternoon, wrote a long letter to Professor Sedgwick about the Bosses. Next day he brought Burgess, a professional photographer, to consider the possibility of photographing the Bosses; and, by June 27th, they had decided that they should be photographed. And then, rather oddly, the Diaries go silent about the Bosses until the beginning of January 1869. Events in the intervening period may be the cause of this. Goulburn was away from Norwich for long periods; he had an accident on October 7th, 1867, which incapacitated him for at least 4½ months; and then his father, after a long illness, died at the end of August 1868. On January 4th, 1869, intense interest in the Bosses revives. Scaffolding had been erected to remove the brown-wash with which the stone vaulting had been coated in the early part of the Century; and this gave Goulburn the idea of retaining it to examine and photograph the Bosses. A new photographer was appointed – Mr Sawyer of Sawyer and Bird. So began the intensive study of the Nave Bosses by Goulburn and Symonds, which resulted, in 1876, in the publication of a huge volume on *The Ancient Sculptures in the Roof of Norwich Cathedral*; and, with this, was combined *A History of the See of Norwich from its foundation to the Dissolution of the Monasteries* by Goulburn and Henry Hailstone, Esq., Jun. This volume was dedicated to: The Revd Edward White Benson, D.D., Chancellor of Lincoln Cathedral, Goulburn's former assistant-master at Rugby, and, in 1883, to become Archbishop of Canterbury.

When he was recovering from his accident of October 1867, Goulburn conceived the idea of translating from Latin the letters and sermons of the Founder of Norwich Cathedral, and writing his biography. Almost straightaway he and Symonds embarked upon this task of translation. Every moment they could seize at any time of the day, either together or separately, they worked at it. Eventually, in 1878, two volumes of 'The Life, Letters and Sermons of Bishop Herbert de Losinga' were published, and dedicated to the Bishop of Norwich, the Honourable and Right Reverend John Thomas Pelham 'who by Simplicity and Godly Sincerity, Fervent Piety, and Labours, unostentatious and unwearied, in the oversight of his large Diocese, has illustrated the See which Herbert de Losinga founded. These Literary Remains of his Predecessor are, by his kind permission, Inscribed, with Sentiments of Veneration for his Office, and Esteem and Affection for his Person.'

Goulburn's third major work, published in 1892, three years after he had retired, was the Biography of his friend, John William Burgon, Dean of Chichester 1876–88. Burgon was an old fashioned High Churchman and writer, 'famous for his support of a long series of lost causes'. Goulburn visited him in Chichester from time to time, and for many years, had been accumulating notes and material.

(f)   *The Bishop*

John Thomas Pelham was a very tall and commanding personality, and a hard-working Bishop. The Pelhams had come over from Normany with the Conquerer, and had lived in Sussex for at least 700 years. It is unusual for the Incumbent of a small country Parish (Bergh Apton) for 15 years, to return to the same Diocese five years later as its Bishop. But Pelham certainly had the advantage of knowing his Diocese and many of the Clergy right from the beginning. Throughout his Episcopate of 36 years, he spent many days and weekends in the Rural Deaneries with his Clergy, who were very much aware of their Bishop's energy and drive. He was a strong Evangelical, but with a fair and tolerant outlook.

Goulburn came to Norwich determined that his relationship with his Bishop was always going to be good. The Bishop came to the Cathedral Services regularly, and Goulburn made a point of keeping him fully informed of any changes or alterations he hoped to make. When the Dean wanted to introduce *Hymns Ancient and Modern* (first published in 1861) as the Cathedral's regular hymn book, he hears that the Bishop had expressed disapproval of it, so he dropped the proposal. But in February 1874, he *did* introduce the S.P.C.K. Hymnbook. However, *Hymns Ancient and Modern* did eventually come into use in the Cathedral. In December 1883, Colonel Phillips, Commanding Officer of the Regiment then stationed in Norwich asked if he might present Hymn Books to the Cathedral for the use of the soldiers. ' "The Ancient and Modern", he said, was the authorised hymnbook for the army'. When Goulburn wanted a Processional Hymn at one of the Diocesan Choirs' Festivals in the Cathedral, the Bishop objected, so Goulburn cancelled the Procession – but, later on we *do* find processions taking place – As Bishop and Dean got to know each other better over the years, an atmosphere of mutual respect and acceptance of each others ways developed. On Sunday, February 8th, 1874, at 8 a.m., Goulburn records in his Diary: 'we sang for the first time the "Sanctus" and the "Gloria" – I fear the Bishop did not like it'. The Dean respected the Bishop highly, but, just now and then, he did find it difficult to suppress a very slight ripple of irritation: 'Oh, what want of effusiveness in the good Bishop's character!'. And writing to Canon Heaviside after he had announced his resignation, he said: 'I have lived next door to our Bishop for 22 years in the most perfectly good relations, concurring in many of his views, venerating his goodness, and trying to imitate his example.'

(g)   *Arthur Penryn Stanley*

When Goulburn's appointment to Rugby School had been announced, a member of staff wrote to his sister: 'Tait is going to leave us in a few days now. Then we shall have the *pleasure* of seeing Goulburn, for I believe from all accounts he is a very mild fellow.'[11] Mild, tolerant and caring he was for his very difficult and aggravating father (who died in 1868). On the other hand, if he felt strongly about something, he would firmly maintain his position and fight for it to the bitter end.

Arthur Penryn Stanley and Goulburn had been lifelong friends since their undergraduate days at Oxford, in spite of very deep theological differences. Stanley had become Dean of Westminster two years before Goulburn had gone to Norwich, and he died in 1881 of erysipelas, at the age of 66. He was small, learned, active in all things for the good of the Church. He exercised a wide influence, and was a charming personality. Stanley's theology was 'liberal'; Goulburn's of a more 'orthodox' type. In 1872, Stanley was appointed a Select Preacher of the University of Oxford. Goulburn decided that *he* had to resign his appointment as a Select Preacher. Writing to the Vice-Chancellor, he said: 'If the pulpit of the University is to be turned into a vehicle for conveying to our youth a nerveless religion, without the sinew and bone of doctrine, a religion which can hardly be called faith so much as a mere Christianised morality, I, for one, must decline to stand there'. Then he wrote privately to Stanley, telling him of his resignation, and expressing the hope that this would not interrupt their friendship. Stanley replied: 'Many thanks for your kind letter, kind and cordial as always. You may be assured that the differences of opinion, which we have discussed ever since the days when we travelled together from Geneva to Athens, have never diminished my regard for you and, I trust, never will'. And at the end of the letter he says: 'I cannot refrain from adding the pleasure it gives me to think that what you write and preach has a lasting and edifying effect on those to whom I have no access, just as probably there are those to whom I have access, from whom you produce no result.'[12]

Goulburn was very moved by Stanley's death. He wrote in the Diary on July 19, 1881: 'The sad news of Stanley's death appeared in "the Times" this morning – I can think of nothing else ... I can't get Stanley's death off my mind'. On the Sunday after, and the day before his funeral at Westminster Abbey, the Canon-in-residence, Canon Robinson, should have been the preacher. Goulburn writes on July 21st: 'After Bkst. went to the Master,

11. J. B. Hope Simpson, *Rugby Since Arnold* (Macmillan 1868), p. 22.
12. Letter from A. P. Stanley (Dean of Westminster) dated December 2nd, 1872. In a Collection of 32 Letters written to Goulburn by leading Ecclesiastics given to the Editor by Mr Bryan Gipps, and now in the Library of the Dean and Chapter of Norwich.

and, on his expressing a wish that I shd. do so, I consented to preach the Sermon next Sunday afternoon, mentioning Stanley'. In a Sermon of almost 4,400 words, Goulburn spent the first part expounding, theologically, the text, 'Whom gave himself for us'; the next part of it eulogising Stanley: 'No one shall say that one of his oldest friends, as I claim to be, witheld from his surpassing abilities and great moral worth that tribute of affectionate admiration, which is indisputably their due. His intellectual gifts were as varied as they were brilliant ... And then there was that intense vivacity and interest in actual life ... His high moral endowments were hardly inferior to his intellectual. Never perhaps did a man from boyhood upwards have a conscience more void of offence. The stern virtues of honesty, integrity, and love of truth, were in him blended with a playful affectionateness of disposition, which gave his character a grace and charm quite irresistible.' And then Goulburn, mentioning Stanley only once, went on to expound orthodox Christianity.

The Sermon was published and raised a whirlwind of hostile, as well as favourable criticism. Goulburn was accused of being harsh and heartless; Stanley's friends were offended by Goulburn's denunciation of his theology; J. W. Burgon, on the other hand, objected to Goulburn's appreciation and praise of Stanley's personality. But William Alexander (then Bishop of Derry, later to be Primate of the Church of Ireland, and an occasional Special Preacher in Norwich Cathedral) said that nothing could have excelled the Sermon. Goulburn's own comment was: 'Being in the pulpit, my conscience would not really allow me to prophesy nothing but smooth things'. Nine years later Goulburn wrote to a relation offering him a copy of Stanley's *Life and Letters*: 'To me they are intensely interesting from the circumstances of my association with him in early days. Heretic as he was, I yet have a soft part in my heart for him. He was the cleverest little chap in the world, and the most socially agreeable. It grieved me in later life to protest against his grievous unsoundness as a theologian, if, indeed, he can be called a theologian at all.'

(h) *The Lynn and Fakenham Railway*
Goulburn was a frequent railway traveller and he enjoyed going by train. But he referred to the Lynn and Fakenham line as 'this horrid railway' – and justifiably so, because it wanted to run a line through the Close! Berdmore Compton says that it also planned to demolish the Ethelbert Gate, but Goulburn does not

specifically state this in the Diaries. Between January 1st, 1881 and January 28th, 1883, he waged the greatest campaign of his career to stop it – and only just succeeded.

The details of the campaign may be read in the Diaries between these dates. On January 1st, 1881, Goulburn received a plan showing the possible route of a proposed railway line for the Lynn and Fakenham Company through the Close. On the 13th, an official of the Great Eastern Railway Company asked him to sign a memorial against this proposed line, which he did. At a Chapter Meeting on March 25th, it was 'agreed to thank G.E.R. for their helping us to exclude a railway from the Close'. And that was thought to be the end of the matter.

Eight months later, on Sunday, November 20th, Goulburn writes in his Diary: 'Heard to my great grief that the railway threatens again the invasion of the Close'. And so the battle began. On December 1st, Goulburn and Heaviside went to London to see a Mr Parkes and Lord Claude Hamilton at Liverpool Street and 'agreed to join the G.E.R. Company in opposing, we not to bear any expense beyond £200'. After once again getting the plan of the route, Goulburn went to the Mayor of Norwich (William Hunter), and asked him 'to feel the pulse of the Town Council about the proposed Railway'.

In February 1882, the original petition was revised and re-adapted to the altered circumstances. The Bishop wished the Dean and Chapter success, but declined to sign. Goulburn 'felt much depressed'. He and Dr Bensley, the chapter Clerk, drew up a letter to send to the Newspapers. And then the campaign really gathered momentum. On February 16th, Goulburn left Norwich at 7.30 a.m. for London, and noticed in the *Eastern Daily Press* that the 'Lynn and Fakenham Bill' was read in the Commons for the first time the previous night. Again he saw the G.E.R. officials; also Sir John Mowbray, M.P., Chairman of the House of Commons Committee of Selection and Committee of Standing Orders, at the Ecclesiastical Commissioners; Mr Knight Watson and Mr Milman of the Society of Antiquaries; and A. J. B. Beresford Hope, M.P. and prominent Churchman. For the next six or seven weeks Goulburn largely commuted between Norwich and London, seeing everybody he could think of who might be helpful, often several times, and writing to a widening circle of people.

On Monday, February 20th, he called on Sir Stafford North-cote, M.P., Conservative Leader of the Opposition in the

Commons; and on Lord Salisbury, Leader of the Opposition in the Lords (and former Chairman of the Gt Eastern Railway). Next day he met Mr Parkes and Lord Claude Hamilton, with a group of M.P.s at Liverpool Street, to plan the opposition to the Second Reading in the Commons. On the 27th, he met Mr John Walter, M.P., Chief proprietor of *The Times*, who promised that his letter on the subject would be published. Back in Norwich (while still writing numerous letters to London) he drafted a letter to send to all M.P.s of Cathedral Cities, and to the Cathedrals Establishment Commissioners. On March 7th he wrote to the Prime Minister (Gladstone) – and received an almost immediate reply – and to all the Deans of Cathedrals, and to the Institute of Architects.

On Saturday, March 11th he was back in London again. 'I walked down to Downing Street and left my cards at Mr Gladstone's; neither he nor Mrs G. were at home, or I shd. have gone in'. On Monday (13th) he 'prepared questions for Parke's Council of War', and saw a number of M.P.s about the strategy to be adopted. On March 22nd, there was a 'Leader' in the *Standard* against the 'Lynn and Fakenham Bill'. He wrote to Canon Robinson, asking him to organise a Petition from the Cambridge Heads of Colleges (which was duly received) and also to the Vice-Chancellor. On the 23rd he received a telegram to say that the Debate on the Second Reading was fixed for Tuesday, the 28th. But, on Monday 27th it was announced that the Speaker had postponed 'Lynn and Fakenham' till Friday (31st). Goulburn now had his allies in London employ a Railway Surveyor (to whom he paid a £50 fee) to draw up a professional Report against the scheme.

On Wednesday, March 29th, Sir H. Drummond Wolff. M.P., reported to Goulburn that Joseph Chamberlain, President of the Board of Trade, and in the Cabinet, would be against them; 'we had much better compromise; could we not offer cheap our land on the other side of the river'. Goulburn would not consider it. 'In the eveng. a letter from Sir F. Drummond Wolff, saying the enemy were going to make an offer of compromise, wh. he wd. bring to me about 2 p.m. at my Club [i.e. on the 31st], I declined seeing him, however, and wrote instead'. On the 31st seats were found for Goulburn and Canon Nisbet in the gallery of the House of Commons. Finally, at the end of the debate on the Bill, Professor Lyon Playfair (Liberal M.P. and Deputy Speaker) proposed that Article 6 be withdrawn, so that the Bill could pass its Second

Reading, and this was accepted. It would appear that the Close was saved.

But, it was not quite the end.

Seven months later, on October 23rd while staying at Aynhoe, Goulburn 'got a letter from Heaviside ... telling me about another proposed invasion of the Close at the bottom of Felton's garden'. Then, on November 21st, in Brighton, 'received a letter from Bensly, enclosing me the announcement of the new proposal of the Lynn and Fakenham to pass a railway thro' the Close – answered this, and wrote to Parkes for an interview at Liverpool Street'. Back in Norwich, on December 1st, 'after Mg. Church went to Bensly's Office, and learned that Elmer had received no plans of the proposed route of the Lynn and Fakenham; so we went in a fly to the Clerk of the Peace's Office in Surrey Street, to inspect the plans deposited yesterday, and there learned, to my great joy, that the line of deviation is to pass *outside* the Close thro' the field separating us from the Vinegar Works ... wrote to Parkes, telling him what had occurred, and that, we having now no *locus standi*, our opposition must collapse'. But there seemed to be a new development during December. On December 30th 'a meeting of Mr Bayliss with the three Canons and myself at the Chapter Office – We agreed to memorialize Parliament against the L. & F. Railway on the ground that they have not given us notice that they mean to take a slice of Cooper's ground – The *petitioning* to be left for "after consideration" – we are disposed to petition, unless they will insert a clause in their Bill, pledging themselves never to ask powers to go thro' the Close'. It looks as if they would not agree to this, for, on January 6th. 'At Mr Bensly's Office we met Mr Bayliss, and sealed our memorial agst. the Lynn and Fakenham'. However, on January 28th, 1883, Goulburn heard from Mr Parkes that the Lynn and Fakenham Railway had abandoned the whole project.

(i) *Walks and Health*

Part of Goulburn's daily routine was his long walks (probably five or six miles) during which he must have covered every road and path leading out of Norwich, often out one way and back another. Out to Eaton, to Earlham, to Costessey, to Sprowston and Rackheath, to Thorpe (usually through Harvey and Birkbeck grounds, for which he had a key), to Lakenham. He had a particular fascination for the 12th Century site of the martyrdom of young St William of Norwich, and for the 15th Century Lollards' Pit. Whenever he could he took his visitors a walk which included these sites. In particular, he loved walking on Mousehold Heath. In 1866, just before Goulburn's arrival in Norwich, the Dean and Chapter had entered into an arrangement for conveying the 200 acres of Mousehold Heath to the Corporation for the purpose of a public Park or recreation ground. In June 1880, this arrangement was finalised in an agreement between the Ecclesiastical Commissioners and the Norwich Town Council.

Goulburn always preferred to take someone with him on his walks – friends, relatives, his Canons, the Precentor, the Chapter Clerk, visiting preachers, anyone who would come. Frequently, they were occasions for business or theological discussion; and for his colleagues in the Cathedral, they were a more relaxed way of working out a problem, or discussing a plan, than sitting across a table from each other. If he did have to go alone, he took a book, or *The Times*, and could often be seen going along, say, the Newmarket Road, reading, or meditating the next Sermon, though, as well, greeting friends and acquaintances and stopping for a chat. He must have been a familiar figure in and around Norwich. In very poor weather he walked up and down his garden, or the Library, for an hour or more.

It must have been this daily, lengthy exercise which kept him going to his 80th year, because, frequently, he was ill, especially during the night; and he had bouts of illness. The astonishing thing was that, after a perfectly dreadful sleepless night, he was usually able to carry on with his normal duties next day. Frequently, he called his doctor (at £1. 1s. a time). In Norwich, it was Dr Johnson until he died in 1874; and then it was Dr Muriel. In London, his very long-standing Dr Morgan (Morgiana, he called him) usually had a visit from him every time he was in London; and he had yet another doctor in Brighton. He absorbed a variety of medicines and advice prescribed by all of them. The indications are that he had some sort of nervous disorder, and possibly ulcers. Julia also suffered what then were called 'bilious attacks', and often had to lie down with severe headaches, probably migraine.

(j) *Daily Life and Work*
Reading through the Diaries, it is difficult to see the justification for the remark of Herbert Leeds in his *Life of Dean Lefroy*: 'He [Dean Lefroy] was following as Dean a scholarly gentleman who

had all but lived the life of a recluse'.[13] Goulburn *was* scholarly; he bought and read books continually; he read periodicals (like the *Quarterly Review* and the *Edinburgh Review*); he consulted sources in the British Museum Reading Room, the Bodleian Library, Oxford, and the Cambridge University Library; he wrote many books and booklets, including major new works; his royalties were an indication of how wide a public he was reaching; he was a preacher, very much in demand, both within his Diocese, and far beyond it; he kept in touch with his contemporary world, by reading, thoroughly each day, *The Times* or *The Guardian*, or some other newspaper. He was regular at the Daily Services of the Cathedral, and the three, sometimes four, Sunday Services. If illness, or something prevented him, he and Julia usually read the Service together in the Deanery.

At the same time, he was also a very sociable person, with an enormous circle of friends and acquaintances. Wherever he went – London, his Club there, on holiday at a German Spa or a British resort, or in the villages around Aynhoe, where so many of Julia's relations lived – he talked to people and often made new friends. The Deanery became, virtually, 'Open House'. In the Diaries, he frequently records the names of the guests at the large number of Dinner Parties which he attended, and also at those which he himself gave in the Deanery. His guests usually numbered between 15 and 20. There was nearly always a number of people staying at the Deanery – friends and relations, visiting preachers and lecturers, candidates for various posts. Luncheon gradually developed into an 'Open Meal'. As well as expected guests, there were often others, old and young, who dropped in casually. Julia used to run 'Bees' in the Deanery (a social gathering to carry out a particular task); some were for 'Matrons' and others for 'Maidens'. Occasionally, Goulburn read to them while they worked.

Of course, all the extensive entertaining and the casual luncheons would not have been possible without a staff of servants; and the extensive entertaining and servants would not have been possible without a dean with considerable private means in addition to his stipend.

Under the Ecclesiastical Commissioners Act of 1840, the Stipends of Deans and Residentiary Canons were fixed. Deans (other than the Deans of Durham, St Paul's, Westminster and

---

13. Herbert Leeds, 'Life of Dean Lefroy' (Jarrold & Sons 1909), p. 24.

Manchester, who received more) had a stipend of £1000 a year – considerably less than the Bishop, considerably more than the average Incumbent; and a great deal more than the average working man. The Dean and Chapter's Stipends depended, to a large extent, on the income from their property, and so, in some years (as recorded in the Diaries) stipends fell short of the official amount. But Goulburn was little affected by such reductions. He probably had an inheritance from his own mother, who died in 1823; he had legacies from relatives, and from friends, such as Mr and Mrs William Gibbs of Tyntesfield, and Bullivant in Exeter; he had a considerable one from his father in 1868; and, eventually, in 1877, he received his brother Frederic's inheritance. Frederic had been a Fellow of All Souls, Oxford; but he seems to have developed a mental disorder and epilepsy, and he lived in a private nursing home at Ticehurst, Sussex, run by two doctors. Goulburn had responsibility for 'poor Fred's' money after their father's death, paying £375 a year to the home.

With, at least, six or seven servants (a coachman, a footman, a cook, and four maids) he and Julia would have been free of domestic duties. When they travelled on holiday, either at home or abroad, Julia always had her Lady's Maid, Rose (who would appear to have spent her life with them, right into their retirement), and also one of the manservants to look after the luggage.

But Goulburn had neither Secretary nor Typewriter. Before Augusta was married, she sometimes wrote letters at his dictation, as also did Frederica Franks and Julia. But, in the main, he wrote all his own letters and had a very large correspondence. The posts were seven days a week, numerous and fast. Typewriters had been produced from the 1870s and were invading British offices by the 1880s. There is no record of him having a telephone, although they were rapidly being installed also by the 1880s. There is, however, one instance in the Diaries of him using a telephone. Telegrams were his main means of quick communication.

He felt a strong pastoral responsibility for the families of his Cathedral staff, and others living in the Close. He often dropped in to talk to their wives and children; he and Ju would sometimes take the children to the Circus; they had parties in the Deanery for them; and the children seemed to feel quite free to wander into the Deanery when they felt inclined to do so. Especially, Goulburn visited the sick, the dying, the bereaved who were in any way connected with the Cathedral. The Dean and Chapter were patrons to twelve Livings in the city, and, among those outside it, of the very large Parish of Gt Yarmouth, and of St Margaret's and St Nicholas', King's Lynn. Goulburn always showed a special interest in all the Dean and Chapter parishes and in the clergy in charge of them. He was always ready to accept preaching engagements in them, and discuss and deal with their problems. He was particularly conscientious about choosing the right man for each, as also for each office in the Cathedral, and he spent long periods of enquiry in accomplishing this. Evenings at the Deanery, usually with visitors, rarely with Julia alone, were often spent with him reading aloud – it might be a Trollope or Dickens novel, a Sermon, an article from a periodical or *The Times*, or from a theological book. In his earlier period in Norwich he had often given a talk to groups on the art of 'Reading Aloud', and this was later published as a booklet. An evening alone with Julia was so rare that he always recorded it. When he was away from home on his own, even for one night, he always wrote to her daily.

(k) *The Cathedral, the Chapter, and the City*

Goulburn was very conscious of his own shortcomings. One of these was the business side of the Chapter's responsibilities; it terrified him, especially as he grew older, and he relied very much on Canon Heaviside to guide him through its intricacies. Yet his last official act as Dean was to complete the sale of two of the Chapter's considerable estates to the Ecclesiastical Commissioners. In his last year as Dean he acknowledged that he should have been more actively involved in the life of the City. But he took comfort from the fact that Canon Heaviside, his Vice-dean, had always taken a very active part in City affairs, events, and committees; as did also his close friend, Hinds Howell, an Honorary Canon, and Editor of the excellent Norwich Diocesan Calendar. Perhaps he underestimated the natural contact which existed between Cathedral and City, and his own part in it. When the Judges came for the Assizes, he called on them, invited them to a representative dinner party, welcomed them to a Cathedral Service, and, in turn, went to dinner with them, Not infrequently the Mayor and Corporation (who quite often were Churchmen and involved in Church Societies) attended special Services in the Cathedral. Goulburn was on friendly terms with leading families in the City – the Gurneys, the Birkbecks, the Bignolds, the Harveys, the Pattesons. Lady Harvey and Mr Birkbeck (in the Thorpe area) gave him keys to private gates so that he could walk through their grounds. He was a member of the Norfolk Club; President of the Archaeological Society, and a keen member of it; a Governor of King Edward VI School; a Trustee of the Gt Hospital; he rarely missed the Norwich Oxford Society dinner. When the British Association for the Advancement of Science visited Norwich in 1868; when the National Fisheries Exhibition was held in Norwich in 1881, and the Royal Agricultural Show in 1886 – on all three occasions he arranged special Services in the Cathedral and made sure that they were well publicised. In more specifically Church circles he was Chairman of the Diocesan Teachers' Training Institution; President of Norfolk and Suffolk Church Choral Association; President of the Churchman's Club; President of the Diocesan Association of Ringers; he was fully involved in the Annual Services in the Cathedral and the Annual Meetings (in St Andrew's Hall or Noverre's Rooms) of the various Overseas and Home Missionary Societies, especially those of S.P.G. Every January, when the Bishop invited the Residentiary and Honorary Canons to the Palace, it was the custom for Goulburn to read a paper on a subject of present concern, followed by a general discussion.

On November 12th, 1871, when the Revd B. J. Armstrong of Dereham was staying with the Bishop for the weekend, he recorded in his Diary that he had attended 8 a.m. Matins, 'a miserably small congregation. Again with the Bishop to the 11 o'clock Service (Litany and Holy Communion). The Church very full ... I was preacher ... Accompanied his Lordship for the third time to the Cathedral at 3.30, where there was a vast congregation to hear the Dean preach for the Hospital.'[14]

Goulburn put great effort into organising special Courses in the Cathedral for Advent and Lent. The most successful, and sustained, of these Courses was his 'Argumentative Discourses in Defence and Confirmation of the Faith', which ran, in eight series from Lent 1871 to Advent 1876. His intention was to have the best possible Speakers, and, initially, he achieved this. The Bishop of Peterborough (Magee), and the Bishop of Derry (Alexander) were both famous preachers. Bishop Magee took the first four Discourses, Goulburn the next four, and Bishop Alexander a further four. So far, there were large congregations for all of them. But then he had difficulty in getting the Speakers

---

14. H. B. J. Armstrong (Ed.), *A Norfolk Diary* (G. G. Harrap & Co. Ltd., 1949), p. 163.

he really wanted, and so the Course lapsed for the year 1873, but resumed again in 1874, when the Speakers were good for their subject, but did not have the same reputation to attract quite so large congregations. Altogether there were 24 Discourse which, eventually, were published in Book form. (See Appendix 8).

Goulburn had a friendly relationship with the Priests of Willow Lane and Wymer Street Roman Catholic Churches; but that with the Free Church Ministers was a little more distant. On June 21st, 1887, when the Queen's Golden Jubilee was marked by a special Service in the Cathedral with the Band of the 19th Hussars and the singing of the Coronation Anthem, Goulburn invited all the Free Church Ministers of the city, who, at their own request, sat together as a group. But he was sorry that they had not worn their gowns.

(l) *Holidays*

Under the Ecclesiastical Commissioners Act 1840, periods of residence were fixed for Deans at eight months, and for Residentiary Canons at three months. Goulburn was fortunate, from 1873, in having two Residentiary Canons (Heaviside and Archdeacon Nevill) who were permanent residents in the Close. He would like to have seen the resident period for all Canons become eight months. He himself was usually away from Norwich for the total of four months he was allowed. He had two periods of about 1½ months each – one would be to drink the waters at a German Spa (like Homburg), or at an English Spa (like Harrogate); or to spend a holiday in Scotland. The other would be taken up going the rounds of the villages surrounding Aynhoe, staying with various relations and friends. In both periods it was quite likely that he would end up with a fortnight in Brighton, where, eventually, he bought a house. He would make up the fourth month by two or three day visits to London, or by preaching engagements in Parish Churches or Cathedrals. But, always during his absence from home, he kept regularly in touch with Norwich by letter (or telegram), and often dealt with business and problems in this way. Especially in London he often managed to accomplish a certain amount of Dean and Chapter business. And whether at the Chaplaincy Churches abroad, or at Parish Churches where he was staying, he expected to be invited to preach and help. So he always took a number of sermons with him, and also continued to write new ones.

Retirement

When Goulburn decided, in the Autumn of 1888, to retire, he thought first of moving to London, and was looking at a house in Montagu Square, near the British Museum. Writing to his cousin, Louisa Thomas, he said that it 'is about the size we want ... with more room for books than many London Houses have. This is essential to me, for my books have accumulated enormously in the last twenty-two years, and the Benedictine Fathers and the Baronius (with his Contimators) which my St John's Congregation gave me when I left them, constitute a Library in themselves'. He goes on to say: 'Ju's state makes me a little uneasy. She is not ill; and yet that she is not right is clear to those who know her, from her staying indoors, complaining of various ailments, and sending for doctors – things entirely foreign to her habits ... It seems to puzzle the doctors ... they give her tonics. The tonics bring on feverish symptoms ... There is something wrong in her circulation, wh, they seem not to understand.'

He then says: 'I should like, when we are settled, to try to help and instruct young men who are seeking Holy Orders ... However, I leave all that till we have settled in our new house ...'[15]

On April 23rd, 1889, Goulburn, now 71, retired, not to London, but to Brighton. In 1873, he had sold his London house for £3943, and bought instead, 14 Lansdowne Place, Brighton. Now, he sold this house and, instead, bought 'Leydenburg', 50 The Drive, West Brighton, which they promptly re-named 'Aynhoe'. To his friend, Canon Constantine Frere he wrote that it was a great wrench to leave Norwich, but a number of considerations pointed in the direction of retirement: 'the heavier pressure both of illness and worries as years multiply; my being out of sympathy with many of those changes which are clamoured for in the Cathedral system, and which I see coming in';[16] Julia's health; his own lack of business acumen. And, of course, he looked forward to greater leisure to study and write, and especially to complete his last major work, the *Life of Burgon*, who had died in April 1888, at the age of 75. His letters to his cousin Louisa in 1890 and 1891, are full of reference to *Burgon*, which was eventually published in December 1891–January 1892.

In May 1889, two articles by Goulburn on 'The Lessons of my Decanate' were published in *The Guardian*. In the first, he

---

15. Letter dated October 9, 1888, from a collection of personal family letters of Goulburn's kindly lent to me by Mr Bryan Gipps.
16. Quoted in Berdmore Compton, *Memoir of Dean Goulburn* (1899), p. 94.

stressed four points: (1) The enormous importance of 'Harmony' among members of the Cathedral body, and between them and their Bishop. (2) The steady rise of Cathedrals to 'a higher and nobler consciousness of their own responsibilites' since the Act of 1840 (which had reformed Cathedral bodies). (3) The growth, during the past 20 years, of Special Services at Church Seasons (particularly at Advent and Lent) with eminent preachers. And he specially mentioned the 'Argumentative Discourses in Defence and Confirmation of the Faith' which had attracted large congregations to hear 'sound and reliable, but at the same time easy and popular arguments' for the Christian Faith, and then were published at a price within the reach of all. Finally, (4) the experiment of 'Peoples Services', borrowed from the practice of Gloucester Cathedral. The Norwich Cathedral body was not 'enamoured of them', but they had been a success. They consisted of popular anthems and extracts from oratorios, interspersed with hymns, 'the whole being prefaced with two Collects and the Lord's Prayer, and concluded with a Collect and the Benediction'. The result was a thronged Nave (men and women) many failing to get in.

In the second Article, Goulburn suggested alterations which he thinks desirable. Twenty years ago, he and the Chapter had opted, in exchange for the estates they possessed, to be re-endowed with new estates by the Ecclesiastical Commissioners which would give them a more reliable income for stipends, etc. Now, he thought, it would be better if the Commissioners kept the estates and paid the stipends.

He also wanted to see reforms relating to Precentors, Lay Clerks and Minor Canons. Precentors 'should be conversant with music as a science'; no one over 50 'should be able to join or remain in a Choir'; the office of Lay Clerk should be made terminable at 50; so should that of Minor Canon; a small portion of the stipend of a Lay Clerk should be taken for insurance, to accumulate at interest as an insurance; and a Lay Clerk should be a probationer for the first year. He saw no reason why active work in the Diocese should not be carried out by one or more of the Canons, as a Canon Missioner, or Educational Canon powered by the worship, study, prayer and meditation of his three months' residence.

Finally, he thought that both the Lectionary and the Bible translation should have been amended rather than revised.

The Goulburns remained in Brighton until the second half of

1893, when they moved to Tunbridge Wells, chiefly for Julia's health, which was very poor. She seems to have become very tense and nervy. On August 4th, 1896, when they went for the day to Eyhorne to visit Gerard and Gussie, Gerard noted in his Diary: 'she full of fidgets about trains and other little nothings. I fear the good Dean is worried to death'.[17] When his sister Mary ('Pom') visited the Goulburns on January 4th, 1897, 'she found the old folk anything but well; the Dean much pulled down and Aunt Julia making herself ill with anxiety'.[18] The Goulburns appeared to have moved first to 3 Calverley Terrace, and then, during 1894, to 12 Calverley Park Gardens, which, again they renamed 'Aynhoe'. A photograph shows a very large substantial house in its own grounds (still there today, though with additions). There they kept a staff of four, a footman, a cook, the faithful Rose and another maidservant.

Goulburn continued to preach regularly in different churches and in different styles, in order to adapt to different congregations. Occasionally, he spent a few days in London; but, chiefly, the time was spent in his study, or writing letters, or at the Daily Services, and in looking after Julia. On their Golden Wedding Day, December 11th, 1895, he wrote a long poem to her, covering, in different sections, the places where they had lived. He wrote to friends quite often – to his cousin, Louisa Thomas, reminiscing about their childhood days in Brighton; to a Norwich friend he wrote: 'I often look back to my Norwich days and my kind friends there ... with great interest and affection.' When Mrs Pelham died in 1893, he wrote a long, sympathetic letter to the Bishop (living in retirement at Thorpe), and ended it 'Your affectionate and still dutiful Dean'. His last public act was, with Archdeacon Denison (formerly Archdeacon of Taunton and a strong High Churchman), and other colleagues, to draw up a 'Declaration of the Truth of Holy Scripture'.

On Sunday, May 2nd, 1897, he had been to Holy Communion at St James' Church, Tunbridge Wells. That evening he went up to bed about 10 o'clock, while Julia prepared a drink for him. Before she could bring it to him, he had died. Gerard and Gussie came at once, next morning, to stay with Gerard's sister, Laura ('Lolotte') who also lived in Tunbridge Wells. In his Diary, Gerard spoke of 'dear kind loving Uncle Edward'.[19] There was a

---

17. Diary of Gerard Thomas, August 4th, 1896 (In the possession of Mr Bryan Gipps).
18. Ditto – January 4th, 1897.
19. Diary of Gerard Thomas, May 3rd, 1897.

short funeral Service at St James' Church on Thursday May 6th, the Church to which Goulburn had recently presented new Altar Rails. The main Funeral Service was at Aynhoe the next day at 2 o'clock, and coinciding with this, a Memorial Service in Norwich Cathedral. The Service at Aynhoe, and the Interment, were taken by Julia's brother Frederick ('The Dean' as Goulburn always called him), perhaps his closest friend. There were large numbers of the Cartwright family present, and some Goulburn relatives. Dr Bensly, the Cathedral Chapter Clerk came from Norwich. On Good Friday, 1898, a Memorial Window in St James', Tunbridge Wells, was dedicated to him. The subject is the Sermon on the Mount, and the lower panels represent our Lord blessing little children. At Rugby School Chapel one of the windows which he gave, while Headmaster, was in need of restoration, and friends and former pupils took the opportunity of adding a Commemorative Inscription in Latin below it. The reredos in All Saints' Church, Hollingbourne, Kent, Gerard's and Gussie's Parish Church, is a memorial to him. Finally, Julia (who outlived him by six years) and Augusta, in 1899, had two windows of St Michael and St Gabriel dedicated to his memory in Aynhoe Parish Church (St Michael's).

THE DIARIES

THE VERY REVEREND EDWARD MEYRICK GOULBURN, M.A., D.C.L., D.D. (1818–1897)

DEAN OF NORWICH (December 4th, 1866–April 3rd, 1889)

Goulburn was installed in Norwich Cathedral on December 4th, 1866, but he did not come to live in the Deanery in Norwich until February 27th, 1867. He remained also, officially, Vicar of St John's, Paddington, until June 4th, 1867, arranging for his Curates to be in charge of the Parish. He had done this in order to facilitate his successor, Emilius Bayley. But, as Dean of Norwich, he was now, ex officio, a Member of Convocation, and so he was able to attend the Meeting of Convocation in London from February 12th to 15th. It was on the third day that the demand by the Anglican Church in Canada (made in 1865) for a Conference of all the Bishops of the Anglican Communion was considered. It resulted in the Archbishop of Canterbury (Charles Longley) calling the First Lambeth Conference in September 1867, attended by 76 Bishops.

••

Before moving to Norwich, the Goulburns spent a week's holiday at Horton, four miles south-east of Northampton, with the Revd Sir Henry Gunning and his wife, Mary, who was Julia Goulburn's much older step-sister.

••

DIARY

1867

FEBRUARY

Wednesday 27 From Horton to NORWICH
Rose at 6.30 – Bkfst. at 8 – Left Horton by fly[1] for Billing Road Station at 8.45 – Left Billing at 9.20 – Had to get Norwich tickets at Peterboro' – Spent an hour at Ely, during wh. we saw the beautiful Cathedral – Got to Norwich about 4 p.m. – the house very nice and comfortable – of course, a bundle of letters – one from the Bp. asking me to preach at his Ordination – answered some of them after dinner – Can. Heaviside[2] came in before dinner, and put me up to several things.

1. A light one-horse covered carriage, plying for hire.
2. Residentiary Canon of Norwich since 1860, and a firm friend and strong support to Goulburn during his 23 years as Dean.

Thursday 28

Cathedral Service twice – After the first, Heaviside showed me a letter of Mrs. Archdall's, about providing for his residence in April, and talking about resignation[1] – We had the Chapter meeting at 1 at Heaviside's House – Canon Robinson[2] attended, and the audit was adjourned to March 26; Kitson[3] was too unwell to attend – In the evening I wrote to Jane Russell about the dimensions of Communts. kneelers – Mr. Patteson[4] attended the Afternoon Service for Heaviside, the latter being engaged as a guardian of the Workhouse – Heaviside took me to see the Choristers' School, a poor mean cottage on the way to the ferry – I asked the master for a time-table – Very tired in the evening.

1. George Archdall, D.D. (or Archdall-Gratwicke), Master of Emmanuel College, Cambridge, and Residentiary Canon of Norwich since 1842. He did resign soon afterwards, and was replaced by Canon John Nisbet, M.A., who remained until his death in 1892.
2. Charles Robinson, D.D., became Master of St Catherine's College, Cambridge in 1861, and annexed to the Mastership was a Residentiary Canonry of Norwich. He also was with Goulburn during the whole of his 23 years.
3. John Kitson, Esq, was the Chapter Clerk; one of the two Diocesan Registrars; and also a Secretary to the Bishop.
4. W. F. Patteson was Vicar of St. Helen's and Chaplain to the Great Hospital. He was one of the two Rural Deans of Norwich. Hon. Canon 1860. Goulburn called him 'Oyster Pattie'.

MARCH

Friday 1

Cathedral Service twice – All day in the study arranging Books – After Morning Service, went w. Heaviside to Mr. Kitson's (who had a bad cough), and discussed with him the Unthank affair, and several other matters, wh. he had to lay before the Chapter – In the afternoon, when Ju[1] & Gussie[1] were out, the Sheriff[2] of Norwich called to explain why he could not dine with us on the 27th. (He is the great Shawl Manufacturer, and offered to show us the Shawls) – The Precentor & Mrs. Symonds[3] called about ½ past 3, and I showed them Richmond's picture of Ju and Fan.[4] – after 2d. Service took a walk across the Ferry by the banks of the Wensum, and over the draw-bridge, and returned by the Castle – Headache in the evening.

1. Goulburn almost invariably called his wife (Julia) 'Ju', sometimes 'Auntie', occasionally 'Judy'. Their niece (Augusta) he called 'Gussie' or similar nicknames. She was the daughter of Stephen, Julia's step-brother. Her mother died in 1853, shortly after her birth, and her father in 1862. Goulburn was her Guardian, and she was nine when she came to live with them early in 1863. They treated her as a loving, and much loved, daughter. She died in 1949, aged 95.
2. W.H. Clabburn, Esq, of Clabburn Sons and Crisp, Pitt Street.
3. The Revd Henry Symonds had been Precentor and Minor Canon since 1844 (he was only three years younger than Goulburn). He became co-author with him of the two major works on the 'Bosses' and on 'Losinga' over a period of some 12 years. With his love of nicknames, Goulburn called him the 'Pinseter', and, later, the 'Pin'
4. Frances (Mrs Boulton), Julia's full sister, and only a year or two older, who died of erysipelas and pleurisy in January 1864.

Saturday 2

In bed (with headache) till 9.30 – did not go to Morning Service – At 11.15 went with Can. Heaviside to the Training School[1], & took the Chair at the Meeting – There was the Bp.[2], Archdn. Bouverie[3], Archn. Omerod[3], Messrs. Hopper, Ormsby, Mr. Howes, M.P., Sir John Boileau[4], & Mr. Cufaude Davie, the Chaplain – afterwards Heaviside showed me the 'Ambulatory' – went with him to a Tailors, to order a greatcoat – home to luncheon – arranged Books – Archdn. Omerod called, & described the men we had met in the morning – also Mr. Bulmer[5] – also Mr. & Mrs. Ripley[6] (of St. Giles) – went to Aftern. Service, & afterwards Heaviside and I experimented on the Eagle, moving it to that part of the Church, where we thot. the reader wd. best be heard – In the evening, Mr. Johnson[7] called & Ju asked his advice about her ear – Gussie ran away in a fright – I looked over Proof sheets, & sent them to Frederica[8] – I was this day elected a member of the Norfolk Club[9].

1. The Norwich Diocesan Training Institution (for Teachers) founded 1839, was in St. George's Plain, not far from the Close, since 1853.
2. The Hon. and Rt Revd John Pelham, D.D., Bishop of Norwich since 1857.
3. Archdeacons: Bouverie of Norfolk; Omerod of Suffolk.
4. The Squire of Ketteringham. (See Owen Chadwick, "Victorian Miniature").
5. The Revd E. Bulmer, a Minor Canon (i.e. Cathedral Curate) 1865–1900.
6. Vicar of St Giles', Norwich, then the leading Evangelical Church in the City. The Ripleys lived in Earlham Hall, Mrs Ripley having inherited it from her first husband, John Gurney.
7. The Goulburn's Doctor, who often attended the Cathedral.
8. Frederica Franks, a parishioner of St John's, Paddington, who continued to be Goulburn's contact with his London publisher, sometimes compiling indexes, and doing secretarial work for him.
9. Then in rented premises on Guildhall Hill. In 1887, purchased 17, Upper King St for £3,600, and 108 years later it is still there.

Sunday 3   Quinquagesima   Morning: The Precentor
           Aftern.: Rev. Canon Heaviside

Bitterly cold – The Precentor in the morning preached of the 1st. vv. of 1 Cor. 13; the Canon in the Afternoon on "Whosoever exalteth himself shall be abased" – both Sermons much above average – The Eagle in its new position seemed to answer very well as regards hearing, but it must stand higher than it does at present – there were about 30 communicants at the H.C. in the morning; the draughts in the afternoon very severe.

Wednesday 6   ASH WEDNESDAY

First Service at 8 – The Bishop there at 8, also at 11 – At 11 I preached (after the Litany) my Sermon on the Commination Service – there was a fair sprinkling of people – a talk with Heaviside afterwards about Robinson's canonical residence, wh. is impeded by his tenant's prospect of confinement in the end of April – then about the prevention of draughts in the Church – went to the Peoples' entrance with Mr. Brown[1] – between Churches at length got my study into something like order – after the Afternoon Service walked with Heaviside towards Mousehold Heath, and lionised the Hospital[2] – the House looks very nice.

> 1. Mr J.H. Brown (Goulburn sometimes spells him with an 'e') was the *local* Architect of the Dean and Chapter, living in the Close.
> 2. The Great Hospital (founded in 1249 by the then Bishop of Norwich) is a residential home (small flats, etc.) for the aged of Norwich, with sick care, when necessary. It was, and is, just outside the walls of the Cathedral Close.

Sunday 10   Lent I   Mg.: Anna the Prophetess (New)
  Aftern.: The devil sinneth from the beginning (St. John's 61)

Rose at 6 – went with Ju in fly to Lakenham Church (St. Mark's) – made acquaintance with, and helped, Mr. Garry[1], and his Curate, Mr. Leach – about 40 communts., the majority of whom were men – returned about nine – A miserable rainy, chilly day. Preached twice, as above – Read part of a Sermon of Woodward's on the Immac. Conception – Fraulein[2] & Gussie dined w. us.

> 1. Goulburn liked to know and support the clergy and parishes in the gift of the Dean and Chapter. The Revd N.T. Garry was in his late 30s. He had become Vicar of St Mark's in 1861 and remained there until 1873.
> 2. Augusta's German Governess had been recommended to the Goulburns by his friend, Wm. Alexander (husband of Frances, the Hymn-writer) who, in October 1867, became Bishop of Derry. She remained a long-standing friend of the Goulburns.

March 1867   45

Tuesday 12   Mr Scott's examination of the Cathedral
Attended both Services – almost all day in the Cathedral with Scott[1], Heaviside, Symonds, and one or 2 of the officials – The Heavisides dined here at night with Mr. Scott.

> 1. Sir George Gilbert Scott, Architect-in-Chief (Grandfather of Sir Giles Gilbert Scott)

Wednesday 13
At 1.25 left Norwich for Yarmouth – Cold most intense – Colvin[1] came to escort us to the Church – there were six or seven clergy there – I preached on the "Mental Process of Temptation" from James 1, 14 (St. John's, 1863) – found our hotel (the Victoria) most comfortable – wrote to my father in the evening.

> 1. The Revd J.W. Colvin, the Senior of five Curates of St Nicholas' Church, Gt Yarmouth, another Dean and Chapter Living. Seating capacity was given as 2,900. The Vicar was Canon N.R. Nevill (who, in 1873, became a Residentiary Canon, and, the following year, Archdeacon of Norfolk).

Thursday 14
Returned from Yarmouth by the train at 9.25 a.m. wh. reached Norwich at 10.25 – walked w. Ju to call on (1) Chancellor Evans[1] (2) Mr. Meyrick – saw Mrs. & Myra Meyrick (3) the Precentor, whom we saw, but not Mrs. Symonds – I looked in on Mr. Muller[2], but found him engaged with a Bridal Party – home to luncheon – talk to Heaviside about the warming – Buck[3] & Symonds dined here.

> 1. The Worshipful Charles Evans, Esq, M.A, Chancellor of the Diocese since 1845.
> 2. The Revd J.S. Muller, Minor Canon 1865–72, one of four Minor Canons.
> 3. Dr Zachariah Buck, Organist of Norwich Cathedral 1819–1877. Famed as a trainer of Organists and Choirs.

Saturday 16   From Norwich to London
                       My Testimonial presented
Left Norwich at 10.45 – got to London at 3.45 – found my father ailing from a chill – at 5.45 went to the School & made an address of thanks for my beautiful Testimonial – 85 handsome volumes[1] and a Tea Service – Mr. Powell requested us to print my 'Farewell Addresses', to wh. I assented. At 7.15 my father's family dinner – fourteen in all.

> 1. These volumes (in Latin) are now in the Library of the Dean and Chapter of Norwich, given by Julia when Goulburn died in 1897.

Monday 18   London to Norwich
Left London at 10 – arrived here at 4 – sleet and snow all the way – Bedesmen[1] came to ask for their Xmas shilling a head – I wrote to Canon Robinson & Chanc. Evans before dinner, about the residence of the former, and after dinner to dear Mr. Gibbs.[2]

> 1. Poor pensioners in almshouses who received a stipend of c.£12 to £15 a year, and were expected to attend the daily Services and keep the Cathedral clean, ring bells, etc. There were six at Norwich Cathedral.
> 2. William Gibbs, Esq., was a very wealthy parishioner and philanthropist of St John's, Paddington (when in his London house), who liked Goulburn, built a Chapel of Ease (St Michael's) within St John's Parish, and endowed it. His main residence was Tyntesfield, near Bristol, to which he invited the Goulburns from time to time. When Goulburn asked him, he also gave sums of money to, at least, two Dean and Chapter parishes in Norwich to help either with increased endowment or repairs.

Tuesday 19   1st. Singing Lesson
Attended both Services – At 11.15 had my first singing Lesson[1] with Dr. Buck – liked it very much – then went to Jessopp[2], and talked about the Dean's field – he lionised me over the Grammar School – walked in the cloister conning my music from 3 to 4 – after Aftern. Service, Mr. Woodcock the warmer, arrived in the Church – we left him there.

> 1. Goulburn had an excellent speaking voice. A contemporary (F.T. Hibgame) says: "Dean Goulburn was the most beautiful reader I ever heard in my life". But he was poor at intoning, so he took regular lessons from Dr. Buck.
> 2. Augustus Jessopp, D.D. was Headmaster of the King Edward VI Grammar School (within the Close) from 1859–79 (and an outstanding Headmaster); then Rector of Scarning for almost 30 years, and author of several historical works centred on East Anglia.

Wednesday 20 First meeting of Lay Clerks at the Deanery
Dr. Howson called, and we had a talk about Deaconesses & Deaneries – after luncheon went with Ju to lionise the Cathedral – then across the Ferry, & into the town – bought a letter weight[1] and a photog[1]. of Dean Pellew – in the evening came 9 Lay Clerks, 3 Boys (Livock, Pearce, Manning)[2], Can. and Mrs. Heaviside, the Precentor & Dr. Buck – the Precentor sang a most touching little English song – I read:

1. E.A. Poe's Bells.
2. Scene in King John. Arthur & Hubert.
3. The Three Horses.
4. Nongong pan.
5. Go Mary, go & call the cattle home.
6. How's my Boy?

1. The letter weight cost 9s. and the photo 1s.
2. Entertainment of Lay Clerks, Choir Boys, etc. at the Deanery was a regular feature of Goulburn's 23 years in Norwich. He often gave a lecture on "Reading Aloud" (which was eventually published).

Thursday 21   Norwich to Lynn
Went to Lynn at 3.5 p.m. – after our arrival at Lynn[1] had tea with Mr. Wodehouse & his mother, & met Mr. W. Hay Gurney[2] & others – I preached at St. Nicholas' Church[1] on the Lent Sunday Lessons – The Service was beautifully done – In the evening a tea party.

1. St Margaret's with St Nicholas', King's Lynn was another Dean and Chapter Living.
2. Mr Hay Gurney was a friend of the Prince of Wales. Along with Lord Suffield he was often to be seen walking in the Norwich Streets with the Prince.

Saturday 23   Judges open the Commission
Sent notice to the Bishop of the time at wh, the Judges wd. come – Attended Church both times – after Mg. Service, Mr. Cufaude Davie[1] came for signatures to cheques – went to Dr. Buck's & had my lesson – home to luncheon – corrected Proof Sheets – went to the Judges' Lodgings with Heaviside at 2.50 – The Bp., Heaviside, & I paid a visit to Mr. Justice Willes – Baron Martin was not there – After Afternoon Service, heard the Boys practise the harmonised confession.

1. The Revd W. Cufaude Davie was Superintendent of the general training of the students of the Diocesan Training Institution (for Schoolmistresses); of the Model Schools; and also Secretary and Chaplain (1857–75). He had been a Master at Eton, and Headmaster of Yarmouth Grammar School.

Sunday 24   Lent 3   Assize Sunday
In the morning, Baron Martin & Justice Willes came in state to Church, with the High Sheriff, Mayor[1], etc. – The Sheriff's Chaplain (Rev. Mr. Burrows) preached on "Rulers are not a terror to good works, but to the evil" – a modest, good Sermon – The Bishop was here – The Anthem at the afternoon Service was beautiful – walked in the Close w. Ju, Fraulein, Gussie, met the Heavisides, Col. & Mrs. Douglas, The Mayor, Dr. Buck, & Mr. Jessop.

1. F.E. Watson, Esq., Solicitor, who did outstanding work for the Church of England Young Men's Society in Norwich.

Monday 25   Annunciation of the B.V.M.
Dined with the Judges

Sent off my titlepage to the Printers – disappointed at not finding a Celebration at the Commn. in the Morning – Afterwards entrusted our Eagle to a man to mend, and looked over the Church in reference to the Stoves – wrote to Scott about the Stoves – went w. Ju and Mrs. Heaviside to call on the Watsons at Thickthorn – saw the ladies – I walked back lionising Eaton Church, meeting the Mayor en route – dined with the Judges, the Bishop, the 2 Marshals, the Sheriff's Chaplain, & Sir Samuel Bignold[1].

   1. 3rd son of the founder of the Norwich Union: Sheriff, Freeman, Alderman, Mayor (three times), Magistrate, for a short time M.P. for Norwich. Formed the Yarn Co. in 1836, to give employment to the poor.

Wednesday 27   Dinner to the Judges

Went with Heaviside to the Bishop's – he asked me to take the Sunday Morg. Sermons in July, and to give an address to the Clergy ordained by him on June 4 – the latter I assented to only conditionally – prepared for the Judges – Our party on the whole went off well – the Judges and Sheriff came in costume – Justice Willes thinks lightly of our Church – Talk about Capital Punishment.

Friday 29

Attended Morning Service – afterwards arranged for the Gallery being thrown open next Sunday – walked with the Precentor thro' Carrow & Bracondale & Trowse to Crown Point – practised singing in the Church with the Choir – Sent French[1] and Risley[1] their stipend today.

   1. The two Curates at St John's, Paddington.

Sunday 31   Lent 4

Preached in the morning at St. Giles[1] for the debt on the Restoration – there was a good congregation – I saw the 4 Choristers, Camplin, Godwin, Smith & another after their dinner, & gave them a little instruction in the Lord's Prayer.

   1. Yet another Dean and Chapter Living.

APRIL

Saturday 6   Training School

After Service a meeting at the Training School, at wh. I presided – We directed Mr. Davie to write to Mr. Lingen about the girl who is said to have copied – the Bp. & Heaviside were at the Hospital[1] meeting.

1. The Clergy were very prominent and numerous on the Boards and Committees of the Norfolk and Norwich Hospital, ever since the idea of a Hospital was put forward by the then Bishop of Norwich in 1758, and the foundation stone laid in 1771. Between the early 1850s and the late 1890s, the Chairman and Vice-Chairman of the Board of Management was always a Clergyman. Canon A.C. Copeman of St Andrew's was Chairman of the Building Committee of the new Hospital in the 1870s.

Sunday 7   Lent 5

At Communn. about 50 communicants – the Boys came to me at 2 o'clock, and I explained the 1st. answer in Overall's[1] part of the Catechism, but did not enlarge sufficiently on the Baptismal Commission – My father[2] went to the Cathedral in the afternoon, & was much pleased with the size of the Congregation, etc. – I spoke to the Servants[3] on the Sentences & Exhortation.

1. John Overall had been Regius Professor of Theology at Cambridge. He drew up the section on the Sacraments in the B.C.P. Catechism. He became Bishop of Norwich in 1618, but died the following year at the age of 59.
2. Goulbourn's father and Cousin, Mary Chetwynd, were staying at the Deanery from March 30th to April 9th.
3. Goulburn had no Secretary or Telephone, but wrote by hand, received, and promptly answered some hundreds of letters a year; but he had a retinue of servants, at least six, which made it possible for him rarely to refer to the domestic scene, and to have frequent large dinner parties, luncheons, and guests. When they travelled long distances, they usually took a man to buy the tickets and look after the luggage, and a lady's maid for Julia. From time to time, Goulburn gave the servants religious instruction, and prepared some of them for Confirmation.

Monday 8

Walked with the Precentor 1st. to Mr. Clabburn's Shawl factory, where we met Ju and MAC, and lionised the shawls and looms – then took a walk with the Precentor to one of Mr. Hinds Howell's[1] livings – in coming back, lionised St. Lawrence's & inspected Mr. Hildyard's[2] copes and chasubles, etc. etc.

1. Canon Hinds Howell was Rector of Drayton with Hellesdon from 1855 to 1899, a good Parish Priest, and also very involved in many Diocesan Boards and Committees; for 40 years an examplary Editor of the Norwich Diocesan Calendar, which is a mine of information on Church and State for the later local historian. They had walked to Hellesdon, then with a population of 496. H.H. had a Curate to look after it.

2. The Revd A.E. Hildyard, Rector of St. Lawrence's, Norwich, had been an Evangelical, and was an excellent preacher. In his short time in Norwich, Father Ignatius had converted him to being a High Churchman, and crucifix, banners, vestments, incense, became the norm at St Lawrence's. Apparently, in the evening, the Churchyard gates had to be locked on a Sunday at 6.30 pm (for the 7 pm Service) as, by that time, the building was packed to capacity.

Sunday 21   EASTER SUNDAY
Dr. Buck came in and gave me a little trial at singing before the 9 o'clock Service – on both occasions I got on *tolerably* well, wavering once or twice; but not at all to my own satisfaction – there is too short an interval between the 2 morning Services – 10 struck as we were closing the 1st. Service, but then we had the Athanasian Creed and the Easter Hymn sung – We had rather less than 50 communts. in the morning – Two copies of my new Publication arrived today[1], one of them I sent to the Bp – Scott's estimate also arrived today; that for substantial repairs is heavy: £12,000.

1. The Postal Service was remarkable. Norwich Main Post Office was open from 7 am to 9.55 pm, and on Sundays from 7 am to 10 am There were five deliveries on weekdays, and two on Sundays, even on Easter Day and Christmas Day.

Monday 22   From Norwich to Cambridge
Left Norwich with Kitson at 7.30 a.m. – a long Chapter meeting[1] here at Can. Robinson's house, in which we discussed the proposition of the Commissioners[2], the division of the Services consequent on the introduction of the Weekly Communions, the throwing open of the Church, the better education of the Choristers, and other subjects, from 10.30 to 3.15 – then Kitson and I were lionised by Professor Sedgwick, 1st. to King's Chapel, his own Geological Museum, and St. John's new Chapel – Heaviside then met us, and he took me to Sidney Sussex College, and introduced me to Mrs. Phelps & Miss Phelps – then I walked home, buying a microscope for little Dustkins en route.

1. Occasionally, Goulburn held a Chapter meeting in Cambridge, in order to be able to include Professor Sedgwick (a very famous Geologist), and Canon Robinson, when they were unable to get to Norwich.
2. There was an on-going discussion with the Ecclesiastical Commissioners on the commutation of the Chapter's land and property.

Tuesday 23   From Cambridge to Norwich
Left Cambridge by the train nominally at 10; but there were excursionists going to Newmarket, whose trains delayed us more

than ½ an hour – Mr. Johnson called at 3 p.m. and seemed to think me in danger of mumps.

Sunday 28
Not well today – The Mg. Service in the Cathedral was beautiful – I afterwards talked to the Boys on "What meant thou by this word Sacrament?" – I am going to speak to the Servants about the General Confession – Fraulein says that the Afternoon Service in the Cathedral was more beautiful than any she had ever heard.

MAY

Thursday 2 Went to Ipswich & back
Wrote after Bkfst. to the Bp. (who is in London) about the new Hymn Book, and to Mr. Raikes of the S.P.G. – Left Norwich at 11.15 – read the Guardian in the carriage – found Mr. Chwarden Westrop at the station – he took me to his house, where I was met by Mr. Gaye[1] of St. Matthew's, and conducted to the Church – a very scanty congregation – the Service was intoned, & there was a surpliced choir – My Sermon did not seem to tell – Collection about £19 – afterwards dined with Mr. & Mrs. Gaye, the County Court Judge, Physician, Solicitor, two Churchwardens of the Church – Left Ipswich at 6.48 & reached the Close as the clock struck 9 p.m.

> 1. The Revd C. Gaye had been Rector of St Matthew's since 1848. Ipswich was in the Diocese of Norwich, which included most of Suffolk until the formation of the Diocese of St Edmundsbury and Ipswich in 1914.

Friday 3
At Morning Prayer, sung the whole Litany, but got terribly flat – went with the Precentor to the Library[1], and got some knowledge of the Books there – at Luncheon came Mr. Gillett of Runham, Mr. Bensley[2], and the Precentor, & we discussed the MSS. in the Treasury, and took Mr. Gillett there – at 3 went with Ju to call on Sir Henry Stracy[3], whom we found at home.

> 1. At this time (and until 1913) the Dean and Chapter's Library was in the Upper Close in the building numbered seven today, and next to Dr Buck's house.
> 2. W.T. Bensly, Esq., LL.D, was Diocesan Deputy Registrar, and, in 1869 on Kitson's death, succeeded him as Chapter Clerk and Bishop's Secretary.
> 3. Sir Henry Stracey of Rackheath Hall.

Saturday 4

I wrote several letters: Sir G. Baker about painting the Church; Scott with a piece of Greek prose; Lloyd Bruce, declining an invitation to Peterboro' Choral; Secy. of National Society, etc. etc. – After luncheon walked to the depot of S.P.C.K. to buy prayers for Choristers – called on the Heavisides to welcome them back – an eulogy of my Book in John Bull – Poor Fraulein received today sudden intelligence of the death of her mother.

Sunday 5

I tried the Litany at Morning Service, but was very nervous, in consequence of the Organist's omitting to give me the note, as I had asked him to do, and introduced a false note into the suffrages – The Mayor & Corporn. came in state to the Church, but left before the celebration – Afterwards I gave a Book of Prayer to each of the little Choristers – At Aftern. Service there was a grand Anthem from "the Creation": "Let there be light" – Walked in the Garden – a talk with poor Fraulein – walked to St. Mary Coslany with Ju – preached there extem. – There was Cathedral Service, w. the exception of the intoning of the Minister – they sang Dr. Buck's music to Bishp Hind's[1] hymn – the singing was too long, & the Sermon also.

> 1. Samuel Hinds was Bishop of Norwich 1849–57. In 1834 he had written "Sonnets and other short Poems". At his enthronement, Dr Buck had composed a tune for one of these, "Come hither, Angel tongues invite". Canon Hinds Howell was his younger step-brother. Their mother had, unusually, given him as his only Christian name, the surname of her first husband.

Wednesday 8

In the middle of Bkfst. came H. Lee Warner with a Rugby Boy; they breakfasted with us – read the Times & a pamphlet on 'Absolution' by Orby Shipley – after 2d Church, went with Canon Robinson over the rooms which it is proposed to make a school for the singing Boys – he seemed to acquiesce in the proposed appropriation of them – 'Auntie' excused herself from dining with the Bp. – I took the Heavisides there, and we had a large party.

Thursday 9   S.P.G.[1] Anniversary

Attended the Cathedral 3 times – at noon we had about 70 communicants – There was a good congregation at 3 p.m. Collected (at noon & 3 p.m.) something near upon £70.

> 1. Society for the Propagation of the Gospel in Foreign Parts (founded 1701).

●●●

Goulburn left Norwich on Tuesday, May 21, to preach at Peterborough Cathedral Choral Festival next day, returning to Norwich on Friday, May 24.

●●●

Monday 27
Ju ill and in bed w. headache – a note from Heaviside, advising to consult the Bp. before the processional hymn is adopted – I wrote to Buck about it – left Norwich at 11.5; got to Ipswich at 1.13 – there Mr. Williams[1] met me, and went on with my bust at one of the Rooms in the Station. [*He went on to stay at Eyke Rectory, near Woodbridge, preaching in the Church next morning, and then returning to Norwich.*]

> 1. On April 29, Goulburn had replied to the request of the Ipswich sculptor, agreeing.

Thursday 30   ASCENSION DAY
Mg. (Cathedral) Imaginary Ascension with Christ,
    and practical application.
A letter about the Rugby Tercentenary, & another from the Deaconess' Institution – The music & chanting at the Mg. Service were not satisfactory – After the Service saw Kitson, and went thro' with him most of the E.C. questions – then luncheon – afterwards walked with Sophia & Frederica to Harvey's Bank[1]; (2) Stacy's[3], Church printing; (3) Chapter Library: showed them the Nuremberg Chronicle[2], and left them there, to go to Church – Evening Service much better performed – met Buck & Symonds & went into the Doctor's house, where he showed me a metronome[4] – dined with the Heavisides and met Sir H. Stracey, the Keppels[5], Fellowess[6] of Honingham, Ripleys, etc. etc.

> 1. Harvey and Hudson's Crown Bank: Founded 1865; failed 1870. Later became the G.P.O. at the top of Prince of Wales Road.
> 2. By Hartmann Schedel: published 1493 (in German); very large format. A History of the World from the Creation. This copy presented by Charles Trimnell, Bishop of Norwich, 1708–21.
> 3. Local Printer in the Haymarket.
> 4. Invented and used in Austria since c. 1815.
> 5. The Hon. the Revd E.S. Keppell, Rector of Quidenham since 1824, and the Revd W.A.W. Keppell, Rector of Haynford since 1837.
> 6. The Revd T.L. Fellowes, Vicar of Honingham since 1866.

JUNE

Sunday 1
Rode Captain Blake's horse on trial to Earlham Hall – had luncheon w. the Ripleys, and returned by 3 o'clock – I wrote to Cap. Blake declining his horse – after dinner read the Chronicle of Barset[1] to the ladies.

> 1. Only recently published.

Monday 3
Captain Blake wrote, saying that the Coachman had bought his horse for me – after a confab. w. the Coachman, wrote to Capn. Blake, asking what he would demand for taking the horse back again – went to Buck for a lesson at 2.30 – then to Aftern. Church – afterwards practice with the Choir – the Dean[1] (who arrived at 4) came in to the practice w. Ju. – An evening with the Dean, who spun a magnetic Japanese top.

> 1. 'The Dean', Julia's youngest brother, Frederick Cartwright, was Rector of the family Living of Aynhoe (Northants.) from 1862, following the death of his older step-brother, Stephen, that year. He remained Rector until his death in 1906, aged 88. Goulburn's nickname for him is due to the fact that he had been Rural Dean from 1844 to 1862, when Vicar of Oakley, Bucks.

Tuesday 4   Day of the June Audit
The Audit began after morng. Church, and did not end till 4.30 p.m. – Sedgwick, Robinson, Heaviside present.
1. We ratified our acceptance of the terms of the E. Comm. [*About commutation.*]
2. Settled the Services to be in Summer at 8 and 5, in winter at 9 and 4.
3. Made a slight increase in the Stipends both of Subsacrists and Vergers, and agreed to throw the Church open from Service to Service.
4. Arranged that Alden[1] should have the offer of the vacant Lay Clerk's house.
5. Decided to give £5 to the Dean of Ely's musical Scheme.
6. Decided to accept Barnard & Bishop's[2] scheme for warming the Church.
7. An increase of pay to the Choristers and Layclerks for the extra Service on Sunday.
8. Decided to take the Norman Chamber as a Choristers' School Room.[3]

9. Decided to open another *grille* in the Cloister opposite to the existing one.
10. Question of more efficiently cleaning the church postponed, till we shd. know more of Scott's plans.

In the evening there were 17 at dinner.

> 1. Henry W. Alden was the Master in the Choir School, and a Layclerk; later he resigned the Mastership and became Subsacristan. Altogether, he served the Cathedral for 41 years, dying, aged 73, as the result of an accident on Dec. 26, 1901.
> 2. Established in 1826 as a small Ironmonger's Shop behind Norwich Market Place, this firm, by the 1860s, was employing a workforce of 400. The 'Norwich Gates' at Sandringham were their work, given by the people of Norfolk and Norwich in 1864 as a wedding present to the Prince of Wales. With a number of 20th Century mergers, it still exists today.
> 3. Previously to the 'poor mean cottage on the way to the ferry', the Choir School had been in the rooms above the Ethelbert Gate.

••

Next day (June 5th) Goulburn went up to London to attend Convocation, sitting for the three days, June 5th to 7th, and also to see the Ecclesiastical Commissioners and the Architect-in-Chief on Cathedral business. He returned home on the 8th.

••

Wednesday 5   From Norwich to London

Started by the 7.30 train, with Ju, Frederica, Phia, Willie, Dean – we dropped them at Ely for the Festival – Heaviside got into the carriage at Cambridge – got to town at 11 – I went at once to Scott's about the warming; he questioned whether the E.C. would allow us to use the 11,000£ restoring the Choir – I went to Yool[1], who took us to Chalk[1], who comforted me about it – but Mr. Christian[1], whom also Yool took me to see, said the conditions would be very stringent – then I went to Convocation & found Heaviside there, and told him – we left Convocn. and went into the Abbey to inspect the warming – and then went again to Scott.

> 1. All Officials in the Ecclesiastical Commissioners' Office.

Thursday 6

Started with my father in his carriage to go to Westminster – put on my gown at Nepean's[1] – was present at the opening of the Session – a debate as to whether the requirements of Sponsors being communicants should be dropped – I spoke against it in very few words – Sat by Stanley – came out with Heaviside during the recess, & walked with him to the Bounty Board[2], to try to find the Bp.; but in vain – then we parted, and I went to Club, had luncheon, chatted to C. Clerke & Nepean, & wrote letters: (1) Bp. of Norwich (2) Barnard & Bishop (3) Ju[3] ... (5) Capn. Blake, sending him £10 for the trial of his horse.

> 1. Evan Nepean, Canon of Westminster; Chaplain to the Queen. Had been Rector of Heydon, Norfolk, 1831–61.
> 2. The medieval dues which the Pope had collected from the English Clergy had been annexed to the Crown by Henry VIII. Queen Anne gave this money to form a fund known as 'Queen Anne's Bounty' to augment the stipends of the poorer clergy. In 1948, this body was joined to the Ecclesiastical Commissioners to form the Church Commissioners.
> 3. When away, he wrote to Julia almost daily, and often on the day he left home.

Friday 7
Rose at 6.30 – went to St. John's – I walked back with Mr. Gibbs to his house, and saw Albinia on her birthday – then to Sir G. Baker with whom I finished up my accounts[1] – went thence to Bkfst. at Seymour Street – went to Convocation – there met, & spoke to, little Stan[2]. & Dean of Ely[3] – there was a discussion on the propriety of petitioning the Archbp. to have the Convocation opened with H.C. – Dean of Ely made an admirable speech – I said a word recommending that the H.C. Service should *not* be in Latin.

> 1. He had officially resigned from St John's Paddington, on June 4th. Hence, "finished up my accounts".
> 2. A.P. Stanley, Dean of Westminster, was only 5ft 5¼ ins To Goulburn he was usually 'little Stan'.
> 3. The Very Revd Harvey Goodwin. Two years later, he was to become Bishop of Carlisle.

Sunday 9   WHIT SUNDAY
First day of the permanent division of Services – the musical part very well done – a beautiful chant for the 68th. Psalm – I saw the Choristers at 2; and also began an address for the Bishop's Ordinees on the 19th.

Monday 10
Bought a pony for Gussie today (£20) which she rode.

Tuesday 11
   Collection in Cathedral for Norfolk and Norwich Hospital
We made the Hospital collection in the Church, & I presented it at the Altar – The Bishop seemed to be out of spirit in his Sermon – unfortunately we began the Service 5 min. before the Mayor &

corporation filed in – wrote to (1) Prof. Willis, asking hints about the rolls in the Treasury[1]. (2) Jane Russell[2], thanking for her kneelers, wh. appeared in the Cathedral for the 1st. time today. (3) The Mayor, apologising for beginning the Service before his appearance.

1. The Account Rolls of Norwich Cathedral Priory (dating from 13th Century); the Revd Professor R. Willis, M.A., F.R.S., Jacksonian Professor of Natural Experimental Philosophy at Cambridge.
2. A parishioner of St John's, Paddington, to whom he had written about hassocks, soon after arriving in Norwich.

Friday 14

Worked with the Precentor at our descriptive card[1] of the Cathedral till Luncheon – then into the Cathedral, where we went to the Clerestory & examined the bosses[2] of Choir & Transept.

1. For visitors – They revised it from time to time.
2. This is the first mention of Goulburn's and Symond's interest in the Bosses. Though it was nine years work on those in the *Nave*, which resulted in the very large publication of 1876.

Sunday 16   TRINITY SUNDAY

The singing at the early Service was beautiful, specially that of Heber's Trinity Hymn[1] – The 11 o'clock Service lasted till 1.30! – after my Sermon to the Candidates for Orders, of whom there were eight, I explained the reason of the change in the hour of Service – I did not instruct the Choristers today, having to read the Articles with the Lay Clerks (Thouless, Minns, Smith, Mears) after Afternoon Service.

1. "Holy, holy, holy! Lord God Almighty!" by Reginald Heber, Bishop of Calcutta (1823–26), who died in 1826 at the age of 43.

Friday 21

Attended Church twice – In the morning worked with the Precentor at my descriptive Card of the Cathedral – then read over in the Church itself what we had written – then luncheon – and then a call with Ju & Gussie on Fan. Pelham[1], who was out – then went with Ju to Burgess, who took my photograph – then with Burgess to the Cathedral to consider about the possibility of photographing the bosses.

1. Fanny Pelham was the Bishop's only daughter (he had three sons). She never married. Later on, she was President of the Young Women's Club, Palace Plain; Vice-President, and then President, of the Diocesan Girls' Friendly Society (after its foundation in 1875). When the Bishop retired, they went to live in Thorpe in 1893. But, within two years, both her parents had died, and she lived in 16, The Close, until her own death in 1916.

On Monday, June 24, Goulburn went to Ely to attend the inauguration of the new Cathedral Organ.

Wednesday 26
A Deputation, headed by Dr. Gale, waited on me to explain the principles of the Temperance Alliance – went to the Luncheon at the Grammar School with the Jessopps – the Speeches had taken place; and the Prizes had been given – healths of the Examiners, Headmaster, Mayor, myself, the Boys (the last proposed by the Pinseter) – a walk round by Carrow Bridge – then to Kitson's office, to seal the agreement never to let the Close again on beneficial leases.

Thursday 27 Dined with the Ripleys at Earlham
Ju confined to her room all day – in the morning began a second Sermon – Then a gentleman [called] who asked me to become a V.P. of the Archaeological Society[1] – dined at Earlham Hall – met Mr. & Mrs. Lohne, Mr. Buxton & Mrs. Buxton, Capn. and Mrs. Boileau, & the Birkbecks[2]. [He also paid an Archaeological Society Subscription of 7s. 6d.]

1. The Norfolk and Norwich Archaeological Society established 1845. Goulburn V.P. and then President from 1870.
2. Members of three well-known Norfolk families: Buxtons, Boileaus, Birkbecks.

Sunday 30
A lovely day – Church 3 times – Between the 2d & 3d Services I worked with M. Gosch at his Danish translation[1] – I saw the Lay Clerks and finished with them the Articles – A pleasant evening with M. & Mme. Gosch, talking over Inspiration, the authority of the Church, and other subjects – spoke to the Servants about the rubric wh, prescribes the Daily Lessons.

1. Some of Goulburn's books were translated into other languages.

JULY

Saturday 6
Drew up Choristers' Examination Papers – after Luncheon, a walk with Bulmer to the site of St. William's Chapel[1] on Mousehold Heath, & back thro' Lady Harvey's grounds – At Afternoon Service the 4 Lay Clerks (Mears, Smith, Minns, Thouless) having taken the Oaths & made their subscriptions in the Vestry, were admitted.

1. Supposed Christian boy victim of a Jewish ritual murder in the 12th Century. Goulburn frequently took his visitors to visit the site, and also the site of the Lollards' Pit.

Wednesday 10   Fireworks & Supper for the Choristers
To the Pinseter's, to draw up a form for the Admission of Choristers – found the Boys playing in my garden afterwards without permission, which made me wroth – We had supper for them at 8, and from 9 to 10 the fireworks.

Thursday 18
In the morning Julia's inflamed eye was worse – I finished a Sermon (in Library) – then came home & worked at my Music, & sat with Ju – A Chapter Meeting at 1 – settled to give the Choristers surplices – went with Heaviside to Barnard and Bishop about our warming & a formal contract for it – then home, & read to Ju 'the Times' – Little Dustkins had the little Gurneys & Amy Douglas to tea, being her birthday – she had all sorts of presents – smelling bottles in a case from Mrs. Heaviside, & a fur purse from Florence Boyrenson. [*Augusta was now 14.*]

Tuesday 23   Norwich Choral Festival
Ju got up, but did not appear; Gussie also was ailing & did not come to the Festival[1] – To Luncheon there came the Stracey girls and Lady [*blank*], the Burtons, Lady Margaret Vincent, Mr. & Mrs. and Ly. Marion Springfield, and Mr. Manning – I shewed the Ladies our pew – I preached on the power of Music from 2 Kings, 3.

1. This was the 7th Annual Festival of the Norfolk and Suffolk Church Choral Association, the primary object of which was: "the encouragement and extension of Congregational Singing, the improvement of Church Choirs, and the supply of Choral Aid on special occasions." On this occasion there were 42 Choirs present. In 1875 Goulburn became President.

Wednesday 24   Examination commenced
At 9.30, a Chapter[1], attended by Mr. Wright about (1) the security for Stannard (Cushion) in letting the Eaton Hall Farm. (2) Mr. Weston's application for some ground for a separate School – then the examination of Choristers till Luncheon Time (Dictation and History of Joseph) – after Luncheon (from 2.30 to 4.15): Geography – Then drove Mr. Wright to Eaton, inspected the ground for the proposed new School – called on Mr. Weston to talk it over.

1. The management of their farms and land, and the relationship with their tenants, was often a major item of most Chapter Meetings. Goulburn felt out of his depths in this sphere, especially as he grew older. The Dean and Chapter's income depended considerably on this source, but they were frequently lenient to the tenant in difficulty, by reducing the rent. He was much more in his element, setting and correcting Exam. Papers. For the next three days the subjects covered were: St Mark's gospel; Grammar; Music (Paper and Viva Voce); Arithmetic; Viva Voce Scriptures; Reading Aloud; and Church Catechism.

Tuesday 30

Service twice – At 10 began the washing of Goldwell[1] and of Herbert Losinga's[2] slab – After Evg. Church came the distribution of the Prizes – Sedgwick came in the middle of it – Buck also was there, and Julia and Mrs. Heaviside.

1. Goldwell's tomb is in the second bay on the South side of the Presbytery. He was Bishop of Norwich 1472–99.
2. Herbert de Losinga, the Founder, was Bishop of Norwich 1091–1119. His burial place is in the middle of the Presbytery, opposite the High Altar, marked by a black marble slab. Six iron candlesticks (made by Eric Stevenson of Wroxham), linked by white ropes, now surround it. Previously, the slab had been the top of a table tomb.

• •

The Goulburns, with Augusta, now go on holiday for the whole of August and September. At this time, Deans were permitted to be absent for a total of four months in the year. It must be said, however, that Goulburn never divorced himself completely from the affairs of the Cathedral. He continued to prepare Sermons, to preach in various churches, at home and abroad, and to carry on correspondence relating to the work and needs of the Cathedral. On this occasion, the holiday took them to (1) London (July 31–Aug. 8); (2) Tyntesfield, near Bristol (Aug. 8–17); (3) Edgcott (Aug. 17–24); (4) Aynhoe (Aug. 24–31); (5) On his own to Salisbury (Aug. 31–Sept. 3) to preach in the Cathedral on the Sunday. (6) Back to Aynhoe (Sept. 3–9), preaching in Banbury Parish Church on the Sunday morning, and in Aynhoe Church in the afternoon. (7) Southsea (Sept. 9–28). (8) Back to Aynhoe (Sept. 28–30); then, (9) Wolverhampton (Sept. 30–Oct. 3) to preach at the Opening Service of the Church Congress on Oct. 1; finally, back to Norwich (Oct. 3).

TYNTESFIELD: The main home and estate of his friend William Gibbs and family.
EDGCOTT: Home of some of Julia's relations.
AYNHOE: Julia's former home. They always stayed with her brother at the Rectory.
SOUTHSEA: Where Goulburn's father, and other relations, were on holiday.

• •

AUGUST

Saturday 3 To Ticehurst [*while in London*]
Rose at 6.40 – Bkfst. at 8 – Started with Ju for Ticehurst at 9.5 a.m. – there about noon – Fred[1] much as usual – fits less violent and fewer – On our return my Father met us at the Station – I walked home, stopping at Club *en route* – found Elkerton arrived with a bundle of letters.

> 1. Goulburn's younger brother, Frederick Anderleet Goulburn, M.A., had been a Fellow of All Souls' College, Oxford. He appears to have become mentally ill, and to have fairly frequent epileptic fits. He was in a private Mental Home (Ridgeway, Ticehurst, Surrey) run by Dr Hayes Newington and Dr Samuel Newington. It is referred to in the Diaries as "bright and comfortable". Goulburn and his father, usually separately, visited him at regular intervals. By 1869, the Home was costing £375 per year. 'Poor Fred' died in 1877 at the age of 57.

Friday 9 At Tyntesfield
Prayers at 8.30 – No letters – after Bkfst. took a long walk (reading Andrews's Devns.) on the brow of the hill wh. overlooks the place – then came in, and worked away at my Family Prayers[1] with Ju – Archdn. Lee[2] & his party came to Luncheon here – afterwards Mr. Gibbs[3], Prescott, the Archdeacon, & I walked up to the Cricket Ground to see the match between Belmont and Lansdowne (Bath) Club – a quiet dinner; and a delightful Family Evening Service at 10.

> 1. Goulburn was preparing a new book with this title.
> 2. The Ven. W. Lee, D.D., Archdeacon of Dublin.
> 3. Mr William Gibbs had an Oratory in the house where daily Services were held. He was at present engaged in the building of a new Church at Clyst St George, on the outskirts of Exeter. In 1873 he was to lay the foundation stone of the Chapel of Keble College, Oxford, another of his gifts; while in 1878 the Hall and Library of the College were opened, the gift of his two sons Anthony and Henry.

Saturday 17 From Tyntesfield to Edgcott
Prayers at 8 – Left Tyntesfield about 9.45 with the Baring Young party in Mr. Gibb's Omnibus[1], wh. took us to Bourton – This was a bad arrangement, as we had to get fresh tickets at Bristol – When we arrived at Banbury, we found our servants & luggage had been left behind – Sophie & Phia[2] were there, & they took Ju to Chacombe, from wh. place she was brought by Mary Aubrey in her carriage – I walked to Edgcott, and was overtaken en route by the 3 mounted children, Judy, Fanny, Chauncy – Afterwards met Aubrey[3], and then he and I met 'Tim' – George & Mrs. Blake came in with the luggage at dinner time, having been detained 2

hours at Oxford – We feel the agreeableness of the change of air from Tyntesfield.

1. The Omnibus for public transport, introduced in 1829, carried 12 passengers inside a cramped compartment, and 10 outside on an upper deck, and was drawn by three horses. This is more likely to be the smaller version introduced in 1849, which carried 12 inside and three outside, and was drawn by two horses.
2. Sophie Willes (nee Cartwright), step-sister of Julia, and her daughter, Phia, of Astrop House, Northants.
3. Richard Aubrey Cartwright, Julia's eldest full brother, had inherited Edgcott House from his mother Julia (nee Aubrey), where he lived with his wife Maey (nee Fremantle), and his four children, Aubrey, Judy, Fanny, Chauncey.

Sunday 25   **At Aynhoe**
Lane preached in the morning on "Concerning Spirl. gifts B., I wd. not have you ignorant". I in the afternoon on the "Tears of Christ" – Mrs. Bevill Ramsay, Tom & Bitta, and Mrs. Eden of Eydon came over – the Fullertons were all there – the heat was intolerable – afterwards Tom took me over to Newbottle in his vehicle (with Lili[1] and Frances) – there I saw the two other children, & the pictures of the whole family – thence walked with Tom to Kgs. Sutton, where I saw Sophie, Phia, W. Willes & Brucie Boy – thence with Tom & Fred back to Aynhoe – Tom & Bitta[2] dined here.

1. One of Julia's eldest step-brothers, Sir Thomas Cartwright, was a Diplomat. He married Countess Elizabeth von Sandizell, eldest daughter of a Bavarian Nobleman. She was 19, tiny, weighed only 6½ stone, and was always called 'Lili'. She dominated the Cartwright family until her death in 1902, aged 97. When Thomas was on his diplomatic missions, he left Lili at Aynhoe Park, and she spent her time doing excellent, detailed paintings of the rooms and building. They had two sons, William and Thomas. When William inherited Aynhoe Park on his father's death in 1850, Lili moved to Leamington.
2. Thomas (Tom) married Lady Elizabeth Leslie-Melville, heiress of the 8th Earl of Lever and Melville, and took the name Leslie-Melville-Cartwright. They lived at Newbottle Manor, and had four children. Lady Elizabeth was always called 'Bitta'.

SEPTEMBER

Thursday 5   [*At Aynhoe, after returning from Salisbury*]
An ominous letter from MAC[1] in the morning as to my father's[2] state – I answered it to him, and then went on with my Sermon – Another letter from MAC urging us to come to Southsea as soon as we could – we settled that I could not go on account of the Banbury engagement, but that Ju was to go on Saturday with Gussie.

1. His father, and also his cousin Mary Chetwynd, were on holiday at Southsea.
2. Edward Goulburn was a Sergeant-at-Law, for a time a Welsh Judge, for two years Tory M.P. for Leicester, and from 1842 Commissioner of the Court of Bankruptcy. He was now a very sick man, and a difficult one, but the Dean treated him with the greatest care, affection and concern.

Monday 9   Aynhoe to Southsea thro' London

Left Aynhoe and the dear Dean at 8 – At the Station got a letter from Ju announcing my Father to be better – I went by London and there dismissed George[1] to his grandmother's at Deddington – In passing thro' I saw Shoveller[2] about our house – got there about 2 p.m. – My Father met me at Station, and brot. me here – we are in the flat over him and MAC.

1. George Drake, his manservant (to whom he gave £1 for expenses).
2. About selling the house lived in when Vicar of St John's, Paddington.

Tuesday 10   At Southsea

Walked an hour before Bkfst. to make some purchases, and then to the pier – engaged in the morning with correcting my 'Family Prayers' – Afterwards drove with my father to the Docks – saw the Glasgow (under repair for dry-rot) – the Nelson (built 1814; cut down to make a training ship) – the Duncan, and the Scorpion (a ship ordered by the Confederates, but detained & purchased by our Government); she is a turret ship – also went over the Hector an iron-clad – came back & walked from the pier with Ju and Gussie – in the evening read aloud the 'Times' comment on the Report of the Ritualistic Commission.[1]

1. The Ritual Commission, set up in 1867, to enquire into the differences of ceremonial practices in the C. of E., had issued its first Report on the question of Eucharistic Vestments.

Friday 13   Southsea

Walked to the pier before Bkfst. – went out for a sail, and went round the Neapolitan Ship, the Warrior and the Terrible – returned before luncheon – after luncheon MAC & Gussie went to Ryde by Steamer; Ju with my father to Anglesyville – I walked to the ferry leading to Haylin's Island, and back by the beach – saw the allotment gardens of the soldiers, and some rifle shooting at the butts by Captain Cuff and another.

Saturday 14   [*Southsea*]

Read aloud in the Evening a contemptuous article in the Times on the Lambeth Episcopal Conference.

Wednesday 18   [*Southsea*]
Walked before Bkfst. with Gussie to a Dolly Shop, and then to the Pier – after Bkfst. wrote to Gregory[1] of Lambeth, and revised my contemplated Pamphlet on the Lectionary – After luncheon went w. little Dustkins in a boat to (1) The D. of Wellington – Commander Curtis kindly showed us everything, and Capn. Hancock's children showed Gussie their Russian rabbits – my father rather poorly in the evening.

   1. Canon R. Gregory, Proctor for the Chapter of St Paul's Cathedral, London.

Thursday 26   At Southsea
Expedition to Shanklin with dearest Gussie; leaving by the 11.30 boat from the Southsea Pier, & returning by the 4.9 p.m. from the Ryde pier – We dined at Shanklin after seeing the Chine[2] – in coming back, we met Burrows[1], his wife & child, on the pier; also Julia Somerville in the Steamboat – My father very much out of sorts – Gussie and I played ball at the Shanklin Station & kept up 725.

   1. The Revd L.F. Burrows, Assistant-Master at Rugby School (1859–72), appointed by Goulburn, shortly before he resigned.
   2. Chine = deep fissure in the wall of a cliff. At Shanklin one with gardens bordering a stream.

• •

From Monday, September 30 to Thursday, October 3, Goulburn was at the Annual Meeting of the Church Congress at Wolverhampton, where he was the Preacher at the Opening Service on Tuesday, October 1.

• •

OCTOBER

Tuesday 1   [*At Wolverhampton*][1]
Walked to the robing room (after Bkfst.) with Mr. Ryder – there spoke to Bishops of London[2], Rochester[3], Nova Scotia[4], Arkansas[5], Archdn. Sandford[6] & several others – there was a procession from the Room to the Church, wh. was thronged – afterwards walked with the Bp. of Oxford[7] about the town – & thence to the opening meeting[1] about the state of the Church in Staffordshire – Hinds Howell carried me off to the reception Room, & made me write to the Bp. of Illionois[8] for a Sermon – then answered other letters – then walked home to a dinner at 5 – Two-thirds of the party went to the Evening, but left Archdn. Fearon & Mr. & Mrs. Herrick; and we had a very pleasant evening.

1. The Church Congress: An unofficial gathering of Anglican Clergy and Laity, originating from a small gathering in Cambridge in 1861, which became a Congress in Oxford in 1862, and, thereafter, met in various cities annually. From 1863, unusually for the time, ladies were allowed to attend all meetings, but did not customarily speak in the debates!
2. The Rt Hon. and Rt Revd Archibald Campbell Tait (Gulburn's immediate predecessor as Headmaster of Rugby), and next year to become Archbishop of Canterbury.
3. The Rt Revd Thomas Legh Claughton, newly enthroned.
4. The Rt Revd Hibbert Binny (since 1851).
5. The Rt Revd H.C. Lay (since 1861).
6. Archdeacon of Coventry (since 1851).
7. The Rt Revd Samual Wilberforce, one of whose Chaplains Goulburn had been in 1847.
8. The Rt Revd H.J. Whitehouse (since 1851).

Wednesday 2   At Wolverhampton
The Archdeacon & Mrs. Moore showed us her drawings of the Egyptian temples, & those of Mr. Hinckes – then wrote to … (3) John Bull, sending the MS. of my Sermon[1] – after luncheon walked into Whampton with the Archdn. Moore[2] & the Bp. of Ely, and attended the 2 o'clock meeting on Church Education – met Ju & the rest of our party at the Refreshment Room (Corn Exchange) and after refreshment there, went with Bunsen & Ju to the Ritual Exhibition – then to the Evening Meeting on Church Missions where after speeches from Archdn. Grant, Lord Nelson, Mr. Marson & Others, the Bp. of New Zealand[3] made the speech of the Evening.

1. His Sermon at the Opening Service.
2. The Archdeacon of Stafford since 1856, and the Goulburns' host in Wolverhampton.
3. The Rt Revd George Augustus Selwyn (since 1841); greatly influenced the development of the colonial church; became Bishop of Lichfield in 1868; Selwyn College, Cambridge, is a memorial to him.

Thursday 3   From Whampton (thro' London) to Norwich
Left Whampton at 8.40 – got to London about 1 – went down to Yool and found him & ascertained his "temporary financial arrangements" – he took me to Mr. Howes – then after ordering a hat and coat, joined Ju at the G.W.R. Hotel[1], where we dined – thence we went to the G.E. Station[2] & arrived here by 5 o'clock express – I crossed to the Heavisides, who were dining at the Palace, and wrote an account of my interview with Yool.

1. Paddington.
2. Liverpool Street (Great Eastern Railway).

Friday 4
Interview w. Heaviside, & then with Sedgwick & Kitson on our affairs – then wrote to Robinson & others – At 2 there was a sealing of deeds at Kitson's Office – thence Heaviside and I walked to the Barracks, to visit Col. Fitzwygram[1] – he walked back with us to the Cathedral, which we showed him – then he came in to see Ju, and staid till the Evening Service.

> 1. The Officer in command of the Regiment then stationed there. There was a good relationship between the Cathedral and the Commanding Officers at the Barracks, a Military Band playing, from time to time, in the Close.

• •

From **Monday, October 7, 1867** until **Wednesday, February 26, 1868**, Goulburn made no normal entries in his Diary, except for 44 financial entries which he made from time to time during this period. This was due to the accident on **October 7**, when he fell coming out of the house of Miss Morse, an elderly lady whom he visited regularly, and he was largely incapacitated for the next few months. The financial entries show nine payments to Dr Eade*, but none to Dr Johnson, though Dr Johnson, who had been ill, had resumed attendance again by February 1868.

*Dr (later Sir Peter) Eade was a distinguished Physician of the Norfolk and Norwich Hospital. During the latter part of his long life, he had a very distinguished civic career in Norwich: Sheriff, then three times Mayor, twice Deputy Mayor, and an Honorary Freeman of the City.

• •

1868

FEBRUARY

Wednesday 26   ASH WEDNESDAY
Preached on, "Fill ye up, then, the measure of your Father".
I resume my Journal, after suspending it for 4½ months – Today for the first time I dressed in my dressing room, and appeared at Bkfst. with Ju, Fraulein, & Gussie in the Library – The 2d Service of the Cathedral was at 11 o'clock, and I preached as above between the Litany and Commination Service[1], adding a few words explanatory of the Commination, wh. was read from the Pulpit by 'the Precursor' – "Rock of Ages" was sung without the Organ very sweetly – The high stool, rod and curtain wh. Johnson & Symonds had prepared for me in the Precentor's Stall, answered admirably – Afterwards, took a turn in the Bath Chair, and called on Miss Morse[2], who came to the door and chatted with me – at 3 came the Pinseter, and we did some collating of Losinga.

   1. Penitential Service, with a list of God's judgements against sinners, for Ash Wednesday. In Book of Common Prayer since 1549.
   2. The lady at whose house he had had his accident.

Thursday 27
In bed till Johnson came to examine my leg, which he did about 10 o'clock, & said he would come now only at intervals – Adjourned audit at eleven o'clock – we saw Mr. Browne, and ordered a new bay & its two flanking buttresses to be faced with Caen stone at an expence of £96.10 – Nisbet[1] took a most affectionate leave of me after the Chapter.

   1. Canon J.M. Nisbet had been Chaplain to Archbishop Sumner 1848–1862 (i.e. for the whole of the Archepiscopte); in 1867 he became a Residentiary Canon of Norwich in place of Archdall-Gratwicke, and remained in this office until his death in 1892. At the same time he was Rector of St. Giles-in-the-Field, London, and when not in his three months' residence in Norwich, lived at 16, Bedford Square, London. Thus, from time to time, he was able to be a go-between for Chapter business with (e.g.) the Ecclesiastical Commissioners.

Friday 28
B.C.[1] sent two Sermons on 'the Incense', and Wordsworth[2] an address about Colenso[3] to be sent, when signed, to the Upper House of Convocation – At 10 o'clock went out in Bath Chair – met Canon Nisbet who called my attention to the disharmony which would be made in the appearance of the Cathedral if the

worst bay and buttresses were gone on with, omitting the bays wh. come next in order to that already restored – Mr. Browne came to me on the subject just before 3 p.m. – Col. Fitzwygram paid a long visit, & wished the band to play in the Upper Close tomorrow – this is to be at 1.30 p.m.

> 1. Berdmore Compton, Goulburn's Assistant-Master at Rugby; now, Rector of St Paul's, Covent Garden; in 1899, he wrote Goulburn's 'Memoir'.
> 2. Christopher Wordsworth (nephew of the Poet), at present Archdeacon of Westminster; next year to be Bishop of Lincoln.
> 3. Vicar of Forncett St Mary, Norfolk, 1846–53; 1st. Bishop of Natal 1853–63, when he was deposed by his Metropolitan for the views he expressed in Biblical Commentaries. Colenso challenged the jurisdiction of the Metropolitan, and was upheld in this by the Judicial Committee of the Privy Council; in 1866 he was excommunicated by the Metropolitan. Controversy continued until Colenso's death 1883.

Saturday 29

A letter from Stan. asking a Sermon in the Abbey for Dr. Cather's institution – also from Salmon[1], telling me of his engagement to Emma Hill – after Tea at 7, worked with Julia at our Losinga translation.

> 1. Curate of St Michael's, Paddington, 1862–72.

MARCH

Sunday 1   Lent I   Satan's study of individual character, as seen in our Lord's temptation.

Ju went to Church at 8, but at 11 staid at home & read the Service with me – then came the Precentor for the H.C. – I asked him to send my alms to the Seaford Seaside Hospital – after luncheon at 2 prepared for Church – was wheeled to the entrance of the Choir, & there walked – Chanted down to the Psalms – Got through my Sermon with great ease – a very large congregation – read some of the article on 'Choirs' in the Contemporary Review to Ju and Fraulein.

Tuesday 3

Ju in bed all day from sick headache – A pleasant letter from Stan[1]. apologizing for his attack on me at Rugby – this I answered – Precentor came in at 4.30 & we worked on Losinga till nearly 7.

> 1. Dean Stanley and Dean Goulburn had a high personal regard and affection for each other since their undergraduate days; but, theologically, they differed profoundly, and said so openly. When they did, they always exchanged notes affirming their mutual personal friendship.

Thursday 5

In the morning I began a Sermon for Sunday – in the midst of it Heaviside & Hinds Howell paid a kind and agreeable visit – went out with Ju in the carriage at 2.45 – called at Earlham Hall & other places – called on Dr. Eade[1] – While Ju was with the Miss Eades, he came down & talked to me at the door of the carriage – then home – worked at Losinga till dinner with the Pinseter – after dinner read the Convocation Debates in the Guardian – also, began correcting my Family Prayers.

> 1. Dr (later Sir Peter) Eade, lived in a large house at the corner of Upper St Giles Street and Bethel Street, opposite St Giles Church. He did not marry Ellen Ling (nee Rump), a widow, until he was 47, but they had 43 years together.

Friday 6

Heaviside sent in a letter of Nisbet's, descriptive of his interview with Mr. Howes and Yool, in which they told him that the Chancellor is going to introduce a bill[1] to legalise past Commutations, wout. saying anything about future ones – When I was up Heaviside came & talked it over, and talked also about the expediency of our being here during the Association Week[2] – I wrote to the three absent Canons; to Stanley, asking what they are going to do at Westminster; to Dean of Cork[3] asking him to preach here during the Association Week; to Bp. of Oxford, asking him to come to us then; to Dr. Buck about his new Anthem, and some others. Bp. of Winchester[4] has had a paralytic stroke – After dinner read Stanley on the Eastern Church.

> 1. This became the Ecclesiastical Commission Act of 1868.
> 2. The British Association for the Advancement of Science was to meet in Norwich in August. Special Services and Preachers were being arranged for the Cathedral on Sunday, August 23, and other days, and Goulburn intended to be present and preach.
> 3. Very Revd A.W. Edwards, M.A.
> 4. The Rt Revd Charles Richard Sumner (had been Bishop of Winchester for 41 years).

Saturday 7

At luncheon, Heaviside came in – We talked about the Assize Dinner, and about the Bp. of Winchester – soon after, when Ju had gone to the Cathedral, came Mr Copeman[1] and Mr Edward Harvey, to consult as to getting up a meeting, with great me as speaker, to open the Churchman's Club[2] – I recommended waiting till the week of the British Association, but said I wd. write to Sir R. Palmer for them, if they wished it – After Church came the Pinseter, and we had some comfortable work at Herbert, and went into tea with Gussie, who had Fanny Pelham & Fraulein Valentine with her – read John Bull, Times, Illustrated News.

1. The Revd A.C. Copeman (later Hon. Canon) was Vicar of St Andrew's, Norwich, until his death in 1896. He was a qualified Medical Doctor, but had been ordained very soon after qualifying. Was a chief founder of the Norfolk and Suffolk Church Choral Association and one of its two Secretaries; later, Chairman of the Building Committee of the new Norfolk and Norwich Hospital during the 70s. His older brother was a Physician at the Hospital, and lived in the Cathedral Close.
2. The Churchman's Club (founded 1868) was due largely to the efforts of the Revd F. Meyrick, Rector of Blickling from 1868. Rooms were in the Market area of the city and had Reading Room and Library; classes on various subjects; and a Cricket Club. President: Dean Goulburn, and he had 15 Vice-Presidents, including the Mayor, Sheriff, three M.P.s and Archdeacons.

Sunday 8   Lent 2

Ju staid at home w. me in the morning & we read the Morning Service, and a Sermon of Burgon's – then, when Gussie came back from Church, dictated to her a short Lecture for the Choristers on the 1st. word of the Apostles' Creed – Luncheon at 2 – I got on pretty well in the Cathedral – my Sermon was 6 min. shorter than that of last Sunday (in all 14 min.) – Mr. Campbell Wodehouse died this morning – I got a letter from Dr. B. asking the Living for his Son.[1]

1. Dr Buck's son, the Revd G.P. Buck (ordained 1866) did get the Living of Alderford with Attlebridge where he remained until 1873. Of two other sons, Dr Henry Buck was a Surgeon, and Sir Edward Buck a Government of India Official.

Tuesday 10

Last night the Ld. Chancellor brot. in his bill to legalise the 18 commutations wh. have taken place.

Wednesday 11

Looked over Hook's Abyss & other books in preparation for my Lay Clerks tonight – Kitson came in, & I showed him a letter I recd. from Stanley this morning (to the effect that they mean to wait, to see whether an Act will not be brot. in this Session, clearly legalising such schemes as ours) – a letter from Dean of Cork, agreeing to be our guest at the Brit. Association – at 8 came Lay Clerks – I gave a lecture on the life & times of Herbert Losinga.

Tuesday 17
Salmon & Risley both wrote this morning, each asking me to unite him with his second love. Risley[1] marries Martina Crawley Boevey, Salmon Emma Hill.

> 1. The Revd W.C. Risley had been Goulburn's Curate at St John's, and was now, as was the Revd R.I. Salmon, a Curate of St Michael's, Paddington. Risley eventually became Rural Dean of Buckingham, and Salmon a Prebendary of Chichester.

Thursday 19   From Norwich to Yarmouth
We left Norwich in our carriage at 11.45 – As far as Acle the country is fairly pretty; but afterwards the road called Acle Turnpike is the deadest, weariest I ever travelled – nothing to be seen for 8 miles but one or two black sails on the Yare and the Bure, wh. lie on the right and left hand very sluggishly – Before arriving at Acle, we passed Blofield Church and Birlingham St. Peter's[1] (?), with a wretched octagonal turret, and a chancel higher than the nave – I noticed that the lower panes of the E. window of Acle Church were taken out – they seemed to be putting in painted glass – Acle Church seemed a fine one, & the village very tidy and clean – the brilliant cleanness of the windows in all the villages, and in this town also, surprised us both – we find comfortable rooms here, looking south, & have sent our carriage home – after a walk upon the Marine Parade, the first I had taken for 5½ months, we took a fly to Gorleston, stopping in the town to buy a map, etc.

> 1. Burlingham St Peter is now a ruin, some of its best fittings having been transferred to Burlingham St Andrew.

Friday 20   At Yarmouth
I wrote to Roundel Palmer[1], w. my petition for the Churchman's Club – In the morning we drove to the Nelson column, wh. is really very fine – Britannia with the trident and wreath is represented <u>coming from the sea</u> in triumph – beneath the globe wh. supports her are Caryatides with wreaths, etc. – on the plinth the names of Nelson's victories, etc. etc. – also got out at the fishwharf, & walked and saw the <u>swills</u> or large wicker baskets used for carrying the herrings, and one or two <u>trolls</u> which are driven thro' the rows like ancient war-chariots – After luncheon we went to Caister Castle, a fine & extensive ruin, with a modern mansion in it where Mr. Bond lives – in coming back by the N. Denes, we noticed the queer skeleton windmills, going at a rapid rate, which pump up the water, & drain the ground in some way I cannot understand.

1. Sir Roundell Palmer, Barrister, M.P.; devoted member of the C. of E. and High Churchman; Liberal; Solicitor-General 1861; Attorney-General 1863–66; later Lord Chancellor. Wrote of Ecclesiastical matters, and composed several hymns; became 1st. Earl of Selborne.

Saturday 21

In the morning walked on the Wellington Pier – a lovely day, wind SSW – then in a Bath Chair to see St. John's Church, and St. Nicholas Church – the former is that of the Beachmen; the interior is somewhat dark w. painted glass, but very nice; there is a peculiar kind of Mosaic as an altar piece, neither picture nor pattern – In St. Nicholas' Church[1], we saw the whalebone chair, the curious Library table in the vestry, and the painted window in honour of Sarah Martin the dressmaker, who devoted much time & toil to reforming the condition of the prisoners in Yarmouth Gaol – it is a noble Church, 1005 feet larger in Area than St. Michael's, Coventry, but has a poverty stricken look – (S. Martin's window has the 4 subjects of our Lord giving the Keys to St. Peter; Dorcas; the Good Samaritan; the angel delivering St. Peter from prison) – In the afternoon went in fly to Fritton broad & decoy – we sent in our cards to Mr. Brightman, who at present lives on the broad, & whose cottage is most romantic; and they allowed us to drive up to the house, & then walk down to the side of the decoy – In the evening read Strickland's Matilda of Scotland.

1. St Nicholas', the largest parish church in England, was destroyed by fire during the 1939–45 War, and fully restored 1957–60 under Mr Stephen Dykes Bower, while Canon Gilbert Thurlow (later Dean of Gloucester) was Vicar.

Sunday 22   Lent 4   At Yarmouth

Went twice to Church – in the morning at St. John's (the Beachmen's Church), in the afternoon at St. Andrew's (the Wherrymen's) – we were delighted w. both Services – At St. John's the singing (tho' not good) was very hearty – Mr. Harrison preached – He was quite extempore, & used a good deal of action – In the afternoon it was a School Service – the Clergyman in the Lessons ejaculated to the Children, sometimes by name, to keep up their attention – Before dinner, exhorted thereto by 2 letters from Heaviside, I wrote a long letter to Gathorne Hardy[1], begging him to get a clause facilitating Commutations, inserted into the Chancellor's Bill.

1. At this time he was M.P. for Oxford University and Home Secretary. In 1878 he was made a Viscount, and in 1892 the 1st. Lord Cranbrook.

March 1868

Monday 23   At Yarmouth

On going out this morning in a bath-chair, met Mr. Charles Morse[1], & his two children – he recommended our going to see an old room in the Star Hotel[2] on the quay – we did so – it is an Elizabethan room, beautifully wainscoted, & w. most curious pendents on the roof – the door is a kind of lobby – there is a throne in the room, an old chair belonging to the Freemasons; & a picture of Nelson, by some quaker – The landlord seemed interested in the antiquities of his house, wh. formerly belonged to some merchant prince of E. Anglia – at 2 we went in our carriage (wh. rejoined us here on Saturday) to Burgh Castle, and roosted under a projecting coign in a violent hailstorm – the regularity with wh. the bricks are laid makes it one of the most interesting relics of Roman masonry in the country – it is attributed to Publ. Ostorius, after his victory over the Iceni – In the evening we read Strickland's[3] Life of Margaret of Scotland & finished it.

   1. The Revd C. Morse, Rector of St Michael at Plea, and Vicar of St Mary Coslany, Norwich.
   2. There is still a Star Hotel on the quay at Gt Yarmouth.
   3. Agnes Strickland (1796–1874), wrote "Lives of the Queens of England" (1840–41), and "Lives of the Queens of Scotland and English Princesses" (1850–59). In both of these her sister Elizabeth collaborated. Agnes was a historian, educated by her father.

Thursday 26

A mild day, very blowy in the morning – at 2 p.m. called on Mrs. Nevill – she advised Ju to go to Martham Church[1], wh. we did – It has been beautifully restored by Mrs. Dawson in memory of her husband – an east window by Hardman; one of the subjects was our Lord's being fed by Angels in the wilderness, in wh. rabbits are introduced – The lilies round the tomb of Mr. Dawson are beautifully carved – The font is octagonal, & w. the same subjects as ours at Norwich: 7 sacraments & in the 8th. panel our Lord coming to judgement w. 2 trumpet angels.

   1. Martham was a Dean and Chapter Living.

Saturday 28   From Yarmouth to Norwich

Left Yarmouth at 9.55; arrived at Norwich at 1 – My father & Mrs. Bowles[1] arrived at about 5.10 p.m. via Ipswich.

   1. The Bowles were friends of Goulburn's father. When Mrs Bowles became a widow, and then Goulburn senior became a widower, Mrs Bowles became the latter's housekeeper at Seymour Street, London.

APRIL

Wednesday 1

After Bkfst. walked with Heaviside in the Cloister, to inspect the present system of draining; then a conference with Kitson – wrote an answer to Chalk, he having officially communicated to me that H.M. had approved the Report on our case made by the Lords of the Judicial Commee. – Read Gathorne Hardy's gallant defence of the Irish Church[1] last night – also Dr. Phillimore's[2] judgement on Ritualism last Saturday.

> 1. There was much concern in many quarters about the projected Disestablishment of the Church of Ireland.
> 2. Robert Joseph Phillimore was Dean of Arches (i.e. the Lay Judge in the Court of Arches, which is the Consistory Court of the Province of Canterbury). In the recent case against the Revd A.H. Mackonochie, Phillimore delivered judgement declaring the legality of altar lights and of kneeling during the Prayer of Consecration.

Sunday 12   EASTER DAY
Aftern.: The Easter Collect. "I have set before thee an open door".

Did not go to Church at 8 – At 11 I went, and chanted the Litany – the Bp. preached – I received the H.C. from the Bp. and the Precentor in my Stall – poor Ju had been in bed all day with bilious headache – I received from Frederica today a book (Newman's Poems); from Fraulein a pretty flower; from 'Little Dustkins' an illuminated text ('Believe and Live'); and from my Ju a band-case[1] – In the afternoon we had a good congregation – Preached as above – After Service Col. Fitzwygram came to bid me 'Goodbye'.

> 1. i.e. a case for a pair of strips ('bands') hanging down in front of the collar as part of clerical dress.

Monday 13

Heaviside called, while the Choristers were here looking for Easter Eggs in the garden; then they had oranges & 6d. each – The blind women[1] came here to tea, & I looked in on them; little D. sang to them – I went to Service at 5 – had some tea in the School Room with Georgie Cubitt and Ada Hansell – In the evening read aloud to Ju the Dream of Gerontius.

> 1. Probably from the Institution for the Indigent Blind, in Magdalen Street, founded by Thomas Tawell – himself blind.

Tuesday 14

At 8 o'clock the Boys [Choir] came, and we played first at: 1. Bran-tub. 2. Bullet pudding. 3. Shooting the ball into the mouth. Then Supper; Dr. Buck and the Precentor had supper with us – Dr. Buck had to send away Smith, whom he caught truanting, and forbidden to come. But Smith had come not expecting to see the Doctor!

Wednesday 15

A letter from the Bp. announcing that he had made Mr. Hopper[1] Archdeacon of Norwich – wrote to Lord John Manners[2], sending him a copy of my 'Personal Religion'.

> 1. The Revd A.M. Hopper had been Rector of Starston (near Harleston) since 1845 (of which he was the Patron). As Archdeacon he continued as Incumbent until his death in 1878.
> 2. Politician; held office in various Conservative Ministries between 1852 and 1892. In 1888 became Duke of Rutland.

Thursday 16

At 8½ o'clock came the Lay Clerks – We had a pleasant supper at 9¼ – After Prayers they took their leave.

Monday 20

After luncheon, Heaviside & Robinson called – I consulted them about giving the Lay Clerks something more for weekly practice – we agreed on a shilling a week.

• •

From **Tuesday, April 12** until **Saturday, May 30**, the Goulburns were in London because of his father's serious illness, which seemed to follow the pattern of improvement and relapse. Dr Morgan called almost daily, and sometimes twice in the day. At the same time, Goulburn continued to do Cathedral business in London, and keep in regular touch with Norwich.

• •

MAY

Sunday 3

Did not go to Church, alas!
In the afternoon, intended to go to Wells Street with Mr. Gibbs[1], but Morgan[2], having intimated the necessity of a nurse for my father, Mr. Gibbs took me 1st. to St. John's House (a Sisterhood) and, there being no nurse ready for tonight, then to Hans Place, Walton Place, Mrs. Willey's, where I could not find one for tonight, but engaged with one for tomorrow.

1. Mr William Gibbs, the Goulburn's staunch and wealthy friend, was very helpful to them, taking them about in his carriage regularly.
2. Dr Morgan was the Goulburns' long-standing doctor in London. Almost every time Goulburn visited London he called on the doctor, and usually obtained treatment or a prescription.

Wednesday 6

In the morning wrote to V.C.[1] of Oxford, begging off my Whitsun Day Sermon there – luncheon with Mr. Gibbs – he took me to my Club[2], from wh. (with the assistance of George) I walked home – met Mr. & Mrs. Ogle[3] of Sedgeford in Hyde Park – also saw Charles Clerke at the Club – he had come (as they too had) from the great Irish Church Meeting[4].

1. Vice-Chancellor. Goulburn was a Select Preacher.
2. United University Club, Pall Mall East, S.W. When in London he, almost invariably, visited his Club.
3. Vicar of Sedgeford, Norfolk.
4. Proposed Disestablishment of the Church of Ireland caused fears about a similar outcome for the Church of England.

Tuesday 19

Ju's birthday – sent up to her in the morning H. Hunt's[1] picture of the Doctors in the Temple – I went to Prescott Hewett, who examined my leg, & was satisfied w. my progress – then to Bell & Daldy, where I bought Giraldus Cambrensis and H. of Huntingdon – thence to Brit. Museum, where (under the kind auspices of Mr. Bond) I worked till 4 p.m. – then Ju fetched me home.

1. W. Holman Hunt, English Painter (1827–1910). With D.G. Rossetti and J.E. Millais (all three at the beginning of their 20s) and four others, he formed the Pre-Raphaelite Brotherhood, which sought to purify art by a return to the truth and seriousness of the early Renaissance. His popular and best-known picture is the 'Light of the World'.

Friday 29

A very oppressive day, with a vehement and alarming thunderstorm about 1.30 – We persuaded my father to give up two of his horses, and I gave orders accordingly – Frederica came to Bkfst., and said Goodbye – I had luncheon with the Gibbses during the storm – went to Tatham & Proctor's[1] at ½p.4; read over my new will and signed it – Ju and MAC. fetched me in the carriage & we went to the Ho. of Charity, and I saw the Warden about our little Chorister Pearse, and saw also the blind Mr. Walpole – Ju and I walked home from Regent Street.

1. His solicitors.

JUNE

Monday 1 [*Back in Norwich since May 30*]
Attended Service twice – After Bkfst. I went (1) with the Pinseter to Mr. Burgess's, where we had a page of Losinga's Sermons photographed (2) to Can. Robinson's; saw him and Mrs. R. (3) Kitson's, with whom I had a long talk – After luncheon called w. Ju on the Bishop and saw him and Mrs. Pelham – then a drive to Thickthorne; Mr. Watson not at home – Mr. Johnson called on our return.

Wednesday 3
Started for Cambridge with Pinseter at ½p.7 – Went to the Library at C.C.C.[1] & examined the Consuetudinarium[2] till about 1 p.m. – then returned to the Bull to luncheon – then to the Univ. Library – Mr. Bradshaw <u>most</u> kind, & explained to us many difficulties in the Corpus MS. – arranged our information chronologically after dinner.

1. Corpus Christi College.
2. A Consuetudinarium or Customary was a book containing (1) the rites and ceremonies for the Services, and/or (2) the rules and customs of discipline, of a particular monastery, cathedral, or religious order. This was necessary in the Middle Ages when there was a variety of local differences.

Sunday 7 **TRINITY SUNDAY**
"Thine own vineyard have I not kept".
Preached an Ordination Serm. as above, having the 6 Candidates (4 Deacons, 2 Priests) <u>opposite</u> to me – we were out about ½p.1 – Can. Robinson preached in the afternoon – After the Service came Buck, the Precentor and Hansell[1] to talk over the sad affair of Mr. Chamberlain[2] – We had the poor Boy, Kendall up and examined him – In the evening was overwhelmed by indigestion & went to bed.

1. Solicitor in the Close.
2. A Master at the King Edward VI Grammar School; he was suspected of molesting one of the Cathedral Choir Boys, Kendall.

Tuesday 9
Dr. Buck came in with fresh discoveries about this wretched business of Kendall's – then we had to go to Dr. Buck's, there to meet Mr. Kendall, the father, Mr. Gunton's Coachman.

Wednesday 10
After Bkfst. received & listened to Rev. Mr. Davidson, a friend of Mr. Chamberlain's – then began my Memoir of Herbert in the Library, receiving there a visit from Dr. Buck – After Afternoon Service, heard the singing of Grosse, the boy from St. George's Chapel, Windsor – Grosse sang well: "Hear my Prayer".

Thursday 11   St Barnabas
In the morning Dr. Buck met the Pinseter and myself in the Library & read the correspondence about Grosse, wh. had passed between the D. of Windsor & the Boy's Father – We determined to take him.

Saturday 13
In bed, my leg being swollen, till 10 – then got up – Mr. Johnson looked in about 12, & prescribed Calomel – Can. Robinson called – then came Heaviside – then Dr. Buck, to tell me that Mr. Kendall, pere, had been stealing his master's pears – [*afternoon*] Service – afterwards admitted the new Chorister, Richard Thomas Grosse, & gave an address to the Boys – then a little work with the Pinseter at Losinga – then tea in the garden with Emily Symonds, Ada Hansell, Amy Douglas, Thorpe Pats., Norwich Pats[1]., Frauleins Snell & Andler – a letter from Lou[2] at Oxford – I wrote for her to the Warden of Merton, V.C. of Oxford, & Charles Clerke.

1. Children of the Close and City, Augusta's friends. 'Pats' = Pattesons.
2. It seems to have been a matter of obtaining four tickets for a University occasion for his cousin, Louisa Thomas, and three other members of her family.

Sunday 14
A letter from Mr. Chamberlayne, w. I afterwards put into Mr. Hansell's hands.

Tuesday 16
Service twice – In the morg. looked over the old Books in the deanery Study Cupboard with the Pinseter & began a Register – Mrs. Carver called, to ask me to give her my influence at a meeting of the Assn. for Widows & Unmarried drs. of deceased Clergymen – after luncheon, called on Mr. Hansell, w. Mr. Chamberlyne's letter [*another one*] – he said he would answer it for me – then to Dr. Buck's – went with him to the lodging-house keeper, where Mr. Chamberlyne lodged – received a most severe

letter from the D. of Windsor[1], rebuking me for the admission of the new Chorister – this I answered in the Evening.

> 1. The Hon. and Very Revd Gerald Valerian Wellesley, Registrar of the Order of the Garter.

Thursday 18

After Bkfst. hard at work cataloguing the Dean's Books[1]; I was joined by the Pinseter – At luncheon (1) Mrs. Wright (2) Mrs. Fraser Tytler (3) Mr. Drake, Senr., Junr. & Miss Drake (4) Mr. & Mrs. & Ada Hansell – Mrs. Fraser Tytler sang very beautifully the Snowstorm, and a Serenade of Gounod's, and The fashion of this world passeth away.

> 1. He had found, in a cupboard in the Deanery Study, the library of Humphrey Prideaux (1648–1724), who had been Dean of Norwich from 1702–24. The three vols. of Dean Prideaux's Diaries (covering the years 1694–1724) are in the Norfolk Record Office; Microfilm in the Dean and Chapter's Library.

Thursday 25   Audit

At Church twice – we sealed a number of leases, and talked over (1) Stipends of Minor Cs. (2) Pew Rents of S. Stephen's (3) The answer to Yool's letter, yesterday received by Kitson – I did not get away till 4.30 – after Church the Pinseter and I examined into Livock's conduct, and finding that the charges of drunkenness and lying were substantiated, had him caned by Alden[1] – Fearside also was caned, and Butler and Livock were excluded from the Firework Supper on Thursday next – A dinner party [*ten guests listed*].

> 1. See June 4, 1867 (Note 1)

Sunday 28

Present at all three Services – Can. Robinson in the morning preached on "O Lord, revive thy work in the midst of the years", in the prophecy of Habakkuk – I read the Prayers for the D. of Edinburgh[1] & the Abyssinian Victory[2] (reference to both wh. was made in the Sermon) on all three occasions – Between the Services I wrote a short Lecture for the Choristers, and gave it to them at 5 o'clock.

> 1. Queen Victoria's second son, the Duke of Edinburgh (a Naval Officer) was shot in the back at Sydney, Australia, by a Fenian towards the end of April. (Fenian = Irish Republican Brotherhood). It would appear that he had not yet fully recovered.
> 2. On Jan. 2, a British Expedition entered Ethiopia (Abyssinia) to release hostages held by Emperor Theodore; on April 13, the British (under Sir R. Napier) stormed Magdala and released hostages. Now Napier had captured Magdai (the Capital) and the Emperor Theodore committed suicide.

JULY

Thursday 2
At work upon MSS. in the Deanery during the Morning – In the afternoon a walk with Muller[1] on Mousehold Heath – On our return, looked in upon the Bedesmen, etc. at dinner in our Servants Hall – Dined with Robinson.

1. The Revd J.S. Muller, ordained in 1859, was a Minor Canon of Norwich from 1865–72. From 1862–65 he had been Dean Pellew's Curate at Gt Chart, Kent (a Living which Goulburn's predecessor held in plurality).

•••

His father's declining health took Goulburn to London from July 7 to 11, and also enabled him to study documents in the British Museum, relative to his work on Bishop Losinga, and to further negotiate with the Ecclesiastical Commissioners on the subject of commutation and loans.

•••

Thursday 9
Went to Quebec Chapel in the morning – B.C. called, & had a long chat about his Deaconesses[1], & about the mode of printing the new S.P.C.K. New Test. – I met Heaviside & Nisbet at the E.C. – Lord Chichester[2] & Mr. Howes[3] were there – Nisbet walked with me to the Mus. – as I was eating an ice at St. James's Hall, Nepean joined me, & we walked together to Brook Street – then home.

1. The first Deaconess in the Church of England (Miss Elizabeth Ferard) was dedicated to her work by A.C. Tait, then Bishop of London in 1861.
2. Elder brother of the Bishop of Norwich.
3. Edward Howes, Esq., M.P. for South Norfolk. Both Commissioners.

Saturday 11   From London to Norwich
Left Seymour St. at 7; did not get to Norwich till 1.30 – found Gussie & Fraulein waiting w. the Carriage – rather a scramble to get ready in time – At Church we had Hon. Can. Hinds Howell, Oys. Patteson[1], and Groome[2]; also Heaviside (as well as Robinson) who returned last night – preached on "the Doctrine of Sacred Places" – got only £17[3] – attended the Practice – Gussie & Fraulein dined with me, & in the Evening I worked at the 'Authorities for H.L.'s Life'. [*Julia had remained in London.*]

1. See February 28, 1867 (Note 4).
2. The Revd R.H. Groome was Editor of 'Christian Advocate and Review' 1861–66, and became Archdeacon of Suffolk 1869–87.

3. It was the Jubilee Service (50 years) for the Incorporated Church Building Society. Established in 1818 in thanksgiving for the victory of Waterloo, £1.000,000 was given by the Government, followed in 1824 by a further £500,000; large subscriptions also came from the King and others; and also continuing subscriptions. Between 1818 and 1833, £6,000,000 was spent on new Church buildings. A Norwich branch was founded in 1836; Canon Heaviside was now its Treasurer, and Symonds, the Precentor, one of its Secretaries.

••

Goulburn returned to London on July 14 until July 29, during which his father was very ill, but, once more, seemed to rally. Two days before leaving for Norwich, Goulburn was ill with what must have been a mild form of Cholera. There had been four major epidemics of Cholera in Britain between 1831 and 1866, killing a total of c. 140,000 people. Effective treatment was not developed until the 20th. Century.

••

Friday 31

All the morning drawing up Choristers' Examination – In the afternoon, Bensly[1] came, & showed us the charter of Herbert's giving Frange to the Monastery.

1. W.T. Bensly, Esq., LL.D., Deputy Registrar and Assistant Secretary to the Bishop.

AUGUST

Monday 3

In the morning a viva voce Exam. of the Boys on the Lawn, the Pinseter assisting – After Evening Service, set the boys a lesson in dictation – In the evening at 9.30 went with Sedgwick to the Judges Lodging, & saw Mr. Justice Keating[1].

1. Sir Henry S. Keating, Judge of Common Pleas, 1859–75.

Tuesday 4

Service for the Judges at 10 this morning – Mr. Talbot (the Sheriff's Chaplain) preached on "the Powers that be are ordained, etc." – Before the Judges came, I mooted to the Mayor[1] the question of his attending an opening Service for the British Association – Afterwards Boys' examination (St. Luke's Gospel) till Luncheon – After Evening Service, Examn. in English Grammar – read to Ju some of the Review of Fitzgerald's Life of Garrick in the Quarterly.

1. J.J. Colman, Esq.,: Partner with his uncle of J. and J. Colman until 1851, then Head; Leader of city Liberals; Sheriff 1862; later M.P.; Magistrate; Deputy Lieut. 1880; Alderman 1896; Hon. Freeman 1893.

Wednesday 5
Examn. in Old Test. in the Morning – Geography in the Afternoon – Taken unwell in the Evening.

Thursday 6
Unwell all day – The Judges and High Sheriff came to dine at 7.30 – Boys examined in Apostles' Creed, etc. etc. & Arithmetic.

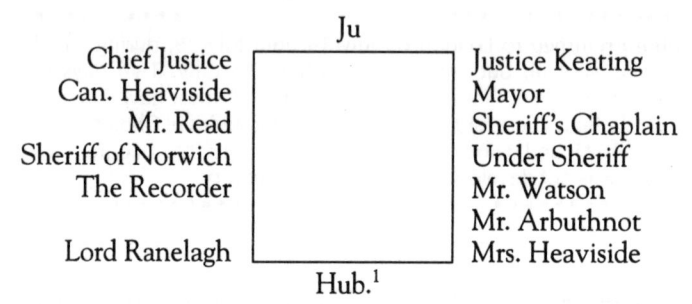

	Ju	
Chief Justice		Justice Keating
Can. Heaviside		Mayor
Mr. Read		Sheriff's Chaplain
Sheriff of Norwich		Under Sheriff
The Recorder		Mr. Watson
		Mr. Arbuthnot
Lord Ranelagh		Mrs. Heaviside
	Hub.[1]	

Dinner in the Library.

1. Julia usually called Goulburn 'Hub' or 'Old Hub', and he always recorded himself on dinner party lists in this way.

• •

Because of his father's declining condition and death on August 24, Goulburn was not back in Norwich until September 5 (having left on August 10) – and then only for a few days before going on a belated holiday to Brighton and the Aynhoe area. He had arranged, with enthusiasm, the special Sunday Services and Preachers in the Cathedral for the Sunday (Aug. 23) of the visit of the British Association for the Advancement of Science. The Dean of Cork preached at the Morning Service, and, in the absence of Goulburn, Canon Heaviside preached at the Afternoon Service. The Collection taken for the Norfolk and Norwich Hospital was £100. 5s.

• •

Wednesday 19
My father had not been so well today – He seems exceedingly depressed, has slept much – He asked for Prayer in the afternoon, and we prayed with him.

Friday 21
At 1 p.m. went w. MAC. and Bullivant to hear Father Ignatius[1] preach at S. Nicholas Acons & S. Edmund King – He read the Litany, & preached on "When my Ω is overwhelmed, lead me to the rock". (Psalm 61) – much gesticulation – had luncheon at the Oxf. & Cambridge – then home in Cab – my father much better.

1. Father Ignatius = the Revd Joseph Leycester Lyne (Deacon). He was determined to restore the Benedictine Order in the Church of England. In 1864–65, he acquired a large dilapidated house at the top of Elm Hill, and, with his followers, established his Monastery. Not recognised by the Bishop, and causing considerable stir in Norwich, the project failed. He was a gifted Mission Preacher, but his folly, obstinacy, and self-righteousness continually brought disaster.

Saturday 22

The morning being very rainy, & my voice no better, we resolved to give up going to Norwich, & telegraphed accordingly – In the afternoon a decided change for the worse came over my dear Father – the phlegm gurgled in his throat, he looked, and talked wildly, & we were much alarmed – Dr. Dodd came, & seemed to think it a hopeless case – Afterwards Dr. Fly Smith, who prescribed mustard poultices and medicine to loosen the phlegm, and thought he might rally – he does seem a little better (10.15).

Sunday 23

My dear Father has been sinking all the day – he however joined in & seemed thankful for the Litany in the morning, and the Psalms & Collects in the Evening – Dr. Fly Smith has called 3 times; he considers the case hopeless.

Monday 24   St Bartholomew

My dearest Father breathed his last at 1.30 a.m. – All the day writing letters – In the afternoon, attended Church at Wells Street[1], walking there & back.

1. St Andrew's, Wells Street, built in 1846.

Tuesday 25

Letters in the morning till Luncheon Time – Then in carriage to Tatham's, with whom I had a long business interview – Walked home – Wrote a Memoir of my Father for "the Illustrated News"[1].

1. The "Illustrated London News" began publication in 1842.

Wednesday 26

I cleaned out the secret drawers, and looked over some of the papers of my Father – At 2 p.m. called on Mr. Jason Smith (I had first been to T. & P's to take them the Banker's Book, etc. etc.) – I walked back & wrote letters about the Dublin Congress, taking Dr. Fly Smith's advice not to go there – In the evening at 8 Ju, MAC, & I went to St Cyprian's & heard a 'fancy Service', beginning with the Lord's Prayer.

Saturday 29   St John Baptist
My dearest Father's funeral – Present: Lord Chetwynd, Dick & Charlie C., H. Stapylton and his son, Fazakerley, Col. & F. Goulburn, Rokeby, Spence M., Aubrey, Gerard Thomas[1], Sir W. Clerke and myself – Nepean (his train being late) only arrived in time to take the latter part of the Office.

> 1. Now aged 20, but who was to marry Gussie twelve years later.

SEPTEMBER

Tuesday 8   [*Briefly back in Norwich*]
Went to Church twice – Attended the Christening of 'Mary Stewart Robinson'[1] in the afternoon at 4; I am her Sponsor – After Service Prizes were given away to Choristers, Sedgwick, Heaviside, Robinson, and the Ladies attending.

> 1. Canon Robinson's youngest child.

Wednesday 9   From Norwich to London
Left Norwich at 7.30 – Gussie & Rose we dropped at Cambridge – wrote to Morgan for his account – At 2 p.m. went to Gosling's[1] and paid in £46 for the Carriages and horses – then to Freshfields, where I made an affadavit about my mother-in-law's personalty – he then showed me a deed appointing me upon my father's death the principal of my Brother's[2] fortune – went to Tatham to inform him of this, but did not find him in – In the Evening, looked over & destroyed papers.

> 1. Gosling and Sharpe, 19, Fleet Street, his Bankers in London.
> 2. See August 3, 1867 (Note 1)

Saturday 12   Got into Lodgings at Brighton
Dined at the Bedford at 5 p.m. and afterwards moved into Mrs. Brown's Lodgings[1], 24, Mar. Parade – Corrected proofs of my Family Prayers in the morning – in the afternoon went out for a long walk with Ju – met Dr. O'Brien, who had just returned from Malvern – met also W. Stapylton, taking his 3 brats to Mr. Malden's School.

> 1. The Goulburn's had arrived in Brighton the day before and stayed at the Bedford Hotel. It was their almost invariable custom, whether in the British Isles or abroad, to stay for a night or two at a good hotel, and, if staying longer, to move into much less expensive lodgings. Goulburn's friends, family and acquaintances were so numerous and widespread that he usually met someone he knew wherever he went.

Sunday 13   At Brighton
Went thrice to Church.
1. St. Stephen's Montpelier Place – Dean of Chichester[1] preached very well on "Come unto Me" – he pointed out that the 'coming' was something distinct from faith, & represented Christian exertion.
2. St. Peter's. Mr. Ashley (late of St. Peter Mancroft) preached on these words in Job which speak of the decay of mountains & rocks & also of things wh. grow out of the earth.
3. St James's – this was a play rather than a Service – thurifer, crucifer, ceroferarii, banner, priest in gorgeous copes – Mr. Purchas wears a mustache without a beard[2] – He preached on "As Moses lifted up the serpent, etc." – he seemed to say that until he organised his Services, Brighton was a spirl. wilderness, but that it was he who 1st. raised the Cross & preached Christ crucified – He described the forging of the brasen serpent – crash, crash, crash, & then a plunge into the hissing stream, & then it was finished.[2] So Christ was fashioned & prepared, then plunged into Jordan in Bm., & then finished on the Cross, etc. etc.

> 1. The Very Revd Walter Farquhar Hook had been Vicar of Leeds 1837–59, and a famous Church builder there, then Dean of Chichester. He wrote: 'A Church Dictionary' (1842); 'A Dictionary of Ecclesiastical Biography' (8 vols. 1845–52); the 'Lives of the Archbishops of Canterbury' (12 vols. 1860–76). When Goulburn had been offered the Deanery of Norwich, he went to Chichester to discuss with Hook the work of a Dean.
> 2. When the Editor, who then had a moustache, was being interviewed by the fully-bearded Bishop of Down before his ordination in 1942, he was told: "Take it off. You can have it all like me, or nothing at all".

Thursday 24
In the morg. received a letter from Proctor, stating that the Copyhold Property at Hadham must go to Fred – In the afternoon drove with Ju to Hurstpierpoint – we were taken over the College Chapel by Dr. Lowe; a sister of Dr. Lowe's wife, Miss Coleridge, was there, and also Mr. & Mrs. Woodard, the son of the Provost[1].

> 1. The Revd Nathaniel Woodard (1811–91) from his ordination in 1841 was convinced that there should be Public Schools to provide a sound middle-class education on a definite Anglican basis. Founded Lancing (1848); Hurstpierpoint (1850), and several other 'Woodard Society' Schools. Became a Canon-Residentiary of Manchester (1870), and Hon. DCL. of Oxford in the same year. Sub-Dean of Manchester (1881).

Monday 28   From Brighton to London
           From London to Ayhoe

Left Brighton at 9.45, arriving in London 11.5 – Saw Col. & Mrs. Knox at Seymour Street, & gave him the Lease of the House – left London at 2 – C. Clerke[1] joined us at Oxford – there dined here besides C. Clerke, Mr. Risley[2], Sophie, Phia, Willy Willes, Tom, Bitta[3].

> 1. Goulburn once referred to Charles Clerke, Archdeacon of Oxford, as a cousin.
> 2. Father of the Curate of St Michael's, Paddington.
> 3. Sophia Willes was a step-sister of Julia, with her daughter Phia and son Willy; Tom Leslie-Melville-Cartwright ('Lili's 2nd son) and his wife, Lady Elizabeth (Bitta), lived at Newbottle Manor.

OCTOBER

Monday 5   At Aynhoe

Dean went out shooting – Risley & his wife came to luncheon here – afterwards we went across to show them the pictures at the Great House[1] – thence I fetched away Dugdale's Monasticon[2].

> 1. Aynhoe Park (the Great House) belonged to Willy Cartwright, son of Sir Thomas (died 1850) and Lady Cartwright ('Lili'), now living in Leamington Spa. Willy needed to let it and he and his wife lived either abroad or in a Cottage on the estate. In Julia's youth the 'Great House' had a staff of 20 to 30 Servants.
> 2. Sir Wm. Dugdale (1605–86), Garter King-of-Arms, brought out the first volume of 'Monasticum Anglicanum' (with Roger Dodsworth) in 1655, 2nd vol. in 1661, and 3rd vol. in 1673. They contained a vast collection of monastic charters and other sources relating to the history of English Monasteries and Collegiate Churches in the Middle Ages.

Wednesday 7   At Aynhoe

Worked at Herbert L. and wrote a good long piece – Walked with the Dean to Croughton & Charlton – Miss Egerton & the little girls were here for several hours – they brot. the announcement of Matthew's[1] intended marriage to Mrs. Robb's Fraulein – the Evening Papers announce the appointment of Magee[2] to the See of Peterboro'; & of Mansel[3] to the Deanery of St. Paul's.

> 1. Matthew Boulton (of Gt Tew Park) had been married to Julia's sister Frances (Fan.) who died in 1864, leaving two young daughters, Meanne and Ethel.
> 2. William Connor Magee, ordained 1845; Rector of Enniskillen; Dean of Cork (1864–68); Bishop of Peterborough (1868–91); Archbishop of York (1891), but died that same year.
> 3. Henry Longueville Mansel (1820–71); High Churchman; Professor of Ecclesiastical History, Oxford, 1866–68; Dean of St Paul's (1868–71).

Thursday 22   At Edgcott
Wrote Sermon in the morning – A bundle of letters in the evening – one from the Precentor, containing the announcement of the Chancellor's[1] sudden & awful death.

> 1. The Worshipful Charles Evans (Chancellor of the Diocese since 1845). He fell from his horse, on his head, at Earlham and was killed. As Chairman of the Board of Guardians, he was on his way to visit the Workhouse. He was 70.

Tuesday 27   From Edgcott to Rugby [*via Leamington*]
Left Edgcott with Judy at 8.45 a.m. – bought Judy Tennyson's[1] Maud & In Memor.; and then went on to the Dentist's (Mr. Jepson) where I left her – then to Lili's where I met the Genl.[2] who told me about Fairfax's proposed candidature for the County – then went to dizzy Gunning, & saw also Mrs. G., Lucie, Jessie & Isabella – sat there an hour – then back to luncheon with Lili – Judy had some stuff in her teeth wh. burns out the nerve – at 4 left Leamington for Rugby in the same carriage with Blackwood – Dr. Temple[3] met me at the Station, & we walked together to the School House – A large party at dinner, consisting of Mr. & Mrs. Huchinson, Arnold[5] & Mrs. A., Mr. Moultrie & daughter, Maggie Arnold, Kitchiner[6], Ernest Sandford, Benson[4], Bowden Smith[5], B.C.[5] & others.

> 1. Alfred Tennyson, a son of the Rectory, was made Poet Laur. in 1850, on the death of Wordsworth; pub. 'In Memoriam' (1850), 'Maud' (1855). Made a peer in 1884.
> 2. Lt.-General Wm. Cartwright, Julia's step-brother, who fought at Waterloo. Fairfax, his son, became M.P. for South Northants.
> 3. Frederick Temple, Goulburn's successor as Headmaster, in 1869 became Bishop of Exeter (and later Archbishop of Canterbury). Each felt a slight unease in each other's company – the new Headmaster and the old; the contributor to 'Essays and Reviews' (1860), and the critic of the book.
> 4. E.W. Benson (now Headmaster of Wellington School) and to be Temple's predecessor as Archbishop of Canterbury.
> 5. Charles Arnold, E.W. Benson, Philip Bowden Smith, and Berdmore Compton had all been Assistant-Masters under Goulburn.
> 6. F.E. Kitchener, Assistant-Master appointed by Temple, became Headmaster in 1874 of the new High School at Newcastle-under-Lyme. [The occasion was the Tercentenary of the School]

Wednesday 28   St. Simon & St. Jude   At Rugby
Walked after Bkfst. with Mr. Moberly[2] to see Mr. Buckoll[1] – rung but no one came – Walked with Benson to see Mrs. Sidgwick[2] – Church at 11.30 – Buckoll read the Prayers, and Dr. Temple the Commn. Service – I preached on James 5, 17 – Coming out, saw Mr. Sale – walked with Burrows to Arnold's House, where we had

luncheon (with a large party) at the Boys' Dinner – then walked with B.C. to see (1) the Buckolls. (2) Stomach & his dr. (3) Billington & K. Ashton. (4) Gilbert, Shoemaker – met Hands, walked with Arnold, Burrows, & B.C. – then to tea with Arnold – came home & wrote to Ju – a pleasant evening – Thoades maj. Ernest Sandford, Mrs. Sedgwick, Lee Warner[2] & the Burrows[2] – also John Sandford.

1. H.J. Buckoll had served (for 45 years) under six Headmasters.
2. C.E. Moberly, Arthur Sidgwick, The Revd F.L. Burrows, Henry Lee Warner, were all current Assistant-Masters.

NOVEMBER

Tuesday 3
A pleasant day – H.C. in the Cathedral for the Pastoral Work Association[1] – Nisbet, Bulmer, Symonds and I officiated – Afterwards I read at the Clerical Rooms my paper on 'Confession' – It was well received, and several questions were asked me by Garry, Mr. Gurdon, Mr. Hoste, Mr. Cooper, Mr. Clement Smith and others – afterwards received at luncheon the Archdeacon of Norwich[2], Mr. Garry and Sweet (who also had bkfst. with us) – After 2d Service at the Cath. I walked with Nisbet in the dark – Sweet dined with us and left us at 8.

1. Founded in 1863 to gather Clergy, from town and country, to discuss pastoral work together.
2. The Ven. A.M. Hopper.

Friday 6
After Morning Service went with Nisbet to Heavisides, & talked over the proposed absorption of our Fabric Fund[1] by the E. Cm. – thence to Kitson's – went to Harvey's Bank[2] to get some Rugby Townhall shares cashed – then walked in Cloisters – then 2d Church – wrote my Lecture on the Bible for an hour – Read in the Evg. Hall's 'Hard Measure' – wrote to Benson sending him Losinga's Letters – Prepared for press my paper on Private Confession.

1. The Fund contained £2,800.
2. Harveys and Hudsons Crown Bank moved, in 1865, from 17, Upper King Street (the premises now occupied by the Norfolk Club) to the great new building at the top of Prince of Wales Road. But, in 1870, the Bank failed and Sir Robert Harvey, the Senior Partner, committed suicide. The goodwill of the Bank was bought by Gurney's Bank and customers transferred to it. The building later became the G.P.O.

November 1868

Monday 9
After Afternoon Service had a talk in the vestry with the Pinseter & old Smith about the search for H. Losinga's coffin.

Tuesday 17   Polling Day
Was at the Poll today, at the opening of it, with Nisbet – we both plumped for Stracey[1] – After Mg. Church began a Sermon for Sunday – At 1.30 went to the Palace to meet the Eastern Bps. – Only Lincoln[2], Rochester[2], and Ely[2] there – Sat between Miss Borelase & Mrs. Heaviside – A talk with Bp. of Rochester about Josephus; with our Bp. about Magee's Sermon – he was not there, having to do homage to the Queen – afterwards a walk with Nisbet & Hinds Howell on the Thorpe Road – After Service came news of the result of the Election:

         Sir H. Sytracey[1] 4509
         Sir W. Russell[1] 4492
         Tillett 4349

A very pleasant evening, singing songs with Gussie.
The 3 Bps. were at Evening Service in the Cathedral.

1. Sir Henry Stracey (Conservative) of Rackheath Hall, Norwich, and Sir W. Russell (Liberal) of Charlton Hall, Gloucestershire, were both elected to Parliament, there being two members for Norwich. The Liberals had an overall majority of 112 seats, with over half a million more votes than the Conservatives. W.E. Gladstone became Prime Minister.
2. The three Bishops were: The Rt Revd John Jackson (Lincoln); The Rt Rev. Legh Claughton (Rochester); The Rt Revd Edward H, Browne (Ely).
3. Jewish Historian (c.37–c.100.)

Thursday 19   Service in Cathedral for Churchman's Club[1].
In the morning finished a Sermon – At 2 o'clock finished with the Precentor our table of Coincidences – then walked with him – a waggon, run away with by a shy horse, nearly went over us, and bolted against a lamp post, which it upset – nobody hurt – Attended 5 o'clock Service – Dinner at 6, Heavisides, Nisbets, Matchett, Meyrick, Garry, Archdeacon, with our 4 selves twelve – The Archdn. of Norwich preached on "Buy the truth, & sell it not".

1. Founded largely through the efforts of the Revd F. Meyrick, recently become Rector of Blickling. Rooms in Upper Walk, Market Place, with Reading Room and Library. Classes on various subjects. Cricket Club formed. Patron: the Bishop; President: the Dean.

Saturday 21
Resumed the translation of H.L.'s letters at the Pinseter's house – After luncheon. & before 2d Church, went to call on the Bp. – mentioned to him (1) the proposed Evening Services in Advent (2) the proposed exhumation of H.L. – After 2d Church, Practice – then arranged with the Pinseter the hymns for the special Advent Services.

•••
From Saturday, November 28, Goulburn was in London, staying with Berdmore Compton, preaching at his Church on Sunday, at Quebec Chapel on Monday, and going to Ticehurst to see his brother 'poor Fred', on Tuesday (Dec. 1). Back to Norwich on 2nd.
•••

DECEMBER

Tuesday 1   To Ticehurst & back to London
Left London by the 9.30 train – left my rug[1] behind, & being cold bought a new one <u>en route</u> – Luncheon with Fred, as usual – Saw Dr. S. and Mr. Alexander Newington – returned to London by 4.33; foolishly stopped at Cannon Street & got out there – bought a fairing[1] for Gussie – came home & settled my accounts – saw Wilson the House Agent in Albion Street about letting our house to a Mr. Lee (Barrister).

   1. The rug cost £1; Gussie's present 16s 6d.

Thursday 3   Evening party of Lay Clerks
At home all day by Johnson's advice – I wrote letters, and prepared for my reading tonight – At 8 o'clock came our guests; Canon & Mrs. Nisbet, Mrs. Wright w. her sister Mrs. Pretyman, her niece Mrs. Hayes, and her grand-niece, Mary Hayes, Miss Cubitt & Miss Georgie – Messrs. Cox, Hare, Thouless, Love, Edwards, young Livock & Grosse, Mr. Mann, Dr. Buck, Mr. & Mrs. Pinseter, etc. etc. – On the whole, it went off well; Mrs. Hayes played a beautiful piece called the 'Russian Bells'.

Friday 4   **1st. Advent Service**
Went to Church at 10, but not at 5 – Thought over my Sermon in the morning – In the aftn. walked on Mousehold Heath, & met Jessopp in returning – He is disgusted with the iniquities of the Trustees of the Grammar School – Litany in the Cathedral at 8 – I preached on 'Prophecy a light shining in a dark place'.

Saturday 5

From Norwich to <u>Yarmouth</u> [to preach on Sunday morning] Cathedral in the Morning – Afterwards meeting at the Training School, where were Bp., of Mauritius[1], our Bp. Hinds Howell, Ormsby, etc. etc. – Hinds Howell came afterwards to Luncheon – at 3.35 I started for Yarmouth – Colvin[2] was asked to meet me at dinner – A pleasant evening – Dreadful ghost-story told by Mrs. Nevill[3].

1. The Rt Revd V.W. Ryan, first Bishop of Mauritius (since 1854).
2. The Revd J.W. Colvin, Senior Curate of Gt Yarmouth; later (1873–85) Vicar of St. Mark, Lakenham.
3. Wife of the Vicar, an Hon. Canon, later to become Residential Canon and Archdeacon of Norfolk.

Monday 7   Second Reading with Lay Clerks (See Dec. 3)

All day long looking over passages to read aloud – Read Burn's Cotter's Saturday night, and the last scene in Othello – H. Howell[1] victorious over Patteson by 120 – In the afternoon with the Pinseter on Mousehold, & then went to the Blind Asylum[2].

1. Canon Hinds Howell becomes a Proctor in Convocation. 26 years later he is one of the two oldest, long-serving members of the House.
2. Institution for the Indigent Blind in Magdalen Street (building now demolished).

Thursday 10   Audit Dinner

In the morning, and also in the afternoon, worked at Losinga with the 'Pinseter' – In the evening the Audit Dinner [*ten guests*]. The Lay clerks came to me this morning, Mr. Burton being spokesman, to solicit an increase of stipend.

Friday 11

A long Audit, beginning at 11, not ending till 4 – Sedgwick, Heaviside, Nisbet, Kitson & myself – we raised the stipend of the Precentor, and agreed to give the Lay Clerks 9d. instead of 6d., for every Service they attend – I had a short walk with Nisbet on the Thorpe Road – At 8 I preached on 'the perspective of Prophecy' – The Congregation very good – Guss & Fraulein bought for me, to give to Ju (on this our wedding day) a musical box combined with a Photographic Album.

Monday 14

Unwell the early part of the day – No Church – However I held a Chapter, at which we considered the Commutation Scheme[1], and decided that Kitson shd. write to the E.C. to ask their account for the coming year – Walked with Phia on Mousehold

Heath; came home, and wrote to Rokeby, in answer to his sad letter of yesterday morning (anniversary Lady R's death) – also to the Secy of the Church of E. Young Men's Society[2] about Professor Rolleston's[3] Lectures.

> 1. The Dean and Chapter spent a great deal of time discussing, among themselves and with officials of the Ecclesiastical Commissioners, the Commutation Scheme for their estates. Looking back much later, Goulburn thought it might have been more satisfactory if the Commissioners had kept the estates and paid their stipends, etc. from the proceeds.
> 2. This very successful Society (still in existence) had its rooms in St Peter's Street. Object: "To band together Churchmen in Christian friendship and effort. and to provide them with facilities for mutual improvement and profitable recreation". It had a Reading Room with periodicals and newspapers, and a very large, and ever-growing, Library. Classes; Lectures; Discussions, etc.
> 3. George Rolleston, M.D. (1829–81): Linacre Professor of Anatomy and Physiology at Oxford 1860–81. Published 'Forms of Animal Life' 1870.

Wednesday 16
At 6 a dinner party, embracing Meyrick, Mr. & Mrs. Fox, the Symond's, and <u>Professor Rolleston</u> – At 8 we adjourned to the Professor's Lectures on the Animals of the Bible wh. was most interesting.

Friday 18   3rd Advent Service
At ½p.11 gave the prizes at the Grammar School – I spoke to them of poor Cotton's view of Emulation, and my differences from him – also of the necessity of working in youth – Afterwards Mr. Johnson, in acknowledging Jessopp's reference to him, spoke of Emulation as attaching to animals, and said that we ought always to be learners, even when "on the shady side of 40" – I was feeling very unwell and consulted him afterwards – A lesson with Buck at 2 p.m. – came home and took a little repose – In the evening at the Cath. I preached to a full Church on "The reviviscence of the Jewish fig-tree a sign of the End" Tho' unwell, I found my ideas flow better than last time.

> 1. = the endeavour to equal or surpass others in actions or qualities.

Sunday 20   Advent 4   Ordination Sunday
At Church 3 times – At 11 o'clock Mr. Perowne[1] preached the Ordination Sermon on "Blessed is that servant, whom his lord, when he cometh, shall find so doing" – The Service lasted 2½ hours – N.B. <u>Another time, the people must be retained in Church by giving out a short hymn, without any pause, immediately after the Sermon during wh. we go to the Altar.</u>

Gave a lesson to the Boys after Aftern. Service on Psalm 3 – Between Services walked with Dustkins & Cousin Kittoms on Mousehold Heath – In the evening read out loud. a Sermon of Newman's on Reverence, and finished 'little Meg's Children' – Spoke to the Servants on the 1st. part of the Ep. for Xmas Day.

> 1. T.T. Perowne (at this time Vicar of Stalbridge, Dorset) had been an examining Chaplain to the Bishop of Norwich since 1862. In 1874 he became Rector of Redenhall with Harleston, and in 1878, Archdeacon of Norwich.

Wednesday 23
Church twice – Chanted the Litany in the morning, and broke down – chanted also in the evening – After Mg. Service, arranged about the New Year Services with the Precentor, and drew up a code of Fines for the Choristers – then read one of Liddon's[1] Sermons on the 'Lessons of the Holy Manger' – After Luncheon, Mrs. & Miss Johnson called about the discomforts of the Cathedral Gallery – then I called on Stacy[2]; and then had my lesson at Dr. Buck's, with Mr. Minns – went into the town to purchase Xmas presents for Ju, Fraulein, MAC. & Cousin Kittoms – then home for second Service.

> 1. H.P. Liddon, Liberal High Church Theologian; Prebendary of Salisbury 1866; Canon of St Paul's 1870; Ireland Professor of Exigesis at Oxford 1870–82.
> 2. His local Printer in the Haymarket.

Thursday 24
(Drew at Harvey's on Dec. 22, £10 for Christmas as Gratuities, & today £5 more)

	£.	s.	d.
7s. Gratuities to 8 Lay Clerks	2.	16.	
Same to 6 Bedes	2.	2.	
Same to 2 Vergers		14.	
Do. to 2 Subsacris.		14.	
Do. to Gatekeeper		7.	
Do. to Schoolmaster		7.	
Inkstand for School		5.	6
Mr. Minns for his help	1.	0.	0
Feltham as Ferrym.	1.	0.	0
Walker for Water, etc.		10.	
Gave Gus		10.	
Cake for Gus		3.	
Game for neighbours		4.	
Gratu. to Bellows Blower		7.	
	£10.	19.	6

Service 3ce – a pleasant day – After Morning Service distributed the Gratuities – then practice in the Cathedral – then went to St. Matthew's School – there spoke to the old folks who received the cake & blankets – home to Luncheon – walked in the Cloisters meditating Sermon – then to the Plain Service, at which Bulmer read the Lessons – Preached in the evening on the necessity of meditation (Ps. 119, 97); and set them a meditation on the Incarnation – Afterwards read aloud the Ritualistic Judgement in Martin v. Mackonochie[1].

> 1. A.H. Mackonochie, Vicar of St Albans, Holburn, was a devoted Parish Priest and a 'Ritualist'; was constantly prosecuted by the 'Church Association'. On this occasion the Court of Arches ruled that candles and the mixed Chalice could not be regarded as illegal; but the Privy Council reversed the judgement.

Friday 25   CHRISTMAS DAY
Communicated at 8 o'clock, and left the Church after the Sermon at the later Service – After Afternoon Service the 13 Choristers came to be bunned, shillinged, & Mincepied – In the Afternoon, I wrote to Meyrick explaining my refusal to lend the Choristers for Sir F. Ouseley's[1] – The Bishop preached in the Morning – an excellent Sermon.

> 1. Sir Frederick Ouseley, Bart. (1825–89), Mus. Doc. Oxford, Professor of Music at Oxford and Precentor of Hereford 1855; founded St Michael's College, Tenbury 1857; Canon of Hereford 1886; composed a sacred Cantata; two Oratorios; and much Church and secular music.

Saturday 26   St Stephen
A long consultation with Symonds and Buck after the afternoon Service as to what answer I should give to Meyrick's letter about my refusal of the Choristers – Resolved to grant them – wrote to Meyrick – Emily[1] came to tea with Gussie.

> 1. Emily Symonds, the Precentor's daughter.

Sunday 27
I had a pleasing letter from Meyrick, thanking for the concession I had made about the Choristers. [*and Meyrick, V. of Blickling, came to the large Dinner Party at the Deanery on the 28th.*]

Wednesday 30
Unwell – did not get up till 10 – sent for Johnson – Lee Warner (James) looked in at 1 p.m., and had luncheon with us – Pinseter came & worked with me afterwards upon a most interesting letter

of Benson's, which contained emendations of H.L.'s letter – In the evening worked at H.L., read the Arabian Nights, & got a Sermon into shape.

Thursday 31
At Service three times.
After Mg. Prayer a visit to Heaviside.
Losinga with the Pinseter till Luncheon time.
Then a walk thro' Lady Harvey's grounds and on to Mousehold.
Then wrote letters to the Dean of York & others.
Boys fidgetting in Organ Gallery at 5 o'clock Service.
Preached at 8 o'clock to a large number of people on "Speak unto the children of Israel that they go forward".
– "The impossibility of being stationary in moral life".
1. Because character is continually in process of formation.
2. Bec. moral life extends over so wide an area.
3. Bec. there is in us a strong Gravitation to evil.
4. Bec. there are external foes – Satan and his angels.

1869
JANUARY

Friday 1   Circumcision

Early Communion at 8, the Bp. celebrating – Choristers sang 'O God our help in ages past', and the 'Gloria' at Gospel, and were dismissed after Nicene Creed – Second Service at 11, full choral – I walked on Mousehold Heath, reading Aladdin – Dinner at 2 o'clock – The Boys, Symonds, & Buck came in afterwards, & we had Magic Lantern, with slides of Aladdin (whose story I told), Robinson Crusoe, the Abyssinian War, etc. etc. – Supper at 8 – Dismissed them all with a 6d. each.

Monday 4

Church twice – worked at the 2d Report of the Ritual Commission[1], trying to see its bearings – After Morning Church, went to call on Mr. Lestrange about the Bosses – Then a walk; called on the Pinseter to talk over (1) the idea of having a second weekly Sermon at the Cath. in Lent – thought over names of people who might be asked to preach – (3) The Cathedral Bosses; shall we attempt to restore them ? – In the evening worked at Losinga.

> 1. The Royal Commission on Ritual set up in 1867. The first Report, also in 1867, was about Vestments; the 2nd Report (this one) was about incense and lights.

Friday 8

After luncheon a pleasant walk w. Canon Nisbet in Mr. Birkbeck's grounds[1]; beautiful view from a ruined pigeon-house on a knoll – At 9 p.m. went to Mrs. Blake's night School at the Boys' Model School – spoke to the Factory Girls upon their advantages and their trials.

> 1. At this time, much of the Thorpe area consisted of two Harvey and one Birkbeck estates. Lady Harvey of Mousehold House (widow of Sir Robert J. Harvey) and also Mr Wm Birbeck of 'The Grove' (later High House) gave Goulburn a key so that he could walk through their grounds.

Sunday 10   Mg.: at S. Peter per Mountergate:
         St Luke 2, 46 – Christ's regard for the Temple.
Preached at St. Peter-per-Mountergate as above – We got £16 odd – what they want to pay off their Church debt is £22. 10. 3d. – After we arrived at home, Mr. Fox came about his brother, who has been a dissenting Minister, but thinks of joining the Church

– In the afternoon, Nisbet preached an <u>admirable</u> Sermon on the Samaritan woman, & our Lord's dealing with her conscience – The Boys came afterwards, and I took them in Psalm 6.

Monday 11

Service twice – Gussie's friends came at 4 and staid till 10 – In the evening they acted a Charade (Cat-as(s)-trophy), and then we all played at Post – There were two Barkers[1], 2 Hy. Pattesons[2], 2 John Pats[3]., Amy Douglas, Myra Meyrick[4].

1. From St Martin-at-Palace Vicarage.
2. Henry Patteston was head of Pockthorpe Brewery; Sheriff 1858: D.L. for Norfolk 1859; J.P., Mayor (1862). Goulburn called him 'Chicken Pattie'.
3. John, Henry's elder brother, had become Rector of Thorpe in 1867. 'Jippattie'.
4. The Revd F. Meyrick had become Rector of Blickling in 1868.

Wednesday 13

In the morning considered the subject of my Oxford Sermon – After luncheon walked with Nisbet on the S. Giles' Road; we talked about the fundamental principle of sin: Selfishness or Lawlessness? – I went to see Heaviside afterwards – then to the School to hear the Trial-boys sing for the choristership – Watts & Davies will fill the next vacancies; Livock's voice is failing – In the evening wrote to the Bp. of Lichfield about Prescott[1], whose qualifications for the See of New Zealand he wished to know – Poppet[2] stupid with the dissipation of last night.

1. G.F. Prescott, ordained in 1853, was Curate of St John's, Paddington, when Goulburn became Incumbent in 1859; he became Curate of St Michael's, Paddington in 1861, and then Incumbent in 1864, where he remained until 1901. Was Rural Dean of Paddington.
2. 'Gussie' (now 15½) had been at a party at the Henry Pattesons.

Thursday 14

The Judge arrives for the trial of the Election Petiton
The Pinseter came at noon, and we chose Lenten hymns till Luncheon time; he had luncheon here – after that I walked to Stacy's house, and thence to Harvey's Bank to pay in Augusta's £120[1] – then with the Bishop & Nisbet to the Judge's[2] – he did not want Service at the Cathedral – looked over little Dustkins marks for the day – a dinner party, which went off well.

Ju

The Bishop	Sir Hy. Stracy
Mr. Penrice	Mrs. Nisbet
Mrs. Gurney Buxton	Col. Bishop
Can. Nisbet	Mr. Gurney Buxton
Ly. Stracy	Mrs. Penrice

O.H.

1. Augusta had an income from her mother's estate, which Goulburn, as her Guardian, managed.
2. At the General Election on November 17, 1868, Sir Henry Stracey (Con.) had come top of the poll, and he and Sir W. Russell (Lib.) were the two M.P.s for Norwich. Now, Sir Henry's election was declared void on the ground of bribery by his agents; and J.H. Tillett (Lib.) was eventually elected to the vacancy.

Monday 18

After luncheon walked w. Pinseter on the heath – Then arranged with him the Lenten Hymns – Gussie went to a Lantern party given by the Mayor – In the evening came the report of the Judgement in the election petition – Stracey unseated.

Tuesday 26

A chapter Meeting at wh. we (1) sealed the Commutn. Scheme (2) ordered the restoration of the failing buttresses on the N. side of the Church with Ketton Stone[1] – (3) ordered the mending of the floor, & making good of the lath & plaster at the window of Alden's house – Pinseter came in the afternoon, & we went on with our work – In the evening looked over S.P.G. reports, & meditated Sermons for Sundays in Lent.

1. Butter-coloured stone from Ketton, near Stamford, which has been quarried there since Roman times.

Thursday 28   Sir F. Ouseley's Lecture

After morning Service, had to hear a dispute between Walker and Dr. Buck about the blowing for the Practice – then made notes for Sermons in the first week of Lent – After luncheon a walk with Heaviside thro' Ly. Harvey's grounds and on Mousehold – Sir F. Ouseley[1] came while we were in Aftn. Church – At dinner (6 o'clock):

Ju

Can. Heaviside	Sir F. Ouseley
Mrs. Nisbet	Pinseter
Mrs. Pinseter	Mrs. Barchard
Miss Barchard	Can. Nisbet

O.H.

Sir F. Ouseley's lecture excellent, and well attended.
The diflt. parts of Choral Service:
1. Monotone   2. Inflected Respond.   3. Psalms.
4. The Services.   5. The Anthem.

> 1. See December 25, 1868 (Note 1).

••

On Saturday afternoon, January 30, Goulburn (and Ju) went to stay with Archdeacon Bouverie, at Denton, and preached twice for him on Sunday, returning to Norwich on Monday afternoon.
••

FEBRUARY

Monday 1   From Denton to Norwich
In the morning, visited the Archdeacon's School and the porch of his Church in wh. there are some curious bosses, one representing our Lord's laying down the natural body & putting on the spiritual body – then after luncheon, drove to Sir Shafto Adair's park at Flixton (Parcum meum apud Homersfield) – then to the Station, where we took leave of the Bouveries – got here just in time for the 5 p.m. Service.

••
Next day (Tues.) Goulburn travelled to Aynhoe, where he preached in the evening, gave a 'Penny Reading' on the Wednesday; travelled on to Oxford on Saturday (6th), and, as 'Select Preacher', gave the University Sermon on Sunday morning, returning to Norwich on Monday.
••

Saturday 6   From Aynhoe to Oxford
Left Aynhoe at 8.27 a.m. – When in Oxford went to the Bodleian, & talked with Cox about Losinga. (2) Called on Rev. – Ogilvie at Mr. Simm's & talked to him about the Dean's[1] Curacy. (3) Met Rector of Exeter[2] & talked to him on the same subject – (4) Called on Burgon[3] on the same subject – (5) bought a present for little D. at Spier's. (6) took my watch to Rowell's – Luncheon with the V.C.[4] in my room in the afternoon – Chapel in the evening at 5 – A large party, at wh. I sat between Mrs. Clerke & Mr. Bernard[5] – also Professor Bright[6], Mr. John Griffith[7], Warden of M.[8], & Lady Anstruther, & many others – after dinner Bonamy Price[9] fastened on me, with his theory for saving the Ch. of England.

1. His brother-in-law, the Revd Freddy Cartwright, Vicar of Aynhoe.
2. The Revd J.P. Lightfoot, D.D.
3. Vicar of the University Church of St Mary (until 1876).
4. Canon F.K. Leighton, D.D., Warden of All Souls.
5. Chichele Professor of International Law.
6. Regius Professor of International Law.
7. The Revd John Griffiths, M.A., (Wadham), Keeper of the Archives.
8. R. Bullock-Marsham, Esq., D.C.L., Warden of Merton.
9. Bonamy Price, Esq., M.A. (Worcester) Drummonds Professor of Political Economy.

Sunday 7   At Oxford

Preached the 'Humility Sermon' on "When thou art bidden of any man to a <u>wedding</u>", in the morning – called upon Woollcombe[1] & upon the Warden of Merton – at 2 attended Dr. Miller's Sermon on "The Grace of God which bringeth salvation" – Then called on C. Clerke & Mrs. Clerke – Service twice in All Souls Chapel – dined in hall w. the Vicechancellor – In the evening came to tea at the V.C.'s, Dr. Miller, Woollcombe, Master of Balliol[2], Montagu Burrows[3], & Mr. Tyrrwhitt.

1. The Revd T. Woollcombe, Fellow of Balliol.
2. The Revd Robert Scott, D.D.
3. Chichele Professor of Modern History 1862–1905. Helped to found Keble College 1870.

• •

Around February 14, Valentines seemed to have been freely exchanged within the Goulburn household (and beyond) – On Feb. 11, Goulburn bought some 10s. worth, spent a further 10s. 6d on the 12th, and 11s on the 13th. He records: "Valentines coming in all the evening".

• •

Wednesday 24   St Matthias

After morning Service, I was alone (disturbed only by a visit from Johnson), but made no way with work – After luncheon, went to the School, and set the Boys a piece of dictation, and a letter – Looked over the Grammar Paper with the Pinseter; during which a letter from Nisbet arrived, saying he had offered St. Paul's [*Norwich*] to the P. – The P. seemed cool about it – Read aloud to Ju a little of the Qu. Review of Lord Campbell's[1] Lives of Ld. Lyndhurst & Ld. Brougham.

1. John Campbell, son of the Minister of Cupar-Fife, became Lord Campbell and Lord Chancellor. He wrote the Lives of two of his predecessors, Lord Brougham and John S. Copley (Lord Lyndhurst). But the 'Lives' not published until all three had died.

MARCH

Tuesday 2

After Mg. Service, did two of Losinga's Letters w. Pinseter – After luncheon attended the Grammar School meeting with Heaviside – Mr. Long[1] of Spixworth in the Chair – Mr. Pinder, Master of the Commercial School[2], applied to us for the appointment of a new master – Heaviside and I took a walk upon Mousehold, in which we got thoroughly wet – Changed before Church – Wrote to the Chief Justice of the C. Pleas, who proposes to dine here on Good Friday!! – In the evening read Gladstone's great speech on the Irish Church disestablishment.

1. John Long, Esq., of Spixworth Park, an Old Boy, generous benefactor and Life Governor of the School.
2. King Edward VI Commercial School, to train boys for careers in industry and trade, was established in 1859, to be separated from the King Edward VI Grammar School with traditional academic education. The fees for the first, one guinea per quarter; for the second, three guineas per quarter.

Monday 8

A day at home – Did not rise till 10 being unwell – Worked with the Pinseter at Losinga in the afternoon – In the evening the Heavisides and the Symondses dined here, and I acted charades w. the Children and Emily – 1st. word: Mer-cury.
(1) 'Mer' – Sea Sick Frenchman.
(2) Gussie currying a horse.
(3) Maudie (as Mercury) stealing from Lucy (as Apollo) the herds of Admetus. (Gussie, Emily, & me).
II. Bar-rack.
(1) Burglar filing thro' a bar, and robbing Gussie in bed.
(2) Gussie examined on the rack.
(3) Emily drummed out of a regiment in Barrack Yard.

Thursday 11

At 11 went to a meeting in the Clerical Rooms[1] of the Committee of Diocesan Schools – Nevill, Ormsby, Hinds Howell, Heaviside, Nelson there – After luncheon, went there again to Burton's Commee. of the Church Association[2] – Meyrick, Mr. F. Watson & others addressed the meeting on the form wh. the petition about the Irish Church should take – Afterwards I took a walk – In the evening Dr. Buck dined there, & Mr. & Mrs. Symonds came at 8 – Acted a Charade with the children and Emily.

1. Rooms over the Ethelbert Gate, formerly used, before the 'poor mean cottage' as the Choir School.
2. 'The Church Association': "For the purpose of maintaining the present doctrinal basis of the Established Church ... and to counteract the efforts now being made to pervert her teaching on essential points of the Christian faith, or assimilate her Services to those of the Church of Rome".

Friday 19

Service three times – A very rainy day – Losinga in the morning w. Pinseter – In the afternoon walked about the Cathed. meditating a Sermon – Paid my first visit to the Bosses, in company w. Spawle[1] and Browne[1] – The colours are almost perfect – Read Ju Disraeli's speech against Disestablishment[2] & Disendowment of Irish Church.

1. Goulburn was a little careless about the correct spelling of names. Barthlomew *Spaul* was the local Builder in the close, and J.H. Brown was the local Architect, also in the Close, both employed by the Chapter.
2. The proposed Disestablishment of the Church of Ireland caused great concern to many English Churchmen. The Act of Disestablishment received the Royal Assent on July 26, 1869 but was not to come into operation until January 1, 1871.

Tuesday 23

Lectured in the afternoon on St. Peter cutting off Malchus' ear – In the morning mounted to the bosses[1] with the Pinseter and Bulmer – then worked at Losinga with the Pinseter – In the afternoon a walk with Heaviside – Read in the evening the speeches of Roundel Palmer[2], Lowe[3], and others, about the Irish Church question.

1. Scaffolding had been erected in the Nave to be able to view the Bosses properly, and moved from one archway to another when required.
2. See March 20, 1868 (Note 1).
3. The Rt Hon. Robert Lowe, Chancellor of the Exchequer.

Wednesday 24   Judges' entry

Went w. Heaviside to meet the Judges, Chief Justice Bovill[1] and Baron Pygott[2], at the Station at 4 o'clock – they arrived at the Cathedral about 4.50 – 'Uncle Bartie' preached for 20 min. on the 'Sufferings of Christ' – At the 8 o'clock Service, Heaviside preached a good Sermon on the 'Penitent Thief' – Read Gathorne Hardy's[3] Speech.

1. Sir Wim. Bovill, Solicitor General and Chief Justice of Common Pleas.
2. Sir Gillery Pigott, Baron of the Exchequer since 1863.
3. Gathorne Gathorne-Hardy: Home Secretary in previous Conservative Government; now in opposition. Warmly attacked Irish Church Disestablishment Bill. In 1878 became 1st Earl of Cranbrook.

Friday 26   **GOOD FRIDAY**
Four Services – (1) 8 a.m. (2) 11 a.m. (3) 5 p.m. (4) 8 p.m.
The 2 Judges came in state to No. 2 – I walked in the afternoon on Mousehold Heath (solus) – In the Evening preached on 'The Impenitent Thief' to an overflow congregation.

Sunday 28   **EASTER DAY**
    Mg.: "The exceeding greatness of His power"
Service three times – I preached in the morning as above – We had about 130 Communicants. Heaviside preached in the afternoon on the Resurrection; I intoned the Service.

Monday 29   Assize Dinner at home
In the morning, examined the Boys Surplices, Books, etc, with the Pinseter – then a walk – wrote ½ a letter to Benson.
In the Evening at 7.30 there dined here:
(1) Chief Justice Bovill & Baron Pygott. (2) Their Marshals. (3) The Heavisides (4) Sir T. Beauchamp and Chaplain ('Uncle Bartie'). (5) O'Malley (Recorder) and Under Sheriff (Blake). (6) Mr. Howes and Mr. Reade. [*The M.P.s for South Norfolk.*] (7) Mr. F. Walpole and Mr. Watson [*The Hon. F. Walpole, M.P. for North Norfolk.*] (8) Colonel Bishop and Sir S. Bignold. (9) Colonel Cockburn – with 2 selves, *nineteen*. Sat between Mrs. H. and Sir T. Beauchamp.

Tuesday 30
After Mg. Service, gave a 'jobation'[1] to the Lay Clerks about their unwilingness to attend practices gratuitously – then read the Class List, and gave the Prizes to the Boys – then with Heaviside to Kitson's Office, where we had much talk about our Incomes under the new system[2] – then we went together to Barnard & Bishop, to set the warming in motion again – in the evening the Choristers came & played at (1) Bob Apple (2) Bran Tub (3) throwing into the mouth – Ada was here, and the Pinseter, and Em'ly, & Dr. Buck.

   1. 'Jobation' = scolding (allusion to the scolding of Job's friends).
   2. Under the Ecclesiastical Commission Act 1868 which ratified the agreements made with the various Chapters about Commutation.

Wednesday 31   Reading & Singing in the Evening
Prepared my reading for the Evening – Then took a walk on Mousehold – Took Ju and Gussie up the scaffold in the Cathedral

– An Evening Party at 7, lasting from 7 to 10.30 – The Rolfes, Robt. Wrights, Cadges, Mrs. Blake and daughter, Hansells (father, Bessy, Ada), Cubitts, Symondses, Mullers, Bulmers, Dr. Buck, Mr. Mann and Boys – I read (after a little dissertation on the merits of Shakspere): (1) Maud Muller. (2) Lea Dreams. (3) Mrs. H.V. Elliott's Nonsense. (4) Speeches of Brutus and Antony in J, Caesar. Grosse and Campling did "Where are you going to, my pretty maid", Minns doing the echo.

APRIL

Monday 5 From Norwich to London
Left Norwich by train at 7.30 a.m. – Mr. Vincent[1] and Mr. Jessopp in the same carriage with me – went:
(1) to the Bank, to get dividend on Fred's legacy[2].
(2) Court of Bankruptcy, to see Wright, and the Law Library[2].
(3) Van Voorst, Paternoster Row, to talk about H. Losinga.
(4) Gozzie's[4] to draw £10, & talk over Executor Business.
(5) Stevens and Norton, Chancery Lane, to tell them to make an estimate of what they will give for the Law Library.
(6) Parker, West Stand, to talk about H. Losinga.
(7) The Club[3] – wrote to Ju – had luncheon. Then, walked to
(8) Rivington's – he gave me some hope about my Books.
(9) Mr. Redgrave's, Offices of K. Museum – a talk about the Bosses.
(10) John Pollen's, 11, Pembridge Crescent – not at home.
(11) Blessed Bartie's – saw her.
(12) to Garlant's Hotel, Suffolk Street, where found old Sedgwick for a few moments.
(13) MAC. to dinner – Met Robert, Dick, and Mr. Chetwynd.

   1. The Revd Wm. Vincent was Rector of Postwick 1864–87, and also a J.P. Later, he became a Baronet.
   2. Goulburn was intent on clearing up his father's estate, selling his Law books, and administering the affairs of his brother, 'poor Fred'.
   3. United University Club, Pall Mall East. Occasionally, Goulburn would like to have taken Julia to luncheon, but women were not allowed on the premises.
   4. 'Gozzie's' = Goslings and Sharpe, Bankers, 19, Fleet Street, London.

• •
Goulburn continued with his business in London until Thursday (April 8) when he went to Horton St Mary, 4 miles from Northampton, to stay with the Revd Sir Henry Gunning and his wife, Mary (Julia's step-sister). Julia was already there. They both remained at Horton (with two day trips to London) until April 28.
• •

Thursday 29

Recd. an invitation from the Abp. for the 10th., to meet the deans, and discuss some "salutary changes in our Cathedral system" – A call from Mr. Raikes, who went with Heaviside & me to the Church Building meeting[1] – Only Symonds present besides ourselves – Mr. Pringle[2] called at 1.30, to talk over the answer from E.C. about the augmentation of S. James's Living – he had luncheon with us – then came dear Archdeacon & Mrs. Bouverie[3] – drew up a circular to send round about the photographs of the bosses – then Church – Sawyer, jun. came at 6, and he, the Pinseter, and I discussed the whole question of the bosses – Coachee came in to resign the post of Subsacrist.

1. The Norwich Diocesan Church Building Society had been founded in 1836 (18 years after the Parent Society). In 1869 it gave grants totalling £210 to 10 churches in Norfolk, and a further £50 to three churches in Suffolk.
2. The Revd A.D. Pringle, Vicar of St James's, Norwich with Pockthorpe, A Dean and Chapter Living.
3. Archdeacon of Norfolk 1850–69. Resigned because of ill-health, but remained Rector of Denton until his death in 1877, aged 81. He founded the Archdeacon Bouverie Fund for Invalided Clergy in Norfolk, by giving £1,500, and hoping that others would also give additional amounts.

Friday 30

At 10 o'clock came Mr. Furse the painter, and I went up to the roof with him and the Pinseter, and got from him a rough estimate of what he would charge for repainting: 15 shgs. a day, and a fortnight doing each Bay (this would be £9 for each bay, and £125 for the whole 14) – but query, does this include the materials? – then called on Mrs. Robinson – Sedgwick called and was very lively and charming – At 8 preached at St. Margaret's.

MAY

Saturday 1   St. Philip and St. James

A very bad night – did not get up till ½ p.11 – Went to Church at 3; installed Archdeacon Blakelock[1] – Hopper was there, but Can. Robinson had forgotten the time.

1. As Archdeacon of Norfolk. Continued as Rector of Gimingham of which he had been Incumbent since 1835.

Monday 3

At ½ p.11 ascended with the Pinseter to the Bosses, and took notes of them, using opera Glass and looking glass – then at I met the 2 Canons, & Barnard, & Mr. Browne on the N. side of the

Church, to consult about the Boiler question – walked on Mousehold, & in returning met Emily on her pony and the Pinseter walking – In the evening drew up heads of a Sermon for Thursday, and (Julia writing) dictated to her a description of the Bosses.

Thursday 6   ASCENSION DAY
    At 8 p.m.: The Heavenly Silence, the Incense,
        and the Fire cast on the Earth. Rev. 8, 1.
Services at 10 a.m. and 8 p.m. – No Sermon, but a celebration in the morning – Afterwards went up with the Pinseter, Heaviside and Robinson, to the Bosses – Corrected on the spot what I had written on the Bosses – <u>told Spaul to paint one of them on trial</u> – After luncheon, a walk in the garden till it rained – then read over again (in the Pinseter's presence) the explanation of the bosses to Mr. L'Estrange – Preached at the 8 o'clock Service a very long Sermon, but I felt interested in my subject.

Monday 10   S.P.G. Meeting
H.C. (very few) at 12 – Afternoon Service at 3 – We dined at 5 … in all 13 – Meeting at 7.30 in Noverre's Rooms – Bishop of Colombo[1], Mr. Chamberlain of the Newfoundland Mission, Bp. of Oxford, and myself, spoke – The Mayor[2] in the Chair – The Bp., Archdeacon of Norfolk, & Nelson in the house.

   1. The Rt Revd P.C. Claughton, Bishop of Colombo (Ceylon) since 1862.
   2. E.K. Harvey, Esq., Alderman and Magistrate; brother of Sir Robert Harvey whose Crown Bank failed in 1870, and also a Director of this Bank.

• •
Archibald Campbell Tait became Archbishop of Canterbury in 1869. He had been a Fellow of Balliol College, Oxford, and Goulburn's immediate predecessor as Headmaster of Rugby. Oxford celebrated the Primacy by inviting the Archbishop on Saturday and Sunday, May 15 and 16 (Whit Sunday). Goulburn was invited to be the Preacher in St. Mary's (the University Church) on the afternoon of Whit Sunday.
• •

Sunday 16   **Aftn.:** at St. Mary's: The Heavenly Silence
        and the proceedings thereupon. Rev. 8, 1st. 5 verses.
The Archbishop preached in the morning on "Where the Spirit of the Lord is, there is liberty" – Preached in the afternoon as above; then walked with F. Compton to Professor Stubb's[1], and consulted him on my difficulties about Losinga – then to New College Chapel, where I was to meet Mrs. Leighton – then to All

Souls, with Mrs. Leighton and Mrs. Harrington – a large dinner in Hall, before wh. an address of congratulation was presented to the Apb. by the Warden.

> 1. William Stubbs (1825–1901): Regius Professor of History at Oxford 1866–84, and then Bishop of Chester, and Bishop of Oxford 1888.

Wednesday 19   Auntie's Birthday
Two Services – At Breakfast Frederica's[1] flowers, mirror, and corona lucis, with all our presents, were displayed on the table – Afterwards I went to the Library and there worked on my description of the Bosses and at the Nuremberg Chronicle[2] – After luncheon, took Frederica to the Bosses & afterwards to the Chap. Library – then walked with her & Ju across the Ferry to Kitson's, who was out – Then home to Aftn. Service – It being Auntie's Birthday, Emily, Gus. & Fraulein dined with us.

> 1. Frederica Franks (London) was a close friend and helper of the Goulburn's for, at least, 35 years, never failing to remember their birthdays, wedding anniversaries, and all other occasions when presents were given. At Goulburn's interment at Aynhoe on May 7, 1897, there was a wreath from her.
> 2. Nuremberg Chronicle (1493): A history of the world from the Creation, by Hartmann Schedel, with many woodcuts by Wohlgemuth, German painter and engraver.

Thursday 20
In the morning began an account of the Cathedral for my photographic work – Worked at the Library – after luncheon, walked to Col. Cubitt's at Earlham, to leave our 3 cards (Heaviside's, Robinson's, and my own) on Mr. Justice Blackburn – came home by Eaton – sent over to Robinson's for the Bp. of Argyll's[1] perusal:
  Neville's, 'Heavenly Father'.
  Shairp's Essay on Keble.
  Bp. Armstrong's Life.
  Box's Recollection of Oxford, lent me by Hinds Howell.

> 1. The Rt Revd Alexander Ewing, D.D., D.C.L. (Bishop of Argyll since 1847), and Lady Alice Ewing, were staying with the Robinsons for a few days.

Monday 24
In the morning in the Library preparing for Lecture this evening, and Sermon on Wednesday – also reading about Dunwich in Suckling[1] – called on the Bishop & had a talk with him – After luncheon called on the Bishop of Argyll; saw him in his bedroom; he seemed to think that Brother Lawrence[2] had re-awakened Ly. Alice's Roman sympathies – Church at 2 o'clock p.m. – afterwards gave the Boys & Lay Clerks cake & wine to drink the

Queen's health[3] – At 8 p.m. gave my Lecture on 'Reading Aloud' at St. Paul's School – School was very well filled.

> 1. Alfred Inigo Suckling (1796–1856), 'History and Antiquities of Suffolk', 1846–48.
> 2. Brother Lawrence of the Ressurection (Nicholas Heman: c.1605–91); Carmelite Lay Brother and Mystic. Had charge of the kitchen, and led a life of almost constant recollection; his writings were brought together in two volumes after his death. He was a favourite of Goulburn's. Modern selection under the title, *The Practice of the Presence of God*.
> 3. It was Queen Victoria's 50th Birthday.

Wednesday 26 Visit to Yarmouth

At 1.30 started with Frederica for Yarmouth – The Mayor (Mr. Nightingale) brot. us from the carriage in his station [*means "from the station in his carriage"!*] – Preached a long & tedious Sermon – then we all adjourned to the ground, where I laid the stone[1], using the silver trowel, wh. I ought not to have done.

> 1. Foundation stone of new Church of St James, Yarmouth.

Saturday 29 Hospital Sermon

The Hospital Sermon[1] at 3 p.m. was poorly attended, and we only collected £48. 13. 6 – The Bp. was there, & Robinson, & Heaviside, and the three Minor Canons; Mr. Nelson, Mr. Copeman & other Governors, and the Mayor in state.

> 1. In 1773 it was decided that the Anniversary Sermon for the Norfolk and Norwich Hospital be preached by the Dean of Norwich each year on August 6. This continued for many years, but eventually lapsed. In 1866 it was decided that an Annual Hospital Sermon should be preached in the Cathedral; and the Mayor and Corporation, the Governors, the convalescent patients, and county families, should be specially invited to attend.

JUNE

Tuesday 8 Conservative Meeting at St. Andrew's Hall[1]

Went to the meeting at 8 with Heaviside – Sir S. Bignold[2] in the Chair – Mr. Sedgwick (the Deputation).

> 1. There were about 2,000 people present to adopt a Petition against the Irish Church Bill to be sent to the House of Lords.
> 2. Norwich Union; three times Mayor; Alderman; M.P.; insisted that there should be alternate Whig and Tory Mayors and Sheriffs.

• •

On June 12 Goulburn went to London, preaching, on the Sunday (13) in two London Churches; On Monday he went, by train, to Bury St Edmunds, where, on Tuesday morning, he preached in St James' Church, then in the Diocese of Ely, now the Cathedral of the Diocese of St Edmundsbury and Ipswich (formed in 1914). That afternoon he returned to Norwich.

• •

Thursday 17

Raining all day, so that I could not get out, but played battledore & shuttlecock with 'Phia & Guskins – In the morning wrote many letters, and prepared a Sermon for Sunday – In the afternoon arrived 12 copies of my letter to the Abps[1]. – In the evening read 'Barchester Towers' to the Ladies.

> 1. The two Archbishops had (after a meeting with Deans) sent a letter to all Deans asking for their views, and that of their Chapters, on changes in the Cathedral system, especially in their own particular Cathedral. Goulburn replied with an 'Open Letter' opposing change at the present time, but advocating improvements in the present system.

Tuesday 29   St. Peter

After Bkfst. commenced a Sermon in the Library – After luncheon, the Bedesmen[1] came to their dinner; I said Grace, & spoke a few words to them – Then walked with Bulmer to call on Garry[2]; we saw Mrs. Garry – Wrote to (1) Rivington, sending an instalment of Sermons for publication – Gussie & the children dined with us; after wh. they dressed up a 'Ghost' to put on 'cousin Mary Chetwynd's bed.

> 1. There were six Bedesmen living in an almshouse; they had a small stipend (about £12 to £15 per year) and duties such as cleaning the Cathedral, being on duty at the door during a Service, or tolling a bell.
> 2. Vicar of St Mark's, Lakenham (Dean and Chapter Living).

Wednesday 30

The Vergers and Subsacrists had tea here – read in the Evening the debate in the Lords about the Amendments to Irish Church Bill.

JULY

Sunday 4

(1) Of active work, and the spirit it should be done in
Church twice at the Cathedral, once at Heigham – Preached as above – At two o'clock saw Kett, Atkins, Minns about their Confirmation – Grosse did not come – Little Gus did her Sermon very well today [*she was now 16*] & got 2s. 6d. for it – In the evening I preached extem. on Love of God – There was a large congregation – In the Cathedral in the morning we had a very large congregation, and many more communicts. than usual.

Wednesday 21

In the morning wrote Sermon, and two or three letters – After luncheon went with Heaviside to Training School – Hinds Howell and Ormsby were there – we agreed to recommend three modes of raising Subscriptions: 1. Sermons. 2. Asking each assisted Incumbent to make himself responsible for 10sh. 3. Private application to Laymen in Diocese who do'nt subscribe – after dinner prepared a Sermon for Kessingland.

Thursday 22

In the morning prepared my Sermon for Kessingland[1] – then called on Sidney & Henry Pelham[2] – found them going out to their cricket – asked them to dinner – then visited the Bosses, & saw Spaull – then wrote to Lou, and looked over Proof Sheets – Left Norwich with Ju and Bullivant at 1.50 – Hinds Howell in the same carriage with us – A nice Service at Kessingland, after wh. they collected upward of £40 – Dr. Buck was there – Mr. Crosse[3] and several clergy – We and Bullivant returned to Lowestoft, where we sauntered about, dined, and then returned to Norwich by the 8.20 p.m. train.

> 1. The occasion at Kessingland was for the Parish Schools Building Fund. The Diocesan Calendar (Editor: Hinds Howell, and usually accurate) states that the Collection was £70.
> 2. Henry Pelham, the Bishop's eldest son, is 23 and has just become a Fellow of Trinity College, Oxford (later to become Professor of Ancient History at Oxford, and then President of Trinity College); Sidney, the second son, is 20 and an Oxford Cricket 'Blue' (later to hold various offices in the Diocese including that of Archdeacon of Norfolk).
> 3. The Revd A.B. Crosse had been Rector of Kessingland since 1865; in 1881 he became Archdeacon of Furness, but, in 1893, returned to Norwich as a Residentiary Canon and Vicar of St Peter Permountergate.

Friday 23

To the School at 11.45, where I set the boys to write a letter on the Cathedral, while I worked at Proof Sheets & at letters for the Training School – After luncheon called on Mrs. Wright, & recd. from her £2 for the Training School.

Saturday 24

In the morning Losingised in the Library – Mrs. Wright came to give me £3 more as a <u>donation</u> for the Training School – At ½p.12 examined the Choristers in the O.T. – After luncheon, went to Dr. Buck (now wigless)[1] and had a lesson till Churchtime – After Church, Practice (with Muller & Buck) – Then a game at single wicket with Gussie – In the evening worked at Exam. Papers, and wrote 3 letters canvasing for Training School to Col. Blomfield, Sir Henry Stracey, Rev. Wm. Stracey.

> 1. For many years Dr Buck had worn a brown wig. It was said that he had promised his wife that, on reaching 70, he would give it up. A resident of the Close records that at the 8 am Service on a Sunday in July 1869 (probably the 25th) there appeared a stranger whom he realised eventually was Dr Buck. "The brown wig had vanished, never to return, and in its stead was seen his own sparse grey hair". He had been 70 in September 1868.

AUGUST

Monday 2
Before Aftern. Service admitted Litchfield Subsacrist, and Walker, Beadle and Bellows Blower – After the Service gave the prizes to the Choristers, and announced to them their fines for the ½ year – Prepared for journey all the morning – Called on the Bishop & saw him.

• •

On August 3, the Goulburns left Norwich (with three Servants, including the very long-serving and faithful Rose) for London; moving to Betchworth House (nr Reigate) – the home of Goulburn's Uncle's Family – from August 7 to 9.
August 9 to October 12 have no entries: During this period the Goulburns were in Bad Kissingen (East of Frankfurt-on-Main) – In his entry for October 13, Goulburn writes: "For Intermediate Journal between Aug. 8 and Oct. 13, see the two Kissingen Books". [*These are not in the Dean and Chapter's Library.*] However, accounts of holidays at other German Spas appear in later Diaries.
• •

Wednesday 4　　　　　In London
In the morning went with Ju to Kensal Green, and saw my father's monument, and those of the Chetwynds – thence to Tatham's; saw Proctor, and settled with him to offer Newington £375 per ann. for Fred. – then to Goslings to get my Circular Notes and letter of Credit – thence to the Club (getting an opera hat in the way) – I have written today begging letters for Training School to Sir Geo. Nugent, Sir. R. Harvey, Sir R.S. Adair, Sir E.S. Gooch, Lord Stradbroke, Lord Rendlesham.

Thursday 5　　From London to Ticehurst and back
Left London with Ju at 9.28 a.m. (by rail) – Got back to our own house again at 5 p.m. – Fred much as usual – I had a conversation with Newington and expressed my surprise at his claim for a larger payment – He said the expenses of his establishment had

increased much since his father's time, and Fred had a separate room, & required man to prevent him going into the rooms of others – I agreed to pay in future £375 per annum = £93. 15 quarterly.

Friday 6
Wrote Training School letters before Bkfst. and again at Club – wrote to Symonds, sending him Sutton's letter about the colouring used for the Bosses – called at S.E.R. station to enquire about luggage to Kissingen.

Saturday 7   From London to Betchworth
Gussie left us at 2 – then Ju and I walked to Rivington's where I gave in my Proof Sheets – then to the Charing Cross Station where we despatched to Frankfurt our Box with the Losinga literature[1] – Got to Betchworth[2] about 6.

> 1. It is understandable that he took his Losinga documents with him for such a long period away from home, but rather incredible that he risked sending them ahead.
> 2. Goulburn's uncle, Henry Goulburn, purchased Betchworth House in 1816, five years after his marriage to the Hon. Jane Montagu, and this became the family seat of this branch of the Goulburns. In fact, they were the only descendants of Munbee Goulburn to carry the name through the greater part of the 20th Century. But no longer are there Goulburns at Betchworth.

OCTOBER

Wednesday 13
First day after our return to Norwich – Busied in opening Letters & Parcels, in writing, and settling for a winter's Campaign – Service in St. Luke's Chapel twice – The Aftern. Service was attended by the Bp. of British Columbia[1] – I went over the hotwater apparatus with Heaviside, & into the roof with the Precentor – The scaffold is under a new bay, where the subjects seem to be in some cases repeated twice – Thus with the sacrifice of Isaac – In the afternoon, I called on Johnson[2], & saw his sister Mrs. Fitch, and then on Kitson – both very ill.

> 1. The Rt Revd George Hills, D.D., 1st Bishop of British Columbia (later Metropolitan); formerly Vicar of Yarmouth 1848–59; Hon. Canon of Norwich from 1850; eventually retired to Suffolk (Vicar of Parham 1892–95).
> 2. The Goulburn's former G.P.

Thursday 14 Five Societies and Oxford Dinner
At the meeting in Noverre's Rooms at 12 (noon) Mr. Sewell Reade[1] opened the Ball, speaking for the Church's Home Work – I seconded him – then came the Bishop of Columbia, and Bp. of Labuan[2] on the Church's Mission work – Our Bp. closed w. a word of dissent from my view of people's getting tired of the Church of England because she is the via media – At the Oxford dinner there were about 30 guests – I was supported by the Bishop of Labuan and Canon Woodford – Got home about 9.30.

    1. Clare Sewell Read (1826–1905) farmed family estate in Norfolk from 1854–96; Con. M.P. for South Norfolk; Chairman of Farmers' Club.
    2. Labuan and Sarawak = Borneo. The Rt Revd Walter Chambers (Bishop 1869–81).

Friday 15
After luncheon I walked with Ju & Gus. to enquire after Kitson[1], who was unable to see me – Bensly, whom we met coming out, had just got our cheques signed – then I went to Johnson's[2], and sat with him – he too is very poorly.

    1. The Chapter Clerk.
    2. The Family Doctor.

Wednesday 20 Preached at S. Peter's Mancroft at 8 p.m.
    to the Churchman's Club on 'Church Principles'
Kitson died at 8 o'clock this morning – Cathedral Service only in the morning – Afterwards walked out to see Johnson, and found him sitting up, and talking gaily – Returned & went to luncheon with Heaviside, and talked over our future arrangements as to Chapter Clerk – Then home – I walked on Mousehold, & back by Thorpe Road, enquiring after Mrs. Kitson on my road home – Met Henry Martin again, who had broken his mast against the Bridge, and had to pay 2 shillings for it – Preached at S. Peter Mancroft a Sermon on Principles.

Thursday 21
Went with the Pinseter to the Jesus Chapel, and speculated upon its restoration.

Sunday 24 Mg.: Ye <u>are</u> come to the spirits of just men made
    perfect. (on occasion of Mr. Kitson's death)
Large congregations both Morning and Afternoon – Heaviside in the Afternoon preached on "The days of our age are 3 score years and ten, etc. etc. – He alluded to Lord Derby's[1] death as well as

that of Kitson – Between the Services I saw the Choristers & gave them questions.

> 1. Edward G.G.S. Stanley, 14th Earl of Derby, had been Prime Minister three times, resigning in 1868.

Monday 25   Kitson's Funeral
Started alone in the carriage at 9.15 – Read Archer Butter's Sermons on 'Church Education in Ireland' en route – Reached Reedham Church at 12 – A pretty rural Church yard – Mrs. Kitson got thro' pretty well – Present: the Pentagamist General Prior, Mr. Turned, Mr. Bensly, Mr. Payne, Mr. Leathes (Son of the Incumbent) – There was a little fracas between Mr. Leathe's[1] Curate and Mr. Payne[2] – At about 2 o'clock we returned; and when we got into the high road (about 5 miles from Norwich) Mr. Payne and I (for he accompanied me) got out and walked – Got to Norwich during the Anthem at about 5.40 and went into the Cath. and told Heaviside my news.

> 1. The Revd C.H. Leathes had just arrived as Rector of Reedham with Freethorpe, a family Living, where he remained for the rest of his life.
> 2. The Revd J.H. Payne, Vicar of Earlham and Rector of Colney.

• •

On Wednesday, October 27, Goulburn went to London to lay the foundation stone (on the Thursday) of a School for St Michael's Church, Paddington. This Church had been built and endowed by the wealthy, and ever-generous, Mr Gibbs, who was now providing the means to build the School. Goulburn dined with Berdmore Compton (Rector of St Paul's, Covent Garden), both nights in London, but slept in the house which he still owned in Westbourne Terrace. He returned to Norwich on October 29.

• •

NOVEMBER

Monday 15
Service twice – After Morning Service, paid Spaull for cleaning 2 Bosses (£51).

Monday 22
Walk with Nisbet to the Mayor's[1] at Eaton Grove, & to Mr. Henry Morgan, the Sheriff's – Papers contain a bad account of the Abp. of Cant[2]. – announce Hayman's[3] election to Rugby on Saturday – In the afternoon Losinga w. the Pinseter; & in the evening finished anotating the second Sermon – The two Willeses arrived today, precursors of the Dean tomorrow.

1. At this time, the Mayor's year of Office was from November to November; so Goulburn was visiting the new Mayor, Augustus F.C. Bolingbroke, and also the new Sheriff.
2. Archbishop Tait (in office 1868–82) suffered from periodic illnesses. Between March 6 and April 8, 1856, he had lost five of his children, varying in age from 10 years to 1½ years. This had profoundly affected him; and before the end of his life his only son was to die in 1878, and his wife 6 months later.
3. Henry Hayman was Headmaster of Rugby School from 1870–74, but even before taking up residence, his appointment met with formidable opposition from various quarters, and this continued throughout his period as Headmaster, culminating in his dismissal. For the remaining 30 years of his life he was Rector of Aldingham in Lancashire.

Wednesday 24

After Mg. Service, walked with the dean to lionise (1) St. Peter Mancroft's (2) St. Stephen's – found the new organ being erected (3) St. Gregory's – then took him to Club[1], & there left him – then called at the Palace & saw the Bishop – then luncheon – afternoon work with Pinseter till Church time – The Dean & W. Willes sat in the Presbytery, but did not hear well – Gussie frightened Emma by dressing up Willie & putting him in the housemaid's closet.

1. The Norfolk Club.

DECEMBER

Friday 10   2nd. Advent Lecture

Intended to preach tonight on the two Antediluvian Prophesies; but only got through the first – So I adjourned the subject announced for next Friday till Christmas Eve, and for next Friday announced the prophecy of Enoch – The Church was very full – In the morning I answered a very kind letter from Temple[1] – Received a strange letter from C. Arnold, grumbling about Hayman having used for Rugby (wout. leave) Testimonials, etc. he had obtained for other Schools.

1. The Revd Frederick Temple, Goulburn's successor as Headmaster of Rugby, was now leaving to become Bishop of Exeter.

Tuesday 14   Adjourned Audit

The Audit occupied from 11 to nearly 2 – I then entertained the party to luncheon, Sedgwick, Heaviside, Nisbet, Browne, Bensly – The Ladies not with us – The chief subjects of discussion were the proposed alterations in and about the Cathedral wh. Browne had advised us to make etc. – After they were gone, I took a walk;

saw the Pinseter, and gave him B.C.'s hymnbook to study – In the evening read some of Pendennis[1] to the Ladies.

> 1. 'The History of Pendennis' by W.M. Thackeray, had, like so many 19th Century novels, come out in monthly parts (with illustrations by Thackeray) from November 1848 to December 1850.

Tuesday 21   **St. Thomas**

Service in the Morning only – After it, Fred G.[1], Mr. Kingscote, Mr. Browne and I went up to the roof and examined Spaull's work – Then a little work with the Precentor at Herbert Losinga, and in re-casting for the year 1870 the 'Various Rules and Uses' – At 3 went to the Grammar School, and presided at the Prize Giving – There was a very nice little Concert, at which a most beautiful piece 'Oh Lady fair' was admirably sung.

> 1. Frederic Goulburn, Goulburn's cousin, son of his Uncle Henry of Betchworth, and his wife Jemima (nee the Hon. Jemima Sondes), who was also at the Deanery.

Friday 24

Preached extemp. in the Evening at 8 on Ps. 19, 4, 5, 6,; its applicability to Xmas Day – We had Choral Evensong at 8, and a very large congregation – <u>In the morning</u> I worked at a Sermon for Sunday – In the afternoon bought a dress for Fraulein, & then took a walk – I met Pringle, who asked me to attend the National Education Meeting on Wednesday. I gave my Christmas gratuities today, of wh. here is a list:

	£.	s.				
8 Lay Clerks	2.	16	£22.	3		
6 Bedesmen	2.	2	£10.	4.	6	(as below)
2 Vergers		14	£11.	18.	6	
2 Subsacrists		14		3		Bonbon Box
Gatekeeper		7	£11.	15.	6	
Schoolmaster		7	£8.	7		
Ferryman	1.		£1.	17.	6	Dress for Fraulein
Bellows Blower		7	£10.	4.	6	
	£8.	7				

Saturday 25   **CHRISTMAS DAY**
     Mg.: The Sympathy of Christ feminine
At the 8 a.m. Communion there were 33 Communts. – Symonds, Muller & I officiated – Bulmer, Heaviside, Nisbet, took the later – I preached in the morning as above – Much time occupied in rewriting a Sermon for tomorrow – after luncheon, visited little Em'ly, & walked with the Pinseter – The two Frauleins had their Xmas with us – I have had a present of Romola from Kate C., shaving cloth from Frederica, penwiper from Fraulein Anna, case for Sermon Notes from <u>little D</u> – am very tired!

Friday 31
     Evg.: The Angels' oath that there shd. be Time no longer.
Was at all 3 Services – In the morning Losingised with the Pinseter – Dined at 2 – Walked in Garden – Service was at 8 – I got thro' without much discomfort, tho' the subject was a little hard – Very tired afterwards –
And so ends the year!

1873

JANUARY

Wednesday 1   **Circumcision**

H.C. in the Choir at 8 a.m. – The Bp., Nisbet, Symonds, Medley[1] being there (but not H. who was unwell) – I spoke aft the Nicene Creed on "Let there be lights in the firmament of heaven" – there were about 60 Communts. – There was some hitch about the organ-playing both in the opening hymn and in the Nicene Creed – The Choristers were in their usual places, and were withdrawn after the Address – After Bkfst. I took Brooke[2] to call on the Bishop; we saw there Sydney, Herbert[3], & Fanny – then took Brooke into the Presbytery, & showed him the aspidal Chapels – Morning Prayer was at 11 (no Commn. Service) – afterwards took a short walk with the 'Pin' on the Thorpe Road, discussing what must be said to 'Hailstone'[4] – After luncheon answered letters; and wrote to the Bp. with our revised 'Scheme'.

> 1. The Revd E.S. Medley had been ordained in Canada and had been Curate of St Stephen, New Brunswick (1863–65) and then Rector to 1872, when he came to England to be a Minor Canon (i.e. Curate) of Norwich Cathedral until 1877. He was also Precentor 1874–77, after Symonds becam Rector of Tivetshall.
> 2. Brooke appears to have been a student attending Lectures by Symonds.
> 3. The Bishop's second and third Sons, and his only daughter. Herbert (1855–81), the youngest son was an Oxford Rowing Blue, Curate of St Philip's, Heigham from 1878, and, in 1881, was killed in a mountain accident in Switzerland.
> 4. Edward Hailstone, Esq., co-operated with Goulburn in writing 'A History of the See of Norwich', which was included in the Bosses Book published in 1876.

Thursday 2

The Choristers came at 6.30; also the Pin, Mrs. Symonds, Little Em'ly [*Symonds*], & little May Morse – Medley dressed as a Postmistress, and gave out the letters admirably, after wh. we had some games wh. consisted chiefly in rushing about & kicking up a dust – At 8 a cold supper in the Library (the games were in the Dining Room) – All went about 9 p.m.

Monday 6   EPIPHANY

After both Services held an examination into the conduct of Mears, who had been accused of irreverence, laughing & talking, by the Miss Robbinses of Shropham – the examination brot. out a charge agst. the chorister Smith of having handed up to the Layclerks a photograph of himself during Service last week.

Tuesday 7

After Church, at wh. Mr. Hailstone was present, the Pin and I went to the School, and prescribed the caning of little Smith – 15 cuts – then we took Mr. Hailstone up to the Bosses; then over the Presbytery, etc. – then I gave him some notes wh. I had drawn up for his work – after luncheon I took him a walk to St William's Chapel on Mousehold Heath – We had dinner at 6.30 – Afterwards Ju, Buskins, MAC. & Hailstone went to Mr. (Professor) Seeley's[1] Lecture at the Grammar School on the two Pitts – they did not much like it – they said that, when it was over, Sir H. Stracey, who took the Chair after Mr. Walpole's departure, made an attack on the Lecturer for speaking in an 'oracular' style and not giving sufficient credit to William Pitt for patriotism – Prof. Seeley replied with warmth – Sir S. Bignold was present; the Pelhams were there.

> 1. J.R. Seeley was Regius Professor of Modern History at Cambridge 1869–95; Knighted 1894.

Wednesday 8

A letter from Nisbet, saying that the Eccl. Commissioners look black at our proposal to sink part of the 'Barrack Money' in the improvement of Canonry Houses – another from Hinds Howell about the meeting on the 25th, about Ath. Creed[1] – rode with little Buskins [*now 19½*] on the Thorpe Road – In coming back her pony kicked, and we had to walk the horses – Whitwell Elwin[2] called after luncheon with the 'Pin' – we took him into the Cath. and he was delighted with the effect of the Norman piers, wh. he is sure are quite correct – then the Pin and I (at his house) looked over proofs of the Boss book – Georgie Cubitt dined here, and she, Buskins and Auntie, went to Chick. Pattie's[3] Ball – I read Middlemarch[4] to MAC. – it is very disagreeable.

> 1. During the previous few years efforts had been made in the C. of E. to have it removed from the Service or pruned, especially of the 'damnatory clauses'. In 1872 Goulburn had preached a Sermon in defence of it, and he continued to defend it.
> 2. The Revd Whitwell Elvin (1816–1900); Rector of family living of Booton 1849–1900, where he rebuilt the Parish Church to his own design. Editor of 'Quarterly Review' 1853–60. Goulburn was consulting him about some of the Cathedral restoration work.
> 3. Henry Patteson, Esq., Head of Pockthorpe Brewery.
> 4. George Eliot, 'Middlemarch: A Study of Provincial Life'. Published 1871–72.

January 1873

Thursday 9
Culfaude Davie[1] came up to the office, and laid before us the objection made by some solicitor to our new Training School Buildings, as overlooking certain premises.

> 1. See March 23, 1867 (Note 1)

Saturday 11
After Mg. Service I met Mr. Gunn at the Choristers' School, and inspected with him what he considers to be the Saxon wall in the Cloisters; (characteristics of Saxon Architecture are according to him (1) Brick, rubble & flint used instead of free stone as material (2) Long and short work at angles of buildings (3) Circular windows splayed inside and out (4) Gable headed windows (5) Herring-bone work round arches) – looked over proofs, and wrote to Proctor & to Mr. Crosse[1] about his window in St Luke's Chapel – Read to the 'Bee-girls' (Ada, Bessie, Mary Wallace, Lottie Wallace), 'Vanity Fair'.

> 1. The children of John Green Crosse (1790–1850), Surgeon of the Norfolk and Norwich Hospital, and his wife Dorothy (who died in 1870) – both buried in the Cloisters – erected a stained glass window in St Luke's Chapel to their memory. Of his eight children (four sons and four daughters) two sons were ordained; one became a Surgeon; one a Lawyer; two daughters married Clergymen; one daughter (Lavinia) became the first Mother Superior of the Community of All Hallows, Ditchingham; and the eldest daughter lived to the age of 95 (1913).

Tuesday 14
I ... called on 'Pin' to thank him for examining the Boys in their Scripture, and on Medley, to enquire about Mrs. M. – Cadge and the other doctor who have seen her today, say that the disease has made great progress since the autumn.

Wednesday 15
After Mg. Service, saw Brown for a moment about the new tiles round the Upper Close, wh. have been twice pulled up – talked w. some of the Police about it – went on till Luncheon time with my Paper on Ath. Creed – then went with Ju and MAC. to see Professor Pepper's[1] exhibition of Faust, and then of the Cabinet in wh. persons vanished & reappeared.

> 1. John Henry Pepper (1821–1900) was an analytical Chemist. In 1862 he began to exhibit an optical illusion known as 'Pepper's Ghost', invented, in 1858, by Henry Dircks, a Civil Engineer. Pepper published popular scientific works and other writings.

Monday 20 To Cambridge and back
Started w. Heaviside and Bensly at 7.15 a.m., and got to Cambridge about 9.30 a.m. – Went to the Phelpsses[1], who gave us a luxurious breakfast; and the Master of Sidney gave me his Pamphlet on College Endowments – Then to Sedgwick's rooms – we found him far too feeble and infirm to attend to any business, and the sight of him lying upon his sofa asleep was ghastly – We discussed the qun. of how to get the money for restoring the Cloister, and determined on going to Chancery for leave to deal with Barrack money rather than to E.C. for a slice of the £12,000 – About the hydrants nothing we thot. cd. be done till Ayris sent in his report – We had a sumptuous luncheon, champagne, Burgundy, etc. at 2, when the Professor brightened up a little – After considering a letter of Matchet's and some small matters about Middleton, we went to see the Master's hydrants playing on his College – Then Bensly and I looked in at St John's Chapel, & caught the congregation breaking up from the Evening Service – Then to Sedgwick's[2] again, to take leave of him – then to Catherine Lodge, where Bensly & I had tea with the Robinsons & saw the children – left Cambridge at 6.30.

1. Robert Phelps had been Master of Sidney Sussex since 1843.
2. Professor Sedgwick died a week later.

Tuesday 21
After Mg. Service, worked at Ath. Creed paper till Luncheon in the little Sitting Room – At 1.30 came a Mr. Jardine (son of Sir W. Jardine)[1] Meyrick's Curate at Blicking, to ask for the living of Hempstead; recommended by Mr. Fielden of Baconsthorpe – He had luncheon with us, as also had Bensly – After Church came Mr. Ram[2] to talk about the interludes for Thursday Evening; to consult me about the investment of the endowment for St John's, Timberhill; and also about Mr. Noverre's offer of getting up a voluntary orchestra.

1. Sir Wm. Jardine was a well-known naturalist and writer; 7th Baronet; had edited 'Naturalists' Library' 1833–45, and had been joint Editor of 'Edinburgh Philosophical Journal. Was now 73.
2. The Revd E. Ram, Vicar of St John's, Timberhill since 1871, where he remained into the next Century. Became Chaplain of the Norfolk County Asylum from 1874.

January 1873

Thursday 23 Lecture on 'Reading Aloud'[1] for the Churchman's Club

Felt unwell, & was in bed till nearly 10 a.m. – Finished the rough draught of my paper on the Ath. Creed – Service at 5 p.m. – Heard there from Heaviside that Sedgwick is worse, and has been in bed since we saw him – Mrs. Sedgwick had heard from John that Paget had telegraphed for 'Isabella' – Went to the Lecture at 8 – Noverre's Rooms full; Sir S. Bignold presided – The Heavisides there, and Mr. Johnson, and many others whom we knew.

> 1. This is, probably, Goulburn's favourite and most frequently given Lecture. On this occasion, he had four musical interludes interspersed between the eight Readings.

Saturday 25 Ath. Creed meeting

After Service, went w. Heaviside to Training School – We considered what censure was to be inflicted on two girls who had not passed Can. Norris's Exam. – Hinds Howell came into luncheon – He and I went to the meeting about the Ath. Creed together – A Mr. Mason, a layman, made an earnest speech, and the Rev. Mr. Armstrong an admirable one – Went to Church & gave a Sermonette – then called on the Medleys – found them both sitting in their bedrooms – He asked me to administer H.C. to his wife on Wednesday at 11.15 p.m. [a.m.] – Answered letters all the evening.

Monday 27 Death of Sedgwick

At about 7.30 arrived a telegram, saying that Sedgwick died at 1 a.m. – I sent it across to Heaviside, to break it to Mrs. S., and wrote to the Bp with the news.

Tuesday 28

After luncheon called upon Mrs. Sedgwick, & talked to her; and also visited the Medleys – I met 'the little Ensors'[1] at the Medleys.

> 1. Those whom Goulburn had known as children, he often continued to refer to as 'little' into adulthood, – Augusta, for example.

Wednesday 29 Meeting of Hon. Canons at the Palace

At 4 o'clock there were several Hon. Canons present – The 3 Archdeacons & Archdn. Bouverie were both at Service and the meeting – Afterwards at the Palace, the Bp. seemed not as strong as usual – He gave an opening address – I read my paper, wh. was too long[1] – Afterwards Hopper, Blakelock, Blyth, Everard, and

Groome spoke; and the Bishop concluded the discussion before dinner, wh. was at 7.45 – I sat between the Bishop and dear Archdeacon Bouverie – it was a very pleasant party.

1. In defence of the Athansian Creed.

Friday 31 From Norwich to London
Left Norwich at 7.15; alone all the way – Went first to Rivington's, & put into his hands my pamphlet about the Ath. Creed – thence to Tatham's – Proctor gave me but little help about investments, and told me I must have a codicil to my will, to leave Ju the proceeds of the House – then to Gozzie, with whom also I talked over investments – Sharpe recommends Indian railways – thence to Club, where I had luncheon, wrote to Ju, and saw the Dean – thence walked to Park Street – the Dean came in to get a Platform Ticket for the Ath. Creed meeting – We dined at 5; and at ½p. 7 I met the Dean at the Club & went with him to St. James's Hall[1] – Meeting crowded – The <u>worst</u> places on the Platform, behind the speakers – Heard the speeches of K. Hucks Gibbs, <u>B.C.</u>, Lord Salisbury[2], Sir Perceval ?, Sir Alwyne Compton[3], and went out while a representative of the working classes was speaking; so that we missed Liddon[4]! Glad to get out; it was intensely hot & gaseous.

1. Probably the Hall of St James' Church, Piccadilly.
2. Politician and writer; opposed Disestablishment of Church of Ireland; Chancellor of Oxford University; future Prime Minister.
3. The Revd *Lord* Alwyne Compton, then Rector of Castle Ashby; high church views; in 1886 to become Bishop of Ely.
4. See December 23, 1868 (Note 1).

FEBRUARY

Saturday 1 Sedgwick's Funeral
Left King's Cross at 9 o'clock after breakfasting here at 8 – When I arrived at Catherine Lodge [*Cambridge*], I found Mrs. R. in distress for fear I should be late; she gave me coffee and hurried me off to Trinity – we met in the rooms under Sedgwick's; there were Heaviside, Robinson, Bensly, Leonard Sedgwick, young Adam the representative & others – Nisbet & Robinson bore the pall. Heaviside and I followed – when we passed the Master's Lodge, an immense train swept out to join us – The Choristers sang very sweetly – The Master of Trinity[1] read the commital to the earth, and the two last prayers, under some emotion; all the rest was choral – I walked a little back with Dr. Phelps of Sidney – then went to the Master's, who gave luncheon to me & Nisbet

& Perowne[2] – I took Nisbet in my fly to the train, w. another gentleman – Got to MAC's about 4 p.m.; wrote to my Ju.

1. The Revd William H. Thompson, D.D.
2. The Revd T.T. Perowne, B.D., who became Archdeacon of Norwich in 1878.

Friday 7
The corrected proof of my pamphlet arrived by the Morning Post – After Mg. Service saw Price about a charge of incivility made against him by Mr. Barnard of Catton – then went w Brown and Spaull to inspect the hoarding, & mounted into the old relic-chamber, and saw the frescos[1] on the walls there – had luncheon with Heaviside; Bensly joined us there – after luncheon we discussed the hydrants and the application to Chancery, and resolved to ask for money to carry out Ayris's plan, wh, will be the most we shall want – then went home & prepared the final revise of my Pamphlet; and wrote a list of people to whom it is to be sent.

1. Early 14th Century work – Chamber now known as 'The Treasury'.

Sunday 9   Septuagesima
At Church three times – Bitterly cold; and in the afternoon sleet falling – Between Churches I sat with Mrs. Medley; told her the story of Tacy & Whewell, and also of the man in spl. trouble who had tacked texts to his bed-curtains; read a little devotional poem to her – came home & went to Church, and preached on the character of S. John the Evangelist, with a termination about Sedgwick. Read in Smith's Dictionary of the Bible.

Monday 10   The Nevills first visit
Had a very bad night, and did not rise till 8 o'clock, too late, for Family Prayers – a dreadful day of cold, sleet, & other discomfort – The Nevills[1] arrived in Service time – afterwards I had a long confab. with him, turning principally on the Residence question, wh. he suggested an adroit method of solving – then I took them both to the Sedgwicks – the Nevills were shocked by the house – they had luncheon here.

1. Canon H.R. Nevill, Vicar of Yarmouth, had been offered the Residentiary Canonry vacant by the death of Sedgwick.

Tuesday 11

My Birthday – After a suffering night, rose not till 8 – Birthday presents: Ju an envelope Box; Buskins miniature views of the Cathedral; Bartie an eyeglass chain; Frederica a lamp shade – a letter from MAC., promising me her Newman's 'Romanism & Popular Protestantism' – At Church there was a grand surprise for us; for there was the hoarding down, and the fragment of the throne[1] thrown open, and the effect magnificent – after Church wrote to Frederica, MAC., Hinds Howell (with an amusing poem & series of caricatures wh. Garry had sent me, representing Duport as seeking admission to the Oxford Club dinner) and others – Mr. Dixon called to explain that the clock could not strike tomorrow – The hairdresser came at 6.30.[2]

> 1. The ancient Bishop's throne (stone) behind (and above) the High Altar, which had come from the previous Cathedral at North Elmham, and probably from Thetford before it.
> 2. More often Goulburn *went* to the hairdresser, but the charge seemed to be the same: 1/-.

Wednesday 12

Unwell, and in bed till 10 a.m. – Mr. Johnson came in and prescribed no drink but 'milk' – At luncheon saw Mr. Fitch[1], and we talked over the frescos (or rather wall-paintings) in the relic-chamber, and agreed to ask Mr. Winter what he would copy them for – Also agreed to postpone the Archaelogical Meeting, on account of the death of Mr. Manning's[1] wife (she was of unsound mind) – then came Heaviside, and I told him all about the Nevill's visit – then I wrote divers letters (1) (2) (3) (4) to the Mayor, Sheriff, F.E. Watson, Fitch, recommedning Mr. Stalter, Junr. as City Surveyor & Engineer, etc. (5) old Mrs. Tyndale, about her criticism of my Sermon … (8) Bensly, about my having had Income Tax to pay on my works twice, etc. – In the evening arranged the subject of my Lenten Lectures.

> 1. Robert Fitch, Esq., F.S.A., F.G.S., was Treasurer and Joint Sec. of the Norfolk and Norwich Archeological Society (of which Goulburn was President). The Revd C.R. Manning, Rector of Diss, was the other Joint Sec.

Thursday 13

In the evening the Valentines dropped in: Gussie was in an unusual state of excitement – I got a bottle of 'Old Prasearete' from Mrs. Heaviside, a case of photographs of Fecamp Abbey (with verses) from the Pin, and a pen-wiper with a dog upon it, probably from 'little Emily'.

Friday 14

Letters not in till 12.30, it being Valentine's day[1] – looked over some of the Boss Book Proofs – I took the Proof's to the Pin's – found him better, and talked with him over the level, and the new Altar in the Cath. – Then called on Lestrange to consult him on the subject of wooden Norman Altars – He told me there was a wooden altar of the year 800 in the Willow Lane Chapel[2]; and then he walked with me to see it – We found at the Priest's house in Willow Lane Father Amherst, Brother of the titular Bp. of Northampton, who had succeeded Costello – He took me into the Chapel, and we saw the Altar, wh. seemed to be of hollow wood.

1. So far as cards and presents were concerned, St Valentine's Day was almost like another Christmas Day.
2. The Jeuits were in charge of Willow Lane Roman Catholic Church (1829–1850); the secular Clergy 1850–1894. When the new Church of St John was ready for use, Willow Lane then became a R.C. School.

• •

From Saturday to Monday (15–17) Goulburn was in London, preaching at St Mark's, Shoreditch on the Sunday morning, and at St Paul's Cathedral in the evening. On Monday, he went on to Oxford, seeing a number of University personages, and also a young undergraduate connection of his, Henry Stapleton. Leaving Oxford on Wednesday, he stayed overnight at Aynhoe, returning to Norwich on Thursday (20).

• •

Wednesday 26   ASH WEDNESDAY

Services at 8 a.m., 11 a.m., 8 p.m. – At 11 the Lay Clerks made a collection for the N. & N. Hospital during the Offertory Sentences – I preached before commencing the Commination Service – Afterwards a walk w. the Pin on Mousehold, in the course of wh. I told him of Medley's suspecting that he (the Pin) did not like Medley's interference with the Choristers.

Friday 28

After Mg. Service walked with Medley (after 1st. visiting the East End with him & Heaviside, and inspecting the painting of the Quatrefoil window & Jesus Chapel) – he told me much about the Choristers and their homes – Mrs M. suffers very sadly.

MARCH

Sunday 2   **Lent I**
"In all points tempted like as we are, yet wout. sin".
Introduction to Lectures on X's Temptation (Short notes)
A lovely afternoon – Service thrice – Bp. present each time – East End of the Church looked lovely; the salmon colour on the quatrefoil window, etc. answers admirably – After luncheon, a turn in the garden – Then called on poor Mrs. Medley, & prayed with her, and heard her husband sing her one of Neale's[1] Hymns – At 3.30 preached as above – Afterwards took a walk on the Thorpe road, & was joined & accompanied by Dr. Jessopp – In the evening read Borrow's Sermons, Andrewes[2], Bengel[3], & Daniel Bagot.

1. The Revd J.M. Neale (1818–66): "the most learned hymnologist and liturgiologist of his time"; author of many well-known hymns; for 20 years Warden of Sackville College, East Grinstead, a refuge for indigent old men; founded other beneficent agencies; author of books in Church History and Theology.
2. The Rt Revd Lancelot Andrewes (1555–1626), Bishop of Winchester. Influential in forming a distinctive Anglican perspective "reasonable in outlook and Catholic in tone".
3. J.A. Bengel (1687–1752): Lutheran N.T. Scholar and Professor, in Germany.

••

On Saturday, March 8, Goulburn travelled to Peterborough to stay with the Dean (Augustus Saunders) and preach in the Cathedral on Sunday evening. "The Cathedral was very full" and was impressed by the Services "well and most reverently done". He returned to Norwich on Monday (10).
••

Monday 10   From Peterboro' to Norwich
I had an hour & 10 min. at Ely, & went and had luncheon at the Deanery – In returning to Norwich, I found all well, and only one letter from Garry, asking me to support him in an application for increase of Stipend to St Mark's on ground of population[1] – I went to Church, and afterwards wrote a letter for him to the Eccl. Commissrs. – At about 6 p.m. on our coming out of Church, there was violent hail, & tremendous crash of thunder, & vivid lightning wh. nearly struck Heaviside!!

1. Population of Parish of St Mark, Lakenham, was then 3,958. It would appear that this increase was not forthcoming, for, later in the year, the Revd N.T. Garry became Vicar of Speenhamland, Newbury, Berks.; in 1875, Rector of St Mary's, Reading, where he remained for 22 years, becoming an Hon. Canon of Oxford in 1884, and Rural Dean of Reading for the whole 22 years.

Wednesday 12   To Yarmouth and back

At 1.30, took train for Yarmouth – in the train was Hy. Patteson & Col. Fitzroy, going down about the Harbour-Commission, with whom I talked – Ministers beaten last night on the Irish Univ. Bill[1] by a majority of three – Arrived at Yarmouth, I first met Colvin, who walked about with me in search of Nevill – afterwards a walk with Nevill on the Parade, in wh. we discussed the proposed subdivision of Yarmouth (to which he is very averse), and how the money for his house[2] is to be raised – Church Service at 7.30 – With a Sermon only 7½ pages, wh. lasted about 18 min., I just got out in time to catch the 8.40 train — got back at 9.40.

1. The Irish University Bill 1873 proposed that the Queen's Colleges at Belfast, Cork and Galway be amalgamated with the ancient (1591) University Foundation of Trinity College, Dublin, to form the University of Ireland, endowed partly from the revenues of Trinity. There were to be no Chairs for Theology, Moral Philosophy, or Modern History. The scheme was assailed from every quarter. 43 of Gladstone's Liberal M.P.s voted against their own Government.
2. The house Nevill would occupy in the Close as the new Residentiary Canon.

Thursday 13

There dined here, to eat Sir H. Stracey's swan, Heaviside & Mrs. H., Dr, & Mrs. Jessopp, and Ada Hansell, and the Pin & Mrs. Symonds – a billet doux from Johnson in the midst of dinner-time announced that Gladstone had resigned[1] – After morning Service we (H. & I) went to Bensly's Office, to talk over what was to be done about raising the £600 for Nevill's house – I was to write to the E.C. and ask whether they would probably let us have part of the £12,000 reserved for the Cathedral for Hydrants – This I did in the Afternoon, and had a heavy time writing letters – After Evening Service, Mr. Dixon came to purge himself about the mal-practices of the clock.

1. But he returned as Prime Minister the following day.

Friday 14

After Bkfst. went to Gurney's Bank, to give notice of my intention to withdraw Mr. Gibbs'[1] £1000 Benefaction to St. John's, Timberhill in 14 days time.

1. Goulburn's generous London Benefactor had also, because of his regard for the Dean, extended his charity to Norwich, and was to do so again.

Saturday 15

Went to visit Mrs. Medley – There was a change for the worse in the night – She seemed extremely feeble; Medley keeps up wonderfully – Then went to Bensly's Office, where Heaviside & the Master soon joined me in Chapter – (1) We sealed a power of Attorney to sell out & get some ready money for the expences of the Establishment (2) Talked over the removal of Bathurst's Statue (3) exchange of Glebe at Scalby[1] (4) Division of Scalby (5) Brown's Plans for Robinson's house and for the Cloister, etc. etc.

1. Parish in Diocese of York, of which the Dean and Chapter were Patrons – still are.

Friday 21   The Doctrine of the Trinity

A miserable day, cold, rain and snow all day long – While the 'Pin' and I were at work, Mr. Paterson came in, the foreman of Cooke of York; he had examined the clock & chimes, and found nothing materially wrong with the exception of the rope of the 'going clock' being rusted – I ordered a new rope, wh. is to be covered with mixed tar and lard – In the evening preached as above.

Saturday 22

Poor Mrs. Medley died at 10 a.m. this morning, after receiving the H.C. at 8 a.m. – As I walked to the Guildhall, where there was a Hospital Meeting, under the Presidency of the Mayor, to determine about Hospital Sunday, the Medical Charities wh. should come in for a share of the spoil, who shd. form the Managing Commee., etc. etc. etc. – the Dissenting Ministers (Barrett[1] at the head of them) wanted to have the upper hand of the Managing Commee. – I was obliged to go before the end.

1. The Revd George Barrett (1839–1916), Editor of the 'Congregational Hymnal', Minister of Princes Street Congregational Church.

Thursday 27

At noon went to Bensly's Office to talk over and settle about some letters wh. had arrived from Nevill and Nisbet – We went over Robinson's garden & Nisbet's back premises with Brown & Bensly, and settled not to re-roof that part of the Cloister where Robinson's house now stands, wh. will make a difference of £300 in the expence (asphalt instead of oak & lead) – Went down to Lakenham at 8; there gave an address on the frequency of

Communion: the Bible rule, the P.B. rule – finished at 9.20 – Poor Mrs. Medley's funeral took place this morning at 8; a most lovely spring day – there was the H.C. at the funeral, and garlands of flowers, & 4 hymns sung by Choristers & Lay Clerks – Boys much affected.

Friday 28
A most lovely day – after Mg. Service (1) worked with the 'Pin' at Losinga. (2) went with him up to the Tower, to see the arch wh. has recently been opened into the Presbytery West Wall. The 3 arches there have been blocked with plaister and then painted – made an abstract of my Sermon 'the Fatherhood of God' for the 'Norfolk Chronicle'.

APRIL

Tuesday 1
Heaviside had a letter today from Genl. Elphinstone, saying Prince Arthur had asked for a Royal Chaplaincy for him, but it was now determined not to bestow these favours on Canons!! – after second Service, wrote to (1) Nisbet & Robinson about our conduct in refce. to Sedgwick Memorial (2) Hailstone, sending him his first remittance of £10. 10.

Thursday 3
Long letters from Nisbet & Robinson about Sedgwick Memorial – The former wants an exclusively Cathedral Memorial, raised by ourselves & the County; the latter wants that we shd. subscribe as individuals, not as a body – he says that all Cambridge people are at sixes & sevens as to their own memorial – Wrote to Mrs. Mortimer (nee Karslake) about eternal Punishment; to Mr. Philip Wills about the Atonement of Christ – after dinner corrected Proofs of my book on the Church and Gospel of Childhood.

Sunday 13   EASTER SUNDAY
The Morning Service (Celebration and all) lasted till about 1.20, beginning at 10.30 –
1. At opening, Easter Hymn with harps accompaniment.
2. High Prayers throughout.
5. Short Anthem of Elvey's after 3d Collect.
6. Tallis's Litany
7. Easter Introit.
8. Gounod's Nicene Creed with the harp.

9. A few notes only before the Sermon – Bidding Prayer omitted – The longer Exhortation at the Communion omitted both at the first & second Celebrations. No singing at all at the early Celebran, at wh. we had 60 Communicants – It lasted till 8.56 a.m. – at the later Celebration, there were 104 Commts. – At Evg. Prayer: 1st. Easter Hymn with harp.

Tuesday 15
Heaviside came to tell me of his successful visit to N. Elmham yesterday, where the P. of Wales laid the foundation stone of the Norfolk College, and of the Prince having asked him to Sandringham for Friday, Saturday, and Sunday (he is to preach on Sunday) – At 2d. Service we had the Nicene Creed on the 2 harps, and an astonishing congregation for a weekday.

Wednesday 16
After Mg. Prayer took Arnold[1] over the Presbytery, etc. etc. until it was time for the Archaeological Meeting at the Guildhall, when we walked up there – Sir F.B.[2] was made a V.p. – I read a short paper on the mural paintings of the vaulted relic-chamber in our N. Choir aisle – (Ju ill and in bed all day) – Mr. Gunn read a Paper on the W. cloister wall, wh. he pronounces to be Saxon.

    1. Probably C.T. Arnold, a Housemaster at Rugby School.
    2. Sir Francis Boileau, of Ketteringham Hall.

Friday 18
After Mg. Service went with the Pin into the Jesus Chapel, to see the relics of an early English (plaister) rere-dos wh. have been discovered there – Found there by Bensly – then took a ride to Beeston Hall, the miser's house, and thence to Rackheath, where called upon Sir H. Stracey – After Evening Service gave the Boys their prizes.

• •

On Saturday, April 19, Goulburn went to London, next day going on to Brighton where he joined Julia and Gussie, remaining there until April 30. From Brighton they went to stay at Horton with the Revd Sir Henry Gunning and his wife Mary, Julia's step-sister, until May 17. Gulburn often worked on his Lecture on 'Church and State', keeping up his correspondence with Norwich (and others). He was anxious to fill the Living of St Peter-per-Mountergate and wrote to the Bishop of Norwich, enquiring whether his nephew, John Pelham, Curate at Lowestoft would be interested. Apparently he was not. He was also unsuccessful with others about whom he enquired before returning to Norwich on May 17.

• •

Saturday 19 From Norwich to London by 7.15 a.m. train
Gave orders to Goslings to buy with the £6000 gained from the purchase of my Rugby house[1] £6000 stock in Russian 5 per Cents Loan of 1872 (Div. payable April 1, Nov. 1) – they are now said to be at 91½ or 92 per Cent – After reaching Town, called at ... (7) Proctor about Rugby house, wh. Trustees have agreed to buy.

> 1. In 1851, soon after Goulburn had become Headmaster of Rugby, he built, at his own expense, a new Boarding House, known as School Field. Now, 22 years later, he sold to the School Trustees "the interest which he possessed in the house in School Field" for £6000. This was only the second Boarding House actually *owned* by the School.

Sunday 20
At 11 I went to Nisbet's Church[1], where I preached on St. Peter's re-instatement in the Apostleship – thence in cab to my Club – had luncheon and read over my Sermon – Then to St. James's[2] arriving before the doors were open – a very fair congregation.

> 1. St Giles-in-the-Fields.
> 2. St James's, Paddington, the 'Parish Church' of Paddington, the vicar being the Patron of St John's.

Wednesday 23   [*In Brighton*]
Took a long walk with Bigge to see an ice vessel (the St. Helena of Chrstiania) being unloaded – The blocks of ice are brought up from the bottom with a clamp, and each of them is weighed, & the weight registered, before it is thrown into the waggon; we went on board and looked on; then we continued our walk – found Ju & Gussie settled in 13, Regency Square[1], & very comfortable – did not feel quite up to the mark.

> 1. It was, usually, the Goulburn's custom when away from home, to stay for one or two nights at a hotel, and then to find, and move into, less expensive lodgings.

Thursday 24   [*In Brighton*]
To Mr. Wilkinson's, the house agent in North Street, who gave me a card for 14, Lansdowne Place; I went over it, and really think it may suit us – then went home to send Ju to see it – It is to be sold for £2,100 – very like Sussex Gardens – After dinner read the Guardian, & Lothair.

Monday 28
A much better night after calomel – After Bkfst. completed the entire MS. of my 'Gospel of the Childhood'[1], wrote 23 labels for presentation copies of my book on the Church – wrote also to the

Abp. of Cant.² – A letter from Heaviside giving an account of the aberrations of Medley³ – went out in the morning – went out again with Ju and saw Mr. Wilkinson about 14, Lansdowne Place; he introduced us to Mr. Lainson, to whom I gave a commission to survey the house for me.

1. 5000 copies of each of these books were printed. The 'Gospel of the Childhood' went into a 2nd. Edition.
2. The Most Revd Archibald C. Tait.
3. Edward Medley (ordained 1863), Minor Canon, seems to have gone to pieces after the death of his wife (she was probably in her late 20s or early 30s.). In 1877, he became a Residentiary Canon and Precentor of St Andrew's Cathedral., Inverness, but returned to the Diocese of Norwich in 1886, to be Vicar of St Gregory, Norwich; then Hopton; then, finally, Rector of Postwick from 1894. All these were Dean and Chapter Livings.

MAY

Monday 19   [*In Norwich*]
In the morning an interview w. Stacy¹, whose children have had low fever from an open drain – also w. Spaull, who has done nothing towards painting the roof, as having received no order – worked with the Pin at H.L. at his house from 10 a.m. to 1 p.m. – then signed some agreements at Bensly's Office about 'the Dean's field' – he came here, and I put into his hand the agreement about the Brighton house – This is my Ju's birthday; I gave her a travelling case, and she had letters from Frederica & B. Bartie.

1. His Norwich printer in the Haymarket.

Saturday 24
At 1.30 Ripley¹ came to luncheon, and gave me an account of the catastrophe at Martham².

1. The Revd W.N. Ripley, Vicar of St Giles, Norwich.
2. On April 5, Martham Church had been struck by lightning, doing considerable damage, both to the Tower and the Clock, as well as to the buttresses at the south-east angle. St Giles and Martham were both Dean and Chapter Livings. Ripley's interest in Martham was because his father-in-law had been Rector.

Sunday 25
After a night of pain and suffering, started for Aylsham at about 8.30 a.m. – En Route meditated my Sermon, wh. was on "Take this child away & nurse it for me", for the Day and Sunday Schools – Mg. Service was at 10.45 – Mr. Aitken assumed 'the dorsal¹ position' in the Commn. Service; had a handsomely

worked stole, etc.; his Curate looked as if he came out of an ecclesiastical bandbox – My Sermon was long; we collected about £10 – Mr. Aitken's open carriage took me to Blickling where I met Mrs. Parmeter, Meyrick's sister, & his curate, who had luncheon with us – After luncheon, they took me into the library[2], a most curious & interesting room of the date 1620; saw there beautiful illuminated MSS. of the Bible, and Coverdale's Bible – we had afternoon Service in the dining room, nicely fitted up as a Chapel – drove back to Aylsham in Mr. Aitken's carriage –I set off for Norwich about 5 – read Marshall on Sancrification en route.

1. 'Dorsal' = An ornamental cloth hung at the back of an Altar. It would appear to mean that the Celebrant faced East with his back to the congregation.
2. It is not clear whether this was the library in the Rectory or in Blickling Hall (Long Gallery). I think the latter, because of Goulburn's remarks about the room, the fact that the present building was erected c.1620, and that the Library does contain two copies of the Coverdale Bible and a variety of illuminated Bibles. The widowed Lady Lothian was probably away from home. The Revd F. Meyrick had been Rector since 1868.

Tuesday 27 Lecture on Church[1]

We went to the Lecture at 8 – the hall was thronged; it lasted about two hours – Thanks to the Lecturer [*Goulburn*] proposed by Utten Browne[2], seconded by C.S. Reade[3] – Thanks to the Sheriff for presiding proposed by Dr. Jessopp, seconded by Mr. Winter (*not* of Swaffham) – Just before I was starting came in Butterfield[4], and accompanied me to the Lecture.

1. This was the fourth in a series of Lectures, inaugurated by the Diocesan Church Defence Association, on 'The Principles of the Established Church', all in St Andrew's Hall. The previous ones had been on April 27, May 12, and May 19, given by different Lecturers. This one, by Goulburn, was entitled 'The Established Church'.
2. Staunch Tory and High Churchman; also a serious student of History. Mayor 1860–61.
3. See October 14, 1869 (Note 1).
4. William Butterfield (1814–1900), famous Architect of various Church, University and School Buildings.

Wednesday 28

Devoted the morning to Butterfield; went with him, the Master, & the Pin, 1st. to the Relic Chapel; then to the face of the Tower Arch, and last to the Bosses – no foundation of a stone staircase to the Relic Chapel discovered.

Saturday 31

Medley & his Captain Brother called at about 2.15 – Medley came again with Choristers at 6.30, & presented a handsome paten and chalice, all jewelled, with chalice veils, etc. in memory of his wife – The Archauntie Lili[1], & the Auntie of Aunties arrived at 4.15.

> 1. Lady Cartwright (former Austrian Countess) widowed step-sisterin-law of Julia.

JUNE

Sunday 1   WHIT SUNDAY
Medley's new Paten & chalice used for the first time – 11 a.m.: A tremendous crush, what with the Hon. Artillery Company, our own volunteers, & the Mayor & Corporation – A Sermon from the Bishop – Lili went a second time to Willow Lane[1] at 6.30.

> 1. Roman Catholic Church off St Giles.

Monday 2
Service twice – <u>Not</u> choral at 5 p.m., the Lay Clerks and Choristers claiming a holiday for Queen's Birthday.

Tuesday 3   Audit
The audit began at 10.15, and kept Bensly & me till quite time to dress for dinner at 7.30 – The chief subjects were the disposal of the Capitular Benefices, the question of the two Canonical Houses (Nisbet's and Nevill's), and the Restoration of the Cloister – At 7.30 dined here, the Bishop, Bensly, four Canons, Mrs. Heaviside, Mr. Hotson, and Dr. Buck (with Hen. & Kitty Stapylton, Lili, Ju and self) 15 – Ke and Buskins dined upstairs.

Sunday 8   TRINITY SUNDAY
Service three times, 8 a.m., 11 a.m., 3.30 p.m.
After the anthem at 11 a.m., I preached (unduly long) from notes on "If any man speak, let him speak as the Oracles of God" – 5 Deacons and 3 Priests ordained – It was not over (thro' my long Sermon) till 2.30 – I felt quite tired – at 3.30 the Master preached a most admirable Sermon; only 20 min. long – Afterwards I took a turn w. Bullivant, in the course of which he offered me £200 for a new altar!

Monday 9
At 10 went over the Cathedral w. Spaull, the Pin, and Bullivant, and ordered the removal of Bishop Bathurst's statue[1] at a cost of £15.

> 1. The Statue, the seated figure of Bishop Bathurst, is now in a corner of the North transept.

•••

Goulburn went to Aynhoe on June 10 for the funeral of General William Cartwright, aged 76, who had fought at Waterloo. He was Julia's stepbrother. Goulburn returned to Norwich on the 11th; and then on Saturday (14) he went to Aynhoe again to preach on the Sunday, returning to London on Monday (16). Preparations were now put in hand for their long holiday on the continent, mainly at Marienbad to drink the waters. They would not be back in Norwich until August 2.

•••

Monday 16
At 10.45, I left Aynhoe for London, having to stop in Oxford ¼ of an hour – got here at 2.15 – drove to (Ogle's) Grosvenor Hotel, Park Street, and was thunderstruck at finding no rooms for the name of Goulburn – drove to Grosvenor Hotel, Victoria Station, but found no room at all <u>there</u> – then went to the Langham Hotel, but there was none there – thence to S. Pancras Station, where met Ju & Gussie, & announced the startling tidings that we could get no rooms – However, on going again to Ogle's, it appeared that the rooms had been ordered in the name of Dean of Norwich! – thence to Club, to enquire about a courier recommended by Stan. – thence to the Deanery of Westminster – his courier was engaged, but I got there the address of the Courier's Office (12, Bury Street, St. James's) and went there, & made an appointment to see two couriers in the morning – thence to Dr. Weber's, where I met Ju – He threw overboard Vichy, & told us to go to Marienbad!!

Tuesday 17   In London, preparing for going abroad
No courier appearing from Dr. Weber, Ju and I went to the Courier's Office, 12, Bury St., St James', and saw one Genevay who refused to come with us under £18 Guas. for six weeks plus 5 fr. a day – went to Cook's Excursion Office <u>opposite</u> 98, Fleet Street – telegraphed to Blake[1] to hold himself in readiness – went to Italian Courier's Office, 38 Golden Square, & there made an engagement to see a courier tomorrow – I ordered a Passport at Gaze's Tourists' Office, & sent my keys to Bensly, & an acct. of my Sermon [*Sun., June 15*] to Npton Herald.

   1. The servant in Norwich who usually travelled with him looking after the luggage, etc.

Wednesday 18   In London
Engaged by recommendation of Porter at Club, Mr. J. Schutz as Courier, 9, Shelgate Road, Northcote Road, Battersea Rise –

decided upon taking Schutz as Courier for £12 a month + 3s. a day while at Marienbad[1] – Schutz appeared in the evening.

> 1. Foreign travel in the Victorian period became commonplace for the middles classes, revolutionised by railway and steamship; and one of the enthusiasms was "taking the cure" in Continental Spas such as Marienbad, Baden Baden, etc.

●●

THURSDAY, JUNE 19:   London to Brussels, via Dover and Calais.
FRIDAY, JUNE 20:   Brussels to Coblenz.

●●

Saturday 21   From Coblenz to Homburg
Left Coblenz about 11 a.m. and got to Homburg about 3 p.m. – I had a bath, and then went to see Melia[1]; and saw also the Baron & Ernst, who is the image of his mother – dined w. Ju at the Table d'hote – Melia came in afterwards.

> 1. Amelia (nee Goldsmid – de Visme) (1814–81), was Goulburn's first Cousin, the daughter of his (real) mother's sister – In 1861, she married, as his second wife, the Baron Leopold von Grempf. Ernst was the son of the Baron's first wife, Jane Bowles, also English, and was Godfather to E. Bryan Gipps (1910–) of Egerton House, Kent, who has supplied letters, photographs and information relating to the family.

Monday 23   From Homburg to Frankfurt
Thunder and heavy showers – after Bkfst. called at Ld. Warwick's lodgings – Ld. W. then walked with me to see Ju at our hotel – we found Melia sitting with her – Melia called again at 6 p.m., and at 7.15 accompanied us to the Station where were the Baron & Ernst, to say Adieu.

Tuesday 24   From Frankfurt to Marienbad
A long day of rail, beginning at 6.15 a.m. and ending not until 7.15 p.m. – we got up at 3.30 a.m. wh. was an effort – We met and were, part of the way, in the same carriage w. Mr. Fred Micklethwaite,[1] & Mr. Talbot, brother of the illustrious Ned's[2] – had much talk with the latter – On arriving here, we discovered we had left Julia's Box behind, either at Eger or perhaps at Asch, where is the Austrian <u>douane</u> – We had a scanty dinner at Klinger's hotel, in the midst of an awful racket, but felt the air refreshing & reviving.

> 1. The Micklethwaite family were centred at Taverham Hall and Hickling Hall, Norfolk, and were patrons of these parishes; the Revd S.N. Micklethwaite was Vicar of Hickling 1849–89.

2. Edward Stuart Talbot (1844–1934) was the first Warden of Keble College, Oxford 1869–88; Vicar of Leeds 1889; Bishop successively of Rochester, Southwark, and Winchester.

•••
From June 24 to July 22, the Goulburns were in Marienbad, drinking the waters, supervised by a local doctor, and meeting friends, relations and acquaintances.
•••

Wednesday 25 At Marienbad
Ju's box did not appear till 10.30 – We sent to our Doctor, and waited for him all the morning long, but he did not come – we read German in Boileau's book, and also read the 2d lessons of the day in the German Testament, and made sundry notes thereon – dinner at the 2 p.m. Table d'Hote: Soup (vegetables & bits of suet floating about), roast beef, really tender doe venison, asparagus white chopped & boiled looking like maccaroni – no fish, no potatoes, and in the way of sweets only a Banbury cake <u>boiled</u> – after dinner we took a walk – then came Dr. Ott, & prescribed 2 6 ounce glasses of the Krenzbrunnen at 6 a.m. with 4 or 5 hours walking – no coffee at night, but soup and eggs – only <u>wafer</u> bread, and no <u>rahm</u> or cream – only ¼ of a bottle of Voslaner Wein at dinner; for more wd. produce irritation.

Saturday 28 At Marienbad
I had two very nice walks with Ju, during the morning, one reading 'Antony and Cleopatra' on the road – We went to Mecsere Temple, and Friedrich's Stein, where was a latin inscription wh. I am ashamed to say I could not decipher* – In the afternoon we strayed into the Lutheran Church, where I have promised to give a Service tomorrow – They were decorating it for the Anniversary of the Church tomorrow – a German Fraulein talked to us in English; we were shown the Surplice and Communion Vessels for the English Service – it seemed a nice Church – I walked with Micklethwaite after my second glass, and we strolled into the Church where children were singing at the Mass, and little boys with satchels where standing round the altar, two of whom were kneeling barefooted & seemed to be in disgrace.

* I find it commemorative of the visits of Frederick King of Saxony in 1824 and 1835, whose health was reestablished at these waters, and acquired a great knowledge of its botany.

Sunday 29   At Marienbad

We sat in the balcony in the morning reading a conference of Lacordaire – then we read our Morning Service – We had Service in the English[1] Church at 4 – Evening Prayer, and a Sermon (wh. I preached from the Lutheran Pulpit) – Mr. Micklethwaite, Mr. Talbot, & Lady Ashburton were there, and we collected about 25 florins[2] for the Lutheran Church, as a kind of acknowledgement – The congregation did not exceed 30 or 31.

    1. He must mean 'Lutheran' Church.
    2. = £2. 10s.

Monday 30

I was at the Krenzbrunnen drinking four glasses for the first time at 5.30 this morning – (Dr. Ott called yesterday, and directed me to change my 2 glasses into four) – when our potations were over, we went lodging hunting[1] – After reading our Lessons, I called on Micklethwaite & Talbot – then we walked up to the pine-forest on the road to Atto's Hohe, and there sat reading the account in 'The Times' of the Tichborne trial[2] – After dinner Ju did not feel equal to the Convent of Tepi with us – Mr. M. & Mr. T., and I went in a Zweispanny – the quadrangle of the convent seemed dirty, but the Church is handsome (tho' gaudy) and the drive was beautiful – We saw in the Church of Marienbad this morning H.C. given to a woman without any celebration[3].

    1. The Goulburns were not too happy with their accommodation. They stayed in Klinger's Hotel from June 24 to July 1, changing from the Top to the Ground floor on June 29. But on July 1, they moved to Hotel Wemar, remaining there although finding the accommodation cramped.
    2. Since 1866, Arthur Orton had claimed the Tichborne baronetcy and estates. Orton was the youngest son of a Butcher at Wapping. Lady Tichborne, widow of the 10th. Baronet professed to recognise in him her long-lost son, reported to have been drowned at sea. His court case collapsed, he was arrested for perjury, sentenced to 14 years penal servitude; released 1884; died in poverty 1895.
    3. Presumably, for some reason, she was receiving the Reserved Sacrament.

JULY

Sunday 6

After Bkfst. and some reading, etc. we mounted to the pine-woods where I read to Ju one of Lacordaire's Conferences[1] – At 12.30 we had our Litany and Celebration in the Lutheran Church – It was just over by 2 p.m. – About 28 persons were present, of whom 22 communicated – We used the Calvinistic Bread, wh. is biscuit bread marked in Squares so as to break easily; you are obliged to chew it – the wine used was a sweet white wine – we dined at our hotel; then rest before 2d Service at 5 – this 2d Service lasted till 6.

> 1. Henri Lacordaire (1802–61) French Dominican Preacher; attracted attention by his Sermons (Conferences) at Notre Dame Cathedral and other places.

Monday 7

Took my first cup at 5.50 – The drinkers more numerous than ever – Ju and I went into the Church, and witnessed part of the Children's Mass – After Bkfst. we read our Lessons – then came the Verwahrer or Custodian of the Church, with his account – He charged 5 gulden for his own Services; 1 gulden for the wine; 30 kr. for the bread, 40 for the Organ-Blower, in all 6.70^1 – This I paid, and took his receipt for it – After dinner at 3.15, we ordered a landau^2, and drove (with Mr. Micklewaite and Talbot, whom we asked to accompany us) to Kuttenplann where Lili's cousin lives, and back.

> 1. = 13s. 5d.
> 2. A four wheeled horse-drawn carriage with two folding hoods that meet over the passenger compartment.

Tuesday 8

After dinner went down to meet the Aubreys^1, & brought them all up here in the 'Bus – Mary, Aubrey, Bertie, Gordon – Aubrey had some dinner, and then he & I adjourned to a pine wood & talked, till it was time for the 6 p.m. Glass – After wh. we all sat on the Promenade, while band played, & Mr. Micklethwaite came up & talked to Aubrey. [*The Aubreys left at 6 a.m. next morning.*]

> 1. Richard Aubrey Cartwright and Mary (nee Fremantle) and their two children. Julia's oldest *full* brother.

Sunday 13

I had two Services today as on last Sunday: Litany and H.C. at 12.30, and Evening Prayer with a Sermon at 5 – In the morning there was but a small congregation, only 9 communts. (myself included) – We used the Lutheran double wafer stamped with the Cross – The whole lasted from 12.30 to about 1.50 – I think there were about 30 people in the afternoon, hardly as many as 20 in the morning.

Monday 14

Then [*afternoon*] came the Lutheran Pastor & Clerk – the latter handed in his little bill, and the former I gave all the balance – Then we went out and called on Lady Ashburton, and found her in a most charming room filled with books at Halbridyer's Hans.

Monday 21   Last Day at Marienbad!

After the worst night of heartburn I have yet had, rose at 5.50 – after Bkfst. wrote [*a number of letters listed*] – then came Dr. Ott on his final visit – the diet of this place to be carried on for three weeks – I gave him 60 Guldens, 30 for each of us – soon after came the Sexton, and I paid him his small account, and made up the English Church Service Book. (Collected on the four Sundays 143 Gu. 92 Kr. – Expences of English Service 15 Gu. 35 Kr. – Balance given partly for the maintenance of Lutheran Services, partly for the sick poor: 128 Gu. 57 Kr.) – then went to make purchases with Ju.

Tuesday 22   From Marienbad to Wurzburg

Left Marienbad about 7.10 & arrived at Wurzburg at 5.40 – At Lichenfels we saw on one side of the stream the Monastery of Banz, founded (like that of Norwich) in 1096, but (unlike that of Norwich) not dissolved till 1803 – opposite to it is the Church of <u>Vierzehn Heiligen</u> much more modern; the great place of pilgrimage for these parts.

Wednesday 23   From Wurzburg to Mayence

At 8 we took a lionising walk and visited the Cathedral, where prayers for a deceased priest were being said with great solemnity – The chief officiant intoned beautifully – The chalice and paten, with the birretta and the stole, were laid upon the coffin – We saw the statues of those Bps. of Wurzburg who were princes of the empire, and carry the sword in the right and the pastoral staff in the left – then we went into the Neue Munster & into its crypt, where is the shrine of St. Kilian[1] the Apostle of Franconia, screened by a red curtain, thro' wh. a bright light shines – There is a beautiful pulpit – We left Wurzburg at 1.30 ... and got to Mainz about 5.30.

1. Died c. 689. A native of Ireland, went as a missionary to the Franks; headquarters at Wurzburg; converted the Ruler and most of the population, before being put to death in the Ruler's absence, by his wife.

July 1873

Thursday 24 From Mentz [Mainz] to Cologne

Our voyage on the Steamer from Mayence to Cologne was delightful in point of weather – no sun, and yet not a drop of rain – but an American came up, and after commenting on my sight which enabled me to read my Diamond Shakespeare, he abruptly informed me of the Bishop of Winchester's[1] death by a fall from his horse – I was much distressed and shocked, and thought of it all the day afterwards, tho' I have not been able to see the paper wh. describes it – We left Mayence about 9 and got to Cologne about 6 – we strayed into the Cathedral and heard Vespers, & a young priest preaching – at 11 o'clock we left Cologne by the night train, and by Schutz's paying two Thalers had a carriage to ourselves.

> 1. The sudden death of the Rt Revd Samuel Wilberforce, Bishop of Oxford 1845–69, and of Winchester from 1869, affected Goulburn considerably, because he had been the Bishop's Chaplain when he was in charge of the Parish of Holywell, Oxford, and had a high regard for him. The Bishop was 68.

Friday 25 St. James

Arrived at the Hotel de Flandre, Brussels, at about 6 a.m. – Rose about ½p.9 and got to Bkfst about 10.35 – Then read in yesterday's Times some comments on the Bp. of Winchester's death – Went into the Town and studied the pulpit of St. Gudule[1] – went into the Church of S. Jacques next our hotel, where the singing this morning at 9 a.m. and aftern. at 4 p.m. sounded magnificent.

> 1. St. Gudule (died c. 712) was a woman saint. She is the Patroness of Brussels, where her remains are buried in the principal Church there, which has been dedicated to her.

Sunday 27 [In London]

I went to St. Paul's in the morning alone & heard Bp. Claughton[1] preach on "Look not every man on his own things" – the unselfishness of the late Bishop's character, and the influence it gave him – I walked thence to Westminster and had luncheon with the Leightons[2] and Archdn. Bickersteth[3] – got from them tickets for the evening – walked thence to MAC's; we dined there at 5, and all 3 went to the Abbey for the Evening Service, and heard Canon Kinsley preach to an overflowing congregation.

> 1. The Rt Revd Piers C. Claughton was Archdeacon of London – From 1862–71 he had been Bishop of Colombo (Ceylon).
> 2. The Revd Dr Francis Leighton, Warden of All Souls, Oxford, had, in 1868, in addition become a Residentiary Canon of Westminster.
> 3. Archdeacon of Buckingham, and Prolocutor of the Lower House of the Convocation of Canterbury.

Monday 28
Saw Lord Chichester at Club, who told me that the E.C. did not think we had given the Minor Canons in our scheme a sufficient pull upon our preferment, but that they agreed with us that "the same Diocese" meant any one diocese in England or Wales – I walked home, and saw in the evening Mr. Shoveller about our house, and Morgan, who thot. I had done quite wrong in going to Marienbad, and was too much reduced.

AUGUST

Sunday 3   First day at Norwich after return home
Assize Sermon.
Service 3ce. at 8, at 11, at 3.30 – Judge Cleasby[1] came in state at 11 and Mr. du Chair[2] preached an admirable Sermon, on "Prepare to meet thy God" [*relating it to the Great Assize*] – Read to the Servants a most striking Sermon of Burgon's on the last vv. of the Gospel of the Day.

   1. Sir Anthony Cleasby (1804–79); Baron of the Exchequer 1868–78.
   2. The Revd F.B. *de* Chair, Curate of Morley (nr Wymondham), and then Rector from 1878–98; Organ. Sec. for Norfolk for S.P.G. 1874–82; R.D. of Hingham 1891–1901; of Norwich from 1901; Hon. Canon 1892.

Friday 8
Then came the Canons to the Chapter at ½p.2 – We ordered the restoration of the Upper Arcade, a new roof (oak & lead) for the vacant space over what was once the Master's House at an expence of £705; and I ordered the restoration of the old refectory[1] staircase at an expence of £61.17 – we also agreed to apply to the Watch Committee about the disorderly persons in the Close – also agreed to go to Q.A.B.[2] for a loan for Nevill's house on security of Corporate Property – Bensly and I were kept till near ½p.7, recording.

   1. The Refectory was on the south side of the Cloisters and had been 160 ft long and 34 ft wide (E.Fernie, "An Architectural History of Norwich Cathedral", Clarendon Press 1993).
   2. Queen Anne's Bounty: Set up in 1704 by Queen Anne with revenues confiscated by Henry VIII, now to be used to augment the Livings of poor clergy; from 1777, it could make loans; from 1803, it could be used towards building and repair of parsonage houses, etc. Between 1809 and 1820 it received grants of over £1,000,000 from Parliament. In 1948, it was united with the Ecclesiastical Commissioners to form the 'Church Commissiones for England'.

Saturday 22

After Bkfst. went to the Library, and worked at the proof of Hailstone's October Chapter till luncheon – then entertained the Venables[1] (6 of them) at luncheon – went with them into the Cathedral, & lionised a little before Service – After Service lionised them further over the Cathedral and took them into the Palace Gardens, where we met young Lee Warner[2] and his wife (Blake Humfrey's dr.) – then brought them home to tea, after which they took leave – then wrote numberless letters – Ethel and Meanne[3] arrived, but their boxes had gone on to Lowestoft – however they were recovered in the evening – Cousin Mary Chetwynd arrived at about ½p.9

1. The Revd George Venables was, at this time, Vicar of St Matthew's, Leicester. He became Vicar of Gt Yarmouth from 1874–86.
2. During the 19th and early 20th Centuries, the Lee Warners, as Patrons and Incumbents, were connected with Gt and Lt Walsingham.
3. See October 7, 1868 (Note 1).

Tuesday 26

After Bkfst. practised with Mr. Minns[1] for the evening – Ju helped me in my Boss Book till the 'Pin' came, and then we finished the Bosses of the 8th. Bay !! – At 1.10 I drove down to the Guildhall to present the petition for keeping publics closed at 11, and not extending the hours till 12 – met there Canon Dalton[2], Mr. Baldwin of St. Stephen's, and others – When we were admitted Mr. Utten-Brown was in the chair – Mr. Chittock made a long speech for the rival petition, and then I held forth for ours, but omitted to say that at Liverpool they close at 10, at Hull 10.30 p.m.

1. One of the Lay Clerks.
2. Popular Priest of the Roman Catholic Chapel in Wymer Street.

SEPTEMBER

Friday 5

Nevill spoke in the morng. of the importance of having in the Cathedral non-evidential Sermons – settled matters with Spaul, Browne, and Stacy before leaving – The Pin worked at indexing with me till 1 – then I made preparations for departure – went into the Church to direct Spaull about stripping the glazed arches of Lady Chapel – Bensly joined me there, and then Mr. Day (a master of Eton) and his wife – these I lionised over our works – then called on & saw Miss Cubitt – called on and saw the Heavisides – then Second Service – Dr. Buck came in afterwards,

September–October 1873

and we agreed to expel Smith – then saw Bush and the other man with the Precentor, & made them an offer of staying on at the present time for a ½ year[1].

> 1. As Lay Clerks.

• •

On Saturday, September 6, the Goulburns (and Augusta, now 20) left for Tyntesfield, near Bristol, the home of the Gibbs family, where they stayed until Saturday, September 13th. Mr Gibbs appeared to be very unwell and confined to his house – There was an Oratory attached to it, where a form of Morning Prayer was said every morning at 9 am, Evening Prayer on Sundays, and Family Prayers on weekday evenings. As usual, Goulburn met and talked to many people coming and going, and those who were resident in the vicinity.

From Tyntesfield, the Goulburns went to Edgcott where they stayed until September 20; then to Eydon until September 29; then to Aynhoe until October 7; finally, to Brighton until October 15th (during which time he went for a weekend to Eton to preach in the College Chapel). Eventually, after more than 9½ weeks absence, they returned to Norwich.

• •

Thursday 18   At Edgcott

Letters from Mr. & Miss Reid[1], saying that he would be only too happy to take St. Gregory's – this obliged me to write to him (at Npton) asking him not to decide till he had seen the place, and begging him to go to the Deanery & look at it – I wrote enclosures for the Pin, Bensly, and Mr. White.

> 1. The Revd C.B. Reid *did* accept St Gregory's, Norwich.

Friday 19   At Edgcott

Last day at Edgcott – It is Aubrey & Mary's Silver Weddingday, and they had many beautiful presents, one particularly of a silver coal-scuttle from Sir T. and Ly. Fremantle[1] (for sugar), and a silver mirror from Mrs Charles Fremantle – Anne Attenbury and 'Tedda' came in after dessert to drink their healths.

> 1. Sir Thomas and Lady Freemantle were Mary Cartwright's parents. Sir Thomas (1798–1890), had been an M.P.; a Treasury Secretary; Secretary at War; Chief Secretary for Ireland 1845–46; Chairman of the Board of Customs until 1873. In 1874, he became the 1st Baron Cottesloe.

OCTOBER

Tuesday 7   From Aynhoe to Brighton

Service at 8 a.m. – A rainy, dreary day – Left Aynhoe at 10.40 – At Oxford we joined Bitta's party, & had Ursie in our carriage –

In London we had 2 hours – I went to Grove, fishmonger, to order venison for Oxford Dinner[1]; then to Le Gassick's for clothes; to the Club where I had a chat w. good Sir R. Kindersley; to Rivington's where I ordered Bennett's[2] book & Haydn's[3] Dates; & to the Chiropodist's – we had a saloon carriage coming down to Brighton, carrying besides ourselves Bitta, Lili, Marion, Frances, Ursie, Fraulein Linder, & Miss Carr, a maid of honour – we find our house very nice[4], & have had a snug dinner here.

1. The Norwich Oxford Society Dinner on October 16.
2. Sir Wm. Sterndale Bennett, Composer, Professor of Music at Cambridge, permanent Conductor of Philharmonic Society's Concerts; Principal of Academy of Music. Book: 'Chorale Book for England'. Died 1875.
3. Joseph Haydn (died 1856) compiled a 'Dictionary of Dates' in 1841, and 'Book of Dignities' in 1851.
4. In June he had bought 14, Landsdowne Place, Brighton.

Wednsday 15   Brighton to Norwich
Left Brighton after Bkfst. at 9.45 a.m. – On arriving in Town, went to Butterfield, who promised to come here in Novr.; paid for my Venison, saw Proctor ... about the sale of Westb. Terrace[1] – came home by 5 o'clock train – arrived 9.30.

1. The house which the Goulburns vacated when they moved from London to Norwich.

Thursday 16
Arranged papers & books before Bkfst. – After Bkfst. answered my letters – then took a walk thro' the Harvey grounds – called on Symonds, Buck, Bensly, Heaviside, but found none of them at home – at 3 p.m. went into Church, & found not only the Bp. there, but the 2 Canons, the 3 Archdeacons, Ormsby, & H. Howell – then went to the Oxford dinner at 5 – neither Nisbet was there, nor Cooke, nor Jessopp, yet we had a pleasant evening – Garry's[1] health was drunk on the proposal of H. Howell, wh. he made with great feeling.

1 The Revd Nicholas Garry (Queen's Coll., Oxford) had been Vicar of St Mark's, Lakenham, from 1861–73; he was now moving to be Vicar of Speenhamland, Newbury, Berks., and, eventually, he would be Rural Dean of Reading and an Hon. Canon of Christ Church, Oxford.

Saturday 18   St. Luke
After Service we had our meeting about the Bush affair – we agreed that it was best to dismiss Bush on the ground of his health not being strong enough for the choir, but at the same time, if he wished it, to make an examination into his conduct & the

charges against him – he did not seem to wish it, so I paid him his stipend and dismissed him[1] – called on Nisbet to say how the matter had ended – also on Symonds, then on Medley – then returning home to luncheon found a letter from Symonds[2] about Tivetshall – sat down at once & wrote a strong letter about him to Mr. Walpole, recommending him as the right man – This I gave him to read.

> 1. In his Open Letter of June 7th, 1869, to the Archbishops, Goulburn had advocated "The providing retirement pensions for ... Lay-Clerks who are incapacitated for their duties by age and infirmity". So one would hope that the dismissal was also accompanied by concern for the Lay-Clerk's future.
> 2. Henry Symonds had been at the Cathedral for some 30 years as Curate, Minor Canon and Precentor. He was an Oxford Graduate and was only some three years younger than Goulburn. He went to Tivetshall in 1874 to be there for 19 years. He still continued to work closely with Goulburn until 'The Bosses' and 'Losinga' were finished. He must have been a competent Latin scholar because a major part of the work on Losinga was the translation from latin of the Letters and Sermons.

Tuesday 21

A long and wearisome Chapter, lasting (for me and Bensly) from 11 down to 3.45 without interruption – Came home and sorted papers, and had an interview with a gentleman about 'Hospital Sunday' and the arrangements in the 'Cathedral' – Wrote to B.C.[1] (who had accepted All Saints, Margaret Street) and to Bullivant – In the evening Gussie made a transcript of my letter to 'The Guardian' about Lay Clerkships.[2]

> 1. The Revd Berdmore Compton, Goulburn's long-standing friend, who, eventually, wrote his 'Memoir' in 1899, was Vicar of All Saints', Margaret Street, London, for thirteen years.
> 2. A few days previously, Goulburn had suggested the idea of students of Theology becoming Lay Clerks; he now publicised it.

Thursday 23

Raining hard all day, so that I could not get out – After Service, went with Medley to see Sir Noel Paton's[1] picture of 'Mors, janua vitae' – At 8 went to the Sheriff's[2] Lecture against Darwinism; most interesting it was, and well attended – It was in St. Giles's School Room – I presided.

> 1. Sir Joseph Noel Paton (1821–91); exhibited at Royal Academy. Painted mythological or historial scenes, and religious pictures such as this ('Death, a Door to Life') in 1866.
> 2. Dr (later Sir Frederick) Bateman, M.D., F.R.C.P.

Monday 27

After luncheon a Chapter at 2 p.m. at wh. we sealed the Lease of Land to tramway company[1], settled about the parcel of ground to be held as a garden by Nevill – At 5 p.m. Service admitted the new Bedesman – had a letter from John Gott[2], saying that he was appointed to Leeds.

> 1. No tram ran in Norwich until 1900.
> 2. John Gott had been Curate of St Nicholas, Gt Yarmouth 1857–61; then in charge of St Andrew's, Gt Yarmouth 1861–66; Perpetual Curate of Bramley, Leeds 1866–73; now appointed Vicar of Leeds 1873–86; later, Dean of Worcester 1886–91; and then, Dean and Bishop of Truro 1891–1906.

Thursday 30

At Lynn – Went (with my Ju) at 8.20 a.m. – Choral Fetival in S. Nicholas Chapel at 2.45 p.m. – Left Lynn at 5 p.m. and did not get to Norwich till past 8 – here I found a bundle of letters awaiting me – the most interesting of them was from Mr. Walpole, enclosing one to Symonds, offering him Tivetshall – also a letter from Thirtle in Bank Street, offering to buy the Living for "an excellent clergyman" of strict Low Church principles – and one for the Bishop, exposing Thirtle – I called at the 'Pin's' and left the letter for him – he was not at home.

Friday 31

Communicated by letter to the Bp. Mr. Walpole's offer of Tivetshall to 'Pin', and Mr. Thirtle's atrocious offer[1] – After Church was in the Church for 2½ hours, superintending the preparations for the Confirmation, wh. were only just finished before they were wanted – At luncheon found Mr. Reid, Mr. Hansell, and Mr. Stannard – In came Mr. Skeggs, a youth reading at King's College, who had seen my letter in the Guardian, and came to offer himself as Lay Clerk – I asked him to stay the night[2] – looked in at the church to see that all was right; saw the Bp. for 2 minutes – did not attend the Confirmation; wrote my letters, and worked also at my Sermonette – Mr. Skeggs and the 'Pin' were at dinner – The 'Pin' did not think he had voice enough for a layclerk – So I told him this before we went to bed.

> 1. It is not stated which Living Mr Thirtle wanted to purchase, clearly a Dean and Chapter one, so possibly, St Gregory or St Peter per Mountergate, both of which were about to be filled.
> 2. Goulburn was always scrupulous in giving hospitality and travel expences to anyone he had for interview, as he did in this case.

NOVEMBER

Monday 3
After Mg. Service, worked in the Library at <u>Saturday Sermonette</u> – At 1.45 Mr. Reid[1] came to luncheon, and told me about the rival factions (Tock v. White) at St. Gregory's, and asked my advice on several points – At 2 came Mrs. Copeman[2] to say that her son-in-law, Mr. Skey, would be glad to accept the Precentorship here – (He has been Precentor of Bristol) – then I took a walk with Dr. Buck on Mousehold in wh. we discussed the steps to be taken about the Precentorship and the Layclerkship.

   1. The Revd C.B. Reid was to be instituted at St Gregory's on November 22.
   2. The wife of the Vicar of St Andrew's, Norwich. The Revd Frederick Skey had been Curate of Gt Yarmouth 1859–60.

Tuesday 4
Started with Hinds Howell for Ditchingham at 8 – I preached there on "Seest thou these great buildings?" "Church Decoration" – met there Archdn. & Mrs. Bouverie[1], and Admiral & Mrs. Eden, the former shocked by the ritualist costumes wh. abounded[2] – walked 3 miles back; got home about 4 – answered my letters before dinner time – The Jessopps, Wm. Cookes, Hinds Howells, Reids, Mr. Garry and Miss Vesey, & Medley, dined here.

   1. Archdeacon Bouverie had retired as Archdeacon of Norfolk in 1869.
   2. The occasion was the reopening of the Parish Church (St Mary's) after restoration. W.E. Scudamore had been Rector since 1839 and very much involved in the formation and support of the Community of All Hallows, Ditchingham.

Wednesday 5
'The Gospel of the Childhood' having arrived, I wrote the names of the Choristers in it, and gave copies to 8 of them after Church – A policeman called to say it would be dangerous to light a bonfire in my field, Mr. Barnard having filled a cottage adjacent with petroleum – So I was obliged to forbid them.

DECEMBER
••
Goulburn became ill on Thursday, November 6, and made no further entries in his Diary until Wenesday, December 3, 1873. Recently, Augusta had been acting as a part-time Secretary and writing some of his letters for him.
••

Thursday 4 Norwich to Grosvenor Hotel, Park St. (Ogle's) Rose at 7 p.m. [a.m.] – read Family Prayers at 8.30 a.m. for the first time since my illness – Muriel[1] came in about 10, and then Bensly – I signed the Chapter Book for the latter and explained to him that we had ordered (levelling) in the cloister – We left our house at 10.20; Ke and Buskins went w. us as far as Cambridge, where they were met by Sirett – (Rose[2] with us) – I read the Guardian, Times and Eastern Daily Press – got to London about 3.15 – it was getting quite dark – left Rose to follow in another Cab with the luggage – found a letter from Prof. Mayor[3], consenting to lecture for Churchman's Club on the 12th. – read to Julia 1st. the report of Prof. Max Muller's[4] Lecture in the Nave of the Abbey (Times) and 2d the report of the Wilberforce Memorial meeting in the 'Guardian' – Papers more interesting than usual – Morgiana came in about 5 p.m. and ordered me some quinine for tomorrow.

1. Their Norwich Doctor in place of Johnson.
2. Julia's very long-serving Lady's Maid, who usually accompanied them, and continued with them into their retirement.
3. The Revd Professor John Mayor, Prof. of Latin at Cambridge.
4. Prof. Friedrich Max Muller (1823–1900), German Academic who settled in England; Orientalist and Philologist; the first Prof. of Philology at Oxford; Curator of the Bodleian Library.

Friday 5
Bkfst. at 9; then paid our bill for the night and read the 'Times' – an acct. of the English subjects executed in Cuba as stokers & firemen of the 'Virginius' – Went out in a hired brougham (after taking my quinine) at 10.30 – 1st. with Ju to Brit. Museum to hunt up such subjects as <u>Scutage</u>, <u>Dalmatic</u>, Schale Crinicon; consulted Blomefield, Pitscens, Vestiarium Xtianum, Palmer's Origines, Hook's Ch. Dictionary, etc. – Ju was delighted then to see Holman Hunt's[1] picture at 39B, Old Bond Street – very disappointing at first sight; the Saviour seems as if he were stretching himself after a day's work amongst the shavings – It is called 'the Shadow of Death' – then to Gosling's – My balance was announced as being £4970, but then this includes £3943. 7. 2 paid in by Proctor on acct. of London House; and 2 large sums, (£43 & £15), drawn yesterday the cheques could not have been presented for – Morgiana called & prescribed continued quinine, occasional calomel, & Vichy water – read Act I King Lear aloud.

1. See May 19, 1868 (Note 1). One of his less well-known paintings.

Saturday 6   From London to Brighton
Bkfst. at 9 – Paid my Bill afterwards & paid (by a cheque) for 2 doz. of 'Begbie's Port' – walked to Floris's for toothbrushes, and then walked nearly to Charing X, when we remembered that Brighton trains start from Victoria – took a cab there in some commotion – however, we were quite in time – read 'John Bull' and 'Illustrated News' in the train; arrived about 3 – first MAC called, then Hen. Gunning, and then MCG[1], who had been at a concert at the <u>aquarium</u> – we dined here at 7, finding everything in our house very comfortable – in the evening came a letter from the Brit. Museum with instructions how to get a reader's ticket; and another from Fred. Goulburn[2], announcing his appointment to Chairmanship of Customs – I find here documents from Bensly, and a letter from Dr. Pope, proposing himself for Yarmouth.

1. MCG = Mary Catherine, Lady Gunning, Julia's step-sister.
2. Goulburn's nephew, son of his late Uncle Henry.

Sunday 7   Advent 2   At Brighton
Rose at 6.45 and was dressed about 7.45 – we had a cup of coffee, & then set off in a very comfortable fly (ordered over night) for St. Peter's, where 'Treacher's Brighton Record' informed us that the H.C. was to be administered at 8.30 a.m. – we got there at 8.15 and found the Clergyman in the midst of the Church Militant Prayer – They had begun at 8, as young Shelley, who greeted us after the Service, told me – there was a most creditable no. of communicants, but all huddled together absurdly eno' at the extreme W. end of the Church beneath the Organ Gallery – young Mr. Hanna read, I thought, too fast – we got away before 9 o'clock struck – afterwards we read the Morning Prayer & Communion Service thro' – then about noon we went out, and walked up and down the Promenade in the sun for about an hour – At 3 o'clock the Archauntie Grannie called for us and we all went (MAC., Mary Aubrey, Mary & H.G., and young Aubrey) to St. Andrew's (Mr. Winham's) – the organ quite shook my nerves, like setting one's teeth on edge. The Sermon was on "the Grace of God wh. bringeth salvation, teaching us, etc. etc.", but I could not listen to it – sat it thro' with difficulty, & came home & fell asleep.

Monday 8   At Brighton
Aubrey & I had a delicious sunny walk along the Parade, looking in at Waterloo St. to order 'the Times', and at an ornament shop to buy a Photograph stand for Ju[1] – we returned after ½p.12 – found a letter from Wood, refusing Yarmouth – wrote to Mr. Crosse, who had announced to us the arrival of his window for St. Luke's chapel[2] – we made up our Bankers' Books and agreed to purchase (for £4440) £4000 worth of Gt Indian Penin. Railway Stock – this I directed Goslings to do, transferring to him from my account w. B. of E. £240 – After dinner read to Ju the 3d Act of Lear, & corrected Proofs of Boss Book.

   1. For their 28th Wedding Anniversary on December 11.
   2. See Note under January 11, 1873.

Thursday 11   At Brighton
Bkfst. at 9, after our Family Prayers – wrote to Buskins, thanking for her almanc; to Frederica, thanking for her views of Canterbury and her Vanity Fair, both wh. arrived this morning as wedding presents – (Ju gave me a new ring, and I to her a ring and a stand for 3 photographs) – also wrote to Bullivant, thanking for a turkey, etc. – In the evening Arthur Wagner, Aubrey & Mary Aubrey dined here, & a very pleasant evening we had.

Friday 19   At Brighton
My hat, wh. had gone for repairs, etc. to Carrick's, 87, Kings' Road, had not returned when I wanted to go out – bought a turkey for Mr. Bayley at Crawther's, 14, Western Road – gave a young man a shilling for picking up 14 shgs. wh. I had dropped into a basket of eggs in the shop – then home – wrote to Heaviside, asking him to distribute my Xmas gratuities, and sending him a cheque for £10 for that purpose – I offered the living[1] to the Rev. Geo. Venables – after dinner read 'Little Dorrit' to the ladies – This morning came from Heaviside an 'E.C. Daily Press' giving a ghastly account of the child-murder at our Bp's Palace[2].

   1. Gt Yarmouth (where he remained for 12 years).
   2. The mutilated body of a new-born baby was found concealed in the bedroom of Emily Francis, a new maid at the Bishop's Palace, who had come from London only a week before.

Sunday 21   Advent 4 St. Thomas   [*At Brighton*]
At 7.45 went to St. Paul's (in a fly) with Ju at 8 – red stoles & a magnificent chasuble – we were back by 9 – at 10.45 we went

again – had Morning Prayer, with fancy Psalms (145 and 3 follg.) – Immediately after the 3rd. Collect the preacher went to the pulpit, & preached: "Ye observe days, & months, & years. etc." – he was very controversial, & I thot. rather bitter – came away before H.C. Service began, with a headache, & glad to get out – we were much squeezed – after luncheon Ju & I walked on the esplanade in front, & met Mr. Thursby, who talked on the Vestaments & many other matters – came in & read afternoon Service, & began a Sermon of Dr. Evans's – saw James[1] on his return from Church, & went w. him thro' the Sacraments in the Catechism – <u>Morgiana</u> called! & said I was much better, but he wd. say I had better not get back to work till Feb. 1 – I wanted him to stay to dinner, but he was obliged to return – After dinner read Massingberd's[2] Hist. of the Reformation Chap. 1 aloud to the Ladies.

1. One of the Servants.
2. Francis C. Massingberd (1800–72); Chancellor and Canon of Lincoln; Proctor in Convocation; wrote 'English History of the Leaders of the Reformation' (1842).

Tuesday 23   At Brighton
Dr. Hayman's[1] long letter, in reply to his dismissal, in 'Times' this morning; read it before going out – then went out and bought Xmas presents for Ju and MAC. at the wood carving establishment, in King's Road (a portfolio w. chamois, and a daggar containing pen, pencil, paperknife, etc. etc.) – returned & wrote Ipswich lecture – a letter from Heaviside at mid-day, summoning Chapter (as V.D.) for 31st. inst., chiefly about the loan for Nevill's house – also formal notice from Bensly – wrote to Groome agreeing to lecture at Ipswich on 3d Feb., and to Buskins, sending P.O. for £1, and a 'stomach's sake' Christmas card – then read Hayman's letter & the 'Times' Article to Ju in her bedroom.

1. Henry Hayman, Headmaster in turn of three previous Schools became Headmaster of Rugby in November 1869, and was the centre of controversy until his dismissal in December 1873 by the Governing Body, "such removal to take effect from 7th Day of April next".

Wednesday 24   At Brighton
After Bkfst. (at wh. appeared a large envelope from Nisbet, with a report upon the expenditure, and comments thereon from Robinson); and also a wooded spectacle case as a gift from Fraulein; and also £25 from Goslings – walked to make two or three small purchases & have a hair cut, & went on w. Ipswich

Lecture, wh, seems interminable – wrote to Nisbet, sending cheque for Harp Platform, & acknowledging <u>his</u> cheque for H.C. alms – I wrote some verses to Kate, thanking her for a toothbrush rack she had sent me, and also to E. Ram, saying he had better fix the grnl. meeting of the Chman's Club without reference to me.

Thursday 25   CHRISTMAS DAY   At Brighton

At Bkfst. came presents, 2 magnificent vases from Frederica, a card-case & almanac from MAC. (to whom I gave a daggar containg pen, pencil, knife, paper knife) – a muffler from Auntie – letters from (1) the Pin, about Elwin's view of Butterfield's plans, etc. etc. (2) the Bp. about the Cathedral body meeting at the Palace – a most dreary day, most dispiriting – we took a fly & went to St. Peter's Church – I thot. the Service rather dreary – Bullivant's turkey, a splendid one, at dinner.

Friday 26   St. Stephen   At Brighton

At Bkfst. presents from Frederica (views of Chichester and Rochester), and Buskins (a thermometer, broken <u>en route</u>) – At midday, came letters from Venables, saying that he is going to Yarmouth on Tuesday, but cannot yet decide – H. Patteson asking subscription to S. James's Schools, and a crowd of others – then I wrote to Nisbet my criticism of his Treasurer's report, and to Heaviside my judgement on another proposal to be made in Chapter on the 30th. inst.

Saturday 27   St. John   At Brighton

By the midday post came a letter from Nisbet, returning my cheque; another from Sweet, offering 3 Sermons in the Cathedral during Lent; another from <u>Howarth</u>[1] offering hospitality at Ipswich – went out – after my return wrote to (1) Bp. of Norwich about his thesis for the Cathedral body; 'Chicken Pattie'[2] with subscn. (£3) to S. James's School; Spaull about his charges, and Mr. Crosse's window; the Lord Chancellor's Visitors (official enquiries about Fred)[3] – Mr. Howarth, accepting invitation to Ipswich.

1. Rector of Whitton with Thurleston since 1835.
2. = Henry Patteson: Head of Pockthorpe Brewery; former Sheriff and Mayor; associated witn many philanthropic enterprises and local institutions; had lifelong practice of going to Church twice every Sunday.
3. Goulburn's brother ('poor Fred') in a Home at Ticehurst, Surrey.

Monday 29 At Brighton

A letter from Heaviside, informing me that the Commts. at both Communions on Christmas Day only amounted to 70 (last year 120) – Ju took an early stroll with me, and we discussed the knotty point when we shd. leave this place.

• •

In spite of Dr Morgan's advice that he should not return to work till February 1, Goulburn decided to leave Brighton on January 6, 1874, and, after a few days in London, to return to Norwich on Saturday, January 10.

During 1873, he had been absent from Norwich 152 days, and, officially, off work in Norwich for a further 27 days. The 152 days of absence were made up of 45 in Brighton; 37 abroad, mostly in Marienbad drinking the waters; 26 in Aynhoe and its neighbouring villages; 17 at Horton; 12 in London; 7 at Tyntesfield, and 8 on preaching engagements (and one family funeral) overnight from Norwich.

It should be made clear, however, that, during these 152 days, Cathedral business was done, especially in London; he kept in very close touch by letter with Cathedral business in Norwich where Heaviside (as Vice-Dean) was in charge; he continued to write Sermons; to work on his books and pamphlets, and to check proofs, also preaching and taking part in Services where he happened to be.

The first 10 days of 1874 are spent in Brighton and London, ending his period of convalescence, before returning to Norwich.

• •

1874

JANUARY

Thursday 1   Circumcision.   At Brighton
Ju came down to Bkfst. with the sealskin purse I had given her – Ju and MAC. went to Church and H.C. at St. Andrew's, Waterloo Street – After luncheon went out with Ju – returned Mr. Trocke's books; left a 'Personal Religion' at Mr. Thursby's[1], after writing in it; paid a wine bill at Hedges & Butler's (£4. 2); ordered a 'Gospel of the Childhood' for Mrs. Thursby at Treacher's – walked with Ju to Bristol Hotel by the cliff, and then back by the 'Madeira Walk' – coming home we met (to our surprise) the Master[2]! – He, Mrs. R., & Ludie came here Monday, and are at 9 (or 19 ?), Goldsmid Road.

> 1. Their son had been the Rector of Berg Apton, Norfolk, since 1864, had recently become the Patron, and a Thursby is still listed as Patron today (1995). This was the Parish of which Bishop Pelham had been Rector from 1837 to 1852.
> 2. Canon Robinson.

Friday 2   At Brighton
Rose, as usual, at 8 – A very wet and very warm day, almost too warm for fires – No letters at Bkfst. and no newspapers – I went out after Bkfst. and called at the newspaper shop to expostulate – sea roaring, rain drizzling, roads dirty – another letter coming in from Burrow, and representing that my testimonial made him out to be too 'Churchy', I re-wrote it, and sent him another.

Monday 5   At Brighton
Last day at Brighton – A letter from Mr. Venables, accepting Yarmouth, and sending me his Bishop's letter thereanent.

Tuesday 6   THE EPIPHANY   From Brighton to London
Left Brighton at 7.30 – read a County Sussex Paper – At Tunbridge Wells took a <u>Cab</u> to Ticehurst, where we arrived about 11.30 – found Fred much the same – Newington says he has left off writing – Ju thot. he muttered & laughed to himself more than at the last occasion of her seeing him – Newington came in and sat there, and was eloquent about the effects of an ⅛th. of a grain of Podophylline daily for a fortnight – also gave us a most wonderful account of a Canon of York, who has a monomania that he cannot eat, & is fed by a stomach pump, and was recovered from an attack of inanition by having a whole bottle of

champagne, & another of brandy, poured into him – we left Ticehurst at 2.20 p.m. and Wadhurst (in train) at 3.10, and got to Ogle's Grosvenor Hotel, Park St., at about 5 – Morgan came in & said I had a nervous tongue, and must walk a great deal at Norwich, & work as little as possible – Oh! how can I do it!

Thursday 8
A dull rainy day – no letters at Bkfst. – read the 'Times' in wh. there seemed to be nothing interesting – walked to (1) the Brit. Museum, & there got a reading ticket for 6 months (2) Rivington's, where I saw Mr. Septimus R. – heard that 3000 of the Gospel of the Childhood had sold, and 2000 of the Catholic Church (5000 of each printed) – gave instructions for a new edition of former – (3) Club: wrote to Miss Nisbet, whom I had met in Gt. Russell St. & who asked Gussie's address – then fell asleep over 'Broyden's Catholic Safeguards' – the Dean came in, & talked about 100 things, and asked me to go with him to Maskelyne[1] & Cooke's entertainment – we had luncheon together – then I went (in cab) to Proctor about my Will, & got into a worry about my affairs there – came away in Cab & drove to the Egyptian Hall, where the Dean was waiting for me – MAC., lit. Buskins, & Ju, were there – the conjuring was 1st. rate, specially the floating of Mrs. Maskelyne in the air and the decapitation trick – little Buskins went w. the Dean to the Opera at 8 p.m.

1. The famous John Maskelyne, co-founder with George Cooke, of London's 'Egyptian Hall', 'a Hall of Mystery', had been a watchmaker. They leased the Egyptian Hall for three months, but remained for 31 years. When his partner died in 1904, with his new partner, David Devant, Maskelyne moved, in 1905, his 'Home of Magic' to St George's Hall. He devoted much energy to exposing spiritualistic frauds. Died 1917.

Saturday 10   [*Return to Norwich*]
Rose at 8 – aft. Bkfst. went in Cab to Morgan's, and asked him about taking on strychnine[1], which he advised – a muddy dirty day – left London at 11.30 – read Hayman's letter in this day's paper, and the Exter reredos case – got here about 3.30, & found nothing but a vast lot of pamphlets, and letters from (1) Ld. Warwick about Hayman, etc. (2) Bullivant offering £200 to the Cathedral as a thankoffering for my recovery (3) The Bp. telling me the Surrogates[2] are appointed by the Chancellor.

1. Very poisonous alkaloid extracted from an Indian tree and much favoured by early crime-writers. At this time it was used in small quanities as a stimulant of the central nervous system and the appetite. Certainly would not be prescribed today.
2. Clergymen appointed, as the Bishop's deputy, to grant licences for marriages without banns.

Monday 12

A letter arrived today from Dr. Collis[1], asking for an expression of sympathy & moral support for Dr. Hayman – I have not yet answered it.

> 1. John Day Collis, D.D., an old Rugbeian; for 25 years, until 1867, Headmaster of Bromsgrove School; at this time Vicar of Stratford-upon-Avon.

Tuesday 13

Rose at 7.45 – Ju read the Prayers for me – a letter from the Bp. of London asking a Sermon for his Fund – I answered this, and also wrote to Dr. Collis, refusing to sign the Hayman testimonial[1], and answered our Bp., promising to preach in the Cathedral next Sunday – all this before Morning Church – after that, took a walk (by myself) on the Castle Hill – then to Stacy's – then to Bensly's – then to see Miss Cubitts – then home to luncheon – then the 'Pin' came, and I walked and talked with him for about 1½ hours round Castle Hill – then went to his house and drew up the Church Card, etc. about the Festivals for 1864 [1874] – then home, & found Mr. Ram – He let me off attending the Genl. Meeting of Churchman's Club, but wanted our consent to the repairs of his Church[2], wh. he said were violently opposed by one of the Churchwardens, against whom he meditates an action for brawling.

> 1. As a former Headmaster of Rugby, it was difficult for Goulburn, publicly, to take sides.
> 2. St John's, Timberhill.

Thursday 15

After Mg. Service, walked in the kitchen garden till 11.45, when Ju came to take me to the Jenny Lind[1] meeting in 'Pottergate Street' – Sir S. Bignold, Hinds Howell, Dr. Bateman[2] & Mr. Hansell were there, and the Mayor presided – I had to propose the appointment of the same ladies on the Committee – Mention was made of poor Johnson[3] & of Donald Dalrymple – E.K. Harvey was there – It resolved on the suggestions of the Sheriff to raise a fund for Orthopaedic instruments – there was some talk as to whether cast-off instruments of that sort were of any use – Ju and I returning met H. Howell, and asked him & his wife to luncheon – Went to Aftern. Service – afterwards wrote to Bp. about the institution of Venables, and arranged my Regent Classics on their shelves; a vol. of Cicero missing.

1. Jenny Lind (Mrs Johanna Maria Lind-Goldschmidt 1820–87), Swedish singer and actress, became a friend of Bishop Stanley and his family. In 1849, she gave two Concerts in St Andrew's Hall for charity. And in 1853, it was decided to found a Children's Hospital in Pottergate, where it remained until 1898, when J.J. Colman donated a new site on Unthank Road, in memory of his wife. By 1982, its transference to the site of the Norfolk and Norwich Hospital was completed. After making her last appearance in public in 1883, Jenny Lind (who had become a naturalized British subject in 1859) became Professor of Singing at the Royal College of Music.
2. Dr (later Sir Frederic) Bateman, a leading Physician and consultant at Norfolk and Norwich Hospital.
3. Dr Johnson, the Goulburn's G.P., died on January 13th.

Saturday 17

Wrote a codicil to my Sermon about poor Johnson – I wrote a letter to Davie, excusing myself from attendance at Training School meeting – sent it by Heaviside – after Service saw Bensly about (1) the sum voted for the present to Symonds ... (3) the orders made at Chapter in my absence, which I approved – borrowed from him Phillimore's Law.

Monday 19

Worked before Bkfst. at a Paper for the Bp's meeting, and made some way w. it – after Bkfst. (at wh. Ju was present) saw Stacy about my Ipswich Lecture, & ordered from him a Wordsworth's Gr. Testament for the 'Pin' (£5. 5)[1] – After Mg. Church walked up & down the Library, looking over the Hymnary & other Hymn Books – After ¾ths. of an hour walking, went to the Pin's to discuss the question about what Hymns we shd. use in the Cathedral – determined after an hour's conversation the S.P.C.K. Hymn Book – I returned to luncheon – At 2 p.m. took the carriage with the Pin to Thickthorne Lodge Gate, having previously called at the S.P.C.K. depository, where we ascertained that the old Hymn Book with B.C.'s New Appendix is one thing, and the newly arranged Book another – we walked back from Thickthorne, a distance of just four miles; got back about 4.30 – went to Evening Service – I wrote to Bullivant, to thank him for the £200 to the Cathedral – also to Mr. Walter Browne, and to Capn. Dawes, declining to sign the memorial about Hayman requesting the Governing Body to reconsider their decision.

1. A leaving present for Symonds, the Precentor, as he becomes Rector of Tivetshall.

January 1874

Tuesday 20   Mr. Johnson's Funeral

At 10.45 started in the carriage for the funeral[1] – arrived at the end of a long string of carriages – got into the Chapel as Ripley was in the middle of the Psalm – I took the Service at the Grave – it was damp underfoot, but a very mild & beautiful day – after the ceremony returned to take off my gown, etc. and then took a walk for 1½ hours on the Newmarket Road; met Canon Dalton[2], & had a few words with him – Auntie went to a Christmas tree at Mr. Rivett's[3] School, and heard Bp. Gallaway address the children, and did not get back till 7.50, when we dined.

1. At St Giles' Church.
2. Roman Catholic Priest of Wymer Street Roman Catholic Church.
3. The Revd A.W.L. Rivett, Vicar of St Martin-at-Palace. (His third Christian name was 'Lovely').

Wednesday 21

After Bkfst. saw a poor woman sent by Copeman, who having kept her money in her house since the failure of Harvey's Bank, was robbed of £100 by housebreakers –[1] After Service took a turn on the Newmarket Road and round by Unthank's – Mr. Barwell met me as I was returning, and made me come into the refectory, and explained that he thot. the level of the old floor was nearly 10 feet below the present soil – He himself got down into the trench wh. had been dug, with a ladder – got ½ an hour's writing at my paper before luncheon – then came Mr. Vincent[2] evidently wishing to know about the Precentorship – he stayed a long time (probably had intended to propose himself – a letter from Dr. Jebb recd. this aftern. asks me to support a measure of his in Convocation.

1. It is very typically 'Goulburn the Diarist' to make an entry like this, and not record the outcome. Based on many instances of his treatment of people in need and beggars, I feel sure that he would have been sympathetic and, in this instance, generous. Harvey's Crown Bank had failed in 1870.
2. The Revd Wm. Vincent had been Rector of Postwick for 10 years, and was to continue there for another 13, during the latter period inheriting a baronetcy. In 1887, some 30 years after ordination, he returned to Leatherhead, Surrey where he was a J.P. and a D.L. for Surrey.

Thursday 22

After Service went with the 'Pin' to view the excavations in the Refectory – He does not think the level to be as low as that wh. Mr. Barwell assigns to it – then took a walk on Ipswich, & back by Newmarket Road, meditating on an inscription for the volumes the D. & C. are to give to the 'Pin' – Bp. Gallaway[1] & Miss Button, Mrs. Wortley, Kate Hansell, the Symondses &

January 1874 161

Medley had luncheon here – The Bishop showed us Zulu Prayerbook, Psalms, etc. and talked about Colenso, etc. etc. – we liked him much – After Service, wrote to Proctor expostulating w. him for charging me Commission on the sale of Westb. Terrace House, whereas it had been previously charged by Hooper & Shoveller – made 1st. draught of inscription for the Pin's books.

    1. The Rt Revd H. Gallaway was Bishop of St John's, Kaffraria 1873–86.

Friday 23   'The Loving Cup'
After Church, walked round the kitchen garden till it was time to go to 'the Loving Cup' – Heaviside and I went together – the troops and volunteers were drawn up in the Market place, where there was a great crowd – Heaviside & I went up into the Club[1] where we found Mr. du Chair (Sen.) and Mrs. D.C. – also two young men – the volunteers fired salutes – then we went into the Guild hall, where we were jammed very close together – I got between Sir Henry Harvey and Mr. (I forgot the name, a Conservative, son of the old Chapter Clerk) – I was close also to Sir S. Bignold, to Chicken Patty, and to Col. Boileau – I, Mr. Gould[2], Canon Dalton, had to return thanks for the Clergy and 'Ministers'; Col. Tower and Col. Bolieau for the Army and Volunteers[3] – We looked over Nevill's house in returning, wh. is immensely large – Bensly came to luncheon – Afterwards Ju and I took him to Mr. Ninham's, to advise upon certain points in the arms of the Deans, wh. are being done beautifully – Mr. Cox called & explained his circumstances – I promised to pay this year the threequarters of his boy's Schooling.

    1. The Norfolk Club.
    2. The Revd George Gould, Minister of St Mary's Baptist Church.
    3. Today the Duke of Edinburgh (the Queen's second Son) married, in St Petersburg, the daughter of Tsar Alexander II. The 3rd Dragoon Guards and the Volunteers paraded in Norwich Market Place; at a special meeting of the Town Council congratulatory addresses were adopted, and the 'Loving Cup' was passed around. At night there was a fireworks display on Castle Meadow; on the 27th the Mayor gave a 'Soiree' in St Andrew's Hall. This was the first marriage link between the British and Russian Royal Families.

Saturday 24
I sent for a fly, and drove 1st. to Mr. Pinder's Commercial School, where I paid him £3. 13. 6 for young Cox's Schooling till the end of the year – the boys came to the Deanery at 5 p.m. & we drank the healths of the royal bride & bridegroom, and of the Queen & Russian Emperor – they had each 6d. from me, and a slice of cake, and crackers, and a minced pie.

Tuesday 27

Cold still continued – Wrote to (1) the Mayor, excusing myself from his Soiree Musicale tonight – (2) The Bp. excusing myself from dining with him tomorrow – (3) Dr. Jessopp thanking him for Father Walpole's[1] Letters, etc. (4) Dr. Hannah[2], asking the subject of his Lent Argumentative Discourses. (5) Bp. of Peterboro', consulting him about an application for money, to wh. he was said to have responded. (6) Dixon, clockmaker, about the deranged chimes – tried to make out the very confused plot of 'Little Dorrit'.

1. Father Henry Walpole (1558–1595): Educated at Norwich and Cambridge; joined the Jesuits (1584); ordained Priest (1588); Chaplain in the Spanish Army in Flanders (1589–91); sent to England (1593); arrested in Yorkshire (1593); prisoner in the Tower of London Feb. 1594–Mar. 1595; tried and executed at York.
2. John Julius Hannah, ordained 1867; Lecturer 1871–75; Vicar of St Nicholas', Brighton 1875–87; Vicar of Brighton 1887–1902; Dean of Chichester 1902.

Wednesday 28

Went to Service at four – not as many Hon. Canons as usual – at the Palace[1] I read my paper on 'Revivals or Missions', and the Archdeacons, Howorth, Potter, Nevill, and Ryle[2] spoke, the latter admirably.

1. Annual Meeting of Dean, Archdeacons, Residentiary and Hon. Canons at the Palace.
2. In 1880, Canon J.C. Ryle, at the age of 64, a strong Evangelical, became the first Bishop of Liverpool, remaining there for 20 years. For the previous 36 he had been, first, Rector of Helmngham, Suffolk, and then, Vicar of Stradbroke.

Friday 30

After Service, Mr. Powell, Hardman's artist, appears, and Mr. Lee Warner[1] and I went w. him to the reliquary chamber and examined the mural paintings – I gave Mr. Powell an order to suggest a subject for a memorial window to Sedgwick – Archdeacon Groome joined us, and made out the name of Ricardus Abbas, on the vaulting of the reliquary.

1. The Revd John Lee Warner, Vicar of Gt Walsingham.

Saturday 31

After Service had a wearying Chapter, which lasted till 1.45 – all sorts of subjects: Symonds' books exhibited; Counsel's opinion to be taken about the affairs of the Tramway Company – Yarmouth sealed – agreement with waterworks signed – rules made in my absence confirmed – questions of new lightning-conductor discussed – question of sufficient resistance to clock-weights in case of their falling; and other matters, wh. seemed very wearing – I read some regulations wh. I had drawn up about the sittings in the Cathedral, & wh., in the main, were approved – Walked round the garden till 3 o'clock Service – afterwards called on Bulmer, and walked with him on Thorpe Road, and made him the offer of the Librarianship – came in and wrote to Proctor, paying him £114 odd for his work in selling the Rugby and Westbourne Terrace houses.

FEBRUARY

The East Suffolk Branch of the Diocesan Church Defence Association had arranged a Series of three Lectures. Goulburn spent from February 2 to 4 with the Rector of Whitton (on the outskirts of Ipswich) and, on Feb. 3, delivered the first of these in the Town Hall, Ipswich, entitled: 'The duty of the Civil Magistrate to the Christian Religion and the Christian Church'. The Chairman was the Lord Lieutenant of Suffolk, the Earl of Stradbroke.

Wednesday 4
Immediately after getting to Norwich I voted, seeing no one near the polling place, but Mr. Bayley of Stoke Holy Cross.

Thursday 5
After Service went to Mr. Tuck's, who laid before me the particulars of his difference w. Mr. Reid[1] – he averred that Reid had made changes not specified in his original programme (in which Mr. T. had acquiesced), and that so far from Mr. T.'s opposing the design of a school, he had offered to subscribe towards carrying one on in a hired house, tho' he thot. Mr. Reid's scheme of using the cottage at the back of the Church, presented legal difficulties – After calling on Mr. Reid (whom I could not find) I took a walk on Unthank's Road & Newmarket Rd. – coming back met Lucy Bignold & Bensly – found Mr. Davies[2] waiting for me; he had plans of his parsonage for me to sign our assent to – the announcement of the result of the election[3] came in: 1. Colman. 2. Huddleston. 3. Tillett. 4. Stracey.

1. See November 3, 1873 – St Gregory's.
2. Vicar of St James', Norwich.
3. J.J. Colman (Lib.) and J.W. Huddleston, Q.C. (Con.) elected M.P.s for Norwich. Liberal Government (Gladstone) defeated. Conservative Government (Disraeli) in with overall majority.

February 1874

Friday 6
I wrote to Ld. Warwick (recommending Blake[1] for Rugby) and to Blake himself.

> 1. The Revd T.W. Jex-Blake (1832–1915), Principal of Cheltenham College, did become Headmaster of Rugby (1874–87) following the Hayman disaster. From 1891–1910, he was Dean of Wells. The Earl of Warwick was a Trustee of the School and, later, a Governor, but resigned during 1874.

Saturday 7
After dinner came a letter from Miss Drake to Dr Buck, declining to help in the singing tomorrow morning, because singing is out of place in an early celebration.

Sunday 8   Sexagesima
Service thrice – Only the Bp., Medley, & self present at 8 – we sang for the 1st. time the 'Sanctus' and 'Gloria' – I fear the Bp. did not like it – I suppose there may have been about 14 commts. – Service lasted just an hour.

Monday 9
Read some of 'Bingham's Antiquities' before Bkfst. – After Bkfst. an interview w. Nevill about the mode of providing money for his house – then called on the Bp. to ask whether he saw any objection to my introducing Mr. Venables by a Service at Yarmouth – he did not – then a walk on Mousehold – In the evening read aloud some of Dicken's Life[1], & saw Mr. Davies, who asked whether the Chapter wd. subscribe to his Parsonage improvements.

> 1. Charles Dickens had died in 1870. Goulburn was probably reading from the Biography written (and completed in 1874) by John Forster, historian and biographer.

Wednesday 11
Studied Jer. Taylor, etc. before Bkfst. – Birthday presents from Auntie (Candlesticks); Buskins (Writing Case); Mrs. Atterbury, a hyacinth & a cineraria; MAC. (Letter Case) and (later in the day) Photog. views of Winches. Cath. from Frederica – letters from Robinson and Nisbet about tomorrow's business – from Dr. Hannah, about his Apologetic Sermon & some criticisms of my Family Prayers from a gentleman in Liverpool – also from Bartie enclosing a chain for eyeglass – After Service, before wh. Nevill gave me a newly published volume of his Sermons, called on the Bp. & told him what we thought of doing about Nevill's house, &

also of my meaning to propose the S.P.C.K. Hymnbook for use in the Cath. – found little Em'ly at luncheon here; she talked of a 'contortionist' at the Circus, who ate a piece of meat fastened on a spur which he raised on his heel from behind – from 3.30 to 5.30 worked with the Pin at the Bosses, and finished the 10th. Bay.

Thursday 12   Chapter Meeting
The morning was occupied with a Chapter Meeting – Election of Robinson as Proctor – Draughting of a new statute, annexing Nevill's house to his Canonry for 35 years – Order for S.P.C.K. hymn book.

Friday 13
Went to Afternoon Church – afterwards wrote out a letter to Bulmer, informing him of my intention to appoint Medley Precentor – Heaviside advices me to cancel one sentence of it, and I have done so.
    I have had two valentines – one a bell for my Study from the 'Pin'; the other a China allumette case, borne by a toad, from Heaviside, I think.

Monday 16
Rose (after a very sleepless night) at 7.30 – Bkfst. in my room; and afterwards concluded my Sermon on Auricular Confession – came down to luncheon – at 2 drove with Heaviside in the Carriage to Rackheath – Saw Sir H. Stracey who bears his defeat very well, but is <u>galled</u> by it – Medley called on me, and showed me a severe review in the 'Union Review' of my book on the Childhood of our Lord – I wrote to Mr. Gibbs[1], thanking him for the £100 he had sent for Mr. Davies.

    1. Goulburn had written to William Gibbs about St James' Parsonage.

Wednesday 18   **ASH WEDNESDAY**
Three Services at 8, 11, and 4 p.m. – At 4 I preached my Sermon on Auricular Confession, which lasted until about 5.20 – at 5.30 Mr. Davies arrived, and I told him of Mr. Gibbs munificent conduct – I answered today at some length a letter from Mr. Scudamore[1], thanking him for his 'Incense for the Altar' – In the evening an awkward letter from Mr. Venables, saying that there is absolutely no income at Yarmouth to which he is entitled.

    1. Rector of Ditchingham 1839–81. High Churchman. Published 'Steps to the Altar' (1846), 'Incense for the Altar' (1874). Strong supporter of All Hallows Community.

••
Goulburn was in London from Tuesday, February 24 to Thursday, February 26, for discussions with officials of Queen Anne's Bounty, with the Ecclesiastical Commissioners, and to preach the first of a series of Lent Sermons on the Lord's Prayer at St Paul's Cathedral on the Tuesday evening.
••

Wednesday 25 At Grosvenor Hotel, Park Street
At 10 went to see Mr. Butterfield[1] & settled to adopt his plan for the altar, omitting the reredos – he did not like the idea of putting an organ in the reliquary, & advised that the well should be closed up again – thence (2) to the Eccl. Commission. where I saw Mowbray, Pringle, Yool – they have no objection whatever to hand over the rectorial rights & tithes to the incumbent in the case of Yarmouth – went to Club, & wrote to Venables, and also to Bensly as to what had passed – then at 2 came Mr. Tompson[2]; I suggested that if he would write a letter to me, pledging himself to remain 5 years with us, unless there were some grave cause (to be approved by myself) for his resigning, I do not feel that I shd. have any right to keep him with us, if at a great disadvantage to himself – then to the Bounty Board, where I discovered I was a Governor – Aston informed me that if we cd. get a new Statue annexing Nevill's house to his stall (for no determinate no. of years), they will make the loan on the usual terms.

    1. Wm. Butterfield (1814–1900), famous Architect.
    2. A new Master for the Cathedral Choir School.

Saturday 28
After Mg. Service I took the Wordsworth's Gr. Test. (after writing the inscription in it) wh. we are to give the Pin to Bensly's Office – then took a walk on Mousehold – then visited Mrs. Page who seems to be sinking fast, & in constant pain – after luncheon young Price called to ask me how he would continue to get an Oxford education most cheaply – I tried him in Latin and Greek, & wrote to Woollcombe about him – wrote to Mr. Tompson, definitely closing with him as Layclerk & Schoolmaster – wrote also to Medley, promising to renew his appointment as Precentor, if he gives satisfaction.

MARCH

Monday 2
All the working part of the day, occupied w. correcting Mr. Hailstone's MS. of Pandulph[1] – after Mg. Church went w. Medley to receive Gussie's halfyearly money (£60) at Gurney's – then walked with Medley on Mousehold discussing with him his various Precentorian plans – One of these is the getting the Layclerks' and Choristers' vestry turned into one, as a room where the whole Choir mt. sit and get ready for Service – another was the getting new Bibles & Prayer Books for the Boys – another, the proposal that he (Medley) shd, rinse the Communion Vessels after Service, etc. etc. – wrote to Mr. Tompson particulars about Alden's house – answered Mr. Scudamore's letter about private forms of Absolution – after dinner, read the Tichborne Summing up[2], Verdict, Sentence – made preparation for going tomorrow.

> 1. Pandulph Masca was Bishop of Norwich 1222–1226.
> 2. The Tichborne claimant, after a long and costly period of litigation, was now finally exposed as a butcher named Thomas Castro, and sentenced to 14 years' penal servitude for perjury.

Tuesday 3   From Nowich to London
On arriving at the Station at ¼p.7 a.m., found I had left behind in a book £55 of Gussie's money, recd. yesterday, wh. I meant to pay in to Goslings' – sent back Blake for it, but he did not re-appear – On arriving in town, went straight to MAC's with my luggage – then, having agreed to dine with her at 5 p.m. took cab for an hour and went to poulterer's, watchmaker's, hatters, tailor's, B. of England (to pay in Lady Blomfield's Cheque), spectacle-maker's, Gozzie's (there drew for £10), then Club, where wrote to Ju; then to Chiropodist's, who rather hurt me; then to B.C.'s[1]; had some luncheon with them, and talk about the Mission, Haslam, etc. – then to Eccl. Commission – back to Club, & wrote the result to Venables & Nevill – At 7.5 we started for St. Paul's – there was a much larger congregation this time, & Canon Gregory was present.

> 1. His friend, and former Assistant-Master at Rugby, Berdmore Compton, now Vicar of all Saints, Margaret Street.

[*Goulburn returned to Norwich on Wednesday, March 4*]

Friday 6
Drew up before Bkfst. a 'form of admission of Minor Canon' – After Mg. Service had a delicious walk – Then called on Spaull about the preparation of the Church next week for 'Argumentative Discourses' – talked with him about the purchase of the pulpit in the Nave.[1]

> 1. It would appear that Goulburn is beginning to think about the presentation of a new Nave Pulpit, which took place eventually at the end of June 1891.

• •

Goulburn spent from Saturday, March 7 to Tuesday, March 10, at Peterborough, preaching in the Cathedral on the Sunday evening. He stayed overnight in London on Tuesday, returning to Norwich on Wednesday, March 11, having preached the third of his Series to Sermons on the Lord's Prayer in St Paul's Cathedral on the Tuesday evening.

• •

Wednesday 11   From London to Norwich
Walked to Club, & wrote to Bp. of Norwich, F. Grutt, Esqre., Dr. Coghlan, and corrected press of the 'Office for Minor Canons' – had luncheon, & then walked to vestry of Chapel Royal, where dressed for the Levee – got away by 3 p.m. – went back to Club & read Dickens's Life till it was time to start for St. Pancras – returned by 5 p.m. train – found Ju and Gussie all right.

Friday 13
After Morning Service, saw the Police, Bensly, Symonds, Hansell, Stannard, Forman, Medley and others, about the Sunday arrangements – At 2 o'clock went to Chapter Office, and (1) assigned to Nevill his house (2) accepted Symond's resignation, (3) apointed Medley Precentor – Then went with Bensly to the Bauchun Chapel[1], & climbing the ladder inspected the Bosses – then to the Layclerk's vestry, which it is proposed by Medley to throw into that of the Minor Canons – then to see Miss Agnes Cubitt, and then Mrs. Page who suffers grievously – dinner at 5; Service at 8 – Nevill preached on Death – Afterwards he communicated to me the News that the Bishop had offered him the Archdeaconry of Norfolk on the resignation of Blakelock.

> 1. The Bauchon Chapel of our Lady of Pity was given by William Bauchon, Granarius of the Monastery in the 14th Century.

Saturday 14

After Morning Service, looked into the Church to see the arrangements – At 2½ p.m. met Moore[1] in the Chapter Office, where he took the Oaths – admitted him after the Service with the Form wh. I had prepared for the occasion.

> 1. As a Minor Canon. Ordained in 1862, W.T. Moore had been Vicar of St John-de-Sepulchre, Norwich, since 1865. He continued as this for a further two years; then, from 1876–94 became full-time at the Cathedral, and also Vicar of St. Mary-in-the-Marsh from 1879.

Sunday 15   Lent 4

Service at 8, 11, 7 p.m. – We dined at 2 – Afterwards Dr. Coghlan retired to his room – I went into the Church, to see that things were going on right – We had the Service at 7; full Evening Prayer with an Anthem, & a prayer before and after the Sermon – Dr. Coghlan[1] preached a striking Sermon, too condensed perhaps in its thot. to be taken in by all at the moment, but just what was wanted, and wh. will be very telling in print.

> 1. This was Discourse No 13 of the 'Argumentative Discourses in Defence and Confirmation of the Faith'. It was entitled 'The importance of the Evidences of Christianity', and given by the Revd Dr J.C. Coghlan, D.D., Incumbent of St Peter's, Vere Street, London. From 1871 to 1876, 24 Discourses were given by a variety of Speakers, and, when completed, all 24 were bound together in a small hardback book in 1876. As they were given, each had been published and sold at 1d.

Monday 16

Chapter Meeting at 2 p.m. – we had a good deal of business, about the repairs of Little's farm; about Newman's farm at Eaton; about the clock weights and Ligthning conductor – and four seals, 3 in re Nevill's house, 1 sealing to Mr. Lepelley the living of St. George's Colegate – Mr. Walpole[1] came to speak to us about the Tramway company, wh. he thot. would go on – afterwards wrote to R.G. Wilberforce (sending £50 for S. London Mission House), (2) Meadow's, permitting a dedication of some Ch. Music to me – after dinner prepared for departure.

> 1. The Hon. F. Walpole, M.P. for North Norfolk.

● ●

From Tuesday, March 17 to Saturday, March 21, Goulburn was in London, preaching again at St Paul's Cathedral in the Sreies he was giving there on the Lord's Prayer.

● ●

March 1874

Saturday 21   From London to Norwich

After Bkfst. went to Baily's in Mt. Street to buy a green goose[1] for the Judges – read the Times & Spectator in the train – at Cambridge I had a few moments chat with Mr. Reid, & then Dr. Hannah got into my carriage, & we chatted all the way to Norwich – then took Dr. H. round the Cathedral.

> 1. The goose cost 10s. 6d. Goulburn frequently bought his poultry and game birds in London and brought them back to Norwich. It is puzzling he did not buy them in Norwich. Occasionally, he brought back venison, which probably was not obtainable in Norwich.

Sunday 22   Lent 5

Rose at 6.15 – went to the early Commn. – about 23 communicants – a fine morning, but the day very rainy – At 11 o'clock Neville preached a very good Sermon – afterwards went with Dr. Hannah into the Nave to inspect the arrangements – Dinner at 2 – afterwards walked with Dr. Hannah in the cloister, & then took him up to the Castle Hill – Dr. Hannah preached a very striking argumentative Sermon[1] on 'Who will show us any good?' with a touching & eloquent practical conclusion – The singing at the end went very well indeed – a very interesting tho' fatiguing day.

> 1. This was the 14th Argumentative Discourse and was entitled 'The Divine Basis of Morality'. The Revd John Hannah, D.C.L., was Vicar of Brighton. He had been Rector of Edinburgh Academy 1847–54; Principal of Glenalmond 1854–70; and he was Vicar of Brighton 1870–87, and Archdeacon of Lewes 1876–88.

Monday 23

After luncheon came Sinyanki, the clerical missionary to the Jews, w, letters from Pusey & Liddon, and new interpretations of the O.T. hard passages – a letter from Bulmer about the M.C.'s vestry; and from Venables; the E.C. have as yet done nothing in regard to Yarmouth[1]!

> 1. i.e. about a stipend for Venables.

• •

On Tuesday, March 24, Goulburn again went to London to preach the fifth, and last, Sermon on the Lord's Prayer at St Paul's Cathedral, returning home the next day.

• •

Wednesday 25   **The Annunciation**

Attended early Communion with the Dean and Mrs. Church[1] at 8 a.m. – I signed my receipt for £20, in payment of my Sermons, and handed it over to their Cathedral Fund – took my leave &

walked to E.C., in Whitehall Place, where I had a satisfactory conversation about Yarmouth with Pringle – left St. Pancras at 4.35 p.m.; got to Norwich at 9, and found Ju and Gussie well.

> 1. The Very Revd R.W. Church: Lived abroad until he was 13; Fellow of Oriel College, Oxford 1838–52; Deacon 1839; Priest 1852; formed lasting friendship with Newman; Select Preacher at Oxford; Dean of St Paul's 1871–90. Author of a 'History of the Oxford Movement', published posthumously, 1891.

Thursday 26

After Bkfst., came Nevill, to tell me of Traxton's delinquencies last eveing; then a poor woman to talk to me about the 'Benevolent Fund'; and then Traxton himself, whom I suspended till Monday – went in to see Mrs. Page, but only saw the children – the poor lady had asked Mr. Williams to give her something to put an end to her existence – went to the Grammar School Meet'n to appoint a Commee. at 3 p.m. – went with Nevill to meet Judges (Blackburn and Brett) at their Lodgings – they were very gracious; they came to the Cathedral at 5.10, but there was no Assize Sermon – Took the Bp. to the Dinner of High Sheriff at 7.

Friday 27

Medley asked leave to have the Choir at Lakenham, to sing at Mrs. M's grave.

Saturday 27

The Judges dined here – (with our 3 selves, 19 in all).

	Ju	Bishop	
Judge Blackburn			Judge Brett
Heaviside			Sir Samuel [Bignold]
			Mr. Coaks
Colman			Judge Brett's Marshal
Judge Blackburn's Marshal			Sheriff of Norwich (Chamberlin)
Rev. Mr. Fellowes			Recorder
The Mayor			Buskins
			High Sheriff
	Dean	Mrs. Heaviside	

Sunday 29   PALM SUNDAY

At 11 came the Judges in state – an enormous crowd – Mr. Fellowes preached on the qualification *of* Jewish judges, "able men, hating covetousness, etc.".

Monday 30
Saw Mrs. Dugdale and filled up her application to the Benevolent Association – I talked with Medley & Spaull about the proposed new arrangements of Lay Clerk's Vestry, etc. etc. – At 2 Chapter Meeting – We sealed a power of Attorney for sale at £789. 15. 10 Consols to meet temporary pressure arising from delay in receipt of money from Chancery – Also for sale of £54. 4 Consols to pay costs of new buildings on Little's farm at Middleton – Agreed that Nevill should be Librarian at a Stipend of £10 pr. ann. – Agreed that Traxton should be made to apologise and reprimanded tomorrow, and that for 6 months his stipend be paid to his wife – Agreed that Medley's proposition about Lay Clerks & M.C.s vestries should stand over till the June Audit – Agreed that Service be at 10 a.m. on weekdays during April – I saw Mr. Tompson & told him he mt. let his house for one year – Then <u>Lichfield and Alden took the oath as Subsacrists</u> – Then at 5 o'clock Service I gave my Sermonette; and afterwards the Subsacrists were admitted.

Tuesday 31
After 11 a.m. Service came the sentence upon Traxton in the Consistory Court[1] – he apologised to Nevill, & was reprimanded – Then Medley and I walked up to Darken's to see a harmonium wh. it is proposed to use at early Communion on Sunday – Then (taking a fly) we went to see Mrs. Medley's monument – then I took Medley back to the Cath., and myself went in the fly to call on Mr. Justice Brett – then the fly took me out on to the St. Giles road to the cemetery – then I walked back by Dereham Road, and in coming back gave my 13 Schoolboard votes to Heaviside.

> 1. The Bishop's Court for the administration of ecclesiastical law within his own Diocese. The Judge is the Chancellor, except when the Bishop reserves to himself the power to try certain cases. Traxton was a Lay Clerk. His 'delinquencies' took place on the evening of Wednesday, March 25th, but we are not told what they were.

APRIL

Sunday 5   **EASTER SUNDAY**
Attended all four Services: 8 a.m., 11 a.m., 3.30 p.m., 7 p.m.
A walk with Mrs. Symonds in Lady Harvey's grounds – All the singing today had gone off thoroughly well – Gounod's Nicene Creed beautiful and beautifully executed.

Wednesday 8

After Mg. Service, went up to the Bosses, to finish my part of Bay 13 – joined there by Medley, Pin, and Guy – the former came to ask whether he could be spared for 3 weeks from Monday next – at 2 went to the 'Pin's', and took a walk with him on Ipswich road, and back by Bracondale – as we returned by Moore's house, I looked in and told him of Medley's wish to go next week and of the necessity of his being in readiness to help Bulmer.

Thursday 9

After Mg. Service, Nevill mentioned a scheme in wh. Scudamore is interested of founding a brotherhood of Preachers in the Diocese of Ely.

Saturday 11

Unwell, and in bed till 9.15 – Then rose and wrote a short Sermon on the Collect for tomorrow – Medley & Buck called: they had had a difference which they wished me to adjust – Medley, insisting that the Boys by singing out of time, were putting the Choir out, had stopped them, and so given Buck offence – I ruled that the Precentor was to preside at rehearsals, while Dr. Buck in <u>teaching</u> the Boys was not to be interfered with.

Monday 13

Rose at 6 – wrote some letters before Bkfst. – afterwards to Rev. Mr. Webb, Principal of Codrington College[1], Barbadoes, who had consulted me as to the legitimacy of Bp. Mitchinson's election – then, with Buskin's help, sent circulars to a great many of the members of the Cathedral Congregation, assigning them sittings, etc. – Heaviside came in after luncheon to say 'Goodbye' – Muriel[2] also looked in and sent me a gargle – I have seen no one else, and have not stirred out the whole day, having a heavy cold.

1. General Christopher Codrington, former Governor of the Leeward Islands, died in 1710 leaving his estates and a sizable fortune to S.P.G. to found a College in Barbados to train men for the ministry. The Church was established in Barbados in 1824, but when disestablishment came to the West Indies in 1870, the Barbadians insisted on keeping an established Church, and so it became the only Established Church in the Anglican Communion outside England. Bishop Mitchinson became Bishop of Barbados in 1873 (until 1882). The Principal was probably discussing a problem which arose out of the situation of unilateral Establishment.
2. Dr Muriel was now the Goulburn's G.P. in place of the late Dr Johnson.

•••

The Goulburns now began a round of visits to relations and friends, leaving Norwich on Tuesday, April 14, and returning on Monday, May 11. They stayed at Horton, with Henry and Mary Gunning, until April 28; then moved to Aynhoe, staying at the Rectory with 'the Dean' (Frederick) until May 9; and then stopping for two nights in London before returning to Norwich.

•••

Sunday 19   *At Horton*

Walked to Piddington, where Mr. Gough preached on "I am the good shepherd" – He spoke of the union of Christendom: Greek, Roman and Anglican, and said that the baptized were safe, if they remain in the condition in wh. Bm.[1] has placed them (but who does ?).

    1. Bm. = Baptism.

Monday 20   *At Horton*

A communication from Nevill, announcing the happy end of Mrs. Nevill's confinement, and the very precarious condition of one of the turrets in the West End of the Cathedral – I wrote to Mr. Brown, Moore, & Nevill.

MAY

Sunday 10   *Rogation Sunday*

In reading the Lessons it struck me that a good Sermon might be made fr. the 2d. Mg. Lesson (New Lect.) on the introduction of Nathanael to Christ – Christ's searching knowledge of those who approach him in prayer – After Bkfst. at the Club, I drew out some notes of this, & took them to Church[1], with the Ascension Day Sermon (written) – Archdn. Sinclair seemed rather feeble – prayers were read in the old-fashioned way – I preached the <u>new</u> Sermon – afterwards went with Mr. C. Greenway, Bath Place, into the Burying ground to see the De Visme[2] vault, wh. is well restored.

    1. St Mary Abbots, Kensington Church Street.
    2. Goulburn's mother's family.

Monday 11   *From London to Norwich*

After Bkfst. at the Club, answered several letters, a budget of which I received from Julia this morning – at 11, James and I started for Bishopgate Street[1] in Cab, and came home via Colchester & Ipswich – in the evening engaged in answering letters, correcting proofs of Boss Book, new edition of H.C. Church – Lili played at Chess with 'Gussie'.

> 1. Bishopgate Street = Liverpool Street Station.

Tuesday 12

Rose at ½p.6, & from 7 to ½p.8 engaged in arranging papers & books, etc. etc. – I imagined I had lost the Sermon I had written on Enoch, but Blake found it wrapped in my hood and stole – After Service long talks with Robinson, Bensly, Tompson – then a walk with the Pin on Mousehold, during wh. we corrected finally 2 sheets of H.L. – then an interview with Spaull about the arrangement for Nave Services[1] – then began answering my letters – Heaviside called, and also Nevill with his little girl, to say (1) that Mrs. N. wished to be churched at the Altar; (2) would I consent to stand Godfather to his child? – After dinner read to Ju (while Lili & Buskins played chess) the debate in the Lords on the Abp's Bill[2].

> 1. Because of restoration work in other parts of the Cathedral.
> 2. The Public Worship Regulation Bill (1874) which became law.

Wednesday 13

A miserable day – After Mg. Service went with Master, Browne, Spaull, Tompson into the Nave, to consult about permanent desks for the choristers.

Sunday 17   Nevill's reading in day, as Archn.

At 11 a.m. the Bishop, three Canons & Self at Church – Nevill read in – Mr. Rowlandson preached on Psalm 8 – Afterwards he sat with me, till he took his departure at 1.30 p.m. – Dinner (Dr. Caldwell[1] being with us) at 2 – about ½p.4 I took Dr. Caldwell the usual round in Lady H's grounds – the whole populan. of Norwich seemed to have turned out to enjoy the fine weather – Coffee at ½p.5 – went to Trinity, Heigham, at 7 – preached for Mr. Rust on Eph. 4, 7–13, an expository lecture for S.P.G. – Mr. Rust spoke very highly of Moore's labour in his Parish – On our return, Dr. Caldwell showed us an Indian book, an Indian stylus, and many curious paintings of Indians, done on talk[2] a sort of slate, wh. scales off in glossy sheets.

> 1. This Sunday, there were Sermons in many Churches in Norwich and suburbs for S.P.G. The Revd Dr Caldwell was a S.P.G. missionary from India. He also spoke at the S.P.G. Anniversary Meeting in St Andrew's Hall on Tuesday.
> 2. Should be talc! This was a magnesian mineral, consisting of broad, flat, smooth, plates, translucent, and often transparent when in very thin plates. It was used in many parts of India at that time as a substitute for window-glass.

Tuesday 19

A heavy day – Three Services in Church – after luncheon took a stroll with Dr. Caldwell on the walls of the Castle – At 7.15, Bussie, Dr. Caldwell & I walked down to St. Andrew's Hall – Bp. of Sasketchewan[1] & Dr. C. spoke, the latter very simple and nice, the former with head-splitting loudness.

> 1. The Rt Revd J. McLean, D.D., newly-consecrated Bishop of the newly-formed Diocese of Sasketchewan, where he remained for 13 years.

Wednesday 20   Archaeological Meeting, noon.
Bp's Meeting at the Palace in the Evening

At 12, I attended the Meeting of the N. & N. Archaeological Society – Fitch, Manning, Sir F. Boileau, Carthew, Arthur Copeman and several others were there – Fred Watson dropped in – I read the description of the hole in the roof of the Nave[1] from Proofsheets of Boss Book – Mr. Gunn commented upon it – Bensly gave a most interesting account of the Sanctuary Map of Norwich[2], with a tracing – Went with the Master to the Bp's Palace at 8[3], to meet the Parochial Clergy, etc. etc. – Question: How to gain a pastoral influence over men, especially young men ? Hussey, Dixon & Colvin read papers; and then the Master spoke; and then I and Nevill; and then Mr. Marston & others.

> 1. "In the tenth bay of the vault the sequence of bosses is broken by a large hole. It is thought that this was for lowering and swinging the figure of an angel holding a censer. The fifteenth century accounts contain entries for paints for the 'Censing Angel', but do not say where it was" (Ethelreda Sansbury, 'An Historical Guide to Norwich Cathedral' (Revised Edition 1994).
> 2. Dr Bensly had a tracing of a Map of Norwich in the Record Office, London, dated 1541, earlier than any known, and apparently intended to show the bounds of Sanctuary, in which convicted persons might take refuge.
> 3. On May 20 and 21 the Bishop had Meetings at the Palace of all those who had been ordained during his Episcopate (i.e. since 1857) – On the Wednesday, the Meetings were in the afternoon and evening; and on Thursday, they attended Morning Prayer in the Cathedral at 8 am, and Holy Communion in the Palace Chapel at 11 am, with Sermon by the Bishop.

Thursday 21

Mg. prayer at 8, with a large attendance of young men, and 'Veni Creator' as the Anthem – There dined here, Father Amherst[1], Pin & Mrs. Pin, Rust & Mrs. Rust, & the Master, & Dr. Buck – 11 with ourselves – Sat between Lili and Mrs. Pin.

> 1. When Lili (Lady Cartwright) was staying at the Deanery in Norwich she attended the Roman Catholic Church in Willow Lane, and Goulburn, out of courteous regard for her had asked the Priest, Father Amherst, to dinner.

Thursday 28
Nevill's Christening (the name Dorothy Catherine) took place at 12.30 – The Bp. was there; Fanny[1] & Gussie godmothers – at 1.15 the Bkfst. to wh. the Heavisides and the godmothers came.

> 1. Fanny Pelham, the Bishop's daughter.

JUNE

Saturday 6 From Norwich, thro' London, to Reading
Left Norwich at 7 a.m. for Bishopgate – There parted from Blake[1], sending him to St. Dunstan's, to leave H.H. Gibbs Ms. Vulgate, there – went to St. Paul's Deanery, & had a satisfactory conversation with Church[2], and agreed to change the Memorial to the Queen into an address to the Abp., wh. I am to concoct – Then to Gozzie's to draw for £10 – Then to Butterfield, where I inspected & approved plans and estimates – then to Club – Then went to try to catch the 4.50 train at Paddington – too late – did not find Blake; hopped into the 5.15 train – When we got to Reading, Blake was not there – A pleasant dinner with the Custs[3].

> 1. His manservant.
> 2. See March 25, 1874 (Note 1)
> 3. The Revd Arthur Purey-Cust, Vicar of St Mary the Virgin, Reading (1862–75). He became Archdeacon of Buckingham (1875–80), and Dean of York in 1880. Goulburn had come to preach for him at 11 am on Sunday morning.

Monday 8
A busy day – Left Reading at 8.35 – sent Blake on to Norwich – Bought books for Miss Hautenville and Ella Purey-Cust – Then went to Church's & conferred with him & Lake – then Lake and I went to Lambeth, & saw the Arcbp. and induced him to say he wd. see what cd. be done about withdrawing Cathedrals from the requirement of a Faculty[1] – I returned to St. Paul's and there saw Lord Blachford, who suggested to me a much neater mode of draughting our alteration – I returned to Club and thence sent a special messenger to Lambeth with the amendment advised by Lord Blatchford – Left London by the 5 p.m. train – very warm & dusty – found all well at home.

> 1. Goulburn (and other deans) wanted the assessment of repairs, furnishings, etc. for Cathedrals to remain as the responsibility of Deans and Chapters, and not be the subject of a Faculty from an external body – e.g. the Bishop.

Wednesday 10

After Mg. Service, took a fly to the Eaton footpath; thence walked very circuitously to Swardeston Common, and thence by Ipswich road home – when I got to the Market Place, so tired that I took another Cab – worked away at the Bosses till dinner time – Ke & Buskins at 9.45 went to a ball at the Sedgwicks – I had an interview with Mr. Sothon today; he said Mr. Sawyer[1] wants in the last number of Boss Book to give photographs of the Seals of the Bishops.

> 1. The Photographer of the Bosses.

Tuesday 23

After Mg. Service, at ½p.11 went on the Box of carriage to Tivetshall[1]; A, of As', Auntie, little Boultons[2] inside; in the pony carriage, Buskins & Ke – did not arrive till nearly 2 – little Emily on her pony met us when we were past Long Stratton – Had luncheon with the Pin, and saw his house, bosquet[3], lawn, croquet ground, kitchen garden, fish stews[4], etc. etc. etc. – I went back in his pony carriage to the Station to meet the 3.45 train; got to Norwich at 4.25 – Then afternoon Service – thought over a Sermon for tomorrow until the ladies returned – dinner at 7.30.

> 1. Tivertshall St Mary with St Margaret had a population then of 610, and is about 15 miles south of Norwich.
> 2. Meanne and Ethel Boulton, Julia's nieces.
> 3. bosquet = thicket or small dense group of trees.
> 4. Fish ponds or tanks.

Monday 29

Large luncheon party: Colbeck[1] & Mrs. C.; little Wallaces; the Pin and Guy and Mrs. Symonds – In the afternoon worked at Bosses with Pin till 6.30 – After Morning Church I called on Mrs. Nevill, who showed me some banners with wh. she wishes to have the Eastern Arches of the Cathedral decorated.

> 1. The Revd W.R. Colbeck, Vicar of Fressingfield, Suffolk, since 1845.

JULY

Saturday 4

After Mg. Service, at which was no M.C. (Medley having taken his departure at 7 a.m., and Bulmer not being appraised that he had done so) I read out the Class List to the Choristers in the presence of Dr. Buck and Mr. Tompson – then a discussion w. him, Spaull, & Tompson about the proposed alterations in the

Classrooms and Chorister School, by wh. the latter is to be turned into our Vestry – ordered Spaull to make an estimate for it – then rowed with the Master to Thorpe & back – At 2d Service we just ended the Thanksgiving as the clock struck 4 – Burton called afterwards and came & sat in the garden, talking about the Abp's Bill, wh, he thinks will be strangled in the Commons – Before dinner, the hairdresser – After dinner, Scudamore's 'Notitia'.

Friday 10   The Archaeological Excursion
Left Norwich with Ju, Ke, Bensly, and Mr. Vincent at 7 a.m. & returned to it at 8 p.m. – Visited Tofts Church, Great and Little Weasenham, Great and Little Massingham, Harpely, Rudham, and then went to Cranmer Hall – At Massingham, Arnold received us, & introduced us to Lady Charlotte A. and his daughter – At Harpley, Mr. & Mrs. Herbert Jones and Sir Willoughby[1] were with us and explained the Church – Mr. Carthew was not there, having had a bad fit of paralysis; nor Mr. Gunn – We met Mr. Elers of West Winch & Mr. Sewell of Yaxley – the last informed me that sealed altars, such as we have in Norwich Cathedral, are of very rare occurence, the only other English specimen being at St. David's – We dined on our return, and went to bed early.

    1. Sir Willoughby Jones, Bart., was Lord of the Manor of Sculthorpe, Patron of the Living, and lived at Cranmer Hall, Sculthorpe.

Saturday 11
Heaviside called for me at 11.30, and we went to the Training School – present Durrant, Ormesby, Blofield, Nevill, Davie, Heaviside & self – we ordered some repairs & painting in the holidays – In the Afternoon Service a young man carried out fainting – afterwards showed the Church to Mrs. and Lady Butler – then took them to our Garden Party, where were the Bignolds, Synges, Wallaces, Reads, & others – Bullivant arrived and Frederica – Woollcombe (late for his train) sleeps at Inn tonight.

Tuesday 14   Choral Festival[1]
At Mg. Service admission of the Bedesman Bailey – Afterwards went with Woollcombe round the Church – then wrote some of Sunday Sermonette – then Walsham How[2] & Miss Hinds Howell arrived – lionised Walsham How over the Cathedral – at ½p.3 was the Service wh. was performed fairly, and the Sermon wh. was first rate – W. How went back with Hinds Howell – went out into the garden to look for comet, but in vain.

1. This was the 15th Annual Festival of the Norfolk and Suffolk Church Choral Association. There were 615 voices representing 32 Choirs and the congregation was much larger than the previous year.
2. William Walsham How was now Hon. Canon of St Asaph and Rector of Whittington, Shropshire; later, to be Bishop of Bedford (Suffragan of London) 1879; 1st. Bishop of Wakefield 1888; Hymn writer and author.

Thursday 16

Before Morning Service called on Heaviside – he was very exultant about the <u>furor</u> shown in the H. of C. last night in favour of the Abp's Bill – read last night's debate in 'the Times'.

Saturday 18

After Mg. Service went into the Town with Woollcombe & Frederica, and then called on 'Oyster Pattie';[1] saw his Church, his Hospital, his pictures – At second Service, the Master announced that the Cathedrals had been thrust into the Bill last night by the H. of C.

1. 'Oyster Pattie' = Canon W.F. Patteson, Vicar of St. Helen's, Chaplain of the Great Hospital, and, jointly with the Revd A.C. Copeman, Rural Dean of Norwich.

Wednesday 22

After luncheon called on Bensly, & arranged to have a Chapter after Service this evening about the separation of Cloughton from Scalby[1] – wrote to Bishop of Winchester about George Willes, & to Archdeacon Kaye; also to Chs. Arnold[2], with a (last) receipt for rent from Rugby house – then Aftern. Service; and after that met Robinson & Nevill in Chapter, and agreed to consent to the making over £36 per ann. of the Vicarial tithe of Scalby to Cloughton – A dinner party in the Library.

1. Two parishes in the Diocese of York of which the Dean and Chapter of Norwich were Patrons. The Dean and Chapter are still Patrons of Scalby, and the Vicar of Scalby is Patron of Cloughton.
2. Charles Arnold (an authority on German literature and art) had been Housemaster of School Field House since 1841. This was the House which Goulburn had bought for the School and had recently sold it back to it.

Tuesday 28

Finished revising proofs of Boss book – put them in Stacy's hand – A Chapter after 11, which lasted (as far as I & Bensly were concerned) till nearly 6 – resolved not at present to enter upon the conversion of the Choristers' School into a vestry, as being too much for our finances – I communicated this to Medley.

The Hon. Mrs E. Goulburn, nee Catherine Montagu, Dean Goulburn's step-mother. An unfinished sketch, c. 1830.

Edward Goulburn's first letter (end portion) written to Louisa Goldsmid, later Thomas, c. 1823.

Augusta ('Gussie') Thomas, nee Cartwright (Goulburn was her Guardian). Photo by T. Fall, Portman Square.

Edward Meyrick Goulburn in his early middle years. Photo by Hennah & Kent, Brighton.

AUGUST

The Goulburns were away from home from Saturday, August 1 to Wednesday, October 21: At *York* (From August 1–3); at *Glasgow* (From August 3–5); at *Oban* (from August 5–12); *Killin* (August 12–13); *Pitlochry* (August 13–15); *Edinburgh* (August 15–19); *London* (August 19–22); *Tyntesfield* (August 22–September 5); *Edgcott* (September 5–12); *Eydon* (September 12–21); *Aynhoe* (September 21–October 5); *London* (October 5–8); *Brighton* (October 8–17); *London* (October 17–18); *Brighton* (October 18–21): Back to Norwich October 21.
On holiday, Goulburn's entries are always more expansive and detailed.

Saturday 1 From Norwich to York (Royal Station Hotel)
We left Norwich (kissing farewells to the little Nevills & Robinsons) by 10.40 train – I read in the Train E. Counties Press, Globe, Times & Church's 'Sacred Poetry of Sacred Religions' – Nice weather for travelling, cool & rainy – At Ely, where we must have staid 1¾ths. hours, I went into the Cathedral, observed the Font, wh. was <u>not</u> leaded inside; the emblems of the Evangelists on the four sides were <u>all</u> winged – then went up to see G. Parry at work on the Lantern, painting censing angels on panels; he expressed himself delighted with a sculpture found in the Lantern, wh. he feared mt. represent God the Father, but was proved to be the 2d Person by the scar in the side – on returning to Station had a long talk with omnibus driver, who told me many things – <u>At length</u> up came the train for Peterboro', where we had to wait about ¾ths. of an hour – got a cup of tea – Gt. Northern Stations' superiority over Gt. Eastern struck us very much indeed – then came on to York; it was nearly 8 when we arrived! Ordered tea for Ju & Gus, & dinner for me – The inn very clean & good, and the manager good, but they are long in bringing things & we have not yet seen the Bill.

Sunday 2   Spent at York
Ju and I went to the Minister for the ½p.10 Service, which including the H.C. Service, was not over till 1.5 – The singing <u>squally</u> & bad; the Services ugly & long; the organ loud; the conduct of singers and officials reverent; the Sermon by the High Sheriff's Chaplain [*it was Assize Sunday*] – The two judges staid for the H.C., as the redgowned Corporation did not – Afterwards Ju and I walked in the grounds of St. Mary's Abbey wh. was delicious; and there I sat till it was time for 4 p.m. Service, to wh. I went – the anthem beautiful, but badly sung.

Monday 3   From York to Glasgow
Breakfast at 7.45; left the Station at 9 – I read the Saturday Review – We came by N. Allerton, Darlington, Durham (where we had a grand view of the Cathedral & Castle), Gateshead & Newcastle where we looked down from the Bridge upon the town at an immense depth below; Morpeth, Alnwick, and Berwick (where we crossed the Tweed, & entered Scotland) – then Dunbar, and then Edinburgh, where amidst hurry & confusion we had to change carriages – A young engineer in command of the train, let himself into the carriage with us – He described himself as belonging to Guildford in Surrey; as detesting the coldness of the Presbyterian Services; as helping on an Episcopalian Choir; as now making trial on this line of a new brake; as having been to Edinburgh twice previously today on this business, in order to qualify himself to make his report – he said that on the N. Eastern line they had once tried how fast they could go; the utmost rate of speed attained was 15 miles in 12 minutes – he pointed out to us at Linlithgow the palace where Q. Mary Stuart was born, & the Church where she was baptized; also the ruins of the tower in wh. Lord Darnley had slept the night before his assassination – the Queen's Hotel at Glasgow, where we are seems fairly good – we have only 2 bedrooms, a small one for Gussie & Rose; and a sitting Room looking out on George Square – we had a very good dinner at a 6 o'clock Table d'Hote, and at a separate table by ourselves – Then Auntie & I walked up to the Cathedral, and went upon the Bridge of Sighs (across the Molendiner Burn) towards the Necropolis.

Tuesday 4   At Glasgow
Found that last night Dean of Chester[1] had sent up his card after we had retired, asking for an interview before he started for D. of Argyll's – he appeared after Bkfst., and wanted me to sign a petition to the Abp. of Canterbury, against any permission being conceded to use the Eastward position and to wear vestments – I on the whole declined, at wh. he seemed disappointed – then I went out alone, and walked to the West End Park (the aristocratic quarter) where the ground and flowers are beautiful, the ground sloping down to the R. Kelvin – then I went to the University, built by Gilbert Scott[2], overlooking the Park, & was lionised over it by a worthy Scot who showed me the library, room used as a Chapel, & classrooms, etc. – There is as yet no actual Chapel – On the 4 Sundays of the month, there is alternately Kirk Service, U.P. Service, Free Kirk, & Episcopalian; and

when the H.C. is celebrated halfyearly, it is according to all the three 1st. of these Communions! This is Principal Caird's[3] doing – took a fly to the Broomielaw – Disappointed on account of the immense length of sheds wh. line & disfigure the riverside – then back to the Queen's Hotel – Had a 3 hours fly – drove 1st. to the Cathedral – the crypt and architecture are really striking; so is the Chapter House – I hardly think the Munich glass appropriate – then we went on to W. End Park, with wh. Ju & Guss were delighted; then to the Queen's Park on the S. of the river, which is charming; borders of yellow and lilac heartease with a line of perilla & white stocks between – then drove back to the Broomielaw – a city of snobs w. lovely surroundings and a Cathedral worthy of belonging to a better Communion than the Kirk.

1. The Very Revd John Saul Howson, D.D., Dean of Chester 1867–85.
2. Glasgow University had been founded in 1451 by William Turnbull, Bishop of Glasgow. The buildings referred to were designed by Sir George Gilbert Scott (1811–78) about 1865.
3. Professor John Caird, D.D. (1820–98) was Professor of Theology at Glasgow University from 1862; and then Principal from 1873. His chief writings were an 'Introduction to the Philosophy of Religion' (1880) and the Gifford Lectures 'The Fundamental Ideas of Christianity' which were published in 1899, after his death.

Wednesday 5 From the Queen's Hotel, Glasgow, to Craig-ard Hotel, Oban

We left Glasgow at 8 by the Union Railway, and had a most comfortable day – read the Times in the railway to Greenock, but after that farewell to all reading – the boat was crowded, so that there was hardly standing-room – In parts of the voyage the sea was rough: the boat lurched & rolled – Ju was very uncomfortable – rain fell incessantly, and drove us down into the cabin where we had to sit upon one another – there was only one gleam of sunshine, and that was when we got on board the little steam tug wh. with band playing (a mockery of our misery) was to take us thro' the Crinan Canal, with its 15 locks, from Ardrishaig to Crinan – At Crinan we got on board the mail steamer, which was an improvement – We left Ardrishaig about 2 p.m., were 2 hours in the Crinan Canal, and 2 hours more from Crinan to Oban in mail steamer – We got here about 6.15, having left Glaswow at 8, 10½ hours & most wearisome ones from the throng, the rain, the wind[1] – The 'Craig-ard' at Oban is beautifully clean & comfortable – Everybody was very civil – We dined at table d'hote at 6.30.

1. The Goulburns' complicated and lengthy journey would have been improved some six years later, with the coming of the Railway to Oban in 1880. Today the rail journey from Glasgow to Oban takes about 3 hours.

Thursday 6 At Oban

After Bkfst. saw our Landlady; had an understanding with Mrs. McLaurin about prices: (Sitting room – gaseous – 6s.; large bedroom 5s.; small bedroom 3s.; maid's bedroom 2s.; Table d'hote dinner 4s. 6d.; Bkfst. 2s. 6d.) – then Ju and Gussie went out to look for lodgings[1], & shortly after I went out – Ju and I strolled up to Miss McPhail's lodging, wh. was recommended; but we found it small, & rather dirty – then I took a hill stroll, and after crossing one or two fences, I reached a height, whence I commanded Loch Etive & Dunstaffnage Castle on one side, & the Bay of Oban on the other – it was very lovely, & I came down delighted – After luncheon, Auntie & I drove to Dunstaffnage[2] in a little one-horse double gig, I sitting in front with the driver – It was beautiful – we saw the recess in the keep of the Castle, in wh. the stone of coronation was kept, while Dunstaffnage was the seat of the Monarchy (afterwards brought to Scone, and thence to the Abbey by Edward Longshanks) – also the ancient cemetery in what was the Cathedral precinct, made solemn by a thick grove – it is very solemn & ghostlike – the Castle stands on an enormous (not very high) knob of rock – In coming home we stopped short of Oban, and Ju & I roamed about the hills, getting now & then into sloppy ground – At dinner, I heard of the 'Serpent of Loch-nill' and made up my mind to visit it – Coming upstairs we met (to our gt. delight) Sir George Baker! Read the 'Lord of the Isles' in the evening.

1. It was the Goulburn's custom to stay in a hotel for the first day or two, and then seek cheaper lodgings. In this case, however, they remained at 'Craig-ard'.
2. Originally a MacDougall Castle, it was taken by Robert the Bruce in 1308, who made it a Royal Castle and put it in the care of the Campbells of Argyll. The early Scots had brought the Stone of Destiny from Ireland to Dunstaffnage Castle. In the 9th Century the Stone was moved to Scone (near Perth) where the Kings of Scotland were crowned. In 1296, Edward I (of England) took the Stone to London (Westminster Abbey). In 1746 Flora MacDonald was kept here for a few days as a state prisoner on her way to London.

Friday 7 At Oban

Bkfst. at the Table d'hote with Sir G. Baker and party – agreed to walk with him to the Saurian mound on the border of Loch Nell[1] – went to the Book-seller, & succeeded in borrowing from him an account in Good Words of 1872 of the Serpent Mound[2] – after luncheon there was rain, but Sir Geo. Baker and I accomplished our visit to the mound in an open fly – we could not see Ben-Cruachan & his three peaks; he had enveloped himself in mist – he is to be seen from the cairn on the serpent's head, looking due east – The place is supposed to be a relic of Druitical worship in wh. both the serpent and the sun figured – we walked back, & were caught by a heavy shower, the effects of wh, however, soon dried off us – got back at 6 – I forgot to say that yesterday at Dunstaffnage I saw on the walls a cannon taken from the Spanish Armada, one of the vessels of wh. had been wrecked on the coast near – It was bronze, had a sort of Verdigris colour, and had a latin inscription giving the maker's name, "Costa (?) me fecit".

> 1. = 'Loch of the Swans'; 2 miles long and ½ a mile wide.
> 2. The Serpent Mound is formed of boulders, some 80 yds. in length, and in the form of an elongated letter S.

Saturday 8   At Oban

After Bkfst. we arranged with the Bakers to go with them to Dunstaffnage – Gussie & the Miss Bakers went with Lady Baker in the morning, and spent a long day at Dunstaffnage painting – Sir Geo., Ju and I went at 1.30 – After seeing the lions, we waited for the ladies to finish their painting, and then all rowed across Loch Etive in a boat – then we all walked home, having frequent showers, but not the worse for it – In the evening got Thursday's Times, announcing that the Commons have accepted the elimination from the P.W. Bill[1] of the appeal to the Abp., and Friday's giving the decision of the Exeter Reredos case by Dean of Arches – The name of the maker of the Dutch gun from the Armada, preserved at Dunstattnage, is <u>Koster</u>.

> 1. Public Worship Regulation Act.

Sunday 9   At Oban

Rose at 7.15, hoping to able to go to the early Communion at 8 a.m. (to which Gussie and the Miss Bakers went), but the servants were all so late ("they always had a good sleep on the Sabbath") that it became impossible – The Bkfst. was not till 9.30 – I went into the Vestry, to offer to read Prayers for the old clergyman, but he had got assistance already – he asked me to preach in the evening at 6.30[1] – The Service was very well done; the reader read in the accents of the Abp. of Canterbury[2]; but I could not always follow the Highland accent – Dinner was at 4, and it was a very 'close fit', 42 people in all.

1. In 1847, when Alexander Ewing was appointed Bishop of Argyll and the Isles, there were only six Episcopal congregations in the Diocese. Soon after he arranged for Services to be held in a house in Oban, afterwards in the Caledonian Hotel, then in an old Masonic Hall, and finally, in 1863, the first stone of a Church building was laid.
2. Archbishop Tait was Scottish, brought up as a Presbyterian. He is regarded as an outstanding Archbishop of Canterbury from 1868–82. In 1856, within a period of 4½ weeks, he lost 5 children (aged 10 to 1½ years), and a remaining son, and also his wife, died four years before him. He had been Goulburn's immediate predecessor as Headmaster of Rugby.

Monday 10   To Iona and Staffa

Started at 8 with Sir Geo Baker for Staffa and Iona – Drenching rain when we started, when we returned, and during our stay at Staffa – We went, not by Tobermory, and took Iona first[1] – it was very interesting – there was an enclosed place where the kings had been interred, but now other gravestones were laid upon it – The beautiful pattern work upon the stone coffins, as also on Macleane's Cross & St. Martin's Cross (in the Cathedral yard) struck me much – The base of the latter is of red granite – There is a tombstone of the last Prioress (Princeps Anna) in the nunnery Chapel, on wh. the lady is pourtrayed with clasped (?) hands – The arches of the nave of the Cathedral are round-headed Norman – it must have [been] a very elegant building – We saw two or three Bishops' Tombstones, on wh. they are represented in the full episcopal attire, very like Goldwell[2], only with the chasuble – Staffa was a failure; after landing in pouring rain, we had to walk a mile to the steps leading to Fingal's cave[3]; & when we arrived at the bottom of these steps, Sir Geo. & I thot. we would go no further, on the good sense of wh. several of those who did go congratulated us – there was on board the Austrian Consul-General, Baron Schreiner (?), Mr. Max Gregor, the great Hungarian wine-merchant, and a young Mr. Dasent, known to Sir George – There was a Yankee clergyman, who talked about my Sermon of yesterday, and several others with whom we struck up a temporary acquaintance – We were told at Iona that those warriors, who appear in the sculptures with a galley on their shields are supposed to be of Danish extraction.

1. They sailed down the Firth of Lorne, and along the south coast of the Island of Mull to Iona on its south-west corner.
2. James Goldwell was Bishop of Norwich from 1472–1499. His tomb is on the south side of the Presbytery.
3. Staffa is only ¾ths of a mile long by ¼th of a mile broad (at its widest)!

Tuesday 11   Last Day at Oban
Misty all day, and raining till the afternoon – went out in the morning to take places in the coach for Tyndrum tomorrow – supposed I had taken 4 inside places by the 10.30 coach, but it turned out I could not have them, and we are obliged to start at 8 a.m. – came in and revised for the press my two remaining Sermons on the Eucharist, and then took them to the post myself – then read Bp. of Argyll's Book on Iona, etc. till it left off raining – and then sauntered on to Dunolly[1] Castle – it would have been really superb the lake and coast scenery with the little yachts flying about; lovely, if the weather would but give it a chance – came back & went on with 'Iona' – dinner at half past six – we were promoted to the head of the table[2].

> 1. Dunollie Castle, on the promontory north of Oban, is the ancient stronghold of the MacDougalls, the Lords of Lorn, and is still owned by the Chief of the Clan MacDougall. Today only the keep and some fragments of other buildings remain. Behind the Castle is the residence of the Chief.
> 2. The Goulburn's Bill for four of them, for five days, at Craig-ard Hotel was £14. 16s.; four seats on the Coach from Oban to Tyndrum were £3. 4s. For the eleven days they had already been away from home the cost had been £59. 12.; i.e. £5. 8. 4d. per day (for four).

Wednesday 12   From Oban to Tyndrum & thence to Killin
A pouring day – We left Oban by the Tyndrum Coach at 8 a.m., having sighted Dean of Chester in a Tarbet coach – the coach was a newfashioned one, with <u>five</u> places (a close cram) inside, all abreast, and glass at the sides – however, we were only four inside, Ju, Gussie, a foreign lady's maid and myself – Rose was outside – The country was fine, specially the pass of Brander, but enjoyment of it precluded by the torrents wh. fell – we recognised the castle[1] in the midst of Loch Awe, wh. seemed to us grander from the heights above than viewed from the low ground, as we did formerly – Got to Tryndrum in drenching rain, & there took an hour's rail to this place, Killin – the luxury of a railway appreciated after the straight back and close fit of a coach – We dined at a separate Table at the Table d'Hote, and then strolled out to see the country wh. is wild and dreary – The Dochart comes dashing thro' the place grandly enough, numberless small cataracts falling into it – Kitchener[2], one of the Rugby masters, is in this hotel, & came to see us in the evening.

> 1. Kilchurn Castle. The 15th century Castle was owned by the Campbells of Breadalbane, but has been uninhabited since the 1740s.
> 2. F.E. Kitchener was both an old Rugbeian, and also an Assistant Master appointed by Goulburn's successor, Frederick Temple. In this year (1874) he was moving to the new High School at Newcastle-under-Lyme as Headmaster.

Thursday 13 [Pitlochry]

The hotel at Killin dirty and dismal, not to be recommended, tho' the people are civil – At 1.30 we started in the coach for Aberfeldy – We went by the north side of the lake to Taymouth, and had a glimpse of the castle[1] – arrived at Pitlochry by train from Aberfeldy at 6.30 – house, inconviently full, but the people most civil and obliging – wrote to Mr. Gibbs, to ask whether he can receive us next week.

> 1. Taymouth Castle: Built in 1801, it replaced a much older structure.

Friday 14

Dismal rain in the morning – Engaged myself in writing a letter to Woollcombe, as the preface to my forthcoming Chapters – finished it by luncheon time – Received a telegram from Fleming's Palace Hotel, Edinburgh, saying that rooms will be kept for tomorrow night – Also a letter from Rivington, acknowledging the receipt of my last two Chaps., and enclosing my publishing account (£830 in my favour) – At 2 we drove to Killicrankie Pass, and there got out and saw the 'Queen's View' of the falls of the Garry – then drove to the 'Queen's View' of Loch Tummel, a quieter scene – on the whole the afternoon was fair – returned at 5.45 o'c and then took a stroll round the village of Pitlochry, & went into a Knick Knack and ornament shop – on our return, to my surprise and pleasure we met Shairp[1] – he came in and we had a pleasant chat about his Books, St. Andrew's, and B.C. and other matters – dined at ½p.6 – read aloud afterwards two cantos of Lord of the Isles.

> 1. John Campbell Shairp was a Presbyterian whom Goulburn held in the greatest esteem and affection. He had been Goulburn's Assistant-Master at Rugby; Professor of Latin at St Andrew's University 1861–72; Principal of United College, St Andrew's from 1868, and was to be Professor of Poetry at Oxford 1877–85; LL.D. Edinburgh 1884.

Saturday 15   From Pitlochry to Edinburgh

Rainy morning, as usual – at 11.14 started for Edinburgh; had nearly an hour to stop in Perth – I read 'Lord of the Isles'; rather tired when we got here (Fleming's Palace Hotel) – most comfortable apartments and most excellent dinner; far the best hotel we have been at – After dinner we took a walk to the top of the Calton Hill, wh. was very refreshing.

Sunday 16   At Edinburgh

A fine day – went to St. Paul's Church[1] at 11 o'clock – Dean Montgomery read prayers very solemnly & well; and a Dr. Gordon preached (from some Chapel in London) – the whole Service was most creditably performed; the preacher's manner & delivery a little affected – came back, & settled to stay here (at the Palace Hotel) till Wednesday – then to Church at St. Paul's a second time (½p.2) – A deacon read Prayers, with his scarf crossed over his breast – A Missionary Clergyman preached about Missions – afterwards I went into the vestry & spoke for a moment to the Dean – then I went to call on the Bishop[2] at 1, Atholl Place – I did not see the Bp., but met him as I was walking back to my Hotel – He asked us to dinner tomorrow – Table d'hote here at 5 – Afterwards Ju & I got wet in visiting the Iron Church, & to no purpose, for the Church was so full there was no standing room.

    1. St Paul's, York Place. Is a copy of King's College Chapel, Cambridge. The Rector was the Very Revd J.F. Montgomery, Dean of Edinburgh.
    2. The Rt Revd Henry Cotterhill, D.D.

Monday 17   At Edinburgh

After drawing for £15 at the Bar [*of the Hotel*], & writing to Stacy, & Mr. Hailstone, we drove to and lionised Holyrood – The bloodstains of Rizzio are nearly effaced – I think the Chapel, in wh. Chas. I was crowned, is the most striking feature – I could not see any pure Norman architecture, though there are some round-headed arches <u>intersecting</u>, wh. I suppose wd. be <u>late</u> Norman – We saw some beautiful Jacobean tables, wh. wd. make good Communion Tables – Later in the day at 1.40 we went in train to Roslyn Chapel[1] & back – The profuse decorations are very lovely indeed; the architraves are very striking – The virtues portrayed in the architrave near the 'Prentice's Pillar[2]' are: the good Bishop giving instruction, guiding the blind, clothing the naked, feeding the hungry, visiting the sick, visiting the prisoners, burying the dead; St. Peter at the end, receiving them all into heaven – the vices I could not entirely make out; there is the careless Bishop, drunkeness, anger with the halberd, the miser w. his hands in his pocket, the envious man with the grapes, the lovers embracing, & Satan coming out of an alligator's mouth to hook them all in – we returned in a carriage w. inquisitive Yankees – bought 'Dora Wordsworth' at a bookseller's shop – Dined with Bishop Cotterill at 7 p.m.

1. Rosslyn Chapel (The Collegiate Church of St Matthew, Roslin), built by Sir Wm. St Clair between 1450 and 1486. "One of the most strikingly beautiful pre-Reformation churches in Europe". It is only the choir of the projected Collegiate Church which Sir William had intended. Severely damaged at the Revolution of 1688, in was restored in 1862. It is now a Cathedral Mission Church of the Episcopal Church.
2. The 'Prentice's Pillar' is said to have been constructed by an apprentice in the absence of his master, who, on his return, was so envious of it, that he killed the apprentice with a mallet.

Tuesday 18   Last day at Edinburgh
After Bkfst. took a walk in the Morng., calling on Dean Montgomery, but not finding him at home – then walked right round the Castle Hill – went into the great hall wh. corresponds to our Westminster Hall (where I observed the likeness of Ld. Moncrieff's portrait to Revd G.R. Moncrieff of Ball.) – went into Dr Nesbit's Church in the nave of St Gile's Cathedral, & saw the place where John Knox's pulpit stood – It is truly wretched – the Choir, wh. is used as the State Church, and where the Ld. High Commissioner attends Service, has been better treated, the new pulpit being low & moved to the side – Into the choir we all went in the afternoon – I walked on, passing J. Knox's house (wh. is not opened today) & passing also Moray House, the curious old residence of the former regent, now converted into Free Church Schools! – to Holyrood – thence walked to the Antiquarian Museum & saw John Knox's pulpit, Janet Geddes's stool, some queer mummies, royal & episcopal seals, etc. – then home for luncheon – at 1.50 hired a fly by the hour – lionised the Castle, Regalia, little room in wh. James I was born, etc. etc. – then drove round Salisbury Crags – Ju & I walked a little way towards Arthur's Seat & left Buskins & Rose to do the rest – we then ended our drive by calling on the Cotterhills, but did not find them at home.

Wednesday 19   From Edinburgh to London
Left Edinburgh at 10.30 and arrived in London by express at 8 p.m. – We stopped at York a quarter of an hour – I read the Times, Spectator, Pall Mall, and Lay of the last Minstrel – We found decent rooms, for wh. we had telegraphed, at G.W.R. – The expenditure of every day of our tour, including today's expenditure (perhaps the heaviest of all) amounts to: £111. 17. 6. But to this must be added 16s. 6, the price of our rooms tonight and (say) 10s. the price of our supper.

              £111. 17. 7.
                1. 6. 6
              ─────────────
              £113. 4.   for nineteen days[1].

Now 19 days at £5. 19. 1 per diem comes to £113. 2. 7.
Therefore we have spent nearly £6 per diem.

> 1. This was for Goulburn, Julia, Buskins, and Rose the maid. It falls into perspective if we realise that this was more than the annual stipend of some Curates, and more than twice the wage of an agricultural worker *for two years*.

Friday 21   [*In London*]
In the morning, after arranging what was to go back to Norwich, I went out – read the article in Fraser on 'Who wrote Shakspere?' – after Luncheon, walked to Wardour Street, and looked into several shops in quest of an altar-table for the Cathedral – then went to Tintie's & there waited till Buskins and Auntie came in – then, leaving Buskins with Tintie, we went together to inspect the Tables I had looked at – We ended by ordering a table to be made from an ancient model wh. pleased us, but wh. was itself too small.

• •

On August 22, Augusta (Buskins), having gone to stay at King's Sutton, the Goulburns went on a fortnight's visit to the Gibbs' at Tyntesfield (near Bristol). On September 5 they rejoined Buskins at Edgcott, moving on to Eydon on September 12, and then to Aynhoe on September 21, remaining there until October 5.

• •

SEPTEMBER

Saturday 5   [*From Tyntesfield to Edgcott*]
Had Bkfst. at 8 – Attended Chapel Service at 8.30 – Mr. Boyd officiated very devoutly – shortly after we took our leave – it was a lovely morning – We had to change at Bristol; and at Oxford we had about an hour to spare – Part of this we employed in seeing Keble[1]; the Chapel will be certainly very imposing.

> 1. After John Keble's death in 1866, it was resolved to found a College in his memory. With money raised by public subscription, building was begun in 1868, the Architect being William Butterfield (1814–1900), himself a follower of the Oxford Movement. The foundation stone of the Chapel was laid, in 1873, by Goulburn's friend, William Gibbs of Tyntesfield, the donor, with whom the Goulburns had just been staying. The Hall and Library, completed in 1878, were the gifts of William Gibbs' two sons, Anthony and Henry.

Saturday 12   Removed to Eydon

I had an alarming letter from Heaviside about the West End, saying that Brown is desirous of having another opinion as to the necessity of taking down the Western gable; and another from Hinds Howell, asking me to remember the 15th. Oct. for the Oxford Dinner – answered Heaviside that an opinion might be got from Blomfield, Scott, or Nessfield.

• •

It is quite incredible that Goulburn makes no mention in his Diary of the horrific railway accident at Thorpe on the evening of September 10, 1874. He was at Edgcott until September 12, when he received this letter from Heaviside, and also the one from Hinds Howell, These must have been posted on September 11, but no mention seems to have been made in them about the disaster. Moreover Goulburn read regularly the 'Times' and the 'Guardian' in which some account must have been given.

The trains involved were the 8.40 pm from Yarmouth, due in Norwich at 9.40 pm, and the down express from Norwich to Yarmouth which should have left at 9.10 pm, but was delayed owing to the late arrival of the London train at 9.23 pm. The Yarmouth to Norwich train left Brundall at 9.25 pm; the Norwich to Yarmouth train left Norwich (Thorpe) some minutes later on the same line. They met head-on at speed at the East Bridge of Thorpe. Carriages were piled on top of each other, the rear carriage of the down train hanging from the bridge over the river, and one or two passengers were thrown into the river. Some carriages toppled down the bank.

The immediate casualty list stated that 17 people had been killed and more than 30 injured; that 27 were admitted to the Norfolk and Norwich Hospital and the less severely injured taken home. But, by the end of October, the number of deaths was given as 26. There was a very heavy rainstorm at the time.

Both Train Drivers and both Firemen were killed; also the Revd Henry and Mrs. Stacey (formerly Independent Minister, Beccles); and Surgeon, Mr W. Bransby Francis, who died a few weeks later. Dr (later Sir Peter) Eade, Physician, was in one of the badly smashed carriages, but he was thrown out on to the wet grass of a meadow. At first, he was stunned and unconscious, but, when he recovered, he attended to the bleeding from his head, managed to get to the house of a friend nearby, and then returned to help. Later, he sent a letter to the 'British Medical Journal' giving an account of his experience both from a medical and a personal point of view.

The Bishop issued a circular to the Clergy of the City and Suburbs, asking them to commend to the prayers of their congregations on the following Sunday, the injured and the families who had been bereaved. And on that Sunday, the Bishop himself preached at the Afternoon Service in the Cathedral to a crowded congregation.

September-October 1874   193

A Thorpe Collision Fund was opened for the Widows and Orphans of the victims. The Railway employees gave one day's pay. By November 21 subscriptions amounted to c. £3000. R.H. Mottram in 'Portrait of an Unknown Victorian' says that claims for compensation amounted to over £40,000, and the Relief Fund for sufferers, administered by Gurney's Bank, continued for 30 years. Mr George England of Freethorpe, sent a donation of £100 to the Norfolk and Norwich Hospital, as a thank-offering for his escape from injury in the accident.

●●●

Saturday 19   At Eydon
Went to Church at 8 – At Bkfst., a letter from Heaviside, saying they had chosen Seddon[1] to give an opinion on the West end, and asking my consent – this I walked over to Morton Pinkey to give.

1. Later, J.P. Seddon, an Architect who restored and built churches in London and Norfolk, was the designer of the carved Pulpit in the Presbytery given as a memorial to Goulburn.

OCTOBER

Tuesday 6
Left London for Wadhurst by the 8.55 train – got to Fred's about noon – found him looking well, but, we thought, graver and more muttering to himself than usual; his memory wonderful as always – Newington finds that the removal of skybalm remedies the lumbago – We got back at 5 – I went to the Club to look at the evening papers, and then walked home.

●●

On October 8, the Goulburns moved to Brighton, where he was to read a Paper next day to the Church Congress then meeting there. Unfortunately, that evening he had, by mistake, torn up his Paper and thrown it into the fire. He had, however, sent an advance copy to the Press.

●●

Friday 9   Paper at Brighton Congress
My torn Ms. being almost unreadable, I got up at 8 a.m. and went to the Office of the Sussex Daily News in North St., where, after some delay, I got a proof of my Paper, printed on slips – read it first in the Dome and then in the Corn Hall.

●●

They remained in Brighton, at 14, Lansdown Place, which he had bought in June, until their return to Norwich on October 21.

●●

Wednesday 21   From Brighton to Norwich
The Dentist[1] (Mr. Wood) came at 7.45 a.m. – he lanced my gums again, but did not extract – Left Brighton by express (no 2d class) at 8.45 – met Mr. & Mrs. Micklethwaite at the S. Pancras Station, and also Lucy Hansell[2], returning home after a 9 months absence – she got into the same carriage with us – Agonies of pain in the evening from toothache.

>   1. Some 16 days earlier, he had gone to a Dentist in London (Mr. Eskell), who filled two teeth and advised him to have a plate for gaps; later he extracted a front tooth. Goulburn continued to have severe toothache, and went to another Dentist (Dr Pritchard) in Brighton; and, just before leaving Brighton, to yet another Dentist (Mr Wood).
>   2. Daughter of Henry Hansell, Registrar of the Archdeaconry of Norfolk.

Thursday 22   Five Societies Sermon[1]
Sent for Mr. White, having had a sleepless night from pain – He came at about noon – strongly recommended my not losing the tooth, but having it dressed with chloral wh. wd. tan the nerve – He put in such a dressing wh. eased me – I was enabled to go to Church in time for the Sermon, preach it, and come away again – I declined to go to the Oxford dinner, from fear of catching cold, but the Pin has gone.

>   1. The Five Societies: Addtional Curates' Soc.; Diocesan Church Building Soc.; The National (School) Soc.; S.P.C.K.; S.P.G. Each year (usually in Oct.) a Sermon was preached on behalf of each Society in turn. This year Goulburn preached for the Diocesan Church Building Soc.

Friday 23
After luncheon went to Mr. White's, who again applied carbolic acid to my tooth – Medley dined here, and talked about the new organ[1], the alterations in Choir Vestry, the 8 boys who want to be confirmed, etc. etc.

>   1. The Choir Organ had been presented by Julia.

Saturday 24
Went to the M.C.s and Lay Clerks' Vestry to see the lavatory & other improvements – Went to the Bp's, to bring before him the case of the 8 Choristers (7 under age) who petition for Confirmation[1] – he saw Medley afterwards, and decided not to confirm the boys.

>   1. In 1859, the Bishop had circulated the Rural Deaneries about the age of Confirmation, which then appeared to be c. 16. The majority of Deaneries considered that a great proportion of those who became regular communicants were 16+ when confirmed, but they did not think that, if 16 were

made the minimum age, the number or standard of Communicants would be increased. They were against limiting the age to 16+, but they did consider that pre-Confirmation Classes for 14+ would be desirable and possible on Sundays.

Monday 26   Chapter on the W. front
After Service a short interview with Medley about Mr. Tompson – then a Chapter in wh. the Woodham Walter Cottages, and the West front were considered – a letter was read from the Master proposing to do nothing till the audit – we thought it necessary, however, to order the W. gable to be immediately taken down – all further operations and the question about ways & means being postponed till the Audit – the difft. methods of raising the wind[1] here, however, copiously discussed – The W. Walter cottages were to be built after Sir W. Jones's type, with porches added – Colman's proposal to purchase off us at a high price the Carrow meadows was referred to the Eccll. Commissrs. – Chapter ended for the Canons about 2.45; me & Bensly about 3.45 – then I walked in the Kitchen Garden, reading John Bull – in the evening read to Ju the article in Edinburgh on Renan's Antichrist[2].

1. 'raising the wind' = obtaining the necessary funds.
2. J.E. Renan (1823–92) French philosopher, theologian and historian; abandoned traditional faith; published 'The Life of Jesus' which undermined the superantural aspects of Christ's Life and teachings.

Tuesday 27
Inteview w. Lichfield <u>before</u> & Daniels <u>after</u> Church about the keeping clean of the M.C.'s vestry – went with Ju to Mr. White, who thinks that the teeth in my right jaw only give trouble from indigestion – he stopped the bad tooth with osteo.

Thursday 29
After Morning Service saw the Bedesmen and the Police, and made arrangements for the Confirmation – also saw Medley, and went with him into the Presbytery, to consider the place of the new Organ.

Friday 30   Day of the Confirmation
After Bkfst. saw Spaull for a few minutes about the arrangements – After Morning Service saw T.W., Hansell and some others – then went to St. Gregory's Church, to inspect the repairs, etc. – Mr. Reid and a very zealous Churchwarden showed me the Church – the Miss Reids were there – did not attend the

Confirmation, but wrote a Sermonette while they were in Church – The 'Pin' and Guy came in at 2.35, just before his Confirmation – We dined alone, and I read Ju a review in the Quarterly on the Strikes & lock-out[1].

1. At Gt Massingham.

NOVEMBER

Monday 2   Buskins arrives

E.G. Arnold & Lady Charlotte breakfasted with us, and gave an account of the strikes at Gt. Massingham, etc. – after Mg. Church, assembled the 3 Canons in the Presbytery, to consider of the Bay in wh. the Organ should be placed, etc. – We thought it might go in the Northern Bay, without any alteration to the workman's entrance beyond that of hanging the inner door, so as to make it swing, and lining the crack with leather – then we talked about the lighting conductor, as to whether the old one (thro' the weathercock) had not better be taken down, etc. – Buskins arrived at 4.15 – Mr. Hull[1] called about the Confirmation; he had presented several candidates under the age, whom the Bp. had confirmed, but had written him a letter, begging him not to do so again – what was he to do? I recommended him seeking an interview with the Bishop, and explaining in each case the 'special reason'.

1. The Revd W.B. Hull, Rector of St Peter Hungate, Norwich.

Tuesday 3

After Mg. Service, a walk with Medley on Mousehold – Buck and he agreeing that the Organ wd. certainly be injured in the North bay without some protection from the draught, Medley and I went to Spaull after our walk, to arrange about the glazing of the arch – then I called at Heaviside's, and had luncheon with them – they were very bright – the Prince[1] had dined with them last night, to celebrate Heaviside's birthday – dined with the Watsons.

1. The Prince of Wales (later Edward VII).

Wednesday 4

After Morning Service, a long visit from Sir S. Bignold, to induce me to ask Rust the Stonemason to vote with his party in the Corporation, where the Conservatives have now a majority of two only – This I declined to do[1].

1. While Goulburn's inclination was Conservative, he had avowed in a pre-election Sermon in July 1870, that "as a minister of Jesus Christ I know no politics".

Saturday 7

At 11.15 read over Buskins release of Robert, and witnessed her signature to it and to certain powers of Attorney – Robert at dinner[1].

> 1. In 1864, Goulburn had become Augusta's (Buskins') legal guardian, "and became guarantee for Robert in administering to Gussy's mother's will". Augusta was 21 on July 18, 1874, and so became independent of Robert Cartwright, her uncle, a Barrister, who was Julia's step-brother.

Wednesday 11

Went to Bensly, whom I saw at Brown's Office – desired Brown to obtain answers to certain questions about the West front, and to prepare plans for reconstructing the gables and pinnacles – these he promised to get ready by Monday 23 – Dinner at the Palace to meet Duke of Cornwall[1] – There were the Henry Birkbecks, Gurney Buxtons, the John Gurneys, Colonel Hale, Mr. Maurice Fitzgerald, Co. & Mrs. Boileau, Miss Boileau, the Nisbets, the Heavisides & ourselves – I sat between Mrs. Gurney Buxton and Fanny Pelham – the latter was taken down by the Prince, who sat between her & Mrs. Nisbet – It was all over early – I had a good deal of talk with the Bishop, & very pleasant talk – H.R.H. said he had passed me in the street several times.

> 1. The Prince of Wales took his seat in the House of Lords in 1861 as Duke of Cornwall. After Sandringham was purchased in 1863, he was often to be seen in Norwich streets. Frederick Hibgame recollects that he "was a familiar figure in Norwich streets, and was frequently to be seen walking between Lord Suffield and Mr Hay Gurney".

Thursday 12

Snow lay on the ground – After Mg. Service thot of taking a walk, but casually going in to see Heaviside, he reminded me that I was due at the Training School reception of the Examiners (Canon Tinling & Mr. Synge)[1] – Before this, wh. did not take place till noon I had time to call at E.K. Harvey's and leave cards on his appointment as Mayor – The room was full at the Training Institution; all three Archdeacons and many others – Can. Tinling hinted that with sixty pupils we ought to have more than three governesses – hereupon we took counsel, & determined to have another mistress, and appointed a Commee. to consider of it, 2 Archdeacons, Heaviside, & Hinds Howell, etc. – did not get back till 2 – at luncheon had Canon Tinling, Colbeck, Ormsby, Hinds Howell – stories about Henry of Exeter – Dined at Shottesham, & met Lord & Lady Abinger, Sir H. & Miss Stracey, Mr. Wraughton, etc. etc.

> 1. The Revd F. Synge was Her Majesty's Inspector of Schools in Norfolk.

Monday 16

After Mg. Service, drew up the 'Agenda' Paper with Bensly – Heaviside and Brown went to inspect the stones wh. had fallen from the W. side of the N. Transept; they are columns of the arcading of the pinnacle – Heaviside sent a resolution to reconsider our resolution a year ago about the Early Commn. on Minor festivals – hereon I wrote him a letter, asking him to reconsider his resolution – Went out with Nisbet (after inspecting the debris of the N. Transept) on the Newmarket Rd.; but before reaching it was obliged to return in a fly! (We had passed Colenso[1] in the street) – After 2d Service saw Medley about (a) Plan of new Organ (b) Advent Services & Hymns (c) his proposal about Chorister's Apprentice Fee.

> 1. J.W. Colenso had been Vicar of Forncett St Mary, Norfolk, 1846–53; published Mathematical Textbooks; became Bishop of Natal in 1853; taught some Zulus printing; produced Zulu Grammar, Dictionary, Reading Books and translation of New Testament, and some O.T. Books; in 1863 was deposed by Archbishop of Capetown for his liberal and unorthodox views; Judical Comm. of Privy Council declared in his favour, but his Archbishop excommunicated him in 1866 and appointed a successor in 1869; he retained the affection of the Diocese; legally he retained the endowments of the See; denounced the Zulu War in 1879; died in 1883, aged 69.

Tuesday 17

Mr. Ram[1] called at 4.15 and asked me to be on the Commee. for getting up an Art Exhibition in Norwich, the proceeds to go to his Church restoration – I consented – After dinner Auntie and Buskins went to the Evanses, to see a play ('the Orange Blossoms') acted by the little Evanses & the little Wallaces.

> 1. The Revd E. Ram was Vicar of St John Timberhill, Chaplain of the County Lunatic Asylum, Thorpe, and one of the Secs. of the Churchman's Club, of which the Dean was President. Goulburn always liked to help and support the parishes of which the Dean and Chapter were Patrons.

Friday 20

Called on Buck, but did not find him willing to see me (he has lost his son[1] in America, Mr. Herbert Buck) – Have had a great shock – My own Ju, after dining with us, left the drawing room very faint, and fell down on the landing; I did not know it for some minutes – when I first saw her on her bed, she did not seem herself – I sent for Muriel, who thinks it is only stomach, but says she is very thin from taking too much of aperients & eating too little.

1. This was Dr Buck's youngest of four sons, who was accidently drowned in America. He also had two daughters. His first wife (whom he married in 1819, and had eight children, three of whom died in infancy) died young. He married his second wife in 1832, and she died in 1873.

Saturday 21

Ju passed a good night & is much better – Mr. Muriel came again at 9.30, & reported well of Ju – After Mg. Service, I went with Nisbet, Spaull, & Bensly to see the staircase in the W. front of the Cathedral, in wh. it is proposed to keep the hose; and thence to the room over the S. side of the Cloister, wh. there has been some choice of using as a Museum for Antiquities – At 3 o'clock Service Mr. Clark[1] (of North Wooton) was installed Hon. Can. – I gave a rather briefer Sermonette than usual – came home, and after writing a few letters, joined the 'Bee' and read them Lyndon's Tale of the French Revolution.

1. The Revd W.W. Clarke had been Rector of North Wooton since 1834.

Thursday 26

At 3 o'clock took the chair at Seyyid Mustafa Ben-Yosuf's Lecture – Hinds Howell there, & Mr. Nevill, and Mr. Morgan, and Arthur Copeman – said a few words at opening & closing – Mustafa's voice beautiful, and his attitudes graceful – texts illustrated were "Like as the eyes of servants look unto the hands, etc."; "Thy word is a lantern unto my feet, etc. "Over Edom will I cast out my shoe, etc."; "My horn is exalted, etc." – very interesting & constructive – a large audience in Noverre's rooms – came home and prepared for a party in Library – with our two selves 16.

Monday 30   St. Andrew

Nevill came in, & asked for authority from D. & C. to stop the building higher of the wall wh. divides him from the Consistory Court – Then came a letter from Nisbet, explaining that he had had an alarming account of his Mother's health, & had telegraphed to know whether to go to her – so he could not come at 11 – But Nevill was there and read a lesson – I spoke for ¾ths. of an hour – then read Ernest Hawkin's Prayer for Missions & allowed a few minutes for secret prayer before giving the Benediction[1] – after it was over, called on and took leave of Nisbet.

1. Day of Intercession for Foreign Missions, observed throughout the Diocese. This was a Meeting for prayer and exhortation in Noverre's Rooms.

DECEMBER

Tuesday 1 Audit Day

Service in the monring at 8; Neville and Master there – Afterwards we all went to inspect that portion of the facade of the West front, wh. had been recently dininterred – then Bkfst. – Chapter Meeting at 9 – Medley sworn in as Precentor – a long day of it – we came to the conclusion as to the West front, to order nothing more at present than an investigation as to whether under Alnwick's[1] doorway there are traces of the old Norman one; then we shall see our way more clearly – Heaviside did not press his motion about the discontinuance of the Communion on Minor Festivals – There came to the dinner Heaviside & Mrs. H., Nevill, Hotson, Medley, Moore, Robt. Wright, Bensly, besides the Robinsons – Blanche Daniell sung beautifully – News of poor Mrs. Nisbet's death was telegraphed by the Canon to his wife in the evening.

> 1. William Alnwick was Bishop of Norwich 1426–36; and Bishop of Lincoln 1436–49. Helped to found Eton School and King's College, Cambridge. He "began alterations which internally have left the great west door set in a Norman arch with a four-centred one built inside it". (E. Sansbury, 'Historical Guide to Norwich Cathedral' (Revised Ed. 1994)

Thursday 3

I called on Mr. & Mrs. George Buck[1] – Poor Dr. Buck seems to be failing – then to Sawyer's and Stacey's to look for a Cabinet Portrait of Dr. Pellew – then walked on Newmarket and Eaton Roads – went to Medley's for a little practice; talked with him over the Organist question – Mrs. Nevill called with sad news – it had been telegraphed from Shadwell Court that Georgie Heaviside had met with an accident in shooting – Heaviside had gone off at once to be with him – I wrote to him & Mrs. Heaviside – A telegram from Heaviside to his wife saying that Georgie had been shot in the buttocks, but 'no danger'.

> 1. The Revd George Buck (one of Dr Buck's sons), at present Rector of Ashbury, Devon; from 1875–82 to be Vicar of Arminghall, Norfolk; and from 1882 Rector of Belaugh. Dr Buck was now 76, but he did not retire for another three years. Because of rheumatism in the fingers he did not play the Organ in his latter years, this being done by his articled pupils; but he was a renowned trainer of organists and choristers.

Wednesday 9

At home the whole day with a cold – Henry Patteson came in about 9 to escort Buskins and young Aubrey to the Ball at the Boileaus at Ketteringham, where the Prince is to be.

Friday 11   Our wedding day
Not up till 10, waking with a sore throat – Present of a 'Blotter' from Frederica, and an envelope case from Ke, and an almanac from Buskins – wrote my acknowledgements to the two first – wrote also to Dr. Bunnett[1] my permission to him to inscribe an anthem to me.

> 1. Edward Bunnett, Mus. Doc., F.R.C.O.: Pupil and assistant of Dr Buck; brilliant musical career; Chorister and Organist at Concerts in St Andrew's Hall; when former, sang with Jenny Lind; from 1880, Organist of St Peter Mancroft.

••

On Saturday, December 12, Goulburn went to Peterborough to preach in the Cathedral on Sunday evening. On Monday, he travelled from Peterborough to London; and on Tuesday (15) returned to Norwich.
••

Sunday 13   Advent 3   At Peterboro'
Rose at 8 – went w. the Dean after Bkfst. to H.P.G.'s, to consult him as to how the Peterboro' Chapter do their repairs of the South Side – Members of the Chapter lend; or they borrow of the Bankers – Late for Morning Church – I went afterwards to the Palace, & had luncheon there; and afterwards a long interesting walk with the Bishop.

Wednesday 16   H.R.H. distributes Prizes at the G. School
Snow & frost all day – After Church the 3 Canons & Bensly came to the Deanery, and I gave them (or rather read) an account of my interview w. Gates and Pringle[1], and told them I shd. think about offering them a loan of the £5000 necessary – Then 1st. Heaviside, and then Nevill and I, hastened off to the Prizegiving at the Grammar School – the Bishop, Mayor, Sheriff, Heaviside, Mr. Bailey of Stoke holy X, Colman, Sewell Read, myself and one or two others met in the Jessopp's drawing room – Col. Hale also there – H.R.H. not puncutal – everything went off well; the Concert pretty and not too short; Heaviside's[2] speech, in wh. he asked the Prince to preside; then the Prince's speech (simple, fluent, manly & straightforward); then the giving of the Prizes (Ralphey Nevill got one); then the luncheon – I sat between Dr. Jessopp and Mr. Cooke, the County Court Judge – came home & answered my letters.

> 1. Officials of the Ecclesiastical Commissioners Office.
> 2. Chairman of the Governors 1873–90.

December 1874

Friday 18
Preached in the Cathedral my 3d and last Adventure Lecture on 'Jewish Sects in the time of J. the Baptist' – the Bp. was there and his two sons (one of whom, Sydney[1], is to be ordained Priest on Sunday next).

> 1. Apart from his Diaconal year, Sidney (1849–1926) spent 52 years of his ministry in the Diocese of Norwich, during which he was Vicar of St Peter Mancroft, an Hon Canon, Rural Dean of Norwich, Archdeacon of Norfolk, and Chaplain to the Norfolk and Norwich Hospital.

Sunday 20   Advent 4
At home all day, and very depressed & uncomfortable – Sidney Pelham was this day ordained Priest, John Pelham[1], his brother, joining in laying of hands – Mr. Crompton & Two other very elderly men were ordained Deacons – Medley came at about 1 to give me and June the H.C.

> 1. This is a mistake. The Bishop had only three sons. Henry was a distinguished Academic at Oxford, three years older than Sidney (but never ordained). Herbert, the youngest, was not ordained until 1878, and, in 1881, was killed in a mountain accident in Switzerland. The Revd John B. Pelham, ordained three years ago, was, at this time, Curate of St Peter, Lowestoft, and, almost certainly, a cousin.

Monday 21   St. Thomas
Very uncomfortable all day – Saw Heaviside & afterwards Nisbet – The latter is going to dine with the Prince at the Mayor's, & with the Bishop & Nevill – The Ventriloquist came at 8 o'clock – Tompson & Bulmer came to dinner, also Alice Nevill & the little Nevills, & the little Wallaces – The Ventriloquist[1] performed, but I did not feel up to seeing him or his company.

> 1. The Ventriloquist's fee was £1.

Tuesday 22
Much better this morning – Rose at 8 – Muriel called – Buskins is laid up as well as myself – Ju is also rather sore-throaty – I occupied myself in conning over the Life of Bishop Andrewes, and in making alterations (aided by Ju) in the 'Various Rules & Uses' for 1875.

Wednesday 23
Wrote a long letter to Mr. Gibbs, laying the state of our West front before him – I received a long & able letter from the Master, giving his view of the West front question – This I passed on to the Canons.

December 1874

Thursday 24
Rose at 8 a.m. and came down to Bkfst. for the 1st. time – Buskins in bed still – Saw and paid the heads of all departments of the Establishmt. their 7s. for Xmas Dinner – among others, saw Chapman, whose wife, he tells me, has been ill with rheumatic fever for 12 months – wrote to the Master about the fitness of Mr. Wilson (lately presented to Topcroft) for St. Stephen's – walked for exercise in the Library for ¾ths. of an hour.

Friday 25   **CHRISTMAS DAY**
Rose at ½p.6; went to Church at 8; a procesional before the Service – we passed thro' the whole length of the Choir into the Vestry – Medley celebrated, I assisted, and spoke upon John 1, 4 – Jessopp was there and make [*made*] such an awkward movement in taking the Cup that the wine was spilled over my hand – The Boys staid thro' the whole & sang the Sanctus and Gloria in excelsis – Church again at 10.30 – The Bp. preached on the two last verses of the <u>Benedictus</u> – In the afternoon I took a walk round the garden for an hour – did not go to Church, but read the afternoon Service with Ju at home, and a Sermon of Burgon's. A dreadful account in the 'Morning Post' of the accident on the G.W.R. Rail, near Woodstock Road Station at Hampton Gay, whereby 31 lives were lost, among others that of a Rev. Mr. Hook (? a son of the Dean of Chichester's) – Medley & a few choristers came with Chinese lanterns and banners and sung carols in the yard, under Buskin's window – then they had mincepie & elder wine, and then came into the drawing room, and sang 'King Wenceslaus' – Did not go till 9.35 – rather a dreary Christmas.

Saturday 26   **St. Stephen**
Bank holiday – Shops closed[1] – Indoors all day – Did not dress till 2 o'clock – [*He wrote nine letters*] – Nisbet called & was very kind.

    1. Under the Bank Holiday Act of 1871.

Sunday 27   **St. John**
Snow on the ground – A good deal has fallen during the day – Went to Church at 11 and 3.30 – (Ju went to 8 a.m. and 11) – The Bishop preached in the morning – I had a walk about ½p.1–3 p.m. in the (gas-lit) Library, and in a cloak till I got warm – I have written a good piece of a Sermonette for New Year's eve, and have read Foster's Sermon on 'Better is the end of a thing than the beginning', and think of speaking to the Servants on the same

subject this evening – Buskins got up after Morning Church – I wrote to Rev. James Wilson[1] of Town Barningham, offering to appoint him to St. Stephen's on Baldwin's resignation, & to Baldwin.

1. He accepted and was appointed in 1875.

Monday 28   Holy Innocents
Service at 8 – By the post came Dr. Reichel's acceptance of my invitation to him to preach 'Argumentative Discourses' – Service again at 10 – went in for a moment to see Heaviside, & saw his gas stove[1], and promised to lend him our invalid chair for Georgie, if I could find it – then a walk with Mr. Medley, to order a sleigh for him to go out to Drayton – then went w. him to enquire for Sir Saml.[3]; saw Lucy B; her father is worse – he longs to recover – Mr. Fenn has been there, & Mr. Bickersteth is now there – Sir S. expresses his trust in Christ, wh. he says he has had for many years – wrote to Dr. Reichel[2], promising to pray travelling expenses, etc. – Mr. Davies[4] called, and I promised to give him £25 of Mr. Gibbs £500, wh. I must get tomorrow.

1. Experimental Gas Cooking Stoves were exhibited as early as the 1820s, but rarely used in homes until the 1880s. Therefore Canon Heaviside's was an innovation.
2. The Revd Canon Reichel, D.D., was a Canon of St Patrick's Cathedral, Dublin.
3. Sir Samuel Bignold (1791–1875).
4. The Revd A. Davies, Vicar of St James', Norwich.

Tuesday 29
An interview with Mr. Tompson in Medley's presence, the result of which was that I agreed to continue him here, on condition of good conduct, for 10 years, wout. placing him on the foundation – Then walked to Gurney's Bank – then to Miss Bignold's – Sir Samuel rather better – gave her Herrick's 'Litany of the Holy Ghost' to read to him – then a walk on Newmarket & Unthank's Road – fell down on the latter, but not at all hurt.

Wednesday 30
After a very bad night rose at 8 – received a letter from Mr. Fergusson – at 11.15 the full Chapter met – we agreed to wait for Fergusson's report before making any further order about the West front – we had several other small matters to settle, specially about the repository of the hose, the site of Woodham Walter cottages, drainage of cloister, application for lease of Dr. Jessopp's

garden, etc. etc. – they had luncheon here, & then left us – then Bensly and I set to work, & drew out the Minutes for the Chapter Book, and wrote a letter of protest against the proposed augmentation of the Gas works, and a contract between Mr. Tompson & myself for 10 years – then Bensly deciphered for me certain words in Ed. I's patent for the erection of a bridge by the Prior & Convent.

Thursday 31
After a bad night rose at 8; Service at 10 – Afterwards walked up & down the Library in gas-light, to get exercise, and also used Mrs. Pellew's chamber horse – At 1.30 came Medley, Tompson and Bensly, and we signed in my study 3 copies of the agreement between Mr. Tompson and myself, one for Bensly to keep, one for Tompson himself, and one for the Precentor – then we dined together at 2 p.m. – afterwards I gave Medley the resolution of Chapter about the charge for copying our music – then had some examination with Bensly into the question of the bridge wh. Ed. I's Letters Patent authorised the Prior and Convent to build – went to Church at 7 – Bp. there and Nisbet & Nevill – I preached.

1881

JANUARY

Saturday 1 Circumcision
Went with Ju to H.C. at 8, where were Bp., Archdn., & self – spoke after the Nicene Creed – there may have been 25 or 30 commts. – wrote to Mr. Chamberlain who had sent me a plan for the possible route of the proposed railway[1].

> 1. The beginning of the saga of the Lynn and Fakenham Railway attempt to run the railway through the Close to link up City and Thorpe Stations.

Sunday 2
After luncheon a walk with Bartie[1] on the Castle Hill, talking of (1) Tenour [*Tenor*] from Edinburgh Cathl. offering himself to fill Minn's[2] place; (2) dismissal of Meers; (3) Boys' concert on Wednesday.

> 1. The Revd G.W. Barrett, Precentor since 1877.
> 2. Mr Henry Minns, Lay Clerk, committed suicide in the Cathedral on November 22, 1880.

Monday 3
Church at 11 – Bartie and I worked at the two new boards for the 'Uses of the Cathedral' & the 'Gradations of Choral Service' – then came the Choristers with their toy instruments and played under the guidance of Dr. G.

Tuesday 4
At Bkfst. arrived Mr. Gladstone's[1] resignation, wh. took my breath away – after conferring w. H. about it, before and after Mg. Service, went to Nevill, & got his signature to a testimonial for Dr. G. – He advised me to think of Stonex – then went to Gladstone himself; he complained of his house, but was much pleased with our testimonial – Bartie came at 1, & we decided at 1st. that he shd, go to Yarmouth to hear Stonex – then Ju and I drove to Lakenham, to see the baby's monument[2] – on our return Heaviside called, & then Nevill, to tell me that it wd. not do to make enquiries in Yarmouth about Stonex – then, with Bartie, drew out an advertisement for the 'Musical Times'.

> 1. After Dr Buck's resignation as Cathedral organist in 1877 at the age of 79, he was succeeded by Dr F.E. Gladstone.
> 2. Augusta's first child, Louisa Fanny, died soon after birth. She had married Gerard Thomas in 1880. The baby was buried in St Mark's Churchyard, Lakenham.

January 1881

• •
On Wednesday, January 5, the Goulburns left Norwich for London, where they remained until January 10, when they went on to Gt Tew Park, Oxfordshire, for the wedding of Julia's niece, Meanne Boulton. On January 12 they went on to the Rectory at Aynhoe until January 24. They then returned to London, and back to Norwich on January 25.
• •

Friday 7

After a bad night, rose at 8 – Read the acct. of the meeting of Parliat. yesterday – then walked to Club, whence a Cab to Liverpool Street, where found Nevill arrived – a very satisfactory interview with Messrs. Parkes, Curwood, Bayliss, etc.[1]; Ld. Claude H. not there – I called on the Dean of St Paul's – to Club, where had luncheon – then to Rivington's, whence sent books to (1) Abp. Cant. (2) Ayre (3) Dean of St Paul's – then to B.C.'s;[2] saw Frank and Francie; B.C. very energetic about Pelham's Dale[3], & his own red vestments.

  1. Officials of the Great Eastern Railway.
  2. See March 3, 1874 (Note 1).
  3. The Revd Thomas Pelham Dale (1821–92) was Rector of St Vedast's, Foster Lane, London. Protracted legal proceedings against him for ritualistic practices resulted in his being sent to Holloway Gaol in 1880.

Saturday 8

After Bkfst. went in Cab to Morgiana's; says it is nervous depression resulting from worry – prescribed infinitesimal dose of Calomel, etc. – then to little Stan's[1] w. whom I settled that he is to come to Norwich *en route* to Sandringham on Friday next; we talked of 'reconciliation' of Churches – wrote to Rickitt and to Heaviside about Stan's proposed visit to Norwich.

  1. A.P. Stanley, Dean of Westminster, died, six months later, of erysipelas. He was almost three years older than Goulburn. He had never fully recovered from the shock of his wife's death five years before. He and Goulburn had a high personal regard and affection for each other, although, theologically, they were poles apart. Stanley was small in stature, but with an attractive, liberal, generous, and active personality, and a considerable scholar, using all his gifts for the advancement of Christianity.

Tuesday 11   Meanne's[1] Wedding Day

Down at 8.15 to Bkfst., but found no one there – there was a running fire of Bkfst. up to 9.15 – received several applications of Candidates for Organistship; these I answered before the wedding, and sent them on to Bartie – The Cartwrights mustered strong; Lucy and Francis were Bridesmaids – The Wedding began at 11.15, Mr. Mitchell reading the Preface, I the effective part, the Dean taking it up after the 1st. benediction, and Mr. Campbell reading the last prayer & the 2nd. benedn. – I gave an address on the honour put by God on the ordinance of Marriage – afterwards, chatting with various members of the family till the grand Gunterian Banquet at 1.30 – I sat between Mrs. Boulton and Mary A.[2] – had to propose the Bride and Bridgegroom – all seemed to go off very well.

> 1. Meanne Boulton was the elder daughter of Matthew and Frances (nee Fanny Cartwright) Julia's full sister, who died in 1864 of erysipelas. Shortly after her death, Matthew Boulton married a German Governess, Pauline Gleissberg (d. 1911).
> 2. Mrs. Aubrey Cartwright (nee Fremantle), Julia's sister-in-law.

Wednesday 12
A budget of letters, some of them from Organists – I contrived to answer all except one – then read the papers, and listened to Matthew discoursing about Bismarck's raising up trouble for England by his agents both in Ireland and in the Transvaal – after luncheon Ju and I took our leave.

Thursday 13 [At Aynhoe]
Soon after Bkfst. came a man from the G.E.R. Company[1], with the memorial against the proposed new line for me to sign – I signed it, and gave him a Consent Paper for the seal of the Church to be affixed – (Ju is writing invitations to Judges' dinner) – after luncheon Hen-pen[2] and I walked to Newbottle, where at Noble's house we exchanged shoes and stockings – then went to the play, 'My dress boots' and 'Husbands to Order' – Mr. Campbell, Eddie, Ursie, Marion, all acted beautifully; it was really very pretty to see Marion as Mme. Philippeau – Little Lili[3] prompted – afterwards saw great Lili[3] and Buckley, who went with me on the stage – we got home about 7 – there is but a poor acct. of the wedding in the Banbury Guardian, probably from some misunderstanding.

> 1. Throughout the contest with the Lynn and Fakenham Railway, Goulburn had the support of the Great Eastern Railway.
> 2. 'Hen-pen' = Henry Cartwright (1811–91); Colonel in the Grenadier Guards; M.P. for Sount Northants 1858–68; and a J.P.; one of Julia's full brothers. Married Jane Holbech, who had died in 1877.
> 3. 'Great Lili' = Lady Cartwright. 'Little Lili' = her grandchild, Elizabeth, second daughter of her second son, Thomas Leslie-Melville-Cartwright. Little Lili would be 21 at this time.

Tuesday 18 [At Aynhoe]

Incessant snow all day – could not get out, so devoted the day to finishing my paper for the 26th., wh. I did in the rough – Took exercise in the passage, in gt. coat & muffler.

Saturday 22

As cold as ever – rapid walk round garden at noon reading <u>myself</u> on Coll. for 3d. aft. Epiph. – the Dean[1] drove with Mr. Hibbert to Newbottle, to skate – after luncheon, I walked down to the Station, and saw the signal-man in his office – Between Goring and Reading there is only one line, wh. detains the trains – Read some of Tennyson's[2] new vol. to Julia – letters came in at 4, forwarded from Crowson's.

> 1. 'The Dean' = The Revd Freddie Cartwright, Rector of Aynhoe.
> 2. Alfred, Lord Tennyson (1809–92). Possibly 'Ballads and Other Poems' (1880).

Sunday 23   Last Day at Aynhoe

Same weather as heretofore – In the morning I made notes for a Sermon on the weather ("He giveth snow like wool", etc. in Ps. 147, 16 et seq.)

Monday 24

We left Aynhoe at 10, and got to the Station ½ an hour too early – when the train came from Kgs. Sutton, we all got into the same carriage with Tom & Willie Willes[1] – Up to Oxford, there were some stoppages, but after leaving Oxford, all went pretty well; we were only an hour late – went 1st. (in a two horse brougham wh. Willie had telegraphed for) to Morgan's – he prescribed for us, & gave us some whisky toddy – then to Hemingways, and thence here (to Crowson's) – Tom Cartwright dined with us, & was very pleasant.

> 1. Sophia (Sophie) Cartwright (1808–96); Julia's step-sister; married (1831) William Willes of Astrop House, Northants, who died in 1865. They had two sons, Tom and Willie.

Tuesday 25   Conversion of St. Paul

At 11.55 left London for Norwich, where we arrived in tolerable time, notwithstanding the snow – found the most intense cold, & a bundle of letters, wh. it took me all the afternoon & evening to answer, many of them about Organists – Far colder than in London.

Wednesday 26 Meeting of Hon. Cans. at Palace
Colder than ever this morning, a suffering degree of cold – in the morning Bartie called about the Organists – after luncheon Lee Warner called – at 4 I went to Church – Present: Hon. Cans. Johnson, Clark, Copeman, Norgate, Garratt (to whom I was introduced at the Palace), Groome, Hinds Howell, etc. – few comparatively – At 5 was the meeting at wh. spoke the Bp. (admirably), Lee Warner, Norgate, Groome, Nevill, Heaviside (admirably)[1] – I came home in a fly at 7 o'clock.

> 1. The subject under discussion was: "To consider whether any practical measures should be adopted to meet the infedility and indifference to religion which are said to be prevalent".

Friday 28
The welcome tidings appeared in the Daily Press that the promoters of the new line having failed to appear before the 'Examiner in proof of Standing Orders', the project has collapsed.

Monday 31
Heaviside and I began our draft of the New Statues at 11, but did not get to the end of those wh. concern the Dean – H. had luncheon here, then I walked in k. garden more than an hour, reading Times – wrote to several persons who had recommended Organists, especially to Agnes and Rev. H.T. Griffith of Felmingham, who has recommended Dr. Horace Hill.

FEBRUARY

Tuesday 1
Rose at 6.15, and worked at Statutes[1] till 7.30 – Heaviside came at 10, and we worked in the Drawing room till 1 – then we went to Smith's house (late Minn's) with Brown and Thomson, to see what repairs were required – we ordered £20 of substantial repairs – went to Church at 5 (with Nevill & Moore) – Traxton imprisoned in W.C. made such a noise to get out again as greatly disturbed us – at last Alden released him – In the evening read the Times, & went on with the Statutes.

> 1. In 1879 a new Cathedral Commission was appointed which led to requests being made to Deans and Chapters about what changes should be made to their Statutes.

February 1881   211

Wednesday 2   Purification of B.V. Mary
After a very bad night, did not rise till 7.30 – Ju went to H.C. – At 10 p.m. [a.m.] came Heaviside & we worked at Statutes till nearly luncheon time – Telegram from the Dean, announcing Fairfax's death – at 4 went in carriage w. Heaviside & Nevill to Judges' Lodgings. At 7.30 came Mr. Justice Lindley, Mr. Justice Hawkins & Mr. Harcourt (son of Sir W. Vernon H.). [*There followed a dinner party of 20, including the Mayor*]².

> 1. Major Fairfax Cartwright, former M.P. of S. Northants, aged 58.
> 2. The Mayor was Mr Samuel Grimmer, a Wine and Spirit Merchant.

Saturday 5
Drafted one or two Statues by myself – went to the Bp. at 11 and talked with him over the Preaching Rota, and also about the precedence of the Chancellor – at noon went in fly to the Hospital, where there was a full meeting with Ld. Leicester[1] in the Chair, and the Bp. near him – Heaviside[2] made an able & lucid exposition of the matter in hand – Mr. Daines opposed, but Mr. Colman, Gurney Buxton, and Dr. Bateman were favourable – The Bp. proposed, & I seconded, a vote of thanks to the unknown donor who will leave £10,000 (thro' Cadge)[3] at the death of himself and his wife, to replace £10,000 now to be withdrawn from the endowment fund to add to the Builg. Fund.

> 1. The 2nd Earl of Leicester, in his capacity as Lord Lieutenant, became President of the Norfolk and Norwich Hositial in 1846 and held the position until 1909. He supported the Hospital generously and his benefactions and subscriptions amounted to over £50,000.
> 2. Canon Heaviside was Chairman of the Norfolk and Norwich Hospital's Board of Management.
> 3. William Cadge (1822–1903) is commemorated by a window in the North Transept of Norwich Cathedral. He was the leading Surgeon of his day in East Anglia. The window was unveiled by the President of the Royal College of Surgeons, and the ceremony attended by Surgeons from twenty countries. It transpired that Cadge was, himself, the donor of the £10,000.

Monday 7   Norwich thro' London to Aynhoe
Snow was falling lightly (but not lying deep) when I left Norwich at 7.30 with one silent man in the carriage – but on my getting to Aynhoe, it lies ½ a foot deep – read the Daily Press, Times & Daily Telegraph, all with accounts of Thos. Carlyle², who died on Saturday, & of Stanley's Sermon about him yesterday – Got to Club at 11.40 – wrote to Ju and had luncheon – At I left London; at Oxford Robert, who had been by 3rd. Class joined me, & came up in my fly – Fairfax¹ is to be buried in his own <u>new</u> family vault – Willie & his two sons and Robert are here tonight.

1. Fairfax Cartwright (1823–81) was the son of General William Cartwright (1797–1873), who was the second son of William Ralph, Julia's father, by his first wife.
2. Thomas Carlyle (1795–1881), Essayist and Historian.

Tuesday 8   Fairfax's Funeral
Bkfst. w. Fred, Willie, Tommie & Fairfax[1] at 9, during which the body arrived and was placed in the hall – all the morning I spent in writing Sermonette and drafting Statutes, till Aubrey came up to see me in my room & talk about Matthew's appointt. of £5000 of Tutsie's[2] money to Meanne – and then came Hen-pen – At 1.30 was the Funeral wh. (on the representation of Howchin, his servant) took place in the General's vault, not in F's new vault – I read the whole Service – Davenport Bromley, Alderman Ellis, two Mr. Barringtons, two of the Pennants were there, besides almost all the family, w. the exception of Mattathias – in the afternoon walked up & down the garden with the Dean & Fairfax.

1. This Fairfax was Sir Fairfax Cartwright, son of Willie, grandson of Lili. (Died 1928)
2. I think Tutsie must be Fanny, Matthew Boulton's first wife, and mother of Meanne, who died in 1864.

Tuesday 15   [Norwich]
After Mg. Service (with Nevill and Bartie) looked over testimonials of Organists with Bartie, & boiled them down to 12 – called upon Mrs. Heaviside & found Ju there; she showed us all her Valentines – Ju and I hope to read the 12 selected testimonials tonight.

Wednesday 16
Rose at 6.30 and looked over Organists' testimonials before Bkfst. – at Church Nevill and Bartie – then looked over testimonials with Bartie till luncheon; interrupted by Mr. Taylor of Heigham, who came to beg for his new infant School – I promised £5 – in th Evening read 'the Times', and looked over with Auntie the testimonials of Messrs. Bishop & Gaffe.

Thursday 17
After Church a Chapter at Bensly's room – Bartie at luncheon – afterwards we settled to send for (1) Selby of London (2) Caldicott of Worcester (3) Atkinson of Bradford – then we went to Symonds, to place the testimonls. of the 7 best men in his hand – signed 30 Bellringers' Certificates[1].

Dean Goulburn in horse-drawn carriage. Photo by George W. Newman Studio.

Dean Goulburn. Photo by G. C. Bryan Gipps, about 1890-5.

Dean Goulburn's retirement house at Tunbridge Wells.
Photo by G. C. Bryan Gipps, Burwash.

1. The Norwich Diocesan Association of Ringers was established in 1877 "to promote Change-ringing and Belfry Reform", with Goulburn as President, the three Archdeacons as Vice-Presidents, together with six Lay People, including two M.P.s.

Saturday 19   First MAIDEN'S BEE[1] of the Season
After Mg. Church got Nevill & Bartie to witness the execution of a Pr. of Attorney in the vestry about the £5000 appointed by Matta to Meanne – the 3 Pins and Mamie came to luncheon – At 3 Church with Nevill & Moore – Afterwards the first Maid's Bee of the season – Bensly came to announce his having purchased land at Middleton for us yesterday adjoining Mr, Gowing's farm, for £2000, on wh. he had paid deposit of £200.

1. Bee = Social gathering for a specific purpose which will benefit an individual or group. Occasionally, Goulburn would come to read to them as they worked.

Tuesday 22
Soon after luncheon Bp. called – he talked about Mr. Barlee, about Geo Brodrick, and about my dropping the Lent Lectures – then I went to the Hospital where Bugg had just been appointed – Chicken Pattie spoke to me of a copy he had got of Sir T. Browne's[2] book about Norwich – Soon after came Mr. Coldicote[1], with whom I had some talk before 2d Church – shortly after our return came Mr. Selby[1] – I sent him & Mr. Caldicote to dine w. Precentor, & go afterwards to Mr. Harcourt's concert.

1. Organist candidates.
2. Sir Thomas Browne (1605–82): famous Physician and Author; settled in Norwich 1637.

Wednesday 23
After Bkfst. at wh. were Messrs. Selby & Caldicott[1], came Mr. Atkinson, and the whole of the day has been devoted to their trial + the 2 Church Services – we think the last plays with much the greatest feeling; a piece of Mozart's he rendered exquisitely – I am much perplexed – the Pin and Moore, with Mrs. B. & Mrs. M., and Mrs. Symonds & Em'ly were all there – Bensly came in to luncheon – Mr. Selby left us by the 3 p.m. train – Mrs. as well as Mr. Caldicott is to be our guest tonight – The Barties & the Pins (5 in all) dine here; with the two men & ourselves 9.

1. Goulburn paid travel expenses totalling £4. 1. 6 to Selby and Caldicott.

Thursday 24   St. Matthias

Atkinson[1] & Mr. & Mrs. Caldicott at Bkfst. – took leave of them before Mg. Church; of Caldicott in the vestry – drove with Symonds to the turn of Eaton Road, & walked back by St. Giles's Road – Bartie came to luncheon, and afterwards we settled to summon one other candidate, Birch – then Ju and I took Georgie, Alice, & Margie Nevill to the circus – It has fallen off, having a ballet, and exposing the equestrienne to danger by making her jump thro' ignited hoops – am going to have a quiet evening with my Ju – we think of settling something to be done to the Cathedral.

> 1. Goulburn paid travel expenses to Atkinson of £2. 10. Admission to the Circus for two adults and the three children was 12s.

Friday 25

After Mg. Church a Chapter at Bensly's Office about [*a variety of business*] ... (5) I told the Canons all about the 3 selected Organists – A man called Crosske[1] came to beg, to whom I gave something at Bensly's instance.

> 1. He gave Crosske 10s.

Saturday 26

Bartie called, & we talked about slippers for the boys in Church – at 2.40 I went to Bensly's Office, and Mr. Frere[1] took the oaths there, & was installed after the 1st. lesson – a Bee, at wh. I read the 2d Act of Lear – at 7.30 we went to the Palace, and met Mr. & Mrs. Constantine Frere at dinner – a very pleasant evening with them and the Bishop.

> 1. The Revd Constantine Frere had been Rector of Finningham, Stowmarket, since 1847; it was a family Living; he was being installed as an Hon. Canon.

Sunday 27   Quinguagesima

At 11 o'clock Mr. Frere read the Service slowly & not altogether accurately – he then preached ... a Sermon wh. seemed to be very good, but I could not hear it and to follow the argument – I got a letter from the Master intimating darkly something wh. mt. be said agst. Atkinson, & wrote for more information – Symonds came in afterwards & talked about the subject of the Master's letter.

Monday 28

Constant snowstorms throughout the day – little Em'ly came into say Good-bye to me – news in the Times of our defeat in the Transvaal, and of Sir George Colley[1] having been killed – Bartie came to luncheon bringing Mr. Birch the new candidate – also the Pin came – the Pin stayed for the 1st. part of Birch's trial, & expressed himself satisfied – afterwards Birch wrote an answer in my study to Bartie's question – he returned by the 5 o'clock train – we dined at ½p.6 for the sake of the servants, who are going to Ada's concert for the 'Jenny Lind'.

> 1. Major-General Sir George Colley was Governor of Natal from 1880; was defeated and killed by the Boers at Majuba Hill on Feb. 26, in the 1st Boer War.

MARCH

Tuesday 1

Hard frost, bright day – after Mg. Service Auntie & I walked to Lakenham where we met Colvin[1], and inspected our Baby's grave – after luncheon prepared some notes & a Sermon for the morrow, and then wrote to Mr. Maguinness about Atkinson – I got a satisfactory letter about him from the Master this morning.

> 1. Vicar of St Mark's, Lakenham 1873–85.

Friday 4

Rose at 6.30, after the curious explosion of an empty tumbler in the night-time – Read Alford's G.T.[1] – After Morning Ch. walked in the house, reading last night's debate on Candahar[2] in the Lords, and Mr. Dillon's insufferable advocacy of murder & civil war in the H. of C.[3] – Worked at Statutes with Heaviside from 2 to 4.30, Bensly coming in for a few minutes to assist us – Heaviside & I worked in the dg. room, a Matron's Bee being assembled in the Library – Haircutter is coming – Corrected & revised some of the Stat. in the Evening.

> 1. Henry Alford (1810–71) was Goulburn's predecessor at Quebec Chapel. His most important work was an edition of the Greek New Testament during the period 1849–61, in which he united "freshness of treatment with wide learning". He became Dean of Canterbury 1857–71.
> 2. In the 2nd Afghan War, Afghan Forces attacked British troops at Maiwand on July 27, 1880, forcing them to retire to Kandahar. On August 9, 1880, Lord Roberts (in Kabul) with 10,000 picked men, decided to relieve Kandahar and began a march of 318 miles, reaching Kandahar on August 31, and defeating the Afghan forces next day. Now, in 1881, should British Forces evacuate Kandahar? By April 27, 1881, British troops were withdrawn from Afghanistan.

3. At the General Election of April 1880, the Liberals, under Gladstone, had an overall majority of 54; Irish M.P.s numbered 61. In Ireland, the harvest of 1879 had been the worst since the Great Famine; in 1880 there were 2590 agrarian outrages; and between 1874 and 1881, some 10,000 evictions. Irish M.P.s showed their feelings about the situation by obstructing the business of the House of Commons on January 31, 1881, for 41 continuous hours (i.e. until Feb. 2). On March 2, Habeas Corpus Act was suspended in Ireland.

••

From Saturday, March 5, until Tuesday, March 8, the Goulburns were in Peterborough, staying with Canon and Mrs Marsham Argles, so that he could fulfill his engagement to preach in the Cathedral on the Sunday evening.

••

Wednesday 9

Heaviside came at 2.30 & we went on with the Statutes till 4.30 – poor H. much cast down about Georgie[1] – Pom[2] arrived today at 3.50 – Wrote to Hutchinson of Rugby, & to Mr. Capes[3] sending him P.O. order for his architectural book on the Churches of London.

1. His son, still suffering from a shooting accident in early December.
2. Mary Julia Thomas (1846–1914), Goulburn's Cousin on his mother's side.
3. William Wolfe Capes (1834–1914): Oxford University Reader in Ancient History 1870–87; Fellow & Tutor of Hertford College 1876–86; Canon of Hereford 1903–14. Postal Order was for 13s.

Thursday 10

Creeny came for my subsn. to Palestine Exploran. Fund[1] – he had luncheon with us – wrote to (1) Little B. thanking for clock sent by her & Gerard – Am hoping to write this evening some letters settling the organistship, wh. I have determined to give to Atkinson – Pom wrote for me to Birch, Selby and Atkinson – I wrote to Caldicott with my own hand.

1. Fund established in London in 1865 to help the restoring of Palestine to the Jews.

Friday 11

Church at 5 with Nevill, Bartie, Moore – then I saw the 5 uncassocked Lay Clerks, and offered to give them surplices for Easter; but Burton objected on the ground of warmth, and Meers on the ground of the surplice not sitting well; so I withdrew my offer.

Saturday 12

Ju and Pom had luncheon early at 1, and afterwards went to the G.F.S.[1] meeting at the Palace – Old Cox came in to say that he & Thouless were quite willing & desirous to have cassocks – wrote to Frowde for my copies of the Revision of New Testament[2].

1. The Girls Friendly Society, founded in 1875, "to bind together in one Society, ladies as Associates, and Working Girls and Young Women as Members, for mutual help (religious and secular), for sympathy and prayer".
2. The New Testament section of the Revised Version of the Bible, initiated by the Canterbury Convocation in 1870, was published this year. Henry Frowde (1841–1927) was Manager of the London Office of the Oxford University Press 1874–1913.

Monday 14

Rose at 6.30, & began my work at the Statutes, discriminating the sources of them by difft. colours, wh. I carried on till luncheon, & got very tired of it – this morning news arrived of the brutal assassination of the Czar[1].

1. Czar Alexander II (1818–81), known as 'the Liberator', was assassinated in St Petersburgh by a bomb thrown at him by an anarchist. He had brought about the Emancipation of the Serfs in 1861; reformed legal and administrative systems; and built roads and schools. His only daughter, the Grand Duchess Marie, had married the second son of Queen Victoria in 1874.

Saturday 19

Rose at 6.30, and read Shakspere to myself – after Mg. Church went to the garden and read Johnson's Shakspere and the Times – on my return Captain Peckham called & asked permission to bring his squadrom to the Cathl. – then came Hinds Howell & Maimie, who had luncheon here – H.H. told me of Woolcombe's having died worth £13,000, and also of his having proposed to Mrs. Wall – read the 4th. Act of Lear to a large Bee – wrote to (1) the Bishop about Mr. Callis's appointment as Hospital Chaplain.[1]

1. In spite of the large number of Clergy (and the Bishop as ex-officio a Vice-President) on the Board of Management (and Committees), there was no officially-paid Chaplain from its foundation (1771) and throughout the 19th Century. In 1840 and 1888 attempts to appoint a salaried Chaplain failed. In 1873 the "Canons in residence and others of the clergy resident in or near Norwich were requested to perform religious duty in the hospital in rotation". And, of course, patients' own clergy were free to visit. Now, the Revd J. Callis, Rector of Holy Trinity, Heigham is appointed as a part-time Chaplain (which he held for 4 years), not paid by the Hospital, but possibly receiving some remuneration from the Chapel Maintenance Fund.

Friday 25   Annunciation of B.V. Mary

H.C. with Nevill, Bulmer, Bartie at 8, I celebrating: about 12 Commts. – being a Festival of Christ, we had singing – Went again at 11 – afterwards a Chapter at Bensly's Office – we reduced Allen's rent by £70 for the remainder of his lease, and agreed that I or Nevill should go to Frostenden[1] on Thursday next & consult Cap. Vincent about Gilbert & Gray – agreed to thank G.E.R.[2] for their helping us to exclude a railway from the Close – I walked in k. garden reading the Parliamentary Summary & leaders of 'Times'.

1. Four miles north of Southwold, Suffolk.
2. Great Eastern Railway.

APRIL

Friday 1
After the worst of nights, rose not till 7.15 – a Chapter in Bensly's Office, at wh. we received Nevill's report of Gilbert & Gray's farms at Frostenden; and as it appeared, we can keep them both by considerable reductions; such reductions were provisionally agreed to – then we adjourned to Dr. Buck's[1] house to survey dilapidations, & order repairs – Bensly at luncheon – Pom and I drove out, returning by Colney & Earlham Rd., I reading to her (until I fell *fast* asleep) Lord Cairn's speech last night on the peace with the Boers[2] – I walked the last mile or two – then went to Dimmock's to look out engravings for Pom to choose from.

1. Dr Buck had died in August 1879.
2. On April 5, the British recognised an independent Boer Republic of the Transvaal, under the Presidency of Kruger.

Monday 4
Bensly came to luncheon to take leave of Pom – the two maids[1] were baptized this afternoon at 3 in St. Luke's Chapel, Robbins, Rickett, Rose acting as Sponsors.

1. For some weeks, Goulburn had been preparing two of his maids, Laura and Lucy, for Baptism; the three Sponsors were also his servants.

Tuesday 5
Rose at 5.30 and went to London with 'Pom' – Parted from her at St. Pancras – then to Chirop., who operated; then to Graves's, where bought Lionardo's Head of Christ for Lou[1] – went to Club and wrote to Lou – then luncheon – then dressed there for Levee, & went there in Cab – saw no one whom I knew – got out about 3 – went to Meanne, whom I saw – then to Cousin MAC's, whom I found surrounded with 'fashionables'; all took flight when I appeared – sat about an hour with MAC, & then went to St. Pancras for 5 p.m. train – in the same carriage with Hay Gurney, who, when I had heartburn owing to taking tea at Ely, gave me 3 charcoal tablets in a glass of Mansavilla – found Ju all right.

1. His Cousin, Louisa Thomas (nee Goldsmid – de Visme), with whose family he had lived, as a small boy, after his mother's death, and also later. This cousin was eight years older, and lived to be over 100.

For the next nine days (until Good Friday) Goulburn is ill, confined to house for the first six days, until April 13, when he went out in the carriage with Julia, and took a short walk.

Friday 15   GOOD FRIDAY
Read Prayers with Auntie at 11 – At 5 went to Church, & preached for nearly an hour (!) on the 'Goodness and Severity of God', a Sermon extracted from my Vol. of 'Occasional Sermons' – Very busy correcting my 'Collects' for new Edn. which Rivington writes is called for.

Sunday 17   EASTER SUNDAY
After a night of great pain & sickness went to the 8 a.m. (Choral) H.C. with Bartie – 119 commts. – Offert. Colln. about £4. 9 – we were not out till 9.45 a.m. – went again at 11 to Ch. and enjoyed the Service much – the Bishop preached on the vision of the glorified Saviour in Rev. 1; a short, & good Sermon, but no very great reference to the day – At 6, Ju and I had a sort of supper – I tried to read to her Dean Law's account of Bp. Ryder, but I fell asleep – I am feeling dreadfully weary, and hope I may have a better night.

Monday 18
A better night – went to Church at 10 – at ¼p.11 Ju and I and Heaviside, went to the Inauguration of Fisheries Exhibition[1]; waited long for the Royal party – talk with John Gunn about luminous weathercocks, and with Mrs. Henry Birkbeck – after the opening, we drove back and picked up Mrs. Heaviside – then to the Mayor's Dejeuner – talked with Robt. Fellowes, Col. Boileau, Dr. Duckett[2] – speeches from the Mayor, the Prince, Ed. Birkbeck, & Pr. Leopold[3] – very much chilled by standing outside.

> 1. The National Fisheries Exhibition, at the Volunteers Drill Hall (on a corner of Chapel Field Gardens), ran from April 18 to May 7. The Prince and Princess of Wales, and Prince Leopold, were in a procession of carriages from Thorpe Station, escorted by a detachment of the 3rd Hussars to the Exhibition. The party then drove to St Andrew's Hall for lunch with the Mayor (S. Grimmer, Esq.). The Exhibition was visited by 70,000 people. One of the Prizes (£10) was given by the Sheriff, Dr (later Sir Peter) Eade for the best exhibit of 'Dress for a Lifeboat Crew'.
> 2. The Revd Canon Duckett was Priest of St John's Roman Catholic Chapel in the Maddermarket, an eloquent preacher who attracted packed congregations on a Sunday evening.
> 3. The Prince's youngest brother, who died in 1884 at the age of 31.

Tuesday 19

Rose at 6.30 after a night of pain – Bartie came in with Mrs. B. to luncheon at 1.30 – I saw him about several little matters: layclerks' capooks and caps, and <u>a holiday for the Boys</u> one afternoon a week – Eddie Wells, & Do-do, Margie, Henry, Helen Nevill came into a feast of Innocents at 5 p.m.

• •

The Goulburns were absent from Norwich from April 20 to May 21: three nights in London; 11 nights at Aynhoe; three nights in Brighton; three nights in Chichester; then a further 11 nights at their Brighton house, and back to Norwich.

• •

Wednesday 20

Rose after a very bad night at ½p.5 – at 7.30 left Norwich for London with Ju and Rose – took Ju to Crowsons – then to Kempe's[1], he had just returned from the country after being laid by 3 months with <u>neuralgia</u> – met Holford Risley[2] – then to Crowson's, where I went by mistake into Lady Antrim's room at 14, instead of ours at 12.

> 1. Prebendary J.E. Kempe was Rector of St James', Piccadilly 1853–95, and Rural Dean 1855–95.
> 2. Father of Wm. Cotton Risley who had been Goulburn's Curate at St John's, Paddington, and then Curate of St Michael's, Paddington, 1867–76.

Saturday 23

After a very bad night, rose at ½p.7 – Went to Morgiana after Bkfst. who advised me to leave off the milk – called at Hemingway's to get the prescription made up – at 12.30 we set off for Paddington – Left town at 1 – tried to read the Spectator, but was attacked by a bad stitch in the stomach, for wh. Ju got me some brandy at Reading – we had to turn out & wait a quarter of an hour at Oxford – got to Aynhoe about 4 – found the Dean at home, just returned from Banbury – He showed us a great many treasures and curiosities, wh. Fairfax had brought home from Greece – He has had the door leading from his Study into the dining room permanently closed and the space is made into a cupboard with shelves.

Thursday 28 [At Aynhoe]

Pondered over a Sermon for the Bp's day of Humiliation[1] – read the debate of last night about Bradlaugh[2], & Jellett on the 'Efficacy of Prayer' – After luncheon, walked to Souldern & back reading the debate in the York Convocation on the Bp. of Manchester's motion to expunge the Ornament's Rubric[3] – Lili arrived today & dined with us.

> 1. On April 21, the Bishop of Norwich had sent a letter to all Clergy in the Diocese calling for a Day of Humiliation on May 23 (or as close to it as possible) in penitence for the spiritual sickness of the Nation, and the failure of the Church to rise to its opportunities.
> 2. Charles Bradlaugh (1833–91) was a freethinker and radical politician. In 1880 he was elected Liberal M.P. for Northampton, but was not allowed to take his seat until 1886 because, as an atheist he claimed the right to affirm instead of taking the oath.
> 3. Ornaments Rubric: The name for the ruling, inserted in the 1559 Book of Common Prayer, that the ornaments of the Church, and of the Ministers, should be those in use "by the authority of Parliament in the second year of the reign of King Edward VI". This was re-enacted in the 1662 BCP.

Friday 29   [At Aynhoe]
Wrote a letter to Bartie about the terms with Atkinson, and about the day of humiliation, before Bkfst. – After luncheon walked to Newbottle across the fields – saw Frances, little Lili, & Ursie[1] – Marion had gone to join her parents in London – looked on while the Dean, Cap. Unthank, Frances, Ursie, & Miss Mountstephen played lawn tennis – then walked back again – there dined here Mr. & Mrs. Griffith of Croughton, Mr. Hibbert, & Buckley who is in the house – with Lili, Ju, the Dean & myself 8 in all.

> 1. Little Lili (Elizabeth) 22, Marion 20, Frances 19, and Ursie (Ursula) c.18, are all the children of Lili's (Lady Cartwright's) second son, Thomas.

MAY

Wednesday 4   [Aynhoe to Brighton]
Left Aynhoe w. the Dean at 7.30 a.m. – on getting to London, went with Ju to Morgiana's; after waiting saw him & got a prescription out of him – then to Holamby's about stockings; then to Bearnard[1], where I found Ju – then to Rivington's, who will only publish Pamphlets at the author's cost – took our tickets for West Brighton.

> 1. Chiropodist.

Saturday 7   Brighton to Chichester
In the morning came from Gussie <u>the sad tidings of Melia's</u>[1] <u>death</u> – forthwith wrote to Lou – wrote also, before leaving Brighton, to (1) Lady C. Kerrison about Service for G.F.S. (2) Herbert Jones, about Humiliation Service (3) Dean of Salisbury about rules for organist – Left Brighton at 11.30 – got to Chichester about 1.

> 1. See June 21, 1873 (Note 1). She was buried in the Cemetery at Homburg.

Tuesday 17   [*At Brighton*]
Tidings of Burglary in the Close, & of the Master losing £10, & the frames of some pictures – wrote to : (3) A.H. Goose (later in the day) for copies of Humiliation Service – wrote on at my Sermon for humiliation Day till luncheon – after luncheon went to Hedges & Butler & paid our wine bill – bought a photograph of the Revisers, and looked over the Revision[1] in Treacher's Shop; then wrote 2 letters in his reading room, and looked over the papers – Heavy rain; we expect Gerard[2] every moment – He arrived, and dined with us, but does not seem quite well.

    1. Revised Version of New Testament 1881; O.T. not till 1885.
    2. Augusta now 28, Gerard 33. Gerard died in 1900, and Augusta in 1949 (aged 96).

Monday 23   Humiliation Day
Attended Service at 10 with Heaviside, at 5 with Robinson, and at 3 with both of them, Herbert Jones, King, Copeman, Hinds Howell – my Sermon on Deut. 8, 11 etc. down to 18[1] – In the morning I called upon (1) Heaviside (2) Mrs. Nevill (3) Mrs. Robinson (4) Went to Jarrold's to thank him for revised N.T. and order copy of my Boss Book for Mrs. Rose (5) Militia Barracks, to call on Mr. Coldwell, whom I saw, & Mr. Mostyn, who had gone to the Levee.

    1. The Diocesan Calendar comments: "Dean preached to numerous congregation. Services in parishes throughout the Diocese on day preceding and following; Rogation Days largely used."

Tuesday 24
After luncheon, Hardie[1] (my old School house pupil, & Bishop Cotton's Chaplain) called – told me of old Anstey's[2] kind remembrance of me; he lives at Clifton – Ju and I drove to Honingham to enquire for Tom Fellowes – Mrs. Tom would not admit us – we walked back the last two miles, & after calling at Allen's nursery garden for flowers (for Baby's grave), I in walking fast (to get out of a shower) got a sprain – it was painful to me at night.

    1. A.O. Hardy, pupil at Rugby in Goulburn's time, spent 21 years in India, initially as Domestic Chaplain to the Bishop of Calcutta (G.E.L. Cotton) who had been an Assistant-Master at Rugby, also in Goulburn's time, and later Master of Marlborough.
    2. C.A. Anstey had been appointed an Assistant-Master at Rugby in 1819. He was an old Rugbeian and had spent most of his life at Rugby.

May 1881

Wednesday 25
In the morg. unable to do more than hobble; lay with my foot up in the Library, & finished my Sermonette – Muriel sent me a cooling lotion, wh. Ju has often applied – At 4, went out with Ju in the carriage 1st. to S.P.C.K.[1], then to place a floral cross on Baby's grave – met Heaviside in the Close, as we were coming back; sent him some <u>Chablis</u>[2].

> 1. For many years S.P.C.K. had had a Depot in Norwich. In 1811 it was at the house of the Secretary, Canon Brown; then it moved to a room over the Ehelbert Gateway, until 1825. It was at 15, Castle Meadow until 1863, when it moved to St Andrew's Hill. In 1870 it is in Prince's Street; in 1877, at the Haymarket; and, in 1881, when Goulburn visited it, it was at 14, London Street. It sold Bibles, Prayer Books, Tracts, and other books; gave grants, and also gifts of books to Schools and Libraries. At this time the total sale of books from the Norwich Depot varied from 13,000 to 29,000 a year.
> 2. A dry white Burgundy Wine, made near Chablis, about 100 miles S.E. of Paris.

Thursday 26   ASCENSION DAY
Auntie & Fred. went to Church at 8, where Nevill officiated at Choral H.C. and left out the Pr. Preface – Auntie & Frederica went to Ch. at 11; the Bishop & 8 Canons were there – Muriel came at luncheon time & inspected my ankle – at 5 went to Ch. & got into the pulpit at once, & sat there till after the 3rd. Coll. then gave them 8 thots. on the Ascension Day Gospel; then a pause, during wh. I asked them to say silently the 3rd coll. for G. Friday, & the Lord's Prayer, with Missionary intention.

Friday 27
Rose at 6.15 – corrected proofs of 2d Ed. of Collects – at 11 came Bensly & Brown, and we made our preparation for the Audit until luncheon time – Eliza Lichfield came, and I told her to sweep out the soldiers' seats – I read the account of the ransoming for £15,000 of Mr. Suter – Before we went out, the Bp. called for a few minutes – then Frederica, Auntie, & I drove to Cossey to enquire for Ld. Stafford – on coming back, I sent newspapers with my Sermon of Monday to a great many friends – then came the hairdresser, with his speculations about Robinson's robbery.

Monday 30
In the evening at 8 we all went to the meeting at the Ch. of England Young Men's Association Rooms[1] – It was announced that the Bp. had had a bad telegram about Herbert; and consequently I had to take the chair, & explain his absence – Both Mr. French (of Mauitius) and Mr. Kane (our guest) of Melbourne

made interesting speeches – We took Arundel M. home in our fly; and on our arrival it shocked us to hear that a 2d telegram had arrived, announcing Herbert Pelham's[2] death.

> 1. This successful and well-supported Society was then in Little Orford Street, Market Place. All over 16 were eligible for membership. The Lending LIbrary had about 2000 books, and there was also a Reference Library. There were classes for the study of Literature, Latin, French, German, Science, Shorthand, and the Bible; it had Cricket and Football Clubs; a Musical Society; a Chess Club, etc. The two Clerical Secretaries at this time were the Revd J. Patteson, Rector of Thorpe, and the Revd Sidney Pelham, Vicar of St Peter Mancroft.
> 2. Herbert was the Bishop's youngest son, aged 26, and was Curate of St Philip's, Heigham. He had been an Oxford Rowing Blue. He died at Les Avants, Switzerland, from injuries received in a fall when mountain climbing.

Tuesday 31 S.P.G. Day

I attended Service at 10, and gave our prayers for the Bp. and Family – afterwards Mr. Tucker presented himself (he and Dr. Thornton coming here from the Palace), and I went with them to the Conference at 12.15 – a fair gathering there – I made a short allusion to poor Herbert's death – Mr. Tucker's speech was very interesting; he is for encouraging <u>separate</u> Diocesan Funds – When I alluded disparagingly to Theological Colleges[1], there were expressions of dissent – At 3.30 Evensong I took the part after the Anthem, asking Prayers for the Bp's famly – then a hymn, then Dr. Thornton's Sermon (an excellent one on 'Thy kin-come') – Telegram at 6.15 from Gussie to say Mr. <u>Thomas</u>[2] passed away on Monday night.

> 1. Theological Colleges had been established, and had continued to grow in number, during the past 40 years, for the non-graduate and the graduate.
> 2. Her father-in-law, Richard Thomas, aged 89.

JUNE

Saturday 4

Muriel came & bandaged my ankle – at 3 put on my surplice at home, but walked in procession into Church with the Master, Moore, Bartie – read 2d Lesson & preached (longer than usual) – then sat in the garden & wrote to the Bp. – read aloud to Ju in the evening the Memoir of Geo. Stephenson[1] in the 'Illustrated News' – A letter from Buskins today shocking us with the news that Harry Pierson is dead & poor Lolotte[2] a widow! – No particulars at present.

> 1. George Stephenson (1781–1848) Inventor and founder of Railways.
> 2. Laura (nee Thomas) 1848–1930, sister of 'Pom' and Gerard (Augusta's husband), was married to Major Henry Pearson (or Pierson).

Sunday 5 **WHIT SUNDAY**
H.C. with Nevill & Bartie; 68 Communts. – a letter from the Pin, enclosing one to the Bp. for me to send, if I thot. fit – there was an allusion in it to Cleobis & Biton[1] – At 11 I went to my stall at once, & did nothing but give out the anthem and preach on, "It is expedient for you that I go away, for if I go not, etc." – The Bp. was there & John Pelham[2] – Sidney[2] returned last night, & came with Fanny for the later H.C. – Mr. Atkinson played the dead March most beautifully – Heavy rain when we came out – at 3.30 went to the Litany Service – wrote to dear Lou[3] about her 3 fold beareavement.

1. The two Argive brothers mentioned by Solon to Croesus, in Heroditus' story, as among the happiest of mortals. They died young.
2. John Pelham, the Bishop's nephew, Curate-in-Charge of St John, Lowestoft; Sidney, the Bishop's second son, then Vicar of St Peter Mancroft.
3. Goulburn's cousin, Louisa, then 71, widow of Richard Thomas, and mother of 'Lolotte', who had also just become a widow. The third death, that of her grandchild Louisa, Augusta's first daughter.

Saturday 11 **St. Barnabas**
Rose at 5.30; left Norwich w. Ju at 7.30, without any servant – made the pleasing discovery that I had the halves of Ret. Tickets in my purse – read in the train the account of the attempted blowing up of the Town Hall at Liverpool – on arriving we drove to Tallant's, N. Audley Street and found our rooms comfortable, tho' a little dear – then Chirop ... – then to Gozzie's ... – walked back to Club, buying gloves on the way – there had luncheon – then to Fortnums[1] to meet Ju – Ju & I went to the Academy, & the Dore, but the 1st. was disagreeably crowded, & the 2d dark, and the pictures not pleasing – walked to our hotel – Fraulein soon after paid us a visit and announced D. of Argyll's impending wedding to Mrs. Anson – We dine with Hen-pen tonight.

1. The shop founded by a royal footman, William Fortnum (now Fortnum and Mason, in Piccadilly) opposite Burlington House, where the Royal Academy of Arts has been since 1867. By the end of the 1880s some 400,000 people were attending the Summer Exhibition.

Thursday 16 [*London to Tunbridge Wells*]
After Bkfst. went to Morgan, who was glad to hear we had settled to go to T. Wells – then to Winter's to have hair cut & make purchases – then read the 'Times' till noon when it was time to go to Charg. + for the 12.40 train – We found most comfortable rooms at the Calverley – we took a fly for 2 hours, and drove to Rusthall Common, & saw the Toad Rock, and then round by

Speldhurst, and Sir David Solomon's, and Southborough back; the most lovely of drives – the beauty and stillness of the country is wonderfully soothing; we are quite charmed by it – we dined at Table d'Hote at 7, but with a table to ourselves – It is a first-class hotel – In the evening read 'Ivanhoe' aloud.

•••
They travelled to Brighton on June 20, where they remained until June 25, returning to Norwich, via London, on that day (Saturday).
•••

Saturday 25

Left Brighton w. Ju at 8.30, Rose following by the next train – When we got to London, we saw Morgiana, who said that the colchicum & codine wh. Garrod[1] had given me wd. not suit me – He prescribed – we went to Norwich by the 12.2 train from St. Pancras – were alone in the carriage, wh. was a clean one; and, as there was little or no dust & sun, it was the pleasantest journey on the G.E.R. we have ever had – Nevill called to ask me to offer Prayer at the opening of the new wing of the Hospital – I still cough much, and look forward to tomorrow's Sermon with apprehensiveness.

    1. A doctor whom he had visited at 10, Harley Street, London.

Tuesday 28

After Mg. Church came Walker with a church chair wh. he had oiled and Brockbank[1] with Books for Choristers' Exams., and about paying Probationers in Church – then worked at the Statutes in the Library – then Bensly, with the Prior's Seal from Fitch[2] (Fitch himself had called after Mg. Church) – then went out with Master & Bensly in carriage & saw the Town Clerk about the injury done to Close roads by passage of heavy Waggons – then with Robinson to Eaton in carriage to see Mr. Stannard's water wheel – Service again at 5; then Bell ringers' Certificates.

    1. Choir School Master.
    2. Robert Fitch, Esq., F.S.A., F.G.S., Treasurer, and one of the Hon. Secs. of the Norfolk and Norwich Archaeological Society.

Thursday 30

Put together a Lection, w. some Psalms and Prayers for the opening of the wing of the Hospital[1] – at 3.15 we started in our carriage for the Hospital; Mrs. Heaviside, Mrs. Nevill, Ju and I – the Mayor was in the Chair – the new building looked very well – I had to make a short speech, wh. turned upon systematic beneficence – Dr. Eade spoke, & also one of the Surgeons – I walked back just in time for 5 p.m. Serivce.

> 1. The first portion of new buildings of the new Hospital were opened – i.e. the Western Pavilion and Central Administrative Block. About 600 people present. In one of the Wards, light refreshments were provided by Dr Eade, as Sheriff and as Senior Physician of the Hospital.

JULY

Wednesday 13
After Mg. Ch. went up w. Bartie into the Organ-loft, to inspect some obscene scribbling; wrote to Mr. Tancock[1] about it – after luncheon looked over O.T. papers of the Boys & finished them – Heaviside called to say 'Good-bye' (he goes for 10 days tomorrow morg. to London) and walked with me in the shade – wrote to ... (3) E.S. Copeman about the Copeman window[2] – going to read to Ju some of Drelincourt on Death.

> 1. The Revd W.M.O. Tancock, M.A., Headmaster of King Edward VI Grammar School.
> 2. Memorial Window in St Luke's Chapel to Dr Edward Copeman, Physician at the Norfolk and Norwich Hospital, who died in 1880, and was the eldest brother of Canon Arthur Copeman, Vicar of St Andrew's, Norwich. Dr Copeman had, in 1856, written a 'Brief History of the Norfolk and Norwich Hospital', and, in 1876, was President of the British Medical Association. He lived in the Close and the window was given by his three children.

Thursday 14
After Mg. Church went to the School, with Bartie, and heard the Boys' Recitation, and then examined them viva voce in N.T. and Catechism; with an interval for luncheon this lasted till 4 o'clock – tonight the Coulsons, the Wellses, the Master, Lucy Hansell & Bulmer dine here – the intense heat makes it impossible for Mrs. R. to come – The party went off well, tho' the Master & the Mistress were a gt. loss.

Tuesday 19
The sad news of Stanley's[1] death appeared in 'the Times' this morning – I can think of nothing else – in the afternoon I wrote to Mrs. Vaughan a letter of condolence, and found this rather difficult – the intense heat continued, making me very uncomfortable – At ½p.7 came the Choristers, Bartie, Mr. Atkinson, Mary Stewart, & Miss Bywater to supper; after wh. we had some rather good fireworks, attended by the Colensos, Ada & Lucy Hansell; Mr. Thouless & family – they went off very well – I can't get Stanley's death off my mind.

1. A.P. Stanley, Dean of Westminster, 1864–81, and Goulburn had a great affection for each other since their undergraduate days at Balliol, although, theologically, their disagreement was considerable. Mrs Vaughan, wife of the Dean of Llandaff, was Stanley's sister.

Wednesday 20

After luncheon drove out on Sprowston Rd., and returned (walking) over Mousehold Heath, on wh. the brickmaking seemed to have stopped – Fanny Pelham sent me a letter of Aug. Hare's[1] descriptive of Stanley's last moments. When told of his danger: "I am quite satisfied. I have nothing on my mind. I always wished it to be here (at Westminster)" – wrote a line to poor Robert, condoling with him on Kate's[2] death, wh. he announced by a line to Julia this morning.

1. Author and Art Collector; lived mostly in Italy and France.
2. Catherine (Kate), nee Prior, wife of Robert Cartwright, Barrister, stepbrother of Julia.

Thursday 21

After Bkfst. went to the Master, and, on his expressing a wish that I shd. do so, I consented to preach the Sermon next Sunday afternoon, mentioning Stanley[1] – Set to work on this till luncheon time, not going to Church in morng – In the evening read the debates in Convocn. about Stanley, & think of reading the review of Mme. de Stael – Violent sickness before going to bed.

1. Dean Stanley's father had been Bishop of Norwich, 1805–37.

Friday 22

Rose at 6.30 & wrote about 2 pages of my Stanley Sermon before Bkfst. – went on with it after Bkfst. till about luncheon time, when I got thoroughly tired.

Saturday 23

Did not dress for Bkfst., but employed myself in finishing my 'Stanley Sermon', wh. I did about 11 – then came Stacy, to whom I entrusted it, to get part of it into type by the evening – I am rather bad with lumbago – I have received today a very beautiful letter from Mrs. Vaughan.

Sunday 24

Between the Services Heaviside came in, and it was arranged that I should take his ticket for the funeral, and attend tomorrow – then I went on studying my Sermon of ½ of wh. Stacy had sent me a proof – This I preached at 3.30 – it was an exciting and disagreeable business[1].

> 1. Very cursory mention of a Sermon which was to cause considerable controversy. Goulburn's appreciation and praise of Stanley's personality did not please some; while his denunciation of his theology offended Stanley's friends. The Bishop of Derry (Alexander) thought the Sermon excellent.

Monday 25   **St. James**
Went by Ipswich road to Town – to Club for luncheon – at ½p.2, set off for the Abbey – called at the Warden's[1], & was very much shocked to hear he was dangerously ill at Oxford – saw for a moment (1) Harry Jones (2) Burly Hugh (3) Mr. Simkinson, with whom I entered the Abbey & stood in the nave for a mortal 2¾ths. hours – Singing very feeble & poor; organ thundering by way of compension; the whole thing (except the reading of the Lesson wh. Canon Prothero contrived to make us hear) scandalously ill done, and the organisation infamous – got to the Club (after a few words w. Bp. of Peterboro') about 5.45, just in time to write to Ju.

> 1. The Revd F.K. Leighton, Warden of All Souls, Oxford, 1858–81.

AUGUST

Thursday 4   *[Judges Dinner]*
Rose at 6.30 & nearly completed my Saturday lecture – After 11 a.m. Service, a Chapter in Bensly's Office to seal Chancellor Blofield's[1] nomination, but it was'nt ready for us; also a question about keeping in order the Banks at Eaton – It was very wearing – Bensly came into luncheon – afterwards worked at the arrangement of the Table, & wrote notices for all the guests – Judges' lodgings at 4 with Heaviside & Robinson – only Denman appeared – Bessy Hansell & Mrs. Robinson helped us to arrange the Table – Ld. Justice Bramwell & his Marshal did not come – The guests were (1) High Sheriff (2) Mayor (3) (4) Justice Denman & Marshal (5) Heaviside (6) The Master (7) Sir Hn. Stracey (8) Dr. Ede [*Eade*] (9) Mr. Keith, under Sheriff of Norfolk (10) Mr. Willett (11) Bensly (12) Mrs. Heaviside (13) Mrs. Coulson (14) Arundell (15) W.T. Moore (16) Rev. Evans Lombe, the Chaplain.

> 1. John Worlledge, Chancellor of the Diocese, had died in July; he was succeeded by Thomas Calthorpe Blofield, M.A.

Friday 5

After Service I went to Bensly's room, where H. and I had an interview w. Thacker, in the course of wh. we were obliged to yield to him as to a diminution of rent – then went over my notes of yesterday w. Bensly and corrected them – Lucy[1] & Louisa[1] Bignold came to luncheon fresh from Aix-les-Bains & the Engadine, where they had seen Sidney Pelham – Bensly also had luncheon here – dined with the Judges, with Heaviside.

> 1. Daughters of the late Sir Samuel Bignold, Lucy, a tireless worker in good causes.

Monday 8

Moore & Mr. Brockbank attested my signature of powers of attorney in connexion with Melia's affairs – then a talk with Brockbank about Dr. Gladstone's[1] savage treatment of choristers – A letter from Buskins to say Gerard is ill & must go abroad, & to postpone their visit to the autumn.

> 1. The previous organist of the Cathedral who had resigned unexpectedly.

Tuesday 9

Constant rain, and so dark that Gas was required for the Lectern – wrote to the Dean thanking him for some venison – wrote to Sydney Linton[1], sending him cheque for £5. 5 to Herbert Pelham Memorial.

> 1. Vicar of St Philip's, Heigham, unitl 1884 (where Herbert Pelham had been Curate). In 1884, he became the first Bishop of Riverina, New South Wales.

Thursday 11   Oxford Dinner

Arundell arrived at ¼p.4; and at 5 I took him to the Oxford dinner, where he sate on one side of me, and Mr. Courtenay Boyle on the other – The dinner went off well, but it was a weak point that we sat down by daylight – the venison was ill carved, and had but little fat – Nobody spoke but Hinds Howell, Mr. Courtenay Boyle, Arundell, and myself on whom devolved the proposal of the toasts.

Monday 15

To Bkfst. came Mr. & Mrs. Power, who were very entertaining – She described her educational establishment at Ham Common, formerly the house of the Duc de Chartres – To luncheon came the 3 Pins; before they went Mrs. Symonds took it into her head that her husband had better compete for the Bodleian Librarianship – this excited us all a little, and he and I went to the Clerical Rooms[1] to look for a Univ. Calendar – When they were gone, MAC, Ju, Fraulein and I drove to Lakenham, whence Fraulein and I walked to see our Baby's grave – then we went down Bracondale by Colman's[2] factory, over Carrow Bridge, into Thorpe Rd. and back to the Ferry – I wrote to (1) Dr. Acland[3] about the Librarianship.

    1. These were above the Ethelbert Gate.
    2. Jeremiah J. Colman (1830–98) moved his business from Stoke Holy Cross to Carrow, Norwich, in 1856, to manufacture mustard, flour and starch.
    3. Regius Professor of Medicine at Oxford, Radcliffe Librarian, and President of the General Medical Council.

Thursday 18
Wrote to Symonds, enclosing the letter wh. I had this morning from Dr. Acland encouraging S. to stand for the Librarianship – also sent him a letter of introduction to Acland – called at Stacy's, to order Oxf. Univ. Calendar.

Friday 19
Reading all day for my Sermonette on the 27th. inst. – a dreadful rain which will be very bad for the crops – glass going down – Mr. Linton of Sprowston called to have the plans & specifications for his new Parsonage signed – this morning Moore and I (for the first time) divided the Litany in a new way, I taking the deprecations & also the latter part, & he the obsecrations.

Saturday 20
After Mg. Church, & a short talk with Mr. Brockbank[1] about the subjects for Exam. in 1882, went to the Bank to get £10 for Elizth. Parsons – then to see the 2 Lichfields[2], both of whom were in bed – I read to them – then to Mr. Atkinson, who gave me a most interesting lesson on the management of the breath in singing – wrote to … (2) The Pin, telling him what Acland says in his 2d letter (3) Acland, asking him to pay a visit.

    1. Cathedral Choir School Master.
    2. Former Subsacrist.

Sunday 21
H.C. with Moore at 8; several young men present, amg. others Stubbings an old chorister – at 11 we had a tediously long Service, with a very lengthy Anthem of Boyse's ('By the waters'), in the middle of wh. the clock struck noon – however my Sermon was fairly short, and we were out at 12.50 – at 3.30 Heaviside preached a good Sermon – Beethoven beautifully played – afterwards a talk with Mr. Atkinson about next Sunday's Mg. Service, wh. I must shorten as there is to be a Charity Sermon.

Monday 22

Daniells came about the two clocks of the Cath. wh. do not keep together – I answered a letter from Mrs. Symonds, who wants her husband to stand for the Bodleian rather agst. the advice of his brother – Fraulein, Lili & I drove to Eaton School, & thence walked by the farm and the Earlham Road, taking a fly at last.

Thursday 25

Rain all day long – I wrote to Nisbet, Nevill, & Robinson, sending to each of them a copy of the new draft Statutes with a letter, the substance of wh. I told H. before Evening Church, and he seemed to think I had stated the willingness of the Commn. to consider suggestions in too unqualified a manner – So I wrote them after Church.

Friday 26

After Church came Symonds & until luncheon time we were colloguing on his prospects, and drafting a letter for him to send to the Curators – wrote a letter for Symonds to Huertley[1] – afterwards overhauled my wardrobe, giving the old clothes to Robbins.

1. C.A. Huertley, Lady Margaret Professor of Divinity at Oxford.

Saturday 27

Wrote for Symonds to Pusey[1] & Liddon[2] – after Mg. Church, saw Brockbank about tomorrow's collection, and then set to work arranging papers, sorting letters, clearing out cupboard, etc. etc. until luncheon – At 3 p.m. preached to a very good congreation – then walked to Mr. White's, where I had my teeth cleaned – returned about 5.45 – at 6 came the tailor to reform a coat, and at ½p.6 the hairdresser – I am going to advise Symonds this evening to discontinue his canvass – If he were to get it, and then find his health unequal to it, what then?

1. E.B. Pusey, Regius Professor of Hebrew at Oxford and Canon of Christ Church from 1828 (when only 28). Oxford Movement Leader. When he died in1882, his library was bought by friends who founded Pusey House in St Giles to house the books.
2. See December 23, 1868 (Note 1).

Sunday 28

At 11 the Church very full – Preached for the Inc. Ch. Bg. Society[1] – got about £21, wh. is good for us – a full Church again at 3 – Heaviside preached – we had Mendelssohn's 'Hear my Prayer' sung very well by Manning.

1. Incorporated Church Build Society founded 1828; Norwich Diocesan Branch founded 1836. The Diocesan Branch could distribute only about £70 per year, but, by 1881, had helped 278 Parishes in the Diocese.

Monday 29

Sad rainy day, showing that the glass cannot be relied upon, as it is going up – disquieting letter from Robinson about draft Statutes to wh. he objects; from Mrs. Nisbet about her father's impending death; and from Symonds, who seems determined to go on with the Librarianship – after Church saw Quinton & committed to him the letters on my Stanley Sermon to be bound – then to Library to take back books – then to Lichfields, to give them Mr. May's publications & say Goodbye – then to luncheon with the Heavisides to say Goodbye.

• •

On August 30, the Goulburns left Norwich for their long holiday period, this year in Wales and in England. After single nights in London and in Gloucester, they stayed from September 1 to 10 with Lady Hamilton at Llanstephan, about 6 miles south of Carmarthen, on the coast; then 2 nights with the Bishop of Llandaff (the Rt Revd Aldred Ollivant); from September 12 to 22, with the Gibbs at Tyntesfield (near Bristol); one night at Exeter; one night at Winchester; then, from September 26 to October 15, with relations at Eyhorne, Edgcote, Eydon; and from October 15 to 25, at Aynhoe. Then, Brighton from October 25 to November 17, Goulburn having a week-end at Chichester and a day in Eastbourne. Two nights in London, before returning to Norwich on November 19, after an absence of almost 11½ weeks.

• •

Tuesday 30   Norwich to London

We left Norwich while the skies were weeping, at 7.30 – on arriving Ju went to Coulson's – Sharpe told me he had been in treaty about my house at Brighton – Coulson's fare not very good.

Wednesday 31

Wrote letters for Symonds to Canons King[1] and Bright[1], and sent them off to him – we left town at 12 for Gloucester – we lionised the Cathedral, & found the supreme verger in his glory – after dinner I wrote a letter to Canon Stubbs[2], & despatched it to Symonds.

1. Both Canons of Christ Church, Oxford.
2. William Stubbs, at this time Canon of St Paul's, and also Regius Professor of History at Oxford; later, 1884, Bishop of Chester, and 1888, Bishop of Oxford.

SEPTEMBER

Thursday 1   From Gloucester to Llanstephan
Left Gloucester at 9; and arrived at Caermarthen Junction about 2.45; thence it is 9 miles to Ly. Hamilton's; I walked the last three miles of the way – the colours of the sand, sea, foliage, enchanting – we found Miss Wellington in the drawing room, laid on her back with an accident to the <u>tendon Achillis</u>.

Friday 2
In the morning I wrote to ... (3) Dean of Ch. Ch. for Symonds. (4) Symonds.

Saturday 3
A letter from the Bp. about Duport's appointment – this I answered – also wrote to Symonds, enclosing him a letter received from Liddon, who says he is not a Curator.

Monday 5
Having recd. a letter from Pusey discouraging Symond's standing for the Librarianship, I sent this to him, urging him to withdraw; in wh. course I was confirmed by Sir E. Kerrison, who writes to me full of apprehensions for Symonds' health shd. he get it – I answered Sir Edward – sent a copy of my 'Stanley' Sermon to Dr. Pusey – at ½p.2 Ly. Hamilton took me & Ju & Mr. Hoare a drive in the sociable[1] by Coombe Wood, & up Llangunnock Road – Mr. H. and I walked back the last three miles of the way – passed a whole train of vans, carrying back the Baptist school children to Caermarthen from their holiday at Llanstephan.

   1. Sociable: A type of open carriage with two seats facing each other.

Tuesday 6
A dreary soppy day – I wrote ... to ... (3) Symonds, sending him letters from Liddon & Professor Stubbs. (4) Liddon, thanking him for sending me an accurate list of Curators.

Thursday 8
I heard from Nevill at the Rocky Mountains & answered him to Quebec ... (4) Pin, sending him King's & Heurtley's letters – also to G.W.R. station at Paddington, asking permission with my return ticket to stay two nights at Cardiff.

Saturday 10

Before leaving Llanstephan wrote (1) to Symonds, who has at last given up the candidature for Librarianship[1] – left Llanstephen at 11, and Caermarthen at 12.30 – got to Cardiff about 4 – went with Ju over the Castle; very grand & highly decorated, but uncomfortable as a dwelling; 119 stone steps; a peristyle, w. the history of Elijah; a very small chapel with monumental bust to late Lord Bute; summer & winter smoking room; bath & bathroom; banquet hall with the history of Robert, Earl of Gloucester; shutters to the loop-holes, looking like aumbrys or cupboards – well worth seeing – the Bp. after our arrival took us thro' his grounds & round the Cathedral; Canon Harvey joined us on the way – we dined at ½p.7 – Mrs. Vaughan[2] & Mrs. Chas. Stanley[3] came in the evening – Bishop Perry[4] & Mrs. Perry also dined here.

1. The new Bodleian Librarian, appointed in 1882, was Edward Williams Byron Nicholson (1849–1912), aged 33 (so much younger than Symonds). He had been Librarian of London Institution 1873–82; remained at the Bodleian for 30 years. Greatly extended the Library, and wrote on many subjects – Biblical Criticism, Celtic Antiquities, comparative philology, folklore, music, palaeography, numismatics, athletics.
2. Dean Vaughan had been Headmaster of Harrow.
3. The widow of Bishop Stanley's youngest son, Charles Edward, a Captain in the Royal Engineers, who died abroad of fever in 1849.
4. The Rt Revd Charles Perry, 1st Bishop of Melbourne 1849–75. Retired 1876.

Sunday 11

Prayer in the Chapel at 8.45 – I gave Canon Harvey a copy of my Stanley Sermon, but doubt whether he approves – At 11 to the Cathedral, where I sat in the stall next the Dean – Mg. Prayer (very reverently done) down to the 3d Collect – Then the H.C. Service – Bp Perry preached – collection at Off. for C.M.S. – all was most solemn and edifying – then to the Cathl. at 3.30, where the Dean preached admirably.

Monday 12 From Llandaff to Tyntesfield

After Bkfst. the Bishop proposed to me a walk – Nothing can exceed his kindness – We left Llandaff, after a most pleasant visit, about 12.40 – At Gloucester we changed into the Midland line – Mrs. Gibb's[1] carriage was waiting for us at Bristol – Chapel at 6; Dinner at 7.

1. Mr William Gibbs, Goulburn's friend and benefactor, had died, but Mrs Gibbs and his family carried on the tradition which he had established. Before his death he had given Keble College its chapel and laid the foundation stone; his sons Anthony and Henry had given the Hall and Library; Henry restored Aldenham Church and helped to restored St Alban's Abbey; Governor of the Bank of England 1875–77; 1st Baron Aldenham 1896; leading member of English Church Union since 1862.

September 1881

Thursday 22   From Tyntesfield to Exeter

Left Tyntesfield at 11 with Ju and Mr. Hardie in Mrs. Gibb's carriage – Read 'Times' and 'Telegraph' in the train – got to Exeter at about ½p.2 – Attended the Cathedral Service at 3 – Priest Vicar did not intone well – Can. Cook (in residence) read the Second Lesson admirably – afterwards he joined us in the nave and showed us the Bishop Patteson[1] pulpit – then he took us to his house – thence, after having my hair cut & buying a new electric wire brush, Ju and I walked to Bullivant's (3, Lyndhurst Rd., Mt. Radford), and sat with him for an hour – he has a cough, but seems in spirits – we walked back and dined in the Coffee House here (Clarence Hotel).

> 1. Bishop John Patteson (1827–71): Founded the Melanesian Mission and became 1st Bishop of Melansia in 1861 at the age of 34; he spoke 23 languages; he was murdered on the island of Nukapu in 1871.

Friday 23

Went to 10.30 Service at Cathedral – afterwards met Bullivant in the nave & helped him to walk to his carriage (for wh. he pays £2. 5 a week) – then to Canon Cook's where met the Oxford professor of Anglo Saxon[1], who showed me one of Leofric's gifts to his Chapter, a Book of Anglo Saxon poetry; and also a man whom I had examined at Cuddesdon for orders years ago – had luncheon with Bullivant at 1.30 – I called on Archdn. Woollcombe[2], & had a pleasant chat with him.

> 1. The Revd John Earle, M.A. (1824–1903); Philologist; wrote much on Anglo-Saxon, and an accomplished Dante scholar.
> 2. The Ven. Henry Woollcombe, M.A., Archdeacon of Barnstaple since 1865, and a Residentiary Canon of Exeter.

Saturday 24   Fr. Exeter to Winchester

After Bkfst. we called at the Palace, where we saw the Bishop[1], his wife, & child – They showed us the Chapel of the Palace, and after that gave us admission by a side door into the Cathedral – felt rather embarrassed with him; so perhaps did he – at 12.15 we left Exeter for Winchester – raining hard on our arrival at 6.5 p.m. – found an old fashioned but clean & comfortable Inn at 'the George'.

> 1. The Rt Revd Frederick Temple had succeeded Goulburn as Headmaster of Rugby. He had married at the age of 55 and had two sons, William, the second, being born in 1881. So it was possibe for Goulburn to have seen two future Archbishops of Canterbury before him, one a babe in arms!

Sunday 25　　　　　At Winchester
After Bkfst. I went to call at the Deanery, where the Dean[1] most kindly asked Ju & me to luncheon – Service at 11 – Sermon by Canon Carus[2] – celebration – Luncheon at 1.30 at the Deanery – The Dean showed us his study (in the roof of the house), his garden and lime tree avenue, & the roof of his stable wh. was the hall of the Travellers' refectory – we went to Evensong at ½p.3.

    1. The Very Revd J. Bramston, B.D.
    2. Canon W. Carus, M.A., Residentiary Canon since 1851.

Monday 26　　　From Winchester to Eyhorne
Left Winchester (the 'George' inn is a good one) at 8.31 – got to London about 10.45 – Having first found at the Club that members cannot have a lady to luncheon, Ju & I parted – walked to Victoria Station for the 2.40 train, where found Ju & Rose – we found Lou[1] & Buskyn waiting for us (in Lou's new carriage) at Maidstone – Gerard is looking much better & clearer, and our darling also looks well – Pom came across to dinner.

    1. Buskyn's mother-in-law.

OCTOBER

Saturday 1　　　　　[At Edgcote]
Received and read gt. part of 'Oxford Tracts No. 3, "Consecreation *not* Transubstantiation" ' – Wrote to (1) Nisbet about instalments of certain Hon. Cans. (2) Symonds, condoling on his brother's death ... (4) Stacy, for more of my 'Stanley' Sermons.

Friday 7　　　　　[At Eydon]
After Bkfst. wrote to (1) The Master, a letter of sympathy about Mrs. R.[1] and about Janet's death (2) Salisbury Everard, who had written to me to name someone for a small living (3) Peter Hansell, with receipt for rent of School Field (4) Mr. Gunn about his discovery of a diffce. in height of the triforium, etc. etc. – then a stroll in the garden, reading B.C.'s[2] tract on 'Ritual Conformity' – read Arthur Mill's Book, 'Blues & Buffs'.

    1. Mrs Robinson was ill. She died early in January 1882.
    2. B.C. = Berdmore Compton.

Saturday 15   From Eydon to Aynhoe
Rose at 7.30 & saw Hen-pen, Ld. Valentia, Maudie, Eddie, Mr. Kenyon before they began their cub-hunting – Shortly before getting to Charlton, I got out & walked here – The Dean rather out of spirits, we thot. – Mr. Turner came in to speak of the awful accident to the Tew Governess, crushed by the fall of a tree – in the evening looked over the Memoirs of Dean Stanley in Fraser's[1] & in Macmillan.

> 1. 'Fraser's Magazine' (founded 1830) had been edited 1861–74 by J.A. Froude, later Regius Professor of Modern History at Oxford. 'Macmillan's' (1859–1907) was from the publishing house of this name. It serialised the Company's new fiction before publication in book form, but was also noted for its serious articles on politics and religion.

NOVEMBER

Saturday 19   From London to Norwich
At 12 left London for our home – on arriving a vast mass of papers, etc., but comparatively few letters – Mr. Ram[1] called to ask my further advice about his churchyard matter, & I told him to find out from the adversary whether he consented to go into the County Court instead of to the Assizes.

> 1. See January 21, 1873 (Note 2).

Sunday 20
Rose at 6.45, after a bad night – Attended with Ju the 8 a.m. celebration – At 11, Mr. Thompson[1] of Aldeburgh (near Felixstowe) preached – I cd. not hear him; his manner was lugubrious – at 3.30 Nisbet preached – after Church I sent to Heaviside's, & heard, to my great grief, that the Railway threatens again the invasion of the Close – Lord Claud Hamilton[2] is coming in this evening to talk over the railway.

> 1. The Revd Henry Thompson was Vicar of Aldeburgh from 1874 to 1904. After Goulburn's time he became R.D. of Orford; an Hon. Canon of Norwich, and, from 1904, Vicar of Eaton.
> 2. He was connected with the Gt Eastern Railway, which opposed this threat.

Monday 21
Before Bkfst. wrote to ... (2) Proposed translator in Stockholm of 'Personal Religion' – after Mg. Church, went up with Walker & Bartie into gallery to settle about Regimental School sitting there – then (4) to Bensly's Office about the proposed Railway – Nisbet & Nevill came & advised how to answer the letter I had had.

Wednesday 23

Rose at 6.15 and lit my own fire – after Bkfst. came Nevill, to ask me to house Mr. Chambers, the Lecturer of the Church Institution – After Mg. Service went to Bensly's Office, where had an interview with the late Robt. Wright's partner, who seeks the place he held – then worked with Bensly & Brown at the preparation of the <u>Agenda</u> paper till it was time for Bensly to go to luncheon with Mr. Chas. Turner – then on my return Mr. Porter[1], Chaplain of the workhouse called to solicit the Gt. Hospital Chaplaincy – then luncheon to wh. Bartie came; afterwards gave him my scheme of Advent Lectures – wrote to Dr. Duckett[2] & to (2) Rev. Henry Thompson who had written to me about the connexion of Crabbe[3] with Aldeburgh, his parish – a significant letter to Auntie from Little Buskins.

> 1. The Revd Canon W.F. Patteson, Hon. Can., R.D., and, for 57 years, Vicar of St Helen's, and Chaplain to the Gt Hospital, had died on November 14. The Revd A.J. Porter did become the new Chaplain.
> 2. Dr Duckett, Roman Catholic Priest of St John Maddermarket R.C. Chapel.
> 3. George Crabbe (1754–1832), the Poet, had been born in Aldeburgh, Suffolk, and later (1781) had been Curate of Aldeburgh.

Saturday 26

Church at 10 – afterwards a meeting with Nisbet & Nevill at the office to determine as to the answer to be given to Mr. Parkes of the G.E.R. – then a meeting with Nisbet, Nevill & Bensly as to the answer to be given to the letter addressed to Bensly by Mathews, the Lynn & Fakenham Solr. – sent copies to Heaviside – after dinner examined the gt. Coronation bible, over the authenticity of wh. great doubt is thrown by a letter received from John Scrivener[1] today.

> 1. Must mean *Frederick* Scrivener (1813–91) New Testament textual critic – His 'Plain Introduction to the Criticism of the N.T.' listed some 1,700 MSS., while the 4th. (posthumous) edition (Ed. by E. Miller) in 1894, listed over 3,000.

Sunday 27   Advent I

Between Churches, I examined our Coronation Bible and two Prayer Books (1662) from the Chapel Royal, Brighton, & wrote a short mem. of them – then walk in the garden reading Sanday[1] on 'the Gospel of the Second Century' – At 3.30 p.m. Bulmer complained of the people singing out of tune to the Litany.

> 1. William Sandy (1843–1920) N.T. Scholar, later to be, at Oxford, Dean Ireland Professor of Exegesis, and then Lady Margaret Professor of Divinity. The accurate title of this book is: 'The Gospels in the 2nd Century' (1876).

DECEMBER

Thursday 1 Norwich to London
Left Norwich by the 7.30 train – fell in with Heaviside at Cambridge; and on arriving at Liverpool Street, we had our interview with Mr. Parkes, Ld. Claude Hamilton, etc. – as the railway is to go through the Close by the Watergate, agreed join the G.E.R. company in opposing, we not to bear any expence beyond £200 – then we parted – at night embodied in my copy of the Statues the suggestions of Nisbet & Nevill.

Friday 2
At 10.30, after purchasing things for dinner at Bailey's, went in Cab to Delahay Street – Present Sir W. James, Ld. Cranbrook, Ber. Hope, Bp. of Carlisle, Lord Blachford, Abp. of Canterbury[1] – on the whole the discussion of the first draught of Statutes went off very well – we were told to embody the amendments on the 2d draft, & then bring it before the Chapter – we were dismissed about 4.10 p.m.

> 1. Archbishop Tait, in the House of Lords, had suggested a Commission to reform Cathedral Statutes. This was the Commission to which Goulburn was summoned. Sir Wm. James (1807–81) Lord Justice; Lord Cranbrook = G. Gathorne-Hardy (1814–1906), Statesman; Ber. Hope = A.J. Beresford Hope (1820–87), Politician, Churchman and Author; Bishop of Carlisle = Rt Revd Harvey Goodman; Lord Blachford = Frederic Rogers (1811–89) Barrister, Permanent Under-Sec. of State for Colonies 1860–71, Privy Counc.; Archbishop of Canterbury = Archibald Campbell Tait.

••
Goulburn returned to Norwich, with Heaviside, on December 3.
••

Thursday 8
After Church inspected with Nisbet, Brown, & Bensly the garden next to the Choristers' School, and the pavement in front of Mr. Tancock's house – we did not sanction Brown's idea of cutting off an angle of the garden, but ordered the gate to the Choristers' School to be rehung where it was before – then inspected the foundations of campanili[1] opposite Mrs. Wallace's house – we dine alone tonight – what a comfort!

> 1. A separate Bell Tower existed c. 30 ft from the Erpingham Gate. This was often to take heavier bells. It was abolished in the 16th Century. (See A.G.G. Thurlow, M.A., 'The Bells of Norwich Cathedral' in Vol. 29 – Centenary Vol. – of *Norfolk Archaeology*, p. 89.)

December 1881 241

Saturday 10
Warnes, the Beadle came to me, and on my telling him that he must keep clean the walks of the Upper Close Square, or resign, he gave me warning for Lady Day – read aloud Tennyson's 'Queen Mary' to Mrs. Millard, Auntie, Ada, and one of the little Evanses.

Monday 12
A Walk with Nisbet to congratulate Jipattie[1] upon his Hon. Canonry – we saw Mrs. Jipattie for a moment, & then walked back – went to Dimock's to buy a present (wedding day after the fair) for Auntie[2] – chose a candlestick wh. wd. either stand or hang on a wall – received the fatal announcement of the line the railway is to take thro' the Close.

   1. 'Jippattie' = John Patteson, Rector of Thorpe St Andrew since 1867 and R.D. of Blofield.
   2. The Goulburn's 35th Wedding Anniversary had been on Sunday, December 11.

Tuesday 13   A Day of worry and vexation "above strength"
After Mg. Ch. sent for the three Canons to consult about the steps to be taken in reference to the proposed Railway – Agreed that Heavisde and I shd. go to the Mayor[1], wh. we did – He said he wd. feel the pulse of the Town Council about the proposed Railway – then we went to Tillett's[2], who was very gracious, and ended by showing us over the relics of Carrow Abbey, recently unearthed in his grounds.

   1. William Hunter, an Auctioneer. Was Leader of the Norfolk Liberals.
   2. Jacob B. Tillett, a strong Nonconformist, Liberal, twice Mayor of Norwich, and, at this time, an M.P. for Norwich. He lived at Carrow Abbey.

Wednesday 14
After Church walked round k. garden for an hour and a quarter – then went to see Miss Hansell, & tell her the steps wh. had been taken about the Railway – went to luncheon with Heaviside – H. and I then retired and drew up a statement of our wants as to increased Stipends for lay-clerks, for the E.C. and sent it off to Ellicott.

Saturday 17   From Norwich to Wells
Left Norwich with Robbins at 7.15 – Pouring rain all day – the journey from Paddington most uncomfortable: at Swindon the carriages were put on another line; at Witham we had to change, and cross the bridge in torrents of rain; no shelter at Witham

Station of any kind; the whole thing clumsy and frequent stoppages, with the Zummerzet dialect – Lord and Lady Arthur[1] and their daughter & Mr. Gandell[2] (who succeeded us in our Holywell House) received me most kindly, & I was just able to write a line for Ju before the Post went out.

> 1. The Rt Hon. and Rt Revd Lord Arthur Hervey (1808–94), Bishop of Bath and Wells since 1869; 4th son of the 1st Marquis of Bristol; on Committee of Revisers of the Old Testament 1870–84.
> 2. Canon R. Gandell, M.A., a Residentiary Canon of Wells since 1880.

Sunday 18   **Advent 4**
Breakfast in 'the Undercroft'[1] at 8.15 – At 9 Mg. Prayer with the Anthem & State Prayers – at 11 (after an hour's interval) the Ordination, beginning with the Sermon on "ye are the salt of the earth" – not out till 2 – then a hurried dinner in 'the Undercroft' – Service again at 3 – then back to the Palace to 5 o'clock tea with Archdn. Browne, and the Examg. party – old Oxford stories – then to my room to write to Ju and MAC.

> 1. The undercroft or crypt (13th Cent) is beneath the Chapter House off the North Choir Aisle.

Monday 19   Wells to London
Prayer in Chapel at 8.30 – then a pleasant bkfst., after wh. took leave in the Bp's carriage – Train started from Wells at 9.55 – Morgiana's servant met me at the Station, & asked me to call at Morgiana's en route wh. I did – he gave me some mock turtle, & told me to go on w. the colchicum dose.

[He returned to Norwich on Wednesday 21]

Saturday 24
Church at 10; gave away my gratuities afterwards to the Choristers with oranges, mince-pies, etc. etc. – Then a walk with Nisbet over Mousehold – after dinner wrote letters to (1) Mr. Sharpe, thanking for his book on 'Anglo-Catholic Principles' (2) declining Sermon to Cambridge Undergrads. in Lent (3) Thanking Dr. Hale (American) for sending me his brochures about Anglo-Catholic movement.

Sunday 25   **CHRISTMAS DAY**
H.C. (Choral) with Bartie at 8; 64 Communicts., Col. Campbell & his wife among them: out at 9.30 – At the later celebration there were only 52 – after luncheon I walked in the garden,

reading two Sermons of Bp. of Durham[1] & Thring[2] of Uppingham; the latter I did not care for – In the evening read to Ju some papers sent me by a lady about the movement in Persia (among the Jews at Hamadau = Ecbatana) in favour of Christianity.

> 1. The Rt Revd J.B. Lightfoot (leading N.T. Scholar and leading member of Company of Revisers of the New Testament). Bishop of Durham, since 1879.
> 2. The Revd Edward Thring (1821–87): from 1853 Headmaster of Uppingham, where he took the School to a foremost position; wrote several books on English Grammar; had a deep sense of the moral purpose in education; founder of the Headmasters' Conference in 1869; established the first Public School Mission to the London poor.

Tuesday 27   St. John Evangelist
At 3 went to the Gt. Hospital, meeting Heaviside and Davies en route – sat by Symonds – the fight was between Bellman and Porter[1]; the latter succeeded, & I was thankful for it after the character wh. I heard of him from Davies this morning.

> 1. The Revd A.J. Porter was appointed Vicar of St Helen's, and Chaplain of the Gt Hospital. Previously, Chaplain of the Norwich Workhouse.

Thursday 29
At 10 Heaviside & I set to work to embody in our new Draft Statutes the alterations agreed upon with the C.C.[1] – Nisbet came in, and made some pertinent suggestions – Ju and I dined at 6, to enable the Servants to go to the Circus – We completed looking over the Lay Clerks' Testimonials; several of the candidates very illiterate men.

> 1. Cathedral Commission.

1882
JANUARY

Monday 2
Muriel called & causticked my throat before luncheon – at 2.15 Ju and I drove to Drayton, and saw the whole family[1] (excepting Mrs. H.H., junr.) – Maimie's brother swung on the trapeze – they shewed us the presents H.H. had received on his golden wedding day, and also a model of the farm belonging to H.H. junr. in Canterbury settlement – came back just in time to go to Evening Church – afterwards wrote short letter to Mrs. Vaughan, and sent some presents to the little Nevills, & wrote to my hatter in London.

> 1. Hinds Howell's was a much reduced family. By this time, out of five daughters and two sons, only two (Conrad and Agnes) now survived, and Conrad was to pre-decease his father. Hinds Howell's wife, Mary Ann, was to die in 1887. Only their daughter Agnes survived them both until 1912, and it was Agnes who wrote her father's 'Memoir', published in 1899. In 1895, two years before his death, Goulburn had written a Preface to the Memoir. It would appear that Conrad and his family had farmed in the South Island of New Zealand. But now he seemed to have a position in the office of the Ecclesiastical Commissioners. His daughter, Maimie, was living with her grandparents, and often visited the Deanery.

Tuesday 3
Saw old Stone, & told him he must make his boy keep Upper Close tidy – after luncheon came Bartie, & we resolved to send for Wareham from Wimbourne & the Southwell man to try them[1]; Bartie was to make further enquiries about the Hennings – in the evening Ju and I went on with the alterations made by the Reformers in the gospels of the Sarum Missal, and nearly finished the work.

> 1. For the Layclerkship.

Wednesday 4
A letter from the Master, announcing Mrs. Robinson's serious illness (Pleurisy) – after luncheon came Heaviside, and we finished our work upon the statutes – when Rickitt came in he announced Mrs. Robinson's death, the funeral to be on Friday ! – wrote a 2d letter to the Master (having already written in the morng.) – Auntie has been to a children's tea at the Jenny Lind[1].

> 1. The Jenny Lind Infirmary (later Hospital) was still on its original site in Pottergate.

Thursday 5
Writing all day long at a Sermon about poor Mrs. R., but my "chariot wheel drave very heavily", and I am greatly depressed – Poor Robinson's acct. of his wife's death reached me this morning; the funeral is to be at the cemetery here, about 1.45 tomorrow – In the evening I went on writing my Sermon, wh. is heavy work for many reasons.

Friday 6   THE EPIPHANY
In the morning at 10 I did not go to Church, but went on with my Sermon till the time of the funeral – A letter from the Master as well as a telegram, asking me to officiate – I sent a note to Moore[1] by the undertaker, asking permission – at about 12.45, Heaviside, Nevill, and I set forth in our carriage for the Station, and after waiting about 10 min. the funeral arrived; it was a long drive thence to the cemetery, & part of the way in pouring rain – on our return the Master, Mr. Stewart, and the two boys came in, and had luncheon, and sat with us till about 4.10, when after a cup of coffee they went; the Boys very attentive to their father.

> 1. The Revd W.T. Moore had been a Minor Canon (= Cathedral Curate) since 1874, and since 1879 was also Vicar of 'St Mary-in-theMarsh', the non-existent Parish Church of the Close, but using St Luke's Chapel (as still the custom). It was etiquette for Goulburn to ask Moore for permission to take the funeral of one of his (Moore's) parishioners.

Sunday 8
At 11 we had the Anthem, "The souls of the righteous are in the hand of God" (Spohr) and a pleasant Service – My Sermon[1] on poor Mrs. R. was from Luke II, & I Peter III, 4 – The dead March afterwards was beautifully played – It rained torrents in the afternoon, having been in the morning exceedingly cold – Church again at 3.30 – after this wrote a letter of sympathy to poor Robinson.

> 1. The Sermon was entitled 'The Sphere and Duties of Christian Women' (c. 3,800 words), and was later printed in the 'Norfolk Chronicle' for January 14, 1882.

Tuesday 10
Our canddiates for the Layclerkship did not appear at luncheon – at 2 Mr. Cussons from Hull, and Mr. Hatfield from Southwell Minster, were tried – the first had a head voice & will not do; the second had a bad cold, & rather a <u>twang</u> – Hennings did not appear at all – I paid the expences of the two who were tried, & sent them back again.

Monday 16

After Mg. Church I had a visit from Cap. & Mrs. Fielder, complaining of their little son's being turned out of their seat on Sunday by Mr. Stanley the stonemason, at the dictation of Alden – after 2d Service I saw ... Alden about Cap. Fielder's charge, and wrote to the Captain – am going to write to Bulmer to ask him not again to absent himself at Xmas – He re-appeared yesterday.

Tuesday 17

Ju and Pom went to tea in Pottergate Street, given to Ju's children[1], & the girls of the G.F.S. under the management of Bessie Hansell – went to Church at 5 – on my return an interview with Captain Fielder, who came very much offended at my not taking so serious a view of Alden's escapade on Sunday as he had done; he resigned the seats I had allotted him at the Cathedral.

   1. Julia taught a Sunday School class.

Thursday 29

After Evg. Church, came 3 candidates (Cooper, Wellbanks, Gooch) for the gatekeeper's place.

Friday 20

Sat at home till 12.45, by wh. time I had nearly finished my Sunday Sermon – then went to the Bp's to enquire after Mrs. Pelham – her progress is very slow – then to the Heavisides, with whom I had luncheon in their drawing room – heard there that Mrs. H.H.[1] has had a stroke of paralysis.

   1. Mrs Hinds Howell.

Tuesday 24

All day long writing paper for tomorrow – A lovely day, mild, dry, shining – I visited the Bp. at 12.45, & found Mrs. Pelham had a good night – He strongly recommended Fanny Crow, whose husband seeks the gatekeeper's place – She & her husband called at 6 o'clock, and seemed to be suitable people.

Thursday 26

Church at 10 – then the 3 Archdeacons & Heaviside came to talk over the proposed testimonial to the Bp. on the 25th. Anniversary of his Consecreation – we agreed to meet the R. Deans here tomorrow at 11 – home to luncheon – then wrote 3 articles of Sermonette, & then went into the dg. room, where were Knight Bruce, Ada, Heaviside, the Wallaces, all listening to 7 choristers singing, Minns & Young Atkinson playing for them.

Friday 27

At 11 came the Deans Rural & Archdeacons, Uncle Bartie[1] the first of them – a little sparring between H.H. and Heaviside – agreed to present a portrait to the Bp., conditionally on his approval – I undertook to write to Lord Chichester – wrote to Lord Chichester[2] and to the Master – In the evening read the Times about Gambetta's[3] defeat & retirement from office; and corrected my Sermonette.

1. The Revd H.A. Barrett, Rector of Chedgrave and Vicar of Langley, joint Rural Dean of Brooke.
2. The Bishop's elder brother.
3. Leon M. Gambetta (1838–82) French politician; Premier 1881–82; resigned Jan 1882.

Tuesday 31

After Mg. Service set to work to look over the proof of the Statutes, wh. gave me much trouble and worry – Heaviside came in to tell me about (what is supposed to be) smallpox having broken out in the training College[1] – After Service [at 5] I finished and despatched the Statutes.

1. The Education Department had long been dissatisfied with the site of the College: "bad, in a very low and apparently ill-drained part of the city. Two large factories, both very noisy, and one with a bad smell ... stand wall to wall with the College, which, moreover, is a mile from the nearest green field, and has only a small turfed court (completely shut in by high buildings) for a recreation ground ... In this only of all the female colleges, the doctor says, the students do not enjoy good health." (1883 Report).

FEBRUARY

Wednesday 1   Mr. Hewson's trail in the Cathedral

In the morning Gerard and I drove out to Cringleford, to leave a letter for Chicken Pattie[1]; then on to Colney, where we got out, and after looking inside the Church, walked home – At 2 p.m. we had the trial of Mr. Hewson; Symonds, Barrett & Atkinson all thinking there were capabilities in his own voice, we agreed to appoint him; and I told him this after 5 p.m. Service.

1. Henry Stantiforth Patteson, Esq., Head of Pockthorpe Brewery, Churchman; former Mayor.

Thursday 2 Purification of B.V. Mary

We went to the Boys' concert at Noverre's Rooms and heard Cinderella wh. was done with great spirit, but wanted exegesis – I walked home from the first Part, observing the electric light[1] en route.

> 1. Britain lagged behind Europe and America in adopting electric power. The invention, in 1878–79 of the carbon-filament incandescent lamp by Thomas Edison (American) and Joseph Swan (English) rapidly increased the demand for electric lighting.

Friday 3

[He went to preach at St. Michael's, Ipswich and on returning at 6] found a letter from Ld. Chichester, enclosing one from the Bp., in wh. the latter consents to receive a picture from us – So I am going to write to the Committee tonight.

Thursday 9

After Mg. Church a 'solemn monial'[1] in our dining Room, first to Messrs. Smith, Burton, Holden, Brooks, & Brockbank, and then to Brockbank privately – I spoke to him kindly & pastorally, but seemed to make no impression – Mr. Burton asked indignantly why Mr. Thouless & Mr. Cox were not summoned – perhaps the whole thing may do good.

> 1. Monial = Mullion = Stump = (in this case) part of the Choir.

Friday 10

After Mg. Church at wh. Nevill re-appeared, he and I went across to Heaviside, and there settled with him to admit Richmond, junr. to a place among the names of artists submitted to the Bp. – Ju, Buskyns, Gerard, the Pin and self walked down to Carrow and were lionised over the Carrow excavations by Mr. King, the head man at Colman's works – he showed us the museum of curioisities found in the excavations[1]; and, in taking us homewards, showed us the manufacture of tin, wh. is exceedingly interesting – we walked back by the river's bank, where Buskyn's was alarmed by a mule wh. had broken its picket – at dinner came a letter from Bensly, saying that the petition agst. the Lynn & Fakenham line must be very shortly got ready – felt much depressed about this horrid railway.

> 1. There are the remains of the Benedictine Nunnery, founded in 1146. The 19th Century house is built in to the remains of the 16th Century Prioress's lodgings.

Saturday 11

Rose at 6.15, & altered and adapted our Railway petition of last year to the altered circumstances of the new line, wh. it is proposed to carry thro' the Close – worked at our petition till 10.30 – then called upon the Bp. to lay before him the names of the 6 artists (Herrkommer, Holl, Ouless, Richmond (W.), and Watts)[1] and ask him to select one of them to execute his portrait – I told him what I had heard about Watts – at ½p.11 I met Heaviside & Nevill at Bensly's Office, and we went thro' the new petition – at 3 took place the Installation of John Patteson, and I preached afterwards – came home & read the last two Acts of Hamlet to a Maiden's Bee.

1. He lists only five!

Sunday 12   Sexagesima

At 11 'Jippattie' read himself in – We met Ld. Justice Cotton[1] at the West Door; he was very well conducted, & did not say a word while walking up the Nave – the Bp. was there, & Heaviside, & 'Jippattie' – J preached – between Churches Gerard & I took a stroll up Gas Hill & back by the Thorpe Road – on our return found the Lord Justice & his Son here – it appears that I christened the latter at St. John's[2].

1. Sir Henry Cotton (1821–92). Lord Justice of Appeal. Privy Councillor and knighted 1877.
2. St John's, Paddington, where Goulburn was Vicar 1859–67.

Tuesday 14

Took leave of Gerard and little B. after Bkfst. – went into Stacy's, where I saw the plans of St Peter Mancroft, the <u>fleche</u> and the pepper-boxes[1] – Bensly at luncheon – he and I drew out afterwards the heads of a letter to the papers about the railway; this I wrote, while Bensly went to a meeting about St. Peter Mancroft; and when he returned, we went thro' the letter together – I got a letter from the Bp. wishing us success, but declining to sign our petition.

1. Beginning of a major restoration for St P. Mancroft. Last stage of restoring exterior reached with celebrations on April 29, 1883; 'fleche' = slender spire added in 1895.

Thursday 16

Left Norwich at 7.30 a.m. with Ju – observed in the 'Eastern Press' that the 'Lynn & Fakenham Bill' was read a 1st. time last night – an interview with Mr. Parkes on arriving, & w, another official[1] –

they spoke of the Lynn & Fakenham scheme as a bubble scheme wh. was sure to collapse sooner or later – then to Sir John Mowbray[2] at the E.C.; he could only see me for a moment, being engaged with Bp. of St. David's, but appointed me to come tomorrow at ½p.11 – then to the Society of Antiquaries, where I saw Mr. Knight Watson and Milman who is, I think, 'the Governor', and who, with his daughter, visited us last autumn – they were quite sympathetic, and I am to address a formal letter to the council on Tuesday next – thence to Beresford Hope's[3] who was kind, and asked me to luncheon, but did not tell me much.

1. Of the Great Eastern Railway (Liverpool St).
2. Conservative M.P. for Oxford University (1868–99).
3. Conservative M.P. for Cambridge University (1868–87); founded St Augustine's College, Canterbury; took leading part in building of All Saints' Church, Margaret St.

Friday 17   At Crowson's
Walked with Frederica down to 15, Bury Street, where saw Heaviside & communicated to him my proceedings of yesteday – then to Sir John Mowbray, who gave me some good practical advice about opposition to the Railway – then to Club, where wrote to Bensly and Mr. Thompson – then luncheon, after wh. drove to 15, Lombard Street but only <u>not</u> to find Sir John Lubbock[1], who missed his appoint.

1. Banker, Scientist, Author; Liberal M.P. for London University; secured passage of Act for Preservation of Ancient Monuments (1882).

Saturday 18
In a brougham at 11 a.m. I went down to see Heavisde at Bury Street, and after telling him what I had done, & reading him the Bp's letter, choosing Ouless, I drove on to Sir J. Lubbock's, who gave me hopes that he wd. oppose the Bill if asked to do so by the Socy. of Antiquaries – thence to Mr. Knight Watson – not at home – thence to Beresford Hope's – told to come again between 2 & 3 – thence to Mr. Ouless's, to whom Monier Williams[1] was sitting – pleasant chat with him – he shewed me Mr. Kennedy's letter about poor Golightly[2] – thence to Cousin MC's, who gave me luncheon – thence to Beresford Hope, from whom I got a promise to support Lubbock – then to Mr. Talbot's[3] (J.G. 10, Gt. George Street) who was most kind and promised to do all he could – thence to Club,, where began my Memorial to the Socy. of Antiquaries – Also wrote to Bensly & to Parkes – then afer two ineffectual attempts to see Heaviside again, home – in the

evening finished my memorial in the rough, & a letter to Kn. Watson.

1. Monier (later Sir) Monier-Williams (1819–99): Orientalist; Professor of Sanskrit at Oxford; largely founded Indian Institute at Oxford (1883).
2. His old Tutor at Oxford, for whom he had a great affection.
3. Conservative M.P. for Oxford University. (There were 2 M.P.s)

Monday 20 Last day in London
At 10.10 drove in brougham to Heaviside's, whom however I did not find at home – then to Stafford Northcote's with whom I had a short, & not very satisfactory interview – then by Sir S.N.'s[1] advice to Lord Salisbury[2], who promised to mention the matter to Lord Redesdale – then to Liverpool Street, where I had a satisfactory inteview with Mr. Parkes – then to Ly. Hamilton, where Ju had preceeded me to luncheon – thence to call on Knight-Watson, whom I found, and who referred me to Mr. Cavendish Bentinck[3] & others – I sought him & Mr. Borlax at the H. of C., but in vain; the crowd was too great – went to Club and wrote to Mr. Cavendish B., and also to Augustus Franks[4], to be present at Council of Antiquaries tomorrow.

1. Sir Stafford Northcote: Chancellor of the Exchequer 1874–80; Leader of the Opposition to Gladstone's Government in the H. of C. 1880–85; Conservative M.P. for Exeter.
2. Leader of the Opposition in the House of Lords (became Prime Mnister 1886).
3. Rt Hon. G.A.F. Cavendish Bentinck: Conservative M.P. for Whitehaven.
4. Augustus (later Sir) Franks (1826–97): Antiquary; Various official positions in British Museum; presented his collection of ceramics, etc. to British Museum; various Hon. Doctorates.

Tuesday 21 From London to Norwich
We left Crawson's at 10.30 & got to Liverpool Street at 11.10 – At 11.30 Mr. Parkes w. his members of Parliament, & Ld. Claude Hamilton at the head of them came in, & it was agreed that there shd. be opposition and a division taken on the Second Reading – they strongly advised my writing to the 'Times', and Ld. Claude Hamilton is to give me some introductions for next week – we are to have a separate petition & a separate counsel – we got down here by 3.40, & I went to the Office and signed the petition – then home & found H. to whom I narrated my proceedings.

Wednesday 22 **ASH WEDNESDAY**
Did not go to Church in the morning, but thot. of what to say at 11 o'clock Service – afterwards I sat a little with H. and saw Mrs. H. whose eyes are bad – then went on to Nevill's, and told him of

my doings – then home to luncheon; after wh. called on Miss H.[1] and reported progress to her – then a conference with Bensly on my plans for next week – wrote to Ld. Percy[2], Mr. Leighton[3], & Parkes, to make appointts. for next week; am going to write to Mr. Walpole[4] – at dinner time seized with headache, & could eat nothing; went to bed early, and with a swelled tonsil wh. made swallowing painful.

    1. Miss Hansell, who lived in the Close.
    2. An M.P. for Northumberland North (Conservative).
    3. Mr Stanley Leighton: An M.P. for North Shropshire.
    4. Rt Hon. S.H. Walpole (1806–98): An M.P. for Cambridge University. Had been Home Sec. three times; an Ecclesiastical Commissioner; and Chairman of the Gt Western Railway.

Thursday 23
In my dressing-room till 4 o'clock, engaged (1) partly in correcting my letter to 'the Times', wh. Ju had written from my dictation last night before I went to bed (2) in writing to a. Knight Watson, who had reported to me in glowing terms the orders of the Council of Antiquaries – At 6 p.m. saw two candidates for the gate, Rawlings and Hodgsons and made notes about them.

Friday 24   St. Matthias
Wrote to (1) Ld. Percy (2) Mr. Stanley Leighton (3) Mr. Walpole (4) Mr. Reeve – We dined at 6, and went to Church at 8 – there was a very good congregation, quite 200 people, I shd. think – Nevill told me afterwards that we had only 100 hassocks in all.

Saturday 25
At 1 came Hinds Howell, Heaviside, & Nevill, & we talked over 'the Portrait' matter, and agreed that we must wait a little longer to see whether things might not look up as regards the subscriptions – I agreed also with the 2 Canons to call a Chapter for April 13 (Thurs. in Eas. Week) to consider the new Draft Statues and also to order 200 new hassocks – Nevill, Hinds Howell, Maimie had luncheon here.

Monday 27
Not called till 6; drest in hurry – had to wait at Station for express by Ipswich (a Monday Morng. train) wh. does not leave Norwich till 7.50 – only stopped at Stowmarket & Ipswich – on reaching town an interview with Parkes & Fearn – then (Fearn with me) in Cab to Mr. Rees's office – not at home – thence to Club,

whence sent on Cab with my messenger & luggage to Park Street – an interview (satisfactory) with Knight Watson and Milman at Burlington House – thence to Club for Luncheon – then to Mr. Sanley Leighton at the Athaneum – he will be helpful but was not very sympathetic – back to Club, & wrote for appointment to Mr. Tyssen Amhurst[1] & Mr. Gurdon[2] – thence to H. of C. to see Mr. Walpole in the Library; he was all sympathy & kindness – then an interview with Mr. Rees (a coarse looking man) and Mr. Fearn in the lobby – then returned to Club & left in <u>Cab</u> all my maps, photos, statements in Ju's little black handbag! then telegraphed to Norwich for fresh supply – wrote to Ju a letter she mt. show to the Canons.

1. Wm. Amhurst Tyssen-Amherst (1835–1909): conservative M.P. for South-West Norfolk; Bibliophile and Norfolk landowner. Enthusiastic collector of books, works of art, and Egyptian papyri; well-known as cattle-breeder, shot, and yachtsman. In 1892 became 1st Baron Amherst of Hackney.
2. R. Thornhaugh Gordon: Liberal M.P. for South Norfolk.

Tuesday 28
At 8.15 to my gt. relief came a parcel from Bensly containing photogr., Maps, Statements, etc. and all that I wanted – Bkfst. at Mr. Walter's[1] at 9.15 a.m. – Lord Blachford[2] and Sir A. Hobhouse[3] there; I thought the latter rather grand – Walter promised me my letter in 'the Times', but said it would be a great convenience to 'the Times' paper to have a station at Taverham Mills – then went to buy fish for Cousin M.C. – then to Grosvenor Square to Lord Percy; he was most kind, but did not impress me as a man of any power – then to Frank Compton's who took me to call on Mr. Gurdon; he received me most graciously & seemed very favourable.

1. John Walter (1818–94): Chief Proprietor of 'The Times'; Liberal M.P. for Berkshire.
2. Frederic Rogers, Lord Blachford: a founder of 'The Guardian'; Privy Councillor. (1811–94).
3. Sir Arthur Hobhouse (1819–1904): Judge; Member of the Judicial Committee of the Privy Council; later became Baron Hobhouse.

MARCH

Wednesday 1
At 10.15 to Mr. Ber. Hope in a brougham – he was most kind and satisafactory, & sent me across the Park to Col. Makin, whom I did not find at home – thence to the Club, where I found a letter sending me back again to Prince's Gate where I arrived at Mr.

Cubitt's 1 hour too late just as the Queen was passing – He was very kind but in a great hurry – thence to Mr. Goschen's[1] – not at home – thence to Lord John Manners[2]; supercilious, but I think will vote the right way – thence to the Club – luncheon & then wrote a long letter to Mr. E. Stanhope[3], & another long letter to my Ju – my bag is recovered, & is not rifled.

> 1. George Joachim Goschen (1831–1907): Banker (Director of the Bank of England); various Government and Cabinet posts; Liberal M.P. for Ripon; later became 1st. Viscount Goschen.
> 2. Lord John Manners (1818–1906): Conservative M.P. for North Leicestershire; had been a Cabinet Minister; became 7th. Duke of Rutland in 1888.
> 3. The Hon. Edward Stanhope (1840–93): M.P. for Mid-Lincolnshire; Under-Sec. for India 1878–80; later Sec. of Board of Trade (and in Cabinet); and then Sec. for War, etc.

Thursday 2   London to Norwich

Wrote a letter before Bkfst. to Mr. Walter, pointing out that the transport of paper from Taverham will not be facilitated by the line's coming thro' the Close – after Prayers & Bkfst. (alone), called on Goschen, and laid the whole case before him – he seemed to think that the fact of a Bill having been obtained already to bring the Railway into Norwich made all the difference – At Liverpool Street, went to see Parkes & report progess; he very civilly accompanied me to the train – got down to Norwich before 4, and immediately went to Bensly and wrote a P.S. to 'the Times', wh. I hope they will insert – a letter from Nisbet about the Statutes awaiting me – also a very unpleasant anon. letter about Mrs. Alden[1].

> 1. Mr Alden had been, formerly, Master of the Choir School, but was now a Layclerk.

Friday 3

Worked at my notes, and also at a Sermonette for tomorrow till 11.45 – then went out and took a long solitary walk, thinking over my Sermon, on Mousehold and back by Thorpe Road – got back 1.45 – found Bensly at luncheon here, who took me afterwards to call on Mr. Utten Browne[1] at Heigham Grove – he was solemn and grand, but not very sympathetic – thence to Mr. Winter's Office, but he was out – thence to Mr. Fitch's – after a little chat with Mr. Payne of Colney at the door, we saw Mr. Fitch at the door of his shop; he gave us very little help, but asked me to write an answer for him to Knight Watson – home & with my Ju's help wrote to (1) Sir John Lubbock (2) Stanley Leighton (3)

Beresford Hope (4) Stafford Northcote (5) Mr. Talbot (6) Knight Watson, etc. – At 8 a good congregation; better than last time – I preached – very nervous, but thank god much helped[2].

> 1. Wm. John Utten-Brown (1805–93): Woolstapler; Mayor of Norwich 1860–61; staunch Conservative and High Churchman.
> 2. Second in course on Friday Evening Lent Sermons.

Saturday 4

Wrote two letters (with enclosures) before Bkfst., one to Tyssen-Amherst, the other to E. Birkbeck[1] – after Bkfst, walked in k. garden reading Othello – then to the Litchfields[2], with whom I prayed – Mrs. L. is, I think fading away – called on Mr. Bagshaw the fishdealer in St. Mile's, to enquire about the misconduct of a Cathedral official alleged in an anon. letter – At 3 gave a Sermonette – Priscilla Litchfield prayed for – after Church came Copeman saying that the 'Lynn & F. Ry. Contractor' would do anything to accomodate us, short of taking the line out of the Close – read the first Act of Othello at a Bee – then saw Mr. Stacy; & then 2 candidates for the Gate – thought of drafting a letter tonight to the members for Cathedral Cities, trying to interest them – wrote to Sir Robert Buxton[3].

> 1. Edward Brickbeck (1838–1908): Conservative M.P. for North Norfolk; in 1883 Chairman of the Fisheries Exhibition in Norwich; Chairman of the RNLI; knighted in 1886.
> 2. Former Subsacrist in the Cathedral.
> 3. Sir Robert Buxton, Bart., Conservative M.P. for South Norfolk.

Sunday 5   Lent 2

At 11 and 3.30 we prayed for poor Mrs. Litchfield, and gave thanks for the Queen's[1] preservation.

> 1. On March 2, for the fifth time, the Queen's life was threatened by assassination at Windsor, when Roderick Maclean, a lunatic, fired a pistol at her, fortunately without effect.

Monday 6

Before Bkfst. drafted a letter to the members for Cathedral Cities asking them to assist us in opposing the Lynn and Fakenham Bill – all day long engaged about this matter, my Ju helping me so much that we had finished off all Cathedral Members before Bed time – wrote also to ... (4) Ellicott, about a copy of the Statutes for Bensly (I wrote to him before Bkfst., asking him to submit our Close troubles to the Cath. Establishments' commissioners) – I called on Heaviside in the Mg.; he had had a favourable letter from Sir W. Harcourt[1] – hard at work on letters all evening.

1. Sir William Vernon Harcourt (1827–1904): Liberal M.P. for Derby; had been Solicitor-General and Home Secretary. Later became Chancellor of the Exchequer, and Leader of the House of Commons. Declined peerage 1902.

Tuesday 7

Rose at 6.15, drafted a letter for Gladstone, and another for the Deans of Cathedral Churches – wrote out the first, and by the time I had done it, it was time to go with Bensly to the Archaeological Meeting – walked down there side by side with Bensly and Thomson, who talked about taking down the old Ferry Arch in 1852 – there was Fitch, Dr. Jessopp, Col. Bulwer, Mr. Carthew, Bensly and others – I was empowered to draw up a petition to Parliament on behalf of the Committee, agst. the invasion of the Close – in the evening, Ju and I addressed our circular to every Dean of a Cathedral Church – Mr. Gurdon wrote today to recommend no opposition on Second Reading; & Sir J. Lubbock to say he cd. not lead the opposition.

Wednesday 8

Drafted a petition for the Archaeological Society, wh. I went over with Bensly at 3 o'clock – wrote a multitude of letters – in the evening came. to my amazement, a letter from Mr. Gladstone[1], most kind and sympathetic, Govt., he says, but rarely intervene's in Private Bills.

1. The Rt Hon. W.E. Gladstone (1809–98): Liberal Prime Minister 1868–74; 1880–85; 1886; 1892–94.

Thursday 9

Wrote to Mr. Hubbard[1] for an appointt. (before Bkfst.) – wrote to (1) Arundell Mildmay, from whom I got a letter this morning saying that his daughter is sinking. (2) Parkes, making an appointment for 11 on Monday. (3) looked over the petition from our Archaeological Society, & then took it across to Bensly's – after some talk with Bensly, I went to see the Litchfields; Mrs L. seemed rather more alive than at my last visit – after dinner a letter from Burgie[2] asking more circulars, etc. to send to M.P.s – read Shakspere.

1. John G. Hubbard (1805–89): Conservative M.P. for London 1874–87; Director of the Bank of England; P.C.; had built and endowed St Alban's, Holburn; created Baron Addington 1887.
2. Burgon, the Dean of Chichester.

Friday 10
Wrote to Dn. of Ch. Ch.[1] (2) Institute of Architects (3) Dean of Salisbury[2] – wrote to Arundell on the death of his dr., the news of wh. reached us this morning.

1. The Very Revd H.G. Liddell (1811–98): Dean of Christ Church, Oxford 1855–91.
2. The Very Revd George David Boyle (1828–1901): Dean of Salisbury 1880–1901.

Saturday 11   Norwich to Crowson's, 12, Park Street
Ju and I w. Robbins left Norwich at 7.35 – Read in the 'Times' the trial of Dr. Lamson – on arriving Ju and I stopped at Goslings' to get money, and then at Pratts to try on gt. coat and at Frodsham's about her watch – then we parked at the Club – I walked down to Downing Street and left my cards at Mr. Gladstone's; neither he nor Mrs. G. were at home, or I shd. have gone in – then to Club – there in the midst of a long letter to Mr. Gilbert Venables (enclosing him Map, Letters, etc.) I was interrupted by a telegram saying Mr. Hubbard would see me between 1 and 2 – after a rapid luncheon hurried off to Princes's Gate; left Mr. H. a map and a printed letter – he was satisfactory, and asked me to listen to something he was writing in refutation of the lies of the 'Liberation Society' – thence to Institute of Architects in Conduit Street, but cd. find no one at home.

1. Edward Miall (1809–81), a Congregationalist Minister; established the weekly Paper 'Nonconformist' and founded the 'British Anti-State Church Association' in 1844 to campaign for the separation of Church and State, and bring about disestablishment. In 1853, changed to the 'Society for the Liberation of Religion from State Control' = 'The Liberation Society'.

Sunday 12   Lent 3
Walked at 10 to St. Mark's – In the afternoon we walked to St. George's, Hanover Square, for the Afternoon Service at ½p.3 – It was shortened – tidy, but with no great life, the whole lasting 50 min. – returned to Crowson's, & were just beginning to read the Bp. of Derry's 'Leading Ideas of the Gospels' when Meanne and her husband walked in – he promised to help me with some M.P.s.

Monday 13
Prepared questions for Parke's Council of War – At 10 drove to Rees's, and handed in the names wh. Heaviside had given me – thence to Liverpool St. where were only Parkes, Ld. Claude, and Sir H. Tyler (who gave us the 1st. Report of Cath. Commission)

– it was resolved to have a fight on Second Reading, and that Talbot or Hope shd. be asked to move the rejection – he promised to talk it over w. Talbot and Walpole & Hope, & let me know the result – then [*after luncheon*] to the Institute of Architects: but my chat with the secretary did not come to much – then to Club, whence I wrote to (1) Mr. Shaw Lefevre for an interview tomorrow.

Tuesday 14
Saw Mr. Talbot, Mr. Walpole, & Mr. Beresford Hope before leaving Town, and prepared them for a conference with Mr. Stanhope – Ju and I left town by noonday train from Liverpool Street.

Wednesday 15
Wrote to Mr. Salt, (2) Mr. Dalrymple (3) Mr. Shaw Lefevre[1] (sending the documents) – also wrote to Mr. Stanhope, thanking him very much for his having given notice of opposition in such a manner as to protect the Close without negativing the railway – I got his letter this morning – I must send Parkes a copy of Mr. Stanhope's letter.

> 1. The Rt Hon. G.J. Shaw-Lefevre (1831–1928): Liberal M.P. for Reading; formed Commons Preservation Society; had been Sec. of the Board of Trade; Sec. to Admiralty; First Commssioner of Works 1880–83; Postmaster-General (in Cabinet) 1883. A Statesman of extraordinary industry and public spirit.

Thursday 16
Bef. Bkfst. wrote to Stafford Northcote, and also to Mr. Talbot, thanking for his introductions, etc. etc. – Church at 10 with Nevill & Bulmer, – talk afterwards with Bartie in the chapter Office about Boys' caps & cinctures – After luncheon, the day being lovely, walked with Ju on Earlham Road, Heaviside going a certain way with us, and back by Dereham Road thro' the cemetery – we visited the Mistresses'[1] grave, and also that of the Blakes – met Heaviside again on our return; he had seen a paragraph in 'Daily News' about our matter – wrote to Dean of Lichfield[2], sending him maps, etc. (2) Rees, sending him names – after dinner Ju and I chose the Gate keeper, going thro' the testimonials.

> 1. Mrs Robinson.
> 2. The Very Revd Edward Bickersteth (1814–92): Dean of Lichfield 1874–92; Prolocutor of Lower House of the Convocation of Canterbury.

Friday 17

After Bkfst. till luncheon engaged on a letter to the Guardian, which I found <u>very hard</u> – Nevill came in to show me the letter Heaviside had recd. [*from*] Prof. Rogers[1], saying that he will propose that the Bill be read that day 6 months! – after luncheon Bensly and I saw Spruce, and I offered him the gatekeeper's place, wh. he accepted – then went over with Bensly my letter to the 'Guardian' – am beginning to feel over-driven.

> 1. J.E. Thorold Rogers, Liberal M.P. for Southwark; Tooke Professor of Statistics and Economic Science, King's College, London.

• •

After writing "a letter to the Deans, asking them to get their Chapters to sign a petition in our favour", Goulburn left, on Saturday morning, for Peterborough, to preach in the Cathedral on Sunday evening, returning to Norwich on Tuesday afternoon.

• •

Tuesday 21

Got to Norwich about 4, having read the 'Daily Telegraph' <u>en route</u> – found several letters, one huge one from Kensit about Melia's affairs, wh. are now being wound up, & Aubrey's & my trusteeship determining – wrote to Cavendish-Bentinck in answer to a 'confidential' communication about the Lynn & Fakenham (2) Marsham Argles, sending him a draft form of Capitular Petition.

Wednesday 22

Knight Watson sent me yesterday's 'Standard', in wh. is a leader agst. the Lynn and Fakenham Bill – drew up a letter for Bensly to send to Eastern Daily Press correcting their mistake about Stafford Northcote's having presented a petition from <u>our Chapter</u> against 'Lynn and Fakenham' – at 2.15 drove to Mr. Ram's[1] to leave him £6. 10 towards the expences of defending his Churchyard – Church again at 5 – talk w. Daniells afterwards about putting out the Bell earlier.

> 1. See January 21, 1873 (Note 2).

Thursday 23

Wrote to Dr. Vaughan (sending him a MS petition); to the Master; asking for a petition from the Cambridge Heads; to the Vicechancellor of Cambridge[1] – resolved to go to Town on Saturday – wrote a letter to the 'Eastern Daily Press', & to Mr.

Warton & Mr. Rogers – When I was dressing for dinner came a telegram to say that Second Reading (<u>Debate</u>) is fixed for Tuesday next – after dinner wrote to Mr. Gladstone and to Rees – I am glad the αγων is to be over so soon.

> 1. The Revd James Porter, D.D., Master of St Peter's College (Peterhouse), Cambridge.

Friday 24
Wrote a letter to 'the Standard' before Bkfst.; also to Gilbert Venables, asking him to procure its insertion – walked in k. garden, meditating Sermon, for an hour – then to see and pray with the two Litchfields – arranged with Bartie the Holy Week Services – Bensly came in, and urged me to write to Hen. Patteson[1] in view of the meeting of the Town Council on Monday, to petition for the Railway – wh. I did.

> 1. Henry Staniforth Patteson, brother of the Rector of Thorpe St Andrew (John); Deputy Lieutenant; former Sheriff and Mayor of Norwich; Alderman; Churchman; J.P.; strong supporter of good causes; Director of various Businesses and Organisations.

Saturday 25   Annunciation of B.V. Mary
Came to town (St. Pancras) by the early train – Saw Mr. Talbot & Rees, and in the later afternoon Sir W. Vernon Harcourt and Shaw Lefevre.

Monday 27
Started in Brougham at 9.45; went to B. Hope, & had interview with him outside his door – (I left with Hope the petition from Cambridge Heads this morning, to present it) ... (4) Rees, only saw his Secretary, but he was satisfactory (5) Parkes, also satisfactory ... (8) Mr. Stanhope – he was most kind & satisfactory – then to Club for a little luncheon – then (9) to Mr. Warton at St. Stephen's Club; he seemed to take great interest, & was very kind ... then (11) to H. of C. where had a long interview with Prof. Rogers in Tea Room (12) went before Dr. Lyon Playfair[1] (Chairman of Ways & Means) to state our case – then it was announced by Warton that the Speaker had postponed 'Lynn & Fakenham' till Friday – then I authorised Rees to get a railway surveyor on our side for £50.

> 1. Had been Professor of Chemistry at Edinburgh; Liberal M.P. for Universities of Edinburgh and St Andrews; had been Postmaster-General and Deputy Speaker of the H. of C.; knighted 1883; became 1st Baron Playfair in 1892.

Tuesday 28

Cab at 9.30 (1) to Rees's, where met Alfred Williams our engineer, & consulted, & gave him instructions – (2) Club where wrote to several of the Deans; to Sir H. Drummond Wolff[1] asking engagement; to Shairp[2] for a good word with Lyon Playfair.

> 1. Sir Henry Drummond Wolff (1830–1908): Politician and Diplomat; Conservative M.P. for Portsmouth 1880–85; later, British Envoy in Persia, Bucharest, and Madrid.
> 2. John Campbell Shairp: One of Goulburn's Assistant-Masters at Rugby; Principal of United College, St Andrew's 1868–77; Professor of poetry at Oxford 1877–85.

Wednesday 29

Shortly before 10 went to Sir Hardinge Giffard's; he gave me a warm welcome, over his bkfst. table – my godchild came down & sat on my knee, and there was a sweet little girl there too – Sir H.G. most kind; advised me to see Sir Thos. Chambers – asked me to dinner at 8, to wh. I am going – thence I went to Mr. Rees, to make suggestions about improving our 'statement' – thence to Club – then at 12 came Sir H.D. Wolff, & dashed my hopes about Friday entirely – Chamberlain wd. be agst. us; the Government governed by him; all our members agst. us; Town Council agst. us; we had much better compromise – cd. we not offer cheap our land on the other side of the river!! – wrote a long letter to my Ju – then went to buy (1) a purse (2) silk stockings (3) H. de Losinga for Prof. Rogers – Dined with Sir Hardinge Giffard; most pleasant.

Thursday 30

In cab the 1st. thing after Bkfst. to Sir H. Holland's[1], with whom had a most pleasing interview – then to my Club – then to see Heaviside – then to St. George St. where met Alfred Williams, and gave him notes for a short report, saying I wd. come back again at 4 – then to Club, where wrote my letter to 'the Times', and then a long letter to Sir Thos. Chambers – a shorter letter than usual to Ju – then to meet my appointt. with Alfred Williams at 4 – told him to get his report printed, & then left him – in the eveng. a letter from Sir H. Drummond Wolff, saying the enemy were going to make an offer of compromise, wh. he wd. bring to me about 2 p.m. at my Club – I declined seeing him, however, & wrote instead.

> 1. Sir Henry Holland (1825–1914): Conservative M.P. for Midhurst 1874–85; Secretary of State for the Colonies 1888–92; Viscount Knutsford 1895.

Friday 31

Shortly after Bkfst. went to St. Stephen's Club, and there left a letter for Mr. Warton – thence to Rees's, where I met Mr. Williams, and saw the printed copy of his Report – thence to Mr. John Talbot, who was late after last night's debate, but with whom I got a few words before his bkfst. – then to Heaviside's Club, who told me of a conversation he had had with one Cripps, a traitor in the enemy's camp – then to Liverpool Street, where I endeavoured to satisfy Parkes and Fearns as to our honourable conduct, and had a confidential communication with them – partly walked & partly cabbed down to the H. of C. where I met Heaviside & Nisbet, & spoke to Sir H.D. Wolff (evidently in the enemy's interests), Prof. Rogers, Mr. Stanhope, and Mr. Warton, who kindly got Nisbet & me seats in the gallery – Ld. Waveney came in, & promised to do all he cd. for us in the lobby, & I belive he did – Mr. Stanhope, Rogers, Sir J. Kennaway (a nasty speech), Tillett (violent), and lastly Playfair who proposed to the enemy to withdraw Clause 6, and so let the Bill pass second reading – Nisbet & I walked to the telegraph Station whence I telegraphed.

APRIL

Saturday 1

Rose at 6, & wrote before Bkfst. to ... (2) Rees, with £50 for Williams. (3) Mr. Vincent about 'Socy. for the Protection of Ancient Monuments' – after Bkfst. went to see (1) Mr. Stanhope (2) Mr. Talbot (3) Mr. Rees – found and thanked (1) and (2) – (3) I did not see, but his Secretary seemed to think that all went right yesterday evg. – then returned to Park Street, & wrote to Shairp before leaving Town – returned to Norwich by midday train – Mr. Tillett[1] with me in the carriage; he lent me Vinet's 'Etudes Historiques', one Sermon in wh, I read – talked of his nephew, of R.A. Cooper, of the progress of Scepticism, etc. etc. – At Ely Blanche Daniell rushed in & began to congratulate me, etc. whereon Mr. Tillett got out – on getting to Norwich, walked home by the Ferry, and called on Miss Hansell <u>en route</u> up the Close.

> 1. Goulburn had said that Jacob H. Tillett, Liberal M.P. for Norwich, made a 'violent' speech in the debate the previous evening, presumably in favour of the 'Lynn and Fakenham Bill'.

Tuesday 4

After luncheon took a letter to the Bp. of Chichester to the General post; he had telegraphed to me to ask what was done on the occasion of the suicide of a lay clerk in the Cathedral[1] – Church shut up ? Service of reconciliation ? etc. – took fly to go to Stanley, the marble mason's, and see the Iona cross preparing for Mrs. Robinson – on my return began a letter to the Master about the cross & the grave, & also describing our success on Friday – finished my letter to the Master after Church; & also put up some documents on 'Reconciliation of Churches', for the Bp. of Chichester[2].

> 1. In November 1880 one of the Norwich Cathedral Lay Clerks (Henry Minns) hanged himself in the Cathedral. A 'Service of Humiliation' was held in the Cathedral on Friday, November 26, at which Goulburn preached 'On Suicide'.
> 2. The Rt Revd Richard Durnford.

Wendesday 5 Spohr's[1] Oratorio ('Calvary') at 7 p.m.
An enormous throng at 7 p.m. – gave two short addresses on the Oratorio, in the 1st. of wh. I told them something about Philo, who is one of the characters – It was not over till 9.20!

> 1. Ludwig Spohr (1784–1859): German composer, violinist and conductor.

Friday 7   **GOOD FRIDAY**
Instead of going to Church at 8 drew out Sermon Notes for the Evening – completed these notes before Mg. Service at 11 – Bp. there (very chilling, I thot.) and Heaviside & Bartie & Bulmer – told the Bp. about the suicide in Diocese of Chichester.

Sunday 9   **EASTER SUNDAY**
H.C. with 'Bartie at 8 a.m. – 93 commts.; we were out at 9.30 – received from Frederic a volume of Scott Hollands[1] Sermons – Bp. preached at 11 with much more energy and power of voice than has been his wont of late.

> 1. Henry Scott Holland (1847–1918): Theologian and Preacher; Canon of St Paul's 1884–1910; Regius Professor of Divinity at Oxford 1910–18; keenly interested in relating Christian principles to the social and economic problems of human living.

Wednesday 12
Aft. Ch. at 10 w. Heaviside, Bartie, Bulmer, I till luncheon time sat in the vestry, assigning seats (with Alden & Eliza L.) to various applicants – Auntie went to a factory girls' tea in St Paul's School Room – Dinner at 7.45 – Afterwards Auntie & I worked together at annotating B. I, Chap. II of my work on the Gospels.

Friday 14

Rose at 6.30, and read up for a Sermon on Sunday – At 11 Service with Heaviside, Bartie, Bulmer – then a meeting with Heaviside, Nevill, & Hinds Howell – we came to the conclusion that non-givers were to be stimulated by a circular from me, and that nothing could be settled as to the artist, until 11 Deaneries, from whom nothing had been heard, had sent in their subscriptions[1] – At 5 Service again with Heaviside & Bartie – then admission of 5 new choristers, and dismissal of 3 old ones, Hardesty among the latter.

> 1. The matter of the Bishop's portrait.

Monday 17   Last Day at Norwich

The whole of the rest of the morning (after 11) occupied in a Chapter Meeting where we had several worrying bits of business, steps to be taken for letting Gowing's farm at Wingfield, sealing Mr. Sutterby's new lease, determining what to do about the vacated School at Trowse, Mr. Rump's request to lower his rent, etc. etc. – the whole of the afternoon I was distracted about many things – there was a long seance here about the Library Paper and ceiling, Heaviside & Nevill joining in, and all of them settling a very pretty, but expensive paper.

• •

From April 18 to May 20, the Goulburns were on one of their regular visits to friends and relations at Eyhorne (where Gerard and Buskins lived); at Farnham; at Aynhoe; then a period in Brighton and in London, before returning to Norwich on May 20.

• •

Tuesday 18   Norwich to Eyhorne

Left Norwich at 7.30 – Observing in the Eastern Daily Press an announcement that Parliamentary Referees are to hear today an appeal agst. the <u>locus standi</u> of D. & C. opposition to the Railway, I stopped to see Parkes & Fearn at Liverpool Street, who assured me that it is all right, and that the appeal is merely formal – called at Meanne's[1] new home <u>en route</u> to Victoria Stan., but neither of them were at home – Got to Eyhorne about ½p.6 – Lou & Gerard met us at Maidstone; dined with Gerard & Buskins at 7.30, wh. was very pleasant.

> 1. Julia's niece, daughter of her sister Fanny, who died in 1864.

Thursday 20 At Eyhorne
We arranged to go in Lou's carriage at 11 o'clock to Langley (Lolotte, Pom & I) and walk back part of the way – we found Mr. Pusey (the Dr's brother) who showed us his Church, a Butterfield[1] production of 25 years ago (just before All Saints), the lines Butterfield, the colour decorations Butterfield, the window's Hardman's under B's superintendence – a good Chapter in Modern English Architecture – Mr. P. talked about letters J.H.N.[2] had written to Pusey, deploring the speed of infidelity – after luncheon, I dictated to Ju a rough draft of my address to the Bp. on the 25th. anniversary of his consecration.

1. William Butterfield, Architect (1814–1900): Architect of St Augustine's College, Canterbury (1845), Chapel of Balliol College, Oxford (1856–57), All Saints, Margaret Street, London (1859), new buildings at Merton College, Oxford (1864), School buildings at Rugby (1875), and Keble College, Oxford (1876).
2. J.H.N. = John Henry Newman.

Saturday 22 At Eyhorne
Gerard came in, and talked about his will & the fulfilment of the engagements of his marriage contract.

Monday 24
Left Little B's Cottage at 8.15 a.m.; read the 'Times' en route – Arrived in town, Ju and I separated – I went to make small purchases and to see Chirop.; thence to Goslings for money; Club for luncheon – Dressed at Club; Levee at 2 – Met (1) Bp. of Carlisle[1] (2) 'the Luminary', who talked about the flourishing state of the Episcl. Ch. in Scotland (3) Dean of Llandaff[2] – P. of Wales, D. of Connaught, & D. of Cambridge[3] shook hands – Ju called for me at 3.15 – went down to Farnham at 4.

1. The Rt Revd Harvey Goodwin.
2. The Very Revd Charles Vaughan, D.D.
3. Field Marshall and Commander-in Chief of the Army; 2nd Duke of Cambridge. *Not* a member of the Royal Family.

Friday 28 At Aynhoe
Before Bkfst. corrected proof for Stacy of my 'Portrait Address' – afterwards wrote to Hinds Howell (re-enclosing him a sketch of the Bp. by Winter, wh, he sent me this morning), and to the Master on the commencement of his residence, and about the Ascension Day Services – and then set to work at the Statutes & carefully entered in my copy the objections of Nisbet & Robinson.

MAY

Tuesday 2
In the morning wrote to (1) the Bp. about the day of Intercession in the Cathedral – (2) the Master & Bartie on the same subject – I also mentioned to the Bp. Mrs. Henry Chetwynd's case of a Boy for St. John's Foundation School – (3) Rivington's – then worked at the Statues till 12.20 – finding Ju had gone to King's Sutton without me, I walked there (½ by the fields) in ½ an hour – there I sat reading the papers till 8 p.m. – then I walked to Newbottle, and found Lili arrived there – Tom & Bitta were in Church, attending the Baptism of their footman; him I saw for a few minutes, and said a word to him, as Tom wished me to do so – Bitta then drove me & Lili to Aynhoe in her carriage – here I found a letter from Heaviside, announcing that a tree in our garden had fallen into his, breaking part of the wall which separates us.

Sunday 7 [*At Aynhoe*]
Too uncomfortable to go to Church in the morning, but staid at home, and prepared a Sermon on Ananias & Sapphira in reference to the Confirmn. on Tuesday – Holford brot. after Morning Service, the appalling news that Ld. Fredk. Cavendish and his secretary have both been assassinated on reaching Ireland[1] – GOD grant it may not be true.

> 1. In Phoenix Park, Dublin. Lord Frederick was taking up his position as Chief Secretary for Ireland; Thomas Burke had been Under-Secretary for Ireland since 1869. The former was 46, the latter 53.

Tuesday 9
Confirmation at Aynhoe by Bishop Mitchison[1] – a wretched day of pain (rheumatism in the shoulder) and depression – The Bishop's address was most admirable, the best I ever heard next to poor Bishop Wilberforce's – was not well enough to be at the luncheon.

> 1. The Rt Revd John Mitchison, D.D., D.C.L., recently retired as Bishop of Barbados and Windward Isles.

Wednesday 10 Aynhoe to Brighton
Rose in pain at 5.30 and dressed with difficulty – left Aynhoe at 7.30 in fly – got to London (the Dean being in the same carriage with us, and covered with Newspapers) at 10.30 – Ju dropped me at Morgan's, who prescribed for my rheumatism – thence to

London Library, where I could not find what I wanted – thence to Brit. Mus. where 1st. I met Burgon, and then had a long interview with Mr. Thompson & Mr. Scott; they were most kind, & got me all the books I wanted – then to Parker's in Southampton Street, to purchase his 'Introduction to the Revisions of the B.C.P.' – thence to Club for luncheon – Ju called for me at 3 p.m. and we went to see the picture in Conduit Street of our Lord before Pilate – the central figure <u>most</u> unpleasing – some details good – then to Victoria Station, where we took Pulman Tickets – very low in the evening.

Friday 12
Read last night's debate, at wh. (Gladstone & Hartington being absent) Sir W. Harcourt[1] proposed the stringent measures intended to restore security & order in Ireland – I think he did this with dignity – Forster's[2] speech was good – (I wrote also to poor old Litchfield about the loss of his wife) – After luncheon felt very low and depressed – Ju and I took a good walk, calling on the Bigges, and the Hannahs[3], but finding no one at home, and then going, after looking at the S.P.C.K., to Madeira – read aloud to Ju Dicken's Great Expectations in the evening.

1. Home Secretary.
2. Wm. Edward Forster, Lib M.P.: had been Chief Sec. for Ireland 1880–82.
3. John Julius Hannah, Vicar of St Nicholas, Brighton 1875–87; eventually Dean of Chichester from 1902.

•••
The Goulburns left Brighton for Norwich on Wednesday, May 17, stayed in London until May 20. On the evening of Ascension Day (18), he preached in St Paul's Cath.
•••

Saturday 20   From London to Norwich
Frederica came in to see us before we left, and went with us to Cousin Mary's – left St. Pancras at 12 noon – <u>en route</u> I finished 'Great Expectations', a most disagreeable sensational novel, leaving an unpleasant impression – found the ordinary quantum of letters awaiting us; answered several of them before Bedtime – also paid my last instalment to the survey of Western Palestine.

Monday 22
After Bkfst. in my room, wrote several letters, and corrected a good deal of the description of the Cathedral in Jarrold's 'Norwich Guide', nearly finishing it.

Wednesday 24
Church at 10 – Afterwards prepared the 'Agenda' Paper with Bensly & Browne till about 12.30 – then went to the Bp.; he was with Henry Birkbeck[1] – he was very willing that I should take my four Sermons in July instead of August – he also said he was glad that I was to address the G.F.S. in July – then we talked about Bp. Crowther[2], & his proposed visit here the first Sun. in July, & the Bp. told me anecdotes about him – then an interview with Spruce the Beadle at Bensly's Office; he wanted to be made a Constable, but hopes he shall get something for it – at 2.15 the Master and I got a walk on the Newmarket Rd. returning by the Ipswich Rd., but we were covered with dust.

> 1. Henry Birkbeck (1821–95) (of Stoke Holy Cross): Director of Gurney's Bank; Sheriff of Norwich 1853–54; HIgh Sheriff of Norfolk 1860; Chairman Gt Hospital Trustees; Treasurer Norfolk and Norwich Hospital; when he died in 1895, a Memorial Service was held in the Cathedral at the same time as his burial at Stoke Holy Cross.
> 2. Bishop Samuel Crowther (1809–91): Ex-slave rescued by British warship in 1822; Baptised 1825; Ordained 1842; consecrated Bishop of the Niger Territories 1864, the first non-European Anglican Bishop. At his Baptism he had taken the name of a London Vicar. Translated the Bible into Yoruba. Preached in Norwich Cathedral on July 2, 1882.

Thursday 25
S.P.G. Day – Services at 10, 11.15, 3.30 – Pouring with rain all the morning – At the 11.15 H.C. ... sadly few communicants – meeting at Clerical Rooms afterwards, at wh. I presided – Mr. Wright made an interesting speech on his work in Japan – then we had luncheon here; 13 with our two selves – At 3.30 we had the Service at wh. the Bp.[1] preached – afterwards I showed him some of the Misereres and some of the bosses in the Cathedral – then we took a short stroll, to see that part of the Close wh. the railway proposed to save [have] – There dined here 10 with our 2 selves – the dinner went off well; Congregations and Collections at lowest ebb.

> 1. The Rt Revd John Mitchinson.

Tuesday 30
At 11.18 started for Cromer – Trains full of excursionists and dirty people – a long (but a very pretty) drive from Cromer to Holt, where we arrived at about 2 – Miss Girdlestone, Mr. Brumell's[1] niece, acted as lady of the house – there was a Mr. & Mrs. Cooke[2] (rector of Baconsthorpe in succession to Mr. Fielden) and some other clergymen – the singing was rather good,

but there was too much of it, and after the Benedn. Bunnett[3] gave an organ recital, wh. was very wearying – I preached – the recital did not end till 5.10 – our fly was at the Church door, & we got to Cromer only just in time for the train, wh. stopped at every station to take up excursionists – walked from Thorpe Station, reaching home at 8.

1. The Revd E. Brumell had been Rector of Holt since 1853.
2. Goulburn mistook the name: the new Rector of Baconsthorpe was the Revd S.R. Coxe, who had come from a parish in the north of England, and in 1885 returned north, eventually becoming an Hon. Canon of Newcastle-on-Tyne and a Rural Dean.
3. Edward Bunnett, Mus. Doc, F.R.C.O. (1834–1923). Born at Shipdam Norfolk; had been pupil of Dr Buck and later his Assistant Cathedral organist; Organist of St Peter Mancroft; as a young Chorister, he had sung with Jenny Lind and Miss Dolby in a Concert at Norwich; was, for a long period, Chorister and Organist at Concerts in St Andrew's Hall. Composer of anthems, hymns, tunes, carols, a Communion Service in E, vocal and instrumental music.

JUNE

Thursday 1
At 11.15 came Miss Patteson, Miss Hopper and others – the meeting at the Clerical Rooms at 11.30 went off very well – Miss Patteson spoke of the immense elevation of woman by the true Religion – this shown by the Patriarchal women even under a system of polygamy – what she said was very interesting, & very naturally told – a collection afterwards for the Ladies' Assocn. of S.P.G. amounting to £11 – then a large luncheon, 20 people – at ½p.2 almost everyone (Miss Patteson included) went off to the Concert.

Friday 2
In the evening we dined at 6.30 to give our servants an opportunity of hearing Miss Patteson.

Saturday 3
A wretched night of sickness; sent for Muriel, who told me to keep indoors and eat nothing – At 12 I saw Hinds Howell, Heaviside, the Master, Archdn. Perowne, and Mr. Garnier (Groome & Nevill absent) and we settled the corrections to be made in my draft of the Address, and agreed that I was to see Ouless on Wednesday week, & tell him we cd. give no more than £500 tout compris – In the evening read to Ju some of Percy Fitzgerald's Life of George IV.

Sunday 4   TRINITY SUNDAY

Went to Church at 11, and preached the Ordination Sermon on "I will pray with the spirit, & I will pray w. the understanding also", but did not stay afterwards – the Master of Magdalen[1] was sitting on the N. side of the Presbytery, to see his son ordained – went to Church again at 3 – afterwards we went into Heaviside's house, and had 5 o'clock tea there with the Master & Latimer Neville – Violent and awful thunderstorm about 2 p.m. – vivid lighting.

> 1. The Hon. the Revd Latimer Neville, Master of Magdalene College, Cambridge.

Tuesday 6   June General Chapter

General Chapter all the day – very worrying, more so than usual, I thought – Heaviside, Browne, Bensly, the Master had luncheon here – At 3 o'clock Bensly started for the Rhine – Left alone, I made what notes I could – the Bishop, two Heavisides, two Nevills, Willett, Bignold, Bulmer, Atkinson, dined here – the Bishop talked about Mr. Cobbold[1] (author of Mary Catchpole) and his Mesmeric powers – the party went off fairly well – Atkinson played beautifully in the evening, and sang – Georgie Nevill, poor little fellow, had broken two of his fingers with a roller.

> 1. Richard Cobbold (1797–1877): Author; Rector of Wortham, near Diss, Norfolk, for 50 years. He wrote an account of *Margaret* Catchpole, a family servant, transported to Australia for stealing a horse; in Australia, she managed a farm, ran a store, and led a useful life in the community; her letters home formed the basis of Cobbold's book.

Friday 9

After Bkfst. enquired at the Master's house, & found that both he & Miss Old are better[1] – I found a Montreal clergyman waiting for me (with Miss Winter) to ask (1) for a Sermon in the Cathedral for enabling him to prevent his Church being bought by Roman Catholics (2) for a Drawing Room Meeting – both these I declined – wrote to … (2) Montreal Clergyman sending him £3.

> 1. Both Canon Robinson and his housekeeper had had scarlatina. This came in waves between 1830 and 1890 and increased in virulence; it was a particular danger to young children.

Tuesday 13

Majority agst. 2d Reading of Deceased Wife's Sister's Marriage Bill in House of Lords last night only 4 – P. of Wales, Dukes of Cambridge, Edinburgh, Albany, all voted for it; and Duke of Connaught paired for it.

••
On Thursday June 15, Goulburn travelled to Reading to preach at St Mary's Church that evening for the Revd Nicholas Garry, formerly Vicar of St Mark's, Lakenham, Norwich. Next day he went to London and called on Walter Ouless to discuss the Bishop's Portrait. Ouless (1848–1933), exhibited regularly at the Academy 1869–1928. His sitters included Charles Darwin, Cardinal Newman and King Edward VII. He returned to Norwich on Saturday, June 17.
••

Monday 19

Set to work upon a Meditation (for my 'Gospels') for Wednesday before Easter – At 12 (noon) went to Clerical Rooms, & took the chair at the Bp's Portrait Meeting – it was not so troublesome as I had anticipated – Present: Hinds Howell, Groome, Heaviside, Nevill, Burton, Norgate, Wilson (of St Stephen's), Monk (?), Arthur Copeman, Perowne, and Dr Wooley[1] (who had come to us for the meeting, at Bkfst. time) – When it was over Archdn. Perowne & Dr Woolley came to have luncheon here, & coffee afterwards – Then walked with Dr Woolley to Victoria Station[2] but finding ourselves too soon there for his train back at 3.55, we walked on Newmarket Road, till it drew near the time – then returned to the town, where he bought a toy for a child's birthday tomorrow.

    1. The Revd J. Woolley, D.D., was Rector of East Bergholt, Suffolk.
    2. Victoria Station was just beyond the top of St Stephen's Street.

Wednesday 21

Read documents about the G.F.S. before Bkfst. – Ch. at 10 – after Church began my address to the G.F.S. – (after Mg. Church Mr. Gunn took me to the West End, and pointed out how much higher the triforium is on one side than the other – also how much nearer the Norman arcading at the interior of the West End is to the string course on the N. of the West Door than on the South) – Bartie came to luncheon – After luncheon he and I walked to Norwich Tyrol[1] & back by Plumstead Road, talking over what was to be said to Brockbank tomorrow – afterwards we paid a visit to Atkinson at the Choristers' School, & talked it over with him.

    1. This would appear to be a 'nickname' of Goulburn's for the high area above Riverside Road. I have found no mention of the name elsewhere.

Thursday 22

After Church called on the Bp. and settled with him that the day of the address to him shd. be July 24 or 25 – he promised to consider whether he could give Mr. Ouless some days in the month of August – he told me of the dangerous illness of Mrs. Groome, reading part of a letter from the Archdn. – then home – Bartie & Brockbank called, & I gave the latter a lecture on his supercilious behaviour to his colleagues in the Choir – walked in the garden, reading 'the Times' – on my return wrote to Ouless, closing with him for his £525 size.

Thursday 29   St. Peter
At 1 called on the Bp. and talked to him on the subject of having a reporter there on the 25th. – he suggested Martin.

Friday 30
Wrote a letter to the Master[1], trying to make him laugh about Bp. Crowther, the Esquimaux, and the Cherokee – Bartie came to luncheon and we talked over the plan of giving the boys a weekly jaunt during the summer months to Cromer – then I went to Mr. White's, and he stopped two teeth for me in about an hour – then walked on the Unthank, Eaton & Ipswich Rds.

> 1. Canon Robinson still seems to be suffering from the aftermath of scarlatina.

JULY

Saturday 1
Fanny Pelham called for a few words about the Hymns of the G.F.S. Service, and then Ripley[1], to show me a paper wh. it is proposed to put about the Church tomorrow at Bp. Crowther's Sermon – At 12.30 I called on Mr. Atkinson to ask him to let his Son take the Choristers to Cromer on Monday as an experiment for future trips – then home – an interview with Bensly about the money to be given for the Chorister's trip – After calling at Atkinson's, I called at the Palace and saw the Bp. on the question of Service, or no Service, in connection with the reading of the Portrait Address on the 24th.

> 1. The Revd W.N. Ripley, Vicar of St Giles, was one of the Diocesan Secretaries for the Church Missionary Society.

Sunday 2
Went to Mattins at 8 – at 11 preached on 'Almsgiving, Prayer & Fasting' – At 3.30 Service again and Bp. Crowther's Sermon on "Without shedding of blood is no remission" – the value attached

by the Yoruba people to the shedding of blood in sacrifice; story of the martyrdom of Joshua, a Yoruba man, by drowning & striking on the head with a paddle – afterwards the Bp. and Ripley came in here for a cup of tea.

Tuesday 4

Drew up Choristers' Exam. Papers before Bkfst. – Called on Bulmer, & committed to him the Geography & Grammar Papers;' Bartie the Arithmetic; Ju has made a history Paper – then after finishing my Papers, worked on at Gospels, & contrived to finish before night all the 'Introductions' down to Palm Sunday inclusive – After luncheon the carriage took me up to Mr. White's, when I had my teeth cleaned – then a walk reading 'the Times' by the City Gaol[1] (where I met Dr Duckett) into Unthank's, thence into the Newmarket Rd., and thence back by Ipswich Road, & over Castle hill, & by the Post Office[2].

1. The site of the old City Gaol (until 1881) on the approach corner to Earlham Road, would shortly see the beginning of the erection of the Roman Catholic Church of St John the Baptist (completed in 1910) by the Duke of Norfolk (Architect: George Gilbert Scott, Jnr. and – after his early death in 1897 – continued by his brother, John Oldrid Scott). It became a Cathedral in 1976.
2. The Main Post Office, built in 1866 as the Crown Bank (Harvey's and Kerrrison's). The Bank failed in 1870. A year or two later it was bought by the Government as a Post Office. It is now part of Anglia Television.

Thursday 6

After Mg. Prayer with Bartie alone, I looked round with him at the preparations for the G.F.S. Service – At 12 the Service took place, the Bishop, Bartie, Heaviside, Mr. Cooper Johnson, & myself – my Address was too long, & hardly as warm in its temperament (I think) as the Ladies hoped & expected – Heaviside & I had letters from Ellicott today, summoning us for Wednesday next.

Saturday 8

Bensly came in, and we talked about the Grammar School Fields and Horticultural Show[1]; about insignia for Spruce; and about the letter I am to write (and have written tonight) to the E.C. in re site of the pound at Mousehold.

1. The Norfolk and Norwich Horticultural Society had been established in 1829, and held three or four shows a year.

Wednesday 12   From Norwich to London

Left Norwich at ½p.7 with Heaviside & Willie – Left my luggage at Garlants, and thence walked to 13, Delahay Street[1] – Ely was on, and kept us waiting a long time (Dean Merivale and Can. Lowe ?) – Abp. left us, looking very ill, as soon as the two or three important matters referred to by the Bishop & ourselves had been settled – then Ld. Cranbrook[2] took the chair, & we whirled rapidly thro' the remaining suggestions – At the close, in thanking them, I renewed my protest, and Lord C. instructed me when and how to make it – then I left H and went to Club, where had tea, & wrote to my Ju – walked back to Downing Street, & called on Gladstone – not at home.

1. Meeting was about the new Statues. The Rt Hon. and Most Revd Archibald Campbell Tait, died 4½ months later.
2. Gathorne Gathorne-Hardy, Statesman, became Viscount Cranborne 1878; sat on Royal Commission on Cathedral Churches 1879–85; Lord President of the Council 1885–92.

• •
Goulburn returned to Norwich on Thursday, July 13.
• •

Sunday 16

After luncheon called on, and sat with, Litchfield; and then walked to the Market Place to enquire after news, but cd. hear none – 2d Church at 3.30 – We heard by telegram that 'Little b.' was delivered of a daughter[1] at 7 a.m.

1. This was Gussie's second, but first surviving, child, and was named Augusta. She married John Wood and lived until 1958.

Tuesday 18

The 'Pin' came to Bkfst. en route to the Archaeological Excursion – continued my Gospels until 11 – then to School, where Bartie & I examined the Boys 1st. in Dictation, & then concluded the General Bible Exam. – after luncheon, Ju and I went to the School, & examined 1st. in the Recitation; & 2d in reading loud – This ended about 4.20, & then went over the Ferry – In returning we stopped at Foulsham's, to buy watch for the chorister best reported by Precentor, organist, Schoolmaster.

Thursday 20

Mr. Goose[1] came from Hinds Howell to ask me how the Episcopal seal should be stamped on the Book containing the names of subscribers to the Portrait – I recommended postponement till it cd. be done satisfactorily – at ½p.12 came Bartie, & he & I drew up the Class List, arranged who are to have prizes, what are to be the subjects of Exam. in 1883, etc.; and then talked about some anthems wh. he wishes (spite of the Canons) to eliminate, and others wh. he wants to retain – after luncheon, went to Foulsham's[2] to order Minn's name to be engraved on the Prize watch.

1. Agas Goose (Goose and Nudd), 19., Rampant Horse Street and 2, Haymarket, was Bookseller, Stationer, Printer, Bookbinder & Publisher of the very comprehensive Norwich Diocesan Calendar (edited by Canon Hinds Howell). The Haymarket address was also the Depot for the British and Foreign Bible Society.
2. James Foulsham, Watchmaker and Jeweller, 74, Prince of Wales Road.

Saturday 22
Church at 3, alone with Bartie – afterwards gave the Boys the Prizes, and gave Minns his watch – then they all came into the garden, and had strawberries & tea, while Ada, Bartie, & Auntie waited on them – Then they played about, while I read to Ada till 6 o'clock Lord Granville's despatch on Egyptian affairs – The Prize Boys in the three Classes were Dix, Quinton, Briggs.

Monday 24   Presentation of Bp's Portrait
Before Bkfst. meditated what to say before reading the Address – Church at 10 with Bartie – then walk round the k. garden, till it was time to dress for 'the occasion' – Hinds Howell, Groome, Perowne, Nevill, Heaviside came to luncheon – also Symonds arrived – after a talk with Hinds Howell over some small points, amg. other whether John Gunn's subscription was to be received (he having cast off his Orders), we went to luncheon – H.H. showed us the magnificent oaken case he had prepared to contain the Presentation Book – we drove (Heaviside, Woolley, Hinds Howell and I) to the Palace at 2 – there had been a stand-up luncheon in the Dining Room – thence we adjourned to the Drawing Room of the Palace, which was cleared & well arranged – I got thro' my address moderately well, tho' omitting to notice H.H.'s exertions, wh. was a great oblivion – drove home in the carriage – when I had taken off my court costume, I went for a walk with Nisbet, Norwich Tyrol, & back by 'Heart's Ease", where we had to stop during a thunder shower, and I had a glass of milk – Symonds dines & sleeps here tonight.

Wednesday 26
Preparations for departure all day, beginning at 7.30 – I am writing to the Librarian of Merton Coll. to return the College 'Origen' which I have had in my possession for years.

•••

The Goulburns are now away from Norwich until September 4 – 4 nights in London with much activity: correcting proofs from the printer, working in the British Museum, attending to a variety of business matters, seeing a large number of relatives and friends (including a visit to Gerard and Buskins at Eyhorne where the new baby "would not open its eyes"). On July 31, they sailed from Calais with Julia's maid Rose, and then travelled by rail to Brussels. Next day they travelled on to Cologne, and, on Wednesday (2) to Frankfurt, and Homburg, their destination, where they stayed at Mme. Fuch's lodgings, Albion House in the Ferdinand Strasse.

•••

AUGUST

Thursday 3   First Day of the Waters

At 7 went down with Ju to the Elizabethean Brunnen, and I drank my three glasses – came back about 8.30 for Bkfst. – Mr. Clark called with Emma Cartwright, and we agreed we wd. all four dine at the 'Quatre Saisons' – called on Mr. Brigstocke[1] whom with Mrs. Brigstocke I found at home.

> 1. The Revd Claudius Buchanan Brigstocke had been Anglican Chaplain at Homburg since 1869, and would continue until 1900.

Saturday 5

Rose at 6 – drank 5 glasses – As we were returning Ernst met us & walked with us to our lodgings; he is here to be examined by a military commission, to see whether he is fit for service in the army – On my asking him about Milly's[1] grave, he said that Madchen wd. show it to us – there arrived a packet from Rivington's, which I looked over and corrected – we took a fly, & called for Madchen, and went to see poor Milly's grave – the Cemetery much neglected, and very dreary & slovenly – I copied her inscription & that of poor Jane Bowles.

> 1. Amelia Goldsmid, Goulburn's cousin, was the second wife of Baron Leopold von Gremp of Homburg. She died in 1881, aged 67, and was buried in the local cemetery. The Baron's first wife, Jane Bowles (also English), had a son Ernst. The Baron eventually married for a third time – a German.

Tuesday 8

Took my four glasses as usual – we met Emma this morning, and walked with her; also Ld. John Manners[1] accosted me at the Elizabethan Brunnen, and advised me to go to Konigsberg, a ruin wh. he expressed himself delighted with – worked at my Gospels, and got thro' the first revise of 2½ of them – till at last the paper came in and we read the accounts of the engagement on Saturday between our troops under Sir Alison & the Egyptians, and the death of poor Lieut. Howard Vyse[3] – went out for an hour in a fly – then wandered about in the wood – Dined at the 'Russie', where Sir Henry Keating[2] spoke to me, and Mr. Freshfield; then the Butlers came in.

1. Lord John Manners (1818–1906): At present Conservative M.P. for North Leicestershire; Postmaster General 1874–80 and 1886–86; Seventh Duke of Rutland 1888.
2. Sir Henry Keating (1804–88): Barrister; had been Solicitor-General; Judge.
3. In 1881, the Egyptian Army mutinied under one of its Colonels, Arabi Pasha; there was anti-foreign rioting in June 1882 when 50 Europeans were massacred; in July, the British fleet bombarded Alexandria; a British Army landed and, in September destroyed Arabi's army.

Thursday 10

Very stewy day; drank at 7 – afterwards we called on Dr. Hoeber, but this throat was so swollen that he was unable to see us, and we were referred to Dr. Weber – worked with Ju at the Gospels, and finished three of them – then, very exhausted, begin to read 'Coriolanus' – Later in the afternoon went to Dr. Weber's whom I saw, and who advised me cold rubbing, & told me to take Bordeaux in preference to Scharzofberger – am going to work at Hebrew this evening.

Sunday 13

Walked to Dr. Hoeber's; he was better & able to see me, but did not alter my way of going on except to tell me to put a little carb. Potash into my glasses of water – being much tired, did not go to Church again, but read Prayers to Ju, and a Sermon of Borrows – Mrs. Butler walked in between 5 & 6, and persuaded me to go to Dr. Dietz.

Monday 14

After our luncheon, came in Dr. Dietz; he prescribed Bella Donna for me, and told me to leave off the Louisen-Brunnen.

●●●

Goulburn's holiday at Homburg was mainly occupied drinking the waters, vsiting the doctors, meeting old friends and making new acquaintances, walking, visiting places of interest, working on his latest book, correcting proofs from the printer, learning Hebrew, reading Shakspere (his spelling), and, of course, attending the local Services and, sometimes, preaching. On August 24, they left Homburg for Cologne, and the registering of their luggage to Calais, instead of Dover, was to cause trouble on the way home.

●●●

Friday 25   Cologne to Brussels

Left the Victoria Hotel, Cologne, at 8 a.m.; we had a coupe all to ourselves, the guard suggesting to us that we shd. pay him for that privilege, and were only disturbed by our carriage being placed on another line at Verviers; I got out for a moment, and the carriage was gone! – we read the Times, Standard, Telegraph – got to Brussels (Hotel de Flandres) at 2.30, and made an attempt to visit the Palais de Beaux Arts, but it was closed; and to walk about the Town, but it rained all the afternoon, and we were driven to Antony and Cleopatra, wh. I read aloud to Ju.

Saturday 26   Brussels to Dover & Folkestone

Left the Hotel de Flandres in a fly at 7.15 a.m. – We got a 'Times' of yeterday at the Station, wh. with Shakspere, lasted us nearly till we got to Calais – At <u>Bergieux</u> we had to go thro' the formality of opening the small hand-cases wh. we carried with us – At Calais, where we arrived about 12.40, we had to give up our Billet d'Enregistrement, and were assured that our baggage wd, be found on board the Calais-Douvres; but it never appeared; and the only consolation we got from the douanier was that it wd. be forwarded on to Dover by the later boat – However, Ju and I watched the luggage taken out of the later boat, but it was not there, and we had to leave instructions with the Inspector to telegraph us if it arrives by the early boat tomorrow – we had a repast at the Lord Warden of tea for one, cold chicken, & ½ a bott. of St. Julien, for wh. (and washing hands) 15 shgs. was charged!! – took a fly to Folkestone, and got to Pavilion about 7.15 p.m.; the house quite full – they proposed to give Rose a bed out, but Ju prefers her sleeping in our small sitting room.

Sunday 27   At Folkestone

Went to see the Station Master here, who was very kind about the luggage, and promised to communicate w. Dover about it –

Went to the Parish Ch. at 11 – Mr. Woodward preached a very good Sermon, but some of it was inaudible, as was throughout the Communion Service, wh. was full choral, Priest's part and all – At the Celebration, in delivering the Bread the Minister squatted down in a most grotesque manner, & most of those who staid did not communicate; we were not out till ½p.1 – Dinner at Table d'Hote, during wh. the missing baggage appeared; it had been broken open at Customs.

SEPTEMBER

Friday 1   Folkestone to London [*Ogle's Hotel*]
Left Folkestone at 8.45 – read the 'Nineteenth Century' en route – went to Rivington's, & there got last sheets of Vol. I of my 'Gospels' – then to Chirop. – corrected my proofs carefully, and then wrote to Buskins, offering her a small Devotional Library, wh. I had bought at Rivington's for her – then read the 'Church Quarterly' and 'Dublin'.

Saturday 2
Ju went to Eyhorne – had an hour and a half of Hebrew before Ju came in from her visit to Eyhorne, where she found little B. and babe quite well – In the evening read aloud the Times to Ju, and the account of the revolt of the Dublin Police.

Monday 4   From London to Norwich
Elizabeth came in to pay us a visit and told me of Prescott's[1] intention of moving into his Parsonage, & of the subscripn. about to be made to help him in furnishing – we got home about 3.30 – an immense bundle of letters here, tho' we had already received more than one relay – answered most of them (except one from the Pin about Guy in Egypt) before dinner – after dinner for wh. we had Gerard's partridges, began settling down.

   1. The Revd George Frederick Prescott had been one of Goulburn's Curates at St John's, Paddington, until he became Curate of the new Church of St Michael and AA in 1861, and then Vicar from 1864.

Tuesday 5
To Bensly's, where I saw Rees's Bill for £70, and concocted a letter to Curwood, asking the G.E.R. company to bear with us this portion of the expenses of the opposition to the Railway – afterwards we talked of the proposal of the Archaeological Institute to

come to Norwich next year – Church again with Heaviside and Bulmer at 5 – Prayer for the Archbishop[1] and for the War[2].

1. Archbishop Tait was ill and died at the beginning of December.
2. In Egypt.

Friday 8

After Bkfst. went to the Library before Church, to get Westcott's[1] and Blunt's Books on the English Translation of the Bible – Durst[2] called to tell me that his exchange of Lynn was at last arranged (with the Chapter's consent) and to thank me for setting the Bp. of Peterboro' right about him – then came Bensly and Fitch's son about the Memorial to the Mayor & Corpn. of Yarmouth to save the Tolhouse at Yarmouth –

1. Brooke Foss Wescott, Regius Professor of Divinity of Cambridge from 1870, wrote New Testament Commentaries and a 'History of the English Bible' (1868); and many other books on the N.T. and on doctrine. Became Bishop of Durham (1890).
2. The Revd J. Durst became Vicar of Bredhurst, Kent.

Saturday 9

Worked till nearly 1, when Shadwell and young Farrer (son of Th.H.[1]) called, wanting a boat smaller than a yacht, and larger than a wherry, in wh. to go down to Beccles – took them to Bulmer's, who cd. give us no information; then to Feltham's – we met him returning to the Ferry, and he referred us to Thompson and Wright, Boatbuilders in King Street – then I brot. them home to luncheon – afterwards I walked with them to Thompson's in King Street, and left them in Mr. Thompson's hands.

1. Thomas Henry Farrar (1819–99) would have been a contemporary of Goulburn's at Eton and Balliol. He was a Barrister and Civil Servant; created a Baronet 1883 and a Peer 1893.

Sunday 10

H.C. with Moore at 8; about 30 Communicants – a letter from Mrs. Empson asking me to solicit Henry Martin to give her Boy Cecil a Scholarship at Lancing[1] – This I did, and also anwered her letter in the course of the day – At 11 Bulmer preached – After luncheon walked up & down garden, reading Dr. Tait's article agst. the Agnostics on the basis of Christian Morality; then turned to Bythner's Hebrew Grammar.

1. Canon Nathaniel Woodard (1811–91): Founded a number of Public Schools "which would provide a sound middle-class education on a definite Anglican basis". St Nicholas's, Lancing (1848) was among the first.

Monday 11
Church at 5 with Heaviside and Moore – as I was reading the latter part of the Prayers, a stone was thrown in from the Cantoris side, & the broken glass nearly touched Mr. Henson's head – The Medleys, Moores and Benslys dine here tonight.

Saturday 16
An extraordinary letter this morning from a Mrs. Western, dr. of the recently deceased Mr. Pearce[1] of Martham, wishing me to write a notice of him in the papers; this I declined – Church at 10 – last time of reading the <u>Prayer</u> for the War; in the afternoon I read the thanksgiving in the Prayer Book[2] – Church again at 3 w. Heaviside & Bulmer – Bulmer just returned from Tivetshall; the Symondses recd. intelligence this morning from a friend in the War office that Guy is safe & sound – a large n. of people in the Cathedral this afternoon, some of whom came to hear Mendelssohn's 'Hear my prayer' – Sir N. Lindley gave away the prizes for the Oxford & Cambridge Competition[3] today – at dinner a most unpleasant communicn. from Mr. Rogers that Gowing demands much lower terms for the Wingfield farm than we have offered him.

1. The Revd J. Pearse had been Vicar of Martham 1832–76; his daughter, Laura, widow of John Gurney (from whom she inherited Earlham Hall), had married the Revd W.N. Ripley, Vicar of St Giles, Norwich, with both of whom Goulburn was very friendly. So he clearly did not realise that Mrs. Western was Mrs. Ripley's sister.
2. The end of the war in Egypt with the Victory of the English troops.
3. From 1857 Oxford, and 1858 Cambridge, held local Exams. for pre University Students. In 1873, the two Universities established a Joint Board to conduct the Exams. These raised the standard of teaching at the local level, and by the mid-1880s more than 9,000 students were sitting for them. Sir Nathaniel Lindley was, at this time, a Lord Justice of Appeal.

Sunday 17
Finished one of my 'Gospel Instructions' before 11 a.m. – Mr. Norgate preached for the Addl. Curates Socy. – It seemed to be a very unpretending good Sermon – I talked with Heaviside about Gowing's[1] proposals after Church – Norgate had luncheon with us – when he was gone, I went to Nevill, to agree with him on the time for a Chapter Meeting about Gowing's affairs tomorrow – He suggested consulting Sewell Read[2].

1. The Dean and Chapter was often generous to its tenants, lowering rents, from time to time, to meet a tenants difficulties. The case of Gowing seems to have been more complicated than usual.

2. Clare Sewell Read (1826–1905) farmed family estates in Norfolk from 1854–1896; Conservative M.P. for East Norfolk 1865–67; for South Norfolk 1868–80; and for West Norfolk 1884–86; served on several Parliamentary Agricultural Committees; Assistant Commissioner to enquire into agricultural conditions in Canada and America; twice Chairman of Farmers' Club; wrote many agricultural papers.

Monday 18

After Mg. Service with Heaviside and Bulmer, Nevill, Heaviside & I met at Bensly's Office & afterwards hear [here] to consider Gowing's application – We resolved to ask Mr. Sewell's[1] advice, and I was deputed, if possible to see him this afternoon – Then we adjourned to Atkinson's house, with Browne, to hear his complaints about the drainage, new tiling, etc. – came home, & wrote to Mr. Sewell – After luncheon Ju drove me to Mr. Sewell's at Catton, where, as he was not at home, I left my letter – then Ju drove me to Joe Gurney's, whence I made a tour and walked home by King Street, reading the Times, 4½ columns of wh. today are devoted to a life of Pusey[2] – Henry and Lady Gunning[3] arrived at 7 – He is wonderful; preached two Sermons yesterday, and is in excellent spirits.

1. He should, of course, be Mr. *Read.*
2. Canon E.B. Pusey, Tractarian Leader; Regius Professor of Hebrew at Oxford 1828 to 1882; had died on September 16, and was buried in the Nave of Christ Church Cathedral, Oxford.
3. The Revd Sir Henry Gunning's first wife (died 1877) had been Julia's stepsister, Mary. He was now 86.

Tuesday 19

At 12 we had a meeting in my study with Mr. Sewell – His advice was to make the abatement of £50 wh. Gowing required, but to insist on having the most substantial securities – When he had gone, we agreed that Heaviside and Bensly shd. go tomorrow and see Mr. Hazard, and discuss how far an arrangement might be made for another tenant to relieve Gowing of the 70 additional acres wh. we had added to the farm at his request – we shall see what comes of it.

Wednesday 20

At work by 7.15 – read up for a speech this afternoon at the Palestine Exploration Fund[1] – Church at 10 – then a walk in the garden reading the Quarterly Statements of the Fund, but very low, nervous & uncomfortable – Ju and I at 3 went to the meeting, where I had great difficulty in speaking – Mr. James

Rose's speech was not much; a number of identifications of Scriptural localities – Hymns were sung at the beginning & close about the 'heavenly Jerusalem', and a collection made at the close – then church again – Heaviside had returned, having seen Hazard, Gowing, & Hall – The upshot is that they will give us a substantial security, and will not insist upon a certain specific sum being laid our for repairs, etc., but that they cannot give more than £230 rent, and we must be bound to furnish tiles for the drainage, etc. – Payne, Thursby, Atkinson, Ralph & Alice Nevill dine here tonight; a pleasant party; sat between Alice Nevill & Lady Gunning.

> 1. The Palestine Exploration Fund was established in London in 1865 to help finance the effort to restore Palestine to the Jews.

OCTOBER

Tuesday 3

Looked out Sermons to take with me before Bkfst. – afterwards met Heaviside, Nisbet, Nevill, at Bensly's Office on Gowing's Business – we aquiesced in his terms; also decided to varnish the chancel Roof of a Church from wh. we are receiving Rectorial Tithes – then to Bank for money – then to call on the Bp. whom I saw and took leave of – then to Mrs. Nevill's, whom I saw – then to Heaviside's; took leave of him & Mrs. H. just before their luncheon – then home – at ½p.2 a walk with Nisbet on Cromer Rd., and back by the Catton Road – Medley[1] and Ada called, & I gave him 2£ towards his Mission Chapel of wh. he gave me photographs [*also wrote four letters*] – hope to settle tonight who to vote for at the Jenny Lind & also at Eye & Ear Infirmary.

> 1. The Revd E.S. Medley, after five yeasr at Minor Canon and Precentor at Norwich, had moved, in 1877, to St Andrew's Episcopal Cathedral, Inverness, as Canon Res. and Precentor, where he remained until, in 1886, he returned to Norwich (St Gregory's).

• •

From October 4 until November 22, the Goulburns were away from Norwich, first, visiting Goulburns cousins briefly at Betchworth, Surrey (a few miles S.W. of Reigate); and then doing the usual round of Cartwright relations and friends at Edgcote, Eydon, Ayhoe and Eyhorne. Finally, from November 2 to 22, they spent the remainder of the time in Brighton, with a short visit to Chichester.

• •

Friday 6   [*At Betchworth*][1]
Walked from 9.25 to 10.5 before Bkfst. – afterwards went with Sissie to see the Kg.-fisher's nest lined with bones, etc. – then came in and worked at the references to my 'Gospel' – Ju went with the Colonel to Reigate, to make some purchases – After luncheon, we took a walk with the Colonel and Louisa, to see the new weir – then Louisa and I went into the Church, and she told me about their difference with the clergyman – Mr. Ricardo & Henrietta are coming here for the night – also Rev. Mr. Tower, Vicar of Guildford, a 1st. cousin of Louisa's – also Sir Trevor Lawrence, M.P. for Mid-Surrey is to dine here.

1. Betchworth House (between Dorking and Reigate) was the home of Col. Edward Goulburn, son of Henry, elder brother of Goulburn's father. His cousin was two years older. He was married to Louisa (nee Tower). Their daughter Henrietta, was married to Col. Horace Ricardo, of Bramley Park, Guildford. There are, no longer, Goulburns living at Betchworth.

Monday 16   At Eydon
A most lugubrious day, pouring all day – In the morning wrote a long letter to Moore about the Bp's prohibition of an Evening Service in St Luke's Chapel – read the account of the Church Congress at Derby in the 'Guardian' – after luncheon walked with Eddie in torrents of rain towards Byfield, but I turned back in the valley when I found waters over the road – got home with my feet soaked, but in a violent perspiration – read in the Evening the Times, and specially an account of the Julian and Gregorian Kalendars, etc. wh. is hard, but worth reading.

1. Col. Henry Cartwright, Julia's brother, had married Jane (nee Holbech) in 1853. She had died in 1877. Eddie was their son. Goulburn's nickname for Henry was 'Hen-pen'. He was a J.P., and had been M.P. for South Northants 1858–68.
2. The Julian Calendar, devised by Julius Caesar in 46 B.C. was not sufficiently accurate. It was revised by Pope Gregory XIII in 1582, but not adopted in England until 1752. In 1582, the day after Oct. 4 was to be Oct. 15, as an error of ten days had accumulated by then.

• •

While staying at Aynhoe, Goulburn made two days trips, on October 23 and on October 27, to Oxford to work in the Bodleian, to see friends. He also took the opportunity to call to see the Archdeacon's son, Ralph Nevill, at Keble, and Julia's young relation, Stephen Cartwright at Merton. On the first occasion (23) "got a letter from Heaviside on the train, telling me about another invasion of the Close at the bottom of Felton's garden". This is a mistake for Charles *Feltham*, the Dean's Verger, who lived in the Lower Close next to the Ferry.

On November 2 they arrived in Brighton for the final part of their holiday.
• •

NOVEMBER

Saturday 4

Discovered early in the morning that I had not brought any Sermons here – telegraphed to Eydon and recd. reply that they had been left there, and wd. be sent on to Aynhoe – All day occupied, partly in thinking over a passage to preach upon tomorrow, partly in correcting the Press for Rivington's.

Sunday 5

Rose with great heat in my left foot, and most uncomfortable – At 10.30 set out for St. Peter's, taking in our fly M. Aubrey and Emma – Church much improved – Western gallery altogether removed; other galleries truncated – the Archdn.[1] read the Lessons and celebrated; I preached extem. with some difficulty – assisted afterwards at the H.C. – went to the Chapel in Waterloo Street, where they have thrown out a grand domed Chancel; a great improvement.

1. The Ven. John Hannah, D.C.L.

Wednesday 8

Much better than yesterday – Wrote to (1) My tutor[1], about my Book on the Collects, and thanking him for a sight of his verses turning the Collects into English Iambics (2) Rivington's instructing him to send my Tutor a copy (3) Wm. Birkbeck, thanking for a kind letter, permitting me to walk in his grounds – then went for a Postal Order for a clergyman spoken well of by Bp. Claughton.

1. Goulburn always retained a great affection and respect for his old tutor at Oxford, the Revd C.P. Golightly (who was very much a 'character'). In his later years he buried himself in ancient history and had little interest in current affairs, though he liked to preach to rural congregations in language which he felt they could understand.

• •
They returned to Norwich on November 22.
• •

Thursday 23

Rose at 6.5, and thought over something to say to the Pastoral work meeting – Manning called & placed in my hand my paper for the Archaeological Society[1] in type – then at 12 the Pastoral Work Association[2] – Two admirable papers were read by Gibson of Lound, and Wilson of St Stephen's – Nevill, Nisbet, Stracey, Fielding, Hinds, Howell, Venables, Hoste, and others spoke – I summed up, reading the letter I had received from Pringle, and telling them what I had heard from Mr. Tower of Guildford – At 3 I went out & called on (1) Mrs Nisbet (2) Miss Hansell – she had prepared a letter for me, asking my sympathy under an impending operation – This I answered after Afternoon Church – Venables suggestion at the meeting about the Salvation Army, that we should use lay help, organising & putting it under control, was much to the point.

> 1. Norfolk and Norwich Archaelogical Society (founded 1845) was strongly supported by the clergy. Goulburn was President, the Revd C.R. Manning, of Diss, Secretary.
> 2. The Pastoral Work Association had, as its object, to gather together, at stated intervals, Clergy from different parts of the Diocese to consider with each other "in an earnest and quiet spirit, the pastoral work of their common Ministration." Members now numbered 250.

Friday 24

Worked before Bkfst. at the origins & history of the Introits – then Church at 10 – Then worked with Bensly at the Agenda Paper – He went to the Bp. at noon, and I went into the Church with Browne to examine the marble pavement of the Sacrarium where it is worn by the feet, and to inspect the Founder's tomb[1].

> 1. The medieval tomb of the Founder (Bishop Herbert de Losinga) was destroyed during the English Civil War (mid 17th Century); in 1682 a new monument was made (a table tomb) with Latin inscription by Dean Prideaux (as he became in 1702). This, because of inconvenience, was moved by Goulburn and the black marble slab set in the Presbytery in front of the High Altar. In 1980, Canon Claude Palfrey gave six handsome Candlesticks (made by Eric Stevenson of Wroxham) linked together with white ropes, to mark his fifty years of Service in the Cathedral.

Saturday 25

Wrote my first Sermonette on the Introits (the Reverence due to the Holy Communion) beginning at 7 a.m. and ending before luncheon – this was intercalated by my visit to the Bp. at 11.15 – He talked with me over Moore's proposed evening Service, and ended by saying he shd. permit it for six months as an experiment.

DECEMBER

Friday 1

After Mg. Church went to Bensly's Office, & learned there that Elmer had received no plans of the proposed route of the Lynn & Fakenham – so we went in a fly to the Clerk of the Peace's Office in Surrey Street, to inspect the plans deposited yesterday, and there learned, to my great joy, that the line of devision is to pass <u>outside</u> the Close thro' the field separating us from the Vinegar Works – then in returning spoke to Nevill in the Market Place; then I went to Heaviside with the news; then home – wrote to Miss Hansell, & took the letter to her house – there heard the account of her from her servant Harriet, and from Mrs. Howard her sister – then luncheon – Afterwards Ju had the first Matron's Bee of the Season – wrote to Parkes, telling him what had occurred, and that we having now no <u>locus standi</u>, our opposition must collapse.

Sunday 3   **Advent I**
Litany, H.C., Sermon & Celebration at 11 – Perowne preached ... and I am told that he made mention of the Abp[1]., but I cd. not hear him – on coming out we heard that a telegram had arrived annoucing the Abp's death – called at Heaviside's to see whether he cd. remember what we did at the time of Abp. Longley's death – Church at 3; Nisbet preached a Sermon on the Abp. – We had the Dead March beautifully played in the Afternoon, and the Anthem, 'The souls of the righteous' beautifully sung.

    1. Archbishop Campbell Tait.

Tuesday 5   General Chapter Day
Robinson not present – immense worries all day long, & more work than ever – Shoals of letters to swell my misery – At the dinner were the Bp. and Fanny, the Nisbets & Nevills (not Heaviside), Bensly, Bignold (not Willett), the Barties (not Moore), and Bulmer – The Bishop quite facetious; told a most amusing story about Bp. Butler[1] of Chichester.

    1. There was *no* Bishop *Butler* of Chichester! Goulburn was now rather deaf. Could it have been Buckner who was Bishop of Chichester 1798–1824?

Thursday 7
Business again with Bensly lasting from10 a.m. to nearly 3 p.m. – a long interview with Alden[1], and also with Mr. Browne – also at noon went to the Bp. at the Palace, to consult him about the proposed amalgamation of part of Gaywood (Highgate) with Lynn – then a short walk in the garden with Times.

    1. Sub-Sacristan (formerly Choir School Master) living in the Lower Close.

Friday 8
Church at 8 [*p.m.*] Bishop there, Nisbet, Copeman, and all three minor Canons – a good congregation, considering the weather –

preached on the celebrity of the Virgin ("all generations shall call me blessed")[1] – at the end recommended prayer for the guidance of the Queen, etc. in selecting a new Apb. – a silence kept for a space after the Sermon – but I was very much hampered and made uncomfortable by my lamp going out[2] – I must take care this doesn't happen again.

> 1. Friday Evening Advent Sermon.
> 2. Electrification was in its early stages, but Britain lagged behind America and Europe in its adoption.

Saturday 9

In the morning corrected proofs, and had interviews with Spaull & Browne about lighting the pulpit in the Nave – Sermonette on the <u>old</u> Introit at 3 – then took a brief walk, and bought a petroleum lamp which may do for the pulpit – After Aftern. Church saw Yeoman at Bensly's Office, and appointed him 'Beadle of the Poor Men'.

Friday 15

Church with Bulmer & Moore at 10 a.m. – Bulmer complained bitterly of the 'Waits' as disturbing the repose of the Close – Muriel came before luncheon & touched my throat with caustic, and advised me not to go out – Ralphie Nevill called at 4.30, bringing his Bp. Andrewes for me to write his name in – Preparations for departure – I saw Browne & Daniells this morning about the gas stoves placed in the Choristers' vestry, and directed them to be lighted an hour before each Service and put out when the Service commences.

• •
On Saturay (16) Goulburn travelled to Lincoln to preach at an Ordination in the Cathedral on Sunday morning, returning on Monday.
• •

Tuesday 19

In the evening the Mildmays (Arundell[1], Mrs. M. and Bizzie) arrived in time for dinner at 5 – At 7 began the Oratorio (Spoilio's 'Last Judgement') – I gave three addresses on 'Thou', 'Weighed', 'Balances', in the course of it – It struck me as singularly dull, and without a feature of interest; and I was heartily glad when it ended (about 9.30) – Mr. & Mrs. Vincent, and their boy came in afterwards to supper – the Mildmays very charming – a great deal of merriment.

> 1. The Revd C. Arundell St John Mildmay was Rector of Denton from 1879.

Wednesday 20
Prepared a Sermon for Friday – went to Church in the morning with Arundell – wrote one or two letters – Vol. III of Bp. Wilberforce came in, which I began to read – Mrs. Mildmay took her leave at 12, but Arundell stayed till after luncheon – Afterwards Bizzie, Ju, and I went out in the carriage, and drove to the Douglasses, to ask them to our Xmas dinner – then home where wrote two or three more letters – News reached us at dinner of Benson's[1] acceptance of the See of Canterbury – In the evening read Wilberforce's[2] Life.

1. E.F. Benson had been one of Goulburn's Assistant-Masters when he was Headmaster of Rugby, and when Benson was Chancellor of Lincoln Cathedral, Goulburn had dedicated his 'Bosses Book' to him.
2. The Rt Revd Samuel Wilberforce had been Bishop of Oxford, and of Winchester, dying in 1873 after being thrown from his horse. His Biography by A.R. Ashwell and Reginald G. Wilberforce (his son) was published in three volumes during the years 1880-82.

Thursday 21   St. Thomas
Mg. Paper contains an Article on Benson's elevation to the Primacy, and a notice of him – Ordination (4 priests & 6 ? Deacons)[1] at 11 – I took no part – Nisbet preached well – out about 1.25 – Mr. Vincent & Bizzie, and M. and Mme. Gosch[2] came into luncheon (not <u>Gauche</u> but <u>Gosh</u>) – afterwards a fast walk in the garden with the 'Times' – then wrote to (1) Benson, congratn. (2) Church[3], asking his support of Pigot as Organizing Sec of S.P.G. (3) B.C. the same (4) Mr. Bashford, of some place near Acle, sending him £2 for his Church – read the 'Guardian' in the Evening.

1. His numbers are correct.
2. A translator of one of Goulburn's books.
3. Dean of St Paul's, London.

Friday 22

			£.	s.
Gratuities:	(1)	6 Bedesmen	2.	2.
	(2)	8 L. Clerks	2.	16
	(3)	Ferryman	1	
	(4)	2 Vergers		14
			6.	12

Service at 8 [p.m.] with Sermon of St. Mary's Song constructed on the model of Hannah's – Read afterwards a Prayer I had drawn upon the subject of Benson's appointment.

Saturday 23

2 Subsacrists	14
Daniels	7
Walker	7
Spruce	7
Choristers	14
£2.	9

Worked at Sermonette for tonight – then read over, and did not quite like, the alterations proposed by the Cathedl. Commissioners, in the last draught of Statutes – the officials named above came to me for their Christmas gratuities before luncheon – afterwards I went to Heaviside's to confer with him about the Statutes, and we agreed as to what I shd. write back.

Monday 25   CHRISTMAS DAY

With Bartie at 8 a.m. H.C., 106 Communicants, £4. 8 collected – Church at 11 again; I sat in the Mayor's Stall[1] – the Bishop preached – In the afternoon wrote to Lucy Bignold[2] sending her £5 towards St. Stephen's Curate (2) Lake[3], thanking for photograph ... (4) Mary Stewart Robinson[4] (5) Emma Wallace thanking for Card – Bulmer, the Douglasses, and the Nisbets are coming to dinner.

1. He was finding it very difficult to hear Sermons from his own Stall, and so he was frequently using the Mayor's Stall, where he could hear better.
2. Lucy was the daughter of Sir Samuel Bignold, who had died in 1875. She was now 47 and was to live to be 89 in 1924. She lived in Surrey Street all her life, was a leading hostess in the city; President of the local Primrose league; a philanthropist in all sorts of causes; for 60 years she had a Bible Class in her own house every Sunday afternoon for working men; and she also held entertainments for their families; she founded the Police Court Mission.
3. W.C. Lake, Dean of Durham 1869–94, and an old friend of Oxford days.
4. His God-daughter.

Wednesday 27   St. John Evangelist

At Bkfst. an uncomfortable letter from an engineer warning me to back out of the Pusey Meml. meeting tomorrow, wh. determined me to write out the chief part of my speech; and this occupied me all the day till dinner time at 6.15, except from 12 to 1.45, when I walked with Nisbet on the Eaton and Unthank Road – Moore came to luncheon, and talked to me about the S.P.G. local Secretaryship afterwards, wh. he evidently much wishes to get – to dinner came the choristers, the two Barties with a nephew, and Ada with Millicent & Humphry Willett – at 7.30 they all went to the Magic Lantern, and I was left alone, and finished my paper about Pusey.

Thursday 28   Holy Innocents
Pusey Memorial Meeting[1] & Oxford Dinner
Hinds Howell came at 12.30, & had some luncheon before starting – then to the meeting – It was very small, but seemed cordial and agreed – I read the greater part of my Speech – Hinds Howell opened the meeting – Mr. Garnier[2], Revd P.F. Boddington[3], Du Port[4], Revd B.E. Tatham[5] spoke, Garnier & Tatham well – Arthur Copeman was there, Davie, Davies, and Symonds – then to call on Nisbet, who took a short walk with me before going out with the Bishop – shortly after, Arundell Mildmay arrived, & we together went to the dinner – very well attended – The evening went off famously – Symonds was there, and a Mr. Jerrard (who was at the Grammar School & said he had had a letter from me); and a Mr. Fowler Smith, who said he often met me at the Club in London; and Mr. Tancock[6], & many others – Arundell and I got away about 8.45, and came home in a fly.

1. Edward Bouverie Pusey, Professor of Hebrew at Oxford, Canon of Christ Church, and Tractarian Leader, had died on September 16, aged 82.
2. The Revd T. P. Garnier, Rector of Cranworth.
3. The Revd T.F. Boddington, Vicar of Salhouse.
4. Canon J.M. Du Port, Rector of Mattishall.
5. The Revd G.E. Tatham, Vicar of Ryburgh.
6. The Revd O.W. Tancock, Headmaster of King Edward VI Grammar School 1879–90.

Saturday 30
Worked hard at Sermonette all the morning – At 3 o'clock preached it: 'Celestine I and the Nestorian heresy'. – then a meeting of Mr. Bayliss with the three Canons and myself at the chapter Office – We agreed to memorialize Parliament against the L.& F. Railway on the ground that they have not given us notice that they mean to take a slice of Cooper's grounds – The petitioning is to be left for after consideration – we are disposed to petition, unless they will insert a clause in their Bill, pledging themselves never to ask powers to go thro' the Close.

1883

JANUARY

Monday 1   **Circumcision**
Went to H.C. at 8 a.m. – the Bp., Nisbet, & Bartie there – the Boys sang the Introit, Kyrie, & Creed, & then went out – I preached on Rev. III, 20 – <u>much too long</u> – were not out till ½p.9 – in the morning began a Sermon for next Sunday on Wife's Sister's Question[1] – The Bp. in the morg. found the door of the N. Transept locked, & had to go round.

> 1. Goulburn felt very strongly about this question and was much opposed to the Bill, which did not become an Act until 1907.

Saturday 6   **THE EPIPHANY**
H.C. with Ju at 8 a.m.; scarcely anyone there; Nevill and Bartie offd. – Service and Sermonette (on 'Gloria Patri') at 3; Nevill and Bulmer – I found great difficulty in reading my Sermon, and was obliged to remove my spectacles – Afterwards at Bensly's Office we met Mr. Bayliss, and sealed our memorial agst. the Lynn & Fakenham, & I agreed to raise the Insurance of the Deanery to £3000, and of the Canonical Houses to £2500.

Monday 8
Wrote to Bp. of Lincoln[1] about marriage of a man with his mother's husband's daughter (Mr. Kent, Miss Blomfield) – Church again at 5 p.m. at wh. after 1st. Lesson Rose was admitted Bedesman – In the evening looked up about Martin5's[2] dispensation to Fuxius in Thomassin, and read some of Froude's Hist. of England.

> 1. The Rt Revd Christopher Wordsworth, Bishop since 1869.
> 2. Martin V (1368–1431) was Pope from 1417–31. End of Great Schism. He restored Churches and other public buildings in Rome: strengthened the Papal power; increased the influence of the Papacy in England; was a man of simple tastes and free from intrigue.

Tuesday 9
Ch. at 10 with Bartie and Nevill – afterwards a walk to Eaton and back by Uthank Road; most lovely day, bright & cold – met Chicken Pattie[1] (driving) who offered to show me some Missals, etc. – also, when near Fitch's shop, Nevill with whom I walked back – It appears that I left the Library open yesterday, & in the night the policeman went up, locked the upper door, & took the key with him – wrote to (1) Mr. Callis[2], asking Sermon at Cathl.

January 1883 293

(2) Mr. Pigot[3], do. (3) declining Lecture at Sheffield – In the evening tried to read some of Hook's Abps. of Cant.

> 1. Henry Stantiforth Patteston, Head of Pockthorpe Brewery. Former Mayor, etc.
> 2. The Revd J. Callis, Rector of Holy Trinity, Heigham, since 1875.
> 3. The Revd W.M. Pigot, Vicar of Eaton since 1875.

Monday 15

Wrote to Charles H. Shorting (an old Rugby pupil), who asks me to be Godfather to his daughter Agnes – After Mg. Church with Nevill & Moore, walked up to Canon Dalton's[1] to ask him about dispensans. for marriages with dec. wife's sister – He took a good deal of pains with the question.

> 1. Priest of the Roman Catholic Chapel in Wymer Street.

Saturday 20

Rose at 6.15, & prepared my speech for the Afternoon before Bkfst. – Meeting[1] at 12 noon – Clerical Rooms nearly full – Mr. Garnier spoke (very good) and Dr. Allen[2], both trying to answer Mr. Reade[3] – I alas! held forth for ¾ths. of an hour – walked to Furse's, where I talked w. him about the flags in the Cathedral – thence to Norfolk Chron. Office[4], where asked Editor to let me see a proof of my speech – then to the Public Library[5], over wh. Mr. Booty lionised me – then home & wrote 6 letters.

> 1. This was a special meeting of the Diocesan Church Defence Association, with the Bishop in the Chair, to consider the Bill for legalizing Marriage with a deceased wife's Sister. Resolutions were moved against an alteration of the law, and petitions to both Houses of Parliament were drawn up for signature.
> 2. Dr Joseph Allen, M.R.C.S., Surgeon.
> 3. Clare Sewell Read, M.P. (no 'e').
> 4. "The Norfolk Chronicle is the recognised Local Church Organ and has a large circulation amongst the Nobility, Clergy, Gentry; the Learned Professions and the Agricultural and Commerical Classes of the District". (Advertisement in the Norwich Diocesan Calendar).
> 5. The Norfolk and Norwich Library was in the Market Place, just below Lower Goat Lane.

Sunday 21   Septuagesima

Preached at 11 ... the 3d. & last of my Marriage-Law Defence Series – then 2d Church, and Sermon from Nevill about the City Schools – I sent for Spruce, and examined him about the charge agst. him by the Police for leaving the Bishopgate Gate opened last night – he seems to explain it fairly.

Monday 22
Chapter Meeting at 12.30 at wh. we investigate the charge made agst. Spruce by P.C. George Eglen, & with the help of Spaull seemed to make that tho' Spruce had taken the matter into his own hands far too much, and acted most imprudently, a censure & warning wd, be eno' for him – This we gave him, and thanked Eglen.

• •

From Tuedsay, January 23 until Saturday, January 27, the Goulburns are in London, staying at Ogle's Hotel, Park Street. He spent much time discussing the Marriage Law question with Berdmore Compton and others; and he went to Parliament Street to order the Reports of the Marriage Law Commissions. Inevitably, he called on Dr Morgan to pay his bill and to check on his current prescription.

• •

FEBRUARY

Friday 2   **Purification of B.V. Mary**
H.C. at 8 as a Communicant – Harriott there, but not Ju – Church again at 10 – then set out walking with Harriott on Newmarket Rd., but driven to take shelter in Norfolk and Norwich Hospital – there Dr. Bateman[1] found us (in the Pro-Chapel) and most kindly showed us over the wards, in wh. he seemed to take a great pride – My 'Gospels' are nearly at an end – Margie & Alice Nevill dined here; Georgie came in the evening; and they all went off at 8 p.m. to the Choristers' Concert at Noverre Rooms – Read to Ju a little of Vol. III, Wilberforce.

  1. Dr (later Sir Frederick) Bateman, Consultant Surgeon.

Saturday 3
Sat at home reading for my Sermonette on the Psalms, till the Under Sheriff (Mr. Hamond) came to announce the hour of arrival of the Judge – at 3.35 called for Heaviside & the Bp. and took them to the lodgings – we had not long to wait for Mr. Justice Field – I ascertained that he will communicate tomorrow – on my return drew our tickets for the company to find their places:

Bp.	Ju
Mr Justice Field	Mr. Justice Matthew
Heaviside	The Mayor
Mr. Colman	Maudie Fellowes

Mr. Willett	Mr. J. Matthew's Marshal
Under Sheriff	Sheriff of Norwich
Mr. J. Field's Marshal	Dr. Bensly
Harriott	Arthur Copeman
High Sheriff	Lucy Bignold
O.H.	

More lively party than usual, Judges chaffing one another – Mr. Justice Field having taken Mr. Justice Matthew's hat, the other said it was spoliation of the Catholics – Mr. Norman the Sheriff seemed delighted – Maudie Fellowes preferred it to a lady's party.

Friday 9
At ¼ to 1 went in carriage to meet Mr. Hope who came by 1 p.m. train – after luncheon came Mr. Murray, the Sec. of the M.L.D. Union[1], and we all 3 talked in my study, and I told them the story about Sir Thomas Erpingham[2] – then went with them to see Chicken Pattie and Arthur Copeman; the former we met in the Close – then we sat with Arthur Copeman – then we went to the Cathedral, where Ld. Percy & Ld. Beauchamp (having come by the 3.40 train, but missed the carriage) joined us, and I lionised them – then we walked down to the stables to see the part of the Close wh. the rail had proposed to invade – Dinner at 6 – Penrice with us, & Arundell Mildmay – they went off at 7.35 – Miss Fenn came & I went to Church & preached the 1st. Lent lecture on St. John XVII, 5 on 'the loneness of Xt.' – a fair congregation considerg. the meeting & the weather – our gentlemen returned about 9.35, having been disconcerted by roughs at the meeting[3], who wd. not allow any speech but Lord Percy's to be heard – they were <u>most</u> goodhumoured.

1. = Marriage Law Defence Union.
2. Sir Thomas Erpingham (1357–1428): For distinguished war service at home and abroad, he was, in 1399, made Constable of Dover Castle; later, Warden of the Cinque Ports; knighted; elected a Privy Councillor; Chamberlain of the Royal Household, and Marshal of England. He was given various Manors in the Eastern Counties, his chief residence being in Norwich. In 1415 he was with the King at Agincourt. For favouring Lollards (who protested against abuses in the Church), Bishop Dispenser orderd him, as a penance, to build the Erpingham Gate. He and his two successive wives are buried in the Cathedral.
3. The Meeting, in St Andrew's Hall, under the M.L.D.U., was to speak against any alteration of the Marriage law. H.S. Patteson, Esq., ('Chicken Pattie') was in the Chair, and among those who had come to speak was the Rt Hon. A.J.B. Beresford Hope (M.P. for Cambridge University; P.C.; founder of St Augustine's College, Canterbury, and who had a prominent part in building All Saints, Margaret St, London.

Saturday 10

Sat with my three guests, who appeared in the highest possible spirits, while they breakfasted – they went away by the 7.30 train – Arundell Mildmay at bkfst. with us – he amused us very much by his acct. of the meeting last night – Two ruffians, Messrs. Burgess and Crotch, gained their point, and broke up the meeting by cat-calls and shouting – a great disgrace to Norwich – Nobody came to luncheon except Maimie – then came in Chicken Pattie crestfallen, to talk over the defeat of last night.

Sunday 11   Lent I

At 11 the Bp., Nevill & 3 min. Cans. present – Bishop has had four sittings to Ouless[1]; called it 'Vivisection in high Art' – likes Ouless – after luncheon a walk with Harriott, by riverside, over Carrow Bridge, and them clomb the hill and looked at the Baby's grave[2] – cemetery very slovenly – in returning Creeny[3] came out of his Church, and made us look at his method of warming his Church, wh. seemed very good.

> 1. Walter William Ouless (1848–1933): Exhibited regularly at the Academy 1869–1928; recognised as one of the most trustworthy portrait painters of the day. Sitters included Charles Darwin, Cardinal Newman; King Edward VII.
> 2. In the Churchyard of St Mark's, Lakenham.
> 3. Vicar of St Michael at Thorn, Ber Street. Bombed in the Second World War.

Monday 12

After Mg. Church, walked with Harriott to Carrow, and saw Tillett & Colman[1], and the ruins of the Abbey, and the tinworks – the news arrived today of three of the Irish Assassins[2] having been convicted on the evidence of Kavanagh the car-driver – after luncheon ... wrote to ... (3) Hinds Howell about a crozier for Benson – after dinner finished reading Mozley's paper on 'Jewish & Pagan conceptions of Future State'.

> 1. J.J. Colman (1830–98): Head of the internationally-known mustard & starch works at Carrow. Liberal; Sheriff; Mayor; Alderman; Magistrate; Deputy Lieut,; M.P. Tins for the mustard were also manufactured at Carrow.
> 2. The Assassins of Lord Frederick Cavendish and Thomas Burke were members of a recently formed secret society called the Irish National Invincibles.

Thursday 15

After Mg. Church, two Choristers (Bales & Smith maj.) were brot. into the vestry, charged with playing marbles in the north transept, which they said Daniells had told them to do – We examined Daniells, who no doubt spoke to them irritably, and told them to go away from the firehouse – then the boys were publicly caned by Brockbank, and I spoke to all the choristers about Sacrilege – on my return found Mr. Fitch in my Study, waiting to present to me a large paper copy of my paper on the Reliquary Chamber, as also a copy for Benson – a letter from Ld. Waveney about the tramways[1].

    1. Electric Trams came to Norwich eventually in 1900.

Friday 16
At 8 [p.m.] preached on the 1st. clause of John XVII, 6, in the Cathedral – Heaviside, Bulmer, Beartie there – about 280 persons present – beautiful moonlight night.

Monday 19
Went to Cambridge with Ju and Harriott, starting at 7.30 a.m. – a little rain – went first to King's – the Miss Okes'[1] showed us their father's portrait by Herkommer[2] in the Combination Room – then the Chapel – thence we walked to Trinity, where we found old Sedgwick's grave marked by a plain slab with nothing but A.S. and the date upon it – then St John's; we could not get into the Chapel – then the backs of Colleges – then the Round Church – then Magdalen, where we saw Mrs. Neville[3] and talked about her son and Algy Mildmay; she put us in charge of a Mr. [blank], Vicar of St. Giles's, who took us to Jesus, but was unable to get us admission into the Chapel – then to 'St. Opposite's', opposite Jesus, a Church built by Canon Lucock[4] in his incumbency – then we went to 'Master's'[5], where we met at luncheon (1) the sister of Mrs. Money Wigram (2) Dr. Phillips[6], Master of Queen's, a mild old man, & Mrs. Phillips (3) Mr. Carr, fellow of the College (4) another gentleman, who talked about the Colleges of Priests formerly continued within the triangle formed by Bury, Walsingham, and Thetford – after luncheon the Master took us to the Fitzwilliam, & thence to see Queen's, a curious old red brick College – left by the 4.17 train – found only awaiting me letters on the Marriage law from (1) Meyrick (2) Bartie (3) Bp. of London (4) John Talbot.

    1. The Revd Richard Okes, D.D., had been Provost of King's since 1850.
    2. Sir Hubert von Herkomer (1849–1914) was a German-born British artist and director of British silent films. Slade Professor of Fine Arts at Oxford 1889–94.

> 3. The Hon. and Revd Latimer Neville, M.A., had been Master of Magdalene College, Cambridge, since 1853.
> 4. Canon H.M. Lucock (1833–1909) had been Vicar of All Saints, Cambridge, until 1875; was now Principal of Ely Theological College, and a Residentiary Canon of Ely; in 1892 became Dean of Lichfield.
> 5. Canon Robinson, Master of St Catherine's College, Cambridge.
> 6. The Revd Geroge Phillips, D.D., had been President of Queen's College, since 1857.

Wednesday 21

At 7.30 [p.m.] to Trinity, Heigham, with Ju and Harriott, where, after trying to read a written Sermon, and finding it impossible from the faintness of the light, I preached extem: the same Sermon as at Catton in December – Mr. Callis seemed well pleased – Saw Chirop. at 6 p.m. & found he had been Ignatius's[1] 1st. monk.

> 1. Joseph Leycester Lyne, ordained Deacon in 1860, dreamed of re-establishing the Benedictine Order in the Church of England. In 1864 he acquired a building with 40 rooms at the top of Elm Hill, Norwich. Calling himself Father Ignatius, he moved in with his first 'Brothers'. Organisation and finance were chaotic. By 1866, it had collapsed. He was a brilliant mission preacher. If he could have curbed his eccentricity and not antagonised people, he might have succeeded. He spent most of the rest of his life in the Monastery he established at Llanthony, South Wales.

Friday 23

Harriott left us (much regretted) by the 11.10 train – wrote to Durst, and later in the day to Dean of Canterbury about tickets for little Buskyns at the enthronization – went into Church with Brown & Bensly, and saw how the jambs are cut away at the back of Minor Canons' seats – came home and re-wrote my notes for tonight on St. John XVII, 6 – Helped thro' pretty well, but caught a cold by taking my cap[1] off in the middle of the Sermon.

> 1. This is the only mention in the Diaries of Goulburn's wearing a 'cap' while preaching – most probably a biretta.

Monday 26

At 11 the Chapter[1] – Mr. Dale of Lynn could not come – We saw Mr. Waters, and let him off £30 of rent for the remainder of his lease, & expunged the condition about the rent going up to £635 when corn is 50s. in Norwich Market – also we saw Thacker, and arranged to divide with him the proceeds of gravel sold for parish purposes from the newly opened pit on Taggs farm – Mr. Browne came into see us, and we arranged that he with Spaull shd. pay a visit to Peterboro' on Monday & make enquiries there on the subject of their tower. Bensly and I had not finished till 6.

1. Especially in his later years, Goulburn always dreaded the business side of Chapter meetings, but the Dean and Chapter had a sympathetic attitude toward their tenants, often reducing rents and helping in other ways.

Wednesday 28

After Ch. with Nevill, Moore, Bartie, called on Heaviside to show him the budget of Draft Statutes today received from Ellicott – 21 days are to be allowed to elapse from yesterday, and then (if no objection is made before Mar. 20) the Report will be sent down for signature – then looked in at Bensly's Office to tell him to put the Draft Statutes on the Agenda for Mar. 12 – then walk with Bensly (a most lovely day) – Bensly had luncheon here – Then came Nevill to announce the agreement of the Clergy to ask for a combined Service of Humiliation[1] on Friday the 9th. in the Cathedral – then wrote to (1) A. Copeman about this Service (2) Nisbet, & (3) the Master with copies of draft Statutes. (4) Mrs. Holmes about two young men she wishes to get into the Athenaeum (5) Church, on the same subject – After 2d Church wrote to the Bishop about Service of Humiliation – in the evening read Ld. Randolph's Speech at Woodstock, Holford presiding.

1. There had been bad weather and the general failure of Autumn sowing.

MARCH

Thursday 1

Heaviside looked in to make a suggestion that we shd. alter the wording of our insertion into the Preliminary Statement, saying that if a Canonry fell below ¾ths. of its value at the Commutation, the proviso about 8 months' residence might require modification – Then Wm. Cooke with <u>poster</u> about the 'Combined Service' of the 9th.[1] – then luncheon – wrote to Ellicott accg. to Heaviside's suggestion – wrote to (1) Abp. of Cant. thanking him for tickets for the enthronement wh. he promises for little B. (2) little B. – after dinner feeling of indigestion – read the 'Times' – am going to invite Hon. Canons & draw up Service for the 9th.

1. The Bishop sent a letter to all clergy in the Diocese about the Service of Humiliation, and he added: "If you have not alrady invited your Parishioners to unite with you in special humilation and prayer before God, I earnestly exhort you to do so at some time in the present season and before March 18th."

Friday 2

My Ju in bed with influenza, puffy throat, & pains in the joints – Muriel came to see Auntie; her tongue not bad, but temperature rather too high – he forbad her to go tomorrow – I dined alone at 1.30 – then went out & walked to Holmina's & saw her & Holmetta, and shewed them Church's letter about Mr. Enys's election at Athenaeum – and saw the picture of all the great men of science of the day about 1808, 1809, Matthew Boulton[1] among them.

> 1. The father or grandfather of Julia's brother-in-law of that name of Gt Tew Park.

•••

On Saturday (3) Goulburn travelled alone to Peterborough to preach in the Cathedral on the Sunday evening, arriving back in Norwich by 3.40 on Monday.
•••

Monday 5

Found Ju better – found invn. from Ripley to make speech on the opium question[1] on Monday next; acceptance by Dn. Lichfield of Palm Sunday; promise from Ber. Hope to vote for Enys and Commr. Domville – answered all three.

> 1. During the 1800s physicians used opium to treat everything from tuberculosis to diarrhoea, and it was generally used as a home remedy. Up to the Pharmacy Act of 1868, it was sold in most shops, and afterwards with little restriction by Pharmacists. By the latter part of the 19th Century attitudes towards the use of opium were changing. Doctors began to abandon it and home use declined, and its habitual use began to be considered a social evil.

Wednesday 7

A day of worry – frequent snowstorms – Mr. Beloe sent a most disagreeable letter in the morning – He is coming to the Archaeol. Meeting on Tuesday, to ask publicly why he is not appointed on the Committee – then came Bensly, and I asked him about Beloe, & also on the defalcation of our income from the depression in recent years, about wh. the Cath. Commissrs. have enquired – wrote to (1) Beloe ... A letter from Bp. enclosing & suggesting alterations in 'Bill for the making or altering of Cathedral Statutes' – In the evening read Vol. I of Ly. Bloomfields Life' aloud to Ju tonight.

> 1. Lady Georgina Bloomfield (1822–1905): Maid of Honour to Queen Victoria 1841–45; widow of 2nd. Baron Blomfield whom she accompanied on his diplomatic missions. Her newly-published book was 'Reminiscences of Court and Diplomatic Life. (2 vols. 1883).

March 1883

Friday 9   [*Service of Humiliation*][1]

Service at 8 [*p.m.*] – Bishop there, & Nevill, Copeman, Bartie, Bulmer, but <u>not</u> Moore – Alden having removed the instrument for giving the note, the 51st. Psalm hung fire at first – It was chanted by the Choir antiphonally, but on their knees – then Bulmer read the rest of the Commination Service up to the Blessing – then I took the Lesson, and afterwards preached, after reading the Prayer for fine Weather, on, "Jesus saith, Have faith in God" – I was greatly bothered by the light being not strong enough to read a Sermon, parts of wh. were faintly written – Is it my eyes? or the gas? – I wrote to Moore about his absence.

    1. The Service was prayer for God's help in the current depression in agiriculture, due to bad weather and poor harvests in recent years.

Monday 12

From 7.30 to 8.30 commenced a Saturday Sermonette – All the rest of the day a most wearisome Chapter about the Statutes – we saw Mr. Pownall & also Mr. Brereton about the School at Thorpe – also we settled that Munday was to be gardener, and a few other lighter matters, and then adjourned till Wednesday in Easter Week – We refused Mr. Wilson's request to encroach upon the ground railed round on the S. of Erpingham Gate, and wrote to ask the Town Council to let the ground to us at a nominal rent on condition of our keeping it in order.

Tuesday 13

Went to a Commitee Meeting of the Archaeological at Mr. Fitch's[1] where were Sir Will. Vincent, Gunn, Manning[2], Harcourt, Phipson, etc. – We agreed to propose that a body of corresponding members shd. be created, and that Mr. Beloe and Mr. Rye[3] should be proposed in this capacity – then we met in the Public Library, which was adorned with Mr. Creeny's[4] rubbings – After a disagreeable speech from Mr. Beloe, he accepted the corresponding membership, but no one proposed him for the Commee. – then after a short paper of Mrs. Herbert Jones's, Dr. Bennett[5] of Rushford gave an excellent Lecture on the collegiate foundation of Gonville and Caius and several other contemporary ones in the Eastern Counties – then he exhibited very curious deeds in connexion with the Gonville family & that of Sir R. Buxton, found at Shadwell Court – then Mr. Creeny took us round the room, and exhibited his Brasses with much of his usual facetiousness – saw the sketch of St. Christopher recently discovered by Mr. Bolingbroke[6] on the walls of his Church in Norwich – got away about 3.

1. Robert Fitch, Esq., F.S.A., F.G.S., Treasurer, and one of the two Hon. Secs., lived at 'The Woodlands', Dereham Road, Norwich.
2. The Revd C.R. Manning, Rector of Diss was the other Hon. Sec.
3. Walter Rye (1834–1929): A Solicitor in London until, at the age of 56, he retired and came to live in Norfolk. But he had spent all his holidays in Norfolk since the age of 21, and he became deeply involved in it, in writing and action, for the rest of his long life.
4. The Revd W.F. Creeny, Vicar of St Michael at Thorn.
5. The Revd E.K. Bennett, Rector of Brettenham with Rushford, the Patron of the Parish being Sir Robert J. Buxton, M.P. for Norfolk South.
6. The Revd N. Bolingbroke, Vicar of St Ethelred with St Peter Southgate, Norwich.

••

In HOLY WEEK Goulburn preached a series of Sermons on:
        THE PALM – Monday, March 19
        THE FIG TREE – Tuesday, March 20
        THE OLIVE – Wednesday, March 21
        THE VINE – Thursday, March 22
        THE THORN – Good Friday, March 23

••

Monday 26   [*Easter Monday*]
Church at 10 – morning in the Vestry with Eli. Litchfield & Alden[1] arranging the list of sitters in the Cathedral – At luncheon Maimie & Blanche – immediately after, Auntie & they fussed off to the Bazaar[2] – I tried in vain to get one of the MCs to walk wih me, but all were engaged – walked <u>solus</u> – Church again at 5 – Lucy & Agnes Holbech arrived – Cecy G. comes at 6 – at ½p.7 we dined, Mrs. & Miss Penrice, Blanche, Lucie, Agnes Holbech, Cecy. who is very bright and nice, & our two selves – They exhibited their treasures for tomorrow's sale after dinner.

1. Henry W. Alden served the Cathedral for 41 years as Lay Clerk, Master of the Choir Shool, and Sub-Sacrist, dying from an accident on Dec. 26, 1901, aged 73.
2. The Bazaar was in St Andrew's Hall for three days (27, 28, 29) for the Society for the Propagation of the Gospel in Foreign Parts (S.P.G.) and other objects.

Tuesday 27
Our six ladies at Bkfst. – then at noon to the Bazaar, a gay scene – saw and spoke to Mr. & Mrs. Watson, St. Emma, Arundell & Mrs. Mildmay, Mrs. Fellowes, the Mayor, the Sheriff and many others – the Mayor & Sheriff[1] having chained themselves went

to the Platform, & Nevill, Heaviside, Winter, Mr. Bignold, & many others accompanied them – They both spoke well – Afterwards I proposed a vote of thanks to them, wh. Nevill seconded – then the Bazaar was declared open – I purchased a plate with a picture of the Water Gate upon it at Auntie's stall for £1. 1; Cecy. & Maudie worked the flower-stall between them – I left the Bazaar & came home – read the 'Times' in the garden till 2.45 – then went to meeting at Gt. Hospital (where Heaviside, H. Birkbeck, Mr. Geldart, Mr. Barnham, etc.) where we sat in solemn conclave upon veal & mutton & cheeses – home & found a lengthy letter from Frederica full of the Vicar – Church & Nevill & Bulmer at 5 – Boys had no surplices; why I wonder – then this journal.

1. *Mayor:* Charles R. Gilman, Esq. (later Sir). *Sheriff:* Samuel Newman, Esq.

Wednesday 28
Wrote to Rokeby[1], & sending money for Benson's Crosier, before Bkfst. – also prepared for Chapter – afterwards an interview with the Precentor about free education for the Probationers – worked with Bensly till 2.45 – then a drive with Cecy. to Eaton School; walked back by Unthank Road – then landed Cecy. at the bazaar; bought one of Maudie's splashers with swallows on it – home & Church – then letters to Frederica; Church, asking tickets for Frederica for Wilkinson's[2] Consecreation.

1. Henry Robinson-Montague (1798–1883), sixth Baron Rokeby in Irish Peerage; General 1869. Was a connection of Goulburn's through his second step-mother, the Hon. Katherine Montagu.
2. The Rt Revd G.H. Wilkinson, D.D., consecrated Bishop of Truro 1883. Later Bishop of St Andrew's 1893; Primus of the Scottish Episcopal Church 1904. Died 1907. He had been Vicar of St Peter's Pimlico 1870–83.

• •
The Goulburns left Norwich on Tuesday, April 3, to visit London, Aynhoe and Brighton, returning to Norwich on Saturday, April 28.
• •

APRIL

Tuesday 3
Left Norwich with Ju & Rose at 7.15 – Peterboro' Cathedral, & deanery have been threatened with Dynamite – my pocket h. stolen in going down Strand.

Wednesday 4

Auntie & I went to Cowtan's in Oxford Street, to chose a paper for our dining room – Rokeby tells me that the new Dean of Windsor[1] is a failure, & moreover is dying! – walked to London Library to pay my subscription – News from Heaviside by telegram of the death of poor 'Chang'[2] – am writing to the poor Master.

> 1. The Very Revd George Henry Connor (1822–83), Dean of Windsor for only seven months, died a few weeks later.
> 2. A son of Canon Robinson.

Thursday 5

Wrote to Canon King, declining address at Oxford on 'Wife's Sister's Question', also to Monier Williams declining attendance at the opening of the Indian Institute[1] in Oxford – wrote to Heaviside in answer to a letter got from him this morning about Robinson's bereavement.

> 1. Built on the corner of Holywell with Catte Street (and next to Hertford College), the Institute was founded following a proposal by Sir Monier Monier-Williams, Boden Professor of Sanskrit, to provide a meeting place for Europeans to learn about India, and Indians to learn about the West. It was closed in 1968.

Saturday 28

Trial of Michael Fagan & his conviction, in the papers – on arriving in London went to Morgiana's – seemed to think Homburg the best place for us in August – on arriving [in Norwich] found fewer letters than usual – answered one about the vocalion[1] from Mr. Baillie Hamilton – a melancholy one from Heaviside about our affairs.

> 1. Vocalion = A musical instrument like a harmonium with broad reeds, producing sounds like the human voice.

Sunday 29   Rogation Sunday

Took the H.C. at 8 a.m. – Lay by all the day, feeling unwell, and reading various Commentaries on Psalm XXXXIII, as well as the Services of the day – Ju staid at home with me in the afternoon – after Service Heaviside called, & talked about Bensly's being subpoenaed to take all documents about Mousehold Heath[1] to London.

> 1. In June 1880 an agreement was entered into between the Ecclesiastical Commissioners and the Norwich Town Council for carrying into effect an arrangement made in 1866 with the Dean and Chapter of Norwich for conveying Mousehold Heath to the Corporation for the purpose of a

Public Park or Recreation Ground. It became a Public Park of 150 acres and, on May 12, 1886, the Mayor (Mr. John Gurney) opened a new road across it, and dedicated the Heath to the free use of the people of Norwich for ever.

Monday 30

Saw Alden, on the closing of the doors of the Cathedral[1], and on Mr. Preston's stall – Saw Daniells on the first subject – saw Mr. Atkinson, and gave him Hamilton Baillie's [*should be Baillie Hamilton's*] letter on the Vocalion – a long interview with Bensly on his taking our records to London – In the evening appeared our new Servant, Arthur Hinton, from Eydon.

1. Precautions in view of the threat to Peterborough Cathedral. (see April 3).

MAY

Tuesday 1   St. Philip and St. James
Day of Intercession for For. Missions

Wrote a letter to Robinson of welcome – Mr. Muriel came after Bkfst., and touched my throat with caustic – Church with Heaviside at 10.30 – sat with the Heavisides afterwards till luncheon time – then a conference with Yeomans about the attendance of a bedesman daily at the West door of the Cathedral – wrote to (1) Railway Benevolent Institn., sending £10 (2) asking Cadman[1] to come to us for S.P.G. next week (3) Sister Lavinia[2], refusing Cath. Pulpit to 'Father Page' of Poona.

1. Prebendary W. Cadman of St Paul's Catehdral, did come.
2. Presumably means *Mother* Lavinia, founder of the Community of All Hallows, Ditchingham. She was the third daughter of the late John Green Crosse, Surgeon at the Norfolk and Norwich Hospital.

Wednesday 2

After luncheon Ju took me a drive out by Earlham road, & back by Unthank's – she went to a Jenny Lind meeting, I to the Police Office, where I had a talk with Mr. Hitchman[1] about the precautions desirable to secure the Cathedral.

1. Robert Hitchman was the Chief Constable and also Superintendent of the Fire Brigade; Inspector of Hackney Carriages, Common Lodging Houses, explosives, drugs, food, etc. His Office was in the Guildhall.

Tuesday 8

Looked at the S.P.G. 81 Report before Bkfst. – At 11.30 H.C. – about 30 communicants – then the meeting in Clerical Rooms, at wh. Mr. Coode Hore gave an address on his work in <u>British</u>

Guiana – I said a few words about the want of interest shown in the Intervession Day, etc. – afterwards at luncheon, Preb. Cadman, Coode Hore, Hudson, de Chair, Dampier, Winter (pere et fils), Mr. & Mrs. Hillyard of Swannington, Maimie, Agnes and their cousin – at 3.30 Evensong, with an excellent Sermon by Mr. Cadman; solid & good – I like him much – we dine with the Heavisides tonight.

Friday 11
Church at 10 – then a Chapter – (1) Protection of Cathedral from explosives; talk with Browne & Daniell on the subject – (2) Cleaning to begin on Trin. Monday – (3) Question of ground outside Erpingham Gate, to be given to Mr. Wilson – (4) when shd. accounts be made up – Bensly came to luncheon – Afterwards Auntie, litle Do-do, the Master, Bensly & myself, drove to Mr. Miller's of Easton Hall, saw the Miss Millers, who showed us the dilapidated wall of the K. garden – we gave orders to do the dilapidated corner.

Tuesday 15
After Bkfst. worked at Ordination Sermon till about 1 – Mr. Arthur Back[1] called to announce his candidature for the Gt. Hospital Living; he has been Cadman's curate, and is at present holding Melton, till another Incumbent is appointed – after Luncheon drove with the Freemans and Ju to (1) Abraham's Hall in King Street; we saw a curious crypt beneath the house – (2) Mr. Tillett's; he showed us the excavations[2] & was wondrous civil – (3) Stacy's for photographs (4) St. Andrew's hall – (5) the Bishop's Palace; Fanny came to us in the garden, and told us Jessop thought the old ruin was a halting place for processions as they went round the Cathedral.

> 1. He did become Vicar of Cringleford in the gift of the Gt Hospital until 1888, when he became Vicar of Worstead, a Dean and Chapter Living.
> 2. Carrow Abbey.

Thursday 17
At 12.30 went to see Old Lichfield; read a prayer with him – saw the account of the death of Marsham Argle's[1] son – met the Master & Mary Stewart riding, & Ludie on a bicycle, with wh. he afterwards had an accident – wrote to Argles.

> 1. Residentiary Canon of Peterborough with whom Goulburn always stayed when he preached in Peterborough Cathedral.

Monday 21

Hard work with Bensly all the morning at the Agenda – Bensly had luncheon here – I walked in garden with the 'Times' reading about Benvenuto Cellini[1] – wrote to … (3) Dean of York[2] (4) Canon Tinling[3], asking about arrangements for showing the Cathedral at York and Gloucester – received news of my tutor's[4] death from his son.

1. 1500–1571: Italian goldsmith, sculptor, and engraver.
2. The Very Revd Arthur Perceval Pursey-Cust, D.D.
3. Residentiary Canon of Gloucester.
4. The Revd Charles Portales Golightly.

Tuesday 22

A long morning in Bensly's Office, interviewing Daniells, Alden, Forman, & making notes of the duties & payments of Cath. Officials – wrote to … (5) (6) Mrs. Coleridge & her son Francis with my condolences on my Tutor's death.

Wednesday 23

Fanny Pelham called about the inscription on her father's picture – also Mrs. Manning about her chorister-son – wrote, before leaving home, to: (1) Mr. Ouless, about the inscription … (3) Bartie, about Mrs. Manning – left Norwich at 11.15 – got to Rugby about 4.15; ran up to the School House, where we saw Mr. Jex Blake[1], who showed us the Chapel – we saw also Patey[2]; the doctor was not at home – at 5.15 left Rugby – got to Lichfield in an hour – the Dean[3] took us into the Cathedral, & gave me some instruction about preaching – it is very exquisite.

1. T.W. Jex-Blake, Headmaster since 1874, had been one of Goulburn's Assistant-Masters. He resigned in 1886 to become Rector of Alvechurch (near Birmingham), and, in 1891, Dean of Wells.
2. George Edward Patey was School Marshall. The Office of Marshall had been instituted by Goulburn in 1850, when he appointed Patey to be his personal man-of-all work; he was also Chapel Clerk.
3. The Very Revd Edward Bickersteth, D.D.

• •

On Thursday (24) Goulburn preached at a Festival Service in Lichfield Cathedral. He found everyone very kind and friendly, but "the Services too lengthened out, and the organ and music too thunderous and overwhelming". He and Julia returned to London on Saturday (26), and to Norwich on Tuesday, May 29.

• •

Saturday 26

Got to town about 1 – to Club, & wrote to Cinny Montagu, having just read in the paper the account of Rokeby's death – to the Academy with Ju; shoals of people jostling most uncomfortably – neither of us like the Bishop's portrait; the subordinate details are good, but there is not the characteristic expression.

    1. The Ouless Portrait.

Sunday 27

Went off to the Wellington Barracks Chapel – The mosaics are exquisite, the monuments numerous, the music (military) very well done; the hymns well chosen, the Confession read in a *very* low voice, the lessons well read by the Colonel – the Sermon (about & agst. pessimism) one of promise, thoughtful, & interesting; but the preacher had not learned how duly to modulate his voice.

Monday 28

Walked to St. James's for the Levee – The Bishop of Bangor[1] came into the vestry, just as I had done robing – Inside I met Mr. Winslow (my Father's old Registrar) and then Heaviside, who seemed in good spirits – the Prince of Wales & Duke of Cambridge both shook hands with us, & the Duke of Albany was also there – after unrobing walked to Jemima's[2], whom I saw & sat with.

    1. The Rt Revd James Colquhoun Campbell.
    2. Widow of Frederick Goulburn (of Betchworth), a cousin of Goulburn's.

Wednesday 30   [In Norwich]

A conversation with Bartie, who seems to think it impossible to get the choir cleaned before Sunday – finished my Sermonette in the rough, & then went to look into the Choir, & found dust lying over it by the inch – interview with Thomson & Spaull about the cleaning.

JUNE

Friday 1

All the morning with Heaviside in the Library, giving an answer to the last letter of Ellicott – In afternoon, carriage drive – we waited at the West front (Ju, Fraulein, and I) to see the hydrants play, urged by the new engine – After dinner arrived a telegram announcing Bullivant's dangerous illness – perplexed whether to go tomorrow.

Saturday 2   From Norwich to Exeter
Rose at 5.30; and getting a telegram to say that Bullivant was still conscious, left Norwich by 7.30 train – got here about 4.30 – after a wash, went to see Bullivant, who was touched to see me, and I was glad I came; read & prayed with him, and had an account of his state from Miss Whitehouse his great niece – then telegraphed to Ju, and wrote to her, & to MAC. about Bullivant.

Sunday 3   At Exeter
Went to the Cathedral Service at 10 – the Bp. was there – There are several points of usage different from our own – After the Sermon I came out; went to Bullivant's, and found Mr. Porter standing at his door – I administered H.C. to him, his niece, & servant, and had a good deal of conversation with him – it was touching to take leave of him – then walked to Mr. Porter's for luncheon – he drove me in his T cart first to the Telegraph Office, & then to my hotel, where we parted – most kind and obliging he was & truly hospitable – prepared to depart by the 10.20 mail train.

Monday 4
In a sleeping compartment of the G.W.R. all night, on a bed between two other gentlemen – At Swindon got a hard biscuit, wh. disagreed dreadfully – at about 4.10 a.m. reached Paddington, found a bedroom kept for me, and tumbled into bed – started for Nowich by the 12.3 train from St. Pancras; Nisbet in the same carriage.

Tuesday 5   General Chapter
Foreman[1] with us instead of Bensly; he is wonderfully ready and quick – the main thing done was the deciding to write to E.C. for Christian's[2] advice upon Brown's recommendations in the matter of the spire and tower – 1. to throw an iron girder round the base of the spire, at its junction with the Tower. 2. to obliterate the Minor Canons' Stalls & restore the spliced jambs behind them – we interviewed Mr. Going, who came to say he did not want done to his buildings, so much as it appeared by a certain plan that he wd. want; & Mr. Dale[3] of Lynn, who came for our advice as to (1) getting himself released of the charge of £150 on his living for the maintenance of St. John's (2) building a parsonage (3) getting a stipend for a 3d curate, out of the Ecc. Commrs.

1. Byron Foreman, the Chief Clerk in the Dean and Chapter's Office.
2. Senior Architect of the Ecclesiastical Commissioners.
3. The Revd B. Dale, Vicar of St Margaret's, Kings Lynn.

Saturday 6

Drew up a letter to Pringle[1], asking for Christian's inspection of our tower, before Bfst. – at 10 set to work with Foreman, writing letters to Mr. Wilson, declining to give him ground outside Erpingham Gate; and to the ex-chorister Andrews, sending him £1 – at luncheon went to the Master's – Heaviside came in in the middle to get me out, to suggest another & milder form of letter to the E.C., wh, we adopted.

1. Ecclesiastical Commissioners' Official.

Thursday 7

Church at 10 – interview with Foreman afterwards about the permission given me to gravel, etc. the garden of the Lower Close; and with Alden, from whom I made out that each subsacrist makes (or may make) £100 by the fees of visitors, instead of £50, as I had previously calculated.

Saturday 9

Wrote to Miss Whitehouse about Bullivant's death, the news of wh. I received from her before Aftern. Church – Funeral to be on Tuesday next at 4 p.m.

Thursday 14

Mg. Prayer at 10 (quite plain, this being the Choir holiday, when all are gone to Cambridge & are to have their refreshment in the Master's house) – Mr. Gunn called to tell me, as if it were a great discovery, that the eastern arm of our cathedral is deflected toward the north from the straight line of the nave & choir; and the reason – at ½p.2 a short walk with the Master – shortly after arrived little B and Gerard & their babe (as fat as fat can be).

1. Gussie's second baby, Augusta, but now her eldest. Altogether she had seven, five daughters and two sons.

Saturday 16

After Bkfst. called on Heaviside, who quite agrees with me that the step to be taken, if Christian refuses to act, is to call in Fergusson – Church at 10 with the Master & Moore – afterwards went into the Cathedral with Browne, and saw the effects of the cleaning; spoke to Alden abut cleaning the Sacrarium.

Sunday 17
A word with Heaviside & the Master about Christian's letter which I got this morning.

Tuesday 19
Spruce called to receive my communication about him from Chelsea Hospital – he has mistaken the terms on wh. military pensions are granted – I referred him to a man who, he said, had got a pension after 9 years service – At luncheon Miss Drake – afterwards I walked with Gerard (partly in rain) to Willm. Birkbeck's – they were not at home – we found our way back across the fields to Lady Harvey's farm[1] – returned to Thorpe Road and across ferry.

> 1. At this time a very large area from Thorpe Hamlet to Thorpe next Norwich, was the grounds of three large landowners: (1) Lady Harvey, widow of General Sir Robert J. Harvey, who lived in Mousehold House; (2) John Harvey, Esq., and (3) William J. Birkbeck, Esq., who lived in High House (formerly 'The Grove'). Goulburn had been given keys to the grounds of (1) and (3), so that he could walk through. After Lady Harvey's death, the concession was renewed by the new owner.

Wednesday 20   Accession Day[1]
At 10 Service for the Accession with Bulmer & Moore – Bulmer preached – Service lasted 1 hr. 35 min. – Mr. Gunn was there, & the little Hay Gurneys (Scob, Mob & Chitterbob) – there was no 'God save the Queen' played (a real omission) – On coming out, saw in the 'Times' the account of Mr. Betts threatening letter to the Bp., & of his being remanded – afterwards went with Gerard to call at the Palace – then walked with Gerard to the Cemetery & saw Chang's grave, & also that of Elk and Mrs. Lichfield – then to the Police Office, where Mr. Hitchman gave me an account of the capture of Betts, & shewed me his handwriting – 2d Church with the Master & Bulmer at 5, at wh. 'God save the Queen' was twice played.

> 1. Queen Victoria ascended the throne on June 20, 1837.

Friday 22
At 4 went with Ju to the Bp's Training College Garden party – talked to the Bp. about the wife's Sister's Bill in the Lords.

Tuesday 26
About 12.25, as I was engaged in writing came Mr. Lee Warner and the Secy. of the Widows' of Deceased Clergymen Fund, and

begged me to come to the Meeting as there was no one to preside – when I went I found Canon King, Mr. Thursby, Mr. Lee Warner, Mr. Payne of Colney & Uncle Bartie – we resolved no more to continue Mrs. Barker's pension, until she put herself in some Institution for [?] persons of wh. we approve; meeting not over till 2.5 – Walked with Gerard by the riverside to Carrow, where a very intelligent young foreman showed us over the blue factory[1] (it is extracted from the refuse of the mustard by pressure); afterwards the refuse goes to make oil-cake for manure – a letter from George Antony, asking me to attend meeting in St Paul's Chapter House about D.W.S. Bill on Monday next at 2.

1. Where blue bags for laundering are made.

JULY

Monday 2
Leaving my luggage at St Paul's Deanery, went to the meeting on D.W.S.[1] question in the Chapter House – there were G.A.D.,[2] Gregory[3], Archdeacon Harrison[4], Palmer, Hannah, Canon Lowe and others – I staid till 3, and then went off to Liverpool Street – caught the 3.30 train to Norwich (via Ipswich) and got here about 6.45.

1. On June 28, the Deceased Wife's Sister's Bill had been defeated in the House of Lords on the Third Reading by a majority of 145 to 140.
2. G.A. Denison, Archdeacon of Taunton.
3. Canon of St Paul's; later to be Dean.
4. Archdeacon of Maidstone.

Monday 9
Completed Yarmouth Sermon about noon – then went out (1) to Norris's at Charg. X, to see about an old oak chest – (2) to Lovick's[1] to buy some china for Buskynoon[2], her birthday – Buskyns made her selection for a revolving Coffee Service – went to Church – afterwards an inspection of the vestry with Brown & Spaull – saw the original level of the floor, & the filled up well.

1. Lovick and Co., China and Glass Warehouse, 28, St Andrew's Street.
2. A new nick-name for Augusta; her birthday on July 18,

Thursday 12   Yarmouth Choral Festival[1]
Left Norwich with Ju at 12.4 and got to Yarmouth at 12.35 – Venables took me into the Church to try the height of the pulpit – I met there Arundell, who entreated me to be short eno' to let him & his choir get away by the 5.10 train; he seemed to be in a

great fuss – Service began at 3 after a long Processional Hymn – it was over just about 4 – then I preached, cutting my Sermon down (as I went along) to just 20 mins.; it was on Psalm CXLVIII – we left by the 5.40 train via Reedham, a very bad one.

> 1. The Choirs had 398 voices, accompanied by a Band in addition to the Organ.

Friday 13

Set to work on the boys' answers to the Catechism Paper – Muriel came & touched my throat – then came Mr. Ram[1]; the man who before desecrated the Churchyard is about to sell his house by auction, and has advertised the Churchyard as a 'back yard', wh. may take intending purchasers in – then came Brown to hear about Christian's letter of this morning, and to tell me about the discovery of steps in the vestry – Bensly at luncheon – I instructed him about a meeting of Canons to meet Christian on Wednesday next – then to the School to examine the Choristers with Bartie <u>in Viva Voce Bible</u> – Bartie had to go at 4, and then Ju relieved him – then I took a walk – then wrote to (1) Christian (2) Col. Parnell about his substitute for lightning conductor – Ly. Vincent dined here at ½p.7, and at 8.15 went to a meeting of factory girls, and another of shop girls.

> 1. The Revd E. Ram, Vicar of St John Timberhill.

Tuesday 17   A Chapter

A day of worry, as Chapter Days usually are – Rose at 6.15, and got an hour's writing before Bkfst. – After Bkfst. wrote on till 11 – then went across to Bensly's Office – a letter from Jecks about the foreshore on the marshes & his Boathouse thereon – this we committed to the Master to look over – then came Browne with his announcement that the alteration of vestry level with new Door, etc. would cost £100 – we examined the spot together, and determined to ask Christian's opinion tomorrow.

Wednesday 18

Mr. Browne came at ½p.10 to say that they had proceeded so fast with the Vestry after yesterday's Chapter that now to put back the modern level wd. be nearly as expensive as restoring the ancient one – So I was obliged to go on – at 11 Christian arrived, & went over the Tower with Brown – at 1.30 he came to luncheon here with Brown & Bensly – the report he makes is that the figures in the spire matter very little, but that the crushing of one of the columns at the S.W. angle of the tower is very serious indeed – He recommends, before the crushed part is meddled with, a strong timber bracing round the exterior of the tower, with strong iron clamps fixed into it thro' the present eyeholes – these will form a frame holding the tower together – the Chapter was at 2 – Heaviside obliged to go away before the end – after he had gone, the Master gave us a summary of Jeck's letter, wh. he had undertaken to read – then having assisted Bensly in his office to annotate, took a walk with him over Mousehold & back by Plumstead Rd. – wrote to the Abp. of Canty. about the Ecclesiastical Survey of the Possessions of the D. & C. of Norwich made in the time of the Commonwealth.

Monday 23
Preparations for departure – went to buy a paintbox for Mary Stewart; then to say Goodbye to Mrs. Nevill; saw Ralphy whose forehead had been bitten by a gnat – then an interview with Munday about the Close – Mr. White at 4; he stopped a tooth for me – said Goobye to Mary Stewart – then Brown, to whom I gave definite instructions about the vestry (1) to make good the jambs of existing S. Window £5. (2) to put a tiling border round the wooden pavement £10. (3) to restore the two steps at the East End of the Chamber £10 – also instructed him to put 2 new lancet windows in the S. wall of the vestry; one for £13, the other for £15, if the Canons' consent were gained.

• •
The Goulburns are now away from Norwich from Tuesday, July 24 to Saturday, September 1: London for one night; Brussels, Bonn, en route to Homburg, where they stayed from July 28 to August 18; Baden-Baden from August 18 to 22; then Nancy, Rheims, Paris, the latter from August 25 to 27; Folkestone from August 27 to 30; London for two nights, then back to Norwich. Their Courier was Chenaud.
• •

Tuesday 31   [*At Homburg*]
Ju did not go out all morning, having a cold – I at the waters at exactly 7 – met & walked w. Lady Maria Brodie, & was introduced by her to her son & daughter – Afterwards introduced her to Gnl. Milman, who, she thot. cd. help her son – drank my two glasses, & inhaled – then met Lake & walked with him till he was joined by Lord O'Hagan – then home – worked a little at Psalm 119 & made some way – then Hebrew – then Guy Mannering –

went out at about noon, and found the Lakes wandering about in search of lodgings – chatted with them on the bench near the Church – then to return Canon Gibbon's call – not at home, but I met him afterwards, & had some talk – to Brahe's for luncheon; afрer wh. we called on Lord Warwick, & sat with him, trying to amuse him – then home & Hebraized – went with Ju to the Louisen Quelle in the afternoon, and took a glass – the Brigstockes called, & he asked me to preach Sun. afternoon[1].

> 1. The Contintental Spas were almost a home from home, meeting so many people whom one knew or got to know, calling and returning calls, preaching and taking Services, etc. It scarcely seemed like "getting away from it all".

AUGUST

Thursday 2
Saw Lady Trevelyan, who asked us to dine at the 'Russie' with her & Sir Charles[1] tonight – then introduced Canon Gibbon to Lake[2], and 'inhaled' with him – a letter came from Hinds Howell, who has had a squabble with Heaviside about the loan of the Bp's portrait to the Bazaar – I wrote back that I thought the best way would be to present the portrait as soon as the Exhibition[3] closes, and then let the Bp. do as he likes about lending it – an afternoon walk with Ju in the environs, wh. brought us close to the cemetery & Amelia's grave wh. we inspected – it is somewhat slovenly.

> 1. Sir Charles Trevelyan was a former Governor of Madras, and carried out considerable reforms in India; Lady Trevelyan (nee Hannah Macaulay) was the sister of Lord Macaulay, the historian. Their son was Sir George Otto Trevelyan, historian and statesman.
> 2. The Very Revd W.C. Lake, Dean of Durham, had been a friend of Goulburn since their undergraduate days at Balliol College, Oxford, and had been the other candidate when Goulburn became Headmaster of Rugby.
> 3. The Royal Academy Exhibition.

Monday 6
Met Mr. Clark, and also Lake and Bradley[1] – Inhaled side by side with Lake, and afterwards walked homewards with him – he told me about Stanley having left £130,000, £60,000 of wh. is to go to Mrs. Vaughan for her life, and after her death to Bradley – I think of writing to Heaviside[2] tonight – did so, and gave him my full view of the Bp's portrait question, that there would be a certain indelicacy in using it to get money before presenting it to the Bishop.

1. George Granville Bradley had been Assistant Master at Rugby under Goulburn; he was also a close friend of Dean Stanley, and followed him as Dean of Westminster in 1881, immediately previous to which he had been Master of University College, Oxford.
2. Canons Heaviside and Hinds Howell were probably Goulburn's two closest friends and colleagues in Norwich. He resolved the dispute about the Bishop's Portrait in a diplomatic and fair manner.

Tuesday 7
In the morning came a worrying letter from Heaviside about the portrait, begging me to write to Ouless and request him to consign the picture to the 'Bazaar Committee' This I answered ... saying that I must adhere to my resolution announced last night.

Saturday 18   From Homburg to Baden
Rose at 6, and left Homburg about 9 – the Baron & Ernst[1] came to the Station to see us off, & tell us about Eyhorne – Got to Baden about 3.30.

1. The Baron and Ernst would have been staying either with Louisa Thomas (Amelia's elder sister & Gerard's mother); or with Gerard and Augusta. The former is the most likely.

Sunday 19   [At Baden-Baden]
Went with Ju to the 8 a.m. H.C. in a fly – a well appointed Church, with some ritualistic externals, but far preferable to Homburg – I celebrated the H.C., Mr. White assisting – At 11 Ju did not go to Church, being ill – I went in a fly and preached for Mr. White – Dinner at Table d'Hote at 6 with a number of Yankees.

SEPTEMBER

Monday 3   [Back in Norwich]
Began my reasons for declining to sign the Report of the Cathedral Establishments' Commissioners – Wrote to ... (4) Hinds Howell about the time for the presentation of the Bp's portrait – Saw lord (?) Justice Lindley & Lady Lindley who called, and at the same time Mrs. Nevill – saw also Mindy, who complained that Brown gave him too much to do in taking up the grass of the Close.

Thursday 6
Went on with my 'Objections to Draft Statutes' – After Ch. at 10 (Heaviside and Bartie) a meeting here of Hinds Howell,

Heaviside, Nevill, self, about Bp's Portrait – settled to have the presentation Oct. 18 – discussed what to do about the surplus money – one of the Commee. to propose at a Meeting early on the 18th. that it shall be given (as part of the Testimonial to the Bp.) to the fund for the endowment of poor livings – wrote to the Bp. about our proceedings – and also to Bensly, altering our Chapter Day from the 13th. to the 12th.

Friday 7
After Mg. Church Feltham[1] came in to complain that the Ferry now brought him in nothing, and to ask that we wd. help him – I promised to bring the case before the Chapter on Wednesday.

> 1. Charles Feltham was Dean's Verger and Ferryman, and lived adjacent to the Ferry.

Tuesday 11
Muriel called, causticked my throat, and syringed both my ears – after luncheon H. Gunning[1] mounted his horse and took his ride – I walked in the garden, reading 'Times', and was joined by Ju and Lady Gunning – I am expecting Heaviside & Dd. Stewart, to talk over the tower of the Cathedral – Mr. Stewart's account of the Cathedral shows a necessity for doing <u>something</u>, but he recommends pulling it about as little as possible; also rebuilding the jambs behind the Minor Canons' Seats.

> 1. The Revd Sir Henry Gunning was now 86. Julia's stepsister, Mary, the first Lady Gunning, had died in 1877.

Saturday 15
Before Bkfst. corrected proofs of my 'Reasons for not signing Report' – wrote two letters about the living of Wighton, vacant by old Methwold's death yesterday morning, and applied for by the Rev J.H.R. Pilling.

> 1. The Revd J.W. Methwold had been Vicar of Wighton since 1835; J.H.R. Pilling was his Curate, and did, eventually, succeed as Vicar.

• •

On Saturday afternoon (15) he set off by train to Beccles in order to preach at Gillingham (just north of Beccles) in the Norman Church of St Mary, which had been substantially rebuilt in 1858–59, returning to Norwich on Monday.

• •

Monday 17   From Gillingham to Norwich

At 9.30 started for the Station with Mr. Dampier – one of the Cowley Fathers[1] en route to Barsham, was walking up & down the Station – did not get out at Haddiscoe, and was taken to St. Olave's – there got out & had to walk back with my bag, to Haddiscoe – there waited ½ an hour and composed some rhymes, describing the misadventure for Ethel Dampier's 'Gillingham News' – got home about ½p.12 – Heaviside came in afterwards, & then Nevill, to give us the account of his visit to Yarmouth about the marshes – It appears that Jecks made more out of them by £120 than he paid rent to us; also that he sub-let them all – also that they will soon be wanted as building land – good news.

> 1. In 1866, the Revd Richard Meux Benson (1824–1915) founded the Society of St John the Evangelist (S.S.J.E.) in his Parish of Cowley, then a village, though with a new suburb of Oxford beginning to develop towards Cowley, hence 'Cowley Fathers'.

Sunday 23

At 11 we had the Ordination (5 Priests, 5 Deacons) – De Saumarez Smith preached a good Sermon ... of the old School – the Bp. seemed to enjoy it – Church again at 3.30 with Heaviside, Moore, Bartie – H. preached an excellent Sermon on "Can there any good thing come, Etc." – "Come and see" – He said that no painter had ever come up to one's ideal of Christ, but several to one's ideal of the B.V.M.

Monday 24

To the Bp's, and talked with him over the various candidates for Yarmouth: Greenall, Pilling, Evelyn-White and Nevill's candidate at Barningham – He seemed to think that Ferrier wd. not be qualified under the Cathedral Act – the Gunnings went by the 11.15 train today, and, as there was no horse box ready for her, Kitty was left soaking in the rain.

Tuesday 25

Wrote to Genl. Parkes about the conduct of the Station Master yesterday about the horsebox – After luncheon called on Miss Hansell, and was glad to find her downstairs & about – She talked about the proposed canal thro' the Holy Land, wh. she thot. wd. be "almost worse than the railway in the Close" – then to the meeting at the Gt. Hospital, meeting H. Birkbeck en route – Mr. Cox, the Master, asked for an increase of his stipend – some were for it, but Heaviside opposed it, and the motion was lost.

Wednesday 26

After Mg. Service worked at a Sermonette on the Festival of St. Michael's – at luncheon was Gussie Rackham, who described a Salvationist Service held outside her house, in wh. a young man preached with vehemence, while a number of young women danced round him with timbrels.

Friday 28

Interview with Browne at 11, from wh. it appeared that the Vestry will cost me just £50 more than the £100 I contracted for – Paid him £120 (having already given him £100 before going to Homburg) – Muriel called & touched my throat – went to Mr. White's[1] at ½p.4, who stopped a decay for me.

> 1. Richard White and Sons, Dental Surgeons, 26, St Giles Street.

Sunday 30

H.C. with Bartie at 8 – Nevill's[1] Service was at 10.45, but no fly appearing, I was obliged to walk, but found a fly half-way – a very pleasing and reverend [t] Service, and Church beautifully decorated – I preached my Sermon on the Manna as illustrating the petition, "Give us this day our daily bread" – too long; people looked weary – walked home – Cathedral at 3.30 – then came Muriel & touched my throat – then Algie Nevill, with the St. Peter's preaching book for me to sign.

> 1. The Ven. Henry Nevill, as well as being Archdeacon of Norfolk and Residentiary Canon of Norwich Cathedral, was also, at this time, Vicar of St Peter Mancroft.

• •

From October 1 to November 24, the Goulburns took their Autumn break to visit friends and relations, and to stay in their house at Brighton, and also to visit Chichester. Goulburn made a one night return to Norwich on October 17, to be at the Presentation of the Bishop's Portrait on October 18. The Itinerary included: Betchworth (near Reigate, with Goulburn's cousins), Eydon, Edgcote, Aynhoe, Brighton, Chichester, and brief stays in London.

• •

OCTOBER

Tuesday 2   *At Betchworth*

Before Bkfst. took an hour's walk before the house, reading carefully the applications & testimonials for Wighton – After Bkfst. a walk to Brockham by footpath, and back by road, still engaged in the same reading – on my return wrote on the subject to (1) Nevill at Reading about his candidate – (2) Bp. about Mr. Muriel of Stanford (3) Mr. Martin about the Rev J.H.R. Pilling (4) Archdn. Perowne about the same – my mind inclines to Pilling – after luncheon drove with Louisa, Mrs. Hepburn, Ju, to Mrs. Drummond's at Fridley – she had been a member of my congregation at Quebec & St. John's – we walked round her grounds & had 5 o'clock tea.

Saturday 13   From Eydon to Edgcote
Ju had a very bad and disturbed night, and did not come down to Bkfst. – I wrote to Mr. Pilling, offering him the living of Wighton (2) Mr. Rivett, explaining the appointment. (3) The Bishop announcing it to him (4) Mr. Arthur Thomas suggesting Dr. Jessopp and Mr. Pigot as possibly qualified for St. George's, Brighton (Patron, Laurence Peel).

Thursday 18   **St. Luke**
Dressed in my Doctor's scarlet gown, and went to the Palace, where I found an immense throng, and felt very nervous – however I got through pretty well, Hinds Howell unveiling the portrait[1] before I began – I spoke to Nisbet, Heaviside, Dampier, Burton, Griffith, Eded, Herbert Jones, and others; and coming out I came upon Symonds, whom I induced to come & sit with me while I ate my 3 p.m. dinner – left Norwich at 4.40.

> 1. The portrait was ¾ths length. So large a sum had been collected for it, that it was determined to have a copy made of it, to be given to the Diocese, and to be placed in the Palace. It was to commemorate the 25th anniversary of the Bishop's consecration.

NOVEMBER

Friday 2   From Brighton to London return
At 8.45 went to London – called on Morgiana, who advised me not to have the two teeth out; but on my pressing their painfulness gave me a letter to Mr. Vasey of 5, Cavendish Place, to whom I went – after some conversation with a young partner, Mr. Vasey came in, and both agreed that I must lose my wise tooth (doctoring the other) – this was done, but it was excruciating, the tooth breaking in my head, and the fangs having to be dug out – He gave me some brandy, and I recovered.

Wednesday 14 [At Brighton]
At ½p.2 went with Ju to the meeting of the Orphan Boys' Home at the Pavilion – It went off very well; Mr. Vaughan made an excellent speech, as also did Talbot, and Cap. Field made some good practical recommendations about teaching the Boys industrial occupations and emigration, and Dr. Griffith made some suggestions about wiping off the debt – I stupidly omitted to call upon the Boys for their last little song – on our return I wrote to Edith Anderson apologising for this, & offering either a donation of £10 or £15, if nine other persons can be found to offer £15, so as to wipe off the £150 debt.

Wednesday 21 [At Brighton]
Letters in the morning from Mrs. Vaughan at Llandaff, and from Blick[1] about Choral Festival on June 12 – answered both these – then went out, had hair cut, and, in a fly, as it rained hard, went to Glading's – there chose at last a small tea set (price £20) for my Ju's wedding day – Bigge called for me at ½p.2, and we walked to the end of Kemp Town, and back my Madeira – we saw a life boat start with sails, and, on our return, we saw it land again with 8 oars – So ends our Brighton holiday.

> 1. The Revd J.J. Blick, Rector of Wramplingham, Wymondham; the Norfolk and Suffolk Church Choral Association.

Satuday 24 [*London to Norwich*]
Went to Hay's, 6, N. Audley Street, to get brown bread biscuits – left London by the midday train; our carriage quite full of ladies till Cambridge – read the Telegraph, Post, Spectator, Illustrated – found <u>comparatively</u> few letters, but heaps of parcels – wrote to … (6) Genl. Parkes, thanking for the investigation he had made into H. Gunning's horse-box case.

Monday 26
Wrote two letters before Bkfst., one to Miss Hansen, thanking for Norwegian translation of my 'Pursuit of Holiness', and sending her an introduction to Rivington's – A beggar[1] called before Church, whose case I heard; she had lost money by sending it thro' the Post Office – after Church went to see H. for a very few minutes; and afterwards the Bp. with whom I talked over Mr. Venable's suggestion of a clerical retreat at the Cathedral in Ember tide – Bartie came in at 2 about the Advent Services, etc. etc. – All the afternoon with Browne and Benlsy, drawing up

Agenda Paper – Dinner at 7; afterwards drew out with Ju a scheme of Advent Services for this year.

1. He gave her 2s.

Tuesday 27
I went to the meeting of Pastoral work – This threw off with an able and atractive, but not sufficiently balanced paper, by Mr. Williams the new Incumbent of Barsham – then followed another, equally favourable to Retreats – Mr. Williams described a Cowley Retreat (very severe) – there were speeches against, as well as for retreats – one by Mr. Ballance; a speech for by Mr. Sewell of Yaxley – Nisbet spoke well – Mr. Venables of Yarmouth recommended a quiet day for the Clergy in Ember times at the Cathedral, with a special Service, 'the verbiage' taken from the Ordinal – I said that if there was a demand for such a thing in the diocese, and the Bp. concurred, I wd. do my best to make it a success – the Bp. closed with showing how the passages of SS. quoted for retreats had been wrested – this he did well – after rapid luncheon a walk with Bartie to Thorpe to enquire for poor John Patteson & family after the news of yesterday – wrote to him on my return.

Friday 30   St. Andrew
A disquieting letter from Christian, proposing to send his nephew here instead of himself on Tuesday – I answered, after consulting with Heaviside that I shd. be glad to see the nephew & give him bed & board, but requesting him to come early, that he mt. make report to us in the afternoon – worked at Sat. Sermonette till 11.45 – then walked with Nisbet, who I found quite disagreed with what I had done, and thought that a visit from young Christian ought to be declined – We walked to J. Patteson's Rectory to enquire; and then back – at ½p.2 we met at Bensly's Office, and saw Brown, & heard the tale of his interview with Christian, and concluded upon the whole that we wd. let the arrangement for Tuesday (to see young Christian) stand.

DECEMBER

Saturday 1
Church in Morng. – afterwards a little work at Origen & Eusebius in the Library – while I was writing Canon King called, and begged me to take the Chair at the Clergy Widows' Half Yearly

meeting, the Bp. being unable to come – I went there at 12.30 – Can. King read out with gt. emphasis a letter from Mrs. Barker's Son, reproving the Commee. for suspending her pension – We gave Miss Carver an addl. £5 for this year – At 3 Church – then called on Mrs. Nevill, where I found the Lady Mayoress (Mrs. Eade)[1] and Mrs. Bensly, and other ladies came in.

> 1. Dr (later Sir) Peter Eade had been elected Mayor on November 9 for the first time. That evening, he and Mrs. Eade were guests at the Prince of Wales' Birthday Ball at Sandringham.

Monday 3
Rain, cold, darkness all day long – Ch. at 10 – then an interview with Bedesman Rix on the hard treatment he had undergone from Strangroom & Cutlock – then interview with Yeomans to enquire about Rix's complaint – in the afternoon Chapter at 2.15 to receive Bensly's estimates for the past financial year – as far as we cd. see, our incomes this year will be much as they were last; for while receipts are diminished, bills are diminished also – Ch. with Nisbet and Bulmer – then scolded Shangroom & Cutlock, and threatened them with withdrawal of my Xmas gratuity – after dinner read aloud to Ju D. Stewart's Report of his examination of our Cathedral, and signed a batch of Bell ringers' certificates[1].

> 1. The Norwich Diocesan Association of Ringers had been established in 1877, with Goulburn as President.

Tuesday 4   The General Chapter
Henry Christian came and inspected the Cathedral, and we had an interview with him & Browne afterwards – his report went to the absolute necessity of <u>immediate action</u>, although it was more consolatory than I had expected – we gave orders to build up a cemented brick pier in the upper stage of the tower, and to cement the fissures in the lower stages.

Thursday 6
Storms of snow and hail all day long – In the morning Archbold[1] called to tell me of the proposal of the Lords of the Council to withdraw the grant from our Training College unless we erect a new building in a healthier part of the City – found a young clergyman awaiting me (Mr. Fisher) Mr. Lombe's Curate at Swanton Morley, who asked my advice about his conduct on leaving Swanton, Mrs. Lombe having discarded him, and been

unkind to him – I sat him down in the Library to write to the Bishop, asking for an appointment, at wh. he might set himself right – he went away at about 5.45.

> 1. The Revd Thomas Archbold, Principal and Secretary of the Diocesan Training Institution in St George's Plain, from 1875–95. The new building in College Road was opened in 1892. Archbold had been Vice-Principal of Culham College, and Headmaster of the Diocesan Middle School at Burgh.

Friday 7
Wrote to Mr Vincent[1], appointing a day for the meeting of the Socy. for preserving the Memorials of the Dead – wrote also to Mr. Fisher, telling him of Ayre's Curacy being vacant – Snow lying on ground – Bensly came to luncheon & talked over Jessopp's[2] application for leave to search our Registers – Heaviside sends a letter from David Stewart, from wh. it appears that he quite disagrees with the brickwork structure and the tie-bars recommended by Christian.

> 1. The Rector of Postwick became Sir Wm. Vincent, Bart. in 1883. He was also Sec. of the National Society for Preserving the Memorials of the Dead, and an office address in London was also given for him. The national Treasurer was Lt.-Col. Charles E. Bignold, fourth son of Sir Samuel Bignold, and Secretary and Trustee of the Norwich Union.
> 2. The Revd A. Jessopp, D.D., formerly Headmaster of the King Edward VI Grammar School, now Rector of Scarning, as a historian, was gathering material for his books.

Saturday 8
Mrs. Fergusson Davie had luncheon here after a G.F.S. meeting – then Colonel Phillips called, and asked permission to present to the Cathedral Hymn Books for the soldiers – 'The Ancient and Modern', he said, was the authorised hymnbook for the army – He lives at Hill House, Thorp[e].

Sunday 9   Advent 2   New Anthem Book introduced
<u>This was the first day of the New Anthem Book</u> – The Mayor & Corporn. were there in the morning – after dinner saw Edward[1], & talked about BM & the Lord's Supper.

> 1. The new manservant whom he had begun to prepare for Confirmation.

Monday 10
When I was working in the afternoon came Brown, to ask to have the Clock stopped, bec. he thought the fissure in the pier has increased since Henry Christian was here last week! – and then

summonses from Burgon & Mr. Freeling to come to Oxford at 2 on Thurs. to vote agst. the proposed new Examiner in the Rudiments of Faith and Religion, being a Dissenting Minister[1] – Church again – then visited Nevill, to induce him to go to Oxford, but he has no vote! – wrote to (1) Henry Christian about Brown's information – (2) Brown to meet us in Chapter tomorrow.

> 1. The Revd Robert Forman Horton, Congregational Minister (1855–1934) – Had been at New College, Oxford; President of the Union 1877. 1st Class Lit. Hum. 1878; Fellow of New College 1879–86; was not ordained till 1884; eventually became President of the National Free Church Council; great preacher & saintly personality.

Tuesday 11
At Mg. Church Nisbet and Bartie – afterwards a meeting of Chapter at Bensly's Office, at wh. Brown appeared and showed photographs of fissures, and explained his views of what was needed, & of the precariousness of the situation – Nisbet proposed that the Cath. shd. be closed and the Services dropped at once – Heaviside & Bensly had to leave early, the 1st. to go to the Bp. with Archbold about the Training School; the 2d to go to Mr. Smith's funeral at Loddon – It was agreed that I shd. go to the Bishop, & consult him about the dropping of the Services – This I did at 2.10, and sat long with him – he seemed to think (1) that unless Christian himself said the building was unsafe for a congregation to assemble in, we cd. not drop the Services (2) that if the danger were imminent, we sdh. have more indications of it than the opening of a fissure (3) that our plan of consulting an engineer was a wise one – called on Heaviside and told him this; also on Nevill & Nisbet, but they were out – wrote to … (2) the Pin, asking him to go to Oxford on Thursday (3) Hinds Howell, the same (4) Christian asking him to return with Brown tomorrow night, & offering him hospitality – In the evening read some of 'the Times' to dear Auntie; gave her this morng. my weddingpresent, a silver bkfst. Service for one person.

Thursday 13
Left Norwich at 11.35 – change at Cambridge and again at Bletchely – at Bletchley saw Salmon who however was travelling 3d class – arrived at Oxford, I put on my gown in the fly, & got to the Theatre[1] just at 2 p.m. – It was thronged – sat between Hodson (who had lost an eye) and Heurtley – could not see B.C. nor the Pin, nor Hinds Howell – it was over by three – majority

against Horton more than 400![2] took my luggage to the cloak room at the G.W.R. – then to the Union, to write one line to Ju, another to Hinds Howell – frightful confusion at the train before the starting of the G.W.R. express – I was in the same carriage with Mr. Wright, Buskin's neighbour, and talked during the 1h. 25m. of the trajet without ceasing – on arrival in town went to Garlant's & made a toilette – then to Club, where dined side by side with Tom; hard indigestible potatoes.

> 1. The Sheldonian Theatre (Architect: Christopher Wren) built 1669, as a place for the "enactment of university business" and ceremonies. It seats 2000 people.
> 2. The voting on this occasion was: For 155, against 576.

Friday 14
Left London at 9.15 – on my arrival at 1, found a letter from Christian, saying he did not consider it worth while to come down.

Sunday 16   Advent 3
Worked at the Introduction to yesterday's Sermonette before 11 a.m. – The Archdeacon Groome preached – it seemed admirable, but I could not well hear it – the soldiers for the first time used the new Hymn Books provided for the Regiment by the Colonel – At 2.10 (in heavy rain) started for Drayton – the Church beautifully warm and light, and very well cared for – Service charming, quite old-fashioned & simple, but most reverent – preached conversationally on Matt. XXVIII, the Great Commission (for S.P.G.).

Wednesday 19
Went with Ju to the Grammar School – Mr. Colman[1], in the absence of Heaviside, was in the Chair – A fairly good concert, the gem of it being a young boy's (Ommanney's) playing on the violin – then Mr. C. asked me to distribute the prizes, which I did, after Mr. Tancock had read out his lists – I said something to them as to my regret for not having learnt Hebrew & Music in my youth – Burdon got my prize, Archbold the Bp's (for Gt. Test).

> 1. J.J. Colman, Esq., M.P., D.L. (Mustard magnate).

Thursday 20
At 2, 1st. meeting at the Literary Institution of the local Society for preserving Monuments of the Dead – I was elected Chairman

for the year, tho' I gave them notice I should scarcely ever be able to attend – Subscribers to have the publications at a reduced price to be arranged by the Commee., the size to be Imperial Octavo – then to Bensly's Office to hear some Chapter worries – then attended a Feast of Innocents, consisting of the little Nevills, little Moore, little Henry Nisbet – looked into begging circulars for Charities.

Friday 21   St. Thomas
Worked till luncheon at 1st. my Sermon for this evening, to which I made a conclusion, and altered it in various ways; then at my Sermonette, the text of wh. is nearly finished, but the introduction not begun – Yeomans came in, and I told him to summon the Bedesmen for tomorrow at 4 – after luncheon, Auntie drove me out to Thorpe School, and I thence went by the Tyrol & Plumstead Road into the Thorpe Road again – there met the Bp., Nisbet, little Henry, and the Miss Maitlands, and walked back with them – the Bp. and Nisbet called my attention to a paragraph in 'the Times' from the Athenaeum, touching the anxiety felt about our Spire (perhaps emanating from David Stewart ?) – on my return wrote to Christian to furnish me with an answer to the Paragraph, in case one shd. be needed.

Saturday 22
Some tenants came to luncheon – Wiley, Waters, Mr. Miller, Gowing – Forman also came and Nisbet – At 3 o'clock I gave my Sermonette – had appointed to see the Bedesmen afterwards at the Vestry, but the Eastern Daily Press & Norfolk Chronicle having asked Brown for an explanation of the Paragraph wh appeared in 'the Times' about the Cathedral tower and spire, we thot. it prudent to meet at Heaviside's house, to consider of an answer – Nisbet and Heaviside both drafted answers – with some alterations we took Nisbet's – Fraulein arrived at luncheon time today, and dined with us – she gave us an account of Ld. & Lady Roslyn, and their children – I wrote before dinner to (1) Miss Whitehouse, thanking for a turkey, and also advising about a proposed window to Bullivant in St. Leonard's Ch., Exeter.

Monday 24
At 1.15 came the various officers to receive Christmas Gratuities – of the Bedesmen there came Yeomans, Stangroom, Cutlock –

after hearing what Stangroom had to say in reference to the charges of talking with others at the Friday Evening Service, and of being late at his door on Sundays, I decided to withold from him the usual 7s – he was in a pet & said his brother had fallen down dead yesterday all of a sudden – wrote to ... (2) Christian about harmonizing his account of the state of our tower with that given by Brown in the local papers.

Tuesday 25   CHRISTMAS DAY
H.C. at 8 a.m. with Bartie and Moore – it was very well done, but few communts., only 85 – last year there were 106 – At 11 the Bishop preached – much shorter than usual – afterwards I visited Mrs. Heaviside, and thanked her for the bottle of Paxarete wh. she had given me – wrote to 'Pom', thanking for a Xmas card – then called on the Nisbets, & found little Henry deep in his Christmas cards – walked with him and Nisbet & the Miss Maitlands to Thorpe, meeting & greeting the Bp. and John Patteson on our way home – The Nisbets, Miss Nisbet, and the Miss Maitlands dine here tonight; also Bulmer – It went off more merrily than common.

Wednesday 26   St. Stephen
After luncheon went with Ju in carriage to Rackheath – saw Sir H. & Lady Stracey; talked about politicis with him – he showed me a valuable book compiled by his son; notices of the lives of Napoleon's Generals, with engravings posted in – on our return, wrote to ... (3) Cufaude Davie, who tells me he uses my 'Gospels' for Family Prayer ... (5) & (6) sending small sums to 'Refugees for Homeless Children' and to Miss Rye's Emigration Homes for destitute little Girls – We are alone tonight; only Fraulein.

Saturday 29
Ch. at 10 – then in fly to S.P.C.K. to settle what type we shd. have for our Cathedral Prayer Books, to be given by the Society – then to Training Institution Meeting – The letter of expostulation, wh. Heaviside & Archbold had draughted, was read and certain alterations made in it; but none of them seem to think it likely to succeed – all that it can do is to protract for a year or so the existence of the present school.

Sunday 30
At 11, the Bp. preached on the General Judgement quoting almost every text on the subject – I tood up the whole time, & therefore heard much better – In the afternoon Nisbet preached his last Sermon[1] on Psalm LXXXVIII.

1. i.e. the last Sermon of this particular three months term of residence.

Monday 31
At 2.15 went to see the Nisbets, and took leave of Mrs. Nisbet and 'little Henry' – then a walk with Nisbet on the Ipswich Road – came in and wrote (1) to one of Bullivant's Executors about his having lived in Cadogan Place (2) refusing a Sermon in 1884 to Incorpor. Ch. Buildg. Society (3) Blanche Daniell enquiring about 'nervous apnoea'.[1]

1. A temporary inability to breathe.

1886
JANUARY

Friday 1   **Circumcision**
H.C. at 8 a.m. – Choristers went out before the Sermon – about 35 Cmmts. – Bartie came to luncheon; afterwards we worked together at the Rules for Collects, etc. in the year 1886; then took a walk together on Thorpe Road – read a little of 'Christians under the Crescent in Asia' in the evening.

Saturday 2
Church at 10 – Afterwards arranged with Bartie the 'Various Rules and Uses', so as to make it unnecessary to have an annual republication – the Bishop of Pretoria[1] came in before 5 o'clock tea. [*Later, a Dinner Party of guests to meet him*]

> 1. The Rt Revd Henry B. Bousfield, D.D., first Bishop of Pretoria, which was formed out of the Diocese of Bloemfontein. He was Bishop 1878–1902.

Sunday 3
Bp.of Pretoria at Bkfst.; he showed us the photographs of his children – At 3.30 [*he*] preached on "Who goeth a warfare any time at his own charge ?" – he spoke much of the way wh. the Home Church 'injusta noverea' sent forth the Colonial Bishops with supplies for their warfare.

Monday 4
Church at 10 with Nevill and Bartie – then a Chapter at Bensly's Office to hear Brown's justification of himself against Spaull's charges – He, however, on consideration, preferred not going into the subject, but abiding by Christian's report of his work, when he inspects it – the order about finishing the caps of the shafts in the Tower before finally clearing away the scaffolding, etc. was rescinded – when he had gone, I brought before Heaviside & Nevill my plan for the more satisfactory discharge of business by a weekly Chapter; we talked it over, and settled to begin with a fortnightly Chapter – wrote to Robinson and Nevill[1] about the fortnightly Chapter.

> 1. Surely it was *Nisbet* in London, not Nevill, to whom he wrote!

Tuesday 5
After a night of pain and sickness, did not rise till 7.30; Bkfst. in my own room – At 11 Bartie came, and I conferred with him

about the supper for the Guild Boys tomorrow; about the Odd Fellows' Service in the afternoon of next Sunday; about contracting the expenditure of the Cathedral on Music within £30 annually; about dropping two of the Choristers, and dropping also the assistant Organ Blower – it was a beautiful bright day (tho' cold), and I walked on Thorpe, and back by Plumstead Road – At 4.45, the Pin and I set off for the Oxford Dinner – Hinds Howell, I fancied, was not quite so bright as usual – we got away about 8.30 p.m., and found here Maimie, who had been helping Ju with the tea for her schoolgirls.

Wednesday 6   EPIPHANY   Choristers' Guild Dinner
The Pin and Auntie went to H.C. at 8 – At 10 I went to Ch. and found Heaviside there; also Bartie & Bulmer – H. wants the cloister door shut up to protect us from draughts – then went to Stacy's to order a Chapter Note Book; met Peter Hansell, who asked me to draw for the £90 left me by his aunt – in returning I paid the £90 into a separate account at the Bank – at 8 came the Guild Youths, Minns, Hogg, Harding, Pooley, Manning – I admitted Minns formally, and then gave a short address on Habit and the force of it – At ½p.8 dinner, at wh. Mr. & Mrs. Bartie & the Pin helped us – we did not get upstairs till 9.50, and the Bp. of Pretoria came in – Pooley sang, & I read the Irish piece in Tennyson's last, and Arthur & Hubert in Kg. John – the Bp. fast asleep – they all went after Prayers.

Saturday 9
Very ailing; not dressed till luncheon – Mr. Christian and Maimie came to luncheon – at 2.15 Heaviside & Nevill came, and Mr. Christian made to us a most satisfactory report as to the work in the Tower, as to the oak used in the ceiling, as to the work's being executed as cheaply as possible, as to its solidity, and as to the artistic success of the restoration – This we reported to Brown who was pleased – worked the rest of the day at my reminiscences of Golightly.

Sunday 10
Still very ailing; in my room till 2 p.m. writing my reminiscences of Golightly – then dressed and went to the Odd Fellows'[1] Jubilee Service at 3.30 p.m. – a large congregation, tho' not nearly as large as I expected – I sat in the Bishop's chair – Heaviside preached – he made good use of the Second Lesson (Acts VI) the

appeal being for 'the Widows and Orphans' Fund of the Odd Fellows' – Mayor[2] and Corporation there – In the evening despatched my reminiscences of Golightly to 'the Guardian'.

> 1. Friendly Societies grew and flourished from the beginning of the 19th Century. As early as 1801 there were 203 in Norfolk alone. The Manchester Unity of Oddfellows, formed in 1810, rapidly became one of the largest Friendly Societies nationally.
> 2. John Gurney, Esq. He died towards the end of his year of office, aged 41, when on holiday at Cannes.

Tuesday 12

Got letters from Sir G. Prevost, expressing sympathy with my letter to the 'Guardian'; also from Meyrick, approving and returning my counter-address[1] to the Bishop – Heaviside coming in to see me, I showed him the counter-address; he recommended the omission of all allusion to the latitudinarian manifesto – this I did – wrote to Meyrick, to Sir George Prevost[2], and also to Burgon, saying that I thought we must move in the direction of a (<u>general</u>) counter-address, and enclosing Sir G.P.'s letter.

> 1. Goulburn was, at this time, engaged in a campaign against Church Reform, considering that the time for it was not yet, and that all effort should be put into making the system, as it was, as perfect as possible.
> 2. Canon Sir George Prevost, 2nd Baronet, was a Tractarian; Archdeacon of Gloucester 1865–81; Hon. Canon of Gloucester 1859–93; Perpetual Curate of Stinchcombe, Gloucester 1834–93.

Thursday 14

Heaviside came in, and urged upon me to make my paper at the Bishop's meeting[1] the foundation of a pamphlet on Church Reform – At 8 [p.m.] came six Lay Clerks, Cox, Hewson, Holden, Brockbank, Smith, Thouless – two Barties and two Moores – they sang a very pretty Part Song; and then I read Mark Antony's funeral Oration on Jul. Caesar; and afterwards Mr. Howard Taylor's 'Song of a Thorpe Thrush' – Mr. Hewson whistled in accompanying the piano, and very pretty and liquid it was – Evening went off well.

> 1. Bishop's Annual Meeting of Archdeacons, Residentiary and Hon. Canons on January 27.

Friday 15

In the evening came in six signatures to the counter-address, to gladden my heart.

Saturday 16
Received 25 signatures to my 'counter-address' this morning – Margie & Charlie Nevill came into luncheon; was much struck by his good looks and manner – Moore came in to get £2. 2 for my subscription to St. Augustine's Miss. Coll.[1], then wrote a long letter to Ben Harrison, who had thanked me for what I wrote about Golightly – Alden came in, and cringed, and solicited an increase of his stipend on the ground that by the new arrangement both the Subsacrists for half the year are bound to attend every week – after dinner received another bundle of letters wh. I am about to open.

   1. Canterbury.

Sunday 17
At Bkfst. appeared a large no. of signatures to my counter address[1], wh. I arranged afterwards – I have now about 104 signatures – then after luncheon, walked to the Barracks, to call on the Colonel, and ask him not to let his band play in the Close; but he had gone to London.

   1. The Post Office in Norwich made two deliveries of letters on a Sunday.

Monday 18   The first 'Fortnightly Chapter'
About 10 signatures to the counter-address arrived in the morning – Church ... at 10 a.m. – then the Chapter at Bensly's Office – Mr. Daynes[1] had an interview with us about the sale of some of our property on Unthank's Road for building land – the whole thing was rather worrying as usual – Bensly came to luncheon – afterwards he and I went with Auntie, Lottie Wallace, and Margie Nevill, to Eaton Hall – Mr. Snelling[2], whom we found there, lionised us over it – It is nicely fitted up, but oh so cold, and so damp, with new paper and plaistering, that I pitied the Judge – all very pretty in summer, no doubt.

   1. John Daynes, Solicitor, of Bavin and Daynes, Opie House, Castle Meadow.
   2. James G. Snelling, of J.G. Snelling and Sons, Grocers, Wine Merchants, etc., Rampant Horse Street.

Tuesday 19
After luncheon called for Nevill and took him to Eaton Hall, where we found the Judge (Sir H. Hawkins)[1] in a jacket with blue neckcloth, and with his dog 'Jack', of whom he gave some comical anecdotes – we hope to be 12 tonight: Bishop, Judge, Fanny Pelham, Lucy Bignold, Knight Bruce, Colonel Gifford, 2

Nevills, Mr. Nevile (the Marshal), and Bulmer (who kindly comes instead of Heaviside, who fears the cold) – The party went off very well – Bishop quite lively.

> 1. Sir Henry Hawkins (later Lord Brampton): As a barrister, had appeared in many famous cases; Judge, and knighted 1876; unjustly obtained the nickname of 'Hanging Hawkins'; patient and thorough; favoured leniency for first offences; after retirement from bench became a Roman Catholic.

Wendesday 20

At 10 the Bp. and Nevill, Bulmer & Moore, appeared at Church; Morning Prayer ended at about 10.40 – we all waited in our places till the Mayor, etc. appeared; then we met the Judge at the Door – Mr. Upcher of Barnham Broom (not the Sheriff's Chaplain) preached on 'Tekel'[1], a Sermon much above the average, tho' I could not hear it perfectly – wrote to a Mr. Tyler, M.P. for Yarmouth, who had written to me, enclosing a petition to him from the Mayor of Yarmouth and others to apply for better preferment for Venables – after luncheon, went with Ju to the Annual meeting of the Jenny Lind in Pottergate Street; the Bp. in the Chair; his chairmanship most patient, and adroit – There were some words as to whether typhoid fever cases shd. be admitted to the hospital or not – I had to propose a vote of thanks to the Bp. for taking the Chair.

> 1. 'Tekel' = Part of the writing on the wall in the Book of Daniel, Ch. 5, vv.25–28, and its interpretation: "Thou art weighed in the balances, and art found wanting".

Friday 22

Some letters, the chief of wh. were to Mr. Tyler, as to what he shd. do in order to get Mr. Venables[1] some preferment, and to a secretary of the Duke of Buccleuch's as to Mr. Venables's <u>physical</u> capacity for a Church at Melrose – an afternoon of ceaseless letters, some to those Parochial Clergymen whom I am inviting to go with me to present our address to the Bp. on the 26th – Sir H. Hawkins is coming to dinner on Monday, but not to Church on Sunday.

> 1. Canon George Venables had now been Vicar of Gt Yarmouth (Pop. c.37,000) with a staff of Curates, for 12 years; an Hon. Canon since 1881; and Rural Dean of Flegg since 1878.

Tuesday 26

Jessopp, Hull, Porter, Pownal, Elder, Greeny, Bellman, had luncheon here; and in the middle of it came the Judge with Jack and Mr. Neville – I had only just time to say 'Good bye' to him, and then accompanied the above to the Palace in our carriage[1] & a fly – Bp. received us very graciously in the Library and I read & presented to him our Address – He said he wd. answer all at once the three applications wh. had been made to him on the subject – then I went to Stacy's, in carriage, and asked him to put our address into the 'Chronicle'.

> 1. Why on this, and on some other occasions, does Goulburn drive, rather than walk, the very short distance across the Close from the Deanery to the Palace? Perhaps it is a matter of a dignified approach.

Wednesday 27

At 4 we had the Service, at wh. were more Hon. Canons than usual – At 5 the Meeting at the Palace – I read the 1st. part of my paper[1], but it was too long to conclude – it was not liked – the Bishop gently censured it, and I don't think anyone took the jokes w. wh. I opened it – Frere spoke next, and then Heaviside, Copeman, Garrett, Venables, all on difft. sides – Heaviside and I got away at 7.15.

> 1. 'Church Reform – the Inexpediency of attempting it at the Present Time'.

Thursday 28

Wrote to ... (2) Ed. of 'Guardian' proposing to him my 'Paper'.

Saturday 30

I got a letter from the Ed. of the 'Guardian', declining my paper on Church Reform – wrote to ... Noverre[1] consenting to become Patron of an entertainment for the 'Children's Convalescent Home'.

> 1. Noverre Bros., the Assembly Rooms, Theatre Street, were 'Professors of Dancing' (Frank and Richard), and the former also taught the violin.

• •

From Monday, Feburary 1 until Saturday February 6, the Goulburns are in London, staying at Garlants Hotel. There they meet the Dean of Lichfield and Mrs Bickersteth, and also Canon Marsham Argles from Peterborough. Both were up for the consecreation of the Very Revd Lord Alwyne Compton as Bishop of Ely. Goulburn manages to book the Dean as Preacher on Palm Sunday in Norwich Cathedral for the Society for Promoting the Knowledge of Christianity among the Jews; while Marsham Argles books Goulburn for Peterborough Cathedral on the third Sunday in Lent. On Friday the Goulburns have luncheon with Berdmore Compton, Vicar of All Saints, Margaret Street, who tells them how he and eleven others had an interview with the Archbishop of Canterbury to protest against Parochial Church Councils. The Archbishop (Benson) and Compton had been Fellow Assistant-Masters at Rugby under Goulburn.

• •

FEBRUARY

Monday 8
A troublesome Chapter, at wh. there was some diffce. of opinion between Heaviside & Nevill as to the sum we shd. ask for Eaton North Farm (Mr. Daynes having made us an offer of it of 10,500£) – It was agreed that I shd. write to the E.C. asking them to send down a Surveyor, to make enquiry on the spot – This I did after luncheon.

Thursday 11
At 3 a meeting of the unemployed was held in the Market Place by Burgess, but the people dispersed quietly – I had told Spruce to be ready to close the Gates if news arrived of any outrage.

Saturday 13
Have today finished and despatched my letter to 'the Guardian' about Golightly – At luncheon Maimie and Dr. Bates[1], who seems to take kindly to his new duties – account in the 'Times' of the Dilke[2] trial in the Divorce Court, wh. is very scandalous.

> 1. Dr Frank Bates had just come from being Organist of St John's Episcopal Church, Edinburgh, to be the new Cathedral Organist; in which position he remained until 1928.
> 2. Sir Charles Wentworth Dilke, Liberal Politician, Barrister and Author; leader of radical section of Gladstone's Government in the 1800s; Cabinet member; friend of the Prince of Wales, was co-respondent in divorce suit, Crawford v. Crawford and Dilke 1885–86, which was sensationally reported. Rejected by electors of Chelsea, ostracised from public life; but returned as M.P. for Forest of Dean 1892.

Monday 15   Convocation Week
Church at 10 with Heaviside & Moore, Nevill having gone to Town for Convocation – afterwards paid a visit to Bartie, and saw him on a couch in his bedroom with Mrs. Bartie and little Dorothy; talked about his health; he hopes to get to St. Leonard's next week; is to wear the new woolen clothes next his skin – we discussed the prospect of the Clerical Rooms Commee. lending them to Miss Ensor for Sunday Afternoons – I thence went to the Miss Ensors, and told them what had passed on this subject – then a walk with the elder Miss Ensor to the Norwich Tyrol and round by Plumstead Road – declined the Mayor's invitation to attend a meeting on Wendesday for the relief of the unemployed[1].

1. Goulburn had great sympathy for the sick and bereaved; he often gave generously to a beggar, or an individual in need; but to him, and to many Victorians, the mass of the unemployed and the poor seemed to be, in Henry Mayhew's words "a large body of persons of whom the public had less knowledge than the most distant tribes of the earth". (Henry Mayhew, 'London Labour and the London Poor' (1861–62).

Tuesday 16

To the Ensors to announce that they might probably get the Ethelbert Room for 4s. a Sunday – then a walk with Miss Ensor to Lollards' Pit, up Gas Hill, and back by Plumstead Road – after luncheon, wrote to ... (2) Buskins, thanking for Whittier Poems.

Wednesday 17

At 10 Church with Bulmer & Moore – Heaviside did not come, as he was going to the Mayor's Meeting for the 'Relief of the Unemployed' at 12 – a great noise at the end of the Service from taking down the scaffold – Heaviside came in to tell me that he had put down the Dean and Chapter £25 for 'the Unemployed' – went with Ju to call on the Barties; he cannot even now walk, tho' well in himself – when he will be about again who can say ? – Hope to read the proceedings of Convocation tonight.

Thursday 18

Church at 10 with Bulmer – Heaviside meanwhile receiving Mr. Smith (Messrs. Smiths & Gore) and going with him and Bensly to Eaton North Farm – after Church went on with my Sermon for Sunday – H. came in and reported that Mr. Smith said the farm is worth £14,000, and that the E.C. would be themselves glad to buy 60 acres of frontage of it for £9000 – wrote to Captain Rowan, Cullybackey, Belfast, acknowledging the 'Ballymena Observer', giving the acct. of the death of his father and mother, and also the book ('Piety without Ascetism', a compilation of Bp. Jebb's[1] from Scongal, etc.) wh. his father desired in his will shd. be sent to me – also to the Bp. declining to attend the Conference[2].

1. The Rt Revd John Jebb (1775–1833), Bishop of Limerick.
2. Goulburn made a point of being in harmony with the Bishop; but, on this occasion, he considered it to be a matter of principle, not to attend the special meeting of the Diocesan Conference on 'Church Reform'.

Tuesday 23

Heaviside had a letter from Smith and Gore saying that they value Eaton North Farm at £14,000, and shall suggest to the Eccl. Commrs. to offer £9000 for 60 acres of the frongage, & think we ought to get £125 rent for the remaining 75 acres – This I showed to Nevill, and gave him a copy of my C.P.G.[1] Pamphlet, wh. arrived this morning – Ju folded & sent off many of the C.P.G. Pamphlets.

> 1. Charles Portales Golightly.

Thursday 25
Called on the Bp. to talk over the proposed change in the arrangement of Mg. Services on the 1st. Sun. in the month – He seemed to think on the whole that the most satisfactory solution wd. be having the whole Service (say) at 10.30, but shortening the singing and the Sermon – met Nevill on my return and told him what had passed – then to Bartie's, and talked over with him the same subject, and also the advertisement of the Lenten Services – he is able to walk a few steps with two sticks – After luncheon drove with Ju to call on the Burtons[1], and saw all of them; they were very friendly; he talked of Bp. Hinds[2] in terms of great regard – very flushed while there, & a bad attack of heartburn – we walked back fast the last 2½ miles.

> 1. The Revd R.C. Burton, Rector of Taverham since 1850.
> 2. The Rt Revd Samuel Hinds was Bishop of Norwich 1849–57, resigning at the age of 64 on grounds of ill-health, and living to the age of 79. He was the older step-brother of Canon Hinds Howell, who had been named 'Hinds' after the Bishop's father.

Friday 26
A hard day's letter writing incessant – Stacy came at 6, and I told him to calculate the expence of printing the account of objects of interest in the Cathedral as a tract, to be sold to visitors wishing to have it by the man in charge of the desk & book.

Saturday 27
Went to meeting at Training School – afterwards Mr. Christian came in – the Architect who has been discarded has sent in a Bill for £432, £222 of which is for his Plans – Christian says it is an unheard of charge.

MARCH
Monday 1   Fortnightly Chapter
Brown attended the Chapter and reported about the proceeds of the sale of timber used as scaffolding – Alden made an application for increase of payment to Subsacrists for their <u>cicerone</u>[1] duty; but

it was deferred till next time – Bensly came to luncheon, and afterwards we drafted letters to the E.C. & to Daynes, and worked at our notes till ½p.3 when Bensly was obliged to go to catch a train – Hills called to see gaiters on, & try to make them a good fit – this journal in the evening; meditating my Lenten Series, and a Sermon for Ash Wednesday.

> 1. Cicerone = guiding visitors.

Tuesday 2

Rather a thaw; impossible to get out – After Church at 10 walked for 1¾ths. of an hour with greatcoat on in the library – called on Bartie, to talk over Alden and the proposed increase of his <u>cicerone</u> stipend – found him shaven, and sitting in his dining room with his dressing gown on – on my return dear Pom[1] arrived, to the joy of my heart – Mr. Hills called to try on a Reformed gaiter.

> 1. 'Pom' = Mary Julia Thomas (1846–1918), Goulburn's Second Cousin. Unmarried.

Wednesday 3

Another wretched day – Snow lying sparse and light; slush under foot, so as to prevent walking – Mr. Brown brot. me the £7. 16 wh. I was to have for the sale of the timber of the nave scaffold; but also a bill from Spaull for removing the scaffolding, which came to £8. 13. 6 – sent for Spaull, who came and explained that this embraced the removal also of the bridge belonging to himself, for wh. he had charged as a kind of interest upon the materials, wh. had been useless to him all these years – after luncheon went into the Cathedral with Ju and Pom, and inspected her pictures[1], and went up into the Reliquary Chamber – then I went to see Bartie & was there joined by Pom; poor Bartie had gone back, & was looking very forlorn indeed – I looked over with him some of the papers giving Alden's account of his receipt from showing the Cathedral.

> 1. When in Norwich Pom took the opportunity of sketching and painting parts of the interior of the Cathedral.

Tuesday 11

After Ch. with Bulmer & Nevill, it being a fine bright cold day, walked with Auntie thro' Buskin's Spinney (the Hackblocks[1] having kindly given us a key) and then to the site of St. William's chapel on Mousehold, wh. we found untouched – in returning, we came across a number of the unemployed, who seemed to be engaged in making a 2d. road over the Heath![2] On my return, Mr. Greenall of Hardley called to canvas for Shropham – he says he has to live at Loddon, 3 miles from his parish – Mr. Wickham, who had been recommended to us by Dr. Gott, and who had been Wilson's curate at St. Stephen's, also called about Shropham – Bensly and I spent the afternoon in correcting the Visitor's Card of the Cathedral wh. Symonds and I drew up some years ago – wrote to Mr. Goodwin of Adderbury who also had written about Shropham – They are going to abolish the Pass Divinity Examination at Oxford.

> 1. William H. Hackblock of Morgan's Brewery Co Ltd, was now living in Mousehold House, formerly occupied by Lady Harvey, and Goulburn once more had a key to the grounds.
> 2. On May 12, 1886, the Mayor (John Gurney, Esq.) opened the new road across Mousehold Heath, and dedicated the Heath to the free use of the people of Norwich for ever. Goulburn was not present on that occasion because he was on holiday at Aynhoe. Mousehold Heath had originally been the property of the Dean and Chapter.

Monday 15   Fortnightly Chapter

Church at 10 – Alden came in about a new gown; we thot that some of the velvet on the old one was needless – Chapter at 11 at the office – almost unparalleled in its worries – We determined to have Mg. Service on and after Sun. Ap. 4, at 10.45; the Precentor on the 1st. Sun. in the month to have chants for the Canticles instead of Services, and the shortest possible Anthem – also we determined to give the Subsacrists in addition to the £52 salary (for showing the Church) a payment of £10 per cent on the gross annual produce of Visitor's fund – Bensly announced that our annual contribution to the payment of the debt incurred by the Nar Drainage Scheme wd. be about £300 pr. annum! Bensly had to go to town and we broke up about 2 p.m. – wrote to (1) Hinds Howell about Hope's[1] candidature for Shropham[2] – Hope called today after luncheon, & I gave him my Ch. reform Pamphlet – In the evening read 'the Times' and Gladstone's outrageous proposal to expropriate the Irish Landlords at a cost of 200 millions.

> 1. The Revd C.A. Hope had been Canon Hinds Howell's Curate since 1870, concentrating on Hellesdon, which, with the Inmates of the City Asylum, had a population then of 338. He was to continue here until 1892, when eventually, having been ordained 25 years, and almost 50, he became Rector of Taverham, population then 207. (By this time Hellesdon had increased to over 1,000).
> 2. In the end, the new Rector of Shropham was the Revd G.W. Watson, Curate of Heavingham, and son of F.E. Watson, Solicitor, who had been twice Mayor of Norwich.

Wednesday 17

At Church at 10, Nevill told me of Ld. Chichester's[1] death, and I had a letter from the Bishop announcing it – wrote to him condolences, offering him help on Sunday – After luncheon called on Bartie, & talked over various matters – he hopes to get to Lowestoft on Saturday, & back to his work Saturday week.

> 1. Henry Thomas Pelham, 3rd Earl of Chichester, was the elder brother of the Bishop. From 1850 to 1878 he had been head of the Church Estates Committee, and to him were largely due the reforms carried out in the management and distribution of Church revenues.

Saturday 20

Wrote a letter to the Dss. of Grafton about Robins[1], wh. I hope may get him a place there; also an answer to a gentleman who had sent me testimonials for Shropham – Maimie came to luncheon, having got over her attack of gout, & talking faster than ever – also Mr. Dickson at St. Martin-at-Oak, who tried to induce me to become Patron of his Bazaar, but failed; I bought myself off with a promise of £10 – then came Lady A. Compton[2], with the little Chapmans[2], drs. of the Archdeacon, little F's pupils – they went off to Church but Pom and I took a walk thro' Lady Harvey's spinney to Mousehold Heath and Edith's Parade – on my return I saw Walker, and gave him instructions about his duties as Book keeper in the Cathedral, on wh. he enters at Lady Day; also gave him an order upon Hill[3] for a gown – also saw Eliza about the devolution of her duties on others; gave her a Bible and Prayer Book and bade her Adieu – wrote a line to Arundell's son[4] at Bristol, who is to be ordained Priest tomorrow.

> 1. One of Goulburn's servants, who had been with him for some years.
> 2. The wife of the new Bishop of Ely, the Rt Revd Lord Alwyne Compton (son of the 2nd Marquess of Northampton); he is described in the Concise D.N.B. as a "simple, direct preacher of high-Church views; a keen archaeologist, he caused diocesan documents to be arranged and catalogued". The girls were daughters of the Archdeacon of Sudbury (in the Diocese of Ely) the Venerable Frank Chapman.
> 3. Walter Bidwell Hill, tailor and woollen draper, 10, Prince's Street.
> 4. Carew Hervey St John-Mildmay, to become Curate of St Mark's, New Swindon, son of Goulburn's friend, Arundell St John-Mildmay, Rector of Denton since 1879.

Monday 22

Have written today to (1) Dr. Wrenford[1], in refce. to the responsibility of Bps. for admitting improper persons to Holy Orders; (2) Mr. Harper[2] of Stoke; (3) Sir George Pringle, hoping that E.C. would recognise the desirability of securing Mr. Birkbeck' a benefaction to Stoke Vicarage, by complying with his terms – Bensly had luncheon with us, and handed in Coe's[3] estimates for a description of the Cathedral with photographic illustrations – then Pom and I walked to Jarrold's, and got for her Mama an illustrated Milton, & for herself an illustrated Longfellow and an inkstand with a horse's rack as a pentray.

> 1. The Revd T.B. Wrenford, D.D., Vicar of Watton since 1867.
> 2. The Revd. E.J. Harper, Vicar of Stoke Holy Cross since 1884 (of which the Dean and Chapter were Patrons).
> 3. Albert Edward Coe, Photographer and Optician, 32, London Street.

Tuesday 23

Went to Yarmouth with Pom and Ju, starting at 10.50 a.m., and returning by 4.30 p.m. – We went first to the Children's Convalescent Home, which with all its cots is a very charming sight (one "in memory of Ada Hansell" and the other the "Ada Cot")[1] and as clean as a silver penny – there were, however, only two little Boys there, both of them up and dressed, and a third in arms; all plain children – in driving to Mr. Venables'[2] House, we met him, and he took us into his Church, of wh. he did the honours admirably – then we had luncheon at his house with Mrs. Venables and a niece – then we walked to the Tolhouse, over wh. he lionised us – wrote to the Dss. of Grafton about Robins; (2) to George Waldegrave, welcoming him here for the Holy Week; (3) Mr. Fitch, begging him to preserve St. William's Chapel[3] on Mousehold Heath from desecration – After dinner, this journal.

> 1. Miss Ada Hansell, who lived in the Lower Close, had been very concerned about the prospect of a railway through the Close, and Goulburn had kept her informed during the various crises. He liked visiting and talking to her. She had died in 1885.
> 2. Canon George Venables (ordained 1850) was Vicar of Gt Yarmouth 1874–86; Rural Dean of Flegg 1878–87; Member of H.M. Royal Commssion on Patronage; and Rector of Burgh Castle from 1888.
> 3. Goulburn was fascinated by the site of St William's chapel, and the Lollards' Pit (Plaque marking site of latter on Bridge Public House, corner of Riverside Road and Gas Hill).

Wednesday 24

A short interview with Yeomans, instructing him about handing over his desk, etc. to Walker – drew cheques for Mr. Browne for sundry works in the Cathedral, the most substantial of wh. was plastering the soffit[1] of the Western Arch (£5. 10. 3 in all) – read some of Froude's[2] very amusing History in the evening, when a shoal of letters came in.

1. = the underside of the Arch.
2. J.A. Froude, historian and man of letters (1818–94); prolific writer; among his works, 'History of England from Fall of Wolsey to defeat of Spanish Armada', (12 vols. 1856–70). Regius Professor of Modern History at Oxford 1892–94.

Friday 26
Mr. Fitch called, and told me of his successful interview with the Conservators of Mousehold Heath – the Mayor gave an assurance that the site of St. William's Chapel shd. be respected, and even talks of uncovering the foundations at his own expense.

••
On Saturday, March 27, the Goulburns went to Peterborough to stay, as usual, with Canon Argles and his family, and to preach in the Cathedral at 7 p.m. on Sunday, returning to Norwich on Tuesday March 30.
••

Wednesday 31
After Bkfst. went across to Heaviside's – He tells me that Mr. Watson's son was appointed yesterday to the Vicarage of Shropham – after luncheon went in carriage to Harry Bullard's[1], and condoled with Mrs. Bullard on her husband's being deprived of his seat; she thinks the Judges have been unfair to him – Saw Eliza[2] about the Bread at H.C. & purchased her Bread-Cutter.

1. Harry Bullard was the fifth of 10 children of his father, Richard, who founded the Anchor Brewery. He was Mayor of Norwich 1878–79 and 1879–80. In 1886 he contested the Norwich seat in Parliament, and won, but was disqualified on petitition because of his agent's bribery. The citizens were so incensed at this that they paid his court costs. He became Mayor again, for the third time, 1886–7, was knighted by Queen Victoria, and became an M.P. in 1890 and 1895.
2. Eliza Lichfield (see also March 20).

APRIL

Thursday 1
I heard today from Father Boniface of Madresous Abbey, thanking me for H. de Losinga, and telling me his apprehensions about the safety of the Abbey in the present state of Belgium.

Friday 2
At 8 [p.m.] the Servie at wh. I preached on the 2nd. Commandment – It lasted till 9.10 – I strove to shew the 2 opposite errors of Romanism and Quakerism; spoke also about the crucifix.

Saturday 3

After Ch. went to the Barracks[1] and saw Col. Gifford, and announced to him the change in the hour of Service tomorrow & in future – Bartie is better, but his leg still stiff – I begged him to get cassocks & surplices made for Burton and Smith by Easter.

> 1. The *Cavalry* Barracks (built 1791–92) in Pockthorpe; the new Britannia Barracks for Infantry, in the course of being built (1886–87) on Mousehold Heath, on Norwich being made a military depot.

Tuesday 6   Archaeological Meeting

After Church at 10, went to Mr. Fitch's house[1] for the Archaeol. Commee. and thence at noon to the Guildhall for the Annual Meeting – three Papers were read: one by Mr. Hudson on the Court Rolls; a 2d. by Mr. Willins of East Dereham Church; and a letter of Mr. Fielden on a large mortar found at Yarmouth – Ld. Alwyne Compton was elected a member of the Society – It did not end till 2.5 – I brought Dr. Bennet, Manning, and Creeny in here to luncheon – Ju came in, after having luncheon at the Palace with the G.F.S.

> 1. He lived at The Woodlands, Dereham Road (near Junction with Waterworks Rd.)

Wednesday 14

Drove with Ward to the opening of Mousehold Heath, whence we walked back by St. William's Chapel – then we called on Dr. Duckett[1], whom we found at home; he interested us by an account of two clerks at the Bank who had come to him under sceptical difficulties to settle their minds, and whom he was instructing – then home, to luncheon – Ward left us for London after luncheon – then wrote to ... (2) Parker, to send 'Herb. Losinga' to Ward[2] (3) Mr. Barker, sending him £10 for Lakenham Schools.

> 1. Canon Duckett was the "popular Roman Catholic Priest of St John Maddermarket Chapel". A very eloquent preacher, so that "St John's Chapel was crowded to the very doors every Sunday evening" (F.T. Higbane).
> 2. Wilfrid Philip Ward (1856–1916) Biographer and Roman Catholic Apologist; son of W.G. Ward, Goulburn's Tutor at Balliol, Roman Catholic convert.

Thursday 15

I went to Jarrold's to order a Boss Book for Ward (£3. 3); then into Fitch's shop[1], to get a little potion for heart-burn – Fitch's shopman accompanied me to the R.C. Cathedral[2], where he entrusted me to a Mr. Kett (Rattee & Kett) clerk of the works, who kindly showed me over the building.

1. Fitch and Chambers, Dispensing & Family Chemists, 7, Market Place.
2. St John's, on the site of the old City Goal at the beginning of the Earlham Road.

Friday 16

A day of little work, the whole of the morning being spent in going to & returning fr. Drayton (after dropping Auntie and Emma Wallace at the nursery garden) – I saw first Agnes, who is putting a drama with song & Music on the stage; then Maimie, and afterwards Hinds Howell in the village, who told me of the awful accident to the wife and daughter of Johnnie Yonge[1] of Hempstead, both killed suddenly by the horse of their carriage running away and dashing their heads agst. a wall – the Hinds Howells cannot come to dinner with the Dean of L.[2] tomorrow, because one of their horses is dyspeptic – in the evening at 8 my Sermon (on the 3rd. Commt.) was got thro' by me with difficulty, & was long and wearisome.

1. The Revd J.E. Yonge had been Rector of Hempstead with Lesingham (nr Stalham) since 1876.
2. Dean of Lichfield, the Very Revd Edward Bickersteth.

Saturday 17

Did not go to Church in the morg. – sat at home, and determined to divide into 2 my subject for Monday next, throwing the death of Abel on the Tuesday, and omitting the maltreatment of Joseph on the Wednesday – after arranging this, made a short Bill announcing the change, and took it to Stacy's – then to Morning Chronicle Office to ask Martin to report for me next week – Alice & Do-do Nevill came to luncheon – It is Do'do's birthday, just 12 years old! – The Bickersteth's arrived at 6.30 – There dined here the two Nevills, the two Moores & Dr. Bates – I had a racking headache, and was obliged to go to bed before they went.

Sunday 18   PALM SUNDAY

Very poorly still – I went to Church at 3.30 – The Dean sat in my seat, & I with the Canons – He preached on the dry bones in Ezekiel, a scholarlike, well put together Sermon – during the Anthem I came out.

Monday 19
Took leave of our kind guests after hearing from them a sad account of their feuds with their Chapter – in the evening read the end of the Bartlett trial; also the acct. of the assassinn. of the Bishop of Madrid.

Tuesday 20
Unwell and out of sorts all day – about 7 Geroge Waldegrave arrived in a fly – I am afraid he will be very dull here.

• •
In spite of continuing to be unwell, Goulburn (and also Julia) took George Waldegrave on an extensive tour of all the sights during the next seven days.
• •

Sunday 25   **EASTER SUNDAY**
H.C. at 8 – 111 Communicants – I found the exertion of voice necessary, to be very great – Athelstan Riley & John Birkbeck called for a few minutes before the 3.30 Service – To this Auntie, & Geo. Waldegrave and myself went – then thought for ¼ of an hour over what to say at Miss Bensly's wedding on Wednesday – Ju and I are not going to 7 p.m. Evensong, but George is – we shall read our Service at home, when he is gone, and also, I hope a Sermon of Dr. Tait's.

Tuesday 27
George Waldegrave after Bkfst, surprised & horrified me with the account of the fraud in connexion w. Lady Waldegrave's will – he represents himself as at present almost penniless – he left us for Yarmouth at 10.30 – I wrote an introduction for him to Venables.

• •
The Goulburns are absent from Norwich from April 28 to May 29 – 10 nights in London at Ogle's Hotel; 9 nights at Aynhoe; 3 nights at Betchworth; and 9 nights at Brighton. The lengthy period in London was for work at the British Museum.
• •

Wednesday 28   Norwich to Ogle's Hotel
At 11 o'clock I set off for Christchurch, Eaton[1], where I found Bensly & the Bridegroom – The Church was beautifully decorated – Mr. Pigot[2] took half of the Service – I omitted to say "Let us pray" before "O Eternal God", which seemed to throw out the

people – My address to them was on "the mutual society, help, and comfort, wh. the one ought to have [*of*] the other, etc. etc. – did not get back till 12.40 – we left Norwich at 2.45; got to Liverpool Street at 6.

   1. Christchurch was built in 1873 for the city side of Eaton Parish.
   2. The Revd W.M. Pigot (ordained 1865) was Vicar of Eaton 1875–1904; Chaplain of the Norfolk and Norwich Hospital 1875–81; Diocesan Inspector of Schools, Norwich, 1875–90; R.D. of Humbleyard 1897–1904; Hon. Canon of Norwich 1901.

MAY

Wednesday 5   At Ogle's
Carefully studied & made an abstract of the statement Bensly had brot. me about Middleton – At 10.30 walked down to H's Club where met him and Bensly, and conversed over our plans of operations – then Bensly and I walked down to Whitehall Place, Heaviside following in a Cab – Saw Sir J. Mowbray, Sir Geo. Pringle, & Mr. Porter – both our petitions were graciously recd. – We are to draft our petition to have another estate given to us in lieu of Middleton – probably they may give us tithe rent-charge in lieu of it, or a smaller estates & some tithe rent-charge – they evidently bowed to what Yool had said on the subject – As to Stoke[1], I read to them and left them with Harper's letter – they seemed disposed to propose to Birkbeck[2] that he & they shall both give £750 towards the new parsonage, and then acceded to building a new one, and his proposed enlargement of the Ch. yard – took Heaviside and Bensly to luncheon at U.U.C.[3] where the former feasted on salmon Mayonnaise.

   1. The Dean and Chapter were Patrons of Stoke Holy Cross.
   2. Henry Birkbeck, Esq., (1821–95), lived at Stoke Holy Cross in a house built for him in 1852. Successful Banker, Norfolk and Norwich Bank (Barclays); High Sheriff of Norwich 1852–53; Deputy Lieut.; Gave Banquet at Stoke in 1875 to celebrate the centenary of the Bank.
   3. Goulburn's London Club – United Universities.

Saturday 8   From Ogle's to Aynhoe
A letter from B.C.[1], announcing his resignation from All Saints – left London by the train at 1 – met Willie[2] (the Squire) at Oxford, and came on with him here – The Dean[3] had a Lawn tennis-party.

   1. Berdmore Compton had been Vicar of All Saints', Margaret Street, London, for 13 years, and had been ordained for 33. He was now 66. He retired to his estate, Atherstone Hall, Warwickshire, which he had inherited from a distant cousin in 1872. From 1897–1908 he was Prebendary of Caddington Minor at St Paul's Cathedral; he died in 1908 at the age of 88.

2. William Cartwright, Lili's elder son, who had returned, in the 1860s, from his travels abroad to live at Aynhoe.
3. The Revd Frederick Cartwright, Rector of Aynhoe, Goulburn's brother-in-law and probably his closest friend.

Thursday 20
Left Betchworth at 9.40 – on reaching London, we sent the Servants on to Brighton – To Frederica's for luncheon at 2 – Bishop of Brechin[1] and his wife & daughter staying with her – she gave us luncheon, and some coffee – came down in Pulman's car at 3.40 – found many letters here (1) Purey Cust[2], whom I had met at the Club; (2) The Mayor, about the pinnacle of the Cathedral (3) case of conscience about S. Examm. before H.C. (4) do. about Prayer for the Dead (5) From Venables, resigning.

1. The Rt Revd Willoughby Jermyn, D.D., Bishop of Brechin since 1875; in 1886 he became Primus of the Scottish Episcopal Church.
2. The Very Revd Perceval Pury-Cust, Dean of York since 1880.

Friday 21 [*At Brighton*]
Went to Gladings about my watch in the morning, also to buy sealing wax, flowers, etc. and to have hair cut and shampooed at Truefitt's – In the Times of today appears a notice of Dr. Tait's[1] death at Folkestone – He will be a real loss.

1. The late Archbishop of Canterbury had immediately preceded Goulburn as Headmaster of Rugby.

Wednesday 26 <u>At Brighton</u>
All day occupied in writing 'In Memoriam' for Dr. Tait – went out in the morning at 12.45, to buy a present for Buskins & do some little shoppings – the whole of Ginnetes Circus[1] passed me; numberless piebalds drawing brass bands, a bull in an open van ('Baron'), an elephant walking & trumpeting, women gorgeously arrayed on horseback, or in triumphal cars, etc. etc.

1. Performing animals and some acrobatic acts were regular entertainments from the Middle Ages. In the 1840s the circus tent was introduced from America, and as the roads became macadamized, circuses with their large tents went on the road. Queen Victoria's expanding Empire made it possible to import elephants, camels, various wild beasts, thus unlarging the scope and attraction of the Circus show and performance.

Thursday 27
With the help of particulars from Mr. Tait, finished my 'In Memoriam' of Dr. Tait, and despatched it to the 'Guardian' – Wrote also to Mr. Tait, to Miss Atherley (enclosing introduction

to Dean of York), to Heaviside, to Mr. Armytage of Ditchingham, thanking for a book, & to Venables, declining to preach at Yarmouth on July 25 – After luncheon walked with Ju to the Electric Railway[1], wh. took us to Kemp Town, whence we walked back on the top of the Cliff – found the Dean walking on the chain pier[2].

    1. One of the earliest Electric Railways, established in 1883, and running between the Acquarium and Black Rock.
    2. The famous Chain Pier was destroyed in a storm in 1896.

•••
The Goulburns returned to Norwich on Saturday, June 29.
•••

JUNE

Wednesday 2

Worked with Bensly till 12.45 – Soon after came Robins, to explain his parting company with the Duchess of Grafton, and to ask me to allow him to make another reference to me – soon after Mr. Stuart, an Indian Missionary, came to ask for help in fitting up his Church – at 6 o'clock called on the Bp. and talked over with him (1) Yarmouth (2) arrangements for the Visitation (3) arrangements for short Services at the Cathedral during the visit of the Royal Agricultural Socy.[1]

    1. The R.A.S. Show to be held at Whitingham, next to Thorpe St. Andrew, on July 12.

Thursday 3   ASCENSION DAY

Only 22 at the 8 a.m. Celebration – At 11 the Bp., Heaviside & the three M.C.s were there, as well as Robinson; a poor congregation – The Master preached – I am glad to find that my memoir of Dr. Tait in the 'Guardian' read better in its mutilated state than I feared it would.

Friday 4

Called on Heaviside before Mg. Church to consult him about sending an invitation to the Prince of Wales – then an interview with Mrs. Coombe (the new Col's wife) about sittings for herself and her family – also an interview with Mr. Birkbeck, who has give up his scheme of building a <u>new</u> parsonage at Stoke on the other side of the road, and wants me to write to E.C. about the change – I did so later in the day – Bartie and Dr. Bates came to luncheon, and I proposed to them afterwards my scheme for Services in the Agricultural Show week, into wh. they entered.

Saturday 5
In order to prevent any possible collision between the hour of Aftern. Service, and the passing of the troops (19th. Hussars) thro' the Close, we gave out that the latter wd. be at 2.45 instead of 3 – After Church, wrote to Sir D. Probyn, to enquire what arrangement the P. of Wales wd. like to have made as to Service in the Cathedral at the reception – then with Bartie proceeded to draw up a form of Prayer for the Special Services during the Cattle Shew Week – Brown came in in the midst of this, and I gave him directions about the Visitation – the 19th. Hussars passed thro' the Close about 6.30 p.m.

Tuesday 8
Made an engagement for the Freemasons to have a Service at 4 p.m. on July 12 (first day of the Cattle Show) – At 12.10 presided at a meeting of S.P.G. in Clerical Rooms – a very interesting speech was made by Mr. Bhose, an Indian: desirability of having unmarried missionaries; remnants of light even in the heathen; ladies' work among the Zenanas[1], etc. etc. – Mr. Jackson, the Suffolk Organizing Secretary, made a suggestion that on the day of Intercession for Mission there shd. be always a celebration – Mr. Bhose came to luncheon, at wh. were (1) Etheldreda (2) 3 Pins (3) 3 Thursbys (4) Dampier – At 3 the Bishop of Derry[2] preached wh. seemed to be most eloquent & striking – He strained his voice a good deal – We take Heaviside over to Drayton for dinner tonight – Lucy Bignold was there, & Mr. Winter of East Bradenham, and Meyrick, & Mr. & Mrs. Walker, & the Bishop of Derry – I sat between Maimie & Lucy.

1. Zenana = the part of the house for the seclusion of women of high-caste families in India and Iran.
2. The Rt Revd Wm. Alexander, D.D., D.C.L., Bishop of Derry and Raphoe 1867–96; husband of Frances Alexander, the Hymn Writer; from 1896, Archbishop of Armagh, and Primate of All Ireland. He was an eloquent Preacher.

Sunday 13   WHIT SUNDAY
H.C. at 8 with Bartie & Moore; about 50 communicants; we did not get out of Church till 9.20, and I had not much more than time afterwards to count the money, look out the hymns, lessons, etc., etc. – Church again at 10.45 – the Mayor[1] & Corporation attended by a mistake of the Town Clerk – the Bishop's Sermon was from the Gospel, but was to me inaudible – It struck me during the Service that I would try a <u>very short</u> Sermon after the

Litany Service at 3.30 – At 3.30 I delivered this; it was just 12 minutes – Mary Stewart[2] came, and I went on with the Acts of the App. with her – Ju, Sophie, & I all staid at home in the Evening – Reading Cyrus Jay's 'Recollections of William Jay'.

1. John Gurney, Esq.
2. Canon Robinson's daughter, who had been baptised on September 8, 1868, with Goulburn as her Godfather. She would now, therefore, be between 17 and 18 and preparing for Confirmation.

Tuesday 15
At 9.30 came Stacy, and I determined to have only letter press for the Cathedral description, & not photographs – Church at 10 – after this a Chapter, very worrying in some of its details, but shorter than usual – I told the Canons of my plan of special Services in the Agricultural Week, which they approved – our incomes fell off about 100£ for each Canon, 200£ for the Dean last year – Bensly came to luncheon – afterwards we set to work again at the Office, & finished about 4.45 – returning home, I found Blanche Daniell arrived.

Thursday 17
Wrote to ... (3) Bensly in refce. to Dickson's wish to hold Eccles with St Martin's-at-Palace[1] – Bartie came at 12.30, & we made every preparation of Advertisements, Bills, letters to Parochial Clergy in connection with the short Special Services in the Show week – Read aloud in the evening some of Nicholas Nickleby to the ladies.

1. A mistake. The Revd David Dickson was instituted to St Martin-*at-Oak* on March 27, 1885. This was a Dean and Chapter Living, St Martin-at-Palace having the Bishop as Patron. The Eccles referred to is Eccles-next-the-Sea, which had no Church (it was under the beach); a population of 17; and was 20 miles from Norwich.

Friday 18
Days pass, & I seem to get thro' no real work – At 11.10 came Mr. Fitch, to talk over the answer that should be given to the Corporation about the site of St. William in the Wood's Shrine – wrote to ... (3) Mr. Dickson, with Bensly's communication about his holding the living of Eccles.

Tuesday 22   <u>Bishop's Visitation</u>
Wrote an apology to the Bp. for not attending upon him at the H.C. – in the morning completed my proofs of the description of the Cathedral – went to the Cathedral at 12.30, and listened to

the Bp's charge – It lasted nearly till 3 – on my coming out, Venables called, & I brot. him into luncheon – he sat with me, and had some talk about a communn. wh. he wished to make to the Bishop in reference to the position of his successor at St. George's[1]. We shall be alone tonight; only the Greenhills with us.

> 1. Venables had had 6 Curates for St Nicholas'; as Vicar of Gt Yarmouth, he was also the Patron of St Peter's, St John's, St Andrew's and St James', where he appointed a Curate to each; but St George's had Trustees as Patron and a Priest-in-Charge; and here difficulties arose about the relationship of the Vicar of Yarmouth to St George's.

Thursday 24   St. John Baptist
Wrote a letter to be hektographed[1], to the Clergy about giving notice in their Churches of the proposed Services in the week of the Show – Nevill looked in, and we talked about Yarmouth.

> 1. Hectograph = A process for copying type or MS. from a glycerin-coated gelatin master to which the original had been transferred.

Friday 25
After luncheon went by appointment to the Palace, and talked with the Bp. about the Friday Commn. 2. The Show Week Services. 3. Yarmouth: Position of the Vicar in Refce. to St. George's – conference on subdivision – he gave me a copy of letter he had written to Venables in reference to his relation to St. George's.

Tuesday 29   St. Peter
All the morning up to 1 p.m. engaged upon my Agricultural Sermon – then came Bartie to talk about the Bills of the Services during the Show week – went to a Trustees Meeting at the Gt. Hospital.

JULY

Thursday 1
Saw Stacy at 9.30, & placed in his hands the Index[1] with [which] Auntie & I drew up last term – After Church wrote to Mr. Ingram of Lewes about Evening Communions and the term 'Altar' – corrected proofs for Rivingtons – wrote to the Bp. about the H.C. tomorrow – to the Col. about the band on Sundays – after luncheon & the Papers, Ju took me to Mr. White's & left me there, she going on with Miss Ensor to the Bignolds – Mr. White said his last stopping had been a failure, and took it out, & replaced it – he seems to be apprehensive of an emeute[2] tomorrow.

1. The Goulburns had compiled an index for 'The Stranger's Guide to Norwich Cathedral'.
2. = riot.

Friday 2 (Final) Day of the Bishop's Visitation
& of the Norw. Election.

Mg. Prayer ... at 8 – Afterwards went with Heaviside to vote – Town very quiet – After Bkfst. wrote to Miss Hammersley, who had asked me in her trouble for some words of comfort – H.C. at 11.30, preceeding the Visitation – six Ministrants – a great number of Churchwardens – Jessopp in his scarlet grown & black velvet sleeves – when all was ended (about!) I withdrew – Church at 5 p.m. for wh. the Master returned, having voted at Cambridge and here also – a new Anthem of Dr. Bates's – In the evening corrected press of Index of the Stranger's Guide to Norwich Cathedral.

Wednesay 7

Wrote a letter to Gregory[1] before Blfst, asking for suggestions as to a suitable candidate for Yarmouth – then to Nevill's, who promises to enquire about young men of character, energy, and promise with a view to Yarmouth[2] – wrote to Fred. Od. Taylor, declining to subscribe to get the Dutch Church back into the hands of the citizens; also to Mr. Swatman, making him an offer of St. George's, Colegate – went into carriage to Harry Bullard to try to expostulate with him about his petitioning against Colman – nobody at home.

1. Canon Robert Gregory, Canon of St Paul's 1868–90; later Dean.
2. Goulburn had accepted a number of suggestions for candidates to fill the living of Yarmouth, had made some offers (which were rejected) and continued to make numerous enquiries (and offers) from many sources. It was not until October that, finally, he found a suitable candidate who was willing to accept.

Thursday 8

At 11 drove down to Hellesdon, and saw Mrs. Bullard about the petition wh. is spoken of as being got up agst. Mr. Colman[1] – The Secy. at the Brewery consulted about it by telephone[2], said he was sure 'Mr. Harry' would have nothing to do with it – I went and tried to telephone him myself – it was arranged that Harry Bullard shd. call here tomorrow morning – walked home – found the Nevills at dinner, and sat with them and told them what I had done.

1. At the July 1886 General Election, J.J. Colman (lib.) headed the poll, followed by Clare Sewell Read (Con.), both of whom became M.P.s.
2. This is the first mention, in the Diaries, of a Telephone. Previously, in the Victorian era, the telegram (telegraph) had been the only means of rapid communication; the telephone was invented in 1876; gradually the number of subscribers increased until, in 1890, there were about 50,000. There is no indication that Goulburn had one installed in the Deanery.

Friday 9

The Choir are having their outing today at Ely, under the auspices of Bartie and Brockbank – worked at the history of 'the Great Bible' till Harry Bullard called, at about 1 – He does not think of joining a petition agst. Colman, but of getting up a petition for the restoration of his own civic rights by a short Act – After luncheon, Auntie and I went to the Bank to get £10 for Elizabeth Parsons, where we heard of E. Birkbeck's[1] beating Lee Warner by a majority of 500 – then to Dimmock's[2], where we inspected his gallery of Norwich Art – Returning, I read the 'Times' in the garden, till Mrs. Heaviside came in and sat with me, bringing Georgie's Australian badger-dog.

1. Sir Edward Birkbeck (Con.) was M.P. for North Norfolk (knighted this year) had been the originator and Chairman of the Fisheries Exhibition of 1883, and was Chairman of the RNLI.
2. George T. Dimmock, Printseller, Picture Frame Maker, and Dealer in Artists' Materials, 66, London Street.

Saturday 10

Rose at 6.5 – Worked a little then, and after Mg. Church, at my Preface to Liturgical Gospels for Saints' Days – afterwards sent back, after writing my name in it, a volume sent by Monier Williams containing the autographs of subscribers to the Indian Institue[1] at Oxford – Maimie and Miss Howes of Spixworth came to luncheon; afterwards Maimie went out, & returned with the joyful news that Arch[2] was turned out, tho' by the narrow majority of 20! – Then a walk – Ju meanwhile had a Garden Lawn Tennis party & 'at home' – more than 50 people.

1. Was founded, following a proposal by Sir Monier Monier-Williams, Boden Professor of Sanskrit. Built with funds privately collected in India, and Britain to study the West. In 1968, after a celebrated controversy in which the University authorities were accused of betraying the donors, it was appropriated for University offices. The building is situated at the corner of Holywell and Catte Street.
2. Joseph Arch, Lib. M.P. for N.W. Norfolk 1885-6 & 1892-1902. Did more than anyone else of his time to improve conditions of agricultural workers.

Sunday 11
H.C. with Nevill & Bartie at 8 – Read over my Sermon 'the History of Agriculture'[1], Gen. III, 17. 18, 19, in the interval – crowded congregation at 11 – delivered my Sermon with tolerable ease, tho' my throat is anything but right, & I am nervous about it – much too long, full ¾ths. of an hour!! – After luncheon went to see Traxton, and found him much lower than my last visit; could not eat grapes because of the pips – Church again at 3.30 – The Master preached on Heb. III, 17. 18. "Altho' the fig-tree shall not blossom, etc.".

1. The Royal Agricultural Society (formed 1838), held a Show each year, a centre being chosen from a series of 9 districts established in 1841. This Sunday was Goulburn's preparation for, and celebration of, the Show's being held in Norwich, The attendance was 104,909. This was the twelfth best attendance of the previous 26 years.

Monday 12   First day
The short Service at 8 went off very well – The Bishop, and all three Canons, were there – I took the Precentor's stall, and spoke for 5 or 6 min. – It was all finished by 8.28 – At Church again at 10 with Bartie <u>solus</u> – after luncheon, an even downpour, wh. quite forbad our going to the Show, as we had intended – This rain, good for the country, is bad for the Show – Bitta arrived at 3.30 – Lilie, Ursie, Bertie did not arrive till ½p.7.!!

Tuesday 13   Show Week
Service at 8 – rather better than yesterday, in point of attendance – luncheon with Lili who was left behind, Auntie, Bitta, Ursie & Bertie, having gone to the Show – then lionised Lili over the Cathedral – then took her to Traxton's; he seems fading out of life – on our return, Ju & her party had not come home – Church again at 5 with the Master, and Bartie – he told me of an accident in the Showground made by a restless horse who was frightened – Ju, etc. have not yet come home; they have gone to Mr. Colman's 'At home' – I wrote this morning to Ld. Halsbury[1] for an appointment to see him about Harry Bullard.

1. The Lord Chancellor.

Wednesday 14
A day of bustle and unrest – Spoke at 8 a.m. – we had finished by 8.25 – Church at 10 – soon after Symonds called, and left with me his Memoir of Sedgwick, and also a brochure about Bp. Stanley's welcome to Jenny Lind – at 12 started in the carriage

with the three Canons for the Dejeunee at St. Andrew's Hall – In the reception room talked with Sir Peter and Lady Ede [*Eade*], Lord Suffield[1], Ld. Bristol, and Rustum Pasha – at the banquet, my seat was between Lady Ede and Lord Egerton of Tatton; the latter talked about my father, whom he had met at Homburg of yore – after we broke up, I talked with the Duke of Richmond – I got out before the great body of people, and walked home, but found myself baffled in the attempt to buy a present for little Buskyns on her birthday – Church again at 5 – The Dean and Holford are expected, but not yet come – Tom is expected at 10 tonight – At dinner we have Mr. & Mrs. Sam Hoare[2], Mr. Temple an officer; Mrs. Bignold & her Son; also the Master – <u>Col.</u> & Mrs. Bignold came – the Colonel & Sam Hoare polked with Mary Stewart and the other girls most beautifully; also with Miss Old.

1. Lord Suffield (formerly Sir Charles Harbord) was owner of the Gunton Estate, Norfolk.
2. Samuel Hoare, Esq., was M.P. for Norwich; created a Baronet 1899; was connected to the Gurneys and Barclays.

• •

The Show atmosphere continued for the rest of the week, including the special Services in the Cathedral. On Thursday, some of the Deanery houseparty went to the Dog Show, while, in the evening, the Nevills took one of them to the Soiree; on Friday, the 5 o'clock Service was 'plain' because the whole Choir had gone to the Show, and, in the evening, the whole of the Deanery houseparty, except Lili (now 81) and Goulburn, went to the fireworks.

• •

Thursday 22

Before Bkfst. wrote my address of Saturday last for the Show Week Publication – also wrote to Sir D. Probyn to ask the P. of W's sanction for dedicating to him – Church at 10 – then wrote Preface for my forthcoming 'Church Memorial of Agric. Socys. Visit' – wrote to … (2) C.A. Hope[1] about Lake as the new Verger.

1. Canon Hinds Howell's Curate, who looked after Hellesdon, which went with Drayton. Hope had been his Curate since 1870 and was to continue as such until 1892, when he became Rector of Taverham.

Saturday 24

Chapter at 11 – one great subject discussed was the filling of Traxton's place – I said I could not suppress a Statutable Officer but was willing to appoint Walker Verger, to hold the place with his Bookkeepership of Visitors, & relinquishing the Organ

Blowing – In this way the Junior Verger's stipend, it was thought, mt. temporarily be reduced from £52 to £30 – Bensly came to luncheon at 1.30; there was also Maimie & Agnes, who had brot. Mr. Mackeson – He was summoned down to attend the Ladies Home Mission Meeting at Clerical Rooms, but got no audience! He seemed a very nice person.

Monday 26
Changed our plans about going abroad – Rose at 5, and had a long weary day of preparations for depature, tearing letters, filling waste paper baskets with rubbish – shortly after luncheon came Heaviside to say 'Goodbye', and Mr. Kennion[1] who gave me a book of his on the question whether St. Peter was ever at Rome – We heard from Courier Cross in the morning, declining our terms at the last moment, as they don't include board-wages – so we resolved not to go to Homburg, but to Harrogate – I wrote to Pom to meet us there – had interviews with Walker about the Jun. Verger's place, and with Alden and Spencer about the Coronn. Bible[2] – Went to the Chapter Library, and thence in to the Town to purchase waste-paper baskets, and to see Stacy.

   1. The Revd R.W. Kennion, Rector of Acle since 1858.
   2. 'Coronation Bible' (See Jan. 14, 1887, and Appendix 8.)

●●

The Goulburns were away from Norwich from Tuesday, July 27, to Saturday, September 11, spending two nights in London; 20 nights in Harrogate; 3 nights at Ilkley; 2 nights at York; 1 night in London; and 18 nights in Brighton.

●●

Tuesday 27   From Norwich to London
Left Norwich with Ju by the 7.35 train (Rose came by a later train) – arrived, parted from Ju and went to ... (3) London House to consult Bp.[1] on Mr. Donne[2] of Limehouse – hearing that I might just catch him, if I went to Fulham, I took a hansom there, but he had just fled – so I returned to Club, and after luncheon, called again at London House, & caught the Bp, and had a glimpse of Mrs. Temple (very pleasing) – The Bp. doubts whether Donne is a 'big enough' man, but will enquire – returned to Club – wrote to the Bp. certain particulars wh. I had omitted saying – thence to Rivington's – thence to Floris's for toothbrushes, and thence to Ogle's, to find a kind letter from the Abp. of Cant. about Canon Hole – and then Morgiana, who told me to drink the mild sulphur water at Harrogate.

1. The Bishop of London was Frederick Temple, Goulburn's successor as Headmaster of Rugby.
2. The Revd Wm. Donne was Rector of St Anne, Limehouse. He *did* go to Yarmouth where he remained for six years, being also, from 1888, Rural Dean of Flegg. He left Yarmouth in 1892 to become Vicar of Wakefield and Archdeacon of Huddersfield.

Wednesday 28

Called on Lord Halsbury[1] (who is to be Chancellor) and discussed Bullard's case; he advised that the Bill shd. be <u>not general</u>, but a Bullard relief Bill – I saw my godchild – then to the Chirop. who operated – then luncheon for Club [*Club for luncheon!*], where I saw Tom for a moment – I found Ju at MAC's – she had had a long visit from Mrs. Benson, who had brot. a letter & book from the Abp. from [*for*] me.

1. Hardinge Stanley Giffard; M.P. from 1877; Lord Chancellor 1885–86 & 1886–92; Baron 1885; 1st Earl of Halsbury 1898.

Thursday 29   From Ogle's to the Royal Hotel, Harrogate

We left our hotel shortly after 9 for King's Cross, and King's Cross for Harrogate at 10.10, where we arrived via Church Fenton (not York), about 4.30 – Pouring rain – took a fly for a quarter of an hour, and went about lodging-hunting; at last took Welton House (the whole house) for 6 guineas and ½ for a week from Saturday next – The Royal is comfortable and clean, the servants very civil, and we had an excellent private dinner at 7.15, after Table d'Hote – I had read some of Sainsbury's 'Marlborough' today, and like it much – have to write to Harry Bullard about my interview with Ld. Halsbury, and to Sir D. Probyn, who declines to lay before P. of W. my request for permission to dedicate to him, before going to bed.

Friday 30

Another sunless, rainy day – letter from Miss Thursby, asking me to come and see her brother who is dying – then went to 'the Cairn, Ripon Road', and saw and prayed with the poor invalid, who seemed insensible, and hiccoughed every minute; walked home in pouring rain – Oh that Yarmouth were off my mind!

AUGUST

Monday 2   From Royal Hotel to 4, Trafalgar Place
After Bkfst. at the Royal, went with Ju to see Mrs. Firtle's lodgings, where Lady Millicent Bence Jones is on the drawing room

floor – took three rooms for 3 guas. ½ a week[1] – then changed our quarters – strolled into the town thro' a mob gathered to see the bicyclers' races – got a 'Daily Telegraph' and returned to read it – then into the town with Ju and had some 'ices' for luncheon at the shops in the Arcade, where such dainties are sold – then called on Mr. Brownrigg[2], and saw his lovely roses and heartsease – he had gone to a funeral – we walked back, after vain attempts to get a fly, all being engaged to take back the bicyclists – 'Minmisney Pinmisney' and her nephew and her niece's governess, called before dinner.

> 1. Puzzling. There is no indication in the Diary that the arrangement made on July 29 had been cancelled.
> 2. Vicar of St Mary's, Harrogate. His son (R.G.P. Brownrigg) was his Curate.

•••

In many of the entries for the remainder of Goulburn's absence from Nowich, he is dealing with correspondence with, or about, a variety of possible cadidates for Yarmouth, even interviewing one in Harrogate, the same one in Ilkley nine days later, and another in Brighton. I shall, therefore, during this period, omit the references to these numerous candidates.

•••

Tuesday 3
Walked down to the Sulphur Wells, and took a ten ounce glass of mild sulphur – after luncheon on bread & grapes, took a fly with Ju, and went to Ripley, crossing the River Wharfe, wh. seemed picturesque, and passing the village of Killinghall – saw the exterior of the Castle, in wh. Oliver Cromwell slept before Marston Moor (date Philip & Mary), and then went into the Church wh. is under repair at the beginning of a new incumbency – Saw the recumbent effigy (much mutilated) of Sir Thomas Ingilby & his lady, his head reclining on a lamb (or a calf?) – temp. Edwr. III – On our return wrote to … Hinds Howell, who, we hear from Medley, has had a slight stroke of paralysis.

Friday 6
Ju went to Church at 8 – I drank my two glasses of water, and between then strolled into Town – we went to Mr. Brownrigg's lawn tennis party & 5 p.m. tea, where I talked with a clergyman who had been a Bible clerk of All Souls in poor Fred's time[1], and knew some Oxford characters, & had been an attendant at Holywell Ch.

> 1. Goulburn's younger brother, Frederick, who had been a Fellow of All Souls, but became mentally ill, was an epileptic, and until he died in 1877, had been for many years in a Nursing Home at Ticehurst, Sussex.

Sunday 8

Ju went to H.C. at St. Peter's at 8 a.m. – At 11 we both went to St. Mary's, Harrogate, where the Service is hearty, and there is a great deal of singing, & even the responses to the Litany are sung – I preached on 'The first and last miracles of Christ' – the Sermon seemed listened to – went on with my attempt to find out whether the P.B. Psalms are translated from the Hebrew, or from the LXX and Vulgate; evidently in many places from the 2 latter, but by no means always.

Saturday 14

At luncheon came a letter from Buskins, telling us that Gerard's illness has broken out again (inflamation of the colon) at Margate and he is quite unable to move – Lolotte[1] has gone to him and telegraphs that he is a little easier, but dozing, (the consequence of the opiates).

> 1. 'Lolotte' = Laura Pearson (nee Thomas), widow of Major Henry Pearson, and Gerard's twin sister. Both were 38.

Sunday 15

At 11 we all went to St. Mary's, Low Harrogare, where the Prayers were read by Mr. Brownrigg's son, he reading the lessons, I the antecommunion Service – I preached on the duty of giving a tithe of income to God – when I was walking home, Col. Knox accosted me, who succeeded my father in his house in Seymour St. and who is here for his wife's health; and then a young lady called Euphue Maxwell, who had asked me by letter whether my Sermon of last Sunday was in print, and I had answered her as if she was a gentleman – she wanted to know whether giving to the poor would be accepted as tithe – in the afternoon we went to St. Peter's, where the Litany was mumbled thro' in monotone – most unsatisfactory – then went home & read thro' the evening Service with a Sermon of Dr. Tait's.

Monday 16   Visit to Fountains and Ripley [*means Ripon*]

Very slightly improved accounts of Gerard by telegram and post – at 11.55 we started by train for Ripon – thence drove at once to Fountains, thro' Studley grounds, wh. are rather formal – a long and wearying walk to the ruins; lovely they are, when arrived at – got back to Ripon shortly before 3 p.m. – lionised by Verger Benson over Ripon Minster – The great beauty of it seems to be the Misereres – we attended the Service at 4.15, and then afterwards we went to 5 p.m. tea with Canon Holms, who was in residence – they were most kind to us – we returned by the 6.7 p.m., & found letters from Gussie & Lou[1] – I hope neither of them are frightened by Gerard's illness.

> 1. Gerard's mother, and Goulburn's cousin.

Tuesday 17
Pom[1] has resolved to return to her mother tomorrow, Lolotte writing to say that Gerard's complaint is <u>peritonitus</u>; he is, however, going on well.

> 1. Gerard's sister Mary.

Thursday 19   At Middleton Hotel, Ilkley
After luncheon Ju and I drove to Boulton Abbey, with wh. we were charmed, and thot it very superior to Fountains – read to Ju in the evening the 1st. Act of Measure for Measure.

• •

In all the long line of possible candidates for Yarmouth who were written to, and who came and went, Goulburn was very hopeful that the Revd G.C. Fisher, whom he had interviewed twice in Yorkshire, and who had visited Yarmouth incognito, would accept. Again, he was disappointed. Fisher eventually, in 1896, became Suffragen Bishop of Southampton 1896–99; and then Suffragan Bishop of Ipswich 1899–1905. The line of candidates continued, but we shall concentrate on the Revd A.H. Dunn and the Revd Wm. Donne.

• •

Tuesday 24   St. Bartholomew   From London to Brighton
After Bkfst. at Ogle's, went to Goslings to draw for £25 – then to Morgan's; he examined my leg, & called it inflamed varix; told me I must not walk, and prescribed – then to Chirop. who operated, much to my relief – having sent Rose on, we came down to Brighton by the 1.50 (Pulman) – found awaiting me a letter from Fisher, <u>declining Yarmouth</u>!!! – so I am on the tramp again.

Thursday 26
In the morning began my reminiscences of Ward[1], and made some way in them – wrote to … (4) Wilfrid Ward telling him I have begun reminiscences of his father – after dinner wrote to … (4) Nevill, who sends a recommendation (from Bradley) of Mr. Dunn.

> 1. W.G. Ward, who had influenced Goulburn at Balliol College, Oxford, before becoming (in 1845) a Roman Catholic. He died in 1882. His son, Wilfrid, (also a Roman Catholic) later wrote a Biography of his father.

Monday 30
A broiling day – occupied all morning with my 'Ward'; made great way with it – a letter from Archdn. Hessey[1] about Mr. Dunn, giving the highest character of him – what am I to do between Archdn. Hessey's Dunn, Dean Vaughan's Goodwyn, and Archdn. Chapman's Canon Harrison? Acton, Sharrow or Bury?

> 1. The Ven. J.A. Hessey, D.C.L., Archdeacon of Middlesex.

Tuesday 31
I laid before the Dean of Llandaff Archdn. Hessey's recommendation of Mr. Dunn, & Archdn. Chapman's of Mr. Harrison of Bury – we agreed that Yarmouth shd. be offered straight to Dunn, and that I shd. write to the Abp. of York for his view of the qualifications of Mr. Goodwyn of Sharrow – both these letters I wrote before dinner.

SEPTEMBER

Thursday 2
Heard from Mr. Dunn by early post – He is going to consult Dr. Machar, Archdn. Hessey, and the Rector of Clopton, Suffolk[1].

> 1. The Revd S. Hooke had been Curate of Yarmouth 1877–79.

Saturday 4
Intense heat again – Letter [from] Mr. Dunn in the morning, proposing to go down to Canterbury to see Dr. Machar on Monday, & probably to come her[e] on Tuesday, then Yarmouth Wednesday – this I answered – read to Ju some 'Framley Parsonage'.

Tuesday 7   [At Brighton]
Mr. Dunn of Acton appared at 1.45, and after he had had luncheon, we had a long talk about Yarmouth – his single object seems to be whether he can do most good there, or by continuing at Acton – after he was gone we took an hour's drive.

Wednesday 8
Wrote to (1) Bensly, to call a Chapter for Sep. 16 (2) Archdn. Hessey, asking him to advise Dunn to go to Yarmouth (3) Dn. of Llandaff, thanking him for his Ep. to the Philippians, and telling him about Dunn, and my letters from W. Ebor. (4) Sir Harry Verney[1], declining his kind invitation to meet Miss Nightingale. (5). Mr. Dunn, asking him to address me at Norwich.

1. Liberal M.P. until his retirement in 1885, and now 85; Florence Nightingale was still very active in founding Nursing Institutions, etc. and was now 66. She lived to be 90.

Friday 10
Wrote to ... (2) Mr. Dunn, saying I thot. there wd. be no difficulty about his not beginning work at Yarmouth till the end of December.

Monday 13 [Norwich]
Was able to get twice to Church, sitting during the Service with my leg upon the kneeler – the Service was very soothing – Heard from Hinds Howell, enclosing a letter from Conrad, in wh. he eulogises Mr. Dunn, and says he hears that he has accepted Yarmouth – a letter from Mr. Dunn himself, saying that he is grieviously perplexed about it – I answered Hinds Howell, and also wrote to Dunn, saying that, in making up his mind, I hoped he would not lose sight of certain considerations wh. I detailed – after Mg. Church walked in the garden, where I was joined by Nevill, who discussed Mr. Dunn with me, & showed me the letter of Spaull charging Brown with keeping back from the Chapter, King's offer to rebuild the pinnacle at his own expense.

Wednesday 15
Heard by the early post from Mr. Dunn, declining Yarmouth – After Mg. Service, Nevill took a turn with me up and down the garden and we discussed the next steps to be taken about Yarmouth.

Saturday 18
A fine sunshiny, bright, cold day – In the evening wrote to Archdeacon Hessey, asking about Donne of Limehouse – Bp. of London now writes to say he thinks Donne would do – After Afternoon Service, went a drive in the carriage reading a paper of Tricotomy[1] by the son of Mr. Johnson of Saxlingham who has sent it to me – saw Walker and told him what would be his duties & emoluments as Junior Verger – saw also Howlett & promised to appoint him to be Bellows Blower.

1. The divison of man into body, spirit and soul.

Tuesday 21 St. Matthew
Wrote to Miss Hare, thanking her for her contribution in memory of her mother (£10) to the Cathedral; to a clergyman, thanking him for 'Handbook of 39 Articles'.

Wednesday 22
Answered a letter from Gott, in wh. he recommends Rev. N.E. Leigh, Precentor of Leeds Parish Church – also from Dunn, indicating a desire to recant – I told him he might do so, but he must do it by return of post – On returning from my afternoon drive, I found a 2d letter from Mr. Norman of Stafford, still more strongly recommending Mr. Littleton of Penkridge,& one from Archn. Stamer, highly commending the wonderful energy of Mr. Littleton, but calling him impetuous and restless – I answered this last before dinner, asking the Archdn. to sound Littleton as to whether he would accept Y. I think Mr; Littleton wd. d for Y, if he wd. come.

Thursday 23
Few letters today – one to institute for Affections of the Speech, 22, Henrietta Street, Covent Garden, W.C. sending £5. 5, to make me a Life Governor – Some talk after 2d Church about the duties of preparing the Table for Holy Communion, etc.

Friday 24
Letter from Dunn, decling Y. (after a long prose) a second time – thereon telegraphed at once to Stamer[1] 'See Mr. L.' – Nevill came in, and I told him what I had asked Sir Lovelace Stamer to do on getting my telegram – later in the day a charming letter from Sir L.S. saying he would be sure to exact proper assurances from Mr. Littleton, so as not to compromise me – what will come of it?

1. The Venerable Sir Lovelace Stamer (1829–1908): Rector of Stoke-on-Trent 1858–93; Archdeacon of Stoke-on-Trent 1877–88; Bishop Suffragan of Shrewsbury 1888–95.

Saturday 25
Received a telegram from Sir L. Stamer that Mr. L. is favourably disposed towards Yarmouth, and asking me to write to him, as I have done – At luncheon, Mr. & Mrs. Shorthouse (introduced by Lady A. Compton), Mrs. Lucas, and one or two other ladies (Geroge Cubitt too) – I gave the Shorthouses an introducn. to Mrs. Ripley[1], as they wanted to see the house at Earlham – Miss Rolfe, a Ditchingham Sister, and another lady, had 5 o'clock tea here – I am working at the Proofs of my Preface to the Saints' Day Gospels.

1. Widow of John Gurney (who died young), and from whom she inherited Earlham Hall. She married the Revd W.N. Ripley, Vicar of St Giles 1859–85; now Rector of Colney and Vicar of Earlham. They lived at Earlham Hall.

Monday 27

A rainy day – In the morning, wrote to Bensly, asking him to announce a Chapter for Tues. Oct. 5 – Also wrote to Archdn. Gifford[1], who, I fear, has virtually made an offer of Y. to Mr. Donne – After luncheon Browne came in, and I went with him to the Cathedral to inspect the group of shafts wh. it is contemplated to restore opposite the Pulpit – as we were going out, we encountered Professor Mahaffy[2] coming with an introduction from Ly. Alwyne Compton – I managed, walking slowly, to shew him over the Cathedral and Cloister – afterwards he came to 5 p.m. tea, and then went with me to Church (pouring hard) – on my return Ju and I concocted a letter to Mr. Colman, declining[3] to receive some members of the Congregational Union on Oct. 11.

1. Archdeacon of London.
2. The Revd Prof. Sir John Pentland Mahaffy, Professor of Ancient History at Trinity College, Dublin; eventually, Provost of Trinity 1914–19; his "reputation chiefly rests on works dealing with life, literature and history of ancient Greeks ... a remarkably versatile writer of great shrewdness and sagacity". (Concise D.N.B. Vol. II, page 1917).
3. Goulburn frequently uses the phrase "decline to receive", "decline to accept", and one is left wondering if "decline" = "refuse", I do not think it does. Very early on the morning of Oct. 11, the Goulburns would be on their way to London to begin their Autumn Break doing the rounds of family villages. So he would have been unable to meet the Congregationalists.

Tuesday 28

Wrote a long letter to the Bishop asking whether he had any objection to my restoring the shafts of the column opposite his throne – found a letter from Mr. Littleton, putting many queries about Yarmouth, & informing me of several Ritualistic practices he indulges in – I was all the evening answering again – I rather hope now he may _not_ come.

Wednesday 29   St. Michael & All Angels

H.C. at 8 with Ju – Church at 10 and 5 – After luncheon Ju and I drove to the Henry Pattesons[1], to enquire for Mrs. Patteson who had lost her Brother, and thence to Earlham, where Mrs. Ripley[2] kindly came out to me at the door, and introduced Mr. Moule, son of the Bishop of Mid-China – She gave me some beautiful grapes – on our return we found our own Bishop at the door, who came up and talked to me about his Cathedral Confirmation, wh. he wishes to praepone for one day; about Mr. Smith's[3] installation on

Saturday and reading in the following day – he seemed very well and lively.

1. They lived at Cringleford.
2. Canon W.N. Ripley, a leading Evangelical in the city, was a strong supporter of the Church Missionary Society. The Rt Revd G.E. Moule, D.D., was Bishop of Mid-China from 1880; the Ven. A.E. Moule was Archdeacon in Mid-China 1884–94, and again from 1904.
3. Rector of Homersfield, Harleston, to be installed as an Hon. Canon.

Tuesday 30 <u>Chapter</u>
Church twice – Heaviside as lame as a tree with the gout, read the lessons from his stall – This is the last day of his residence – Afterwards a very worrying Chapter – the question of Spaul's yard seems eternal – Thompson's report of the decayed double cottage at Frostenden was the chief business – At 3 Ju and I drove over to Postwick to call – found the V at his door talking with good Louisa in her carriage – Lady Vincent had just lost her baby – The V showed us his two lively little girls, and their half-brother, Francis who, having left Eton, is now studying German under a tutor at Freyberg.

OCTOBER

Monday 4
A most lovely, warm, balmy day – Answered a note from one of Mr. Dunn's Curates, in wh. he tells me that if the Abp. of Cant. would tell Mr. Dunn it is his duty to go to Yarmouth, he would go – received a long letter from Bartie about the Gloucester Cathedral plan of having Organ Recitals in the Nave of the Cathedral, wh. he wishes to follow here; no attempt there to make it a Service, or turn the music and singing to spl. account.

Tuesday 5
The special Chapter at 11 – a great deal of talk and difference of opinion as to the fairness of the E.C.'s proposal of exchanging tithe rent charge with us for Middleton – we determined that Bensly should write to, and afterwards see, Smiths & Gore, to see whether the E.C. mt. be disposed, when the Foldholme marshes fall to them (in 1889) to give them to us together with a certain amt. of tithe rent charge, and until they shall fall, to give us a money payment to represent them – Chapter ended at luncheon time – Mr. Wm. Mathews, Professor of English Literature and Rhetoric in some Amern. University, a wizened squinting man,

very spare, and somewhat fulsome in compliments (introduced by Frederica) had luncheon here – I then took him over the Cathedral, wh. he did not, I thought, much care for – at 3.15 Auntie & I took him in the carriage to N. & N. Hospital, where they saw Sir T. Browne's[1] skull, and then to St. Peter Mancroft's Church – then I took him to see the Lollards' pit, and afterwards sent him back in carriage to his hotel – Auntie had her Sunday School girls at tea.

> 1. Sir Thomas Browne, famous physician and author of the 17th Century, was buried in the Chancel of St Peter Mancroft Church. In 1840, a workman, preparing another grave next to it, unearthed his skull. It was reinterred in 1922 in its proper place.

Thursday 7
Mr. & Mrs. Littleton dined with us last night, and slept here – we like them much (especially her); but he seems much to excitable and susceptible to worry, to do for Yarmouth – I feel sure he won't take it – She came to Church at 10, while he went to Nevill's – I had just a quarter of an hour after Church to take them round to the side chapels, etc. before they started for Yarmouth – came in and wrote receipt for £15 for Grammar School Field, and other small letters – wrote a long letter in answer to enquiries about Eternal Punishment.

Saturday 9
No letter from Mr. Littleton – two letters about Westhall – went to the Palace, and consulted the Bp. about the Candidates for Westhall, telling him that I proposed to offer it to Venables in the first instance – then came Neville and advised that if Donne failed us for Yarmouth, Mackarness should next be tried – a drive with Bartie, in the course of which we discussed his plans for having four Musical Services in Advent.

Sunday 10
At Church thrice – telegraphed to Littleton[1] to let me know his decision – I got a telegram from Littleton 'No'; so immediately wrote to Mr. Donne, and sent the telegram to Nevill – Heaviside called, and we agreed that if Venables does'nt take Westhall[2], it shall be offered to Medley[3]; H. to wait, meanwhile, to see whether Medley wants St. Gregory's.

> 1. The Hon. the Revd Cecil Littleton remained Vicar of Penkridge in Staffs. (a family Living) until 1893, when he became Vicar of St Mary's, Chesterfield, and, in the following year, an Hon. Canon of Southwell Cathedral.

2. Westhall was a village of c. 430, 5 miles NE of Halesworth.
3. The Revd E.S. Medley had been a Minor Canon of Norwich 1872–77, and Precentor 1874–77; he then became a Residentiary Canon and Precentor of St Andrew's Cathedral, Inverness 1877–86. He wanted to return to Norfolk, and he became Vicar of St Gregory's, Norwich in 1886.

Monday 11   From Norwich to Ogle's
Left Norwich with Ju at 7.35 (Rose & luggage by next train) – We left our two umbrellas in the net of a Smoking carriage, out of wh. we moved into another, and so lost them – arrived, I went straight to Brigg, to buy a new umbrella – at Club found a telegram from Mr. Donne (afterwards supplemented by a letter) to the effect that he wd. come to Club tomorrow at 12.30 p.m. – wrote to Hinds Howell about Medley's prospects – on returning to our hotel we found a telegram from Venables, saying that Dunn will now accept Yarmouth.

Tuesday 12
Wrote to Venables, declining to offer it to Dunn[1] a 3d time – then came in Mr. Donne[2]; he had been at Yarmouth, & seen it, and is quite willing to take it – a delightful man, & apparently just the man for the position! Deo Gratias! Deo Gratias! – He had luncheon with me; and then I wrote him a formal letter tendering the living to him – then put a P.S. to Venables, announcing Donne's acceptance – to the Bp. also announcing it, and to Bensly – telegraphed to Nevill to give Donne an appointment in London – cabs all day as it was pouring fast.

1. This is the end of the 'Dunn saga'. The Revd A.H. Dunn remained Vicar of All Saints, Acton, Middlesex, until 1892, when he became Bishop of Quebec, Canada, for the next 23 years.
2. The Revd William Donne remained at Yarmouth until 1892 and was Rural Dean of Flegg 1888–92, when he became Archdeacon of Huddersfield & Vicar of Wakefield. He was Hon. Chaplain to the Queen 1896–98; Chaplain in Ordinary 1898–1901; and Hon. Chap. to King Edward VII from 1901. He was also Hon. Chaplain to the Bishop of Wakefield from 1896.
    (Canon G.R. Winter Vicar of Swaffham, sent Goulburn an epigram of The Dean, the Dunn, and the Donne'.)

•••

On October 11 the Goulburns had embarked on their Autumn Break which would take them once again to visit family and friends at Eyhore, Edgcote, Eydon and Aynhoe. Then, after a overnight return to Norwich for a Chapter Meeting (November 3), a further 16 nights at Brighton, and a final return to Norwich on November 20.
•••

Wednesday 13   From Ogle's Hotel to Edgcott
A letter from Venables, enclosing one from Dunn, offering to take Yarmouth, if I were driven into a corner; answered this before going out – wrote to Nevill at Albury about Donne's appointment; and to Donne himself.

Thursday 14
In the morning draughted some notes for Advent Sermons – after 5 p.m. tea I wrote to Palgrave and Mr. Worlledge letters of introduction to Mr. Donne, and sent them to him, with advice to consult Bp. of London as to dismissing present Yarmouth Curates[1] – after dinner wrote to Venables, offering him Westhall – Letter from Bensly about his interview with the Commissioners.

>   1. Ten out of Venables' eleven Curates were dismissed. In fact, Donne appointed some 13 Curates in their place.

Thursday 21   Eydon
Finished making notes for a third Advent Sermon – Hebrew till the letters came in – one from Venables declining Westhall, and recommending for it Mr. Girling[1], one of the Chapelry curates at Yarmouth, who must, he thinks, be dismissed – this seems not a bad idea, as smoothing Donne's way.

>   1. The Revd G. Girling did go to Westhall. He had been Curate in Charge of St Andrew's, Yarmouth, the Wherryman's Mission Church. He was c. 48. For the first 13 years after his ordination in 1863, he had been a Chaplain in Bengal.

Tuesday 26   Eydon
In the course of the morning Sir H. Dryden called, and gave to Lucie, Mrs. Skeels and myself a conversational Lecture on 'The Crucifix in Art'; no image in connexion with the Cross known till 500 years after Christ; he wanted more information about robed crucifixes, etc. – wrote to Donne from whom I got a letter ... (3) Jarrold ordering my Boss Book for Sir Henry Dryden ... (5) refusing a subscription to a Socy. for Protection of Women & Children (6) in defence of the Free Mason's Service in the Cathedral.

NOVEMBER

Tuesday 2   Aynhoe thro' London to Norwich
Left Aynhoe at 7.30 – on arriving parted from Ju and the Servants and went to Morgiana's, who prescribed – (1) Meat only 2ce a

week (2) Mixture alkaline after meals (3) Calomel lightly on the tongue – got a carriage by myself to Norwich – on arriving wrote to (1) Ju (2) Geo. Girling, offering him Westhall (3) Lord Mayor[1] elect, declining invitation for the 9th. (4) Macmillan with 15s. 8d. for Sarum Breviary. (5) Medley (6) Mrs. Skey, declining a Preface for her book – am going to dine with Heaviside.

> 1. A mistake. The first *Lord* Mayor of Norwich was Dr E.E. Blyth, 1909–10.

Wednesday 3   Norwich to Garlant's Hotel
Chapter at 11 at the Office – Nisbet wanted us to haggle a little more, but on the whole it was thot. wiser not to do this, but to accept E.C.'s offer of Acle Marshes + Rent charge in exchange for Middleton, and we indicated four Rentcharges, Crimplesham, Gt. Plumstead, Hopton, and [blank] wh. we shd. prefer – left Norwich at 3.55, but did not get to London till ½p.8 – found a comfortable room & fire at Garlant's.

Saturday 13   Brighton to Chichester
Before leaving Brighton, wrote (by Donne's suggestion) to the Lord Chancellor, to ask him to give a small Living to Goodrich of Yarmouth, and to Donne to say I had done this – left Brighton at 11.35 – found our dear friends here[1] all well and cheery – after luncheon they took me in their carriage to call at several places, the chief being Lady Victoria Wellesley's, and Goodwood, where we enquiried after the Duke – no one at home anywhere!

> 1. The Very Revd J.W. Burgon, Dean of Chichester, and his family.

Sunday 14
At 10.30 the Service wh, as I staid for the 2d Celebration, was long; my Sermon much too long – at luncheon was not only Mr. Margoliouth[1], but Count Conrad von Zeppelin, a very unassuming, pleasing, and intelligent young man; had some talk with him afterwards – at 3 we had a very delightful Service, and Mr. Margoliouth preached well and solidly on "the Chureh, wh. is his body, the fulness of him, etc.". Eph. 1 – After the Service, Bp. Tufnell[2], Canon Awdry, Archdn. Walker, and their wives came in to afternoon tea.

> 1. The Revd George Margoliouth was, at this time, Organ. Sec. of Parochial Missions to the Jews.
> 2. The Rt Revd E.W. Tufnell had been the 1st Bishop of Brisbane, Australia, retiring 1875, and was now a Residential Canon of Chichester, as were also Canon W. Audry, and the Ven. J.R. Walker, Archdeacon of Chichester.

Monday 22 [Norwich]

After Mg. Service, went with Heaviside to poll for Hotblack[1] to represent our Ward on the Town Council – Bartie came to luncheon, & we had some talk about Brockbank[2] declining to be at the first oratorio on Wednesday 1 Dec. on the ground that he had mistaken the day – also about the Freemason's Service, at wh. Mr. Cholmeley admits his having sunk his voice at saying "thro' Jesus Christ our Lord".

> 1. Geroge S. Hotblack, Esq., of John Hotblack and Sons, Wholesale Boot and Shoe Manufacturers, Mountergate Street.
> 2. One of the Lay Clerks.

Tuesday 23

After Serivce I found Dr. Bateman[1] awaiting me, who carried me off to see a picture of Bp. Bateman[2] done by an artist in the Town Close from an engraving in the last century – the artist had made the crook of the staff pointing inwards (on the authority of the Bps. Seal) not outwards as in the engraving, and had represented him as in the Chapter House of the Cathedral, supposed to be surrounded by Norman aracading, instead of in a room of Trinity Hall, as the engraving represents him – In the afternoon wrote part of a Sermonette for the 1st. oratorio.

> 1. Dr (later Sir Frederick) Bateman: Physician at the Norfolk and Norwich Hospital; his interest in nervous disease gained him an international reputation. Had been Sheriff in 1872; Magistrate; died in 1904 at the age of 80.
> 2. William Bateman, Bishop of Norwich 1344–55; founded Trinity Hall, Cambridge, to train clerics to replace those who had died in the Black Death.

Thursday 25

After Church a most worrying Chapter – on returning to luncheon with Bensly, I found a letter from the Dn. of Winchester, apologizing for short notice of a meeting called for Monday next in London by the Dean of Canterbury, to which the Deans and Canons of all 'landed' Chapters are invited to consider the 'situation', & what can be done to remedy it[1] – I immediately called on the 3 Canons, and it was eventually arranged that Heaviside and Nisbet shd. go to London to attend this meeting.

> 1. In the 19th Century Dean and Chapter income came largely from the property they owned in the Close, and in town and country. The Ecclesiastical Commissioners wanted to take over the Capitular Estates and run them more efficiently. The E.C. would pay an annual income to the Cathedral in exchange for its estates, until it was possible to re-endow it with an estate which would produce an equivalent income. The Depression of the 1880s undermined the scheme. Hence the meeting in London.

Friday 26

After Mg. Church, went to (1) Nevill's, to tell him the arrangements for Heaviside & Nisbet's going to London ... (3) the Chief Constable's Office, to talk about Police protection for the Cloister on the nights of the Oratorios; ... (5) the Post Office, where I had an interview with Mr. Winch about the young man Harcourt, & got the particulars – then home to luncheon – afterwards wrote (1) to the Postmaster General about Mr. Harcourt;[1] (2) The Lord Chancellor, answering his question about St. George's, Bloomsbury ... (4) Conrad Hinds Howell, enquiring about the incomes of Bps.

1. A young Post Office official had asked Goulburn to write to the Postmaster General on his behalf about some trouble which he had incurred inadvertently.

Tuesday 30   St. Andrew

A long seance with Heaviside, in wh, he told me all that had passed yesterday at the Dean of Canterbury's meeting of the Landed Chapters in London – a Committe was formed of the Deans of Cant., Peterboro', Winchester, Canons Nisbet, Crosse, Rawlinson, to draft and present a petition to Ld. Salisbury to bring in a bill enabling the E.C. to relieve the Chapters, whose incomes fall short of the sums fixed at the time of their Commutations – The Deans of Carlisle & Chester said their incomes did not fall short – wrote a letter to Conrad Hinds Howell, from whom I received a most interesting communn. about Bishop's incomes, with an Act & a Report.

DECEMBER

Wednesday 1

The Oratorio at 7.30 went off well; the organization and arrangement, and the conduct of the people perfect – but I confess I was not interested or edified – I constantly kept losing my place in the words, and the body of voice seemed to me not sufficient for the building; and the Oratorio (Spohr's 'Last Judgement') defective in melody; the Overture interminable – I spoke for about 15 min. on "Oh that I had wings like a dove", the yearning of the soul for rest.

Thursday 2

Rose feeling very creaky – at 10 Service – then heavy snow storm came on – at 1 o'clock all the world came to luncheon – I think

21 in all – some talk with the De Satges who staid after the rest had gone to Miss Patteson's Meeting at Noverre's Room, Bishop presiding – the ladies returned from the meeting before Church (at 5) – There dine here tonight ... with our four selves 12.

Monday 6

After Mg. Service wrote a letter giving advice in a sad case of conscience, and then carefully looked over my Chapter Notes and prepared for tomorrow – then some Hebrew – after luncheon called on Medley[1], who took a walk with me – we had some talk about the proposal to restrict the Lay Clerks to a particular fortnight for their holiday, all holidays to be taken together.

1. The Revd E.S. Medley had, this year, become Vicar of St Gregory's.

Wednesday 8

No going to Church except at 7.30 for the Oratorio Service – I saw 'Spaull' about his reading desk and seat, for which he had charged £7. 7, if we purchased, but declined to take anything for the loan; Alden, and told him he must be content with £2 for preparing the sacramental bread, and was to send in the Baker's bill to Nevill – Admitted Bartie and Bulmer Precentor and Sacrist – Bensly had luncheon here – The little Cartwrights came to stay with us till it was time to go to Church – I spoke on "Come unto me, all ye, etc." – then the Choir gave Mozart's 'Requiem' – I stirred up the congregation to give more liberally to the expenses – We got out about 9.15.

Thursday 9

After Church a walk with Nisbet on the Newmarket Rd. – on my return found Hinds Howell here for luncheon; he had come in about making an alteration to his will – worked all the afternoon at letters – sent Mother Adele[1] £5 out of the Communion Alms with £5 of my own; £10 to Mr. Ram for the roof of his Church[2]. (3) Nevill about my interviews with Alden (Eucharistic Bread), and Spaull (Preacher's Chair and Faldstool).

1. Mother Lavinia, Foundress of the Community of All Hallows, Ditchingham, had, as her co-foundress, Mother Adele. It was to her that Goulburn sent his gift of £10.
2. St John, Timberhill.

Saturday 11

Our wedding day – Auntie gave me a writing table candlestick with Lucifers, etc. and a silverine pencilcase and the sweetest possible word on a scrap of paper – I had bought for her at Brighton four pottery flowers in gutta percha – I wrote to Frederica, thanking her for the Bp. of Truro's[1] Book, 'Laws of the Kingdom of Heaven'.

> 1. The Rt Revd George Wilkinson, D.D. Later became Bishop of St Andrew's and Primus of the Episcopal Church of Scotland.

Wednesday 15
Raining all day; unable to get out – Service at 10 with Nisbet, Bartie, Moore – almost all the rest of the day studying the P.B. Version of the Psalms, and placing in parallel col. the LXX, Vulg., Douay. A.V., P.B., R.V., wh. interests me much, but I am going into it as usual too elaborately – Alas! for the Oratorio tonight; the weather is so bad that no attendance can be expected! – However, there was a better attendance than ever before – I returned to my Stall after the Sermon, and was able to hear the singing better, and to follow the words in the Book – The Collection, however was worse than ever.

Tuesday 21   St. Thomas
Church at 10 – then a walk with Bartie on the Thorpe Road, talking about tomorrow's Oratorio and music for the lower orders in the Cathedral (as at Gloucester) – wrote to Bulmer, accepting his dedication [of] Hymn Tunes to me – at 2.30 held a Chapter which lasted till 6 – Waters appeared and asked for reduction; Mr. Wright to talk about the report he had made of the condition of the new marshes; Brown also, in a very excited state on account of his having been kept shivering in the hall – we thot. him flushed with drinking.

Wednesday 22
Answered a letter from B.C. telling me of his journey to Rome, and inveighing agst. Bishop of London[1] for his censure of Beresford Hope and the late Mr. [blank][2] who joined him in building All Saints – also wrote to little Buskins with a present – wrote to Mr. Colman, thanking him for sending £5 towards the collection tonight – Fraulein arrived about 5 p.m. and had some dinner; she seems to be very happy. – Service at 7.30; wretched evening, and the congregation not half it was on the other nights – I gave the address in the middle of the Oratorio, and divided it into two parts, so as to make two breaks in the music – the 'Requiem' is very dreary music, and I am not edified at all.

1. The Rt Hon. and Rt Revd Frederick Temple.
2. Beresford Hope gave the site for All Saints, Margaret Street, London; Henry Tritton gave the external fabric; so this is probably the latter.

Friday 24

Sent two cheques for charitable objects, one for the restoration of a Gilbertine[1] Church – read the news – the Conservatives furious with Lord R. Churchill – Church at 5; I preached my last Advent Lecture. At 11 o'clock today I distributed my Xmas gratuities.

1. Gilbert Sempringham (c.1088–1189), founder of the Order, the Chief of the 13 Houses being at Sempringham (Lincs.). The Order was composed of Nuns who followed the Cistercian Rule, and Augustinian Canons who ministered to them. It was an entirely English Order. Gilbert lived to be over 100. Had retired from his Abbacy before his death.

Saturday 25   CHRISTMAS DAY

Went with little F. and Ju to the Choral H.C. where we had about 62 communicants – I got a present of mittens from Fraulein, & from Frederica Tennyson's new book 'Locksley Hall sixty years after' – Xmas cards from Margie & Charie Nevill – happily a dearth of letters – At 10.45 the Bishop preached on 'The Word was made flesh', but was to me almost inaudible – after luncheon, Ju, Fraulein, and I walked <u>thro'</u> Lady Harvey's grounds[1] and returned by Plumstead Road, a feat I have not performed for many a long day – Wrote ... to a Mr. Joseph Jacobs who has sent the programme of the proposeed Anglo-Jewish Exhibition, asking whether we have exhibits bearing on the history of the Jews in England – There dine here tonight Nisbet, his wife, sister, & son and the two Miss Maitlands and St. Emma.

1. Lady Harvey had died some years before, but Gulbourn still referred to the grounds in this way.

Tuesday 28   Holy Innocents

Howlett called, to ask me to right him as to what he was to receive for looking after Commn. Plate, & helping in the nave, wh. I did by a letter to Bensly – After luncheon, at wh. Archbold[1] looked in to ask me to sign a cheque for Tg. School, walked for an hour in garden, reading the Times – Mrs. Symonds & Miss Evans came in – the Pin has had a sort of formation cut out of his right eye today without being submitted to Chloroform; dreadful pain in all the nerves of head afterwards – Several Innocents came to tea, cakes & Xmas presents – a whole batch of Nevills, the little Moores, Henry Nisbet, etc. etc. – they are to have games in the Library afterwards.

1. Principal of the Diocesan Training Institution for Teachers.

Thursday 30
After Mg. Church a walk with Nisbet on the Newmarket Road – coming back, we called at Mrs. Evans's to enquire for the 'Pin' – found Mr. Robinson[1] there, who said the Pin had better not see anybody for 2 or 3 days; going on favourably – Auntie went to an afternoon Entertainment for the children at the Jenny Lind.

> 1. Haynes Sparrow Robinson, Esq., M.R.C.S., Surgeon, 50, Bethel Street.

Friday 1
Ch. at 10 – then finished off my own Sermon on the Barren Fig Tree, to be distributed between tonight and tomorrow morning – then to Mrs. Evans's to inquire for Symonds – I saw him and Mrs. Symonds, the right eye half open, but the left bandaged – He seemed to be in good spirits, but is not allowed to talk much.

1887

JANUARY

Saturday 1   Circumcision
H.C. at 8 a.m. – I preached from the wooden lectern – about 30 commts. – after Bkfst. wrote a long letter to Mr. Scott of the Museum about his work (names of English Incumbents) – wrote to Mr. Justice Denman[1] thanking him for Iambic Translation of 'Black Eyed Susan', and to Mr. Joseph Cawis about St. William of Norwich – Fraulein and Frederica are with us this evening; I suppose we shall have elder wine.

> 1. George Denman (1819–96): Judge of High Court of Justice, Queen's Bench division 1881–92; published translations in Greek, Latin, and English verse.

Wednesday 5
Snow falling all day – Occupied all day in drawing up Exam. Papers for the Choristers, and in allotting the Exam. between the Minor Canons and myself – Sent a small subscription to Ranworth Church – At 6 the Choristers came to dinner, and Dr. Bates[1] with them – a very pleasant conversation with him afterwards on the hours of Service in the Cathedral, chanting of Minor Canons, etc.

> 1. Dr Bates, Organist during Goulburn's last 3½ years in Norwich, had a liking and affection for him. When, as a rather nervous young Organist he had come for interview, Goulburn's kindly and encouraging welcome had put him at ease, and when he took up the appointment Goulburn gave him much support.

Saturday 8
Nevill still ill[1] – in the morning wrote to ... Bellett, who had asked my authority for the assertion that the Czar is ordained Bp., Priest, & Deacon, at the time of his Coronation – the answer from Stanley's 'Eastern Church', gave me much trouble – Mrs. Pin came to luncheon, and later Maimie and Hinds Howell, who told me he had been offered 2 Bishoprics – wrote to little Buskins, thanking for her Almanac.

> 1. He had Bronchitis.

Monday 10
Nevill ill again – snow and ice everywhere – sent for Thompson & Browne about sweeping & gravelling the Close – wrote ... to Prof. Charteris[1], thanking him for his 'Year Book of the Kirk' – to

Preb. Stephens, signing a petition agst. the publication of Divorce Trails – in the evening Auntie helped me in drawing up some questions on the Ch. Service for the Choristers (from Evan Daniell's Book).

> 1. Prof. A.H. Charteris (1835–1908): Professor of Biblical Criticism, Edinburgh University 1868–98. Moderator of the General Assembly 1892.

Wednesday 12

Heaviside has kindly taken Nevill's residence for him – Charlie Nevill called in the Mg. to tell me that the doctor thinks his father's complaint will turn to gout – after luncheon a walk first in the garden, then in the Cloister – In the latter Bartie joined me, & talked of the popular sacred music & singing wh. they wish to have in the Nave of the Cathedral, after the manner of Gloucester – wrote about the Missions to Seamen, promising a collection in the Cathedral, possibly on a Sunday aftern. in Lent – In the evening arrived the awful news of poor Northcote's[1] sudden death at Ld. Salisbury's – read Froude's History to Auntie.

> 1. Sir Stafford Northcote (1818–87), 1st. Earl of Iddesleigh 1859; Foreign Sec. 1886, but resigned six months later, dying suddenly on the day of his resignation.

Friday 14

Before Bkfst., and all morning, engaged in composing and writing out a letter for the 'Daily Press' about the Coron. Bible[1] – Nevill sent tidings thro' Charlie that the unemployed[2] were breaking windows in the Town, and that the gates had better be shut; instructed Spruce to do this – went up to the Editorial Officer of the Daily Press, and asked the Editor to insert my letter, wh. he will do tomorrow, if he has space – then into the Market Place, where the unwashed were loafing about – met Genl. Cockburn who told me several of them had been seized by the Police – they are Socialists come down from London – then went into Stacy's shop; he had not suffered, but Creeny[3] had had a stone thrown at his head – then went on to Symond's and sat with him, & found him better.

> 1. Goulburn had spent some time on the problem of two Coronation Bibles from the Queen's Coronation (June 28, 1838). The son of the Bishop of Winchester at that time (Bishop Sumner) said that his father possessed the Bible on which Queen Victoria took her Coronation Oaths, and it had been bequeathed to him. On the other hand, Norwich Cathedral possessed a Bible in which Bishop Stanley had written that this was the actual Bible "on which her Majesty Queen Victoria took the usual oaths at her coronation". Eventually Goulburn reached the conclusion that the

Winchester Bible was that on which the Queen had *taken* her oath, and the Norwich Bible that on which she had *signed* her oath.
2. In the 1880s Trade Unionism and Socialism were seen as movements to be profoundly feared by the prosperous section of society, and the unemployed and many of those in poverty were seen as embodying these movements. Goulburn had great sympathy for the unfortunate individual and often helped him or her; but he had little or no sympathy for the 'unemployed' as a body.
3. The Vicar of St Michael at Thorn.

Monday 17

Church alone (with Bartie) at 10 – Heaviside staid at home, to be with Mrs. H. while Willie underwent an operation by Cadge[1] – After Church called on the Bp. to get a little light on the subject (Marriage Laws) which he proposes for his Hon. Can. Meeting – then a walk – in returning looked in at Heaviside's to enquire after Willie; he was under ether, when the operation was done – wrote a long letter to B.C. in answer to his criticism of my Phrase "Christ pleading the merits of His sacrifice".

1. William Cadge (1822–1903): "East Anglia's leading surgeon of the second half of the 19th century" with an international reputation. When, in 1904, a memorial window was dedicated to him in the North Transept of Norwich Cathedral, the ceremony was attended by surgeons from twenty countries. (Dr A. Batty Shaw, 'Norfolk and Norwich Medicine' 1992).

Wednesday 19

Church twice – A heavy cold – First Choristers' Examn. Paper set after Church at 11 (Brockbank sat with the Boys) – then up to see Symonds, who however could not see me, being worse – A thaw, which makes the streets swim with mud, but lovely overhead – A second Exam. Paper set at 2.30 – Went with Ju to a Jenny Lind Genl. Meeting at 3 – Mayor[1] presided & Bp., Hinds Howell, & many others – Mr. Hoare[2] made a very good speech.

1. Sir Harry Bullard.
2. The Revd W.M. Hoare, Rector of Colkirk.

Saturday 22

Attended a meeting called by Winter[1] of East Bradenham at the Clerical Rooms at 12 – Ruri-decanal Secretaries were all invited, but hardly half a dozen came – Hinds Howell was there however, and William Stracey – We talked over the proposed S.P.G. Conferences, and the celebration of Aug. 12 as the Centenary of the Colonial Episcopate[2], but made very little way – Afterwards felt very poorly & much chilled by the temperature of the Clerical Rooms –

1. Diocesan Organizing Sec. of S.P.G. There were some 50 SPG Deanery Secs. throughout the Diocese, of whom only 6 came to this meeting.

2. The Rt Revd Samuel Seabury was the first Bishop of the Protestant Episcopal Church of America, consecrated in 1784 in Aberdeen by Bishops of the Episcopal Church of Scotland. But, the Rt Revd Charles Inglis was *the first colonial Bishop* consecrated by Bishops of the Church of England for Novia Scotia in 1787.

Wednesday 26

Church at 10 – <u>Viva Voce</u> Bible Examination at the School (with Bartie and Auntie) till luncheon time – Canons Venables and Frere at luncheon – then Examn. again till <u>3.15</u> wh. closes the work of the Examination – at 5 went to the Palace in the carriage – a gt. number of Hony. Canons – I read my short Paper, & then Perowne[1] read a very able and clear paper, taking a difft. line from mine – Heaviside and Frere had a little fencing – Winter, Venables, and Frere, went to the Palace to dinner.

1. The Archdeacon of Norwich and Rector of Redenhall.

Saturday 29

At 10 o'clock came Bartie, & we made out the Class List, Prize list, etc. etc. – Church at 3 – then distribution of Prizes in the Vestry – present Nevill, Bartie & Brockbank.

•••

The Goulburns are now away from Norwich for a short break until February 19, visiting relations and friends at Eydon (especially 'Hen-pen' until February 5, and then going to their house at Brighton.

•••

Monday 31   From Norwich to S. Pancras

Left Norwich w. Ju (Rose following by a later train) at 7.30 – arrived, went to Bearnard[1], who operated – then to Club for luncheon – then to Goslings, where drew for £15; and invested the £1000 Chilian Bonds just paid off, in a new Chilian loan wh. only pays 4. 10 instead of 6 pr. Cent – so interest falls off! – had called previously at Pratt's to order greatcoat & two pairs of trousers – after tea and a little reading at Club, walked to Cousin MAC's – then to our Hotel (Ogle's) – am expecting Morgiana every moment – he came, and gave me a course of treatment; am to see him again on Saturday – Tom[2] looked in in the Evening & told us the alarming reports they had recd. of Frances from St. Moritz; he, Bitta. & Marian are crossing tomorrow, to go to her.

1. Chiropodist.
2. Thomas Leslie-Melville-Cartwright and his wife Elizabeth ('Bitta') had five children. Marian, the third, was 26, and Frances the fourth, was 25. Whatever the crisis was now, Frances lived to be 76!

FEBRUARY

Wednesday 2   Purification of the B.V.M.
London to Eydon

Auntie went to H.C. – after Bkfst., walked (in a very keen air) to Club – walked back – Rose had gone out, and our things were not packed – It appeared from Mrs. Ogle that Rose thot. we were not going till tomorrow – so we went at 1.30 from Euston (via Northamp., Blisworth, & Pinkney) leaving her to follow via Banbury – got here about 4.30; found dear Hen-Pen[1] like himself and very much better than we had ventured to hope.

   1. Col. Henry Cartwright (1814–90), one of Julia's brothers.

Saturday 5   Eydon to Brighton
At 10 a.m. we look a loving leave of Hen-pen ... London – straight to Morgiana's who prescribed & to whom I gave Maudie's sensational novelette, 'Dr. Jekyll and Mr. Hyde'[1], wh. I had read in the train – left London for <u>West</u> Brighton at 3.27 – in the evening read to Auntie the celebration of the American Episcopate in Lambeth Palace & Ld. Salisbury's interview with the State directed Colonies Association.

   1. Robert Louis Stevenson, 'The Strange Case of Dr. Jekyll and Mr. Hyde' (1886).

Monday 7   At Brighton
Went out to make small purchases, and bought B. Hannington's[1] Life at Treacher's – then to the Vicarage – saw Mrs. Hannah, & the Archdn., before he started for Convocation – borrowed of him Lightfoot on Coloss. and Hessey's[2], 'Sunday' wh, I am now reading.

   1. E.C. Dawson, 'James Hannington' (Bishop of East Equatorial Africa, who had been murdered in Uganda in 1885). Just published 1887.
   2. The Ven. James Hessey, Archdeacon of Middlesex 1875–92; had been Headmaster of Merchant Taylors' School 1847–70. Bampton Lecturer 1860 on 'Sunday: Its Origin, History, and Present Obligation'.

Monday 14   At Brighton
A gouty wretched day – news from Heaviside of the Unemployed coming into the Cathedral, but going out quietly before the Sermon – wrote to him – also ... (3) to Bartie, sending him my Lenten Bill, wh. is at last complete, all but Barker's[1] subject; (4) Barker, asking him to send his subject to Bartie – I walked to James Anderson's house and back, on my way back

calling at Truefitt's to have my hair cut & shampooed – on my return finished my notes for a 3d. Lenten Lecture on the Xtian Sunday.

>   1. The Revd R.V. Barker, Vicar of St Mark's, Lakenham since 1885.

Wednesday 16   Last day at Brighton

Walking is labour and sorrow to me – went out and got back [my] watch from Glading's, and also bought a photograph easel for Buskins, and some toys for Chucks and Chubbs[1] – Ju and I took a fly 1st. to Henson's, where I had seen a letter weight, wh. I bought her.

>   1. Augusta Thomas's two elder daughters Augusta (5) and Ella (4).

Tuesday 22

Read a gt. part of 'She'[1] – is the whole thing a fiction? – If so, it is a very elaborate, and a stupid one.

>   1. 'She – A History of Adventure': A Novel by Sir H. Rider Haggard (1856–1925), the Norfolk Novelist, just published. 'She' is a mysterious Queen who has the secret of eternal life, 'She-Who-Must-Be-Obeyed'.

Wednesday 23   **ASH WEDNESDAY**

An hour's walk in the garden from 2 to 3.20 wh. seemed to do me good – Nevill looked in for a minute after Mg. Church, to explain about the Cathedral being cold – I read the three Services of the day at home, & found pleasure in doing so – Nevill took the Comminn. Service in the Morg. and Bartie is to preach for me at 5 p.m. – Heaviside joined me in my walk in the garden and we talked about 'She' – he will try and find out whether there is such a potsherd as that of Amenarias – got a letter from little F.[1] sending me an acct. of the restoration of Derry Cathedral; rather interesting.

>   1. Goulburn was very friendly with the Alexanders (Bishop of Derry, later Primate), and his wife Frances (Fanny), the Hymnwriter. Little 'F' is almost certainly Fanny.

Friday 25

Nevill is down again with bronchitis, and I accordingly postponed the Chapter to Wednesday next, to give him time to get better – gave my odds & ends of <u>Agenda</u> to Bensly, who is going over to Plumstead to mark trees on Wiley's farm – news came today of poor John Gurney's[1] death at Cannes – Ripley & Mrs. R. were with him; it is supposed the earthquakes may have hastened his end.

1. John Gurney was the son of Mrs Ripley, wife of Canon W.N. Ripley, by her former marriage. He was 41 when he died, and his father had also died young. He had been Mayor of Norwich 1885–86. In 1883 he had given £500 towards the purchase of the Castle (former prison) by the Corporation. In 1886, when Mayor, he suggested that the Castle become a Museum and offered £5000 for its conversion. He died before giving this sum, but his widow honoured his promise. He had also offered £1000 towards the laying out of Mousehold Heath as a Public Park, when it was conveyed by the Ecclesiastical Commissioners (on behalf of the Dean and Chapter) in 1880, and, as Mayor, in 1886, he had opened a new road across it.

Monday 28

Rose not till 8, after a very bad night – When dressed, I walked in the garden in beautiful sunshine for 1 & ¼ ths. hours – Mr. Donne[1] came and walked by my side for some time (he comes to be admitted Surrogate[2]) & talked about Yarmouth, Mr. Moore, Venables, etc. – soon after came Muriel, and seems to think I must have had steel given me with the strychnine after luncheon – drove with Ju to Drayton, & saw Hinds Howell, Maimie, & Lady Briggs – as we were going away, Agnes drove up (she had returned from taking Conrad to the Station) and we had a good view of the two Tartar Horses – wrote in books to be sent to the Baden Baden Church Lending Library.

1. The Revd W. Donne, the new Vicar of Yarmouth.
2. Surrogate = A Clergyman, or other person, appointed by the Bishop as his deputy to grant licenses for marriage without Banns.

MARCH

Wednesday 2

A Chapter at 11 – not as worrying & lengthy as usual – It was over before luncheon – wrote a line to Miss Marsh thanking for her life of Lord Cairns[1], wh. came this morning, & to Mr. Tancock about a woman recommended by him for the Gt. Hospital[2] – read aloud to Ju in the evening the end of Burke's speech on American Taxation and some of Keightely's History on the American War.

1. Hugh McCalmont Cairns, 1st Earl Cairns, Lord Chancellor 1874–80. Died 1885.
2. The Foundation of the Gt Hospital dates from 1249. In 1835 the ancient Charities of Norwich were placed under two bodies of Trustees: the Church List and the General List. The Gt Hospital came under the former, and new Trustees for it were elected in 1837. The age of admission was raised from 60 to 65, and, in 1858, it was laid down that all those nominated for admission must have lived in the City of Norwich for at least three years – a rule which still stands.

Thursday 3

All the morning spent in writing out fair the Chapter notes of yesterday – Muriel came & touched my throat, rather relieving me – then Bartie, who brot. Music Prizes for me to write the Boys' names in – I told him that we agreed in Chapter that our popular musical Service (after the Gloucester[1] Pattern) might be held in the Cathedral.

> 1. In 1886, Gloucester, successfully, held a number of free performances of sacred music in the Cathedral (including Handel, Beethoven, Mozart and Mendelssohn) which attracted (to put it in 19th Century terms) "all classes of people".

Friday 4

I kept in all day, in very low spirits – Heaviside came in, in a fuss about John Gurney's funeral, to wh. it is arranged that he is to go in our carriage – I wrote a line to Nevill & to the Bp. about the Services this evening; then a line to an American lady Mrs. Coles who has had 1000 copies of the 1st. part of my book on the Devotional Study [of] the Scripture printed "for private distribution" – I grieve to see that Mr. Raikes has got into trouble about an appointment at the Post Office – hoped to be helped thro' this evening – Got thro' pretty well, but was much too long. ('the Ground of the 4th Commt.')

• •

On Saturday, March 5, Goulburn travelled to Barnack, six miles NW of Peterborough, to stay with Canon Argles and his family, and preach in Peterborough Cathedral on Sunday Evening. He returned home on Tuesday (8), arriving at 4 p.m.

• •

Tuesday 8

On arriving wrote to ... (4) Liddon[1], signing a memorial to Abp. of Cant. to give some re-assurance about Bishopric of Jerusalem[2] – Medley called to tell us about his Parish, & asked a subscrn. for Cassocks of his Choristers.

> 1. H.P. Liddon: Canon and then Chancellor of St Paul's Cathedral.
> 2. The Anglican Bishopric in Jerusalem (founded 1841) was beset with difficulties. The first Bishop, nominated by the Church of England died after four years; the King of Prussia had the right to nominate the next Bishop. He nominated a German-speaking Swiss, who was Bishop for 33 years and became the target of much criticism. On his death in 1879, the Church of England chose an Irish Missionary, Barclay, who died within two years. The Bishopric then lapsed for seven years. Against the advice of Chancellor Liddon (who had travelled extensively in Palestine) the Archbishops, in 1887, announced the appointment of a new Bishop *in* Jerusalem, and the Jerusalem and the East Mission came into being to support the Bishopric.

Wednesday 9

After Church Miss Carver came to beg; and then Nevill, to announce Spelman's[1] valuation of the Arminghall Estate (£16,335) – then walked up to Mousehold House, to thank Mr. Hackblock for his key, and by the use of it got through his spinney – neither of them at home – called on Heaviside – H. had heard at the Club[3] of the excellence of Medley's Sermons, the beauty of the singing, and the fulness of the Church – Church again at 5 – afterwards Nevill told me of Colman's[2] declining, thro' Garrett Taylor, to give more than £16,335 – Saw Bensly, and arranged with him to have a Chapter about it on Saturday at 11.

1. H.W. Spelman and Co Auctioneers, Valuers, and Estate Agents, 24, St Giles' Street.
2. J.J. Colman would be interested in this land, because it was just beyond the South-Eastern outskirts of the city, close to Carrow House and Works, and Trowse Mills.
3. Probably the Norfolk Club in the vicinity of the Guildhall, but in process of purchasing 17, Upper King Street, moving there at the end of 1888.

Saturday 12

At 3 Nevill installed Archdeacon Woolley[1], but I was not present – After Church [at 10 a.m.] a short Chapter, principally to agree upon the next step to be taken in the negotiation with Colman for purchase of the Arminghall Estate – agreed that Bensly shd. (en route to the Continent) endeavour to see Smith & Gore & ask them the lowest price wh. E.C. would allow us to take – Margie & Helena Nevill came to luncheon.

1. As Archdeacon of Suffolk, continuing as Rector of East Bergholt.

Friday 18

Heaviside sent across a letter from Nisbet, saying that it was resolved yesterday by the Cathedral Committee to accept gratefully Childer's Cathedral Bill, Smith & Goschen having assured the Deans of Cant. & Peterboro' that we were not likely to get better terms – Hereupon I wrote to Nisbet that I thot. he had exceeded his powers, our Chapter not having consented to Childer's Bill – Ju had a meeting all the morning about some new Refuge, to which came Mrs. Bullard & Ly. Mary Currie & others – Muriel came to me, and pronounces my liver still to be all wrong – I am hoping to be helped thro' tonight, but what if paroxyms of coughing come on? – think of writing to Mr. Dixon about his mistake in making Goodrich of Ely[1] to have been the last ecclesiastic who was Chancellor.

1. Thomas Goodrich, Bishop of Ely (Jan. 1552–July 1553); Stephen Gardiner, Bishop of Winchester (August 1553–Nov. 1555); Nicholas Heath, Archbishop of York (Jan. 1556–Nov. 1558, – the latter being the last.

Sunday 20   Lent 4

Did not go out – Read Mattins and the Commn. Service alone in the drawing room & afterwards Is. Williams[1] on the Ep. & Gosp – Then my own Paper on the Collects – drafted anew the notes of my Lecture for Friday next – Mr. Muriel came before luncheon, with bad news about Mrs. Hansell's State (Ju saw her today) and news that the Bp. starts tomorrow on a Confirm. Tour[2] – Read the Afternoon Service with Ju. In the evening occupied with my two concluding Lenten Lecures.

1. Isaac Williams (1802–65): Tractarian poet and theologian. Wrote a 'Devotional Commentary on the Gospel Narrative' (8 vols.).
2. Bishop Pelham had increased the number of Confirmation Centres from about 25 at the beginning of his Episcopate to about 62 in later years, so that the Candidates would not have to travel so far from home. On average, there were from 3,000 to 4,000 candidates each year, and this, of course, included three quarters of Suffolk in addition to Norfolk. So his Confirmation Tours, lasting several days at a time, could be very trying for a man of 76. But he continued this plan up to his retirement six years later.

Monday 21

I went for ½ an hour in the garden before luncheon, and also for ½ an hour afterwards, during wh. Heaviside joined me, and we agreed that he & Nevill shd. draft a letter to the E.C. asking them whether they wd. allow us to sell the Arminghall Estate for £18,000[1].

1. Pringle, of the Ecclesiastical Commissioners, replied "saying that the E.C. will assent to the sale of Arminghall at any price *not under* £18,000."

APRIL

Saturday 2

Ch. at 10 – then came a letter from Mr. Margoliouth[1], saying he will not be here till 8 – this made me go round to the Barretts, the Moores, and Dr Bates (all of whom had been asked to meet him) to put them all off – Mr. Margoliouth arrived at 8.15.

1. Organising Sec. of Parochial Missions to the Jews Society.

Sunday 3   Palm Sunday

Church at 10.45 – After luncheon went w. Mr. Margoliouth to enquire for the Bp., and then took Mr. M. to see the Lollards Pit

– At 3.30 he preached an excellent Sermon – In the latter part, which was about the Parochial Missions to the Jews, his voice became fainter – He dined with us at 6 and was very pleasant.

Tuesday 5
After Mg. Ch. went in fly with Margoliouth to the Music House[1], and shewed him the chamber in wh. the Jew lived, and the crypt underneath – Mr. Margoliouth left us about 4 o'clock for Yarmouth.

> 1. The Music House, King Street (now part of Wensum Lodge) is the oldest house in Norwich, where, in the 12th Century lived Jurnet and his son Isaac, two of the wealthiest Jews in England.

Friday 8   **GOOD FRIDAY**
Went to Ch. at 8 with Ju – after luncheon, dissatisifed with my existing notes for this evening, & re-wrote half of them – wrote to the Bp. about the Sunday arrangements being made – Hewson called with a telegram saying his father is dying; wd. I lend him £4, as he has not money eno' to go to Ireland – Foolishly (perhaps) I advance him £5 of his Stipend.

Sunday 10   **EASTER DAY**
Did not go to Church at 8 a.m. (Ju went) – Church at 10.45 (with the two Canons, & 3 M.C.s) – I preached on "Touch me not", the Sermon wh. I wrote yesterday morg.; it was about 20 min. – then I celebrated the H.C. assisted by Heaviside, Bulmer & Moore – Church again at 3.30 – One of Handel's long Anthems – Nevill preached with a good deal of life on a text in I. Cor XV.

•••
The Goulburns are away from April 13 to May 18, doing the usual round of friends and relations: London April 13–14; Eyhorne April 14–18; Aynhoe April 18 to May 2 (with a Levee in London on April 25); Edcott May 2–9 (with a day in Leamington with Lili on May 5); Eydon 9–16; London 16–18 and back to Norwich.
•••

Wednesday 13   [*Norwich to London*]
Left Norwich with Ju at ½p.7 – on arriving I went (1) Spratt's, to pay for Stocking (Elastic) – (2) Grant & Cockburn, to try on & have gaiters altered; (3) Club for luncheon – looked over Gam. Parry's Book on Art, Moberly's, Wm of Wykeham, & Mcarthy's 'Ireland since the Union' – thence to Blomfield's to consult him

about a credence & railing for the Cathl. – then to Hotel where found a letter from Vincent[1], announcing his resignation of Postwick; wrote off to Lord Rosebery at once & sent my letter by a messenger to Lansdowne House.

> 1. The Revd Sir Wm. Vincent, Bart., had been ordained for 29 years, and had been Rector of Postwick for 23. He was a J.P. He retired to Leatherhead, Surrey, where he continued to be a J.P., and where he also became a Deputy Lieutenant. Lord Rosebery was the Patron of Postwick.

Thursday 14   From Ogle's to Eyhorne

Left London at 2.45 for Hollingbourne – after tea walked to the dear people in the other house[1], and saw the children who are very flourishing and interesting – Gerard looks pulled, but in excellent spirits – He is said to be going on quite satisfactorily.

> 1. Gerard and Augusta (Buskyns) Thomas and their family. The Goulburns were staying at Eyhorne House, the home of Louisa de Visme Thomas, Goulburn's cousin, and widow of Richard Thomas, Gerard's parents. Gerard and Augusta lived in a house on the estate.

Sunday 17

A happy day – Church at 11 – I admitted little B's child into the Church after first lesson (Ethel Lilian Mary de Visme) – she was as good as gold, and so were Chucks & Chubbs who were present – afterwards I preached on "Galilee the trysting place" – 5 o'clock tea at Gerard's – A light tea here at 7.30; and then a great deal of conversation with Sir F.G.[1] – how tiring is much conversation even when agreeable!

> 1. Sir Frederick Goldsmid (1818–1908) was a Major-General and an accomplished oriental linguist, who carried out important commissions in the East. Gerard, a Barrister, had accompanied him on his Special Mission to Persia. He would have had a family connection with Gerard, whose mother was the daughter of John Louis Goldsmid and Louisa Boscawen Goldsmid (nee de Visme). The latter's husband deserted her and the family, and they changed their name to de Visme.

Monday 18   From Eyhorne thro' London to Aynhoe

Little B came in to take leave of us – Sir F. Goldsmid, tho' he had come down in a 2d class carr. took a first, so that we might travel together – he talked enthusiastically about the Gordon Boys' Home[1] at Fareham, wh. I think I must support – on getting to London I went to Bearnard, and was operated upon – and then to Club, where I got a sight of the facsimile in 'The Times' of Parnell's letter to Egan, excusing himself for denouncing the murder of Ld. F. Cavendish & Mr. Burke in the House – then to MAC's to meet Ju; then to Paddington for 1 p.m. train.

1. The Gordon Boys' homes were founded to perpetuate the memory of Major-General Charles Gordon (1833–85), killed at Khartoum after sustaining a siege for 317 days.

Tuesday 19   At Aynhoe
Wrote to Mrs. Nevill before Bkfst. exhorting her to get a letter from the Bp. to Ld. Rosebery about Nevill's fitness for Postwick – in the mg., after looking at the article on Ld. Shaftesbury in the Edinburgh, & at Parnell's vehement repudiation of the letter to Egan in the 'Times', worked with Ju at preparing Services for the Jubilee[1] – then wrote a long letter to our Bp. about the celebration of the Jubilee in the Cathedral, & also about the Hospital Chaplaincy, to wh. he does not propose to appoint a <u>beneficed</u> clergyman.

1. Queen Victoria's Golden Jubilee (50 years) of her Coronation on June 28, 1837.

Wednesday 20   [At Aynhoe]
Wrote to Heaviside before Bkfst. expressing my idea of Barrett's holding the Hospital Chaplaincy in <u>commendam</u> with the Precentorship – finished drawing out with Ju a Form of Service for 8 a.m. on the Monday, Wednesday, Thursday of the Jubilee Week; than wrote to Bartie enclosing this Service; to Mr. Clarke of St. Michael's, who has applied for the Chaplaincy, & to Mr. Wilson of St. Stephen's, who writes in favour of Mr. Ward.

Thursday 21   [At Aynhoe]
Wrote to (1) Martin, about Sidney Pelham's qualifications for Hospital Chaplain; (2) Rev D. Dickson[1], about his application for the post – Buckley has an idea of writing to the 'Guardian' about two points in the Marriage Service: one, the impropriety of a woman giving the bride away (a patre velamico ejus); the other the still greater impropriety of children officiating as bridesmaids.

1. Vicar of St Martin-at-Oak since 1885.

Friday 22   [At Aynhoe]
A letter from Heaviside about 1. The Training School difficulties[1]. 2. The Bp's view of the Jubilee Service in Cath. 3. The Bp's plan for Hospital Chaplaincy; 4. The popular Music Service, at wh. 4000 [?] people were present; 5. Bishop's view of Vincent's resignation: 6. necessary repairs at Wyllies farm drains; 7. Colman's desire to delay beyond 2 years his settlement for Arminghall Estate.

1. In 1883, the Education Department had complained about the situation and condition of the Diocesan Teachers' Training Institution in St George's Plain. The Dean and Chapter offered two sites for a new College in 1885; but these were not approved. Finally, the Ecclesiastical Commissioners offered a site in College Road which was approved, and the new building was opened in October 1892.

Saturday 23 [At Aynhoe]
Cuckoo heard by the Dean for the 1st. time today – am going to give £20 to the new Fund for Clergy temporary Relief, Sons of Clergy[1].

1. The Sons of the Clergy Corporation was founded in 1655 and is still active today (1995) in helping Clergy and their families in need.

Friday 29 [At Aynhoe]
In the afternoon walked with the dean to Deddington, he reading by the way a Sermon preached by Farrar[1] at St. Paul's, exhibiting the vice and misery of London, together with its enormous wealth concentrated in the hands of a few – very disagreeable reading.

1. Frederic Wm. Farrar, at this time Canon of Westminster and Rector of St Margaret's; later (1895) Dean of Canterbury.

MAY

Thursday 5 From Edgcote to Leamington and back
The ailing tooth last stopped by White giving me pain, I resolved to go to Mr. Jepson at Leamington (33, Warwick Street), and have it out – at 11.25 went in Aubrey's Brougham to Banbury, reading en route Vaughan on the Philippians – finding Mr. Jepson out, I went on to Lili's, and gave her a letter from Ju – then to Mr. Jepson's at 1.30, where I had to wait about ½ an hour – he having tested the tooth strgly. advised its removal, and having applied a burning anodyne, he drew it very skilfully (about 4 seconds & ½) – I had a dreadful pain for a long time aftrwards, wh. he attributes to inflammation of the socket – the face-ache did not go off till I reached Edgcote again – Lili gave me a sumptuous luncheon, and then she and I went (1) to see her 'Shursh'[1]; (2) the Parish Church, where there is a side Altar, as at St. Martin's, Brighton; (3) a picture of Mr. Lewis, representing the Lord's Supper as it was, the Apostles on Oriental Divans round a table only a foot high; our LORD'S face worn, but dignified; he is about to give the sop to Judas who is on his left, St. John being on His right & St. James next to St. John – after a short drive, Lili dropped me at the Station.

1. Roman Catholic. After more than 60 years in England, Lili (Lady Cartwight) had not, apparently, entirely lost her Bavarian accent.

Friday 13 [At Eydon]
In the morning, a letter from Bartie, wh. I answered by sending him a circular both for the Parochial Clergy & for Dissenting Ministers, inviting them to attend Cathl. Jubilee Service on 21st. June – then finished my Ordination Sermon for Trin. Sunday – wrote to Cuf. Davie assenting to 2 Cathedral Services for the 5 Societies on Sept. 15 – also to Pilkington, declining to belong to C. of E. Purity Society[1].

1. Aimed at producing purity among men; a chivalrous respect for womanhood; the preservation of the young from contamination; rescue work; and a higher tone of public opinion. The two Archbishops were its Presidents, all of the English Bishops were Vice-Presidents; and, in the Diocese of Norwich, the Bishop and five clergy formed the Diocesan Committee.

Sunday 15   Rogation Sunday   [At Eydon]
After luncheon read a book of Arthur Hadd on the Apostolical Succession – I am just starting for Ch. to preach on "the flowers appear on the earth: the time of the singing of birds is come, etc." in Cant. II.

Wednesday 18   From Frederica's – home
Wrote to Mrs. Mortimer, answering her letter about Prayers for the Dead – Ju & I left London at 12 & got here by 4 – fewer letters to answer than usual – Mayor determines after all to stay at home on Jubilee Day – many gratified answers from Dissenting Ministers who are much pleased with being asked to Jubilee Service – Frank Grant (quondam Rugby Boy) has sent me his life of Johnson.

Thursday 19   ASCENSION DAY
Celebrated the H.C. at 8 a.m. with Nevill, Bartie & Moore; about 35 Commts. – at 10.45 the Bp. was there, the Master, Heaviside, Nevill, & the three M.C.s – I retired after my Sermon – after luncheon called on the Master, & saw him, Ludie[1] (who is to be ordained on a title from Mr. Blaxland on Trin. Sun) & Mary Stewart & Miss Old – It rained so hard that the Master & I were deprived of a walk – went home, when Heaviside & Willie called and sat some time – afterwards came the Master, & we made a vain attempt to walk, after wh. he sat with me telling me about the vast Organ wh. has been built by Boulton & Paull's[2] foreman,

& is now for sale – church again at 5, with rather a better congregation – preached on 'Civilisation, its use & abuse' – too long.

1. Ludovic Stewart Robinson, to be Curate of St Andrew, Haverstock Hill, N.W.
2. From an Ironmonger's Shop, founded in 1797, Moore and Barnard, on the corner of Lt London Street with London Street, there eventually emerged the giant Manufacturing Firm, Boulton and Paul.

Friday 20
Bartie came at 9.15, & opened his scheme of having the Jubilee Service in the Choir, using only the small organ – we settled the particulars of the Service & singing – wrote to the Mayor, who wishes to ask Bp. of Colchester[1] to his dinner on Tuesday.

1. The Rt Revd Alfred Bloomfield, D.D.

Saturday 21
After Mg. Church (Master, Bulmer) went down to the Precentor's, to communicate to him the letters recd. from Clergy, etc. about the Jubilee, and to discuss arrangements – at 11.45 went to Mr. White's who cleaned one of the back teeth, & took a mould of my mouth – home, and wrote a circular to Hon. Cans. about their stalls on the Jubilee Day – at 3 Church with Master & Bartie – then in carriage to Hellesdon House to see the Mayor & also to Bp. about Jubilee Service arrangements – very much depressed in the evening – sending circulars to Hon. Cans.

Monday 23
A long and worrying Chapter, in wh. it was settled to reverse all the proposals for Jubilee Service made by the Precentor & Bates, and to have the Service in the Nave, and use the great Organ – at 7.30 Ju, Heaviside, and I dined with H.H. to meet the Bp. of Colchester – a very lively evening – Bp. full of humour.

Tuesday 24
Wrote some letters in the morning, and received a remonstrance from Bartie as to our decision of yesterday – S.P.G. meeting at wh. I presided, at 2.15 – Bishop of C. plain & sensible – afterwards a monster luncheon – at 3 the Bp. preached well in an excellent voice on Ps. CVIII, 13 – At 7.30 was the Mayor's Dinner in the Greyfriar's Hill, to which I took the Master & Heaviside – I sat between the High Sheriff & Mr. Sam Hoare[1] – The latter talked about the Bp. of Ripon's Sermon on Sunday at St. Margaret's, and its effect upon Gladstone & Smith – the former (Sir Alfred Jodrell) seems to be right-minded & religious, but delicate – I had

to make a speech for the Bp., Clergy, & Mins. of all denominations wh. I managed to do with tolerable ease.

> 1. Samuel Hoare (in 1899 created a Baronet) was M.P. for Norwich for 20 years; "upright, warm-hearted, and patriotic politician and gentleman" (J.L. Smith-Dampier in 'East Anglian Worthies' – Blackwell 1949). He was a Member of the House of Laymen, and served on the Royal Commission on Ecclesiastical Discipline.

Wednesday 25

At 11.15 came Mr. Jones (Wesleyan), and Mr. McAllan[1], as deputation from Dissenters – they only wanted to be provided w. seats all together – very friendly interview – another harassing Chapter at 12 – Nevill started the idea of having music and choir in the Gallery, wh. seems good – nothing finally arranged – People's Music in the Cathedral at 8 – The Cathedral was crammed, but the music hardly spirited or loud eno' – I went to the extreme East End, but cd. hear very little – Preached a little on 'Fetch me a minstrel'.

> 1. The Revd W.A. McAllan (Presbyterian).

Friday 27

After Mg. Service at 10 saw the Master, Bartie & Bates, to make the final arrangements about the Jubilee Service – agreed to have the singers at the East End, but to have the Organ used for the Voluntary & for the chanting of the Psalm – Lesson to be read in the Nave – Heaviside came in at the end of our Deliberations, and acceded (he had been Prizegiving at the Commercil School).

Saturday 28

Interview with Brown about ... (2) Plan of the Cathedral for circulation – After Church called on Mr. Tancock to ask about his School's coming to Jubilee Service, and for a loan of the room for that day.

Tuesday 31

After Bkfst. Bartie came in to tell me that the Queen of the Sandwich Isds.[1] is coming to the Cathedral on Sunday, and that the Mayor wd. call on me about it – After Service at 10 went to Catton in a fly to call upon Col. Mansel about the Volunteers coming to the Jubilee Service; but he is in London – returned & wrote to him – then meditated a Jubilee Sermon on the 5th. Commt.

> 1. Sandwich Islands is the former name of the Hawaiian Islands. Under native rule until annexed by the U.S.A. in 1898; became the 50th State in 1959.

JUNE

Wednesday 1
A long morning with Bartie drawing up proceedings at the Jubilee Service – a Mr. Greer called, who said his wife was a descendant of Bp. Scambler[1], and that Scambler's heraldic device, a heart perpendicular was to be seen on the small gate giving access to the Bishop's Palace – Spaull in the Boss Book has said it was Lyhart's device – the Mayor called, and told me the particulars of the proposed visit of the Hawaiian Queen on Sunday and Monday – Tancock also called about the proposed rehearsal of the School children in his field on the 20th. June – Mr. Barrett came at 6.20 & talked over his work about the Musical Services for the people.

   1. The Rt Revd Edmund Scambler was Bishop of Norwich from 1586–95.

Saturday 4
A day of great worry – Heaviside called about our meeting the Queen at the West Door of the Nave tomorrow – worried in the evening by thot. about this Royal Visit.

Sunday 5   **TRINITY SUNDAY**
A much happier day – Ch. at 8 with the Bp. & the Candidates and Bartie; but no Canon was present, wh. (to say the least) looked bad – at 10.45 the Ordination, at wh. two of the new Yarmouth Curates were made Deacons, one a Mr. Pemberton – wrote a line to the Mayor about closing the Cathedral tomorrow, when the Queen is to be lionised – Service at 3.30 again, when there was a dense mob, filling the Cathedral and Upper Close – we went to the West Door, with the Mayor & Sheriff, to receive her Hawaiian Majesty (as with the Judges) – very difficult to clear a gangway.

Monday 6
At 11.45 went to lionise the Queen & Princess over the Cathedral – they kept us long waiting – The three Canons were there and Hinds Howell, and little Med., Bensly also, Brown, etc. – It was anything but a success – there was not time to do anything satisfactory, and had there been, communication thro' an imperfectly furnished interpreter wd. have been anything but satisfactory – I contrived, however, to introduce Mrs. Nevill's friend, Miss Haynes – At ½p.2 Ju and I went (in carriage, taking Heaviside) to the Mayor's Dejeuner, where I sat between the

Princess & Mrs. Steward of Rackheath – Princess delighted with Robinson's Sermon, and with some effect of the light at the time the account of our Saviour's Baptism was being read – Mayor proposed the Queen's health, to wh. the Charge d'Affaires responded very well, and then Cotman proposed the Mayor's health.

Monday 13
Wrote to Ly. Iddesleigh, from whom I received a most interesting letter, thanking me for the book I had sent poor Northcote, & wh. he had allowed me to inscribe to him – she is sending me her Book of his occasional pieces – Sent for Mr. Paris (Paris & Scott, Electricians) King St., to ask the probable expense of picking out the lines of the spire in light on the 21st. – £150!!

Wednesday 15
Wrote letters to the 5 Newspapers before Bkfst. – after Mg. Church came Foreman with my public letter for the Papers written out – At luncheon were Revd G.S. Barrett, Bartie, and Cap. Back of the Artillery; after luncheon went into the Cathl., and showed Mr. Barrett & Cap. Back the arrangements – soon after came in Col. Combe, Col. Finch, & an orderly, to whom I shewed their part of the arrangements – shortly after the Pin & Mrs. Pin, & Mr. Copeman[1] called – The latter promised to do what he could to make the Clergy come in surplices – then closed the Ch. and I and Bartie practised while Bates & Sophie listened – we settled that a faldstool placed in the Nave was the place to conduct the Service from – a Church Emigration[2] meeting was held in the Clerical Rooms today, Copeman presiding.

> 1. Canon A.C. Copeman, M.B., LL.D, Vicar of St Andrew's, Norwich; joint Rural Dean of Norwich since 1870; Chairman of the Norwich Board of Guardians; Board of Management of Norfolk and Norwich Hospital; Chairman of its Building Committee in the 1870s; a Founder and Sec. of the Norfolk and Suffolk Choral Association.
> 2. The Church Emigration Society was in constant touch with Clergy in the Colonies, who informed it of opportunities for people who wanted to emigrate. The Society tried to ensure that those whom it helped to emigrate were bona fida Church people, and of good character.

Thursday 16
Later in the afternoon the Mayor came to ask whether I wd. advise him on Sunday Evg. to go in state to the Princes' Street Chapel – on the whole I did so.

Friday 17
Jubilee on the brain! – After Church a short Chapter, in wh. we agreed to give everyone a Jubilee Gift except Timpson's men (amounting in all to £6. 15).

Saturday 18
Saw Mr. Hitchman[1] at the Police Office about the arrangement for Tuesday – the little Moores and Dorothy Bartie came to tea at 5, and Auntie gave them presents – A numerous 5 o'clock tea in the garden, the Berneys, Ensors, little Moores, Dorothy Bartie, etc. etc.

> 1. Robert Hitchman, Esq., Chief Constable, Superintendent of Fire Brigade, Inspector of Hackney Carriages, Common Lodging Houses, explosives, drugs, foods, etc.; his Office was in the Guildhall, Market Place.

Monday 20
At 5 Service again, but plain – then met Bartie & the Stewards to give instructions about tomorrow.

Tuesday 21
Jubilee Day – Up before 6 – corrected proofs of my Jubilee Sermon for the 'Norf. Chronicle' – Everything went off well at ½p.10 – very quiet & Orderly – the Band of the 19th. Hussars very effective – None of the Ministers came in gowns – the Coronation Anthem superb – Bp. did his part admirably – It lasted only ¾ths. of an hour – then went with Pom to the Guildhall, & afterwards to the Mayor's Platform, where the spectacle of the Market Place thronged[1] was very striking, & the singing of 'Home, sweet home', by the children specially touching – then home for a mouthful of luncheon; and then to the Old Men's Hospital, where Auntie gave all the old women a portrait of the Queen – I made them a little speech about the Queen – wrote to the Eastern Daily Press thanking people all round.

> 1. In his Diary, Sir Peter Eade says there were 11,000 children in the Market Place; the Mayor and Corporation paraded to Princes St Congregational Church in the evening; and the city was illuminated, with a display of fireworks.

Wednesday 22   Norwich to London
Left Norwich at 7.30 – found a room at Garlant's – went to Club & wrote to (1) Auntie – then luncheon – shortly after started for Buckingham Palace; met Kempe and his son there – the household gift very ugly – the Queen came in, and shook hands with several of the gentlemen, and kissed a good many of the ladies –

then to Club, where wrote at length to Ju, & also to the Bp. – Pall Mall thronged, & bright with illuminations on my return.[1]

> 1. Being in London, Goulburn missed further Norwich Golden Jubilee activities. The Mayor and Sheriff entertained 1100 of the aged poor in the Agricultural Hall; and, in the evening, the Mayor and Mayoress gave a soiree in St Andrew's Hall. Goulburn returned to Norwich on Friday.

Monday 27

Rose at 6 and wrote to Bensly, and to the Bp., about the Hospital Chaplaincy before Bkfst. – at 12 went with Ju and dear Pom to Yarmouth – Tom's yacht (the Firefly) not heard of at the Signal Station, tho' telegrams awaited him – went to the Donnes, who most hospitably gave us luncheon, and shewed us the new reredos – Mr. Arnold[1], one of the Curates, & Ld. William Cecil[1], another, had luncheon with us, & the latter sate by me – full of views and arguments – went to the Children's Convalescent Home[2]; introduced to Miss Turner, the Matron – then drove along the barren shore line for the breeze, and as we were returning, out rushed Tom Martin, Ursie (accompanied by the Unthanks) who had just time before our return at 5 to lionise us over their charming little yacht, the Firefly – the Firefly starts for Norway at 2 a.m. tomorrow.

> 1. In 1888, the Revd H.J.L. Arnold became Vicar of East Dereham, and in 1902, an Hon. Canon of Norwich; and the Revd Lord Wm. Cecil became Rector of Hatfield, Herts. (in the same year), and Rural Dean of Hertford in 1904.
> 2. Children's Convalescent Home, Euston Road and Marine Parade (North) Gt Yarmouth.

Tuesday 28

Ju is giving a great tea to the old women[1] of the Hospital, and therefore we are not to dine till 8.

> 1. From the Great Hospital.

Thursday 30

Went with Pom and Ju to inspect Bulmer's[1] gallery of pictures, to wh. he has recently added – Mr. Landy Brown called to say he has not nerve to undertake the Hospital Chaplaincy – Ju & Pom w. Heaviside went to the rose-show at Mr. Colman's – hope to read a little more about Kett's rebellion[2] tonight.

> 1. The Revd Edward Bulmer (ordained 1855) was a Minor Canon of the Cathedral for 35 years, 1865–1900. His Obituary said: "He was a good musician and art connoisseur, besides being a well-read man in foreign as well as English literature".
> 2. Robert Kett, a landowner of Wymondham, headed 16,000 insurgents in July 1549, against common land enclosures. They twice captured Norwich. Kett was captured and hanged.

JULY

Saturday 2
After Mg. Church went to the Bp. to discuss the Hospital Chaplaincy – I suggested Archbold[1], and we agreed that I shd. sound him on the subject – after Aftern. Church drove up (with Pom) to Archbold's – his <u>great</u> difficulty is about leaving Burton in the lurch – A garden tea-party: Mrs. Fellowes & Maudie, Hansells, Wallaces, Miss Days, & the Lincoln Miss Barretts.

> 1. The Revd Thomas Archbold, Principal and Secretary of the Diocesan Training Institution, lived in Colegate Street.

Tuesday 12 Garden Party and Sale
All domestic arrangements broken up – At 9.45 left this house & went to Ipswich, Hinds Howell, Feilden, Nevill, Browne, in the same railway carriage – got there about ½ an hour before the presentation to Groome[1] began – he seemed to be touched by our coming, and on the whole gratified – I spoke first & read the Norfolk Address – then Perowne seconded me – then Archn. Woolley spoke and then C. Frere, and the Deputy Mayor of Ipswich, who pressed me to come to luncheon – I had a chat with the Rev. Ruck-Keene, brother of the boy who was at Rugby in my time, & now Chaplain at Nice – Perowne, Nevill, & Mr. Fielden, and I, and H.H. came back in the same carriage – found the Garden Party prospering – I gave my reading 'Sands o' Dee', Browning's 'Three Horses', 'Execution of Louis XVI', 'Forsaken Mennan'; Poe's Bells; Trench's 'Poetry in Words' – 'Hubert & Arthur' – very tired afterwards.

> 1. The Ven. R.H. Groome had been Archdeacon of Suffolk since 1869; he continued as Rector of Monk Soham, where he had been since 1845. Both his fellow Archdeacons Perowne (Norwich) and Nevill (Norfolk) were present at his Presentation; and also his successor Woolley.

Friday 15
Church twice – Interviews afterwards with Mundy about his not been seen eno' at work in the Close; with Spruce about the noise made by children in the Close on Monday nights, when the Volunteers come for their drill – wrote to Mr. Hitchman about this matter, and also to Captain Back.

Monday 18
After Aftern. Service, Bartie came in to discuss with me his taking the living of St. George's, Tombland wh. the inhabitants are memoralising the Bp. to appoint him to.

Thursday 19 Judge's entrance and Choral Festival
At 12.55 went to the Shire hall with the Master in Carriage – Mr. Justice Grove asked that, as the Lodgings were so far out of Town, he might have his Service tomorrow at 10 – Also settled with the Master that Morning Prayer should be at 9.15 (plain) instead of <u>after</u> the Assize Service – this involved my calling (with carriage on Bartie, on the Bp. (where I wrote him a note, & saw Mrs. Pelham for a minute or two), & at Mr. Hansell's Office – Got home about 2, and found luncheon over, & Willie Holbech[1], there, & the preacher, Canon Howell Evans (a <u>Cursal</u> Canon of St. Asaph)[2] – Choral Festival at 3; much better arranged than ever before; but there were very few choirs, & it is evident that the whole thing is going down – Mr. Evans preached on Psalm CXXXIV, 1, 2 – Afterwards tea in the garden with Maimie & her friends & the preacher, & Willie Holbech, and Hinds Howell.

   1. An in-law connection of Julia's.
   2. Was a Proctor in Convocation for the Cathedral Chapter, but not a *Residentiary* Canon.

Friday 22
Mg. Ch. with Master, Bartie, Bulmer, at 10 – then a specially harassing Chapter, at wh. Mr. Clowes appeared & told us we could not hope to get more than 2s. 6d. <u>per acre</u> for Eaton Hall Farm (having got some time back £1. 8) – and that the sum to be paid for Mr. Stannard's improvements cd. not be much less than £300 – we agreed to offer it for sale, with Eaton Hall, and what remains to us of Eaton North Farm, to the E.C., Bensly and I to ask for an interview with them on Tuesday – made notes with Bensly till 4 – then a talk with the Bp. at the Palace in wh. it was settled that Bartie shd. try the duties of Hospital Chaplaincy for six months from Sept. next[1].

   1. In 1879 a Chapel had been built and consecrated at the Norfolk and Norwich Hospital. In 1840, and again in 1888, the suggestion to appoint a *salaried* Chaplain was turned down.

• •

From July 25 to September 3, the Goulburns are away from Norwich on their long Summer Break: In London (2 nights); at Chilton Lodge, nr. Hungerford, Berks. (6 nights); in London (1 night); at Harrogate (16 nights); Durham (3 nights); Ilkley (3 nights); York (2 nights); Brighton (7 nights).
• •

Monday 25   St. James

Left Norwich at 7.45; got to London (with Ju) at 11.15 – went straight to E.C. in Whitehall, where I found Mr. Porter the Financial Secretary & another Secretary – talked the whole matter of Eaton Hall Farm over w. them – they do not pooh-pooh the idea of purchasing it.

Tuesday 26

At 9 went to Club & had bkfst. – then to Whitehall; had a satisfactory interview with Porter – afterwards with Conrad H.H.[1].

> 1. Conrad Hinds Howell appears to have a position in the Ecclesiastical Commissioners' Office.

Thursday 28   At Chilton[1] *[staying with Mr. & Mrs. Butler]*

After Bkfst. (wh. was at 9), I took a delightful stroll down the avenue leading up to the Stables, and then across the grounds to the village and across the river (Kennett) to a chalk scooping in the cliff – rambled in a wood at the back of this scooping – on my return went into the village, and sat down in the School, and heard the Master teaching about the mote & the beam, and then, at his request, put some questions to the children about the Beatitudes – he sent his young son with me, to show me the Church, wh. is very pretty & well cared for; the churchyard, with the monuments of Pophams, Chaloner, Smiths, etc. etc. – Mr. & Mrs. Kitson (the clergyman) came to luncheon.

> 1. A village on a hill, 9 miles N.E. of Oxford.

Friday 29   At Chilton

A letter from Sir J.R. Mowbray refusing to treat w. us for the purchase of Eaton Hall Farm – answered, making an appointment with Mowbray for Wednesday next – wrote to Heaviside sending Mowbray's letter to him – then went with Ju and Mrs. Butler to see the Laundry, Stables, Dairy, etc.

AUGUST

Wednesday 3   From Ogle's Hotel to Harrogate

Wrote to Dr. Bennet,[1] who had proposed an amalgamation of the Chapter w. the City Library; (2) Lieut. Eardley Willmot, who asked me to get up a meeting for the Church House;[2] (3) Ripley, who asked permission for the Bp. of Liverpool[3] to preach in the Cath. on Sep. 2 – at 11 went to Whitehall Place, and had an interview with Sir J. Mowbray and Porter – they advised us strongly not to think of taking Eaton Hall Farm into our own hands, and said the best thing to be done wd. be to sell it, if we cd. do this at a reasonable rate – we left London at 2.30 and after a hot fusty journey got here about 6.15 (Cleveland House, York Place).

1. The Revd E.K. Bennet, D.C.L., Rector of Bunwell since 1885.
2. Archbishop Benson wanted somewhere for the Convocations and the newly formed House of Laity (Canterbury 1885; York 1892) to be brought closer together, even as a single assembly. Hence the idea of Church House, Westminster, the foundation stone of which was laid in 1891. The present Church House replaced it in 1940.
3. The Rt Revd J.C. Ryle, had been Vicar of Stradbroke in the Diocese of Norwich 1861–80; an Hon. Canon 1872–80; before becoming the 1st Bishop of Liverpool in 1880. He was a leading Evangelical.

Monday 8 Pom arrives.

At the waters in the morning met Gibbs and his Son[1] who had had a letter from Tyntesfield, expressing Mrs. Gibbs' wish for a visit – bought soap, etc. and a bottle of champagne to welcome Pom – shortly after Canon Gibbon[2] called, and asked us to a reception on Wednesday afternoon – then Archdeacon Hessey[3] – after luncheon read the 'Times' – wen to Dr. Bealey's at 4, and met <u>en route</u> Clarence Roberts and Mrs. & Miss – C.R. went in to see Dr. Bealey for a moment about a patient whose <u>taste</u> deceived him; a sort of taste-blindness – then Dr. Bealey and I took a walk and returned by the back of this stray, where the air is delicious – then Dr. B. accompanied me to the Station, where Ju joined us; and having waited a few minutes we had the delight of seeing our dear Pom!

1. Son, grandson – and Widow – of the late William Gibbs who had been Goulburn's strong supporter, friend and benefactor at St John's, Paddington, and afterwards.
2. Residentiary Canon of Ripon, and also Vicar of Christ Church, Harrogate.
3. Archdeacon of Middlesex.

•••

While in Harrogate, the Goulburns spent Tuesday (9) in York; in Durham on Saturday (20), they received a telegram from Canon Heaviside telling them of Mrs Heaviside's sudden death; when in Ilkley, they visited Bolton Priory on Tuesday (23).

•••

SEPTEMBER

Saturday 3
Ju and I left Brighton at 8.45 by express – read thro' 'Little Lord Fauntleroy' – a long time at the St. Pancras Station, during wh. I finished Fauntleroy – Left London at 12 – got to Norwich at 3.30 – a letter from Heaviside who left Norwich today – answered this – then walked across to Nevill, and had a long confab. with him about Heaviside, & the residence, and the Eaton Hall Farm negotiations – and also saw Mrs. Nevill, whom Ju had come across to see.

Thursday 8
After Mg. Service (Nevill, Moore) there called a Rev. W. Richard, to ask for pecuniary help – has acted as a Curate (Deacon) to some Incumbent who is dead – wishes to be ordained Priest at Xmas, & is reading with Archbold – I wrote to the Bp. about him, who speaks of it as a sad case – no energy of mind in him or his wife – <u>very</u> <u>poor</u> – am about to send him £3. 0. 0 – wrote to the Mayor asking him to come to Harvest Thanksgiving Service on the 18th.

Friday 9
After Mg. Church finished a second Saturday Sermonette – Mr. Muriel called & found me better – told me to leave off whiskey altogether & to take some Strychinine – Mr. Porter[1] called, & I said I wd. try to help him on Sunday – after luncheon Auntie & I called on Mrs. Bright in Robinson's house, who gave us a bad account of Mrs. Gibbs; some internal tumour; unlikely to recover – afterwards walked with Frederica over the Castle Hill to Mile End Road, & back by Unthank's – Church again at 5 – I am writing out Shairp's[2] letter about Lynn & Fakenham Railway for his Briographer – hope to go on with Antony & Cleopatra this evening.

1. Vicar of St Helen's and Chaplain to the Gt Hospital since 1882.
2. Goulburn was always very pleased that his good friend Professor John Campbell Shairp, although a Scottish Presbyterian, had given him such help and support in his battle to retain the sanctity of an English Cathedral Close.

Monday 12
Church at 10 – Nevill came in afterwards, to ask me to see Bensly about Spaull's[1] house, who is said to be mortgaging our property as well as his own – Bensly came, and had luncheon here – After

luncheon we both went to Nevill's for consultation about advertising Eaton Hall – Conrad Hinds Howell was with Nevill – he thinks that in the scheme of the E.C. for the repayment of Mortgage loans there is a ray of hope – a short walk with Frederica – then wrote to Porter[2] to ascertain our ground about the Mortgage Loan – heard from Heaviside that he intends to return Wednesday Evg; so have called a Chapter for Friday.

> 1. Bartholomew Spaul, Builder, did the Cathedral work of repairs, etc. and lived in the Lower Close.
> 2. Mr. Porter of the Ecclesiastical Commissioners – *not* the Vicar of St Helen's.

Tuesday 13

Before Church poor young Pigot came over from his father[1], to say his mother had died suddenly yesterday evening from syncope induced by violent tooth-ache – asked me to go and see his father, wh. I promised to do – All the morning soaking rain; worked at my notes for Sunday; considered what prayers to use with Pigot – after luncheon it cleared & I drove over to Eaton – the poor man & his family quite stunned with the blow; prayed with him and talked a long time; his sister-in-law Mrs. White with him; 5 children ranging from 18 to 2 yrs. old – on my return read the account of Sir W. Harcourt's[2] speech & glorious defeat last night; 141 maj.

> 1. The Revd W.M. Pigot had been Vicar of Eaton since 1875, and remained until 1904.
> 2. Sir Wm. Harcourt: Liberal M.P. since 1868; Whewell Professor of International Law at Cambridge 1869–87; Solicito-General; Home Secretary 1880; Chancellor of the Exchequer 1886. In opposition after 1886; attacked the Irish coercion policy of Lord Salisbury's Government.

Wednesday 14

Ch. at 10 – interview afterwards w. Spencer about Mr. Hales (37, P. of Wales Road) who misconducts himself by spitting in Church – wrote also to a gentleman in Cromer, who objects to money being taken for shewing the Church – then called at Eaton, driving there in fly – prayed with poor Pigot – walked home – after luncheon wrote to Mr. Hales about his misconduct.

Friday 16

Church at 10 – then a Chapter – we resolved to give Mr. Oakey, or Stannard supported by Oakey, a lease of Eaton Hall Farm for £100 a year, with covenants that by giving 6 months notice we may call in as many acres as we please for building, allotments, etc., in that case diminishing the rent £1 per acre – we also had a talk about Miss Pratt's house; empowered Bensly to reduce the rent to £50.

Sunday 18
After luncheon a walk in the garden, meditating an extemp. Sermon on the 'Lilies of the field' (Gospel of the Day) – this I delivered at 3.30 and brot. before them the subject of the new Altar Rail, Credence, and restoration of the cut away shafts on the North side of the Choir, where the Chancellor's throne was – after Church Ju and I called on, and sat with, Heaviside.

Tuesday 20
After Ch. came Bartie to explain that by the special request of the Commee. of Governors of the NN. Hospital, he had agreed to give a short early Service at the Hospital every Sunday, wh. however he says will not interfere with his Cathedral duties – after luncheon Ju went w. Mrs. Nevill to see Mrs. Heaviside's grave.

Saturday 24
Poor and creaky – sent for and saw Muriel, who touched my heart, etc. – announcement by the 11 o'clock post of dear Mrs. Gibbs's death – Bp. of Salisbury[1] and Mrs. Wordsworth came in and had luncheon with us – lionised the Bp. and Mrs. W. over the Cathedral till 2.45 – then Service – the Bishop returned after the Service & I took them to Goldwell's[2] effigy – then into the Nave, then to call for a few minutes on our Bishop – then we three walked to the Station.

> 1. The Rt. Revd John Wordsworth (1843–1911) – great-nephew of Wm. Wordsworth, the Poet. He was the elder son of Christopher Wordsworth (1807–85), Bishop of Lincoln, who was the son of Christopher Wordsworth (1774–1846), Master of Trinity College, Cambridge, who was the younger brother of William!
> 2. James Goldwell was Bishop of Norwich 1472–99. The Cathedral Spire had been struck by lightning in 1463, and Bishop Goldwell had rebuilt it and it is still standing today. He also had the Presbytery vaulted in stone. 97 of the Bosses in the Presbytery represent Goldwell's name by the picture of a well-head painted gold.

Thursday 29   St. Michael and All Angels
Did not go to Morning H.C.; at the time of Service it poured – we were obliged to go to St. Michael's[1] in a fly – The Church is beautifully restored, and there are wood panel paintings of the 14th.

Century over the Altar – The Service ended after the 3d. Collect – There was a Processional & Recessional in wh., as it was raining, I did not join – Preached extem. (with a written appeal for funds beforehand) on Jacob's ladder – <u>far</u> too long, & I was most uncomfortable with cold feet – home about 12.45 – Venables then called and had luncheon with us – He has been in Ireland visiting Archbp. Lord Plunket[2] – At 3 I took the carriage & drove to Eaton Vicarage to see Pigot – found him over the Sermon he is to preach this evening at St Michael Pleas' – staid but a short time, and then walked back – went to see Heaviside, & had a chat.

1. St Michael at Pleas.
2. Archbishop Lord Plunket (1828–97). Leader of Evangelical party in the Church of Ireland. Archbishop of Dublin 1884; defended Irish Church Establishment.

• •

The Goulburns set out for their Autumn visits to friends and relations: At Betchworth (3 nights); Eydon (9 nights); Edgcote (5 nights); Aynhoe (7 nights); Addington (2 nights); Brighton (14 nights); Chichester (3 nights); and back to Brighton (for 4 nights), returning to Norwich on November 19.

• •

OCTOBER

Thursday 27   From Aynhoe to Addington

Left Aynhoe after Bkfst. at 10.30 – pouring rain – on arriving went to Morgiana, and got a prescription from him – went to the Club and had luncheon – then to the Victoria Station, where met Ju and the Servants, at 3.55 – when we got to East Croydon, the Abp's carriage was waiting for us – we took up Miss Benson in the town – the Palace[1] is about 3 miles drive – we found the Abp. very well, and most exceedingly kind they were – dinner at 8 – I sat between Mrs. Benson & Miss Grosvenor – There were Sir John & Lady Fowler[2], Canon Knollys, Rev. Mr. Fowler, & a gentleman who lives near Lou, & knew all about her – very pleasant evening.

1. The Manor of Croydon had been the summer residence of the Archbishops of Canterbury from Norman times until the middle of the 18th Century. It was sold in 1780; soon after Archbishop Manners Sutton came to Canterbury (1805) the Addington Palace Estate was bought to replace it. It, in turn, was sold in 1897 for £70,000; In 1854, Addington Palace became the home of the Royal School of Church Music (which had been founded in 1927).
2. Sir John Fowler (1817–98): Civil Engineer. In partnership with Sir Benjamin Baker, was mainly responsible for the construction of the Forth Bridge 1882–90.

Friday 28   St. Simon and St. Jude   At Addington
Prayer in the Chapel at 9 – At Bkfst. sat by Lady Fowler and Miss Benson – afterwards Ju went with Canon Knollys to the Church for Holy Communion – I finished my 3d Sermon – then the Archbishop came to take me out for a stroll before luncheon – we went to the Church thro' the kitchen garden, and met Ju & Canon Knollys coming back – the Abp. shewed me Abp. Tait's monument, & then the very pretty Church, & the Monuments in it of several Abps. – then home for luncheon – At dinner the Bp. of Rochester[1] appeared.

> 1. The Rt Revd Anthony Thorold. In 1890 he became Bishop of Winchester.

Saturday 29   From Addington to Brighton
Most affectionate adieu from the Abp. – at 10.45 left Addington in a fly with the servants – at 3.55 left London in a Pulman for Brighton – wrote ... (1) to Mrs. Gibbs's solicitor, acknowledging his letter about Mrs. Gibbs's legacy (£500).

Monday 31   At Brighton
Just as I was going out, Mr. Morris Fuller called – I told him of Mrs. Hinds Howell's death, wh. we heard of today from Maimie – I wrote condolences to Hinds Howell & Maimie.

NOVEMBER

Friday 4
We were dreadfully shocked by the announcement of Edward's[1] sudden death on Wednesday, which we had from Cecy – set to work writing – (1) Poor Louisa[2]; (2) Jane Goulburn,2 (3) Abp. of Cant. asking him to take our local S.P.G. Sermon next year; (4) declining to subscribe a 2d time to the Restoration of the Gilbertine Priory[3] at Old Melton; (5) Precentor, asking him to look into the return for the Churchman's Year Book – Read the account of the Consecration of Truro Cathedral[4] yesterday.

> 1. Col. Edward Goulburn of Betchworth, with whom they had very recently stayed.
> 2. Louisa (nee Tower) is the widow, and Jane the sister of the Colonel.
> 3. An Order founded c 1135 by St Gilbert of Sempringham, composed of Nuns who followed the Cistercian Rule and Augustinian Canons who ministered to them. It was a purely English Order, and never spread to Europe.
> 4. Diocese created 1877; 1st. Bishop, E.W. Benson 1877–83; Cathedral begun 1880; consecrated 1887; completed 1910.

Goulburn travelled to Betchworth for Col. Edward Goulburn's funeral on November 8; and then, on Saturday (12) to Chichester to preach in the Cathedral at 3.30 p.m. on Sunday, and to attend the Installation on Monday afternoon of the Revd F.J. Mount as a Residentiary Canon and Archdeacon of Chichester, returning to Brighton on Tuesday (15).

In his Diary entry for Monday he remarked on "the riots yesterday in Trafalgar Square". On November 8, the Commissioner of Police had banned public meetings in Trafalgar Square. Socialist Groups, Metropolitan Radical Clubs, and the Irish National League determined to defy the order, and, on Sunday (13) four main columns of marchers approached the Square from North, South, East and West. The Square was guarded by 1,500 foot police and 300 mounted constables. On the perimeter were 300 mounted Life Guards, and shortly 300 Grenadier Guards took up position in front of the National Gallery. There were 150 arrests and 200 injured. It was called 'Bloody Sunday'.

Saturday 19   From Brighton thro' London to Norwich
Left Brighton with Ju at 8.45 – Found dense fog in London – Went to Goslings to draw £10, and talk about the new Trustees to my Marriage Settlement[1] – then to St. Pancras where met Ju, long before time – <u>heaps</u> of letters, most of wh. I answered before bedtime; among them Mrs. Gibb's legacy, for wh. I sent a receipt to Antony – Heaviside pledged me today for £50 for the Training School liabilities, wh. I sent to Archbold.

> 1. In 19th Century Britain, a Marriage Dowry consisted of the contribution by the Bride's family toward a fund intended to support and benefit the couple while alive, and the Bride when widowed, and to provide for their children. This was matched by a commitment on the part of the groom to provide her with an income after his death and an allowance during his life.

Thursday 24
A day of harassment and discomfort: have done nothing but write to (1) Mr. Hudson, declining Archaeol. Meeting on Monday Evg. – (2) (3) Antony Gibbs and Stanny Waller, asking them to act as Trustees of Mar. Settlement – At ½p.11 went with Nisbet in the carriage to the fork on the Ipswich Road, whence we walked back – went to the Bank, as they were closing, to pay in Mrs. Gibbs's Legacy.

Saturday 26
In my dressing room till after luncheon – very wretched and unable to put my right foot down – another row about the locking of the Cathedral doors during Service time.

Tuesday 29
Bensly came at 10, after I had been interviewed by two Candidates for the vacant Bedemanship – I gave him £10 to hand to Mr. J.B. Brown, the man whose boathouse was wrecked by the fall of a tree in my field – After luncheon Auntie had a working party.

DECEMBER

Thursday 1
A most disagreeable meeting at the Palace at 8, where I spoke – Ward found fault with Hinds Howell behind his back – several proposals to augment the small Capitular Livings out of the incomes of D. & C. – Socialist tendencies strongly developed – Heaviside & I came back at 9.45 in our carriage.

Friday 2
A wretched day ensuing on a miserable <u>sleepless</u> night, thinking over the disagreeable meeting at the Palace – at 10 rose and dressed, & then walked in Garden – Muriel came to me there; he had been at the meeting last night – then came William Johnson, Mrs. Nevill's candidate for the Bedesmanship; I took down particulars about him – It is a great comfort that I have written my Sermon for tonight – a better congregation than usual, and the seat they contrived in the <u>Nave</u> pulpit most useful.

Tuesday 6
The most dreadfully worrying of all General Chapters during the 21 years of my being Dean of Norwich – The Master did not appear till about 11, but the whole of our available time till about 4.30 was taken up with his lengthy report, devoted to ruthlessly cutting down our expenditure – Some of the suggestions we accepted, but the most of them were trivial, some impracticable – He wanted to abolish the office & stipend of Architect, to wh. we did not assent – At luncheon besides Heaviside and Bensly & Brown was Mr. Gray, our poor farmer at Frostenden, who came to get leave to go on without paying more than £20 (instead of £50) annually. To dinner everybody came except the Barretts – The Bp. very cheerful – Today arrived intelligence from Jemima[1] that Jane G[1]. had had a paralytic stroke and is dying, but may live some hours – This I answered.

> 1. Jemima was the widow of Frederic Goulburn, younger brother of the late Colonel who had died on November 2. Jane Goulburn (unmarried) was the Colonel's sister.

Sunday 11 — Advent 3
Our wedding day – Auntie got a piece of work for a sofa-back from Frederica, and I a pair of bands, with a very loving letter – We went to H.C. together at 8 a.m. and again to Morning Prayer at 10.45, when the Bp. preached – bitterly cold, and a little snow – Having a headache, I did not go in the afternoon to Church; studied St. John XX, 19 to 25, in Steir, Matt. Henry, and other Commentators – Auntie went to Aftern. Service.

Monday 12
Snow lying on the ground; darkness and gloom; did not go out – wrote to (1) Frederica, thanking for bands, & her letter (2) Argles, asking him about the reduction of the stipend of all the officials at Peterboro' by 10 pr. cent; (3) to Rev. Mr. Moffett, an Irish Clergyman, who had asked me whether I called orthodox Dissenters 'Catholics', and kindred questions – this made me look into Pearson[1] and Barrow[2] and other Books – Heaviside called in the aftern. & talked about the attempt of Aubertin to assassinate Jules Ferry[3] – hope to amuse ourselves by reading a little of Oliver [*Twist*].

1. John Pearson (1613–86), Bishop of Chester; wrote his classical 'Exposition of the Creed' in 1659.
2. Isaac Barrow (1630–77): Anglican Divine and Classical Scholar. Professor of Greek at Cambridge. Wrote 'Treatise on the Pope's Supremacy, "a work of outstanding ability".'
3. Jules Ferry (1832–93): French Statesman. Voted against the war with Prussia and was Mayor of Paris during the siege (1870–71). His last Ministry (1883–85) fell through his policy of 'colonial expansion'.

Tuesday 13
Wrote to Henry Frowde[1], thanking for a magnificent new 'Teachers' Bible – Ch. at 11 – in Library till 12 – then went to Nevill and had a 'talkee-talk' about retrenchment of finance, new altar-rail, new pulpit – on my return, wrote to Hitchman to make a Report about the protection of the Cathl. from fire – then luncheon – signed the certificates of several Girls at the Training School – then Bensly came about the marriage settlement, and advised that I shd. write a letter to Aubrey[2] about Ju's charge on the Edgcote Estate, wh. I am doing.

1. Henry Frowde (1841–1927): Publisher; Manager of London Office of Oxford University Press 1874–1913; styled 'Publisher to the University of Oxford' 1883.
2. Richard Aubrey Cartwright (now aged 76), Julia's eldest *full* brother.

Wednesday 14
Letters from (1) Smith & Gores, proposing to call (in re Cooper's meadow) tomorrow; (2) Argles, saying that the Dn. of Peterboro's Income is reduced 33 pr. Cent. – went over to read these to Heaviside before Church – then Church – then a long seance with Bartie till near luncheon time about the Choir, its holiday, pay, efficiency, etc. – Bensly came to luncheon – then an hour's walk, partly in garden, partly in Library.

Thursday 15
At 11 came the three Canons & Bensly and Mr. Smith (Smiths & Gore) to consult about the two acre meadow at Thorpe Hamlet – Mr. S. evidently will advise the E.C. that we shd. endeavour to buy up from Cooper the remainder of his lease, & then treat the whole property as building ground – All, except Heaviside and I, went in the carriage to the ground – At 8 is the People's Service – Service well attended – (upwards of 1000 people).

Sunday 18   Advent 4
Went at 8 to Church with Ju, where were the 14 ordinees – Ju went again at 10.45, but only staid to the end of Archdeacon Woolley's Sermon – then she joined me here, and we read together the Litany & Communion Service, and part of Philip Brooks's Sermon, 'The Candle of the Lord' – after luncheon, walked in the garden for 1¼ hours with my Andrewes – Church at 3.30 – reading also Mr. Joule's criticism of a passage in the Bp. of Ripon's Sermon before H. of Commons, eulogistic of Huxley, Darwin, Tyndall, Spencer.

Thursday 22
Wrote to Secretary of Institute for Speech and Ear Affections to inquire authority for putting my name on the Commee. – walk in garden (bitter cold & slippy) with snow shoes till 12.15.

Friday 23
Church at 10 – then in fly to Mr. White's, who tightened my old block of teeth, and could not find any mischief in two places where I thot it was going on – called at Mrs. Nisbet's – talk about Auricular Confession – then an hour's walk in the garden – then the doling out of seven shillings each to the Officials as Xmas Gartuities – then dinner at ½p.1 with Fraulein & Toddie; talk whether Hinds in 'Hinds Howell' is a Christian or

a Surname – Very small congregation at 8 – So end the Advent Lectures of 1887.

Saturday 24
Got a letter from Secretary of Institution for Diseases of the Throat and Ear, giving a copy of my letter, allowing my name to be placed on the Commee. – sent this on to Mr. C.S. Loch of the Charity Organization[1] – Choristers came for their mince pies & shillings at 11.15 – then an hour's walk in the garden – Service at 3.

> 1. The Charitable Organization Society was set up in 1869 to centralize the increasingly diffuse and inefficient system of private charities. Charles Stewart Loch (1849–1923) was its Secretary from 1875–1914 (knighted 1915). Member of several Royal Commissions; Took Professor of Economic Science and Statistics, King's College, London, 1904–1908.

Sunday 25   **CHRISTMAS DAY**
H.C. at 8 with Nevill and Bartie; it tired me much – At 10.45 the Bishop preached – Mrs. Nevill & Algy came in at ½p.2 bringing me a Florida orange from their plantation there – they told me that Heaviside gives Algy a daily Lecture in the Calculus – Read some of Dr. Stevenson's Lectures sent by Prof. Charteris[1].

> 1. Archibald Hamilton Charteris (1835–1908), M.A., Hon. D.D., LL.D, was a Church of Scotland Minister; Professor of Biblical Criticism, Edinburgh University 1868–98; revived Order of Deaconesses in Scotland; Moderator of General Assembly, 1892.

Monday 26   **St. Stephen**
Did not go to Church at 8, tho' Ju did – At 10 I took the Lessons – walked in the garden for an hour till the snow came on – then went on with one of my January Sermons – wrote to (1) Frederica, thanks for her silver trowel; (2) Heaviside at Sidney[1]; (3) Stacy, ordering a card for 'Various Rules & uses' to be sent to Canon Worlledge[2] of Truro – then the 'Pin' and Guy called – we had a long talk about the proposed new pulpit[3] – also about some memorial to old Buck[4] – A letter from the Bp., asking me to Hon. Can's Meeting for the 25th., and mentioning that he had appointed Dr. Raven Hon Can[5].

> 1. Sidney Sussex College, Cambridge, where he had been, in the 1830s, a Fellow and Tutor.
> 2. Residentiary Canon and Chancellor of Truro Cathedral from 1887.
> 3. The stone pulpit in the Nave which was being given by Goulburn.
> 4. Dr Buck had (for 68 years) been Organist and Choirmaster of Norwich Cathedral, up to 1877. He died in 1879.
> 5. The Revd J.J. Raven, D.D., Incumbent of Fressingfield with Withersdale. He had been Headmaster of Gt Yarmouth Grammar School.

Wednesday 28   Holy Innocents

A long and worrying Chapter – a complaint from the Chief Constable of Spruce's having left all the gates open last night, & being the worse for drink – I sent for him and, in Bensly's presence, gave him a quarter's warning.

Thursday 29

Did not go to Church, but occupied myself in thinking out, and reading up for, what is to be said tonight, & what on Saturday night – at 11.30 walked for an hour in the garden – then came in to meet Mr. Hitchman by appointment; told him our resolutions about committing the Cathedral to the care of his Brigade in regard to fire – also asked him whether he could get some respectable and efficient man to take Spruce's place, wh. he promised to think about – tried to look out a Sermon for the Bp. (who is ill) for New Year's Mg., but cannot find one wh. I have not preached before – Medley & his wife called & were very merry – hope I shall get thro' well this evening – Church more full than last time – I spoke about the worship of Heaven being the model of that upon earth – The Christmas Carol 'Nowell' was beautifully sung – In the Hallelujah Chorus, the voices were not together.

Friday 30

Bartie came to luncheon, & I read him the Chapter Order made on Wednesday last about the holiday of the Choir – At 2.15 drove to Drayton with Auntie and little F. – had a long chat with Hinds Howell[1], who enlarged upon the Hindses and the Howells – on my return, while Auntie and little F. went to a Xmas tree at Jenny Lind, I drew up notes for a short Sermon tomorrow on St. Peter's ladder of Christian Graces.

---

1. Hinds Howell's family had lived in Barbados for 250 years. A son of Thomas Howell, Bishop of Bristol 1644–61, was a Colonel on the Royalist side during the Civil War, and afterwards migrated to the Island of Barbadoes. Canon Hinds Howell's father, Col. Conrade Howell, was Treasurer of the Island. In 1804, he became a widower, with six sons, and three years later, married Elizabeth Thornhill Hinds (nee Rock), widow of Abel Hinds. She had a son and a daughter, the son being Samuel Hinds, Bishop of Norwich 1849–57. By Elizabeth, the Colonel had three daughters and two sons, the elder of whom was Hinds (born 1808) given, as his sole Christian name, the surname of his mother's first husband!

Saturday 31
Did not go to Mg. Church, but sat at home working at my 1st. Epiph. Sermon – in the midst came a letter from Cissy, saying that Jane had passed away yesterday (30th.) at 1 a.m. – At 1 came the four tenants, Mr. Gowing, Mr. Waters (junr.) (the father is dying), Mr. Snelling, Mr. [blank] with Bensly and Foreman, and ate minced pies and drank champagne – I preached at 3 p.m. – very fair congregation – then came into 5 p.m. tea the Pin, Mrs. Symonds, and little Em'ly, the Saint, Lucy Hansell, Kate Medley, Mrs. Bartie; a very merry New Year's party.

APPENDICES

APPENDIX 1

Published Writings and Sermons of Dean Goulburn

+ In the Library of the Dean and Chapter of Norwich
* In the Local Studies Library of Norwich Central Library, Bethel Street (At the time of going to print (December 1995) it was not known if Goulburn's Writings, listed as in the Local Studies Library, survived the fire of 1994.)

(1) Books and Booklets

+   1850 Address to Masters at the beginning of Half-year (at Rugby School).
    1850 Bampton Lectures: 'The Resurrection of the Body'.
    1856 'The Book of Rugby School'.
+ * 1859 'Bacon: the first Principles of his Philosophy stated in Popular Form, and the Application of them to the Study of the Holy Scriptures pointed out' (Lecture in Schoolroom of St Mary's, Marylebone).
+   1860 'Blaise Pascal'. (A Lecture in Exeter Hall, London, to the Y.M.C.A.).
  * 1862 'The Education of the World'.
  * 1862 'Replies to 'Essays and Reviews'.
  * 1863 'The Office of the Holy Communion in the Book of Common Prayer' (2 Vols.)
+ * 1866 'Thoughts on Personal Religion' (New Edition). This had a wide circulation in England, U.S.A. and abroad.
+ * 1866 'The Acts of the Deacons' – A Course of Lectures.
+ * 1867 'The Results of the Writer's Experience of Private Confession'. (Paper to the Pastoral Work Association in Norwich)
+ * 1868 'The Bible' (Lecture to the Churchman's Club in Norwich).
  * 1868 'Popular Objections to the Book of Common Prayer'.
+ * 1869 'The Functions of our Cathedrals'. (An Open Letter to the Archbishops in reply to an Enquiry from them to all Deans of Cathedrals).
  * 1869 'The Pursuit of Holiness'. (This had a wide circulation, with new Editions in 1871 and 1873, and also editions previous to 1869).
+ * 1870 'The Existing Mode of Electing Bishops, and any alteration that may be made therein consistent with the Union of Church and State'. (Paper to the Central Committe of the Church Institution at King's College, London).
  * 1871 'Of the Lierne Vault of the Nave of Norwich Cathedral'.
+ * 1872 'Reasons for neither Mutilating nor Muffling the Athanasian Creed, but retaining it intact in the Services of the Church'.
+ * 1872 'The Great Commission' – Meditations on Home and Foreign Missions'. (Drawn up at the request of the S.P.G.).
+ * 1873 'The Church's Title to her Endowments'. (Lecture in St Andrew's Hall, Norwich).
+   1873 'How may the Church, while holding fast the Doctrine of the Athanasian Creed, show due consideration to those who object to its present Form, or congregational use, and maintain the bond of peace in her Body?' (Paper in Bishop's Palace at gathering of Residentiary & Honorary Canons).

+	*1873	'The Gospel of the Childhood'. (5,000 Copies printed + 2nd Edition).
+	*1873	'The Holy Catholic Church'. (5,000 Copies printed).
+	*1874	'Fasting Communion'.
+	1874	'The Duty of the Civil Magistrate to the Christian Religion and the Christian Church'. (Dialogue Lecture at Ipswich for East Suffolk Defence Institution).
+	*1875	'A Commentary, Expository and Devotional, on the Order of the Administration of the Lord's Supper'.
	*1875	'Authorities for the Life of Herbert de Losinga'.
+	*1876	'The Child Samuel'.
	*1876	'A Manual of Confirmation'.
+	*1876	**'The Ancient Sculptures of the Roof of Norwich Cathedral'.** (With Henry Symonds) and **'A History of the See of Norwich'** (With E. Hailstone).
	*1877	'The New Lectionary Examined with Reasons for its Amendment at the Present Time'. (With C. Wordsworth, Bishop of Lincoln, & J. W. Burgon, Dean of Chichester).
	*1877	'The Christian Doctrine of Prayer'.
	*1878	'A Memorial presented to Lord Beaconsfield'.
+	*1878	**'Life, Letters and Sermons of Bishop Herbert de Losinga'.** (With Henry Symonds)
+	1878	'An Introduction to the Devotional Study of the Holy Scriptures'. (*10th* Edition)
	*1879	'On Preaching' (With J.E. Cooper).
+	*1880	'Everlasting Punishment'. (Lectures).
+	*1880	'The Lord Chancellor's Burial Bill' – Letter to the Bishop of Norwich.
+	*1880	'The Collects of the Day in the Book of Common Prayer'. (2 Vols.).
+	*1881	'The Confessions of a Reticent Dean' – Letter to the Bishop of Lincoln on Ritual Conformity.
	*1882	'The Ousey Memorial'.
	*1883	'Marriage'.
+	1883	'Thoughts on the Liturgical Gospels'. (2 Vols.).
	*1886	'Meditations on the Liturgical Gospels'.
+	1886	'Church Reform, the Inexpediency of Attempting it at the Present Time'. (A Paper at a Meeting called by the Bishop).
+	*1886	'Reminiscences of Charles Pourtales Golightly'.
	*1888	'Three Counsels of the Divine Master for the Conduct of Spiritual Life'. (2 Vols.).
	*1888	'Reasons for not signing "The Report of her Majesty's Commissioners for inquiring into the Condition of Cathedral Churches in England and Wales" upon the Cathedral Church of Norwich'.
+	1889	'The Lessons of my Decanate' – Published in the 'Guardian', and reprinted.
	*1891	'Dean Goulburn's Farewell to Norwich Cathedral'.
	*1892	**'John William Burgon'. (2 Vols.).**
	*1894	'Thoughts on Passages of Holy Scripture'.

(2) Sermons

+ 1853 Sermon in St Mary's, Oxford, for the Radcliff Infirmary, at Installation of the Earl of Derby as Chancellor of the University.
* 1853 Sermons, preached chiefly in the Parish Church of Holywell, Oxford.
+ * 1858 'Learning, a Requisite for the Ministry of the Present Day' (At Ordination in Christ Church Cathedral, Oxford, with the Bishop of Oxford.
+ * 1859 'God keeping and breaking silence'. (Sermons at St Paul's Cathedral, London).
+ * 1859 'Human Instrumentality employed in Man's Salvation'. (Sermon at Ordination in St Paul's Cathedral, London, with the Bishop of London).
+ 1860 'The Kingdom that comes, not with Observation'. (Sermon in St John's, Paddington, for the new Church of St Michael).
+ 1862 'Have Salt in Yourselves'. (Sermon on death of Prebendary J.H. Gurney, Rector of St Mary's Marylebone, with brief Memoir, etc.).
+ 1864 A Pastoral Letter on the Bishop of London's Fund to the members and parishioners of St John's, Paddington, and St Michael's.
+ 1864 An Address to the Sisters of St Peter's Home, Brompton, on the Anniversary of its foundation.
+ 1864 Four Sermons on: The Inspiration of Holy Scripture; The Word of God, a Seed; Experimental Knowledge of the Scriptures – a Dispensation from Inquiry; Everlasting Punishment. (Preached in St John's, Paddington).
+ * 1867 'A Word for the Old Lectionary'.
+ 1867 'The Theory of the Introduction of Music into the Worship of the Church'. (Sermon at 8th Anniversary Festival of Norfolk and Suffolk Church Choral Association in Norwich Cathedral).
+ * 1867 'Farewell Counsels of a Pastor to his Flock'. (Nine Sermons at St John's, Paddington).
+ * 1870 'The Moral Atmosphere of a Contested Election'. (At a Special Service in Norwich Cathedral).
+ 1870 'The Principles of the Cathedral System Vindicated'. Eight Sermons.
+ 1871–1876 'Argumentative Discourses in Defence and Confirmation of the Faith'. These 24 Discourses, divided into 8 Series, by 8 Lectures (one of whom was Dean Goulburn), were given in Norwich Cathedral during these years, and eventually were published as a Book.
+ * 1877 'The Royal Supremacy' (Sermon on Trinity Sunday at Ordination in Norwich Cathedral.
+ * 1881 'Dean Stanley and his Theology'. (Memorial Sermon in Norwich Cathedral on July 24th).
+ * 1882 'On Reading the Prayers and Lessons'. (Sermon at Trinity Sunday Ordinary in Norwich Cathedral).
+ * 1882 'The Sphere and Duties of Christian Women'. (Memorial Sermon in Norwich Cathedral for Mrs. M.C.M. Robinson, wife of Canon Robinson, Residentiary Canon and Master of St Catherine's College, Cambridge).

+ *1884		'Preaching a Sacred Function (Sermon at Trinity Sunday Ordination in Norwich Cathedral).
+ *1885		'Holy Week in Norwich Cathedral'. (7 Lectures).
+ *1886		'A Church Memorial of the Visit of the Royal Agricultural Society to Norwich'. (Two Sermons in the Cathedral on Sunday at beginning of Week).
+	1887	Lectures in Holy Week in Norwich Cathedral.
+ *1887		'How may the Christian Pastor economise his time?' (Sermon at Trinity Sunday Ordination in Norwich Cathedral).
+ *1887		'Submission to Constituted Authority, the Foundation of Social Morality'. (Sermon in Norwich Cathedral on the first day of Jubilee Week (June 19th), and also Hospital Sunday).
+ *1888		'Ministerial Absolution as taught by the Prayer Book'. (Sermon at Trinity Sunday Ordination in Norwich Cathedral).
+	1896	The last Sermon which Goulburn preached on March 27th, 1896.
	*1898	8 Sermons on the Life of St John the Baptist.
+ *1898		'The Lord's prayer'.

(These last two were published after Dean Goulburn's death).

Also

+   A Collection of typed Booklets of Sermons, mostly undated.
+   A Collection of 214 Sermons in MS. in a collection of Note Books.

In 1867 the Dean and Precentor Symonds compiled:
*   'The Stranger's Guide to Norwich Cathedral'.
This was revised and updated from time to time, by Dean Goulburn.

Edward Meyrick Goulburn's first letter (c. 1823, aged 5) to his Cousin Louisa Goldsmid (8 years older), later to be Louisa Thomas. It is written in a very large script between copybook lines, and is likely to have been copied from a storybook or copybook.

> Dear Lou,
> Once upon a time there was a very poor cobbler, who suddenly and unexpectedly came into a large fortune. he was so stupified at first by surprise and excess of pleasure that he was unable to make use of his wealth. just so, am I, but sufficiently myself however to know and feel that I am ever my dear Lou most affecty yrs
>
>   Edward Goulburn

APPENDIX 2

SELECT BIBLIOGRAPHY

14 Volumes of the DIARY OF DEAN GOULBURN between Jan. 1, 1861 and Dec. 31, 1887. (Dean and Chapter Library, Norwich).
NORWICH DIOCESAN CALENDAR AND CLERGY LIST, 1858–1899 (Ed. Canon Hinds Howell) (Norwich Diocesan Office, and Local Studies Library in Norwich Central Library). (*Note: Survived the fire!*)
BURKE'S 'Landed Gentry'.
'THE CONCISE DICTIONARY OF NATIONAL BIOGRAPHY' (Up to 1985) (3 Vols. O.U.P. 1992).
CROCKFORD'S 'Clerical Directory' (1858 onwards).
FAMILY LETTERS written by Goulburn, mostly to his Cousin Louisa Thomas (1858–97). (Lent by Bryan Gipps, Esq., of Egerton Hall, Kent).
32 LETTERS written *to* Goulburn between 1872 and 1876. (Given to the Dean and Chapter Library, Norwich, by Bryan Gipps, Esq.).
BOOKS, BOOKLETS, PRINTED SERMONS by Goulburn (in the Dean and Chapter, Library, Norwich).

ALEXANDER, Eleanor, *Primate Alexander, Archbishop of Armagh* – A Memoir. (Edward Arnold, London, 1913).
ARMSTRONG, H.B.J. (Ed.), *A Norfolk Diary* – Passages from the Diary of the Diary of the Revd Benjamin John Armstrong (Harrap 1949).
ARMSTRONG, H.B.J. (Ed.), *Armstrong's Norfolk Diary*. Further Passages from the Diary of the Revd Benjamin John Armstrong (H. & S. 1963).
BARRETT, Philip, *Barchester – English Cathedral Life in the Nineteenth Century*. (S.P.C.K. 1993).
BARRINGER, Christopher, (Ed.), *Norwich in the Nineteenth Century* (Gliddon 1984).
BATES, Dr Frank, *Reminiscences and Autobiography of a Musician in Retirement*. (Jarrold & Sons 1930).
BECK. A.J., *Norwich Cathedral Library* – Its foundation, destructions and recoveries. (Dean and Chapter of Norwich, 1986).
BIRKBECK, H., *The Birkbecks of Norwich*, (1993).
BULL, Jack (Ed.), *The Story of Keswick Hall Church of England College of Education (1839–1981)*.
CARTWRIGHT-HIGNETT, Elizabeth, *Lili at Aynhoe* – Victorian Life in an English Country House. (Barrie & Jenkins 1989).
COMPTON. Berdmore, *Edward Meyrick Goulburn, D.D., D.C.L., Dean of Norwich* – a Memoir. (John Murray 1899).
EADE, Sir Peter, M.D., *Some Account of the Parish of St Giles, Norwich*. (Jarrold & Sons 1886).
EADE, Sir Peter, M.D., *The Norfolk and Norwich Hospital, 1770–1900*. (Jarrold & Sons 1900).
HARRIES, R., CATERMOLE, P., MACKINTOSH, P., *A History of Norwich School* – King Edward VI School at Norwich (Friends of Norwich School 1991).

HOPE SIMPSON, J.B., *Rugby Since Arnold* – A History of Rugby School from 1842. (Macmillan 1967).

HOWELL, Agnes Rous, *Hinds Howell* – A Memoir (Parker & Co. 1899) (With a Preface by the late Edward Meyrick Goulburn, D.D.).

HIBGAME, Frederick T., *Recollections of Norwich 50 Years Ago*. (Norwich 1919).

KITTON, Frederic G., *Zechariah Buck, Mus. D. Cantor*. – Organist and Master of the Choristers of Norwich Cathedral 1817–1877. (Jarrold & Sons 1899).

LEEDS, H., *Life of Dean Lefroy*. (Jarrold & Sons 1909).

LONG, Sydney, (Ed.), *The Autobiography of Sir Peter Eade, M.D., F.R.C.P. (1825–1915)* – With Selections from his Diary. (Jarrold & Sons 1916).

MITCHELL, Sally (Ed.), *Victorian Britain* – An Encyclopedia. (Garland Publishing Inc., New York & London 1988)

PALGRAVE-MOORE, Patrick, *The Mayors and Lord Mayors of Norwich, 1836–1974*. (Elvery Dowers, Norwich 1978).

PATTESON, Isabella K., *Henry Staniforth Patteson, 1816–1898* – A Memoir.

SMITH-DAMPIER, J.L., *East Anglian Worthies*. (Basil Blackwell, Oxford 1949).

SANSBURY, Ethelreda, *An Historical Guide to Norwich Cathedral* (Revised Edition 1994) (Dean and Chapter of Norwich).

GOULBURN FAMILY TREE

GOULBURNS left the Lancashire-Cheshire border for Jamaica in the 17th Century and were settled there, at Amity Hall, for over 100 years.

George GOULBURN of Amity Hall (Will proved 1748)
├── Edward (of A.H.) m. — *Read of New York*
│   └── Munbee GOULBURN (of A.H. & London) (1756–1793) m. 1782, the Hon. Susan *Chetwynd* d. 1808
│   ├── *Edward (1787–1868) m. (1) 1815 Harriet de Visme (d. 1823)
│   │   ├── Henry (1784–1856) m.1811 the Hon. Jane *Montagu* (Lived at Betchworth)
│   │   │   ├── Henry (1815–1843)
│   │   │   ├── Edward (1816–1887) m.1856 Maria L. Tower (Betchworth)
│   │   │   │   ├── Henrietta m.1877 Col. *Ricardo*
│   │   │   │   └── Henry (Major) 1858–1928
│   │   │   ├── Frederic (1818–1878) m. Hon. Jemima *Sondes*
│   │   │   ├── Cuthbert (Gen., D.S.O.) (1860–1944) m.1902 Grace *Foster* (Betchworth)
│   │   │   │   ├── Edward Henry
│   │   │   │   ├── Nancy Grace (1904–1933)
│   │   │   │   └── Cuthbert (1906–44)
│   │   │   └── Jane (d.1887)
│   │   ├── Edward Meyrick (Dean) (1818–1897) m.1845 **Julia Cartwright** (d.1903)
│   │   │   ├── Arthur (1863–1946)
│   │   │   └── Mary (1862–1930)
│   │   └── Frederic (Col.) (d.1836)
│   │   └── Frederic Anderleet (1820–1877)
│   ├── m. (2) 1825 Hon. Esther *Chetwynd* (d.1829)
│   │   ├── *Edward (1787–1868)
│   │   └── Esther (d.1853) m. 1851 Henry *Chetwynd-Stapleton*
│   │   └── Henry
│   ├── Harriette (d.1830)
│   ├── Susan (d.1836)
│   └── m. (3) 1831 Hon. Catherine Montagu (d.1865)
│   └── *Edward (1787–1868)
└── Henry m. Sister of Brother's Wife & left estate to Nephew.

*Dean Goulburn's father Edward, was married three times

GOULBURN COAT OF ARMS: Argent a Cross between 4 Doves gules.

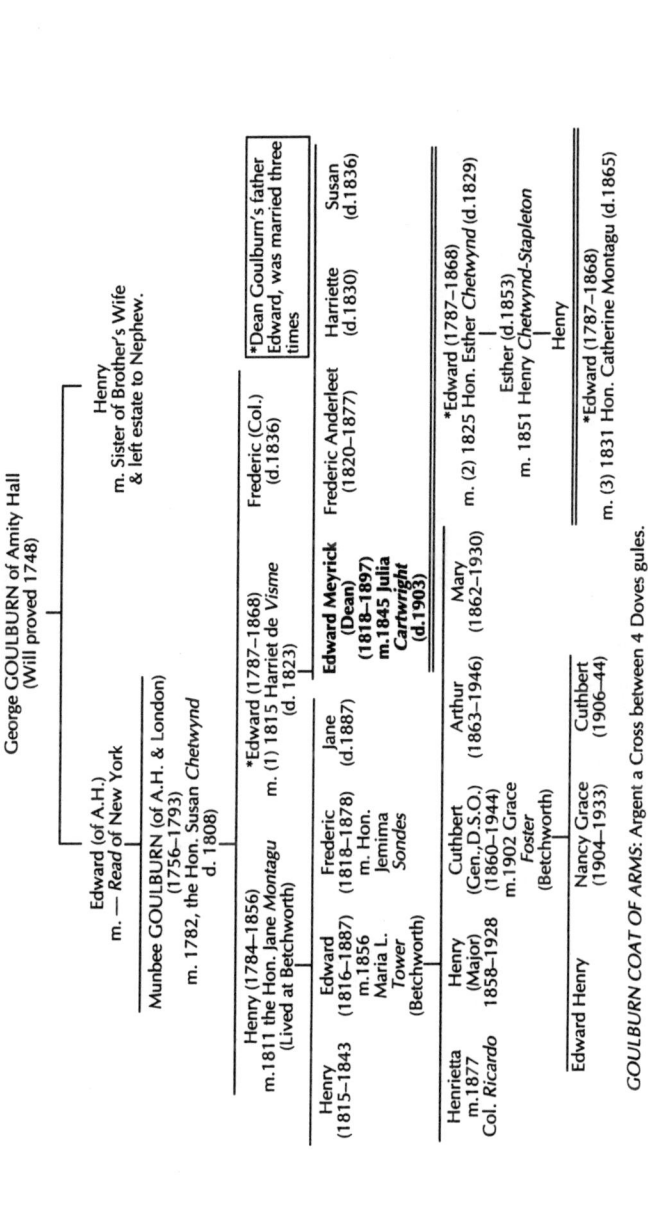

THOMAS FAMILY TREE

Richard THOMAS of Eyhorne House, Hollingbourne, Kent (1792–1881)
m. 1838 Louisa DE VISME*, Daughter of John Louis GOLDSMID.*
(1810–1911)

| Ella de V. Thomas (1840–1926) m. 1860 Rev. John Shaw | Louisa Goulburn Thomas (1843–1926) m. 1863 Henry Gipps Major, 9th Norfolks | Bertha Jardine Thomas (1844–1932) m.1873 Edward Delmar Morgan | Mary Julia Thomas (1846–1918) 'Pom' (Unmar.) | Laura Charlotte Thomas (1848–1930) 'Lolotte' m. Major Henry Pearson (d.1881) | Richard Gerard de V. Thomas (1848–1900) m. 1800 Augusta Emma ('Gussie') Cartwright (1853–1949) |

8 Children
8th: G. Bryan Gipps
(1876–1956)
m. Helen Johner of
Switzerland

E. Bryan Gipps
(1910–
Egerton House, Kent

| Louisa Fanny de V. Thomas (1880–1880) Buried St Mark Lakenham Norwich | Augusta (1882–1958) m. John Wood | Ella (1883–1967) | Lilian (1886–1961) | Richard (1886–1958) m. Eva Sharp | Bertha (1889–1965) | Edward Stephen (1891–1959) m. Frances Thompson |

(Gerard and Augusta Thomas's other six children buried at Hollingbourne.
There are no male descendants with the name 'Thomas').

Note: *John Louis GOLDSMID left his wife Louisa (mother of Louisa (Thomas) and went to America.
His children (by deed poll) took their mother's name 'DE VISME.

E. Bryan GIPPS (See 'Acknowledgements')

GOLDSMID – DE VISME FAMILY TREE

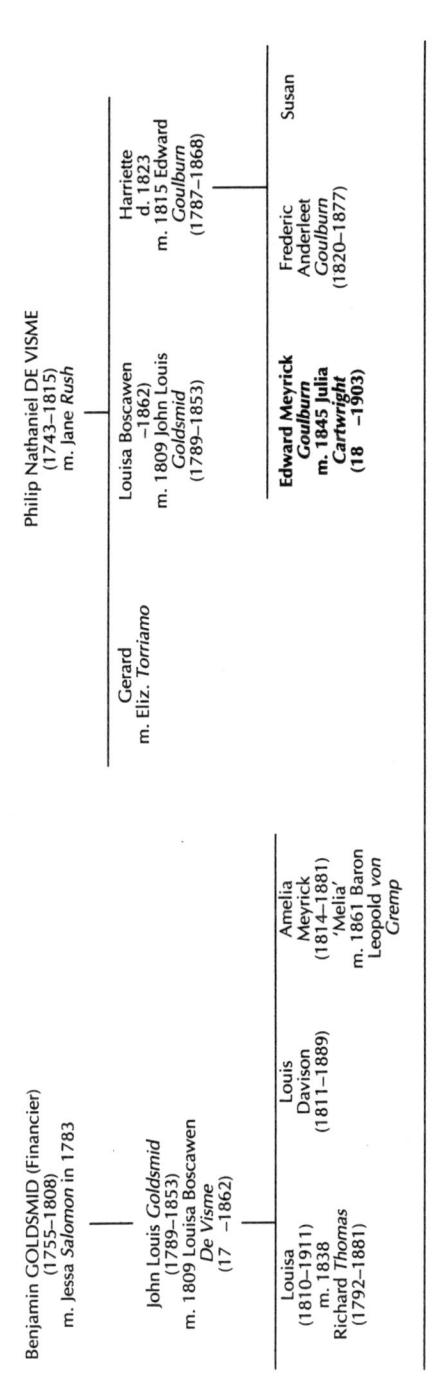

```
Benjamin GOLDSMID (Financier)                              Philip Nathaniel DE VISME
      (1755–1808)                                                 (1743–1815)
m. Jessa Salomon in 1783                                         m. Jane Rush
            |                                          _____|_____
            |                                         |              |                        |
    John Louis Goldsmid ————————————————— Louisa Boscawen       Gerard                  Harriette
       (1789–1853)                           –1862)           m. Eliz. Torriamo          d. 1823
   m. 1809 Louisa Boscawen              m. 1809 John Louis                           m. 1815 Edward
         De Visme                            Goldsmid                                    Goulburn
        (17  –1862)                         (1789–1853)                                (1787–1868)
                                                                                             |
                                                                                   _____|_____
                                                                                  |                    |
                                                                          Frederic                 Susan
                                                                          Anderleet
                                                                          Goulburn
                                                                         (1820–1877)
```

Louisa	Louis	Amelia
(1810–1911)	Davison	Meyrick
m. 1838	(1811–1889)	(1814–1881)
Richard Thomas		'Melia'
(1792–1881)		m. 1861 Baron
		Leopold von
		Gremp

Edward Meyrick Goulburn m. 1845 Julia Cartwright (18 –1903)

*
John Louis GOLDSMID left his wife and family and went to America; the family reverted, by deed poll, to their mother's maiden name of DE VISME.

Louis Davision GOLDSMID (DE VISME) was a Curate at Brighton, but, from 1838, lived under restraint for a mental condition until his death in 1889.

+
Amelia GOLDSMID (DE VISME) was the 2nd. wife of Baron Leopold von Gremp of Homburg, Germany. When she died in 1881 she was buried in the Cemetery there. By his first wife, Jane BOWLES (also English) he had a son, Ernst, who was Godfather to E. Bryan GIPPS (1910–   ) of Egerton House, Egerton, Kent. Baron von Gremp married for a third time – this time a German.

CARTWRIGHT FAMILY TREE

William Ralph CARTWRIGHT (1771–1847) m. (1) Emma Maude (d.1808) daughter of 1st. Viscount Hawarden.
Aynhoe Park, Northants.

1st. Marriage

- Thomas (Sir) (1794–1850) m. 1824, Countess Eliz. von Sandizell ('Lili') (1805–1902)
  - Emma (died (1827).)
  - Wm. Cornwallis (1825–1915) m. Clementine Gaul
    - Fairfax (Sir) (d.1928)
  - Thomas R.B. (1830–1921) m. Eliz. Jane Leslie-Melville (d.1892)
    - 4 daughters

- William (Gen.) (1797–1873) m. 1822 Marianne Jones
  - Fairfax Wm. (1823–1881)
  - Aubrey Agar (Maj.) (d.1854)

- Mary Cath. (d.1877) m.1827, Henry Gunning (Rev. Sir) (d.1885)

- Cornwallis Richard (1801–1870) m.l. Alicia Trower (d.1867) 2. Jane Trower

- Robert (1805–1899) m. Catherine F. Prior

- Stephen Ralph (1806–1862) m. Lady Fanny Hay (d.1853)
  - **Augusta Emma ('Gussie') (1853–1949) m.1880 R. Gerard de Visme *Thomas* (1848–1900)**
  - 7 Children (See Thomas Family Tree (Appendix 2))

- Sophia (1808–1896) m.1831, Wm. Willes (d.1865)

William Ralph CARTWRIGHT (1771–1847) m. (2) Julia Frances AUBREY (in 1810) daughter of Col. Richard Aubrey

2nd. Marriage

- Richard Aubrey (1811–1891) m.1848 Mary Fremantle (d.1885)

- Henry (Col.) (1814–1890) m. 1853 Jane Holbech (d.1877)

- Frances Eliz. (Fanny) (d.1864) m. Matthew *Boulton* 1845 (d.1894)
  - Meanne (d.1934)
  - Ethel (d.1924)

- **Julia (18 –1903) m.1845 Edward Meyrick *Goulburn* (1818–1897)**

- Frederick Wm. (1818–1906) ('The Dean') R. of Aynhoe (1862–1906)

CARTWRIGHT COAT OF ARMS: Ermine a Fess between 3 Fireballs sable fired proper.

APPENDIX 7

Open Letter 'Eight Directions'

In his OPEN LETTER dated June 7th, 1869, to the two Archbishops, in reply to their enquiry addressed to the DEANS of Cathedrals, Gulburn ended by stating Eight Directions in which he thought improvements should run:

(1) A more constant attendance on the Services of the Cathedral by resident members of the Body, *not officially bound to render it*.
(2) An improvement of the income and *status* of the Minor Canons, these being the regular ministers of the Choir, and the conductors of the daily worship. Duties might be assigned to them corresponding to the increase in their remuneration as Pastors of the Precinct, Preachers on Sundays or Festivals, Educators of the Choristers, etc.
(3) Better payment of the Choristers. More attention to their general education, their religious training, and provision for them in after life.
(4) The providing retirement pensions for Minor Canons and Lay-Clerks who are incapicitated for their duties by age and infirmity.
(5) The bringing into greater prominence the feature attaching to Cathedrals of a School of Sacred Music for the Diocese. Could arrangements be made here for gratuitous instruction of the Clergy in the performance of the Choral Service, and in the best mode of teaching and superintending Parish Choirs?
(6) The connexion of a Cathedral with a Theological College, which the Dean and Canons might superintend and give Lectures to.
(7) The emoluments of Canonries to be increased by at least one-fourth of their present income, (to enable the holders of them to maintain, without other help, their position as dignified Clergymen) and this being done, *but not otherwise*.
(8) To enforce from each Canon, as at present from the Dean, a residence of eight months.

APPENDIX 8

'The Augmentative Discourses'

NORWICH CATHEDRAL ARGUMENTATIVE DISCOURES IN DEFENCE AND CONFIRMATION OF THE FAITH 1871–1876

This was probably the most successful, and sustained, Series of Lectures which Gulburn planned. He considered that guardianship of the Christian Faith was one of the special functions of a Cathedral, and it had to be done effectively, so he called upon the most distinguished theologians and speakers he could muster for the Series.

SERIES 1: *The Right Reverend William Connor MAGEE, Lord Bishop of Peterborough*
Tuesday, March 28th, 1871: *Discourse 1: Christianity and Free Thought*
Wednesday, March 29th, 1871: *Discourse 2: Christianity and Scepticism*
Thursday, March 30th, 1871: *Discourse 3: Christianity and Faith.*

SERIES 2: Tuesday, December 12th, 1871: *Discourse 4: The Demonstration of the Spirit.*
The Very Reverend Edward Meyrick GOULBURN, Dean of Norwich
Wednesday, December 13th, 1871: *Discourse 5: Above Reason, not Contrary to it.*
Thursday, December 14th, 1871: *Discourse 6: The Cumulative Argument in favour of Christianity.*

SERIES 3: *Discourse 7: The Athanasian Creed (i)*
Discourse 8: The Athanasian Creed (ii)

SERIES 4: *The Right Reverend William ALEXANDER, Lord Bishop of Derry*
Tuesday, December 17th, 1872: *Discourse 9: Man's Natural Life.*
Wednesday, December 18th, 1872: *Discourse 10: Man's Moral Life.*
Thursday, December 19th, 1872: *Discourse 11: Man's Wedded Life.*
Sunday, December 22nd, 1872: *Discourse 12: Man's Fallen and Redeemed Life.*

SERIES 5: *The Reverend Dr John Cole COGHLAN, Incumbent of St Peter's, Vere Street, London.*
Sunday, March 15th, 1874: *Discourse 13: The Importance of the Evidences of Christianity.*
The Reverend Dr HANNAH, Vicar of Brighton.
Sunday, March 22nd, 1874: *Discourse 14: The Divine Basis of Morality*
The Very Reverend Edward Meyrick GOULBURN, Dean of Norwich.
Sunday, March 29th, 1874: *Discourse 15: God's Demand of Faith a Probation of Mankind.*

SERIES 6: *The Revd Canon REICHEL, D.D., Canon of St Patrick's Dublin.*
Sunday, March 7th, 1875: *Discourse 16: Demonstration of the Being and Fundamental Attributes of God.*

Wednesday, March 10th, 1875: *Discourse 17: The Character of Christ a Sufficient Proof of His Mission and Divinity.*
Sunday, March 14th, 1875: *Discourse 18: The Necessary Limits of Christian Evidences.*

(After the second of his three Discourses, Dr Reichel was recalled to Dublin by a telegram, but did not arrive until after the death of his son; his third Discourse was read for him by Goulburn).

SERIES 7: *The Reverend Prebendary C.A. ROW, M.A., Prebendary of St Paul's Cathedral, London.*
Monday, March 27th, 1876: *Discourse 19: The Adaptations of the Universe as Proving the Existence of an Intelligent Creator.*
Wednesday, March 29th, 1876: *Discourse 20: Hints for the Solution of the Difficulties of Theism. The Immortality of Man.*
Friday, March 31st, 1876: *Discourse 21: Miracles. Jesus Christ in His Divine Person, and His Action on History, the Strongest Proof of His Own Divine Mission.*

SERIES 8: *The Reverend Canon Alfred BARRY, D.D., Principal of King's College, London, and Canon of Worcester.*
Sunday, December 17th, 1876: *Discourse 22: The Christian Doctrine of Prayer.*
Monday, December 18th, 1876: *Discourse 23: Is Prayer Needless?*
Wednesday, December 20th, 1876: *Discourse 24: Is Prayer Useless?*

APPENDIX 9

A note on the costs and prices in the Diary

• •
The Goulburns, being people of affluence, were able to live in a style impossibe for Curates, for most Incumbents without private means, and for a large proportion of the nation whose wages were still less than £150 a year. The earlier Diaries were still in the 'Golden Age' of Victorian prosperity, and the latter in the period of the 'Great Depression'. Throughout these periods, the income and lot of the 'poor', although still pitifully low, were slowly improving, and even in the 'Depression' all who were in work were helped by falling prices.
• •

Railway Travel
Dean Goulburn enjoyed rail travel. His most frequent journeys were to London (via Cambridge or Ipswich), the time taken being just under four hours. The first class fare (he always travelled 1st.) was about £1.15.6d. return. If Julia was also travelling, she had her maid, Rose, and often they had one of the manservants to look after the luggage. He and Rose travelled 2nd. class. Preaching engagements took Goulburn by train from Norwich to Gt Yarmouth (6/9d.R.); to Ipswich (13/3d.R.); to Ely (19/6d.R.); to Cambridge (£1.5.0 R.); to Peterborough (£1.3.6d.R.). An other regular journey was London to Brighton (15/- R.); but the Dean liked to travel in the Pullman Car (and this was an extra 1/6d.); and if the train was an Express, it was a further 2/-. One year the Goulburns, with Gussie and Rose, spent a 19 days holiday in Scotland, travelling Norwich to York, York to Glasgow, and returning Edinburgh to London. The entire cost (travel, hotel, excursions, meals, etc.) came to £113. 4. 0. This is £5.19.9d. per day; and averages £1.9.10d. per person per day.

Travel by Fly or Ferry
The Goulburns had a Carriage, horses and Coachman in Norwich; but, when away from home, they continually used a Fly, which had a minimum charge of 1/-. Sometimes a fly was hired for a long period and charged by the hour. In Glasgow, they hired one for 4 hours and paid 15/6d. On this Scottish holiday the fare on the Ferry from Greenoch to Oban (for all 4) was 14/-.

Hotels and Lodgings
Quite often, the Goulburns stayed for one or two nights in a London Hotel, usually Ogle's 'Grosvenor Hotel' in Park Street (parallel to Park Lane). It is not clear when, and when not, meals are included in the hotel charge, for Goulburn, when on his own, often had breakfast or lunch (costing 1/6d. to 2/-) at his Club, the United Universities in Pall Mall East. The 'Grosvenor' was about £1.5.0 each, per night. In the various hotels where they stayed, the nightly rate ranged from 15s. to £1.14.0. These hotels included: 'The Calverly', Tunbridge Wells; 'The Norfolk', Brighton; 'The Clarence' and 'The George Inn', Exeter; 'The Pavilion', Folkestone; 'The Royal Station', York; 'The Queen's', Glasgow; 'The Palace', Edinburgh; and 'The Craig-ard', Oban. When on a main holiday, either

Appendix 9

in Britain or abroad, they stayed for only two or three nights at a hotel, and then looked for cheaper for lodgings for the remainder of the holiday. Accommodation usually included a sitting-room as well as bedrooms.

Medical and other Professional Attention
Both the Dean and Julia (more often the former) frequently called the doctor, whether in Norwich, London or Brighton (and on holiday too). The doctor's charge (home visit) was always £1.1.0. The dentist also charged £1.1.0, except for a London dentist who charged only 10/6d. The Chiropodist's charge was 5/- (again a home visit), and the hairdresser came for 1/-. It was also 1/- for a shampoo.

Books

		£	s.	d.
(1876)	The Ancient Sculptures of the Roof of Norwich Cathedral	3.	3.	0
(1878)	Life, Letters and Sermons of Bishop Herbert de Losinga (2 vols.)	1.	2.	6
(1880)	The Collects of the Day in the Book of Common Prayer (2 vols.)		11.	4
(1888)	Three Counsels of the Divine Master for the Conduct of Spiritual Life. (2 vols.)		9.	0
(1892)	The Life of John William Burgon (2 vols.)	1.	4.	0
(1898)	The Lord's Prayer		6.	0

Admissions to Entertainments, etc.
Circus: Goulburn, Julia and 3 children of Archdeacon Nevill: Total: 12/-.
Royal Academy Exhibition (London) Admission and Catalogue   3/6d.
Cardiff Castle   2/-.
Waxworks Exhibition (Brighton)   1/-.
Brighton Aquarium   1/-.
Wellington Pier, Gt Yarmouth   1/-.
London Zoo   9d.
Brighton Pier   6d.

Personal Items
Goulburn had a passion for buying *Gloves*. He bought a pair about every other month, ranging in price from 3/- to 7/6d. (average c. 4/-). Umbrellas came next, partly because he kept losing them. They cost from 16/- to £1.0.4. Toothbrushes were a good third, ranging from 1/- to 2/-. Other items, of which he records the price, were: Spectacles 3s. to £1.18.6d.; Hat 6/6d.; Socks 5/-; Boots £1.16.0; Scissors 6/6d.; Handkerchief 2/6d.–3.6d.; Sponge 5/- to £1; Razor 8/6d.; Braces 1/-; Walking Stick 1/6d.; Paper Knife 1/-; Purse 8/6d.; Toothpaste 2/6d.; Opera Glasses 16/6d.; and a Shetland Waistcoat 10/-.

He also bought a Surplice for himself for £2.10.0; a Gown for a Lay Clerk £3.1.0; and Bibles for the Choristers at 1/6d. each.

Obviously, a Servant did most of the household shopping, but Goulburn himself, on occasion, like to buy poultry, meat or game (either in London or Norwich): Turkey £1.2.0; Goose 10/6d.; 2 Fowls 6/6d. each; Quarter of Lamb

18/-; Pheasant 4/6d. and 5/6d.; Hare 5/- and 6/-; Bordeaux Pigeon 3/6d., Crab 2/6d.

We are not told the weight of any of these, but, considering the number of people usually dining at the Deanery, they must have been large birds, etc.

Post Office
The Diaries indicate a fast Postal Service. In Norwich there were six Collections daily (three on Sunday), and five Deliveries daily (two on Sunday). The Head Post Office was open on six days a week from 7 a.m. to 9.55 p.m., and on Sundays from 7 a.m. to 10 a.m. Its Telegram Section was open 24 hours a day, every day. Letter postage was: Up to 1 oz., 1d.; up to 2 ozs. 1½d; and for every additional 2 ozs., ½d. Newspapers were ½d.; and books, up to 2 ozs. were ½d., with every additional 2 ozs., ½d.

••

Set against the value of money, then and now, and taking into account the fact that a large proportion of the population, in the second half of the 19th Century were earning only £2 to £3 a week, these prices are not so different from ours. Some items may be less, other more expensive. In general, the purchasing power of the low paid was very limited.
••